International Tax Law

International Tax Law

Second Edition

Edited By

Andrea Amatucci

Wolters Kluwer
Law & Business

Published by:
Kluwer Law International
PO Box 316
2400 AH Alphen aan den Rijn
The Netherlands
Website: www.kluwerlaw.com

Sold and distributed in North, Central and South America by:
Aspen Publishers, Inc.
7201 McKinney Circle
Frederick, MD 21704
United States of America
Email: customer.service@aspenpublishers.com

Sold and distributed in all other countries by:
Turpin Distribution Services Ltd
Stratton Business Park
Pegasus Drive, Biggleswade
Bedfordshire SG18 8TQ
United Kingdom
Email: kluwerlaw@turpin-distribution.com

Printed on acid-free paper.

ISBN 978-90-411-3727-2

Printed and Bound by CPI Group (UK) Ltd, Croydon, CR0 4YY.

List of Editors and Contributors

Prof. Andrea Amatucci, Professor of Public Finance Law, University of Naples, Italy
Prof. Miguel A. Caamaño Anido, Tax and Finance Law, La Coruña University, Spain
Prof. Gabriel Casado Ollero, Tax and Finance Law, Complutense University, Madrid, Spain
Prof. Nicola d'Amati, Emeritus Professor of Tax Law, University of Bari
Joachim Englisch, Senior Research Assistant, Institute of Tax Law at Cologne University, Germany
Eusebio González, Professor of Tax Law, University of Salamanca
Charles H. Gustafson, Professor of Law, Georgetown University Law Center, Washington, D.C.
Werner C. Haslehner, Fellow, Law Department of the London School of Economics and Political Science, United Kingdom
Prof. Dr. Konosuke Kimura, University-professor (em.), Nihon University, Japan
Joachim Lang, Director, Institute of Tax Law at Cologne University, Germany
Lerke Osterloh, Professor (em.) of Public Law and Tax Law, Goethe University Frankfurt am Main, Justice of the Federal Constitutional Court a.D.
Marion Petri, Professor of Financial Law and Tax Law, Johannes Gutenberg University of Mainz
Roberta Scarpato, LL.M Taxation Law, Boston University
Henning Tappe, Assistant Professor, Institute of Tax Law, University of Muenster
Christoph Trzaskalik, Professor of Public Law and Tax Law, Johannes Gutenberg University of Mainz
Victor Uckmar, Professor Emeritus of Public Finance, University of Genoa
Antonio Vázquez del Rey Villanueva, Professor of Tax Law, University of Navarra

Table of Contents

Preface

The study of international tax law requires knowledge of tax law's evolution. On the threshold of the third millennium, tax law, originating as an independent legal discipline at the beginning of the last century, can now rely on a solid theoretical basis which will undoubtedly enable it to meet the difficult challenges implied in the current processes of internationalization.

The complexities experienced up to now in all contemporary tax law systems, together with the theoretical implications arising from such changes, require prompt reflection on 'new' principles which have emerged in the international legal scholarship. While providing the basis for further investigation, these principles show continuity even when the ongoing processes of internationalization seem to be a pointer to a significant break with the old and consolidated relationship between the action of taxing and sovereignty of States.

As a result, the need is felt by the author to end this transition phase with a comparative analysis conducted by a sample of the best international tax law scholars, providing a systematic review of the fundamental themes of tax law and of the prospects in the near future of tax legislative systems. These systems are grouped according to the major homogeneous legal areas they belong to.

This leads us to perceive that a new systematic function has been acquired in legal theory by tax law, combined with the particular and, in some respects, original processes that have taken place in the development of specific legal systems.

In this context, there have been numerous analytical studies, concentrating on the interrelation between tax law and private law, and the specific types of legal sources according to their classification by legal categories. This has been done by using interpretative methods which require legal institutions to be properly qualified in order to be adapted to technical formulations of tax rules, which are entirely influenced by the underlying economic process.

In celebrating the first centenary of the birth of tax law theory, recognising the progress already achieved in the twentieth century, and which is bound to bear fruit in the present millennium, the events leading to the creation of the various tax systems have stimulated reflections and innovations as regards legal theory, opinions of academic commentators and case law, as well as profound and original legislative approaches, all revolving around the dissolution of those historical constraints which had managed to survive and be consolidated, i.e. the tenacious and strong relationship between the sovereignty of States and taxation.

This has been amply confirmed during the last decades by emphasising, in the context of a far reaching process of globalization, the growing internationalization of tax institutions and relationships with a particular focus on those legal systems – above all those of Member States of the European Union – which pursued the aim of harmonization for years as a prelude to modern forms of unification, which are not only required but guaranteed by methods based on the principle of full subsidiarity. As well as these interesting developments accompanying the start of the new millennium (which is not in contrast with, but complementary to the process of globalization) the crisis and, in some cases, the disintegration of an ideology resting with centralized State, have suggested new forms of aggregation to come to the fore. While being inherently autonomous, these forms are consequently able to propose once again the compulsory system of leviable tax in significantly new terms capable of stimulating the development of hypotheses behind tax levying by relying on new forms, contents and institutions typical of tax law which, on the basis of past experience, evidence specific problems being closely related to the modern day.

The European Community system has been increasingly enriched by topics originating in different contexts in line with the specific features emerging from the various national legal systems. The Community system has proved able to interpret fundamental principles based on common ground, which require tax legal theorists of the modern day to seek (with intelligence and diligence) to ensure that these principles are properly identified and systematized.

In this context, a major emphasis in international tax law is given to the process of fiscal harmonisation in the EU Member States, and the implications of the relevant Treaties for the economic systems in the Americas and the Pacific Rim.

The reader will understand that a survey of the future of this branch of the law, together with the fundamental conceptual framework underlying this volume, does not aim at overcoming or even abandoning the framework which is inherent in the notion of 'tax legal relation' or *rapporto giuridico tributario* (i.e. the legal situation whereby a mere act of levying a specific type of tax leads to an obligatory relation to arise between the taxpayer and the competent body in charge of imposing and collecting the tax), in particular when it comes to the analysis of the objective elements behind it. However, attention has also been focused further ahead by pointing out the correlation with the considerable progress achieved in these specific topics in recent decades, and in similar problems covered in other branches of the law. By harmonizing and correlating the elements mentioned above in relation to the procedures for the implementation of tax rules, the present analysis contains useful considerations on legislative systems which, while undergoing a chaotic process, are a reflection of long-term developments hinting at solid theoretical and practical outcomes in the future.

Looking back to recent achievements, it should be observed that the universal aspects of tax law have enabled schools of thought in various countries to contribute to this theoretical development, often in an independent manner.

The selection of the authors appearing in the present volume was made by taking account of their scientific and theoretical background, so that this volume would provide a useful view of their complex origin.

This is the reason why explicit reference was made to European countries (Germany, Italy and Spain) where, also due to their common, profound cultural and legal traditions based on Roman law, tax law literature had the best chance to consolidate and communicate internally, and produce fruitful results. Today, however, it is being pursued and addressed towards new goals. Scholars, inspired by the teachings and indications already given in the past, are now ready to deal with newly conceived legal frameworks behind tax systems operating in complex and open societies, characterized by major processes of internationalization. We have therefore highlighted analytical studies in tax law emerging in these three homogeneous countries, rather than rely on a partial view of different research experiences gained in many countries of the old continent.

This volume is basically a collection of chapters or summaries of chapters of the work *Trattato di diritto tributario* (appearing in five volumes). This work was edited and coordinated by myself for the German authors (from W. Schick to C. Trzaskalik) and equally for the Spanish authors (from Eusebio González García to others), and was first published in Italian by Cedam in 1994.

At the beginning of the twentieth century, strong premonitions emerged in Germany over the discipline of tax law originating in this country. The first specialized academic text on financial law was published in German by F. von Myrbach-Rheinfeld,[1] together with an essay on tax principles by B. Fuisting.[2] These contributions were coupled with others of equal standing in the tax field which appeared in the area of administrative law texts. From 1915, L. Waldecker, as an independent professor, taught courses in financial and tax law at the University of Berlin. In the years immediately after World War II, tax law studies developed in Germany to serve as a proper legal discipline. These studies, however underwent such a rapid and intensive growth that they acquired a significant level of autonomy in a short time, allowing them to take their place next to other traditional legal disciplines. The 1920s, which coincided almost completely with the period of the Weimar Republic (1919–1933), deserve to be regarded as the golden age of studies in tax law in Germany. The fundamental theoretical contributions made in this decade came, in fact, from A. Hensel's manual,[3] which represented the first systematically organized review of tax law, and the book by O. Bühler[4] which, though less systematic, was of particular importance in terms of the general aspects of tax law being examined. In the same period, significant contributions of scientific value also emerged from research analyses made by German scholars outside the Universities, in particular E. Becker,[5] a judge

1. *Grundriß des Finanzrechts*, Leipzig, 1906.
2. This work, entitled *Grundzüge der Steuerlehre*, was published in 1902.
3. 1st edition in 1924; 2nd edition in 1927; 3rd edition in 1933.
4. *Lehrbuch des Steuerrechts*, I. *Allgemeines Steuerrecht*, Berlin, 1927. Oldenburg, 1990.
5. Cf. M.R. Theissen (ed.), *Gedenkschrift zum 50. Todestag von Dr. H.C. Enno Becker*, 1869–1949.

who was responsible for bringing the 1919 general tax law code *(Reichsabgabenordnung)* into existence[6]. While it is true that the drafting of this code did not have the consensus of H. Nawiasky[7] and L. Waldecker,[8] it was however welcomed by E. Kaufmann,[9] J. Jellinek[10] and O. Bühler,[11] despite the fact that it was not incorporated into a framework of general principles. E. Becker was a supporter of *wirtschaftliche Betrachtungsweise,* which is the essence of the methodology for interpreting tax laws. Together with the tax law theorists in this decade, mention should be made of the work by K. Ball,[12] an equally eminent scholar who was particularly resourceful in including the topic in the overall system. Mention should also be made of the work by H. Dorn,[13] who conducted research on double taxation; as well as R. Grabower[14] and J. Popitz[15] who provided an analysis of the laws instituting taxes on company income and trade. M. Lion[16] provided an in-depth analysis of tax regulations applying to financial statements, while G. Strutz[17] published a manual on tax law. In this decade, works on administrative law[18] no longer devoted space to taxation law.

From 1933 to 1945, during National Socialism, F. Reinhardt[19] outshone all the others. His major contributions included proposals for legislation with his vital role being played within administrative financial authorities. In 1942, the first teaching chair in tax law was established at the University of Cologne, with O. Bühler being appointed there in 1945.

Bühler provided a considerable stimulus to the significantly scientific evolution of tax law which took place in the German Federal Republic, this evolution also being substantiated by the establishment of further teaching chairs in specific fields in the second half of the century.

German scholars of tax law can be divided into two groups, on the basis of their theoretical formation. Some come from the field of public law while others come from civil law. These experts rarely come from the field of criminal law. It is a fact that

6. On this theme see the *From Public Finance Law to Tax Law – Studies in honor of Andrea Amatucci*, Jovene Naples and Editorial Temis Bogotà, 2011. This collection of methodological content consists of seven volumes totaling 5028 pages. The work has contributions by 158 authors, from five continents.
7. *Steuerrechtliche Grundfragen,* München, 1926, p. 8.
8. *Fin. Arch.,* XLII, 1925, pp. 69, 75.
9. *Recht und Wirtschaft,* 1919, p. 211.
10. *Verwaltungsrecht,* 3rd edn, Berlin, 1931.
11. *Lehrbuch des Steuerrechts,* I. *Allgemeines Steuerrecht,* 1927, p. 83.
12. *Steuerrecht und Privatrecht,* 1924, p. 153.
13. Cf. F. Klein, 'Zur Erinnerung an Herbert Dorn', in *StuW,* 1987, p. 97.
14. 13 Cf. A. Pausch, 'Rolf Grabower und die Steuerwissenschaften', in *StuW,* 1973, p 189.
15. Cf. A. Pausch, 'Im Konflikt mit dem Steuerpositivismus. Johannes Popitz; zwischen gesetzlichem Unrecht und übergesetzlichem Recht', in *StuW,* 1985, p. 54.
16. Cf. A. Pausch, 'Max Lion, Pionier des Bilanzsteuerrechts. Aufstieg und Verfolgung eines deutschen Steuerwissenschaftlers jüdischer Abstammung', in *StuW,* 1979, p. 149.
17. *Grundlehren des Steuerrechts,* 1924.
18. Cf. *Vorträge auf der Salzburger Umschulungstagung,* 1941, *Bucherei des Steuerrechts* (edited by Fritz Reinhardt), vol V.
19. Cf. Those who held tax law to come within administrative law area, see: O. Mayer, *Deutsches Verwaltungsrecht,* 3rd edn, 1924, I, paras 27–32; P. Fleiner, *Institutionen des deutschen Verwaltungsrechts,* 8th edn, 1928, para. 27 and W. Jellinek, *Verwaltungsrecht,* 3rd edn, 1931.

German professors of tax law usually deal with other branches of public or private law jointly.

In Germany, it is not easy to identify schools of thought in the area of tax law. Nevertheless, and in line with the full academic independence of German scholars, there are only few of the common elements which are there to evidence, though vaguely, the existence of schools being understood to conduct homogeneous research studies in specific areas in the sense already described above.

Broadly speaking, however, all German scholars are disciples of Klaus Tipke, but they have formed their own opinion and have not propagated Tipke's theories. Notwithstanding this, the University of Cologne, where systematic formulations have been made in this branch of the law, has tended more than other universities to form a school including Klaus Tipke's predecessors, such as Othmar Bühler and Armin Spitaler, whose scientific research and method did not achieve however the importance and reputation gained indeed by the ability and achievement of a teacher of tax law like Klaus Tipke.

The specialized journal *Steuer und Wirtschaft* of the Cologne school, the oldest one, devoted considerable attention, with a flattering book review, to the *Trattato di diritto tributario* on which this volume is based (1997, p. 80).

The Münster school pays special attention to the relationships with constitutional and administrative law. Ottmar Bühler, Klaus Vogel, Paul Kirchhof and Dieter Birk taught at the University of Münster, but they differ considerably from one other in terms of their published research analysis. Obviously, the University of Münster is not the only academic centre where the relationships between tax law and constitutional and administrative law is fully taken into account: there is a difference in quality.

A special analysis of the relationship with private law is made by the Bonn school, whose members are Werner Flume, Wolfang Schön and Brigitte Knobbe-Keuk.

Due to such considerably new amount of research analyses, the reference framework of this volume is further enhanced to provide complete answers to the subject of tax law, which is as yet in a process of constant and active evolution.

The presence of such a considerable amount of authoritative German literature likewise confirms the interest taken by scholars in the progress of the tax discipline and the need for them to carry out comparative analyses with others from different but communicating cultural backgrounds. Despite cultural differences, however, fruitful dialogue among them has never failed. These scholars have devoted considerable attention to the specialized aspects of tax law, though without losing sight of some of the frameworks of tax law which are in common with the institutions of private law or public law.

Let me now mention the names of those contributing to this volume. Joachim Lang, professor from the University of Cologne, a place which is known for providing the oldest tradition of teaching and research in tax law, is the author of a basic manual appearing in the 20th edition published in 2010; and his teacher Tipke,[20] who expanded and revised the manual, thus producing an excellent work in three volumes. Lerke

20. Cf. K. Tipke and J. Lang, *Steuerrecht, ein systematischer Grundriß*, 20th edn, Köln, 2010 and K. Tipke, *Die Steuerrechtsordnung*, in three volumes, Köln, 1993.

Osterloh, a constitutional judge from the University of Frankfurt a/M and Christoph Trzaskalik from the University of Mainz, are known respectively for their research in the areas regarding the relationship between tax law and private law, and the activity of administrative financial authorities.

Also in Italy (the schools of which are analyzed in the first chapter), the first sporadic preparatory approaches to the study of taxation law as a legal discipline come from research contributions made by eminent experts in administrative law at the start of the twentieth century. In fact, O. Ranelletti[21] examined methodically and in detail the legal nature of the *imposta* system (tax), while F. Cammeo[22] did so in the area of the constitutional legitimacy of the system of whatever type of tax. During this stage of scientific research, the description of tax law received little space in the manuals of administrative law.[23]

Ranelletti,[24] A. D. Giannini's teacher,[25] founded the Neapolitan School being inspired as it was by the substantive and uniform nature of financial law, where G. Ingrosso[26] first received his academic training.

The 1930s can be defined as the golden age of tax scholarship in Italy. Considerable stimulus to financial studies should primarily be ascribed to B. Griziotti.[27] Though conducted with an 'integralist' approach typical of the legal and economic studies of the time and rejected by subsequent legal theory, his studies were such as to produce not only eminent economists at the University of Pavia, but also an appropriate tax law school whose leading and representative figure is E. Vanoni.[28] He had the merit of contributing towards research progress, especially on general themes, such as the interpretation of tax law, and of later being the unchallenged protagonist of the modernization process in the Italian tax law system.

M. Pugliese[29] also deserves mention, with his studies on international fiscal law and tax liability, as well as his general contributions. Experts in tax proceedings such

21. 'Natura giuridica dell'imposta', in *Municipio Italiano,* 1898.
22. 'Le tasse e la loro costituzionalità', in *Giur. it.*, 1899, IV, p. 204.
23. S. Romano, *I principi di diritto amministrativo,* Milano, 1912 and L. Meucci, *Istituzioni di diritto am- ministrativo,* Torino, 1909.
24. *Diritto finanziario,* Milano, with a 3rd edition already appearing in 1928.
25. 'La classificazione delle imposte nel diritto tributario', in *Studi dedicati alla memoria di Zanzucchi,* Milano, *Vita e pensiero,* 1927, p. 337, *Istituzioni di diritto tributario,* Milano, I, ed. 1938, and Il *rapporto giuridico d'imposta,* Milano, 1937.
26. Distinguished academics of administrative law continued being attracted by tax law subjects. Cf. Zanobini, 'La sistemazione delle sanzioni fiscali', in *Riv. dir. pubbl.*, 1929, I, p. 500. 'La legge di imposta nel diritto pubblico', in *Riv. dir. pubbl.*, 1911, I, p. 145 and *Istituzioni di diritto finanziario,* II: *Le entrate dello Stato,* Napoli, 1937. In the same context: E. Scandale, *La riscossione delle imposte dirette,* Napoli, 1929; M. di Lorenzo, *Principi di diritto doganale,* Napoli, 1934; F. D'Alessio, *Corso di diritto finanziario,* Napoli, 1937 and G. Tesoro, *Principi di diritto tributario,* Bari, 1938.
27. *Studi di diritto tributario,* Padova, 1931 and 'Per il progresso scientifico degli studi degli ordinamenti finanziari', in *Riv. dir. fin. sc.fin.*, 1937, I, p. 1.
28. *Natura ed interpretazione della legge tributaria,* Padova, 1932 and 'I soggetti passivi del rapporto giuridico tributario', in *Foro It.*, 1935, IV, p. 325. On these general topics: Cutrera, 'La norma tributaria', in *Riv. dir. pubbl.*, 1933, I, p. 596 and 'L'accertamento tributario', in Riv. *dir. pubbl.*, 1935, I, p. 121.
29. *L'imposizione delle imprese di carattere internazionale,* Padova, 1930, *L'obbligazione tributaria,* Padua, 1935 and *Istituzioni di diritto finanziario. Diritto tributario,* Padova, 1937.

as G.A. Micheli[30], who was the editor-in-chief of the tax and financial law review founded by Griziotti, and E. Allorio,[31] together with the eminent expert F. Carnelutti,[32] paved the way to the analysis of court hearings on tax matters.

In the 1950s, the transfer of G.A. Micheli[33], to the chair of tax law at the University of Rome and of E. Allorio to the chair at the University of Milan provided particular stimulus to the theoretical development of tax law. Both of them provided particular stimulus to research and analysis on a topic for which they provided a major theoretical framework. As experts on the law of civil court proceedings, they have significantly influenced the definition of tax trial proceedings and the complex, controversial debate over the burden of proof. Starting from rather approximate initial solutions, they provided a complete system identifying a variety of persons recognized by law as the subjects liable to tax, legal relations and court proceedings allowing legal theory to confidently face the difficulties involved in the functioning of today's tax system.

This process of enrichment of the Neapolitan School was completed with the transfer of V. Romanelli-Grimaldi[34] from the chair of administrative law at the University of Pisa to the chair of economics and financial law at the University of Naples. In contrast with the Pavia school, he returned to the topic of methodology, which had been introduced by the founder of the Neapolitan school, Oreste Ranelletti, inspired by the uniform and substantive nature of financial law,[35] again taken up by G. Ingrosso[36] and which would be continued, with particular attention to constitutional principles, by V. Sica[37] and G. Abbamonte.[38] This active theoretical development was made easier by the inclusion of chairs in tax law in university public competitions starting from the 1960s.

Together with these luminaries there are other significant figures who, though being committed to theoretical work along other independent lines, have been able to establish a dialogue with the experts referred above, thus encouraging a fruitful debate. I am referring, in particular, to the theoretical and practical contribution provided by A. Uckmar,[39] who in this context paved the way to younger academics, starting from his son Victor, who has more than honored the paternal traditions at the University of Genoa through the great prospects offered by the law on registry tax, with the enormous impact of tax law on civil law institutions. Here, I would also like to mention

30. 'Sull'ammissibilità di una decisione allo stato degli atti del processo tributario', in *Riv. dir. fin. sc.fin.*, 1939, II,p. 13.
31. *Diritto processuale tributario,* Milano, 1942.
32. 'Introduzione allo studio del diritto processuale tributario', in *Riv. dir. proc. civ.*, 1932, I, p. 105.
33. He later published an important work, *Corso di diritto tributario,* Torino, 1984.
34. 'Metodologia del diritto finanziario', in *Rass. di dir. pubbl.*, 1960, I, p. 1.
35. *Corso di diritto finanziario,* 3rd edn, Milano, 1927. On the Neapolitan school, see my article 'L'insegnamento del diritto finanziario', in *Riv. dir. fin. sc.fin.*, 1999, p. 492.
36. *Istituzioni di diritto finanziario,* vol. II, *Le entrate dello Stato,* Napoli, 1937.
37. *Bilancio dello Stato e programmazione economica,* Napoli, 1964.
38. *Principi di diritto finanziario,* Napoli, 1975; *Pricipios de Derecho de la Hacienda Pùblica,* Bogotà, 2009 (Spanish translation).
39. *Le leggi del registro,* including three volumes and appendix, Padova, 1928–1931. Cf. also D. Jarach, *Principi per l'applicazione delle tasse di registro,* Padova, 1937.

the valuable contribution provided by Vittorio Berliri[40] to the topic of 'best tax' (or *ottima imposta)* with subsequent analytical contributions by his brother Antonio,[41] who was active in research for a particularly long time at the University of Bologna.

These experts have stimulated in-depth analyses which were conducted in the second half of the last century by increasingly numerous as well as second generation students.

With this solid and complex theoretical basis, this book contains contributions by Italian authors representing the schools of tax law and financial law in the context of the specific topics being dealt with. This volume contains chapters on tax law by myself, as representative of the Neapolitan school, and by Nicola D'Amati (who taught at the University of Bari and is a student of A. D. Giannini) and on international tax law by V. Uckmar, an important figure also outside this school. They share the greatest experience in Italy both on the research and teaching level, having started their respective careers during the 1950s.

F. Sainz de Bujanda undoubtedly has the merit of encouraging research on financial law with particular reference to tax law. The theoretical development of tax law in Spain can be divided into three basic phases.

The first phase was only theoretical in character, basically characterised by contributions from the 1950s and 1960s, and collected in six volumes of the series *Hacienda y Derecho.* In the second part of the 1960s, Bujanda's and other Spanish scholars' research provided significant contributions to the progress of tax legal science.

The second phase was both theoretical and legislative in character, coinciding with the study of the legislative draft of the 1963 (revised in 2003) *Ley General Tributaria.* A Commission worked on this draft for two years, with the participation of eminent tax law experts of the time.

The third phase was theroetical and didactic in character. After 1970 the combined teaching of economics, finance and tax law was abolished, and the first five university chairs embracing only 'financial and tax law' subjects were established. In the 1970s the publication started of Sainz de Bujanda's magnificent work consisting of three volumes.[42]

The consistent and constant scientific evolution in the last thirty years of the twentieth century resulted in research activity being carried out by a growing number of Spanish experts who dealt with all the basic topics of tax law. As regards the Spanish tax law research community, with the contribution of Eusebio Gonzàlez Garcìa, this volume includes authors representing the current tax law schools in Spain. The chapter by E. Gonzàlez Garcìa, which is included in this volume, has been revised by Antonio Vàzquez del Rey.

---

40. 'La giusta imposta. Appunti per un sistema giuridico della pubblica contribuzione. Lineamenti di una riforma organica della finanza ordinaria', in *Annuario di diritto comparato e studi legislativi,* edited by Salvatore Galgano, volume XIX, III; edited by *Istituto di Studi Legislativi,* Rome, 1930–1933.
41. *Il processo tributario amministrativo,* Reggio Emilia, 1940 and *I principi di diritto tributario,* I, Milano, 1952, II, Milano, 1957; III, Milano, 1964.
42. *Sistema de derecho financiero,* Madrid, I, 1977.

The two Spanish tax law schools are included in two categories: the first one is the important school founded by Sainz de Bujanda and includes approximately two-thirds of the academic world evenly distributed in three areas (Andalusia, Valencia and Madrid). The second school groups together the other third of the professors, some of whom are inspired by Calvo Ortega and others by Pérez de Ayala.

This volume is an expression of such a complete scientific reality; in fact, the school of Sainz de Bujanda is represented by Casado Ollero, from the Andalusia school, while the minority area is represented by González Garcìa.

In any case, the reference to the above schools is appropriate also to consider that a Spanish translation of the revised edition of *Trattato di diritto Tributario,* published by Temis Bogotá and edited by myself, did not come as a mere chance. This mirrors the process by which the 'concepts' formulated by the academic Achille Donato Giannini crossed the ocean. They were included in the Spanish *Ley General Tributaria* of 1963, thanks to the Madrid professor Fernando Sainz de Bujanda. This model, thanks to Montevideo professor Ramòn Valdés Costa, was then implemented in the Tax Code (MCTAL, 1967) adopted by many countries in Latin America. The other contemporary line of Italian tax law theorists, developed by the Pavia school, was disseminated in the faculties chaired in Argentina by Mario Pugliese and Dino Jarach, both students of Benvenuto Griziotti.

The author intended to integrate this view of tax law scholarship with the rules of the EU treaties governing the relationships of European tax systems with the other most important economic areas, i.e. the Americas and the Pacific Rim countries. I am sure that the analysis of the effects of the EU Treaty on tax rules on Western and Eastern countries will enable the reader to complete the world panorama provided in this volume.

In the USA, tax law has undergone highly interesting developments.

In this regard, however, I would like to say that tax law and policy became an important element of legal scholarship as early as the 1930's. Since that time, tax law has become increasingly important and complex. Today, tax law is taught in virtually every Law School in the United States, which means that there are professors at every Law School who specialize in tax law and policy. Moreover, there is a question about federal tax law on the Bar Examinations of every state of which I am aware.

While I may sound boastful of my colleagues working in the area of tax law, it is necessary to remind the reader that an important contribution of tax law scholarship in the United States lies in the recognition that a proper understanding of tax law equally depends on a proper understanding and examination of the economic, political and social consequences, whether from a macro or micro point of view.

Charles H. Gustafson, who is an excellent representative of this highly important area of scholarship in international tax law, has been involved in this project. Gustafson is a professor at the Georgetown University Law Center in Washington, D.C. He teaches in various areas of public international law, international trade and investment and federal taxation. He is the co-author of several casebooks on federal income taxation, including his *Taxation of International Transactions* (West 2001, 2nd edition). In this second edition, his chapter has been revised by Roberta Scarpato – LL.M (Legum Magister) in Taxation Law, Boston University.

Gustafson is an active member of the American Law Institute and has served on a number of committees for the American Bar Association.

Before World War II, there was less academic activity being conducted in the area of tax law. Japanese academic research into this field substantially began after 1945, accepting Professor C. Shoup's Tax Mission from the US.

Professor Hiroshi Kaneko is the leading scholar. He is a Professor Emeritus of the Faculty of Law at the Tokyo University. Professor Kaneko is a representative of the IFA, Japanese Branch and a member of Trustees for IBFD. He has already retired from Tokyo University, although he is still committed to academic research activity.

The Shoup Mission recommended university lectures in tax law both at the Tokyo and Kyoto University. The professor who first covered a tax teaching chair at the Tokyo University was Shozaburo Sugimura, with Professor Shuichi Sugai covering the same teaching at the Kyoto University. Professor Kaneko is a successor to Professor Sugimura. Professor Yoshihiro Masui is now in the teaching position which was covered by Professor Kaneko before his retirement.

In Japanese universities, only some law faculties require teachers to lecture in tax law. At the Faculty of Commerce and Business Administration, for example, tax accounting courses are taught by professors of accounting. The academic tax law association is represented by the Japanese Society for Tax Law. The number of members of this association amounts to over 300 and they provide purely academic activities for the public.

Kimura Konosuke[43] has written a chapter dealing with the effects of the EU Treaty on the Pacific Rim countries (Tax Law, International Taxation); he is a significant figure in Asia, being Professor of Law at the Faculty of Law of Keio University and at the Advanced Research Institute for the Sciences and Humanities of Nihon University (Tokyo).

While stressing the aim of providing a complete volume, considerable space has been devoted to the topics which have aroused the greatest research interest in recent decades, in relation to the scholarship trends in specific areas of tax law in general and of international tax law in particular, towards which the various schools are oriented.

43. He is the author of numerous publications. Some of his most recent works are: Interpretation of Law in Japan in the Light of Comparison with Common Law Systems, in: Klaus Vogel (ed.), Interpretation of Tax Law and Treaties and Transfer Pricing in Japan and Germany, Series on International Taxation 20: Luwer Law International. The Hague/London/Boston, 1998/09, p. 1–13; General Theory of Tax Law, Seibun-dou, Tokyo, 1999/04; International Tax Law of Japan, Seibun-dou, Tokyo, 2000/07; The Controversy over the Concept of Corporation Income: Premium Capital Taxation, 9 Keio Law Review, 15–57 (2000); Draft of Administrative Procedure Act 2001, Shinzan-sya, Tokyo, 2001/05; Gewerbestandort Japan Steuerrecht und Steuerpolitik als Instrument der Standortsicherung: Standort im Vergleich zwischen unmitelbarem und mittelbarem Finanzgewerbe, in Zentaro Kitagawa, Junichi Murakami, Hiroshi Shiono (Hrsg), Regulierung, Deregulierung, Liberalisierung, Mohr Siebeck, 2001/10, 67–78; Allocation and Taxation of Head Office Expenses Between the Head Office and its Branches in Other Countries, Gensyo, Taipei 2002/07, 765–807; Automated Clearinghouse Tax in Framework of Clearing Retail Payment Arrangements: Proposed International Tax Rules, RESEARCH PROJECT granted by Scientific Research Foundation, 2003/03, 1–18; Deferred Compensation and Disguised Loans – Current Taxation by 'Time Value of Money' Approach (Note), 522 Tax Jurisprudence (Japan Tax Jurisprudence Association) 29–53.

The authors have each been asked to examine topics on which they conducted specific research analysis.

In preparing this volume, I thought it appropriate to reconcile the need for uniform analytical criteria with independent analytical approaches provided by the authors. Therefore, and in line with the purposes of the volume, I opted for the size of individual contributions to be left up to authors to decide within a previously agreed length of pages, taking account of what they themselves believed the specificity of the theme being dealt with might require in terms of writing length.

This volume is also designed to express the fundamental achievements gained by tax law experts at the end of the first centenary in this discipline, and which have allowed for the opening up of new horizons already in sight at the start of the third millennium.

In this sense, the comparison between the various methodological approaches already adopted and the achievements gained by international tax law scholars in their own country systems of law under investigation, has proved to be extremely useful for the growth of the resources of international research, in which the need for a better knowledge of domestic legislations cannot be disregarded. All the more so in this case, since this comparison may provide further stimulus to bringing the various schools closer together, in such a way as to conduct assessments of the current status of scholarship in other countries.

This is the most useful path for international tax law experts as well as those of other branches of the law to embark upon. There is no doubt that any cooperative and comparative effort made to assess scientific achievements will, as a result, increase the progress of tax law studies globally. It is important that these achievements be assessed closely with the improvement of the methods for analysis and knowledge of the field.

We are familiar with the process which makes it easy for legal theorists to acquire a better knowledge of the purposes behind the command or provision enacted by a legislature and, consequently, the real dimensions of taxation arising out of the fact in this case, thus making it possible for them to come up with careful examination of the legitimate grounds underlying tax levying acts of administrative tax authorities, including, of course, their procedural law aspects.

Incidentally, these are the reasons why a volume like this has been designed for practitioners in the legal profession, i.e. to provide them with adequate and updated information on the basic aspects of international tax law, and to reliably and fully express the theoretical approaches adopted by the relevant schools in this area, as well as to express the main contributions of jurisprudence.

This book is intended to fulfill the above purposes, and at the same time, to provide all the most recent bibliography and jurisprudence references in order to go more deeply into specific topics.

W. Schick, J. Trzaskalik and E. Gonzáles, co-ordinating this volume together with various authors, have the merit of covering new areas of study with the fullest scholarly quality, combining significant contents with improved dialogue between scholars from different nationalities and languages, but inspired by the common purpose of ensuring that the academic discipline they have investigated and acquired knowledge on can advance towards a better, more complete theoretical understanding.

This exciting venture began with the planning of the *Trattato di diritto tributario* and ended with the publication of this work. The first was mostly experienced in the relaxing and understanding company of my wife Mary whose life, dedicated to the family and students, ended due to an incurable illness before this hard task was completed. However, I would like to dedicate the results now achieved to her, being indebted for the affection, comfort and support she was able to provide even when it was she who needed it more.

Acknowledgement

The author would like to thank Angela Andreina Puopolo for her precious support. He also expresses his deep gratitude to the late lamented Professor Rocco Caporale of the St. Johns University of New York for his kind help in making this volume of international relevance and in choosing a publishing house so prestigious and of broad reach.

CHAPTER 1

The Contribution of Economic Analysis of Law to the Tax Law Methodology*

Andrea Amatucci

§1.01 ORESTE RANELLETTI, THE FOUNDER OF THE NEAPOLITAN SCHOOL OF PUBLIC FINANCE LAW

The study of methodology is a delicate preliminary subject on which the precision of any scientific research in the field of law is based. After about half a century of silence the debate on this issue is regaining its strength. This due to the analysis of Oreste Ranelletti's work on its methodological perspective.[1]

* On the current conception of this method, cfr. Lerke Osterloh, methodological problems in Tax Law, in '*From Financial Law to Tax Law (Book in honor of Andrea Amatucci)*, V volumes, Temis (Bogotà) and Jovene (Napoli), 2011.

1. Luigi Ferlazzo Natoli and Gaspare Falsitta were both Sicilians and Professors of Tax Law, in Messina and Pavia respectively. Natoli was born in Messina in 1940, while Falsitta was born in Santa Ninfa (Trapani) in 1933 but moved to Milan in 1958. They are the authors of the first two articles published in the ninth issue (2004) of the *Rivista di Diritto tributario* under the titles of 'La scuola finanziaria napoletana e la genesi del Diritto finanziario' by Ferlazzo Natoli, and 'La sistemazione del Diritto finanziario nella coeva opera di O. Ranelletti e di A.D. Giannini e la data di nascita della' scuola' finanziaria napoletana' by Falsitta. These two articles have reopened the debate on the fundamental question of methodology of Tax Law.
Ferlazzo Natoli, in the first paragraph of his article, explains effectively the relationship (described by German scholars as *roter Faden)* among the different periods of the evolution of philosophical, economic and legal thought in Southern Italy from the fifth century B.C. to the 19th century A.D.
The analysis of Oreste Ranelletti's works and of the other professors who worked after him at the Law Faculty of the University of Naples, gave Natali the opportunity to show that a common cultural background, which had its roots in Magna Grecia, is the starting point of the method with which these Southern professors studied Public Finance Law in the 20th century. It may be helpful here to understand what Falsitta thought about Ranelletti's work. Falsitta (p. 959) says that Ferlazzo Natoli compelled him to write on the same issue on which only some

It is useful to begin our survey with a description of our jurist as given by one of his Professors, from the critique of his works by an eminent scholar and through his own words.

Ranelletti's Professor, Vittorio Scialoja,[2] wrote:

> 'At that time (1889–91) among those students, and today (1930) among these professors, distinguishes himself Oreste Ranelletti..... Young Ranelletti was a typical virtuous man from Abruzzo,[3] a strong and at the same time genteel Region of Italy. He was a man of acute intelligence, extremely diligent in his job, showing a good deal of passion for truth and its findings'.

Erminio Ferrari,[4] another eminent jurist, gives us a useful judgment on him: 'Ranelletti belongs, no doubt, to that group of scholars who supported the use of Law Method even in the study of Public Law...'; 'it is well known that Ranelletti, who was himself a supporter of Law Method, preferred its concrete application to legal studies rather than a theoretical discussion on how to practice it. That is the reason why we have no document on the Method written by Ranelletti'.

---

years earlier Ferlazzo Natoli himself had written an article 'Osservazioni sulla nascita e lo sviluppo scientifico del Diritto tributario in Italia', in *Rass. Trib.*, 2000, I, 353.

Falsitta in a previous article (pp. 365 and 366) had examined Ranelletti's 3rd edition of *Diritto finanziario per l'anno accademico 1927/28* (Tenconi, Milan). Falsitta writes that: 'We do not think that Ranelletti's works represent a real development, especially for the scientific autonomy of the subject, compared to the traditional theories of the period in which they were written'

He points out that Ranelletti makes no clear difference between the different steps of application of Tax Law (the making of a tax law, its application and its interpretation). Ranelletti uses economic categories which he borrows from Adam Smith's Principles, but which have no relationship with Tax Law.

'A first characteristic of his book is therefore the combination of applied Law and the Principles of Public Finance, between Law and Economics'.

2. Falsitta (p. 368) points out that 'Ranelletti makes a mistake when he examines the public nature of Tax relationship: Falsitta judges Ranelletti's work (p. 368) to be rather poor, noting that Ranelletti says little of interest for the future, since he simply summarizes past scientific experience.

   According to Falsitta's 'Osservazioni sulla nascita e lo sviluppo scientifico....' (2000), Ranelletti's book *Diritto finanziario* has no scientific value at all.

   But four years later Falsitta, in his 'La sistemazione del Diritto finanziario... 'gives a completely different judgment on Ranelletti's book. He says that among the scholars of the XIX century, Ranelletti is undoubtedly the one who devoted himself to the study of Finance Law with great passion, writing issues of great scientific value, and he recognizes in him also a great talent in teaching.

   In 'Oreste Ranelletti nel XXX anno del suo insegnamento', published in *Studi di diritto pubblico in onore di Oreste Ranelletti*, Padova, 1931. Vittorio Scialoja was born in Turin in 1856. His father Antonio (1817–1877) was professor for Law and Economics at the University of Turin in the period 1846-48 and Minister for Economics in Garibaldi's government in Naples in 1960 and in the Italian Government from 1865 to 1867.
3. Let us see how Ranelletti describes himself: 'He was born at Celano (Aquila) on 27 January 1868, from an ancient local family. He attended the elementary school in his village, and the high school at the State Ginnasio-Liceo of Aquila, outstanding among all the students of his school and gaining his High School cerificate in July 1887 with the highest grades', 'Oreste Ranelletti nell'Opera sua, 31 December 1955', in Oreste Ranelletti, 'Scritti giuridici scelti', I, *Lo Stato*, Jovene, Napoli, 1992, p. 604.
4. In 'Il percorso di Ranelletti tra monografie e manuali, tra ricerca ed insegnamento', in Oreste Ranelletti, *Scritti giuridici scelti*, XXXIV.

Referring to the application of his own analysis to the field of methodology in Public Finance Law, Ranelletti in his autobiography[5] wrote about himself:

> 'He thought that the first purpose of the Law Faculty was to educate young people to contribute to the formulation of law at the national level. Therefore, he thought that economic and political disciplines had to be studied as well, as a basis of the study of Law, so that students could understand that legal norms find their origin in the social or political needs'.

This way of thinking confers much more importance to the economic and financial disciplines. Ranelletti developed a unitary idea of these subjects and a better understanding of them in everyday life.

Ranelletti thought that the development of a single method to be applied to all branches of Public Finance Law was a fundamental issue. This is due to the fact that there is a strong link between the legislative instruments used by a legislator, in accordance with common logic in Public Finance.

Ranelletti paid particular attention to the relationship between Law and Economics. In keeping with Southern cultural tradition,[6] he was an experimenter of his own Method in its original structure for a better understanding of the role of economy in the study of Public Finance Law, which ought to show organic unity.

Renelletti's substantial and consistent theory of Public Finance Law is based on these premises.

§1.02 THE THREE PHASES OF RANELLETTI'S EXPERIMENTAL METHODOLOGY

Following in the footsteps of his professor Scialoja, Ranelletti studied Private Law and Roman Law at the University of Camerino and left in 1899 to teach at the University of Macerata.

His academic activity from 1905 to 1928 can be divided into three related periods.

In the first period that lasted fourteen years (1905–1919), he taught at the University of Pavia, where he was Professor for Administrative Law, before leaving for Naples.

He published the two volumes of his fundamental work *Principi di Diritto amministrativo. Introduzione e nozioni fondamentali,* (first volume) and *Del Diritto amministrativo in generale, L'organizzazione dellapubblica amministrazione. L'azione amministrativa* (second volume)[7] in 1912 and in 1915 respectively.

5. 'Oreste Ranelletti nell'Opera sua ...', p. 618.
6. See my handbook *L'ordinamento giuridico della finanza pubblica,* 8th edition, Napoli, 2007, p. 1 et seq.; *El ordenamiento jurìdico de la Hacienda Pùblica,* Bogotà, 2008, Spanish translation.
7. These two books may be found in all the main Law Libraries (even at the main Library of the Law Faculty of the University of Naples, shelf marks Massaric 47 inv. 3624 and Massarib 68 inv 3358). As we can gather from their covers, he was Professor of Administrative Law at the University of Pavia at least during the period 1912–1915.
However, it is not just interesting to know how long Ranelletti experimented with his method in each University, but also why he developed it in the way he did. No doubt great influence can

In the Preface to the first volume, Ranelletti thanks 'with all his heart' Francesco Saverio Nitti,[8] Professor of Public Finance at the Law Faculty of the University of Naples, 'for the kind and fiduciary task to write this handbook'.

It was a part of *Scienze giuridiche e sociali,* printed in Naples by Pierro. Nitti's fourth edition of *Scienza delle Finanze* was the first volume of this work. In this work, not only does Ranelletti quote Nitti's work, but also makes reference to another volume that Nitti was working on at that time, namely *Diritto finanziario italiano.*

Nitti's exceptional scientific character fascinated Ranelletti, who shared with him a common cultural background and the same interest for the economical basis of Public Finance Law. This is why Ranelletti accepted Nitti's invitation to contribute to the Neapolitan Series, while he was Professor of Administrative Law at the University of Pavia.[9]

In 1919 Ranelletti left the University of Pavia, where he was President, to go to the University of Naples, to participate in the academic life of the Law Faculty there.

Between 1919 and 1924, while working at the University of Naples, Ranelletti published *Le lezioni di Diritto amministrativo nell'Università di Napoli per gli anni 1920–21,1921–22 e 1922–23.*[10]

Although at the Law Faculty of the University of Naples Ranelletti was a professor appointed to teach only Administrative Law, thanks to his relationship with Nitti, he acquired a profound knowledge of Public Finance Law.[11]

At that time, Professors of Administrative Law also taught the fundamental principles of Public Finance Law, which was considered a part of Administrative Law even though it already had a certain scientific autonomy.

Ranelletti wisely devoted a short part of his course of Administrative Law to Public Finance Law and, in the academic years between 1922–1924, decided to publish the first two editions of *Diritto finanziario* as an integral part of the above quoted *Le lezioni di diritto amministrativo* published in Naples in 1920-23.

These two small volumes represented the first attempt in Italy to give a unitary asset to the scientific subject[12] and were published in a limited number of copies, since they were primarily for the use of students. One of these students, who distinguished

---

be traced to his Southern cultural background, which he acquired from to his family and from attending schools in his Abruzzo.

Furthermore, the fact that in 1912, when he was professor at the University of Pavia, he thanked Nitti, then professor at the University of Naples, for asking him to write an important work for the Neapolitan Series shows how great Ranelletti's interest for the cultural activity of the University of Naples was.

8. Born at Melfi (Potenza) in 1868.
9. Giovanni Giolitti was fascinated by Nitti, who had written *Napoli e la questione meridionale,* (Napoli, Guida, 1904). This is the reason why Giolitti asked Nitti to draft a special law for Naples, which was passed with general consensus in 1904.
10. The first volume was published in 1921 and it deals with Administrative Acts. The other volumes were published in 1923 and in 1924.
11. See my handbook *L'ordinamento giuridico...*, p. 21, where I point out that Ranelletti 'was Professor of Administrative Law at the Law Faculty of the University of Naples until 1924 and that he devoted much of his teaching time also to Public Finance Law'.
12. Before Ranelletti's work F. Von Myrbach Rheinfeld published *Grundriss des Finanzrechts,* Leipzig, 1906 and München, 1916.

himself among the others for his aptitude for research, was Vincenzo Romanelli-Grimaldi, who took notes of Ranelletti's lectures. Later Ranelletti himself used these classroom notes to write the second edition of his work.

The third and last period (1924–28) was spent at the University of Milan. In the first semester of 1924 Ranelletti gave up his chair at the University of Naples because he had been invited by the Italian Ministry of Education to organize the new University of Milan. Thanks to his interest in Public Finance Law, which he had developed with the help of his Neapolitan students, he at once proposed the establishment of a chair of 'Public Finance Law and Public Finance'.

A few months later, he was appointed Professor of this subject for the academic year 1924–1925. As Ranelletti himself wrote:[13] 'after few months of research, since the Faculty could not find anybody who wanted to teach that subject, he was asked to hold that chair..... since he was responsible for the innovation'.

During the academic years 1924–1925 and 1926–1927 Ranelletti worked hard at his new chair. During the other four years he was responsible only for conducting the seminars in Administrative and Public Finance Law. Ranelletti's activity at the Law Faculty of the University of Naples was also the result of his interest in this subject that he had shown while he was working in Pavia, since he had enthusiastically accepted Nitti's invitation to write the two famous volumes *Diritto amministrativo,* which were published in the Neapolitan Series.

He published his *Lezioni di Diritto Finanziario per l'anno acc. 1925–26*[14] at the University of Milan. This was the result of his academic interest and development at the University of Naples to whose cultural tradition he effectively belonged. In fact, Ranelletti could not have gained all the necessary experience during his teaching period in Milan.[15]

On the title page of his *Le lezioni di Diritto finanziario per l'anno acc. 1925–26* there is no mention of a 'first edition' and no edition of this book was printed during the academic year 1926–1927.[16]

Ranelletti's *Lezioni 1926–27,* printed by Tenconi in Milan, in fact, does not deal with Public Finance Law but with the Principles of Public Law. On its cover there is no

13. See his autobiography *Oreste Ranelletti nell'Opera sua...*, p.619.
14. This can be found in the Library of the Law Faculty of the University of Milan in Sala Settecento. Diritto pubblico.
15. Falsitta, 'La sistemazione del Diritto finanziario ...', p. 972, wrote that Ranelletti's passion for Public Finance Law could not suddenly emerge (How could Ranelletti write his *Lezioni di Diritto finanziario per l'anno accademico 1925–1926* without a scientific background on the main issues of this subject?) (p. 973).
16. In one line of his 'La sistemazione del Diritto finanziario ...', p. 970, Falsitta writes of a 'second' edition, without specifying, as he had done for the *Lezioni* (1925-26) and for his third edition, who was the editor and where in the library this otherwise untraceable edition can be found.

indication as to which edition it represents.[17] Ranelletti subsequently published the third edition of his *Diritto finanziario per l'anno acc. 1927–28.*[18]

In short, Ranelletti published only two volumes on this subject in Milan, that is, *Lezioni di Diritto finanziario per l'anno acc. 1925–26* and *Diritto finanziario per l'anno acc. 1927–28.* He considered this latter book as 'the third revised and updated edition' not of his *Lezioni* edited in Milan, but of the preceding Neapolitan edition of *Diritto finanziario.* The *Lezioni* represent the first experiment at building a unitary system of Tax Law, put together using his class notes gathered during his teaching years before moving to Milan.

What is of interest to us here is not which of the two previous editions Ranelletti was referring to, but the content of this third edition, which contains the ultimate development of his theory and brings to completion his efforts in the previous editions.

Ranelletti's methodology differs from that developed by Benvenuto Griziotti during approximately the same period.[19] Griziotti, born in Pa via in 1884, thought that it was quintessential to be financially savvy, that is to be able to grasp the financial phenomenon in its essential aspects and to understand the related political orientations, the structure of the legal system and its economic function.

Griziotti had followed an inclusive approach, on the assumption that the financial phenomenon must be examined in all its aspects. On this basis he developed the so-called 'syncretistic' Method and, in particular, the procedure of functional interpretation.

The difference with Ranelletti's method is clear: he thinks that Law research and Economics research must be distinct from each other. According to Ranelletti, jurists must examine the financial phenomenon from a legal point of view, based however on a good grasp of scientific economy, which, in its own turn, studies the economic aspects of the phenomenon.

17. In *Sala Settecento, Diritto internazionale,* of the Library of the Law Faculty of Milan. Ranelletti, 'Scritti giuridici scelti', I, *Lo Stato,* Jovene, Napoli, 1992, XLII, and *Studi di diritto pubblico in Onore di Oreste Ranelletti,* Padova, 1931, Vol. I, XIX. We may not agree therefore with Falsitta's theory, expressed in 'La sistemazione del Diritto finanziario…', 970, who thinks that Ranelletti published *Lezioni di Diritto finanziario* in 1926–27 as a 'second edition'.

18. Acopy of the 3rd 'revised and updated' edition of his *Diritto finanziario, Corso tenuto nell'anno accademico 1927–28,* Tenconi, Milan, can be found in the Library of the Law Faculty of the University of Naples (shelf mark XII G11, XIV G 41, and another copy at H 1287 Sezione di Finanza Pubblica of the Dipartimento di Scienze Internazionalistiche). Therefore, the 3rd edition of Ranelletti's work, printed by Tenconi in Milan, had a wide distribution and it can still be found in many libraries, in contradiction to what Falsitta states in 'La sistemazione del Diritto finanziario …', p. 989.

19. See Griziotti, 'Sul metodo di ricerca e critica negli studi finanziari', in *La riforma sociale,* n. 2, 1933. His works on methodology were also reprinted in *Studi di scienza delle finanze e diritto finanziario,* Milan, 1956.

§1.03 THE TESTING AND ANALYSIS OF RANELLETTI'S METHODOLOGY, CONDUCTED BY THE SCHOLARS OF THE NEAPOLITAN SCHOOL

Ranelletti's methodology gave birth to a school, which has developed and continued during the 20th century at the University of Naples.

[A] Francesco D'Alessio

Francesco D'Alessio[20] wrote a *Corso di Diritto finanziario,*[21] printed by Jovene in Naples in 1937. As stated on the cover page, he was Professor for Public Finance Law As stated on the cover page, he was Professor for Public Finance Law and Public Finance at the University of Naples.

D'Alessio was the first professor at the Law Faculty of the University of Naples who went on to apply the method developed by the pioneer Ranelletti.[22]

D'Alessio thinks that, within the framework of national Public Law, the interrelationship between taxes, management of income and its distribution must be studied from a social point of view as well as from the point of view of the political choices, which caused them.

Public Finance Law, says D'Alessio, differs from Administrative Law and should be an independent subject in University curricula, not because it is an autonomous branch of Law, but because its aim is to examine in depth and together Public Finance and the rules governing the financial activity of public authorities.

D'Alessio emphasized the reasons why we must distinguish Public Finance Law from Administrative Law: Public Finance Law had not yet achieved scientific autonomy and had some relevant relationship with Public Finance and other political and social sciences on which the legislator founded his choices. Although D'Alessio further developed Ranelletti's methodology, it can be said that both were less interested in developing a method and much more in its concrete application.

---

20. Born at Montescaglioso (Basilicata) in 1886.
21. This book can be found in the Library of the Law Faculty of the University of Naples (shelf mark XIV. G.47). In the first five chapters, the author deals in depth with the general principles of Public Finance Law: 1) Concept - Nature and aims of Public Finance Law; 2) Relationships between Public Finance Law and other branches of the Law; 3) The sources of Public Finance Law; 4) The effects of Public Finance Rules and their interpretation; 5) The subjects of Public Finance Law relationships. Public Finance Administration and its organs. In the sixth chapter, he examines in particular the specific issue of State incomes. We may conclude, therefore, that Falsitta, is incorrect when in 'La sistemazione del Diritto finanziario ...', p. 988, he states that D'Alessio is a member of the Tax Law School, rather than of the Public Finance Law School.
22. Falsitta in 'La sistemazione del Diritto finanziario ...',p. 988, pointed out that 'if we accept the idea of a [Ranelletti method], we may say that D'Alessio is a scholar who may well have accepted this method'. At the same time, Falsitta noticed that D'Alessio did not accept Ranelletti's method as a whole, but modified it according to his own experience and thinking, giving new impulse to its development.

[B] Gustavo Ingrosso

Gustavo Ingrosso[23] was Professor of State Accounting (1943–52) and of Public Finance and Public Finance Law (1949–52) at the Law Faculty of the University of Naples. He published an exhaustive volume, *Diritto finanziario* in Naples in 1954 (printed by Jovene),[24] in which he summarized his previous *Istituzioni di Diritto finanziario*, published in three volumes between 1935 and 1946.

Ingrosso held that the State's financial activity may be considered political from a subjective point of view, but that it also has an objective political connotation because it is functional to the goals of the State.[25] In addition, he states,[26] the procedures used by the State to achieve its goals cannot be examined apart from their economic implications.

He is of the opinion[27] that the State must use the procedures of an economic agent in the pursuit of its goals and needs.

Ingrosso, after describing in detail[28] the political essence of the State's financial activities and the differences between Public Finance and Private Economics, reaches the conclusion that financial management is a *legal activity* and that, therefore,[29] Public Finance Law must have the dignity of a scientific subject.

He explained[30] that as Public Finance Law is based on economic and social grounds, so is Public Finance founded on the knowledge of its concrete application in law, for a better understanding of financial phenomena.

According to Ingrosso,[31] laws are the result of ideas, needs and tendencies with which scholars and experts of Public Finance have confronted themselves, and retain echoes and remnants of their inquiries. At the end he concludes that,[32] although the subject is unitary, the theoretical study of Public Finance Law, which is a genuine Law subject, must be distinct from the other financial subjects, which have a social connotation.

While Griziotti thought that finance was a unitary system to be studied at the same time from a legal and from an economic perspective, Ingrosso paid considerable attention to a complex of financial phenomena that characterize financial economy and that are part of positive law. Ingrosso identified several different financial phenomena, economic in character but governed by financial Law, thus representing a juridical action related to a financial phenomenon. Although he considers the subject from a

23. Born in Gallipoli in Puglia in 1877.
24. This book can be found in the Library of the Law Faculty of the University of Naples. Its content deals with general and special issues of Taxation. As a result we may say that Falsitta, 'La sistemazione del Diritto finanziario….', p. 988, is inaccurate when he states that Ingrosso was a member of the Tax Law School and not of the Public Finance Law School.
25. *Diritto finanziario…*, p. 5.
26. *Ibid.*, p. 6.
27. *Ibid.*, p. 6.
28. *Ibid.*, p. 7.
29. *Ibid.*, p. 8.
30. *Ibid.*, p. 9.
31. *Ibid.*, p. 9.
32. *Ibid.*, p. 10.

unitary perspective, from a theoretical point of view, he makes a distinction between Public Finance Law and Public Finance.

Although he may be using a different terminology, he shares the methodological and conceptual approach of Ranelletti and D'Alessio.

Ranelletti sees in a unitary financial phenomenon distinct legal and financial aspects, and D'Alessio seems to support this point of view. Ingrosso describes as common 'subject' what Ranelletti and D'Alessio had defined as 'phenomenon'.

Ingrosso points out that the State financial activity is instrumental with respect to all other State functions. He derives the scientific autonomy of Public Finance Law from the need to think of economic science as its fundamental basis, as Ranelletti and D'Alessio had already thought. The scientific autonomy of Public Finance Law[33] from Administrative Law has its reason in a methodological criterion of *quantity* (its intrinsic capacity of theoretical increment, due also to didactic necessity) and of *quality*, on the assumption that its development occurs along a consistent guideline. This guideline goes along the principle of organic unity, which in Public Finance Law is represented by the economic factor.

In addition, Ingrosso pointed out some of the fundamental aspects on which the relationships between Tax Law and Public Finance Law are based. He reasons that Tax Law, which is only a part of Public Finance Law, is a particular and specific branch of Law, characterized by *specification* or *particularism*. But it is theoretically and rationally necessary to consider to what extent and in what way taxes are a part of modern economic and social life. By focusing on the specificity and particularity of Tax Law, compared to Public Finance Law, Ingrosso has brought about an important theoretical development, insisting on their common economic basis on Public Finance Law.

It is easy to appreciate the notable progress achieved by Ingrosso's efforts to deepen and connect the search for the economic components of Public Finance Law, whose scientific autonomy he had recognized, in contrast with his predecessor D'Alessio.

D'Alessio and Ingrosso experimented Ranelletti's method and enriched it with their personal contribution, thanks to their analysis of fundamental aspects of Public Finance Law.

[C] Romanelli-Grimaldi

Romanelli-Grimaldi[34] also paid significant attention to the problem of method[35] to be followed in the economic interpretation of Public Finance Law, but reached opposite

33. *Ibid.*, p. 14.
34. Born in Naples in 1904.
35. His lecture 'Metodologia del Diritto finanziario', which was part of the course on 'Scienza delle finanze e diritto finanziario' at the Law Faculty of the University of Naples was published in *Rassegna di Diritto pubblico* in 1960, edited by Alfonso Tesauro, professor of Constitutional Law at the same Faculty. In the first part of this complex lecture he criticized Griziotti's methodology and in the second part he made his contribution to the development of the correct

results to Griziotti's thinking. He arrived at this important outcome thanks to the information on the method that he could find in Ranelletti's, D'Alessio's and Ingrosso's works, who had taught the same subject at the Faculty of Law in the first half of the 20th century.

Ranelletti makes a distinction between Public Finance Law and Public Finance since the first has as its object Public Finance in a legal perspective.[36] As mentioned before, Ranelletti, as well as Griziotti, had a unitary vision of public finance, but, in contrast with Griziotti, Ranelletti thought that Economics was the fundamental basis for a better understanding of the legal aspects of the phenomenon.

Initially Romanelli-Grimaldi accepted Ranelletti's point of view, but later, he questioned the unity of the phenomenon, as did D'Alessio and Ingrosso. He pointed out that the word 'phenomenon' might have two meanings. In a technical perspective, it is something whose cause or origin may be the subject of scientific research. This meaning is suitable in the case of Public Finance, which, as any abstract, mathematical and economic science, has as its object the study of the origin and the interconnections of finance 'per se'.

The 'phenomenon' of Public Finance Law, on the other hand, is 'what appears' in the world of Law, which is different from the real social appearance; by 'finance' jurists understand only a general and exterior identification of the science.

Romanelli-Grimaldi thought that, if Public Finance and Public Finance Law have as the object of their study substantially different purposes, the adoption of Griziotti's 'syncretistic' method creates the drawback of a study that has to do with heterogeneous subjects. He warned that in the conceptual system devised by Griziotti there is the danger that the financial authorities and judges may take advantage of the law, by not applying it or by reforming it, since the will of the interpreter may prevail over that of the legislator, and thus make the interpreter the creator of financial laws. He hoped that Public Finance Law might be separated from Public Finance[37] and become part of the Law of Science.

Romanelli-Grimaldi explained that his rejection of the 'syncretistic' method did not mean the denial of the role of Public Finance and of other social sciences as legitimate disciplines different from Law.

Romanelli-Grimaldi's fundamental idea was to keep a clear distinction between the two different financial phenomena, the first of which was clearly a law phenomenon while the other was an economic phenomenon. He therefore adjusted the method to reflect this distinction and, taking into account Ranelletti's and Griziotti's studies, placed great emphasis on tax obligation and on the functional interpretation of Tax Law.

method. Falsitta, in 'La sistemazione del Diritto finanziario ...', p. 988, is again incorrect when he states that Romanelli-Grimaldi is a member of the Tax Law School, rather than of the Public Finance Law School.

36. See Falsitta, 'La sistemazione del Diritto finanziario....', p. 973.

37. Romanelli-Grimaldi, by supporting the idea of the need to separate Public Finance from Public Finance Law, as Griziotti had already proposed, anticipated the reform that would take place in Italy forty years later.

He rejected, therefore, the antithetical extremisms of stressing the importance of economic aspects, as did Grizotti, as well as of their rejection, as did the formalists.

During his stay at the University of Naples, Romanelli-Grimaldi, using also the notes which Ranelletti had used for the publication of the second edition of his *Diritto finanziario per l'anno accademico 1923–24,* began writing a complete introduction to the reprinting of Ranelletti's work *Diritto finanziario for the academic year 1927–28,* 3rd edition, which was published by Tenconi in Milan.

Unfortunately, he died in 1963, before he/she could finish the writing of the introduction, and, as a consequence, Ranelletti's *Diritto finanziario* was not reprinted.

[D] Vincenzo Sica

Romanelli-Grimaldi's contribution allowed his successors to the Chair of 'Public Finance and Public Finance Law' at the Law Faculty of the University of Naples to follow in his path. They were Vincenzo Sica, Professor of Constitutional Law and Giuseppe Abbamonte, Professor of Constitutional and Administrative Law. Both of them have made important scientific advances. They showed that the substantial and unitary methodological concept has its very roots in the contemporary Constitution, thus giving it a new vitality.

Approaching the issue from an experimental perspective, Vincenzo Sica,[38] wrote a complete work whose title was *Bilancio dello Stato e programmazione economica, Profili giuridici,* Naples, 1964, printed by Liguori.[39]

After conducting an exhaustive analysis of the Constitution, he came to the conclusion that in a modern State the State organization does not have itself as its aim, but is bound to pursue relevant economic objectives, through the use of State accounting, taxes and public expenditures, within the framework of an overall economic policy. The State, therefore, can be examined from the perspective of its economic activities.

[E] Giuseppe Abbamonte

Giuseppe Abbamonte[40] wrote a work of great scientific value, *Corso di Diritto finanziario,*[41] whose title was changed to *Principi di Diritto finanziario*[42] in the following editions. He examined the State's financial activity, as described in the Italian

38. Born at Castel San Giorgio (Salerno) in 1924.
39. This book can be found at the Library of the *Dipartimento di Storia economica* of the University of Naples (coll. SE.059.07.19). Its chapters deal with 1) General Principles. 2) State Accounting. 3) The economic planning. 4) Relationship between State balance sheet and economic planning. Undoubtedly, Falsitta, 'La sistemazione del Diritto finanziario....', p. 988, makes a mistake when he states that even Sica is a member of the Tax Law School and not of the Public Finance Law School.
40. Born in Naples in 1923.
41. Liguori, Napoli, 1969.
42. Liguori, Napoli, 1975. It was last reprinted in 1993 and can be found in the Library of the Law Faculty of the University of Naples (coll. XIV. B. 256).

Constitution, pointing out the importance of political reasons which lead to a choice that takes as many economic and technical implications as possible into account.

Abbamonte examined the non-fiscal purposes of any fiscal rule, paying attention, in the eventuality of a judicial review of its Constitutionality, to the need of researching the consequences of the application of such fiscal rule on the national economy and the relationship between income and expenses.

He dealt with the methodological problem of the relationship between Public Finance and Public Finance Law, paying particular attention to the limits of each discipline. He pointed out the importance of Public Finance to decide whether a law is in accordance with the constitutional principal of equal treatment.[43]

Abbamonte, following on Sica's path, made a significant contribution with his systematic interpretation of the principles of ability-to-pay, gradual ability to pay and substantial equality. In his view their aim is income redistribution, as well as balance and public expenditure, through the coordination between their *ratio* and the reasons, which characterize any State economy.[44]

---

43. Falsitta, 'La sistemazione del Diritto flnanziario ...', p. 986, gives three examples to demonstrate that Neapolitan professors would always be interested in Tax Law more than in Public Finance Law. The first example is Pugliese, who never taught in Naples and who, like his colleague Jarach, moved to Latin America. This is an interesting example for those who wish to study the School of Pavia to ascertain whether Pugliese's *Istituzioni di Diritto finanziario* really dealt with Public Finance Law rather that with Tax Law. However, Falsitta seems to make reference to Pugliese's *Istituzioni di Diritto finanziario - Diritto tributario* published in Padua in 1931. The second example is D'Alessio, professor at the University of Naples. Falsitta himself, as pointed out before, acknowledged his support of Ranelletti's method. Falsitta's third example is Abbamonte (p. 988). According to him, Abbamonte's work deals with Tax Law and not with Public Finance Law, and to support his theory he says that Abbamonte always quotes scholars of Tax Law.
    In reality, after 205 pages in which Abbamonte deals only with Public Finance Law issues, he examines the general issues of Tax Law, from the methodological perspective of Public Finance Law. In the remaining 89 pages there are only five footnotes where he quotes only Thon, Giorgianni, Forti, Russo and De Bono, only two of whom are scholars of Tax Law. Abbamonte, on the contrary, in the first 205 pages of his volume, in which he deals with Public Finance Law, quotes above all scholars of Public Finance Law and of Public Finance, such as Griziotti (12, 35, 193), Ingrosso (44, 122, 125, 127), Romanelli-Grimaldi (36), Sica (8, 127, 135), Talice (127), Buscema (102), Di Renzo (122), Zingali and Amato, (14), D'Avanzo (45), Corano (58), Donvito (58), Petrini (58), Pietro-Boni (58), Provini and Sechi (61), Barna (24), Brochier (24), Laufenburguer (24), Miller (24), Predetti (24), Gangemi (15), Cosciani (29), Vitagliano (30), Pesenti (33), Arena (36), Del Vecchio (36), D'Albergo (36) Pedone (24) and Esposito De Falco (36). Ranelletti's book *Diritto finanziario* has had a profound influence on Abbamonte's volume, who cites him indirectly through Ingrosso, Romanelli-Grimaldi and Sica, who published their works after Ranelletti and before Abbamonte.
    If this explanation is not sufficient to show that Abbamonte's book deals with Public Finance Law, it may be useful to read what Abbamonte says in answer to Mauricio Plazas Vega: 'He ahí el imperativo de profundizar sobre el contexto económico y de tener conciencia sobre la interdisciplinariedad del Derecho Financiero público. De ahí también la miopía de quienes idolatran el Derecho tributario' [Amatucci-D'Amati (ed.), *Historia del Derecho de la Hacíenda Pública y del Derecho Tributario en Italia, El aporte del pensamiento jurídico financiero de la Italia Meridional,* Temis, Bogotà, 2004, XXI.]
    See Abbamonte, *Principi....*, pp. 8, 10, 22 and 26.
44. See in particular Abbamonte, *Principi...*, p. 34. Abbamonte has made a great contribution in the writing of Tax rules in the Spanish Consitution of 1978. See Amatucci, 'La finanza pubblica nella Costituzione spagnola del 1978', in Riv. *dir.fin.sc.fin.*, 1980, I, p. 531.

Abbamonte's best contribution[45] is the construction of the issue of the judicial review of constitutionality through the analysis of the economic effects of the rules of financial law.

In addition, he examined the relationship between Public Finance Law and the other branches of Law, as well as the problem of the administrative sources of Public Finance Law, as well as the most important methodological issue, that is the interpretation of financial rules.

He says that as the legislator, when dealing with Tax Law, uses concepts of Public Finance to make his choices, so the interpreter must use the same concepts for a better understanding of those laws.

Abbamonte thought that the general principles of Public Finance must be similar to those of other branches of Law.[46] At the end of his analysis of the method he came to the conclusion that a 'logical unity in the Public Finance system' exists.[47]

On the basis of his predecessors' works, Abbamonte further developed the method and applied it in the interpretation of fundamental principles. We can say that the major difference between Ranelletti's book and that of Abbamonte's is that the first is the starting point, while the latter is the completion of the development of the method.

Ranelletti, with his scientific and teaching activity laid down the basic principles, which have their roots in the cultural background developed in previous centuries. Ranelletti developed his method over the course of several decades and offered it to the other scholars who supported it and made it more efficient, by applying it or by perfecting his methodology.

The Neapolitan professors of Public Finance and Public Finance Law, in particular, were very interested in Ranelletti's method, since they had the same cultural background in common with Ranelletti. Throughout the 20th century they continued to develop his method, while working at the University of Naples and publishing books and articles dealing with Public Finance Law there.[48]

45. He wrote the famous *Processo costituzionale italiano,* Jovene, Napoli, 1962.
46. Abbamonte, *Principi...,* p. 190.
47. *Ibid.,* Chs III, IV, V, e VI.
48. In contrast to Falsitta's theory, 'La sistemazione del Diritto flnanziario ...', p. 988, Neapolitan Professors were members of the Neapolitan School and not of a vague Italian School. The University of Rosario in Bogotà is publishing in Spanish Ranelletti's and Abbamonte's works, as well as all the works of the Neapolitan School in a special Series, edited by Mauricio Plazas Vega, who has also written an interesting article dealing with the Neapolitan School and published in *Riv.Dir.Fin.eSc.Fin. Dir. Fin.e Sc. Fin.,* 2003, I, p. 104, whose title is 'Il concetto di tributo alla luce del rapporto tra il Diritto fi nanziario pubblico ed il Diritto tributario e tra il Diritto comunitario ed il Diritto nazionale'.

§1.04 THE RELATIONSHIP BETWEEN THE HARD-LINE CONCEPTION OF THE ITALIAN SCHOOL OF PAVIA AND THE SUBSTANTIVE VIEW OF THE SCHOOL OF NAPLES

At the same time, however, an interesting analysis was being conducted at the Universities of Pavia and of Milan, with the Method as its object. This was done thanks to the contribution of famous professors from those Universities.

The creators of the two methodologies of Public Finance Law, that is Benvenuto Griziotti, founder of the School in Pavia, and Oreste Ranelletti, founder of the Neapolitan School, had taught in those Universities since 1920. While the first supported the so-called syncretistic method that upheld the fusion between Economics and Law studies, the latter was in favour of a substantial theory according to which the research activity of a jurist must be kept away from that of an economist, even though Economics is the basis of the Science of Law.

Dino Jarach[49] and Mario Pugliese,[50] two of Grizotti's students, moved to Latin America, where they taught and published some works, which are fundamental for the science of Law in those countries.

Ezio Vanoni,[51] another student of Grizotti, wrote an excellent book on the interpretation of Finance Rule. It is a really interesting methodological analysis of Tax Law made by the same author of *Lezioni di Scienza delle finanze e diritto finanziario.*

Undoubtedly, Ranelletti influenced the professors who taught after him at the Università Cattolica of Milan, through his teachings and his two books on *Diritto finanziario.* We must also mention another famous professor of the University of Milan, who made an important contribution in the field of teaching and research, Achille Donato Giannini, who was born in 1888 in Foggia (Puglia) and who received his Law Degree from the University of Naples in 1909.[52]

It is wrong to think that economic analysis of law is useful only in countries with common law legal systems, where the judges create law[53]. In Europe, indeed, after those first decades, it has been accepted by the Doctrine of countries with civil law legal systems[54].

49. Born in Milan in 1915, from May 1941 he taught at the University of Cordoba and from 1973 at the University of Buenos Aires. His fundamental work is *Finanzas Públicas y Derecho Tributario,* Abeledo Pierrot, Buenos Aires, 2nd edn, 1996.
50. Born in Bologna in 1903, he wrote *Lafinanza edi suoi compiti extrafiscali negli Stati moderni,* Padova, 1932 and *Istituzioni di Diritto finanziario – Diritto tributario,* Padova, 1931.
51. Born at Morbegno (Sondrio) in 1903 he wrote *Natura e interpretazione delle leggi tributarie,* Padova, 1932 and *Lezioni di Scienza delle finanze e diritto finanziario,* Roma, 1934.
52. Arturo Carlo Jemolo, in *Mio caro Giannini, vecchio amico da quarant'anni,* an Introduction to *Studi in onore di Achille Donato Giannini,* Milano, 1961 described him thus: 'Born in Foggia on January 2, 1888, he studied at the Law faculty of Naples, in a period of great splendor for that University. His masters were Enrico Pessina and Federico Persico as well as Carlo Fadda, Pasquale Melucci, Francesco Nitti and Augusto Graziani'.
53. Calabresi, *Cosa è l'analisi economica del diritto?, supra.*
54. Minda, *Teorie postmoderne del diritto,* Bologna, 2001.

Economic Analysis of Law has spread in the European legal systems with a Roman law formation, in which the traditional issue is interpretative[55] and, consequently, the jurist's task is the adoption of a correct method of interpretation. Through Economic Analysis of Law, the economic approach has been fascinating for the Roman law scholars[56] because this method identifies in the social and economic goals of the law the instrument to determine the meaning of the legislative text.

The European jurists, even in a Roman law system which is not based on the 'precedent' rule and in which the result of a ruling sends anyway signals to the natural and legal persons concerned, had already underlined the interactions among economics, sociology and law at the beginning of the twentieth century, although especially with reference to the specific area of the financial legal system, in general, and to the tax one, in particular. At that time, indeed, an interesting scientific experience started in Europe concerning the connections between financial law and economic research because the first one is directly connected with an economic discipline, the Public Finance.

Meaningful is the contribution of the legislation and the doctrine in Germany and Spain as well as the hard-line conception of the School of Pavia and the teleological-economic view of the School of Naples.

In those first decades of the twentieth century, it was believed in Italy that it was necessary to study financial law with the contribution of the public finance but it was not clear how to achieve the cooperation between these sciences.

Benvenuto Griziotti[57], founder of the School of Pavia, developed the hard-line method of the finance law study. Through it the juridical, economic, technical and social aspects of the financial phenomenon must be studied simultaneously by a single scholar, the 'financier', who is jurist, economist, technician and sociologist, together. According to Francesco Forte[58], Griziotti laid the groundwork of Economic Analysis of Law fifty years in advance of his birth in the United States. According to Griziotti, the interdisciplinary work consists in the comprehensive study of financial facts and this brought him to develop the method of functional interpretation of financial law rules. This is a general principle that concerns every juridical branch, such as commercial law and administrative law, which are particularly suitable for economic analysis of law. The teleological interpretation, which aims to consider the purpose pursued by the legislator, is a fundamental part of Griziotti's functional interpretation but it does not represent the only one. The economic element of Griziotti's functional analysis, developed on the methodological level of the study of law, is the *'economic reality principle'*. The juridical institutions must be examined on a substantial level. This is the

55. Cooter Gordley, *Law and Economics in Civil Law Countries*, International Review of Law and Economics, 1991.
56. Alpa, Pulitini, Rodota' and Romani (edited by) *Interpretazione giuridica e analisi economica*, Milano, 1982.
57. *Principi di politica, diritto e scienza delle finanze*, Padova, 1919, *Sul metodo di ricerca e critica negli studi finanziari*, La riforma sociale, n. 2, 1933, republished in Studi di scienza delle finanze e diritto finanziario, II, Milano, 1956, p. 94.
58. *Il contributo seminale di Benvenuto Griziotti all'analisi economica del diritto*, Rivista di Diritto Finanziario e Scienza delle Finanze, 2006, I, p. 435.

valuable contribution brought by Griziotti long before this principle was acknowledged by the Constitution. He used the *adjusting* interpretation, even though the economic reality principle is sufficient to identify 'economic law', which is not rigorously legally defined.

The School of Pavia aroused on the basis of an ideological stimulus, like the School of Chicago. Griziotti's view of the financial phenomenon was politic, whereas the one of his master Luigi Einaudi and of De Viti De Marco was economic and the one of several followers of Vilfredo Pareto was sociological. Einaudi was concerned that the economist could get lost in the tortuous maze of the real cases stated by single laws and could neglect the solution of fundamental problems. Griziotti's studies were inspired by the interventionist State model, so, on the basis of the economic analysis of tax laws, he affirmed their analogical and adjusting interpretation. Einaudi, who inclined towards a liberal State model, was not completely in favour of Griziotti's thesis. Griziotti's economic analysis of law represented, indeed, the result of a brilliant intuition, however, like each groundbreaking contribution, it contained some imperfections: it was founded on an ideological premise, it did not accurately distinguish the de jure *condendo* point of view from the de jure *condito* one and did not accept rigorously juridical positivism and the statutory reserve[59].

The interdisciplinary approach was considered almost an heresy by the Italian jurists, guardians of the dogmatic purity, and by the economists fearful of surrendering to non-scientific contributions and of losing the control of the 'Public Finance and Financial Law' professorships, a subject introduced in the nineteenth century which remained intact until the end of the twentieth century.

The Italian Oreste Ranelletti published a fundamental work of administrative law[60] in Naples, between 1912 and 1915, where he taught the same subject at the local juridical Faculty of University Federico II. Then he became professor of 'Financial Law and Public Finance' at the State university of Milan, where in 1928, he published the third edition of the first Italian financial law handbook[61], in which, despite excluding the fusion between the legal and economic investigation, he underlined their close connection. He specified, indeed, that the economic science must be 'basis and assumption' of financial law studies. This means that Ranelletti's view, like the contemporaneous contributions of Enno Becker and Benvenuto Griziotti, represents the financial legal system built on economic foundations, anticipating the origin of Economic *Analysis of* Law. Consequently juridical research does not merge with the economic one, but has to take the last one into account. Thus Ranelletti, unlike Griziotti, considered a law and economics scholar who studied law, using, however, a juridical method.

Achille Donato Giannini, who had Ranelletti himself as a commissioner of his competitive examination to professorship, was firstly author of three financial law

59. Forte, *Il contributo seminale di Benvenuto Griziotti all'analisi economica del diritto, supra.*
60. *Principi di diritto amministrativo, Introduzione e nozioni fondamentali*, 1st volume, Scienze giuridiche e sociali, Napoli, 1912 and *Del diritto amministrativo in generale. L'organizzazione della Pubblica Amministrazione. L'azione amministrativa*, 2nd volume, ivi, Napoli, 1915.
61. *Diritto finanziario*, 3rd edition, Milano 1928.

handbooks, of which the first was contemporary to the third edition of Ranelletti's financial law volume, and then of several editions of the most famous 'Tax law Institutions'[62].

The investigations of D'Alessio, Ingrosso, Romanelli-Grimaldi, Sica and Abbamonte were not founded on an ideological assumption, they considered only the de jure condito matters and were linked to Positivism and to the statutory reserve principle, increasing the value of the law content according to the logic afterwards expressed by Arthur Kaufmann[63]. The School of Naples refuted the understandable defects present in the broad-minded approach of Griziotti's groundbreaking theory, which represents, however, a valuable introduction and continued to study in depth the theological-economic method[64], which is integrated by Economic Analysis *of* Law, and increased the value of the reason of its existence[65]. The School of Naples refuted also the narrow-minded approach of formalism, which denies each relevance of every economic content of the tax rule. Rightly, Gustavo Zagrebelsky[66] observes that a doctrine completely dosed within legal formulas, without any awareness of the phenomena that guide the normative force, will produce 'eccentric' works of 'mere jurists', without any interest. The economic aims' study of the financial rule and also of the tax rule, allows to understand their real meaning and their applicability to concrete cases, and to fulfil efficiently the constitutionality review function through the verification of their effects.

In Europe[67] in the 1960s and 1970s of the twentieth century, the jurists continued to develop researches of dogmatic nature, with reference to disciplines different from financial law in general and tax law in particular, which were indifferent to the explanations of the juridical phenomenon through the Economic Analysis of *Law* method. Only some of them posed unproductive issues about the alleged conservative nature of this method, which was considered a cultural attitude and that, indeed, in the United States was deeply rooted.

---

62. The 9th and last edition edited by Vincenzo M. Romanelli Grimaldi, was published in Milan in 1965.
63. *Rechtsphilosophie*, 2nd ed., Munchen, 1997.
64. See Fichera, *Imposizione ed extrafiscalità nel sistema costituzionale*, Napoli, 1973; Perrone Capano, *L'imposizione e l'ambiente, Trattato di Diritto tributario* (edited by Amatucci), *Annuario*, Padova, 2001, p. 121; Ingrosso, *Divisione e classificazione nella Scienza giuridica finanziaria*, Napoli, 1977; Pace, *La legge finanziaria*, Napoli, 1983 and Amatucci, *L'interpretazione della norma di diritto finanziario*, Napoli, 1965; *L'interpretazione della legge tributaria, Trattato di Diritto tributario*, (edited by the same author) *Annuario*, Padova, 2001, p. 255; *Funzioni e disciplina del bilancio dello Stato*, Napoli, 1970; *L'ordinamento giuridico della finanza pubblica*, 8th edition, Napoli, 2007.
65. S. Tommaso D'Aquino, professor of Theology at the University of Naples Federico II since 1272, specified that the law does not represent Law itself but a certain reason of law, (*Summa Theologica* I/II: question 57, article 1).
66. *Il diritto mite. Legge, diritto, giustizia*, Torino, 7th ed., 1992.
67. Cooter, Mattei, Monateri, Pardolesi, Ulen, Il *Mercato delle regole. Analisi economica del diritto civile, supra*.

§1.05 THE PAVIA AND MILAN SCHOOLS OF TAX LAW AND THEIR RELATIONSHIP TO RANELLETTI'S SCIENTIFIC ACHIEVEMENTS

In the academic year 1924–1925 Giannini was Professor of 'Tax Law and Public Finance Law' and of 'State Accounting' at the recently founded Law Faculty, of the Università Cattolica of Milan until 1936, when he was appointed Professor of Administrative Law. In 1943 he was given the chair of 'Public Finance and Public Finance Law' at the same Faculty. In 1947 he went back to Puglia, where he was born, to teach at the Law Faculty of the University of Bari where he worked for several years and where he was also Dean until he retired in 1958.[68]

Furthermore, Giorgio Tesoro taught at the University of Bari; he wrote *Appunti di Diritto finanziario,* (Orme, 1936) and an article 'Sull'autonomia del Diritto finanziario', (Bari, 1936). Together with A.D. Giannini, he directed the *Rivista italiana di Diritto finanziario,* published in Bari, which merged in 1940 with *Rivista di Diritto finanziario e scienza delle finanze* directed by Griziotti.

During his stay in Milan A.D. Giannini published three interesting books, that is *Lezioni di Diritto finanziario e tributario,* published in 1927,[69]*Elementi di Diritto finanziario e contabilità di Stato,* (printed by Giuffrè) in 1934,[70] and *Elementi di Diritto finanziario,* (printed also by Giuffrè), in 1945.[71] In his first book he analyses Tax Law and in the second book State Accounting, which together constitute Public Finance Law; in both books he presents a unitary idea of these two subjects and, in his third book, he reviews the same issue in detail.

It is very interesting to examine the relationship between this famous scholar and Ranelletti. A.D. Giannini was born ten years before the publication of Ranelletti's article 'Natura giuridica dell'imposta' in the review *Municipio italiano,* in 1898.[72] A.D. Giannini was appointed Professor of Administrative Law in 1925. On the occasion of his appointment Oreste Ranelletti'[73] delivered a wonderful public lecture. This means that A.D. Giannini's scientific standing was still developing, while Ranelletti's was already mature and huge.

---

68. See Micheli, 'Achille Donato Giannini', in *Riv. dir.fin. sc.fin.,* 1965, I, p. 191.
69. This can be found at the Library of the Università Cattolica, III, 2-H-33, Deposito Centrale, Largo Gemelli, 1,Milano.
70. This can be found at the Library of the Università Cattolica, X-VIII-G-28, Deposito centrale, Largo Gemelli, 1 Milano.
71. This can be found at the same Library of the Università Cattolica, shelf mark Pajardi- DI-460-6, Sala Giurisprudenza, 1st floor, Viale Emilia Parmense, 84 Piacenza. A.D. Giannini's first volume *Lezioni di Diritto finanziario e tributario* printed in 1927 was published at the same time as Ranelletti's work, *Lezioni di Dirittofinanziario per l'anno acc. 1925-26* printed by Tenconi, Milan. Nevertheless Ranelletti had begun working on a Method for Public Finance Law some decades earlier, since his first work on this subject was *Natura giuridica dell'imposta* published 1898; he went on writing 'La distinzione degli atti di impresa e di gestione', in *Studi di diritto in onore di V. Scialoja,* I, Milano, 1905,705, and 'La funzione di controllo della Corte dei Conti', in *Riv. Corte Conti,* 1912, 52, as well as the first two editions of his *Diritto finanziario,* printed for students' use only before A. D. Giannini's book was published in 1927. Falsitta, on the contrary, thinks that Ranelletti's book was not the first work dealing with Public Finance Law, since, in his view, it was published in the same year as Giannini's book (1925–26).
72. Reprinted in *Diritto e pratica tributaria,* 1974, I, p. 789.
73. Arturo Carlo Jemolo, *Mio caro Giannini…*

A.D. Giannini accepted Ranelletti's method.[74] He decided to publish three volumes of *Diritto finanziario* during the years 1927–1945, which constitute the central years of his life (1888–1965). He completed his work while teaching Public Finance Law as well as Tax Law and State Accounting at the Università Cattolica, and also after he was appointed full professor, still at the Università Cattolica, and then at the University of Bari. Giannini's scientific works influenced the Neapolitan School, with which he shared common roots.

A.D. Giannini analysed Tax Law with the Method he himself had created until 1945, when he published his three volumes on *Diritto finanziario.* He wrote some valuable works, such as *La classificazione delle imposte nel Diritto tributario,* in *Studi dedicati alla memoria di Pier Paolo Zanzucchi,* Milan, 1927 and Il *rapporto giuridico di imposta in* 1937. His *Concetti fondamentali del diritto tributario* published in 1956[75] is also very interesting. In the 9th edition of his very famous handbook *Istituzioni di Diritto tributario,*[76] he states that Public Finance Laws is like a guide for the legislator and can sometimes be used for the interpretation of tax statutes; nevertheless, he rejected the so-called functional interpretation supported by Griziotti.

The 9th edition of his *Istituzioni* was published in Milan in 1965. He died in that same year. A serious illness prevented him from studying during the last period of his life. This edition was edited first by Romanelli-Grimaldi,[77] who died in 1963, and then by Enzo Pace,[78] who, in the 1972 edition, added an Appendix dealing with the new Tax System, which was also added to the reprint of the 9th edition.

Giannini's works on Tax Law have a high scientific value, recognized even abroad, thanks to his cultural acumen which he acquired whilst studying Public Finance Law.[79] He has therefore shown the right approach, fitting for a scholar of Tax Law.

Even the great Spanish scholar of Public Finance Law, Sainz de Bujanda,[80] was fascinated by Giannini's works and translated it into Spanish, thus influencing the draft of the *Ley General Tributaria* in 1963. As they prepared their Tax Code for Latin America (MCTAL), this law was considered by professors Valdés Costa,[81] from Uruguay, Gomes De Sousa, from Brazil and Giuliani Fonrouge, from Argentina as an example to be followed. Thanks to Sainz de Bujanda, as well as Pugliese and Jarach, A.D. Giannini's and Griziotti's works were introduced in the above countries, which already had a tradition of Roman Law.

74. A.D. Giannini, Il *rapporto giuridico di imposta,* Milano, 1937, p. 6, deals with the economic effects of taxes. He examines the ultimate aims of taxes, underlining the fact that the fiscal aim is not the only purpose of taxes. According to Falsitta, 'La sistemazione del Diritto finanziario..., however, in his comparison between Ranelletti's book and A.D. Giannini's book (p. 981), Giannini never refers to concepts of Public Finance, nor to Finance Economics.
75. Turin, 1956,46, first volume of the *Trattato di diritto tributario,* in 14 volumes.
76. (p. 10) This book was printed for the first time in 1938 and reprinted several times later.
77. See Riv. *Dir. Fin. e Sc. Fin.,* 1965, I, p. 570.
78. He wrote *Legge finanziaria,* Napoli, 1983.
79. There is therefore no 'disconoscimento' of Public Finance Law, as Falsitta states in 'La sistemazione del Diritto finanziario ...', p. 984.
80. *Sistema de Derecho financiero,* two volumes (1977–1985). The Spanish edition of *Istituzioni di diritto tributario* by A.D. Giannini was published in 1957.
81. C. Valdés de Blengo and Sayagué Areco (ed.), *Codigo tributario,* 4th edn, Montevideo, 1994.

Having received his training in the fashion of Ranelletti's scientific personality, Giannini, in his turn, had a profound influence on the professors who taught after him.

In fact, some very famous Tax Law professors such as Pietro Bodda,[82] Renato Alessi,[83] Enrico Allorio[84] and Enrico De Mita,[85] followed A.D. Giannini's methodology, while teaching Public Finance and Public Finance Law at the Law Faculty of the Università Cattolica.

Instead of simply conducting research in the distinct areas of Law and Finance, they preferred to teach Public Finance Law making sure that they followed a correct methodology in their valuable research dealing with Tax Law.

Therefore, these teachers of Public Finance and Public Finance Law may be said to have created a School,[86] which has made a great contribution to the scientific development of Tax Law thanks to the method developed by A.D.Giannini.

The same teaching and scientific experience (and with the same objectives) was shared by some other Tax Law professors, such as Nicola D' Amati of the University of Bari, where A.D. Giannini spent the last ten years of his academic life; Victor Uckmar of the University of Genoa; Gaetano Liccardo of the Second University of Naples and Andrea Parlato of the University of Palermo. They taught Public Finance and Public Finance Law and they too published fundamental works dealing with Tax Law.

D'Amati, thanks to his direct experience with A.D. Giannini, also wrote an interesting survey on Public Finance Law.

Giannantonio Micheli,[87] the head of the Roman School, lived through the same scientific experience. He was Professor of Tax Law and, together with Luigi Einaudi, A.D. Giannini, Salvatore Scoca and Sergio Steve he was an acute and scrupulous Director of the *Rivista di Diritto finanziario e Scienza delle finanze,* founded by Griziotti. Micheli thought that the study of Tax Law could not be separated from a constant analysis of Public Finance Law and Public Finance.

---

82. Born in 1904, he wrote interesting essays dealing with Tax Law, such as *Alcune opinioni in tema di solve et repete,* Torino, 1933, and Il *sostituto d'imposta,* Milano, 1941.
83. Born in 1905, he, together with Gaetano Stammati, wrote the famous *Istituzioni di Diritto tributario,* Torino, 1956 and *Monopoli fiscali: imposte di fabbricazione: dazi doganali,* Torino, 1956.
84. He wrote the well known book *Diritto processuale tributario,* which was reprinted several times (1942–1953- 1955–1969) and *Nuove riflessioni sulla teoria generale del processo tributario,* 1951.
85. Particularly famous are his works *Principi di Diritto tributario,* Milano, 2002, and *Interesse fiscale e tutela del contribuente,* Milano, 1991.
86. Falsitta, in *La sistemazione del Diritto finanziario*… …, thinks that the effort to be a member of a School is a sort of self attribution of a nobility title, and therefore he condemns the research of leaders, schools and heads. Nevertheless Falsitta, who was professor at the University of Pavia and at the University of Milan, was part of the Milan School, which was founded by Giannini. He gave the following title to the 7th chapter of his book (p. 974): 'The Public Finance Law School of the Università Cattolica del Sacro Cuore di Milano… and the role of'founder'of A.D. Giannini, professor of Public Finance Law at the Cattolica for 16 years and one of the 'pioneers' in the birth of Tax Law Science in our Country'.
87. Born in Milan in 1913, he was professor of Tax Law from 1963 at the University of Rome. He wrote 'Diritto tributario e Diritto finanziario' in the *Enciclopedia del Diritto,* Milano, 1964, and also *Cor so di Diritto tributario,* Torino, 1970, whose 7th edition was printed in 1984.

Another great Tax Law Professor, Antonio Berliri, in his book *Principi di Diritto tributario,* Milan, 1952, p. 81, observed that the study and the knowledge of political and economic phenomena are no doubt useful and sometimes necessary in order to appreciate and take into the right consideration the facts on which the legislator has based his choices. While agreeing with the point of view expressed by Massimo While agreeing with the point of view expressed by Massimo Severo Giannini, in 'L'interpretazione e l'integrazione delle leggi tributarie', in *Riv. dir.fin. sc.fin.*, 1941,I, 197, by Luigi Vittorio Berliri in 'Interpretazione delle leggi tributarie', in *Riv. it.dir.fin.*, 1942,71,16 and by Antonio Uckmar in 'Interpretazione funzionale delle norme tributarie', *inDir. prat. trib.*, 1949,I,184, he strongly criticized Griziotti's theory.

According to Antonio Berliri's theory, economic and political reasons related to a single tax or to the whole tax law system may be relevant only in the search of the real intent of the legislator and of the so-called *'ratio legis'.*

M.S. Giannini pointed out the peculiarity of this theory, which is based on a methodology thanks to which the interpretation (or, better, the general application) of Tax laws must be carried out through the study of Public Finance and of financial politics. This means that, in a given social context, the scholar must study the material facts and the political and economic situation on which Tax Laws are based.

Another famous Tax Law professor, Luigi Vittorio Berliri, wrote an interesting book entitled *La giusta imposta,* reprinted in Milan in 1975. In this work, Berliri pays particular attention to the economic basis of any tax. His book begins with an essay written by a great scholar of Public Finance, Luigi Einaudi, who reminds the reader that he also wrote a book about the 'best tax'.

All these great Tax Law professors of the first generation have written, taught or directed Law reviews dealing with Public Finance Law and Public Finance.

They all studied Tax Law following the correct method they had acquired, thanks to their knowledge of Public Finance Law in relation to Public Finance.

The first financial law handbook in German (Grundriss des Finanzerechts) was written by the Austrian Myrbach Rheinfeld in 1906. In Germany, was fundamental the contribution brought from the teleological view of law by Rudolf von Jhering[88] in 1983. In this theoretical context the *Reichsabgabenordnung* of 1919 states at §.1: *'In the interpretation of tax law it is necessary to consider its purpose, its economic significance and the evolution of the actual situation'*[89]. Thus it was legislatively established the *'wirtschaftliche Betrachtungsweise'*, a way of economic consideration of tax law, half a century before *Economic Analysis of Law* aroused in the United States. In Germany, the 1920s represented the first decade, rightly designated as golden, of the new tax law science, which is the main specialized area of financial law. Klaus Tipke[90] observes that after 1933, Germany lost the relevant position it had reached in the systematic elaboration of financial law, owing to the racial laws. The Abgabenordnung's section one of 1977 states at §.3 that: «*the* achievement of tax *revenues can* constitute *a secondary* purpose'; as a consequence the social and economic aim (extra-tax) is in

88. *Der Zweck in Recht*, Leipzig, 1893, Italian translation: *Lo scopo del diritto*, Torino, 1972.
89. Tipke, Lang, *Steuerrecht*, 19th edition., Koln, 2008, p.155.
90. Die Entwicklung von Forschung und Lehre im Steuerrecht, Steuer und Wirtschaft, n. 3, 1981.

general considered as the primary one. The German Constitutional Court[91] stated that the Constitution acknowledges the concept of tax contained in the Abgabenordnung and that the tax law is legitimate if it is able to pursue purposes of economic and social policy which coincide with the constitutionally guaranteed values. In Germany, indeed, the sociological instrument is considered as a social instance that indicates the factual nature of the data from which the survey is carried. Ira Sache ist Wahrheit represents the legal principle that underlines the factual nature of the truth. The Verhaltnissrnrissigkeit spread as Prinzip or Grundsatz, regarding the adherence to the real fact of the tax assessment procedure.

The Spanish Ley General Tributaria of 1963 states at Art. 4 that taxes are instruments, of economic policy and underlines the economic aims of the tax. Fernando Sainz de Bujanda published in the following two decades a fundamental handbook of financial law[92] which gave impulse to the scientific research about this subject in Spain. On this basis, the interpretatión economica of tax law spread in Spain.

§1.06 METHODOLOGICAL RIGOR AS THE FOUNDATION OF THE SCIENTIFIC AUTONOMY OF TAX LAW

Any rigorous scholar needs, therefore, to study Ranelletti's works and those of the other authors mentioned above, who devoted their research efforts to Public Finance Law.

Knowledge of the evolution of the thinking on this subject since its origins and of its most important developments is extremely useful for methodological research. In Germany *(wirtschaftliche Betrachtungsweise)* and in Spain *(interpretacíon economica)*,[93] important contributions were made to the solution of this preliminary question, thanks to the fact that a sound economic background in Public Finance is considered a basis for all Public Finance Legal Systems.

Taxes always have economic consequences and we must presume that the legislator always take them into account. The aim of taxes is always a fiscal one (to produce an income); but they also have other extra-fiscal objectives guaranteed by the Constitution.[94]

As a consequence, therefore, it is necessary to follow a correct methodology, thanks to which a teleological interpretation of Tax law, which guarantees its right application, can be conducted.

91. See Amatucci, *Konzepte der Besteuerung in Italien und in Deutschland,* Steuer und Wirtschaft, 2007, n. 3 and *La ratio economica del concetto giuridico di tributo,* Rivista di diritto tributario internazionale, 2007, p. 37 and Osterloh, tax law professor at Frankfurt am Mein University and judge of the German Constitutional Court, *Il concetto di tributo, la capacità economica e l'interpretazione economica. Concetti base del diritto fiscale nella giurisprudenza della Corte Costituzionale federale tedesca,* Rivista di diritto internazionale tributario, 2007, p. 17.
92. *El sistema de derecho financiero,* 2 volumes, Madrid, 1977, 1985.
93. Extra-fiscal purposes are allowed by Art. 3 of the German *Abgabenordnung* of 1977 and by Art. 2 of the Spanish *Ley General Tributaria* of 1963–2003.
94. See Franco Fichera, *Imposizione ed extrafiscalità nel sistema costituzionale,* ESI, Napoli, 1973.

The interpreter of Tax Law must be aware of its extra-fiscal aims, which are the basis for a correct taxation.

As far as constitutional legitimacy is concerned, the principle of 'less serious injury' in the ability to contribute also needs to be defined, as well as the flexible relationships with other constitutional rights, such as the principles of proportion, of non-arbitrariness and of solidarity.[95] The scientific autonomy of Tax Law is based above all on its methodological unity. Its principles are the same as those of Public Finance Law.

Undoubtedly, Tax Law has enjoyed scientific autonomy. Its main principles, such as progressiveness, the ability to contribute and substantial equality, are unitary and exclusive with respect to the power of taxation. They can be construed through a method, which is common to Public Finance Law as a whole. Nevertheless, Tax Law has no methodological autonomy.

Therefore, it can be stated that Public Finance Law has absolute scientific autonomy.[96] Tax Law on the other hand has a relative scientific autonomy, since it is founded on unitary principles, but it has no methodological autonomy.

This peculiarity with regard to the autonomy of Tax Law is not surprising: it is a consequence of the relationship that exists between Tax Law, Public Finance Law and Public Finance, and which characterizes the network formed by the various branches of Economics and Law.

The formalistic theory, on the other hand, is based on a non-experimental theory, according to which a Method, which should be the same for all branches of Tax Law and different for all the other parts of Law, in the analysis of Tax Law does not exist.[97] This narrow-minded theory is not the right way to approach the unity of Tax Law, which may be achieved only thanks to the analysis of its common economic contents.

If Tax Law rejects this methodology, it runs the risk of splitting itself into several different technical disciplines, which may be of interest only to lawyers and which are similar to other aspects of fundamental Law.

In this way, other related subjects such as Criminal Tax Law, Tax Procedural Rules, Business Tax Law and International and EU Tax Law can develop and acquire autonomous scientific dignity.

In contrast, the simplified formal perspective, which has no relationship to any methodological analysis, and which is gaining ground, may cause a loss of unity in Tax Law. This is the great challenge that must be faced in this new century. And this is also the reason why it is necessary to keep the debate on methodology alive at all times.

It is a duty incumbent on us, senior professors, to maintain and transmit a vivid representation of the scientific developments achieved by our smart predecessors. We must build an imaginary bridge to unify our past with the new, very long and difficult

95. See my Handbook *L'ordinamento giuridico....*, p. 65 *et seq.*
96. See Manlio Ingrosso, *Divisione e classificazione nella scienza giuridica finanziaria,* Napoli, 1977.
97. See 'L'interpretazione della legge tributaria', in *Trattato di Diritto tributario,* edited by Amatucci, *Annuario,* Padova, 2001, p. 255.

way, which will lead us to the future, so that the debate may develop along this path with the same rigor as in the past.

Thus we will assure that scientific autonomy and unity of Tax Law will be achieved. Only in this way can the development of Tax Law take place, within the framework of the fundamental rights of law and of economic development, of which it is an instrument.

§1.07 THE ORIGINS OF ECONOMIC ANALYSIS OF LAW IN THE UNITED STATES

At the beginning of the 1960s of the 20th century, a movement of thought called *Economic Analysis of Law* or *Law and Economics*[98] arose in the United States. It is now structured around several branches and regards law and economics as self-governing disciplines, even though it acknowledges important points of contact between the two sciences[99]. It is appropriate to consider not the results of the studies of law and economics scholars but especially their methodology[100].

Ronald H. Coase[101] an English economist, taught at the London School of Economics from 1935 to 1951 and then in the United States, where he joined Chicago Law School. His volume about the problem of social cost written in 1960 is one of the main works through which the first generation method of the Economic Analysis of Law was built. In 1991 he was awarded the Nobel Prize for economics.

This phase of the origins[102] of the movement that took the 1960s, dates back to the first law and economics thoughts[103], not only the ones of Coase but, after a short period of time, also the ones of Guido Calabresi[104] professor at Yale Law School. During a tutorial about the economic approach to the juridical phenomenon that took place at the Max Plank Institute of Hamburg in 1965, Calabresi admitted[105], with reference to

98. Sacco, *L'interpretazione*, Le fonti del diritto italiano, 2 *Le fonti non scritte e l'interpretazione*, Trattato di diritto civile, edited by Sacco, Torino, 1999, p. 230.

99. Abrescia, presentation to the volume of Friedman, *L'ordine del diritto. Perchè l'analisi economica può servire al diritto*, Bologna, 2004 translation of *Law's Order. What economy has to do with law and why it matters*, Princeton University, 2000.

100. Sacco, *L'interpretazione*, *supra* p. 230.

101. *The firm, The Market and the Law*, University of Chicago, 1988, Italian translation, *Impresa, mercato e diritto*, Bologna, 1995.

102. *The Origins of Law and Economics*, edited by Parisi, University of Minnesota Law School and University of Bologna and Rowley, The Locke Institute and George Mason University, Cheltenham, 2005, in which half a century of evolution of this method is analysed. Chiassoni, *Law and Economics, l'analisi economica del diritto negli Stati Uniti*, Torino, 1992, p. 300.

103. Remarkable is the contribution to the history of the first decades of the movement given by Veljanovski, *The New Law and Economics. A Research Review*, Oxford, Centre for Socio-Legal Studies, 1982.

104. *The Cost of Accidents*, Yale University, 1970, Italian translation: *Costo degli incidenti e responsabilità civile*, Milano, 1975. Calabresi was born in Milano in 1932. His family moved to the United States in 1939 because his father Massimo, a cardiologist, and his mother Bianca Maria Finzi Contini, a researcher of European literature, decided to leave Italy for political reasons.

105. Calabresi, *Cosa è l'analisi economica del diritto?*, Rivista di diritto finanziario e scienza delle finanze, 2007, I, p. 343.

the pessimistic considerations of the famous jurist Konrad Zweigert, that this approach was not yet a rigorous study of law at that time but he affirmed, wholeheartedly convinced, that it would have become in a short period of time.

The contributions produced at this stage were indeed inadequate, like every scientific innovation, but had the merit of having given impetus to the intense evolution of the movement that they were helping to create.

If an individual is selfish because he maximizes his benefit, only altruism is economically efficient. Coase and Calabresi believed that altruism is a useful parameter for the individual, whom does not always choose the economical solution if the higher cost provides a benefit for other people.

Other contributions, besides those of Coase and Calabresi, characterize particular branches of the movement and come from scholars like Armen Alchian[106], who studied the microeconomics of property rights, Aaron Director[107], who analysed the protection of competition in accordance with the Neoclassical microeconomics of Chicago School, George M. Humprey[108], who examined interest groups and the regulation of private enterprise, Gordon Tullock and the Nobel Prize James Buchanan[109], who developed in depth the public choices and the economic logic of law.

This first generation method considered law as a series of phenomena to interpret, thus causing perplexities in some economists. It followed doubts about the suitability of the economic model to allow the complete knowledge of the juridical phenomenon. However, the reason of this unsuitability was not in the irrationality or inefficiency of law.

The law and economics method has been gradually considered more suited for the analysis of constitutional law[110] and administrative law[111] because it guarantees effectiveness, representation and the forms of government. From administrative law stems financial law, closely connected with financial science, and from financial law emanates tax law especially regarding the federal structures.

Tax law represents thus the last of the three generations which correspond to the cited branches of law in an intense process which involved only the first half of the twentieth century. For this reason, tax law had already aroused a particular interest

106. *Some Economics of Property Rights*, Il Politico, 30, 1965, p. 816.
107. *The Parity of the Economic Market Place*, Journal of Law and Economics, 7, 1964, p. 1.
108. *The Law and Economics of Public Policy: A Plea to Scholars*, Journal of Legal Studies,1, 1972, p. 1.
109. *The logic of the Law*, New York: Basic Books, 1971, with a Postscript After Twenty- Five Years, Fairfax, VA, The George Mason University, Buchanan and Tullock, (Manifesto of Virginia) School of Public Choice, *The Calculus of Consent: Logical Foundations of Constitutional Democracy*, University of Michigan, 1962.
110. *Economics of Constitutional Law*, edited by Epstein, from University of Chicago, Cheltenham, 2009; in this work it is demonstrated the essential role of *Economic Analysis* in the study of Constitutional law.
111. *Economics of Administrative Law*, edited by Ackerman, Economic Approaches to Law series, edited by Posner, United States Court of Appeals for the Seventh Circuit and University of Chicago Law School and Parisi, University of Minnesota Law School and University of Bologna, n. 15, Cheltenham, 2007. It is interesting the reason, contained in this volume, for the interaction among law, economy and political sciences.

since the first developments of this method by Coase[112]. He observed that this system was unable to generate an optimal allocation of resources, despite the legislator's attempts. He analysed taxes as 'Pigouvian instruments' and specified, replying to the criticisms received, that these referred to a tax system based on damage, concerning those who, operating in the area where the damage was produced, caused it and who should have been liable to tax.

The Chicago's formulation of Economic Analysis of Law arose on the basis of an ideological impulse, with regard to the 'interventionism' logic.

Coase and Williamson's Economic Analysis of Law was founded on 'transaction costs', which correspond to aspects of tax technique, namely to the technical and operational element.

Coase observed that even taxes implied, on the one hand costs of assessment, collection, fight against tax evasion and avoidance and, on the other hand, costs of accomplishment and tax planning by the taxpayer.

§1.08 THE EXPANSION PHASE OF ECONOMIC ANALYSIS OF LAW IN THE 1970s

The U.S. movement of thought of second generation, which coincided with the expansion phase[113] of the 1970s, was characterized by a wider interdisciplinary approach, legal and economic, to problems traditionally regarded as juridical. To this second phase took part, in some ways Calabresi and, especially, Richard A. Posner[114], who was professor at the University of Chicago Law School and studied in depth the economic analysis of tax law.

Calabresi represented the normative conception developed at Yale Law School, which was in conflict with the positive view developed by Posner at the University of Chicago Law School[115].

Calabresi believed that the essence of the economic theory application to law was the text analysis, which aimed to know the legal rule that was able to solve effectively and efficiently a legal problem. Posner thought that the economic analysis went beyond this, revealing the inner nature of law, which could in itself be efficient.

Calabresi developed thus a pragmatic, instrumental and axiological conception. Posner, instead, built a view that valued the scientism of. Economic *Analysis of* Law, which was able, renewing positivism, to describe the mechanisms that control the legal

112. *The Problem of Social Cost*, Journal of Law and Economics, 3, 1960, p. 1, republished in Coase, *The Firm, the Market and the Law*, *supra*, p. 283.
113. In the 1970s, a secondary literature of ideological criticism about *Economic Analysis of Law* began to develop. Among the first authors of this tendency: Baker, *The ideology of the Economic Analysis of Law*, Philosophy and Public Affairs, 5, 1975, p. 3.
114. *Economic Analysis of Law*, 1st ed., Boston, 1973, 6th ed., New York, 2003.
115. Posner, *Review of Guido Calabresi, The Cost of Accidents. A legal and Economic Analysis*, University of Chicago Law Review, 1970; Hirsh, Law and Economics: an Introductory Analysis, 1979; Oliver, Law and Economics, Allen and Unwin, London, 1979; Assmann, Kirchner, Schanze, *Okonomische Analyse des Rechts*, Munchen, 1978.

system functioning and to interpret the legal rule through the analogy method and with the contribution of ideologically neutral natural sciences.

Essentially, therefore, Posner accepted, to some extent, the *normative view* of Calabresi[116]. Economic *Analysis of* Law at this stage, pursued the goal of formulating rules which ensured the achievement of transactions (exchanges and allocations of material or intangible resources, like the ground, silence, clean air and freedom of thoughts) able to maximize general welfare. This method, with all its branches, was based on the presumption of scarcity of resources and of welfare maximization. So with the second generation method, rules and economical instruments were used, with a more advanced technique, in the interpretation of law, in order to establish whether the legal rules were correctly applied and efficient, that is able to enhance collective welfare, and whether it was possible to adopt rules more suited to pursue such goals.

First of all, the second generation method of *Economic* Analysis *of Law* proposed the study of the legal reality with a logic closer to the economic one[117]. In this context, tax law assumed particular importance. Economic Analysis *of* Law was indeed considered appropriate especially to fields of law involving the interaction between juridical phenomena and economic ones, using an approach that integrated the investigation instruments developed by economics with the jurist's logic[118].

Posner[119] devoted a chapter to the topic of 'taxation'[120] in his major work concerning this method, observing that 'tax law sometimes tends to change the allocation of resources or the distribution of welfare, but it aims especially to cover expenses related to public services, although inevitably with consequences both on allocation and redistribution'. Indeed, if the legislator pursues only aims of tax revenue, tax law produces uncontrolled non-tax effects (economic and social).

In this sense, emerged on eneous assumptions the primacy of economics upon law, which was considered as a passive object of analysis and perhaps of criticism. In this period in the juridical and economic Faculties of the United States, courses of *Economic Analysis of Law* were introduced, classical courses were adjusted to this method and several specialized legal journals[121] took inspiration from it.

116. Pardolesi, *Luci ed ombre nell'analisi economica del diritto*, Rivista di diritto civile, 1982 and Cooter, Mattei, Monateri, Pardolesi and Ulen, *Il mercato delle regole, Analisi economica del diritto civile*, Bologna, 1999. See also *Analisi economica del diritto*, voice of Digesto civile, Vol. I, Torino, 1987, p. 309, Gallo, *Introduzione al diritto comparato, III, Analisi economica del diritto*, 1998, Chiassoni, *Law and Economics. L'analisi economica del diritto negli Stati Uniti, supra*.
117. Calabresi, *Cosa è l'analisi economica del diritto, supra*.
118. Stigler, *The Law and Economics of Public Policy: A Plea to Scholars*, Journal of Legal Studies, 1, 1972, p. 1.
119. *Economic Analysis of Law, supra*, and Sacco, *L'interpretazione, supra*, p. 159.
120. See Miceli, The Economic Approach to Law, Texas Law Review, 53, 1975, p. 776.
121. Krier, *Review of Richard Posner, Economic Analysis of Law*, University of Pennsylvania Law Review, 122, 1974, p. 1664 and Chiassoni, *Law and economics, l'analisi economica del diritto negli Stati Uniti, supra*, p. 324.

§1.09 THE DEVELOPMENT AND CONSOLIDATION PHASE OF ECONOMIC ANALYSIS OF LAW

In the 1980s, the developing and consolidation phase of the movement started through several factors: the formulation of economically efficient legal rules by some economists, the contribution of economics and law scholars, the adherence of the U.S. Federal Administration to Economic Analysis of Law and the appointment as federal judges for some members of this movement, the ideological criticism of Posner's positive approach and of other expressions of Chicago Law School.

From the reconstruction of the early period of the movement (1960s) and from the debate of the expansion phase of the 1970s between the normative School of Yale Law School, represented by Calabresi, and the positive School of Chicago Law School expressed by Posner, emerge the intuitions of the last author that allowed, in this phase (1980s), the full expression of innovative potentialities, in which the movement itself was rich.

To Coase and Director is dedicated a David Friedman's volume[122], which is particularly relevant for the evolution of Economic Analysis of Law. Born in Chicago, he was an expression of the local Law School and the son of Milton. He was awarded the Nobel Prize for economics in 1976. David Friedman analysed[123] Posner's theories and had the merit of having given rise to this third generation of Economic Analysis of Law, which offers interesting points of meditation.

In the 1980s some new law and economics tendencies were developed. Susan Rose Ackerman[124] performed the economic reformulation of administrative law, from which, as already mentioned, financial and tax law come. It is interesting in particular the choice of the method made by Williamson[125], who conducted 'law economics-organization theory' researches concerning the contractual logic in the transaction costs economics. The researches of the Austro-evolutionist[126] law and economics scholars aimed to refute the criteria of economic efficiency from the inside.

This method applied new economic techniques, such as the game theory or the behavioural economics[127], which have made Economic Analysis of Law much more interesting. The first generation method presumed that the economist doubted about the suitability of the economic model to allow the interpretation of the real world, so he

122. See also *L'ordine del diritto. Perché l'analisi economica può servire al diritto, supra.*
123. Friedman, *Richard Posner,* The New Palgrave Dictionary of Law and Economics, New York, 1998.
124. *Progressive Law and Economics – And the Administrative Law,* Yale Law Journal, 98, 1988.
125. *Economic Organization, Firms, Markets and Policy Control,* New York, 1986, Italian translation *L'organizzazione economica. Imprese, mercati e controllo politico,* Bologna, 1991.
126. Rizzo, *Uncertainty, Subjectivity and the Economic Analysis of Law,* edited by the author himself, *Time*, Uncertainty and Disequilibrium, Lexington, 1979. The economist, researcher at new York University, published other several works about the same subject in 1980 and two others in 1981 and 1982, which aroused particular interest. He adopts the Austrian school method. Hayek, *Individualism and Economic Order,* London and Henley, 1949 and Kirzner, *Competition and Entrepeneurship,* University of Chicago, 1973.
127. *Behavioural Law and Economics,* edited by Rachlinski from Cornell University, Economic Approaches to law Series, Cheltenham, 2009. In the three volumes, interesting writings are selected which involve economics, psychology and law.

tried to build another method without these deficiencies. This premise had not convinced the second generation scholars, and this critical analysis intensified during the third generation phase. The relationship between economics and law has been correctly considered on equal terms; the method guarantees the single and autonomous scientific innovation, so that it makes economics more interesting and law more efficient. The economic model tends to adapt to the juridical phenomenon and to reinvigorate the altruistic logic which animates the redistribution through the public intervention in the economy.

The interdisciplinary research between law and economics is able to facilitate the development of both sciences; a much more refined methodology results from the contact between law and the economic conceptual system. The relationship between the juridical second one is complementary in regard to the first. The fundamental issue consists in the identification of the procedures through which the two approaches manage to operate with synergy.

Law harmonizes with economics, however, after half a century of analysis conducted in the universities of Yale and Chicago, much remains to be studied of the relationship between the two models: economic and juridical. Law appears more efficient and economics seems more interesting.

The role of Economic Analysis *of* Law occupies the general theory of interpretation and its solutions change as a consequence of the conviction about the content of the interpretation procedure.

The analysis directed to refute the adherence to the literal meaning of the rule and each dogmatic axiom aim to revalue the meta juridical factor, whose options affect the solutions. In this way the traditional interpretative approach evolves.

The *Begriffsjurisprudenz* criticized the aprioristic concept in the interpretation of the law by building the concepts, deducing the rules from them and asserting that the foundations are contained in the legal text[128]. This means to eradicate the idea of the objectivity of the text meaning and of the argumentation value.

It is interesting to verify the relationships between *Economic Analysis* of Law and *Begriffsjurisprudenz,* which aimed to allow the text comprehension and the deduction of the rule from the concept, which should come from the popular consciousness. Afterwards it was believed that the concept exists out of the jurist's mind that builds it.

Rational law acts as a model for the legislator to produce positive law and for the interpreter as a source of light to illuminate the text. *Economic* Analysis *of* Law follows some aspects of the rational law criterion, owing to the mechanisms through which it enters law life. Exactly from rational law the principle should be deduced that no juridical criterion is reasonable if it does not allow natural and legal persons, whom the legal rules affect, to make their choices[129].

Therefore, conceptualism does not consider the purposes of institutions and the social reality on which law works and, in this sense, *Economic* Analysis *of* Law is

128. Heck, *Begriffsbildung und Interessenjurisprudenz,* Tubingen, 1932 Larenz, *Methodenlehre der Rechtswissenschaft,* Berlin/Heidelberg/New York, 1991; Wank, *Die Auslegung von Gesetzen. Eine Einfuhrung,* Koln, 2001.
129. Sacco, *L'interpretazione, supra.*

different. Its primary characteristic is rationality and its main purpose is the utilization of the conceptual apparatus obtained from the economic studies to know the reasons of the legal rule existence.

A tricky problem arises at the methodological level because the economic theories, which form part of the issue of public choices, do not have reached a satisfactory level of ripening yet. The law and economics approach, however, can promote the knowledge of the reasons why the juridical system has assumed a certain structure. This method checks the suitability of the legal rule to reach the purposes established by the legislator. It has also the function of affecting the behaviour of natural and legal persons, in order to guarantee the attainment of those specific objectives. Thus the economical modelling facilitates the interpreter in the prediction of the incidence of the legal rule upon the behaviours of natural and legal persons to which it refers. Through this method, the interpreter understands also the possible heterogeneity of the purposes of the legal rules. It is much more easier to give a complete sense to an instrument if the use to which it is devoted is known. The relationship between this method and economics does not consist, thus, in the utilization by the juridical research of a whatsoever theory developed by the economic science; this method accepts the challenge of using the economic theory to form and to know the content of the legal rules.

The aims are identified considering the economic and social policy instrument[130] adopted by the law. The knowledge of the goals pursued by the law is permitted by the analysis of the possible effects[131] derived from its application.

The judge must cooperate to achieve socially useful aims, through informed, predictable and uniform[132] rulings, which consider the effects (of the rules).

Economic Analysis of Law[133] considers, so, necessary the use of the economic logic, not only to allow the legislator to formulate the legal rule evaluating the effects, but also to consent the interpreter to understand the reason of the choice.

The commercial law scholar Francesco Denozza[134], always interested in the applica-don of the postulates of Economic Analysis of Law to the law of economics, observes that the analysis of legal rules effects to achieve the knowledge of their aims, represents an essential step in the activity of the 'legislator's auxiliary' jurist, 'critical of the law' jurist and the 'interpreter of the law' jurist. He notices, nevertheless, that the attention paid from the jurists to the general theme of the evaluation criteria of rules effects is currently poor. These must be interpreted considering the monitoring of the effects through different methodologies. There is a need to orient the interpreter towards the formulation of positive or negative judgments about the effect that rules are able to produce.

130. Cohen, *Ethical Systems and Legal Ideals. An Essay on the Foundations of Legal Criticism*, New York, 1933, Cornell University.
131. Llewellyn, *Some Realism about Realism, Responding to Dean Pound*, Harvard Law Review, 44, 1930-31, p. 1222.
132. Sacco, *L'interpretazione, supra*, p. 252.
133. Abrescia, Presentation to the volume of *Friedman L'ordine del diritto. Perché l'analisi economica può servire al diritto, supra*, pp. 25, 39 and 583.
134. *Norme efficienti. L'analisi economica del diritto*, Milano, 2002, p. 2.

Economic Analysis of Law indicates not only the connections between law and economics. Even social sciences allow the interpreter to perform his function correctly. Since the first half of the twentieth century, the sociological instrument aroused among the jurists a considerable interest. Through the interpreter's mediation, the law expresses a socially widespread aspiration, involving criteria of good faith, custom, guilt, injustice and abuse. The full comprehension of the legal rule can be obtained through an interpretation that considers the social instance of which the legislator is recipient. Economic analysis, dogmatic and social reality support criteria of former 'validity', as they stimulate solutions suggested by the best allocation of the resources, which is a public good, by the jurist's knowledge, which is developed after an evaluative analysis and by the social instance, which is at the basis of each evaluation.

At the end of the twentieth century[135], the belief spread in the doctrine[136] that the guiding principles of the Liberal State are not damaged, considering that the law text suggests to the interpreter to catch the legislator's will through indications offered by society. The interpreter understands the 'nature of things', considered as social reality and fact for investigation purposes, letting them filter through his culture and his values, in order to complete his cognitive process.

Social conscience, however, does not constitute an empty space destined to be filled with the interpreter's ideology. The language analysis and the argumentation Doctrine do not indulge the interpreter with alterations, he has to be aware of the role of the sociological instrument too.

Therefore, it is fundamental the research, even through the study of the effects, of the aims not only economical but also social, which interact among them to allow the knowledge of the legal rule content.

These are not methods, but stages of the unique process in which the method of Economic Analysis of Law is included in whole or in part. This could be not completely efficient but alternative methods are currently deficient.

Thus Friedman redefines the role of Economic Analysis of Law, which is accepted by the most recent law and economics literature, rendering meaningless the debate between the schools of Yale and Chicago. The third generation method is not so different from the second generation one, it only uses new techniques.

Friedman takes inspiration from Coase, but expresses this more advanced conception of Economic Analysis of Law, which can be considered as post Chicago[137].

135. Bobbio, *Uber den Begriff der Natur der Sache,* Archiv fur Rechts - und Sozialphilosophie, 1958, p. 305.
136. Sacco, *L'interpretazione, supra*, p. 244.
137. Abrescia, Presentation to the volume of Friedman, *L'ordine del diritto. Perché l'analisi economica può servire al diritto, supra.*

§1.10 ECONOMIC ANALYSIS OF LAW SHOWS ELEMENTS IN COMMON WITH REALISM

The interpreter experiences the law in his spirit in order to comprehend it. The fervency of life affects the legislator's activity as much as the interpreter's[138] one, who rebuilds the rule of law through representative forms which are sources or objects of juridical assessment[139]. Interpretation identifies the meaning to attribute to the law, which is the result and not the preconceived effect of the interpreter's activity[140]. The problem of the interpreter's closeness to the law can be resolved in '*realistic*' terms, described as 'non cognitive' that is '*sceptic*' and '*realistic*', or in '*formalistic*' terms, considered as 'cognitive' or 'eclectic' in an '*intermediate*' logic.

According to the *realistic* conception, arisen in the United States in the first decades of the twentieth century, interpretation consists in a cognitive and volitional activity, which always involves a decision or a choice, even unconscious, by the interpreter. The legal reasoning must constitute an effective control instrument of the judge's evaluative activity[141].

In the cognitive process, the interpreter expresses value judgments[142] to perceive the ones contained in the rule text in order to declare which is the law meaning. Therefore, interpretation has a creative nature[143].

Juridical studies must be theoretical and practical according to the technological realism, which expresses a functional conception of positive law. Furthermore, the technological realism considers the positive law values and concepts as the continuous product of the activity of the economically and technologically advanced social component[144]. Realism enhances the function of the extra-legal factors in the analysis of law, it considers the legal certainty as relative and the knowledge of the juridical Life real factors as necessary, and is pessimistic about the utilization of general criteria to solve particular issues. Already in 1947, Rodolfo Sacco[145] argued that the legal

138. Gorla, *l'interpretazione del diritto*, Milano, 1941, p. 33.
139. Betti, L'interpretazione della legge e degli atti giuridici, Teoria generale e dogmatica, Milano, 1949, p. 3.
On the non-retroactivity and the authentic interpretation: A. Amatucci, J. Malherbe, P. Daenen, G. Marongiu, F. Amatucci, J. Hey, G. Teixeira, H. Gribnau, M. R. T. Puwels, in *Rivista di diritto tributario internazionale - International Tax Law Review* of La Sapienza University in Rome, founded in 1999, and co-edited by Amatucci, Tejerizo Lopez, Malherbe, Puoti, Sacchetto.
140. Tarello, *L'interpretazione della legge*, Milano, 1980, p. 63.
141. Llewellyn, *Some Realism about Realism, supra*, p. 1239, *The Case Law System in America*, translated by Nickerson, with the introduction of Gewirtz, University of Chicago, 1989; See Schlegel, *American Legal Realism and Empirical Social Science*, Studies in Legal History, University of North Carolina, 1995, in particular the contribution of William Underhill Moore; see Surges and Clark, *Legal Theory and Real Property Mortgages*, 37, Yale Law Journal, 691, 1928; Oliphant, *A Return to Stare Decisis*, American Bar Association Journal, 14, 1928.
142. Caiani, *I giudizi di valore nell'interpretazione giuridica*, Padova, 1954. See Tarello, *Orientamento analitico – linguistica e teoria dell'interpretazione*, Rivista trimestrale di diritto e procedura civile, 1971; Guastini, *L'interpretazione dei documenti normativi, supra*, pp. 4, 44.
143. Bigliazzi-Geri, Breccia, Busnelli and Natoli, *Il sistema giuridico italiano, I, Norma, soggetti e rapporto giuridico*, 1986, p. 58.
144. Cohen, *Trascendental Nonsense and the Functional Approach*, Columbia, Law Review, 35, 1935, p. 809.
145. *Il concetto di interpretazione del diritto*, Torino, 2003.

statement has no objective meaning and its only significance is the one that the interpreter attributes to it. Emilio Betti[146] criticized this position, Joseph Esser[147] agreed about it but only Pier Giuseppe Monateri[148] accepted it giving ample reasons - Currently the conviction is spread of the non-uniqueness of the text meaning [149].

This conviction is based on two reasons.

For starters, the interpretation of law is intrinsically a decisional process. It is not conducted an analysis of the law meaning, but this one is conceptually 'built' deciding its meaning. The legal text contains prearranged stimuli through which the interpreter expresses a spontaneous reaction[150].

Each statute is problematic, as it expresses at least two different meanings. This is due to the plurality of interpretation methods competing with each other[151]; the juridical nature of language which is nebulous owing to the concepts vagueness and to the semantic and pragmatic ambiguity[152]; the semantic context of which the laws are part and that could affect the single laws texts[153]; the doctrine's dogmatic construction[154]; the evolutionary interpretation which catches the change of meaning of the legal text over time and owing to the pluralism of the ethical and normative values, which is caused by the utilization of the interpretation methods and the different

146. *L'interpretazione della legge e degli atti giuridici, supra.*
147. *Grundsatz und Norm in der richterlichen Fortbildung des Privatrechts,* 1974.
148. *Interpretazione del diritto,* Digesto civile, X, 1993.
149. Nerhot, *Il diritto, lo scritto, il senso,* 1992, p. 47; Bigliazzi-Geri, Breccia, Busnelli, Natoli, *Il sistema giuridico italiano, supra,* p. 58; Guastini, *Le fonti del diritto e l'interpretazione,* 1993 Trattato di diritto privato (edited by Judica and Zatti), p. 393; Carcaterra, *L'argomentazione nell'interpretazione giuridica,* Ermeneutica e critica, atti del convegno dei Lincei, 135, 1998, p. 109.
150. See Luzzati, *La vaghezza delle norme, Un'analisi del linguaggio giuridico,* Milano, 1990; JORI, *Semiotica giuridica,* Jori and Pintore, Manuale di teoria generale del diritto, 2nd ed., Torino, 1995, p. 305; Luzzati, *L'interprete e il legislatore,* Milano, 1999; Chiassoni, *L'ineluttabile scetticismo della 'Scuola genovese',* Comanducci and Guastini (edited by), Analisi e diritto, 1998, Ricerche di giurisprudenza analitica, Torino, 1999, p. 21 ss.; Comanducci, *L'interpretazione delle norme giuridiche: la problematica attuale,* Bessone (edited by) Interpretazione e diritto giudiziale. I: Regole, metodi, modelli, Torino, 1999, p. 9 ss.; Schauer, *Le regole del gioco. Un'analisi filosofica delle decisioni prese secondo le regole nel diritto e nella vita quotidiana,* Bologna, 2000; Barberis, *Lo scetticismo immaginario,* Comanducci and Guastini, (edited by), Analisi e diritto 2000. Ricerche di giurisprudenza analitica, Torino, 2001, p. 1.; Chiassoni, *Archimede o Eraclito? Sul primato teorico dello scetticismo, Materiali per una storia della cultura giuridica,* Torino, 31, 2001.
151. See Merkl, *Sul problema dell'interpretazione,* Il duplice volto del diritto, Il sistema kelseniano e altri saggi, Milano, 1987, pp. 255 ss.; Alexy and Dreier, *Statutory Interpretation in the Federal Republic of Germany,* Mac Cormick and Summers (edited by), Interpreting statutes. A comparative Study, Dartmouth, 1991, p. 73.
152. See Luzzati, *La vaghezza delle norme. Un'analisi del linguaggio giuridico, supra;* Endicott, Vagueness in Law, Oxford University, 2000.
153. See Chiassoni, *La giurisprudenza civile. Metodi di interpretazione e tecniche argomentative,* Milano, 1999, p. 597; Velluzzil, *Interpretazione sistematica e prassi giurisprudenziale,* Torino, 2002, p. 123.
154. See Guastini, *Realismo e antirealismo nella teoria dell'interpretazione,* Ragion Pratica, 17, 2001, p. 43 and *Variaciones sobre temas de Carlo Alchourròn y Eugenio Bulygin. Derrotabilidad, lagunas axiològicas y interpretaciòn,* June 2006, §§1-3.

utilization of the same method[155]. The realistic conception develops the right method that leads the interpreter to choose a specific meaning[156]. The intuitional realism is not persuasive, as it affirms that judicial activity_ is strongly affected by the assessment of tax avoidance facts and must achieve not the certainty, but the justice of a single case. Furthermore, it believes that the doctrine cannot anticipate future judgments and the interpretation techniques fulfil a 'smoky' function[157].

It is, well-founded the realistic conception but it cannot be qualified as 'non cognitive Indeed, knowledge involves the creative activity underlined by realism.

Different is the content of the northern realism[158], arisen in the first half of the nineteenth century and developed in Denmark with a significant evolution in Norway. This realism, however, differs from the famous Scandinavian realism arisen in Sweden; about a century separates these conceptions. The northern realism expresses a deep interaction between theory and juridical praxis and gives ample space to the practical considerations in the juridical argumentation. The Scandinavian realism is, instead, part of the wide phenomenon of opposition against formalism because it gives attention to the current events and the material aspects of law, beyond the norms and the concepts which obscure social reality and psychology of law. According to the Norwegian Frede Castberg[159], the justice of the rules content does not mean only rationality or fairness of law. The need of justice of the law's goes beyond: justice is equality, which is absence of abuse. Arbitrariness is the absolute enemy of justice.

Consequently, the other conception, the formalistic one is unfounded. According to this, interpretation is a cognitive activity which consists in finding the 'true' (unique and determined) meaning of the law, which corresponds with the 'true' (unique and determined) will or intention of the legislator. Juridical formalism describes positive law as a coherent and complete system[160]. Its main features are the descriptive nature of the rules, of the values and of the concepts expressed by legal texts and the conviction that, in order to avoid subjective value judgments, people must follow strictly the linguistic formulas chosen by the legislator[161]. As a result, it is possible to distinguish a theoretical interpretative formalism, which consists in a mechanical and not evaluating activity[162], from a normative interpretative formalism[163], which does not allow the judge an evaluating activity. Mechanical juridical elements and the

155. See Alexy and Dreier, *Statutory Interpretation in the Federal Republic of Germany, supra*, p. 78. Alexey, *Teoria dell'argomentazione giuridica. La teoria del discorso razionale come teoria della motivazione giuridica*, Milano, 1998, chap. I.
156. Chiassoni, *Tecnica dell'interpretazione giuridica*, Bologna, 2007.
157. Frank, *Courts on Trial. Myth and Reality in American Justice*, Princeton University, 1949, p. 12.
158. Sepe, *Realismo nordico e diritti umani*, Napoli, 2008.
159. *Philosophy of Law in the Scandinavian Countries*, The American Journal of Comparative Law, 1995, p. 390.
160. Gilmore, *The Ages of American Law*, Yale University, 1977, translated by Mattei (edited by Gambaro and Mattei), *Le grandi epoche del diritto Americano*, Milano, 1988.
161. Guastini, *Dalle fonti alle norme*, Torino, 1990 and Gilmore, *The Ages of American Law, supra*.
162. L. A. Hart, *Il concetto di diritto*, Torino, 1998, translation of *The Concept of Law*, chap. II, Oxford, 1961.
163. Lyons, *Constitutional Interpretation and Original Meaning*, Social Philosophy and Policy, 4, 1987, p. 75.

methodological autonomy of the juridical doctrine characterize formalism[164]. This method, considered in the cognitive sense of faithfulness to a meaning completely and uniquely preconceived to the interpretation, comes to an unreal. conception. The formalistic sentences are unpredictable and subjective. In this sense, formalism is lacking, whereas the School of Pavia has an excess in the utilization of economic concepts in law interpretation. Thus the formalistic reasoning is a socially damaging 'transcendental nonsense'[165] because it is vague and unrelated to any empirical reference. The law methodology must instead be enriched with the contributions of economic and social sciences. The rule of law, correctly considered in a substantial sense, must be faithfully respected, apart from the consequences and the injustice that it causes[166]. The observation of the rule of law requires the comprehension of its real content, especially through the comparison of the effects and the justice related to the different meanings. The interpreter uses all his knowledge, information, aspiration and feelings. Several are the interpretative instruments that help him.

Giovanni Tarello[167] identifies the 'opposite' one, the analogical, the economic, the authoritative, the systematic, the equitable and the one that comes from general principles.

It is possible to derive from the instruments a criterion which enhances the primacy of the extra-juridical reality related to law such as the purpose, interest and value. The interpreter's level of subordination to the law[168] is influenced the adoption of the interpretation code.

The defence of the objective meaning theory led to make recourse to the voluntary idea; asserting that the legislators will is the object of interpretation, even though it is not certainly known. The voluntary theory of the twentieth century's half was opportunely abandoned[169]. The interpreter's faithfulness must be considered as referred to the fundamental values of positive law and, consequently, it is related to the law but in a subsraritial logic[170], full of economic and social contents.

The eclectic or intermediate conception, which represents an interpretation sometimes in realistic terms and sometimes in the formalistic logic, is partially unfounded.

164. Dworkin, *Political Judges and the Rule of Law* (1978), (edited by the same author) A Matter of Principle, 1985, p. 316 and Amatucci, *L'interpretazione della norma di diritto finanziario*, Napoli, 1965.
165. Cohen, *Trascendental Nonsense and the Functional Approach, supra*.
166. Bobbio, *Formalismo giuridico e formalismo etico*, (edited by the same author) Studi sulla teoria generale del diritto, Torino, 1955, p. 145 and Lyons, *On Formal Justice*, Cornell Law Review, 58, 1973, p. 883.
167. *Orientamenti analitico-linguistici e teoria dell'interpretazione*, Rivista trimestrale di Diritto e Procedura Civile, 1971, p. 1.
168. Chiassoni, *Tecnica dell'interpretazione giuridica, supra*.
169. Gorla, *L'interpretazione del diritto, supra*, Sacco, *L'interpretazione, supra*.
170. Zagrebelsky, *Principi e voti. La Corte costituzionale e la politica*, Torino, 2005, p. 59 and Mac Cormick, *Rethoric and the Rule of Law. A Theory of Legal Reasoning*, The Oxford University Press, 2005.

The interpretation should be considered in realistic terms in doubtful cases, in which the interpreter has to choose among several competing meanings[171], or when 'creating' the meaning of the text of law. It should be instead, formalistic in clear cases, when a text of law has a meaning suitable to solve a specific question juris on the basis of semantic rules empirically detectable, through which the text shows a precise meaning, or on the basis of the legislator's will [172].

No text can be considered of doubtful or clear significance with regard to the interpretation process.

'The intermediate conception appears wrong because the legal text interpretation **can never** be formalistic. Knowledge reveals a creative component [173] revaluating the rhetorical nature of legal reasoning, through the pre-comprehension by the interpreter [174], the law-policy of texts antagonistic re-examination, the alternative use of law, the infinitely meaningful nature of texts and through the arbitrariness of the meaning choices in the application of rules (deconstructionism).

Through an ethical-political reason the interpreter affirms the importance of an element over others, which in a voluntary context appears as evidence or clue of the psychological components of law[175].

The problems to which the doctrine pays particular attention are currently the uniqueness or not of the legal text meaning, the nature of the interpreter's activity, of creation or reproduction of texts, and the concept of his faithfulness to the law[176]. Interpretation constitutes a cognitive activity and at the same time an expression of will[177], as among the several meanings the interpreter decides which of them must be attributed to the text of law[178].

---

171. Monateri, *Interpretazione del diritto*, Digesto civile, 4th ed., Vol. X, Torino, 1993; Denozza, *La struttura dell'interpretazione*, Rivista trimestrale di diritto e procedura civile, 1995, p. 1.; Luzzati, *L'interpretazione giuridica*, 1995, Scarpelli and Luzzati, Compendio di filosofia del diritto, Torino, 2001; Diciotti, *Interpretazione della legge e discorso razionale*, Torino, 1999, p. 532; Derrida and Vattimo (edited by), *Diritto, giustizia e interpretazione*, Roma-Bari, 1998; Troper, *Una teoria realista dell'interpretazione*, Materiali per una storia della cultura giuridica, 1999, 29; Villa, *Condizioni per una teoria della interpretazione giuridica*, Velluzzi (edited by) Significato letterale e interpretazione del diritto, Torino, 2000, p. 173.
172. L. A. Hart, *Il concetto di diritto, supra*.
173. Sacco, *L'interpretazione, supra*, p. 244, Derrida and Vattimo (edited by) *Diritto, giustizia e interpretazione, supra*.
174. Gadamer, *Verità e metodo*, Milano, 1995; med. A., *Ermeneutica*, Enciclopedia del novecento, Roma, 1997; Betti, *Ermeneutica come metodica delle Scienze dello spirito*, Roma, 1987; Zaccaria, *L'arte dell'interpretazione*, Padova, 1990; Mengoni, *Ermeneutica e dogmatica giuridica*, Milano, 1996; AA. VV., *Ermeneutica e filosofia analitica. Due concezioni del Diritto a confronto* (edited by Jori), Torino, 1995; Irti, *Testo e contesto*, Padova, 1996; Viola-Zaccaria, *Diritto e interpretazione, supra*, they observe that law is positive only because it is interpreted. Indeed, the execution of the interpretative procedures and the achieved awareness of the inexhaustible *Konkretisierung*, allowed the achievement of valuable methodological acquisitions.
175. Scarpelli, *L'interpretazione (Diritto)*, Grande dizionario enciclopedico. Gli strumenti del sapere contemporaneo, II, I concetti, 2nd ed., Torino, 1997, p. 422.
176. Sacco, *L'interpretazione, supra*.
177. Viola and Zaccaria, *Diritto e interpretazione, Lineamenti di teoria ermeneutica del diritto*, Roma-Bari-Catania, 1999, pp. 113–126.
178. Guastini, *L'interpretazione dei documenti normativi, supra*, pp. 4, 44.

In this way Economic Analysis of Law improves law's expression abilities through the economic science.

So the conception acknowledged by Economic Analysis of Law is connected to the former realism and to the interpretation general theory afterwards developed, which can be accepted if it is considered in a way that does not alter the cognitive nature of interpretation. It is crucial the contribution of the teleological-economic method developed by the School of Naples, which not casually is described as substantial, and equally realist is the Economic Analysis of Law, both are indeed sided against the formalism in support of the Scandinavian realism.

§1.11 EFFICIENCY AND REDISTRIBUTIVE JUSTICE AS SELECTION CRITERIA OF THE REAL LAW TEXT MEANING

Economic Analysis of Law leads to reduce ambiguity establishing exact criteria that help the interpreter[179] with the choice among the several meanings which the text assumes, as acknowledged by realism in the United States and currently more intensively by the general doctrine.

Following the course traced by realism, Economic Analysis of Law provides the interpreter with suitable criteria to make the right choice among the different meanings of a text of law[180], showing 'general welfare'[181] as a value to favour.

'Efficiency and redistributive justice'[182] affect general welfare. Friedman avoids the growth crisis of Economic Analysis of Law getting over the School of Chicago[183], celebrating particularly the role of efficiency and not restricting himself to make critical considerations[184] towards Posner's thought.

Efficiency consists in the enhancement effects of collective welfare, redistributive justice, instead, consists in the fair result of the legal rules, which affect people and the distribution of general welfare.

Jusnaturalism, normative positivism and the sociological view are the three conceptions of law, as Norberto Bobbio[185] observes.

179. Sacco, *L'interpretazione*, *supra*, p. 181.
180. Abrescia, Presentation to the volume of Friedman, *L'ordine del diritto. Perché l'analisi economica può servire al diritto*, *supra*, p. 33.
181. According to S. Tommaso d'Aquino the ethics of virtue constitutes an ability to pursue the purpose, which for the law is *common welfare*. See Schonberg, *Tommaso d'Aquino*, translated by Pietro Kobau, Bologna, 2009, p. 105.
182. Denozza, *Norme efficienti. L'analisi economica del diritto*, *supra*, p. 2.
183. Hatzis, *Norms and Values in Law and Economics*, London, New York, Routledge, 2009.
184. Abrescia, presentation to the volume of Friedman, *L'ordine del diritto. Perché l'analisi economica può servire al diritto*, *supra*, p. 41. Friedman criticizes Posner, on the basis of the following considerations. To start with, the judges could pursue not only efficiency but also egalitarian and redistributive needs. Added to this, the judges could lack a sufficient economic background and even if they had it, the inquiry findings of the procedure could not be able to achieve this result. Thus, the *common law* efficiency thesis is a theoretical possibility and the *ex post* criticisms referred to current law are questionable. The general consideration of the economic aspects of the regulated phenomenon is not part of *Economic Analysis of Law* tasks.
185. *Teoria generale del diritto*, Torino, 1993.

Jusnaturalism considers only normative values and particularly justice, as law justification. Kelsen's normative Positivism considers the rules system of current positive law, apart from the values, and thus justice, and the fact, which gives sense to law. The sociological conception underlines law efficacy with its real connection with society. Alongside this conception is the North American realism that exalts the fact, which gives sense to law, that can give the judge the power to build the law on the basis of this fact, which can be contrary or not to positive law.

So, as observed by Mauricio Plazas Vega[186], the right conception is three-dimensional because this considers together the three inseparable contents of jusnaturalism, normative positivism and the North American realism. The three-dimensional vision takes inspiration from Hegel's dialectic, which connects thesis, antithesis and synthesis, representing law as values, rule and fact.

The redistributive justice value must thus not be the only one considered in the conception of law.

The Constitutions of the main countries guarantee general welfare. Indeed, they aim to satisfy the fundamental needs of a human being projected towards their optimal condition, and to protect economic, social or property rights and cultural rights in addition to the freedom of economic initiative.

Social rights justify the fair limitation of economic rights, which, however, re-expand afterwards in a context of social and economic development. Economic rights can be restricted within a limit but this must guarantee their non confiscation. It is thus protected the equal starting point of individuals that incentivizes the economic initiative, and the direct commitment to the effective protection of economic, social and cultural rights and, for what is possible, the economic development, are stimulated. The State's services in support of those who are not in equal starting conditions must obviously be effective.

Constitutions impose also economic efficiency[187], through which general welfare increases and, through the progressive and substantial equality principles, they guarantee also redistributive justice, which, affecting individuals, distributes general welfare.

Reasonableness, adequacy, proportionality, externality and quality of life are economic concepts at the basis of constitutional values, which constitute the ground of re-distributive justice and efficiency. These protect economic, social and cultural rights, to which the law is subsequently linked.

Economic, social and *cultural* rights have been acknowledged as fundamental rights marked as fundamental rights in the International Covenant adopted by the United Nation Assembly on 16 December 1966 jointly with the Covenant of Civil and Political Rights (both known as New York Covenant).

---

186. *Del realismo al trialismo jurìdico*, 2nd edition, Colombia e Brasile, 2009, p. 54. The author analyses in particolar the North American realism doctrine and *Economic Analysis of Law*.

187. Abrescia, Presentation to the volume of Friedman, *L'ordine del diritto. Perchè l'analisi economica può servire al diritto, supra*, p. 582.

The recognition of economic, social and cultural rights marked, as Norberto Bobbio[188] observed, the transition from a simply liberal or formal democracy to a social democracy.

It is interesting to consider the role of public law disciplines with regard to the fundamental problem of the separation between allocative issues, which regard the ways to maximize the general satisfaction, and redistributive issues, concerning the ways through which this satisfaction can be distributed[189]. This theme was formerly studied by Coase. This method requires the separation of the allocative issues from the redistributive ones, in addition to the scarcity of resources, such as human activities which can generate conflicts.

Each redistributive intervention reduces the efficiency levels. This happens because of the distribution of the maximized general welfare through the allocation, that is the redistribution, or through the correction of an *efficient* rule, *so* that the redistributive services are enhanced.

Generally, a redistributive justice implies a double inefficiency: the one connected to each redistributive form and the one derived from the adoption of an inefficient rule[190].

§1.12 HOW TAX LAW PURSUES PURPOSES OF REDISTRIBUTIVE JUSTICE WITH LESS EFFICIENCY LOSS THAN THE OTHER BRANCHES OF LAW

In the field of the economic public law, tax law plays a leading role because of the interest that it has constantly arisen among the Economic *Analysis* of Law scholars, especially with reference to efficiency and redistributive justice. The negative effects upon efficiency, that is on the welfare increase effects, produced by the redistributive justice policy, which affects individuals and distributes well-being through tax rules, are always less than those caused by different *rules* of law.

The purposes of redistributive justice, which conflict with the efficiency ones, can be better achieved, even though this is not the only solution, through specialized juridical branches, *such as tax law.*

It distributes the general welfare with less damages on the welfare's growth itself. Thus, with the same level of redistributive justice but with more resources coming from the better efficiency, general welfare increases.

The Economic Analysis *of* Law method is particularly efficient for the whole financial law and therefore even for tax law, which is a fundamental component of the first one, because behind this branch of law it exists an economic reason developed by a specific economic science, the public finance. Lerke Osterloh[191] specifies that

188. *Teoria generale della politica*, Torino, 1999, p. 456.
189. Denozza, Norme efficienti. L'analisi economica del diritto, *supra*, p. 8.
190. *Ibid.*, p. 5.
191. *Methodenprobleme im Steuerrecht*, Jahrbuch des offentlichen Rechts der Gegenwart, edited by Peter Haberle, Tubingen, Vol. 56, 2008, p. 151, report held on 28 June 2007 at the Forum of the University of Beirut, Faculty of juridical and economic sciences. Melis, *L'interpretazione nel*

economic disciplines, especially public finance and enterprise tax economics, give a contribution which leaves a mark in the tax law essential content.

The legislator is led to favour the tax instrument in order to pursue purposes of *efficiency* and redistributive justice. Consequently, the interpreter of tax law is more intensively engaged in the research of the meaning which ensures more suitability to pursue the aims of efficiency and redistributive justice.

As Posner observes, the tax phenomenon is juridical and differs from the economic one, even though it is deeply connected to the last one. The juridical and economic methods complement each other but they do not melt. The tax law interpreter rebuilds more easily the legislator's economic choices and understands his ratio and purposes, evaluating the effects and thus the meaning of the rule, as specifies David A. Weisbach[192] from Chicago Law School University. He rebuilds public choices through the economics an law logics especially in the light of Buchanan's contribution. The utilization of this method neither implies a transgressive jump[193] over the boundaries of the tasks traditionally performed by jurists nor there is a withdrawal of the tax legal science in favour of the economic science.

The tax rule allows the wise interpreter to make the correct choice because he is a legal theorist and a practical operator. Through *Economic Analysis of Law*, made even more efficient by financial science, the interpreter identifies the conflicting interests between taxpayer and State in the juridical context established by the tax rule, but not in the sense developed by the *Interessenjurisprudenz*[194].

This method respects the tax law principles but adopts the solution inferred from the criterion based on the costs-benefit analysis.

The tax rule interpreter ensures redistributive justice, evaluating the social costs of public choices and identifying who supports and who benefits of them. The tax technique is one of the transaction costs. The jurist estimates the advantages and the damages referred to the taxpayer and to the State Among the possible solutions he prefers the one that increases the advantages and reduces the damages and allocates both, thus preventing the recipient person from making the translation of the costs

diritto tributario, Padova, 2003; Ferlazzo Natoli, *La teoria dell'interpretazione nel diritto tributario: spunti introduttivi*, Diritto e pratica tributaria, 1996, I, p. 335 and my chapter *L'interpretazione della legge tributaria*, Trattato di diritto tributario, (edited by me), annuario, Padova, 2001, p. 255.

192. *Economics of Tax Law* n. 19, Economic approaches to Law Series, n. 19, edited by Posner, United states Court of appeals for the Seventh Circuit and University of Chicago Law School and Parisi, University of Minnesota Law School and University of Bologna, Cheltenham, 2008. See also the reports of the Workshop *Searching for new Models in the Economic Analysis of Law*, held at the University of Messina from 25 to 27 March 2007 and organized by Giuseppe Sobbrio. These reports, with the introduction of Guido Calabresi, have been gradually published in *Rivista di diritto finanziario e scienza delle finanze* from the third booklet of 2007. ADAMS, *For Good and Evil, - The Impact of Taxes on the course of Civilization*, Maryland, 2008, analyses tax policy, which throughout history is able to direct civilization. The author affirms that the history of tax legal systems make men wise.
193. Denozza, *Norme efficienti. L'analisi economica del diritto, supra*, p. 11.
194. Heck, Gesetzeauslegung und Interessenjurisprudenz, Tubingen, 1914, Begriffsbildung und Interessenjurisprudenz, *supra* and Larenz, Methodenlehre der Rechtswissenschaft, *supra*.

upon other people. Facing multiple solutions, the interpreter of a tax law chooses the one which maximizes the general satisfaction in behalf of the State or the taxpayer.

Thanks to several instruments like social instances, values and Economic Analysis of Law considered in the current motivation of the third generation, the interpreter chooses, among several solutions, the correct one and the more efficient between costs and benefits, without altering the tax rule content with his ideologies, and ensuring efficiency and redistributive justice.

Tax law and economics work together to facilitate the interpreter's activity, who make recourse to a criterion that enhances the analysis of the consequences of different meanings. He chooses on the basis of the effects[195], following a specific criterion given by Public Finance. For the rule application he considers if the effects overlap with the legislative aims, so granting redistributive justice and efficiency of these laws.

The interpreter considers 'the nature of things' that is social reality like the fact. The factual approach must be completely recovered because the fact is particularly source of tax law. in this sense is rightly valorized the fairness of the fact cognitive proceedings by the judge[196], which excludes generalized forms of legal presumptions. He interprets the tax statute depending on his application to the real case and chooses, considering the effects, among several meanings what convinces him more, as it realizes more intensively than the others, redistributive justice[197] and efficiency. The tax statute becomes an instrument through which the Economic Analysis of Law scholars aim to achieve further results concerning the well-being allocation, especially the ability to affect considerably people's behaviour, in order to achieve the purposes that the legal system pursues through the processes of identification of collective choices, reducing economic and social welfare less than other laws. Especially the relief tax rules, like the expenditure rules which acknowledge aids, stimulate specific choices of public interest, such as the establishment of a business in a particular less developed area or a behaviour against pollution. Public finance modelling allows the interpreter of the tax statute to anticipate the real impact on the individuals' behaviour to whom it is addressed[198]. The incentive[199] for efficient behaviour overlaps with the

195. Denozza, *Norme efficienti. L'analisi economica del diritto, supra*, p. 11, states that it cannot reasonably be affirmed that all rules can be interpreted, disregarding systematically the effects produced by the choice of the one or the other possible interpretation.

196. Since the half of the twentieth century it was believed that the judge applies to the real case a rule, of which he has already identified the meaning. Robert Alexy underlines that in 1960 Lorenz had already refuted this right formulation. *Teoria dell'argomentazione giuridica, supra*. See also Sacco, *L'interpretazione, supra*, p. 165.

197. Sacco, *L'interpretazione,* Le fonti del diritto italiano, p. 231, observes that in Italy a group of jurists among the best prepared, favours *Economic Analysis of Law* and outside this group the method leaves the other jurists indifferent or is misunderstood. Some of them affirm that the method favours capital values at the expense of others and other sceptics refute its rigorous and formal argumentation and prefer the logic linked to the mood oriented to the argumentative cunning and debtor of the moralistic emotion and theatricality. In favour of the interpretation inspired by *Economic Analysis of Law* are Alpa, Pulitini, Rodotà and Romani (edited by) 1982, Mattei, *Comparative Law and Economics*, 1987 e med. A., I, Atto e valore, Deridda and Vattimo (edited by) *Diritto, giustizia e interpretazione, supra*.

198. Abrescia, Presentation to the volume of Friedman, *L'ordine del diritto. Perchè l'analisi economica può servire al diritto, supra*, p. 7.

resources allocation to those who will be able to manage them more efficiently, so that the damage to the welfare growth would be smaller.

The economic concepts, guaranteed by redistributive justice and efficiency, allow to know and solve problems of tax law[200].

Where the interpretation of the tax law with the correct traditional method leads to several results, the interpreter, using Economic Analysis of Law in its highest evolution level and complementing this method with the contribution of the European schools, is able to justify the choice of the solution which best realizes redistributive justice with the least damage to efficiency, concerning the effects that this choice produces. It is necessary, of course, to verify the compatibility of the result indicated by this method with the indications drawn from the tax statute, the general principles and the dogmatic because these ones prevail on the method results. Indeed, all these instruments are simultaneously used to reach a unique result, the most suitable for the tax juridical system is chosen. The interpreter of the rules of European tax law must neither take inspiration from the rules of his national legal system nor from the prevailing principles of some other national legal systems. He must consider the effects spread in all Member States, which favouring the four fundamental freedoms and the tax non-discrimination principle, are the basis of collective welfare.

The U.S. Economic *Analysis of* Law purified from the elements which affect the cognitive nature of interpretation, constitutes a useful integration of the economic analysis method built at the beginning of last century by the U.S. realism and the Italian, German and Spanish doctrine, concerning financial law in general and tax law

199. Friedman, *L'ordine del diritto. Perchè l'analisi economica può servire al diritto?*, Bologna, 2004, translation of *Law's Order. What economy has to do with law and why it matters*, Princeton University, 2000.

200. Monica Sofia Safar Diaz, Economic Analysis of Constitutional Law: Application of Economic Theory Under the Public Choice School (Análisis Económico Del Derecho Constitucional: Aplicación De La Teoría Económica Bajo La Escuela De La Elección Pública), in *Revista Derecho del Estado*, No. 23, pp. 175–190, 2009; Mark Geistfeld, Efficiency, Fairness, and the Economic Analysis of Tort Law, in *Theoretical foundations of law and economics*, Mark D. White ed., Cambridge U. Press, 2009, NYU School of Law, Public Law Research Paper No. 09-26, NYU Law and Economics Research Paper No. 09-21, 2009; Eyal Zamir and Barak Medina, Law, Economics, and Morality: constrained Economic Analysis of the Fight Against Terrorism, Law, Economics and Morality, Oxford University Press, Forthcoming, 2009; Anne Van Aaken, Opportunities for and Limits to an Economic Analysis of International Economic Law, Society of International Economic Law (SIEL), Second Biennial Global Conference, University of Barcelona, July 8–10, 2010, U. of St. Gallen Law & Economics Working Paper No. 2010-09; Douglas H. Ginsburg and Eric M. Fraser, The Role of Economic Analysis in Competition Law, in *Getting the balance right: intellectual property, competition law and economics in Asia*, Ian McEwin, ed., Hart Publishing, Forthcoming, 2010; Nicolas F. Diebold, Non-Discrimination and the Pillars of International Economic Law – Comparative Analysis and Building Coherency, Society of International Economic Law (SIEL), Second Biennial Global Conference, University of Barcelona, July 8–10, 2010; Edward Peter Stringham and Mark D. White, Economic Analysis of Tort Law: Austrian and Kantian Perspectives, in *Law and economics: alternative economic approaches to legal and regulatory issues*, Margaret Oppenheimer, Nicholas Mercuro, eds., pp. 374–392. New York: M.E. Sharpe, 2010; Edward Peter Stringham and r. Gonzeles, The Role of Empirical Assumptions in Economic Analysis: On Facts and Counterfactuals in Economic Law, in *Journal des Economistes et des Etudes Humaines*, Vol. 15, N. 1, 2010; Geoffrey P. Miller, *Law and Economics versus Economic Analysis of Law*, NYU Law and Economics Research Paper No. 11-16, New York University (NYU) - School of Law, 2011.

in particular. The tax law science evolves, ensuring an efficient system and redistributive justice, only if it is analysed considering financial law, from which it comes, and which is pervaded by an extra-juridical motivation developed by a specific economic science, which is indispensable for the jurist who is strictly constrained to the correct methodological criterion.

Before juridical rationalism spread, the interpreter only drew the text meaning, but now he controls also the efficiency and the redistributive justice of tax law. This principle, which acts upon individuals to equally distribute welfare, requiring progressive taxes and social expenses, ensures the adequate understanding of tax law, provided that the concept of fair or unfair tax rules is clear. Justice and injustice describe the relationship among tax rules.

Economic *Analysis of* Law gives an important contribution to the clarification of the concept of justice which overlaps with the correspondent constitutional value. Indeed, this method allows the interpretation, constitutionally oriented, of the tax statute[201], so that it tends to determine efficiency and redistributive justice as qualified by the Constitution, in accordance to which the interpreter chooses the correct meaning of the tax rule[202].

The U.S. model of Economic Analysis of Law has now spread around the world[203]. It has reached Latin America, Japan, China[204] and Europe noticing a more favourable reception in Germany, Holland, Switzerland and Scandinavia even for their economic organization. It is not only an uncritical welcoming of a U.S. modelling in the European context. The structural differences among different systems are examined, especially the ones between civil law and common law countries.

Calabresi, referring to the aforementioned comparison with Zweigert of 1965, to whom he had announced that the economic approach to the juridical phenomenon was not a rigorous study at that time, but that it would shortly, observes: '... and after not many years facts have given me reason'[205].

---

201. In this sense is the sentence of the Constitutional Court n. 64 of 14 March 2008, about the criteria for the occupation of public spaces and areas and the sentence of the Court of cassation at united sections n. 26972 of 11 November 2008.
202. It is the case of the jurisprudence of the Court of Cassation itself with united sections (nn. 30052 and 30057 of 23.12.2008), on the basis of which, do not exist in the Constitution and in the European legal system, the principles about law abuse which allow not to consider the cases expressly provided by law, in which tax avoidance can be recognised.
203. *The Law and Economics of Globalization*, edited by Yueh, Cheltenham, 2009.
204. *Economic Analysis of Law in China*, edited by Eger, Faure, and Naigen, Cheltenham, 2007, in which excellent examples of *'Law and Economics'* are contained, which are useful to identify the applicable law in the essential dimensions of economy.
205. *Cosa è l'analisi economica del diritto?, supra.*

CHAPTER 2

Tax Law

Nicola d'Amati

---

§2.01 CONSISTENCY AND SYSTEMATIC NATURE OF TAX RELATIONSHIP IN THE TRADITIONAL DOCTRINE

The doctrine distinguishes between two aspects in tax relationship: one in which the power or sovereignty of the State appears - it consists in withdrawing from private economies the means necessary to form the general fund for the production of other public services – and the other one, *the right to tax*, which is formed by the credit given by the State to the taxpayer as an income tax.[1]

The same year in which Ranelletti held his *Course* at the State University of Milan, Blumenstein formulated the concept of tax relationship. However, it was differentiated into two figures: tax power relationship and tax liability relationship, the former concerning a financial accomplishment by the taxpayer (so-called tax liability relationship), the latter scrutinizing the tax (assessment relationship) and also exercising the individual's right to cooperate with the administration, so as to safeguard his/her interests and to influence the amount of tax.[2]

Buhler combines the two aspects into one,[3] that is, within the sphere of tax relationship.

This does not involve the assumption of tax relationship as a unifying criterion of a particular law sector, as in Barbero's system; he has however considered the legal relationship not as a direct relationship between two subjects, but as a relationship mediated by the legal system: the subjects find themselves in a mutual collaboration,

---

1. O. Ranelletti, *Dir.fin.*, 150 ff., Id., *Nat.giur.*, 32, where we are informed that it is *political law* for the *cause* and for the *title*, but it is *civil law* for the *effect*, the *form* and the *foro*.
2. E. Blumenstein, *Sistema di diritto delle imposte*, Milan, 1954, 9 and ff.
3. The concept is formulated in this way by Giannini, *Ibid.*, who makes it close to the Italian legislation.

sub jure, and the legal relationship takes the form of a *relationship* between a *given subject and the law*.[4]

Precisely, the theorists of this orientation warn that this relationship, taken as a whole, belongs primarily to public law, while tax liability is the same obligation of civil law used by the legal system in tax matters.[5]

Despite it being a formal distinction, the different nature of the two components – excluding the unity of personal duties and financial obligations – also excludes that their entirety can make the whole of taxes a separate branch of public law.

§2.02 THE 'ASSESSMENT': 'TAXATION' ALTERNATIVE IN THE 1930s–1940s DOCTRINE

The traditional doctrine defines the assessment as the act or the series of acts necessary for the verification and evaluation of the different constituents of the tax liability, with the resulting application of the rate and the concrete quantitative determination of the taxpayer's debt.[6] The adjustment notice is done, as a rule, by the Administration itself, according to the forms prescribed by law: between the position of the objective rule and its application to the case, there is an official act that determines the amount owed by the person liable for payment.[7] Tax liability arises from the occurrence of the condition, and the adjustment notice is a condition for the credit pay ability.[8]

To such conception it was opposed that – in most taxes and, in particular, in direct taxes – the tax would arise from the act of taxation.[9] Subsequent writers have considered the problem in a reductive way, asserting that the contrast between the assertion that the tax obligation arises from the condition of the tax and the contrary, and follows only on first approximation the recognition of the moment when tax obligation originates. The issue is more complex, since the declarative theory conforms to the stages through which public revenues pass. *Assessment* relates to all of the government credits, whatever the title, even though there are different ways in which it is carried out (Article 222): direct taxes and other fixed-term revenues are collected through roles issued in each year through the procedures prescribed by the relevant laws and regulations and by the amount of the taxpayer's debt to the State (paragraph 2, letter a). The revenue collection authorized by the budget law must be made through agents designated by the relevant laws and regulations (Article 223, r.d. n. 827 of 1924).

The prospective of Allorio is different: as a proceduralist, he follows Carnelutti's instructions, in the sense that the conception of the tax phenomenon must be considered, from a legal point of view, as a conflict of interests.[10] In a research few

4. D. Barbèro, *Il sistema del diritto privato*, new edn., Turin, 1989, 59 ff.
5. A.D. Giannini, *Istituz*, 73 ff.
6. A.D. Giannini, *Istituz.*, 143 ff.; the references are in the 1960 edition, previous to the writings of Capaccioli and Micheli.
7. A.D. Giannini, *Ibid.*
8. A.D. Giannini, *Istituz..*, 151
9. E. Allorio, *Diritto processuale tributario*, Milan, 1942, 96 ff.
10. F. Carnelutti, *Introduz.allo studio del dir.proc.trib*, in 'Riv.dir.proc.civ.', 1932, 105 ff.

years later, Carnelutti also considers how tax law colleagues have not replied with equal enthusiasm to the reciprocity.[11] Speaking of the complexity of the tax court process and of the plurality of the aspects is unnecessary,[12] given that even today there is a debate whether tax commissions had, from the start, administrative or jurisdictional nature.[13] Nor it is a coincidence that the first response to Carnelutti's solicitation came from a tax consultant and that the subject-matter of the discussion was the administrative tax court process.[14]

But the real treatise on procedural law was to come shortly afterwards, with the *Opera* by Enrico Allorio.[15] The postulate of the normal coincidence of the subject of tax relationships with the subject of the tax case[16] and the reduction of substantial situations into formal actionable acts did not appear clear to all, and the *Opera* was going to meet criticisms and misunderstandings. Among the former, those by Carnacini, about the consideration which sees tax procedural law as an 'accomplished procedural microcosm',[17] do not take into account the dual jurisdiction – ordinary and administrative – of tax litigation. To these criticisms are to be added, in the form of *Postilla*, the criticisms by Griziotti towards the claim that, according to the jurist, formal considerations are decisive (p. 87); such claim would reach results of obvious, but unworthy clarity.[18] Among the latter, there are the supports – not always consistent with the thought of Allorio – of some presumed 'students' who reverse the view of the *Opera*, by considering overriding the substantial aspect, conceived instead by Allorio as the premise of procedural law, in order to let the compulsory relationship matches with the procedural relationship.

The idea of the *Opera* is based on the reconstruction of the Tax Authority, according to the view that the instrumental rule, in establishing a function, can make it *bound*. Such is the function of taxation that finance performs and must perform by enforcing the tax law verified in its real features, with the greatest freedom and the most rigorous means of researching.

Tax procedural law is connected with the substantial institutions, which are the functions and face of tax procedural law and which patently stand out in examining the relationships between the process and the substantial institutions; these relationships express themselves in those ones between tax process and the substantial tax relationship.[19]

The key point is in the concept of taxation, which, in every category of taxes, would be the procedure through which the Tax Authority would find the tax relationship. These are effects that can be appropriately placed in that group of acts ruled in our

11. F. Carnelutti, *Finanza e processo*, in 'Riv.dir.fin.sc.fin.', 1937, I, 243 ff.
12. Cf. N. d'Amati, *Quel memorabile anno 1926 …*, in 'Dir.prat.trib.', 2007, I, 671.
13. Cf. N. d'Amati, *L'eleganza delle origini delle commissioni tributarie*, awaiting publication in 'Studi Parlato'.
14. A. Berliri, *Il processo tributario amministrativo*, Reggio Emilia, 1940, 2 vols.
15. E. Allorio, *Dir.proc.trib.*, Milano, 1942
16. E. Allorio, *Dir.proc.*, 345 ff.
17. T. Carnacini, *Recensione all'Opera dell'Allorio*, in 'Riv.dir.fin.sc.fin.', 1943, I, 192
18. B. Griziotti, *Ibid.*
19. In this sense, E. Allorio, *Dir.proc.*, 79.

system, by distinctive rules distinguished from those that rule jurisdictional proceedings as well as from those related to public administration acts, conversely similar to these ones.[20] This is an aspect that is not far from Allorio's Studies,[21] in order to demonstrate the nearness of the administrative activity to the jurisdictional one.[22]

Allorio's procedural conception makes as the subject of the assessment tax process the right of the person who thinks himself/herself injured by illegitimate taxation to make the tax court revoke the imposition. Taxation by finance and impugnation by the taxpayer are on opposite sides as the two cornerstones of tax procedural law.[23] This connection seems weak in the point where the disputability of the act of taxation is connected with the constitutiveness. Actually, the act of finance could have appeal terms-pending constitutive efficacy, unless it is contested; so constitutiveness is not considered as a feature of the act, as it depends on external and uncertain circumstances.[24]

The phenomenon is defined by the doctrine of administrative cases, which, going back to the origins of the confusion, warns how it is often forgotten that even in legal obligations there is a difference between the source of the obligation and the way in which the application of the *ex lege* creditor's right is regulated. It may therefore happen that the constitutive case of the obligation takes on efficiency with the intervention of an act of the creditor.

In this case, it develops a module in which there would be a declarative ablative procedure that can claim to be an assessment procedure, applied in a subordinate form: the taxpayer fulfils his/her own obligation, just the one that he/she believes to be the extent of the condition; the office will take action at a later date, in order to verify the tax condition assumption, through an office procedure.[25]

In essence, it is the finality of the act, not the constitutiveness, to allow the appeal.

§2.03 THE 1950s PRE-REFORM AND ROLE MEDIATION

The 1960s and 1970s writings on the assessment adopt positions that are highly critical of the traditional doctrine, with the statement that, within the assessment case, the body of knowledge available is little and vague. It is difficult to oppose serious arguments to rough and generic opinions.

More can be said about the state of the assessment doctrine. The ground becomes more solid with the announcement of a committed and proactive writing. Among the whirl of digressions of doubtful relevance, the only concrete point, that seems to pave the way for some solution is the claim that all the activity that forms the assessment is

20. E. Fazzalari, *Giurisdiz.volontaria*, in 'Enc.dir.', vol. XIX, 330 ff.
21. E. Allorio, *Saggio polemico*, etc., in 'Riv.trim.dir.proc.', 1948, 487 ff.
22. E. Allorio, *Dir.proc.*, 11 ff.
23. E. Allorio, *supra*, 123.
24. E. Allorio, *Ibid.*
25. M.S. Giannini, *Dir.amm*, 1267 ff.

generally regarded as inseparable and ever-recurring from the traditional doctrine.[26] The case of tax with assessment would therefore be the one in which the collection (or its completion) is reached following the sequence: declaration, office 'notice', possible agreement, appeals, etc.[27] This conception does not seem to go beyond the mere contrast between the provisions issued in the '50s and the constructions made on the basis of existing laws in the previous decade.

Proceeding with caution, we are reminded that Giannini's *Istituzioni* were published in 1938 – when the existing RD 17 September 1931, No. 1608, and the law 8 June 1936, No. 1231 – with interpretations and amendments of laws on direct taxes, in conjunction with the T.U. 24 August 1877, No. 4021, of the laws on the tax of movable wealth that, in Title VI, regulated the tax determination and collection, whose application was subsequently extended to all direct taxes.

The legislature of 1958, though recasting the previous legislation in the T.U., had given particular emphasis to the new discipline of assessment based on the annual tax return principle, introduced by Article 1, L. 11 January 1951, No. 25, then recast in Article 17, T.U., cit.

During the public finance and financial law course introduction lesson, held at Sacro Cuore Catholic University, Allorio warned how, through the new income annual tax return subject to direct taxes, the legislature had modernized the process of taxation, by touching the tax business in its essential aspect, and by placing itself at the heart, not only of tax law – as it is technically referred to – but of the financial function of the State, of the very life of the State.[28]

The 1950s legislation has gradually accrued other changes, with rules on the assessment, the collection and the penalties. Among the provisions recast in the T.U. of 1958, it has particular relevance in Article 174, which included the definitive registration in the roles of the corresponding taxes, with the taxable income determined under Article 123, by keeping fixed the higher income office assessments of the previous years.

Despite the diversity of situations, there is a common element in Article 174, where the connection between the declared taxable income and the tax is mediated by the roles, and in Articles 123 and 142, which still keep fixed the higher income of the previous assessments. When facing the new legislation, the 1960s and 1970s literature – lacking some dogmatic references able to strengthen innovative positions – found consensus in the criticism of the traditional elaboration, and this often without reconstructing the contents and remaining enmeshed in schemes which have been put in contrast to figures that are specular or just similar, but which have no foundation in the history of law or in the well-established dogmas.

26. E. Capaccioli, *Ibid*
27. E. Capaccioli, *supra*, 10 ff.
28. E. Allorio, *Sulla riforma del procedimento d'imposizione*, etc., in 'Moneta e credito', 1951, 474 ff.

§2.04 AN ALCHEMICAL FORMULA: THE ASSESSMENT AT VARIABLE COMPOSITION

The criticism of the traditional doctrine is based on the supposed rigidity of the assessment set up by the declarative theory. Such theory says that where the law indicates the elements of tax obligation through a general and abstract formula, there is the need of an activity able to ensure: (1) the existence of the material prerequisite, in respect of any individual taxpayer; (2) the correspondence between the material prerequisite and the case law; (3) the monetary value of the condition (tax base).[29] In this way, the formula can join the concrete reality of the single tax relationships. Generally speaking, this construction – that is consistent with the rules in force at that time, is opposed to the fact that, in the case of a tax with assessment, the collection is the result of the sequence: declaration, office 'notice', possible agreement, appeals, etc., with a variable composition,[30] referring to the '50s legislation, which had been cleared up by the T.U. of 1958, by adjusting the assessment (Articles 31 et seq.), in accordance with the principle of the annual tax return.

Although being not intentionally challenging, the term 'sequence', however, refers to an ordered succession of things, which does not really benefit from the notation that it is 'at variable composition'.[31] It is a sort of catenary succession, which may consist of one or more acts, but which cannot change the order of the rings. The declaration can be followed and even replaced or not by the office 'notice', but the office notice cannot precede the declaration; nor can it ignore the fact that the traditional theory had already warned that tax assessment is made of the act or of a coordinated series of acts of a different kind.[32]

The same critical tendency warns that some logical reasons would want the inquiry to be opened by the act that occurs first, that is by the declaration; but, for a sort of gentlemen's agreement, nobody worries about the declaration.[33] It is surprising that, after 15 years from the entry into force of Law No. 25 and then of the T.U. of 1958, and of the laws on direct taxes, nobody is aware of what Allorio had suspected in the very moment in which the law was being enacted: that is, to consider the declaration as the centre point of the financial function of the State.[34]

By reversing the premise, the same position gives strength to the declaration, which, for the purposes of the production of the effect, would have a role equal to that of any other act that might occur, including the assessment notice issued by the office.[35] Just one point is still open: the equivalence of the acts subsumed in the assessment is not compatible with the concept of sequence, which involves a certain chain of the acts, some of which cannot exist without the expectation of at least another one.

29. E. Capaccioli, *Accertamento tributario*, in 'Riv.dir.fin.sc.fin.', 1966, I, 3 ff., spec. 6 ff.
30. E. Capaccioli, *supra*, 10 ff.
31. E. Capaccioli, *Ibid.*
32. A.D. Giannini, *Istituz*, 158.
33. E. Capaccioli, *Ibid.*
34. E. Allorio, *Sulla riforma del procedimento d'imposiz.*, *supra*, 474.
35. E. Capaccioli, *supra*, 27 ff.

After further insistence on the degradation of the studies on assessment, it is claimed that the assessment notice produces a precise and specific effect: the tax base fixing. To achieve this result, it would be enough to remind that, in the traditional doctrine, the tax assessment involves the observation and evaluation of the different elements of the tax liability, including the tax base, with the resulting rate application and the concrete determination of the tax liability.[36]

The theory of the sequence, accepting the category of the 'illiquid element case',[37] seems to approach the traditional doctrine and then to depart with the prediction of the liquidation effect, far from the concept of credit pay ability.[38]

The recognition of the contradiction in the most accepted general doctrine of tax law is transient: on the one hand, the obligation is created by law with the occurrence of the condition, on the other hand, the same obligation is based on the state-administration power which would exclude the direct 'law-fact contact'.

It is also to clarify the importance of the term illiquid 'element', that the theory of the sequence derives from the obligation to compensate; such obligation arises as soon as an injury occurs, resulting in the estimation process,[39] where credit–debt is to be considered liquid not only when it is determined its amount, but also when only mechanical operations of simple arithmetic remain[40] without giving importance to the observation and evaluation of the various constituents of the performance.[41] Anyway, the reference to the agreement between individuals on the amount of any possible compensation is not relevant; except for the recurrent question of the unavailability of tax obligation, the tax base estimation is made by the offices when facing a bound function.[42]

§2.05 (CONTINUED): COMPOSITION AND PROCESS

The doctrine previous to the T.U. of 1958 depicted the agreement as a transactive bilateral negotiation, as a conceptually different condition of the measure; i.e. a transaction, not as a constitutive act of the tax relationship, but as a condition of the unilateral measure of taxation, conceptually distinct from it, although formally joined to it,[43] anticipating the provisions of Article 4 of Law No. 1 of 1945, then recast in Article 34, T.U. 1958, where the composition takes the form of an accession of the taxpayer to the assessment.

In the following editions of the *Opera*, this figure acquires more complex aspects, with the prevalence of the composition, as a misure of taxation that is distinguished from the proper accession of the taxpayer to taxation or, rather, to the quantitative

36. A.D. Giannini, *Ibid.*
37. E. Capaccioli, *supra*, 29, seg.
38. In this sense A.D. Giannini, *supra*, 150 ff.
39. E. Capaccioli, *supra*, 24 ff.
40. E. Capaccioli, *supra*, 26.
41. A.D. Giannini,*Istituz.*, 143.
42. A.D. Giannini,*Istituz.*, 143.
43. E. Allorio, *Dir.proc.*, 1942, 178 ff.

element of the same.[44] The definition does not seem to adhere to the *ratio* of the regulation, which includes the accession of the taxpayer to the tax base determined by the office: it is a measure which occurs when the proper act of taxation has produced its effects, with the assessment of the tax base that the taxpayer has asked for being reviewed. The next measure is an act which, though being authoritarian, contains, entirely or in part, the reasons of the taxpayer, and shows a subtle transactive character.

In the continuation of the sequence, the compositions may be followed, though not necessarily, by the decisions of the tax courts.[45] The view is not entirely accurate, since the tax composition is defined as antithetical to the tax dispute[46] and, if the appeal is pending, the proceedings are extinguished.[47]

The view that there are decisions concerning only the tax base within the proceedings for direct taxes is not even accurate. Such decisions would be equivalent to the declaration, as well as to the 'notice' and to the composition, since they produce an effect of the same type: they define the liquidation of the tax base.[48] The dissent is based on logical rather than legal arguments. The set may consist of elements of any nature, even different from one another, according to a criterion able to recognize whether an object, an entity or an event belongs to it. Internally, there may be subsets, which must include homogeneous elements. Within the theory of the sequence, the assessment tax case is, by definition, the one in which the collection (or its completion) is reached as a result of the declaration, of the office 'notice', of the possible agreement, of the appeal, etc.[49] Therefore, the declaration would have a role equal to that of any other act that may appear: in particular, the office notice. The equivalence of these acts is manifested in terms of the specific legal effect, which characterizes and defines it, being the declaration – like any other act – an act of liquidation of the tax base.[50]

In providing for easy objections, the same view notes that there is nothing to consider the declaration in relation to the act which may follow it and which is configured as a procedural requirement.[51] It is debatable whether, with respect to this, the criterion based on the effects is more appropriate for aggregating the set, but not the opinion that the proposed solution is unavoidable because 'we study the phenomenon that is referred to as "assessment";[52] you cannot, in fact, take as a proof of validity, the assertion that you want to demonstrate'.

The far most prone point of the set-sequence can be found in the decisions which would concern only the tax base, where the dispute and the decision of estimation are always identifiable and distinguishable and, therefore, equivalent to the declaration, the notice, the composition, since they produce an effect of the same type.[53] The

44. E. Allorio, *Dir.proc.*, 1962, 84.
45. E. Capaccioli, *supra*, 11.
46. E. Allorio, *supra*, 176 ff.
47. A.D. Giannini, *Istituz.*, 172.
48. E. Capaccioli, *supra*, 32 ff.
49. E. Capaccioli, *supra*, 10 ff.
50. E. Capaccioli, *supra*, 27.
51. E. Capaccioli, *supra*, 28 ff.
52. E. Capaccioli, *Ibid.*
53. E. Capaccioli, *Ibid.*

specification may be acceptable, although limited to the issues of estimation under the competence of the commissions; but it loses consistency when it is referred to the power of the central commission, which is also extended to the disputes arising from the existence and the assessment of the income mentioned in the previous paragraph (Article 50, TU on the imp. of r.m. of 1877). The central commission is also competent in this matter, within the limits of the criteria by which the commissions have made the estimation.

Therefore, an empty symbol remains within the formulation of the set-sequence. Nor the obstacle would deserve to be bypassed, by including the decisions of the central commission, whose responsibility is, however, of legitimacy. Precisely for what concerns the effects, the obstacle would be unassailable, since in the jurisdictional field it has produced a legal consequence which would mark the jurisdiction with regard to the administration. Such consequence is the *res judicata.*[54]

§2.06 THE TAX PROCEEDINGS AS AN ALTERNATIVE TO THE TAX RELATIONSHIP

It is a little earlier than this one, the theory that has advanced the variable character of the assessment as a tool set up by the law to bring together subjective legal situations having a content that may not be appropriate, such as the tax obligation and the power of taxation, with a view to a final legal effect: the acquisition by the finance of certain services by way of taxes or penalties.[55] Furthermore, the equivalence of the two figures seems to be set to create uncertainties in the way of thinking itself, where we are warned not to consider the tax process as a necessary form of tax enforcement, as it is in the declarative theory.[56]

In any case, the procedural theory complies with a peculiar phenomenon: the application of i.g.e managed with a pattern without the characters of the proceeding, being an instantaneous tax whose fulfilment, contemporary with the occurrence of the case, may also occur with the use of tax symbols (brands) without the provision transforming into an obligation to do.[57]

The critical front line towards this figure is very wide, which the constitutive theory defines as a *tax-free* figure,[58] while a leaning declarative orientation talks about *evasion case*[59] with an expression of doubtful accuracy, as if these taxes are designed to encourage the practice. It is actually a self-assessment,[60] which admits only the next assessment on the accuracy of the accomplishment.

54. E. Allorio, *Nuove*, 513.
55. F. Maffezzoni, *Il procedimento d'imposiz. nell'ige*, Napoli, 1965, 71.
56. A. Fedele, *A proposito di saggi sul procedim.trib.*, in 'Riv.dir.fin.sc.fin', 1971, I, *estr.*, 11 ff., text and note 24.
57. On this question, cf. A. Berliri, *La legge del bollo*, Milan; in a critical way, N. d'Amati, *L'imposta di bollo*, Turin, 1961.
58. E. Allorio, *Dir.proc.*, 92.
59. E. Capaccioli, *L'accert.*, 5.
60. A.D. Giannini, *Istituz.*, 151, *adde*, N. d'Amati, *Autoaccertamento*, in the *Appendice*, in 'Novis.Dig.It.', vol.I.

§2.07 THE 'PURE' DOCTRINE OF THE PROCEDURE

Another approach, through a different formulation, argues that for the declarative approach the tax obligation is created by law, so that all the following acts are moments for the liquidation, i.e. the quantification of the service, although they cannot deny the existence of investigative proceedings equipped for that purpose.[61] It is also noted that, along this line, they would have gone on reducing the tax assessment to a mere administrative act for qualifying the obligation that has already arisen.[62] The analysis stops at the surface of the phenomenon, by mixing declarative theories, which deeply differ from each other; their bond is broken in the point where the procedural conception believes that the traditional doctrine would reduce the activity in which consists the assessment to a mere (administrative) act of liquidation,[63] due to the mere liquidation of the tax base.[64] The traditional doctrine defines, instead, the *assessment* of the tax in a broad sense, as the act or the series of acts necessary for the verification and evaluation of the different constituents of the tax liability, with the consequent application of the rate and the assessment of the taxpayer's debt.[65]

During the construction phase, the procedural theory tends to distinguish the different situations the one from the other, by giving a more specific content, within the framework of the tax rule application procedure, through a procedural pattern which, on the one hand, unifies the sequence of more acts and, on the other hand, it highlights how some legal situations, which would lead to the need for other acts, derive from the accomplishment of these acts.[66]

Disagreeing with the traditional notion of the administrative procedure, being it a sequence of acts and operations linked together, with regard to and at the service of the main act,[67] the procedural theory achieves the process to decompose in a variety of different obligations within tax law by establishing more assessment acts. The critical point is in the unresolved harmonization of the proceedings arising from the need to make different controls on the ways of application of certain taxes, with the payment of services due at different times, however, deriving from a single source: the tax base case that is presented as a closed structure case, which links a variety of situations.[68]

The perspective of the procedural theory is different, which tends to emphasize the conceptions that move from the principle of tax capacity (Article 53, paragraph 1, Constitution) and from the need to ensure the full realization of the tax, both in terms of detection of the condition and of the taxable persons, and in terms of participation in public expenditure, as opposed to the declarative theories deriving from the rule of law (Article 23, Constitution) .[69]

61. G.A. Micheli, *Consideraz.sul procedimento trib.d'accertamento*, in 'Riv.dir.fin.sc.fin.', 1974, I, 620 ff.
62. G.A. Micheli, *Ibid.*
63. G.A. Micheli, *Ibid.*, with references to Capaccioli
64. In this sense, E. Capaccioli, *supra*, 28.
65. A.D. Giannini, *Istituz.*, 143.
66. G.A. Micheli, *Consideraz.*, 625 ff.
67. A.M. Sandulli, *Procedimento amministrativo*, in 'Noviss.Dig.It.', vol. XIII, 1921, spec.1922.
68. N. d'Amati, *Sistema, infra.*
69. A.D. Giannini, *I concetti fondamentali del diritto tributario*, 1956, 159 ff.

The diversification of some theoretical orientations does not seem acceptable on the basis of the juxtaposition of different constitutional principles, all designed to make the tax secure and fair. Moreover, it is due to the traditional doctrine itself the awareness of the fact that there is a certain uniformity in the various tax systems, addressing the legislature primarily to those economic situations which, for their generality and for their suitability to express the citizens' tax capacity, are considered as best suitable for being the basis of taxation.[70]

The linearity of the formulations dating back to the traditional doctrine does not always correspond with the observations of the subsequent literature, where the procedural aspects of tax application are interwoven with substantial situations of dubious connection. Nor the inquiry of tax studies - characterized by more complex and articulated phases of implementation - makes it clearer. Such inquiry would reveal the need for reconstruction, not according to the scheme of a single administrative procedure, but according to the patterns of more administrative proceedings and single acts which are variously connected with each other.[71]

Situations that are torn away from their place are placed in unnatural contexts, such as possible patterns that would occur where the levy is included in proceedings designed to adopt measures or however to achieve results totally uninvolved in tax matters, without indicating the nature and the function. They are, actually, levies on the administrative acts, which are connected with the exercise of a particular public activity, and for which the payment of a specified sum is a condition for the effectiveness of the concession act. The concession act has no effect unless it is complemented by the payment of a certain sum of money.[72] It is a poorly fruitful phenomenon, which ends with the issuing of the act or with the refusal of the concession without the non-existence or the irregularity affecting the measure effectiveness.[73]

Therefore, there is no place for the configuration of the payments themselves as a previous payment, instrumentally designed to the discharge of a future tax obligation with the charging of the amounts paid in advance,[74] nor it could not be allowed the charging of the sums already passed under the taxation authority, and bound to the discharge of a subsequently arisen credit of the same authority.[75]

This reconstruction is based on a hypothesis that can be easily reversed: in the absence of a title, no amount can be paid as a prepayment. The mandatory ablative procedures are different; they have both the privative and the appropriative aspects, as the real procedures. Even the operating rules are different, there not being, in this case, the pre-withdrawal of amounts due as a fee for the request for a public service,

70. A. Fedele, *supra*, 10.
71. A Fedele, *supra*, 13 ff.
72. A.D. Giannini, *Istituz.*, 470 ff.
73. A. Fedele, *supra*, 16 e ff.
74. S. La Rosa, *I tributi di conc.governativa*, etc., in Aa.Vv., *Saggi*, *supra*, 143 ff.
75. A. Fedele, *A propostio di saggi sul procedim.trib.*, *supra*, estr., 18 ff.

personally concerning the person liable for payment.[76] More simply, it is the conduct charge of a person to realize his/her own interest, in order to exercise a right.[77]

Precisely for this feature, no one would be able to find a basis for the taxation authority's obligation to repay, entirely or in part, the amounts paid, if the condition does not occur, i.e. justifies a lower tax service related to the connection of the service with the contribution to public expenditure.[78] It is a question overcome by the magisterial guideline of the same theory, which links again the fee with the demand for a State service which requires a certain activity of the public authority that the law connects with the obligation to pay that tax:[79] a tax which directly refers to the fulfilment of one of the activities of the administration,[80] without references to the tax capacity, as regarding the type of service requested.[81]

§2.08 PROCEDURE AND DIRECT PAYMENT OF THE TAX

The past few decades literature, generally critical of the traditional doctrine, considers the procedure as a unifying framework for all aspects of taxation, similarly to the tax relationship of the traditional doctrine: the duty of declaration takes its origin from the occurrence of the condition. The declaration is required even if no income has been produced during the tax period,[82] shifting the perspective from a substantial level (tax liability) to a formal one (tax return), so as to loosen the bond between the occurrence of the condition and the development of the tax obligation. Article 1, Presidential Decree No. 600 would seem to confirm this view with the provision for each taxpayer's obligation to declare his/her own income (Article 1, Presidential Decree No. 600). The reconstruction is not sensitive to the *ratio* of the rule. The subject of the declaration is the taxpayer's income, regardless of whether a tax debt arises or not.

In any case, it is the income and not the declaration to be the condition, as source of the tax obligation. According to this view, the declarative theories are all reducible to the need to find a point of reference in the statutory reserve (Article 23 of the Constitution) and in the general legislative predetermination of the content of the tax obligation.[83] It is not a very detailed reconstruction of the traditional doctrine, according to which the assessment is instead the subject of a specific administrative activity, which is also regulated by objective law, with all the consequences connecting with the administrative nature of the acts created in this field by the public authority.[84]

Nor do we see the reason to oppose to this view, opinions based on the principle of tax capacity (Article 53 of the Constitution, section 1),[85] ignoring the definition of

76. A.D. Giannini, *Istituz.*, 43.
77. P. Rescigno, *Manuale del dir.priv.*, Napoli, 236.
78. A. Fedele, *supra*, 19 ff.
79. G.A. Micheli, *Corso di dir.trib.*, Turin, 1984, 24 ff.
80. A.D. Giannini, *Istituz.*, 470 ff.
81. A.D. Giannini, *supra;* G.A. Micheli, *Ibid.*
82. G.A. Micheli, *Consideraz*, 629 ff.
83. A. Fedele, *A proposito*, 10.
84. A.D. Giannini, *Istituz.*, 144 ff.
85. A. Fedele, *Ibid.*

condition[86] included in the of direct taxes. The drafting of this text was achieved with the work of several commissions that have followed over the years, in some of which there was also Giannini; the final codification has been achieved by the last commission headed by the lawyer Scoca, who is the editor together with Giannini of a collection of tax laws.[87] It is due to Giannini not only the definition of condition in the formal sense - included in the Consolidated Law of 1958 – but also the supposition that, in the identifying of the condition, the legislature is primarily addressed to those economic situations which show the suitability to express the citizens' tax capacity and which are recommended as the basis of taxation.[88] Therefore, it also falls the view on the separation, or at least on the unnecessary coincidence between the occurrence of the condition and the rise of the tax obligation.[89] Actually, the condition and the tax obligation are perfectly compatible and firmly bound, in the sense that the condition is the source of tax obligation, being it the expression of tax capacity.

Within the procedural theory, the fungibility of the implementation schemes of taxes is considered as an expression of the general plurality of the relationships required in the implementation of each single tax and of the mere possibility of the development of obligations having the tax service as their subject.[90] These are all denier hypotheses, not containing solutions of alternative questions or views to the legally valid formulations of the traditional doctrine.

The question becomes accurate through the view according to which the legislature would make a levy in the case that certain facts occur; these facts are taken as tax capacity rates and they are detached from the overall structure of the tax.[91] Such a withdrawal would not anticipate, therefore, the final act, but it would produce specific effects in relation to the existence and the size of that specific condition considered as to be divorced from the other conditions, whose effects would remain separate from the normal rules for the calculation of the total income.[92]

The two remaining points to be clarified are whether or not there is, in our tax system, a 'partial' condition and what are its specific effects.[93] In the definition of T.U. of 1958, the provisions relating to single taxes indicate the facts and the situations which form the basis of tax obligation (Article 2) independent (Article 3), while Articles 1 and 72, T.U. i.r., indicate the monetary or in kind 'possession' (sic, availability) of income included in the categories specified in Article 6 as a condition of the tax obligation (Article 2, cit.). Therefore, there are no 'partial' conditions but only the condition of the tax on the companies income (Articles 1, 72, TUIR) to which withdrawals are connected. The term *deposit* itself, recurring in the regulations

86. A.D. Giannini, *Istituz.*, 119 ff.; this definition is also present in previous versions.
87. S. Scoca, *Un tentativo di codificaz. delle leggi tribut*, in 'Studi Giannini', Milano, 817, seg. spec. 825.
88. A.D. Giannini, *I conc.*, 159, seg.
89. A. Fantozzi, *Premesse per una teoria generale della successione*, ecc., in Aa.Vv., *Studi, supra*, 87, seg., spec. 121.
90. A. Fedele, *supra*, 8.
91. G.A. Micheli, *Ibid.*
92. G.A. Micheli, *Ibid.*, 639.
93. G.A. Micheli, *supra*, 639-40.

included in Title III (Articles 26–30) of Presidential Decree No. 600, designates an arithmetic calculation to determine a payment *on account of* capital obligations.

Not even the legal technique gives reasons to the same theory: the withholding tax is not levied on the sum received by the taxpayer, but it is deducted by the withholding agent from the amount to be paid to the substituted person. Instead of the sum, the taxpayer receives the certification of the taxation made, with the indication of the corresponding tax credit. It is also uncertain the nature of the taxation that an authoritative approach considers as a private relationship (Bodda, Allorio), while the jurisprudence debates the question whether the disputes between the substituted and the substitute belong to the ordinary jurisdiction or to the tax one, depending on whether one gives priority to the private relationship, from which the income arises, or to the tax nature of the withholding tax.

Another question is whether or not the factors that determine taxes are the signs of tax capacity. Precisely because of the 'partiality' of the condition of the withholding tax, the solution is problematic. Article 53 of the Constitution sets out tax capacity as the measure of the participation of all to public expenditure: a service that, though not defined, is capable of being defined where the withholding tax may not correspond with the final tax and where the taxpayer is not in tax debt, but in tax credit.

Once it has fallen the procedural superstructure, is remains the bareness of the phenomenon: the occasional tax is related to specific legal situations, referring to more complex cases. In the rearrangement of the Unitary State legislation and of the regulations of the fifties – made with the TU of 1958 – Articles 126 and127 have adjusted the direct withholding tax on category A and C / 2 incomes, paid by the State administrations as well as the withholding taxes made by persons or entities that make payments of emoluments subject to r.m.

Thus, emerges the critical point: the levy has a real character, even if it is intended to the fulfilment of a progressive personal income tax. God does not play dice (A. Einstein), but the legislature does. As in the case of Schrödinger's cat – that nobody knows whether he's alive or dead until the box is opened to see if it has remained in its compartment or has gone in the other, releasing the poisonous gas – in the supposition of advance payment, only with the confluence of the occasional levy with the total income, one can know the level of the subject's tax capacity in the contribution to public expenditure. Therefore, tax capacity is defined not in relation to a single taxpayer, but to a certain category of recipients and to a particular type of income, of capital, of labour or self-employment, etc.

The unnatural expansion of the concept of procedure did not make us feel its presence, where it actually is. The view that a final assessment absorbs and cancels the partial tax act[94] overlaps two aspects that must be distinguished: the partial payment, which is absorbed by the total income, and the relative proceeding which, on the contrary, does not follow the events related to the tax base formation. The withholding agents must deliver the certification and electronically transmit to the Internal Revenue Service the tax and contributory data contained in it as well as the additional data

94. G.A. Micheli, *supra*, 640.

necessary for the tax authorities to pay off and control (Article 4, paragraph 3 of Presidential Decree No. 322 of 1998), by identifying possible irregularities in the payment of the tax through the verification of the documents (Articles 36*bis* and 37*bis*). The certificates proving the payment of the withholding taxes and any other document as provided for in the laws are stored, presented and transmitted at the request of the competent authority (Article 4, cit., Paragraph 4).

The procedural view loses the central point about the condition occurrence in the explanation of the so-called anticipation of the levy. Income taxes are 'periodical', in the sense that the de facto situation which one must consider for the right determination of the condition is confined within a space of time defined by the legislature.[95] The concept has been defined by the T.U. of 1958: the tax is due for periods to each of which an autonomous tax obligation corresponds (Article 3), and the T.U. itself sets out the beginning and the end of the tax relationship, providing that the taxes are due from the period in which they occur to the period during which the relevant conditions end (Article 5). Therefore, periodical taxes are open-structure cases,[96] in which the tax debt-credit continuum allows you to define the total income at the end of the period, including the revenues, the costs and any other situation occurring in the same period; once the period has ended, the case becomes a tax source.

The procedural theory, lacking in the knowledge of the periodical tax, has not experienced the duplicity of the phenomenon. When the single revenues are objectively taxable, they are subject to withdrawals, even not coincident with the final level of the taxpayer's tax capacity, but coincident with some ratio criteria, uniform for classes of taxpayers. At the end of the period, the different situations join together as units, in order to form the total income declared by the taxpayer or established by the office, with which it corresponds the net tax due or the tax credit to be collected or deducted in the subsequent tax period.

§2.09 FROM THE 1951 PRE-REFORM TO THE TAX DIRECT PAYMENT

Within the more mature formulation, the tax procedure is defined as a coordinated series of acts of a different kind, some of which are simple material actions, others are negotiation administrative acts or mere legal acts, whose essential lines can be understood through the multiplicity of the rules that regulate the various taxes, to make a rational system.[97] Therefore, it is not accurate the observation that, within the declarative thesis, the tax obligation[98] is basically predetermined only by the principle of legality (Article 23). The general reference to the declarative thesis seems to follow the traditional doctrine, but it actually follows the administrative doctrine,[99] although it is not mentioned, for which the omission of the necessary procedural act redounds in

95. A.D. Giannini, *Istituz*, 134 ff.
96. N. d'Amati, *Sistema istituz.*, 52 ff.; already, Id., *Diritto tributario – Teoria e critica*, Turin, 217 ff.
97. A.D. Giannini, *Istituz.*, 158.
98. A.Fedele, *A proposito*, 10.
99. M.S. Giannini, *supra*, 1267, not quoted by Fedele.

defect of the procedure, not being it introduced by an interest .[100] Within taxation, it may therefore happen that the constituent fact of the *ex lege* obligation does not acquire effectiveness without the intervention of an act of the creditor: in these cases the fact, that is the source of the obligation, takes effect with the intervention of the taxpayer or of the legal creditor's declaration.[101]

The theorists of the procedure, generally disinclined to these conjectures, wonder about the meaning of this legal obligation, which cannot acquire its effects if certain acts by the taxable persons or the p.a. have not been made.[102] But it remains distant the reconstruction according to which the formula would respond to the extent of the so-called assessment, which would have an effect of knowledge of events occurred earlier, in order to attribute them a particularly effectiveness, from which it would follow the ablative effect.[103] In the conjecture of the administrative doctrine, the assessment is a way of regulating the exercise of the creditor's right, by affecting the effectiveness through an act of private autonomy or of the office.[104] This process is part of a particular subtype of declarative effectiveness,[105] i.e. it occurs a form of legal transformation of the situation, which makes the taxation authority's *ex lege* personal right effective.

The procedural theories take positions that are critical of the traditional doctrine, and not always reconstruct accurately its dogmas. According to the theory of the sequence, the assessment defined by the declarative theories is an indissoluble and always recurring activity.[106] The incorrect reconstruction of the assessment scheme of the traditional doctrine affects the critical arguments, sometimes based on regulations that have turned up those existing at the time of the primary formulation. Even if Giannini has remembered the new rules in the editions following the *Istituzioni*, critics have remained bound to the primary or imaginary formulation.

Doubts are strengthened by the claim that the tax relationship arises precisely in the moment when the Tax Authority makes a taxation.[107] However, tax obligation is not *always* expected to arise from taxation.[108]

In the former case, the tax office takes the initiative to assess the tax by ways of regular procedure, in the latter case it makes the necessary investigations to adjust the declaration.[109]

100. M.S. Giannini, *supra*, 934.
101. M.S. Giannini, *supra*, 1266 ff.
102. G.A. Micheli, *supra*, 634.
103. G.A. Micheli, *Ibid.*, text and note, in the same sense as E. Capaccioli, *supra*, 23 ff.
104. M.S. Giannini, *Ibid.*
105. In this sense, A. Falzea, *Efficacia giuridica*, in 'Enc.giur.', vol. XIV, 432 ff., spec. 496 ff.
106. E. Capaccioli, *supra*, 7.
107. G.A. Micheli, *supra*, 623 ff.
108. E. Allorio, *Nuove*, 496.
109. A.D. Giannini, *Istituz.*, 157 e 164.

§2.10 THE NEW FORMS OF THE ADMINISTRATIVE PROCEDURE

The most recent doctrine places the administrative procedure on a new basis, by drawing the attention to the emerging realities in the administrative law state systems, where the relevant theoretical pattern undergoes changes such as to weaken its authoritative traits in favour of the negotiation ones.

Positive law allows, however, some of these acts (including *the assessment notice*) to have a legal protection that is the same as the one related to the administrative measures. It also happens that such law causes legal effects similar to those of the administrative measures. The cornerstone around which these procedures move is certainty. The common structural feature is, therefore, to give certainty to legally relevant facts, being they qualified by law.[110] These procedures consist of two logical moments: the one acquiring the fact, the other externally showing the elements acquired and the relevant legal effects, which the administrative doctrine shows through ways suited to regulate tax affairs.

In the traditional doctrine,[111] the assessment makes the tax debt liquid and collectable while in the administrative doctrine,[112] the office and/or the taxpayer's act makes the tax credit effective.

There is another distinction between legal certainties (the claim made in the act must be considered sure by all) and material certainties, which do not create any tie. Allorio's conception belongs to the former category, according to which the base-situation is the foundation of the tax from an economic point of view, but it is not the constituent of the tax relationship: the act of taxation is the *only* constituent of the tax relationship.[113] The positions of the writers who have subsequently made interventions on the assessment are more vague. The theory of the sequence claims, with a simplistic formulation, that in tax law it would make no sense to search for a rule that gives the office the power to create the legal fact with regard to the condition of the tax obligation. That is, there would be material certainties that would not give the office the power to unilaterally establish the legal profile of the tax obligation, but they would work only for the liquidation of the amount owed by the taxpayer.[114]

Being dubious about the dogmas, the procedural theory considers, on the one hand, the denial, in the tax assessment, of any constitutive effect as a limit of the declarative theory and on the other hand, the reaction to the 'constitutiveness' conception of the assessment as a scaling down of the meaning of the 'assessment' administrative act. The procedural theory illustrates the declarative theory's merely cognitive value, by swinging, in the consequences, between the constitutive theory – as opposed to the declarative theory – and the appreciation of the constitutive theory's results, in the scaling down of the meaning of the assessment administrative act, even

110. In this sense, F.Tedeschini, *Procedimento amministrativo*, in 'Enc.dir.', vol. XXX, 872 ff., spec. 892,ff.
111. A.D. Giannini, *supra*.
112. M.S. Giannini, *supra*.
113. E. Allorio, *Dir.proc.*, 90.
114. E. Capaccioli, *supra*.

though it is claimed that the recognition of events would also have a 'foreclosure' 'significance',[115] not far from the constitutive nature of the act.

§2.11 THE ANNUAL INDIVIDUAL INCOME TAX RETURN AS A TURNING POINT IN THE ASSESSMENT DISCIPLINE

The introduction of the principle of annual individual income tax return, which has deeply changed the assessment discipline, requires a reflection on the condition of the studies, also to connect the various positions with the legislation of the time when they were made.

The new principle does not affect the function of the declaration. The obligation to declare to the tax authority, the de facto conditions to which the law connects the tax obligation, it is established and more or less fully regulated for all taxes to which the regular assessment procedure is applied. Such principle must therefore be regarded as a general principle of the formal tax law.[116] However, its features and functions can change, as it happened under Law No. 25 in 1951, when, with the introduction of the annual income tax return subject to direct taxes, the legislature modernized the process of taxation by placing this declaration at the very heart of the financial function of the State.[117]

The theories developed in the following decades, not always in agreement in defining the concept of assessment of the declarative theory, oscillate between contrasting opinions. It is not far from the traditional doctrine the opinion that the tax case with assessment is the one in which the collection (or completion) is reached as a consequence of several acts: the term, intentionally generic, comes under the catenary logic of the procedure, where the 'variable' feature expresses a simple and even banal conception: that the chain can stop at just one or a few rings or add others.[118] In this way, we do not go beyond the traditional theory, for which, as Giannini warned in the 1960 edition of the *Istittuzioni*, the assessment, in its broadest sense, can be an act or a series of acts.[119]

The other approach notices that the procedural scheme, on the one hand, unifies the sequence of several acts into a unitary purpose; on the other hand, it points out that legal situations derive from the completion of the acts themselves. Such situations, in turn, determine the need to develop other acts,[120] so as to make the unit flexible. It is more complex the schema of the declarative theory, according to which the procedure consists of a coordinated series of acts of different nature, which can be seen through the multiplicity of the regulations governing the various taxes and with which it is possible to create a rational system.[121]

115. G.A. Micheli, *Consideraz.*, pgg. 621 and 623.
116. A.D. Giannini, *I conc.*, 229.
117. E. Allorio, *Sulla riforma del procedimento di imposiz.*, in 'Moneta e credito', 1951, 174 ff.
118. E. Capaccioli, *Ibid.*
119. A.D. Giannini, *Istituz.*, 141.
120. G.A. Micheli, *supra*, 625.
121. A.D- Giannini, *Istituz.*, edn., 1960, 158.

However, during this period, there is a debate clarifying the differences between the latest positions on the consequences of the supposed equivalence of the acts of which the assessment sequence is composed. The one believes that, from a purely logical point of view, the operation made by the administration would not be different from the formulation of the taxpayer's declaration.[122] While the procedural theory limits the convergence, arguing that this perspective would not correspond with the structural and functional identity of the acts.[123] The assessment notice would play a role that is not that of the declaration,[124] though blending its function into the general supervisory capacity that is usually attributed to the public administration.

The approaches are different. The sequence theory argues that in the tax assessment and from the legal effect point of view, the declaration would deserve a role equal to that of any other act that may occur. The declaration would count as an act of liquidation of the tax base as well as the office 'notice',[125] even if this equivalence is not supported by the regulations of the T.U. of 1958, then in force. Article17 provided that anyone who owned incomes or properties subject to tax was required to declare them every year to the financial administration, even though there were no changes (paragraph 1). The taxes recorded in the rolls created by the tax offices (Article 173) corresponded with the tax bases declared by the taxpayer (ex Article 174), and were collected by local or syndicated tax collectors. The liquidation did not derive, therefore, from the taxpayer's activity, but it moved from the work of the office to the tax record in the rolls.

Nor it is worth invoking a different kind of equivalence, in the sense that the incomes declared by the taxpayer, as well as those established by the office, will imply the record in the corresponding tax rolls.

Differently from Article 173, the following Article 174, T.U.i.d., provided for the record in the provisional rolls of the taxes corresponding with the tax bases established by the office. At a legal level, the record in the tax rolls corresponding with the tax base declared by the taxpayer implied the fulfilment of the service, with a releasing effect for the taxpayer, while, if it occurred the adjustment of the tax base declared by the taxpayer, the payment presented itself as a partial fulfilment (Article 1181, Civil Code).

§2.12 ALLORIO'S *'NUOVE RIFLESSIONI'* AND THE SO-CALLED EQUIVALENCE PHENOMENON

The so-called criterion of equivalence of the acts, flattening the effectiveness on the effect, does not allow us to the way it works in the legal reality; these are aspects that Allorio had properly defined. Through an inaccurate reconstruction, the same position claims that Allorio's constitutive conception would have had no relevance in the forties for the prevalence of the declarative theory. The displacement of the original setting into the new positive system would have given rise, therefore, to twists and distortions

122. E. Capaccioli, *supra*, 27; conf., G. Micheli, *Ibid.*, text and note 14.
123. G.A. Micheli, note 14, *supra*.
124. G.A. Micheli, *supra*, 635.
125. E. Capaccioli, *supra*, 27 ff.

creating confusion: on the one hand, because it would make the legal character of the tax obligation live with the administration power, as the tax base; on the other hand, because of the restless flittering *(in the heaven of legal concepts)* of the assessment label, which rests uncertain sometimes on one act, sometimes on the other.

What is more, wherever it stopped, it would have found itself at the edge, since it would have shown its own character on the basis of the original idea, that is in a way abstracted from the reality of the system, so that the traits of the notice and of the other acts would be such that it (the assessment label) could never fit with the various contents in which it had to be dropped.[126] The rough judgment on the conjectures of the traditional doctrine - not exactly rebuilt - on the assessment, is followed by the serious ironies on the constitutive theory, this one neither properly understood. Stopping our attention on the essential points, it must be remembered that Allorio was the first and the one to warn, in the same year of the enactment of Law No. 25 of 1951, about the value of the principle of the annual tax return, which was introduced within the reform of the taxation process.

To meditate on scientific arguments in relation to coherence and systematic nature, on the basis of the new rules, is not about moving thesis that were unreasonable in the previous system into the reformed one, where they would have found a hard application; on the contrary, it has allowed to fill a gap in the previous formulations, even with a value (in a sense) restrictive of those thesis.[127]

As for the unnatural coexistence of two regimes, the (benevolent) critic loses an important point: the duality is in the law, which included the obligation to submit the declaration and, lacking this, the intervention of the office assessment (Articles 17 and 31, T.U.i.d.). In the former case, the adjustment is connected with the declaration; in the latter, it is an administration business, in lieu of the private autonomy act, which is combined with the liquidation effect precisely by the sequence theory, denying in this way the censures made against Allorio's reconstruction. Nor it must be forgotten that both the situations are among the sources of the obligations, which arise from any act or fact suited to produce them in accordance with the legal system (Article 1173, Civil Code).

The opinion that Allorio's description is a first step forward also lacks credibility, so that by bringing the various acts into line, the equivalence can be noticed despite the differences.[128] It is hard to imagine into line acts previously described in the volatility of a label at the edge of different elements, such as the 'possession', which sometimes appeared as a fact sometimes as a right. Moreover, the attribution of these views to Allorio is amazing, which has reconstructed strong and deep connections between substantive and procedural situations, still far from opinions based on simplistic parallelisms that would place the assessment theory close to the agreements for the liquidation of the damage caused by culpable action or omission of an indictable subject.[129] The strong personality of Enrico Allorio, the greatness and the depth of his

126. E. Capaccioli, *supra*, 37 ff.
127. E. Allorio, *Nuove*, 496.
128. E. Capaccioli, *Ibid.*
129. E. Capaccioli, *supra*, 24.

Opera make it not only appropriate, but necessary to keep quiet, according to the teachings of Ludwig Wittgenstein: 'one must keep quiet when there are matters about which he cannot speak.'

The procedural theory detaches itself, by method and content from this view. According to the procedural theory the tax assessment function would be the supremacy exerted to the verification of the taxpayer's declaration or to replace this latter. Despite the proximity, the two assessment forms differ the one from the other, in the sense that the administration intervention is not confined to the application of penalties in the event of a breach of obligations, but it would extend its activities also to the establishment of the *an* and of the *quantum* of the coercive service. The difference between these two aspects is seen in the content as well as in the function.[130] The adjustment has as its subject in a document: the taxpayer's declaration and, in particular, the income declared. In the event of omission of the declaration, it occurs the assessment activity of the office with the discovery of the de facto situations, which are the source of the obligation. The office assessment has, above all, a sanctioning nature[131] when occurring an omissive-commissive behaviour by the taxpayer.

§2.13 THE TAX ASSESSMENT FROM THE COLLECTING POINT OF VIEW

The development of tax legislation has continued without interruption from the system of taxes - defined by the laws of 1864, instituting the direct taxes, largely recast in the T.U. 24 August 1877, No. 4021 - up to the forties. In this system, the assessment procedure ended with the recording in the rolls of the taxes determined by the office; the tax recording without prior assessment appeared flawed and faulty: an act that was no suitable for representing the tax relationship.[132]

The importance of the assessment has raised an inspired debate on its effectiveness. The declarative theory argued that the assessment made the tax credit liquid and collectable,[133] while for the opposite theory, the act of taxation was a constituent of the compulsory relationship.[134] With Law No. 25 of 1951, the development of the legislation has become uneven, due to the principle of the annual tax declaration.

There were different positions before this change. The declarative theory has not met particular difficulties, as the new principle did not affect the *ex lege* nature of the tax debt. Shortly perspicuous, instead, the theories developed in the sixties–seventies, which, deviating from the dogmas of the traditional doctrine, did not experience the discontinuity of the legislation of the fifties, which was transformed by the T.U.imp.dir. 1958 into a unit. The theory of the variable assessment, though suspecting the missed performance of the procedure operating in the forties, it has set the regulations of the fifties against the theoretical constructions following the previous decade legislation.

130. G.A. Micheli, *supra*, 635.
131. G.A. Micheli, *Ibid.*
132. E. Allorio, *Dir.proc.*, 112 ff.
133. A.D. Giannini, *Istituz.*, 143 ff.
134. E. Allorio, *supra*, 96 ff.

Despite this clarification, there are certainly misunderstandings due to the weakness of the connection between the theoretical constructions and the positive system. The point where the deviation clearly occurs is in the opinion that the declaration, as well as the 'notice', is suited to produce the typical effect of the liquidation of the tax base:[135] the equivalence of the liquidation effect. The opinion softens as soon as you remember that, for the T.U.Imp.dir., the taxes corresponding with the tax bases declared by the taxpayer (Article 174) were definitively recorded in the rolls, while for those corresponding with the tax bases assessed by the office, but not yet conclusive, the recording was provisional (Article 175). Apart from the different effectiveness of the tax recording in the rolls, depending on whether the incomes are declared by the taxpayer or assessed by the office, the liquidation occurred when the tax was recorded in the rolls. This aspect shows the most important element, which generally passes unnoticed in tax literature: the shift of the focus of the financial administration's activity from the assessment to the collecting.

Unaware of this perspective, the original formulation of the procedural theory considers the power of taxation adjusted so as to determine the exercise of an activity with a variable content: when the obligation is fulfilled, it is the power to receive what is willingly paid, and the power to make by the court a different and more serious obligation, where the original transfuses and extinguishes.[136] It is a well-known phenomenon: the self-assessment of the traditional doctrine,[137] that is all but a process creating the tax service; such service, instead, fits in many forms of I.g.e application, which represents the subject of Maffezzoni's writing.

This conception has given rise to an approach that is divided into more approaches, each of which takes as its basis one or more aspects of this definition. In the sequence theory, the *variable* assessment begins to develop; it defines taxes without levy as *evasion cases*,[138] as if the self-assessment is intended to this purpose.

The more procedural theory-orthodox approach configures certain advance payments hypothesis, in respect to the condition occurrence, as a case, whose substantial effect is represented by the move of the money property to the tax levying authority.[139] The focus of the conception is in the opinion that the tax administrative procedure should not assume a function similar to that performed, in the declarative thesis, by the so-called tax obligation,[140] implicitly asserting its specular nature with regard to the compulsory relationship.[141]

Nor it has missed the effort to give coherence to the various aspects through a controversial discussion that focuses on the power of taxation: i.e. whether or not it is correct to recognize the exercise of this power only when the act of the p.a. precedes the 'obligation' to pay the tax, while it would not occur when the administration

135. E. Capaccioli, *supra*, 28.
136. F. Maffezzoni, *Il procedimento d'imposizione dell'I.g.e.*, Napoli, 1968, 44.
137. E. Allorio, *Dir.proc.*, 93.
138. E. Capaccioli, 5 ff., e 10 ff.
139. A. Fedele, *supra*, 19.
140. A. Fedele, *supra*, 11.
141. A. Fantozzi, *La successione*, in Aa.Vv., *Il procedimento*, ecc. 118 ff.

controls the payment by the defaulting taxpayer.[142] This question has not been clarified, however, by the observation that these are all manifestations of a taxation power;[143] the limits of this conception are emphasized by the conjecture according to which *when* the financial administration gives rise to an act of taxation, this very act of taxation, in turn, gives rise to the tax relationship even if there is not the exercise of a taxation power.[144]

The assessment of direct taxes was made, in the forties system, by the financial administration, with the ascertainment of the reason of the State credit and of the person of the debtor and the subsequent collection by rolls (Article 222, lett. a, r.d.l. No. 827 of 1924). The principle of the annual tax return has made the office assessment subsidiary, compared to the lacking declaration that is related to the application of penalties.[145]

Another approach of the procedural theory has developed a complex scheme that, on the one hand, unifies the sequence of acts into a unitary purpose and, on the other hand, involves a variety of acts and situations,[146] identifying the assessment effect of the traditional doctrine in the tax liquidation made by the office with the recording of the relevant sum in the rolls. According to this view, the taxpayer's declaration is considered as an act due: a form of generic dutifulness by which the subject would be bound, in order to help the financial administration with the data necessary for the accurate determination of the tax condition and of the tax base.[147]

None of these formulations is compatible with the system of the T.U. of 1958, which deeply changes the previous system with the mediation of the rolls. The mediation was replaced in the seventies by the direct payment of the taxes by the taxpayer's irrevocable bank proxy (Article 3 *bis*), d.p.r. No. 602).

As regards the procedural aspects, the assessment, though giving priority to the ways of collection, verifies the declaration under the twofold aspect of the legality of the declaration, and of the entire compliance.

§2.14 FROM THE TAXATION WITHOUT DECLARATION TO THE DECLARATION WITHOUT TAXATION

Not noticing this step, the procedural theory has observed that according to the traditional doctrine, everything that takes place *before* the fulfilment of the tax levying authority's personal right does not have a legal connotation of its own, even in relation to the fact of having denied the tax assessment any constitutive effect. In this way, the tax assessment would have been reduced to a mere (administrative) act of tax liquidation, that is, of quantification of the obligation already arisen.[148] Although united in the criticisms of the traditional doctrine, another position, equally critical,

142. G.A. Micheli, *Consideraz.*, 623 ff.
143. G.A. Micheli, *Ibid.*
144. In this sense, E. Allorio, *Nuove*, 496.
145. A. D. Giannini, *Istituz.*, 164.
146. G.A. Micheli, *supra*, 625 ff.
147. G.A. Micheli, *supra*, 630.
148. G.A. Micheli, *consideraz.*, 621.

had a very different perspective not realizing that the traditional doctrine was an expression of the forties legislature, in which the tax assessment was the act or the series of acts necessary for the verification and evaluation of the constituents of the tax debt.[149] Instead, the liquidation[150] has found its organic structure with the T.U. imp.dir. which has arranged the fifties legislature in an organic way.

In a study reconstructing the essays included in the set of texts on the tax administrative procedure, the distinction between the traditional doctrine and the procedural theory is related to different constitutional rules. The former, under Article 23, related to the general regulatory predetermination of the tax obligation content, while the other, under Article 53, paragraph 1, related to the principle of tax capacity,[151] as if the two constitutional rules can be applied in an open way.

According to this latter view, the tax condition would have the dual function of event determining the correlative participation to public expenditure, and of parameter for the final determination of the extent of the participation itself.[152] The two aspects are not simply side by side, but related the one to the other, since the latter determines the extent of the former.

It also loses consistency the distinction, within the discipline of each tax, between what is related to the legal mechanisms for the completion of the levy and what is related to the definition of the condition for determining the extent of the participation to public expenditure.[153] The tax condition cannot produce distinct effects: the degree of tax capacity, with the identification of the extent of participation to public expenditure makes the relevant service constitutionally legitimate. Therefore, it occurs the convergence of the two aspects: the source of the tax obligation and the correspondence between the service and the principle of tax capacity, in the sense that the tax liability arises when it occurs the de facto situation established by law as a condition,[154] even if the base-situation cannot be seen as a mere economic foundation of the tax.[155] The *legal* status of the condition, does not consist, however, in the presumptuous constitutiveness of the *taxation act*, but in the activity determining the tax base and the corresponding tax recorded in the rolls (Article 31 T.U.i.d.), [156] whatever is its effectiveness. It should be remembered, in fact, that the condition consists in one of the legal events suitable to produce the obligations in accordance with the legal system, which Article 1175, Civil Code., identifies as sources of the obligations. By combining the two views, it is noticed how the source-fact of the tax liability requires a form that can be solemn, such as the taxpayer's declaration or the financial administration's act,[157] in order to make the tax obligation arisen by law effective (M.S. Giannini). The form may also be free, being it the self-assessment (A.D. Giannini), as well as the

149. A.D. Giannini, *istituz.*, 143.
150. E. Capaccioli, *supra*, 23 ff., incomplete.
151. A. Fedele, *supra*, 10.
152. A. Fedele, *supra*, 7.
153. A. Fedele, *supra*, 7.
154. A.D. Giannini, *Istituz*, 119.
155. E. Allorio, *Dir.proc.*, 87 ff.
156. E. Allorio, *Nuove*, 496.
157. M.S. Giannini, *Dir.amm.*, *infra*.

completely casual application of tax values when the total monetary amount of the marks applied corresponds with the amount due (A. Berliri). This distinction is connected with the different configuration of the condition, depending on whether the taxes are periodical or instantaneous: in the former case, we have a closed-structure case, where the tax, even if assessed at more levels, remains connected with the event that determined its origin. Instead, in the latter case, there is an open-structure condition and the tax is due for calendar years, with each of which an autonomous tax obligation corresponds (Article 7, paragraph 1, T.U.i.r.). Possible taxations, made during the tax period, are elements that contribute, together with other levies and payments, to the development of tax obligation.

According to Article 5, T.U.i.d. taxes are due from the period in which the situations occur to the period when the relevant conditions end; an autonomous tax obligation corresponds with the tax period (Article 3, paragraph 1, T.U.i.d.; Article 7, paragraph 1, T.U.i.r; it arises when the period established by law ends.

Another approach belonging to the same theory has raised the question of the provisional recording of direct taxes in the rolls, *ex* Article 176, T.U. No645, on which the Constitutional Court has expressed itself in judgment No. 77, handed down in 1967. The Court argues that the recording of the tax base of the last but one or last previous year follows the current taxation system, so-called in final, according to which the tax is recorded in the rolls before the period it is referred to, when the income extent, not yet matured, is unknowable and can only be imagined. The arguments of the Constitutional Court did not appear convincing, in the point where the Court invokes the principle of tax capacity.[158] The view of constitutional judges is actually different, since it considers the provisional tax recording in the rolls as not irrational for a technical reason: to avoid the formation of supplementary rolls, thereby not violating, in this respect, Article 53 of the Constitution, nor the principle of equality *ex* Article 3 of the Constitution (judgment No. 77). There are however stronger reasons. It is a longstanding conjecture of our doctrine that there is, within direct taxes, the State right to provide a regular service,[159] depending on the income nature, with the need to determine each period of which the legislature determines the beginning and cessation (Article 5 T.U.i.d.). Article 176, T.U.i.d., should be considered, therefore, not as isolated, but as part of Title X, concerning collection. The recording in the rolls of the taxes corresponding with the income declared by the taxpayer is accompanied by the provisional recording, on the basis of non-definitive assessments (Articles 174-5). The recording provided for by Article 176, cit., is, therefore, a way of assessment and liquidation of the service relating to the corresponding tax period, which does not affect the principle of tax capacity, nor that of equality.

The amenability of the various levies and payments made during the tax period to an overall service, shows how the tax obligation is the only necessary form of the tax, and the general plurality of the obligatory relationships[160] appears relevant only because it works in the execution of each tax. Therefore, the proposed alternatives

158. F. Gallo, *L'imp.sulle assicuraz.*, Turin, 1970.
159. O. Ranelletti, *Natura giur.*, 1898, *supra*, 17 ff.
160. A. Fedele, *supra*, 8 ff.

appear weak, as a total or partial advance payment or as a form of deposit payment,[161] being they phenomena all related to the tax period.

The fifties legislation makes the income tax return central, with the recording in the rolls of the tax corresponding with the income declared by the taxpayer or assessed by the office.[162]

§2.15 CENTRALIZING TAXES

It is very important, the move from the tax collection based on the rolls to the direct payment, made by Article 3*bis*, Presidential Decree No. 600, inserted by Article 3, Presidential Decree No. 920 of 1975, which provides for the payment of IRPEF, then extended to other taxes, to the sections of the State provincial treasury, by the taxpayer's irrevocable delegation to an authorized credit company. As in T.U. of 1958, which provided for the recording in the rolls of the tax corresponding with the income declared, even in the direct payment it takes precedence the income declaration made by the taxpayer.

During the phase of development of the positive system, the method of the *taxpayers declarations* checked and verified by the agents was supposed to better meet the financial administration needs, since the tax authority is not satisfied with the simple taxpayers *declarations*.[163]

This criterion was at the basis of the R.M. tax discipline, which required each person to declare their non- land incomes and made the declaration being verified by the agent,[164] a figure midway between the taxpayer and the administration, in many ways similar to the existing tax agencies. Differently from land taxes, subject to tax on the basis of the census evaluation, the determination of the R.M. tax was based on the taxpayer's tax declaration, verified by the tax inspector. The disputes between the agent and the taxpayer were delegated to special commissions, in order to record the income finally determined in the roll.[165]

Another illustration of 'modernism' is to be found in the municipal federalism. The R.M. tax was due in the municipality in which the taxpayer had his/her residence. The industrial, insurance and business firms, such as the owners of two or more places of the same establishment in different municipalities, were required to make just one declaration in the municipality where they had the establishment or their headquarters, and they paid the tax in the same municipality (Article 13, paragraph 2, No. 4021 of 1877). These are criteria even adopted in the laws that regulate the facilities for the South: the place where the firm has been created or the place where the relevant factory is established.

161. G.A. Micheli, *supra*, 638 ff.
162. E. De Mita, *Le iscrizioni a ruolo*, Milan, 1979, where the awkward formulation is already in the title of the writing.
163. I. Santangelo Spoto, *Imposta*, in 'Dig.it.', 1902–1906, 176 ff.
164. Più ampiamente, O. Quarta, *Commento all'imp.di r.m.*, II, Milan, 1920, 3 ff.
165. O. Quarta, *Ibid.*

It is very complex the procedure for determining the taxpayers income; such procedure intertwines local governments and administrative bodies with the tax commissions. The Provincial Council created or revised the list of the individuals, corporate bodies or corporations subject to the tax; a member of the commission of first instance could take part together with the urban administration to the revision of the taxpayers list in the municipality where the commission itself had its seat, always in an advisory capacity (Articles 33 and 34, T.U., cit.).

The tax inspector could intervene, always in an advisory capacity, to the meetings for the revision of the lists (Article 34, Ult. Paragraph). He sent the taxpayers the declaration form (Article 35, T.U. cit.). The same inspector created, for each municipality, the taxpayers chart, splitting them up according to the various sorts of industries, businesses and professions, with the standards to be determined by regulation and noticing, for each taxpayer, the net income denounced and the one recorded by the inspector or adjusted (Article 38, T.U. cit.).

The difficulty of separating, in this case, the different aspects has led many writers to consider only the activities of the tax courts, to reach the false belief that they would consist in bodies of active administration. There was often the awareness that, subsequently, they would become judicial authorities, though leaving unexplained the structural or functional mechanism by which it may have occurred such a deep change.

The widespread belief that tax commissions had, originally, an administrative nature, is due to the then existing Article 43 of T.U. of 1877, according to which the Commissions of First Instance had always the power to raise the R.M. incomes established by the inspector, when a complaint occurs, or not, by taxpayers and even if they had conformed to the recordings or adjustments made by the inspector. Perhaps, remembering that at the time taxes were applied for quota, some healthy doubts could emerge, at least reading the immediately following article: the commissions of first instance proceed in their judgments by order of classes (Article 44). Now it is reached a logical bridge between several aspects of the tax system, as the legislature had given the judicial bodies office instruments in order to well assess the fairness of their judgment (ex Article 50, paragraph 1, T.U. cit.).

The relevance given to the payment does not want to separate the collection from the other aspects of the overall phenomenon, which is derived from the de facto situation or the base-situation of the tax, being it a *case in point*. Namely, a legal species of the case, which connects the declaration of knowledge of the tax liability with the payment, that is not limited to factuality, and becomes a legal relationship made up of the irrevocable taxpayer's proxy to a banking company, which must provide the certification with the indication of the money order and of the date on which it was received, with a commitment to make the payment in cash on behalf of the taxpayer within five days (Article 3*bis*, cit., paragraph 2). Namely, a private relationship falling into the payment delegation (Article 1269, Civil Code), thus giving the collection an organic and coherent shape.

§2.16 TAX PAYMENT

The persistence in many Italian writers of the authoritarian conceptions pervading the German doctrine, did not allow us to notice that the tax system history is characterized by the 'declaration'–'collection' link, with the consequent problems in the jurisdiction field. The direct payment via bank proxy apparently weakens the important distinction between the two branches of jurisdiction, which was clear in the collection based on rolls, even in the phase when they are created, by recording the taxes corresponding with the incomes declared by the taxpayers. Moreover, the tax jurisdiction includes all the disputes concerning the taxes of every kind and species, including the regional, provincial and municipal ones and the contributions to the National Health Service, as well as the surcharges and the surtaxes, the administrative penalties without reference to the legal situations involved (Article 2, paragraph 1, d.lgs. No. 546 of 1992).

The regulation raises two kinds of problems. We have already seen how tax law is not well defined, nor the notion of tax finds, among those who welcome it, a wide convergence. In order to overcome these uncertainties, many writers dealing with tax jurisdiction have reconstructed the jurisprudence's guidelines, in order to derive common elements from the case study, with the aim of defining the tax legal requirements. The diversity of the methods and approaches followed in the reconstruction did not allow, however, to achieve significant results. But, even if the individuation of the tax notion and of the relevant requirements is reached, the result does not seem satisfying. The tax jurisdiction has as its subject the litigations related to the matter, regardless of whether the discussion is about subjective rights or legitimate interests. Partial readings of Allorio's *Opera* persuaded that the tax process has a challenging nature; this is true,[166] but it is also true that, according to Allorio, the tax process took longer before the ordinary court,[167] also indicating the insurmountable difficulties arising when the differences between the two jurisdictions are not taken into account.[168]

The solution adopted by the legislature is not marked by clarity, since, even if the challenging nature is made explicit by Article 19 – which lists the challengeable acts representing the subject of the appeal – the ritual is characterized by the statutory process. The tax courts apply the rules of the Legislative Decree no. 546 and the rules of the Code of Civil Procedure (Article 1, Paragraph 2). Even the challenging nature totters when going from the title of the regulation to its content: the appeal of the expressed or implied denial of returning taxes (Article 19, paragraph 1, lett.g), from Article 6, l.n. 2248 of 1865, it is considered a subjective right by the doctrine. By excluding any mingling between the two aspects – such as the hybrid formula characterizing the challenging-decisional process – the solution can be found by going to the roots of the issue, warning that Article 6, l.1865 excluded from the courts jurisdiction, among other things, the disputes on direct taxes until the publication of the rolls (paragraph 1), which made, and still makes, the tax credit and the taxpayer's

166. E. Allorio, *supra*, 152 ff.
167. E. Allorio, *supra* 152 ff.
168. E. Allorio, *Nuove*, 504 ff.

right to the repayment of amounts unduly paid a subjective right. The criterion distinguishing the two jurisdictions worked, then, within the sphere of the collection, with reference to the rolls publication.

In the direct tax payment lacks a criterion of equal immediacy, even if it may occur and be seen from a different perspective. The obligation to pay when the tax period ends makes the traditional doctrine live again (according to it, the State credit arises when the condition occurs), but it also gives consistency to the different formulation, according to which the tax service derives from the tax base declared by the taxpayer.[169] These aspects are made unitary by the administrative doctrine, which claims that the *ex lege* tax credit becomes effective through the taxpayer's act (declaration) or through the administration's one (assessment notice). By placing as subject of the tax jurisdiction the matter (Article 2, paragraph 1, Legislative Decree No. 546) instead of the situations, it is not possible to diversify the protection of the legitimate interests, compared to that of the subjective rights. Therefore, if occurring the taxpayer's appeal against the payment notice, there is the appeal of the act under the former aspect, and the demand for repayment in case of unfounded State credit under the latter one. The tax process occurs, sometimes as challenging, sometimes as decisional, up to the extravagant definition of challenging-decisional process. It is a real monster that, at any dispute, goes into crisis for the incompatibility of the two aspects, in terms of the competence and of the evaluation instruments not belonging to the ordinary jurisdiction, but to the special one.[170]

§2.17 PAYMENT CONTROL

In the reconstruction of the taxation act from the collection point of view, some aspects of the dogma of the declarative doctrine live again,[171] with the warning that the abstract relationship becomes effective with the intervention of a private autonomy act.[172] The tax service is determined by the debt recognition made by the taxpayer in the declaration that governs the structure of the interests at stake. The payment is made through the taxpayer's irrevocable proxy to a banking company authorized with a private relationship even if the limitation contained in Article 54, r.d. 26 August 1924 No. 827, relates it, basically, to the collection concessionaires. The view has changed by Article 19, Presidential Decree No. 241 of 1997, which refers not to the State accounting rules, but to the agreement signed between the Ministry of Finance and the Italian bankers' association (A.B.I.).[173]

The company delegated must give the taxpayer a certificate stating, among other things, the commitment to make the payment in cash on behalf of the taxpayer within the next five days (Article 3 -*bis*). This system has allowed us to think that the acceptance of the delegation by the credit company involves the objective and

169. E. Allorio, *Nuove, infra.*
170. E. Allorio, *Nuove, infra.*
171. A.D Giannini, *Istituz., infra.*
172. M.S. Giannini, *supra.*
173. Ampiamente, C.Coco, *La delega bancaria*, etc. 232 ff.

subjective renewal of the tax obligation through the substitution of a non-tax obligation of the bank. Actually, the relationship of the taxpayer with the bank is, from the beginning, a private relationship, as confirmed by the bank's dead stock of the amounts paid by the taxpayers up to five days later.

The tax aspect reappears to appear with the issue of the certificate containing the indication of the amount of the money order and the commitment to make the payment in cash on behalf of the taxpayer. The delegation of the taxpayer to the bank is part of the payment delegation with the bank's obligation to pay the State the sum corresponding with the tax due by that taxpayer (arg. ex Article 1269, paragraph 1).

The payment is a payment that does not necessarily coincide with the fulfilment. The statutory doctrine warns that our system indicates, as a content of the debtor's obligation, a trend behaviour towards the result of the creditor's right fulfilment, which is not a logically essential moment of the actual occurrence of the result,[174] in the sense that the purpose of ensuring the fulfilment of the creditor's expectation may also be lacking.[175] This conception does not touch the obligation, which remains unitary for the mainly instrumental function of the debtor's payment, compared to the fulfilment of the creditor's interest, but it allows to warn that the tax liability, though coinciding with the obligation of civil law,[176] fits into the category of the public subjective rights, in which there are effects which are equal to those occurring in the private relevant rights.[177]

Tax offices verify the declarations submitted by the taxpayers and by the withholding agents, pointing out the possible omissions, and providing for the payment of taxes or of additional taxes due. They also provide for the imposition of fines and for the submission to the judicial authority of the report for the breaches sanctioned by law (Article 31, paragraph 1, Presidential Decree No. 600).

The tax fulfilment control follows two lines. The omitted declaration gives rise to the office assessment (Article 41), while, in cases of incompleteness or inaccuracy of the declaration, the tax authority proceeds to rectify the declaration with a single act (Articles 38 and 40). The assessment notice, which includes the indication of the tax base or of the tax bases assessed, of the tax rates and the taxes paid, etc. must be motivated or it risks nullification (Article 42, first and last paragraph, d.p.r. No. 600).

Like the other acts enumerated in Article 19, Legislative Decree no. 546 of 1992, the assessment notice is challengeable with recourse to tax courts. The regulation also makes clear how the appeal has as its subject the negative assessment of the State claim. The tax jurisdiction does not adopt an opinion, therefore, only on the adequacy of the notice, in relation to the legitimate interests injured by the act, but also on the financial administration claim. The denial, often implied, of returning the sums wrongly collected implies the State non-compliance towards the taxpayer-creditor. The confusion increases when it is perceived that the call for repayment can also be made

174. R. Nicolò, *Adempimento*, in 'Enc.dir.', vol. I, 554 ff.
175. R. Nicolò, *Ibid.*
176. A.D. Giannini, *Istituz*, 76.
177. O. Ranelletti, *Dir.fin.*, 170 ff.

with hierarchical recourse, regulated within collection (spec.artt. 37 and 38, Presidential Decree No. 602).

With the payment control, the tax office verifies that the tax corresponds with the tax base declared by the taxpayer and proceeds to the liquidation of the taxes, contributions and premiums due (Article 36*bis*, paragraph 1). Basing on the data derived from the declarations of the taxpayers and of those in possession of the tax record, the Administration provides, among other things, for correcting the errors made by the taxpayers, for reducing the tax deductions indicated in excess than expected by law, and for controlling the compliance of the data contained in the declaration with the advance or the final payments (paragraph 2).

When the automatic controls, i.e. the controls made by the office, show a result different from the result specified in the declaration, the outcome of the liquidation is communicated to the taxpayer or to the substitute to avoid the error repetition and to allow the regularization of the formal aspects (paragraph 3). Besides verifying the correctness of the taxpayer's behaviour (Article 1175, Civil Code.), the control tends to assess the punctuality of payment and the correspondence with the sum declared.

In return, the office must fulfil its own function by respecting the bonds imposed by the instrumental rules,[178] according to the criterion of the good performance of public administration, based on the principles of collaboration and good faith (L.n. 212, 2000, Article 10, paragraph 1), thus, joining the private aspects with the administrative procedure. It has no basis, therefore, the deviation from the conjecture of the obligation as a necessary form of tax obligation in its fulfilment, that is, of the case of a single tax obligatory relationship for each taxable event.[179] The tedium of the repetition of matters already discussed should be suffered for the need to discuss the cornerstones of the critical approach. The fungibility of the tax fulfilment schemes can have significance only in terms of more schemes for the fulfilment of taxes legislatively established, for each type of tax; not in terms of multiple relationships within the same tax, but of partial advance payments for the tax service. As A.D. Giannini and Enrico Allorio have warned: 'A great chaos would occur in the administration if each taxpayer would pay the tax without following the regulations legislatively governed,[180] even if occasional payments are made to appear as formal procedures.'

Nor is the general opinion of the of the trend plurality of relationships more acceptable, consisting in subjective situations, such as, the tax replacement or the tax liability. In these cases, the obligations of third parties are associated with the debt of the taxpayer. Even the motivation is weak, the general acceptance of the thesis of the identification of the tax with a tax obligation would be entered into crisis when a part of the doctrine had given, in the field of direct taxes, constitutive effectiveness to the declaration, maintaining firm the constitutiveness of the assessment notice.[181] The view is quite different. The declaration has not constitutive effectiveness, being a 'simple (due) recognition of the extent of the taxable base'; to such recognition, (not to

178. E. Allorio, *Dir.proc.*, 132 ff.
179. A. Fedele, *supra*, 8.
180. A.D. Giannini, *Istituz.*, 148 ff.; E. Allorio, *Dir.proc.*, 98 ff.
181. A. Fedele, *Ibid.*

the declaration), the law relates the tax obligation.[182] An *ex lege* obligation, connected with the income declared, while the so-called *taxation* has a function corrective of the declaration.[183] There is, i.e. a partial compliance (Article 1181, Civil Code), which is followed by the financial administration demand for the greater sum due. It is neither conceivable that a plurality of assessments, also subsequent – as in the case of the recording tax – may determine different obligatory relationships.[184] The financial administration acts correspond with different powers of the office; all of these powers have as their subject the case in point from which tax obligation originates.

§2.18 LIQUIDATION

The verification of the tax liability fulfilment by the taxpayer has a two-phase development. In the former phase, the financial administration proceeds to the liquidation of the taxes, the contributions and the premiums due, as well as of the repayments due basing on the declarations submitted by the taxpayers and the withholding agents, of the data and the elements directly inferred from the declarations submitted, by providing, among other things, for correcting the material errors and miscalculations made by the taxpayers (Article 36*bis*, paragraphs 1 and 2, lett. a).

Once these operations are made, the administration controls the compliance with the declaration and the timeliness of the payments of the taxes, the advance and final contributions and premiums of the withholding taxes made by a withholding agent (lett.f). If the two aspects are regular and the payment coincides with the debt recognition made by the taxpayer, the payment is regular although it not necessarily coincides with the fulfilment.

When the automatic controls made show a result different from the one specified in the declaration, i.e. the office controls show a tax or a higher tax, the tax authority proceeds to the adjustment of the declaration and, therefore, of the income declared by the taxpayer, without prejudice to the assessment. The financial administration activity is a form of self-defence, so that the data resulting from the liquidation are considered, to all intents and purposes, as declared by the taxpayer or by the substitute (paragraph 4, Article 36*bis*, 600 DPR).

The tax liquidation, working within the collection by means of rolls (Article 174 ff., T.U.i.d.), has been distorted by the attempt to bring all the assessment features and events to the typical effect of the tax base liquidation,[185] not realizing that the liquidation is made by the office with the recording in the rolls of the collection of the tax corresponding with the income declared. Nor it cannot be seen the fact that the tax liquidation is made without prejudice to the assessment action, under Article 37, Presidential Decree No. 600 (Articles 36*bis* and 37*bis* of the same Decree).

182. E. Allorio, *Nuove*, 496.
183. E. Allorio, *Ibid.*
184. G. Falsitta, *Struttura dell'accertamento*, etc., in AA.VV., *Studi sul procedimento amm.trib.*, 37 ff. spec. 68 ff.
185. E. Capaccioli, *supra*, 28.

The liquidation, in essence, is connected with the income declared by the taxpayers, being they individuals, companies or institutions (Section 37 ff.), while the assessment is the result of a complex office business, which takes the form of the *notice*, containing the details of the taxable base or of the tax bases assessed, of the tax rates applied and the pre/after-deductions taxes, of the withholding taxes and the tax credits (Article 42, paragraph 2, DPR 600).

§2.19 TAX COMPLIANCE

The unification of the formal aspects (regularity of the declaration and of the subsequent submission) and the substantial ones (payment) materializes in the payment, depending on the compliance. The statutory doctrine warns that the debtor's obligation and the creditor's right do not constitute two sides of the same coin: there is no strict mutual implication between the fulfilment of the personal right and the application of the obligation, so that the current occurrence of one of the two situations must necessarily be followed by the occurrence of the other one.[186] The distinction can also be seen in the events concerning tax obligation, for which split payments are expected, as in the case of the withholding tax made by the withholding agent (Article 64, paragraph 1, Presidential Decree No. 600), or in the case of the payment made by the responsible, for events and situations referable exclusively to the taxpayer (paragraph 2).

The real offer is not less complex than it is considered by civil law: once the debt arises *ex lege*, the taxpayer makes, within the required deadline, the tax payment by means of the taxpayer's irrevocable proxy to one of the banks affiliated. Through the certificate issue, the real offer becomes real and concrete; it becomes a payment with the credit company's commitment to make the payment in cash on behalf of the taxpayer (Article 3*bis* DPR 602).

Therefore, it remains valid for the Civil Code as well as for the tax laws, the configuration of the service as a personal service of the debtor, generally aiming at the result of the creditor's right fulfilment, even if the actual occurrence of the result is not an essential moment.[187]

The statutory doctrine does not consider the compliance as a cause of the *extinction* of the creditor's right, but as a cause of the implementation of that right: i.e. the implementation of the obligation content, identified in the personal service of the debtor, who has not been able to negotiate.[188] It is an exact definition, but it is not supported by valid arguments, such as the reference to Article 1191 of the Civil Code, which would exclude the requirement of capacity for the validity of the compliance.[189] The regulation has not, however, a substantive nature, but a procedural one, in the sense that the unenforceability of the payment made to an incapable person avoids the

186. R. Nicolò, *Adempimento (dir.civ.)*, vol. I, 554 ff.
187. R. Nicolò, *Ibid.*
188. R. Nicolò, *supra*, 556 ff.
189. R. Nicolò, *Ibid.*

development of litigations which would lead, however, to the recognition of the compliance validity.

Therefore, the view that sees the compliance as an *act due* is problematical (not negotiating), whose reason and limit is in the obligation previously assumed.[190] The doubts arise from two considerations. The pre-determination implies a regulation that may occur in the negotiation obligation, where the *service*, in a subjective sense, derives from the act. In the case of *ex lege* obligations, the compliance becomes effective with an act of the creditor or of the debtor: the declaration of the taxpayer or the assessment notice issued by the financial administration.

The payment must be made to the creditor or to his representative, that is, to the person specified by the creditor or authorized by law: the fulfilment of tax obligation is governed by the regulations contained in the DPR No. 602. The methods of collection of direct taxes are: (a) direct withholding tax; (b) direct payments to the concessionaire and to the sections of the provincial treasury of the State, (c) recording in the rolls (Article 1). After the inclusion of Article. 3 - *bis*, the payment of the personal income tax, then extended to higher taxes, is made at the sections of the provincial treasury of the State by means of the irrevocable taxpayer's delegation to one of the banks authorized (paragraph 1). The direct payment is the prevailing collection system, while the tax recording in the rolls becomes subsidiary, being used in cases of non-payment or partial fulfilment of the tax due. The collection agent is to be configured as a representative of the State-creditor or as the subject indicated by the same creditor. He then becomes a concessionaire, through a change occurred not only in the name, but in the very figure of the collection agent and in his relevant function, as reflected in the following provision: 'The former provided for collecting taxes and other revenues (Article 1, T.U. No. 1401 of 1992), while the concessionaire "receives" the direct payment, by exercising an active administration activity.'

With the collection reform, implemented by d.l. No. 203 of 2005, the system of the concession assignment was abolished and the collection activity was transferred to the Internal Revenue Service (IRS); it is configured as a public law legal entity (Article 61, l.n. 300 of 1999) and is situated in the category of private institutions, whose activity is accessed by a public interest.[191] The IRS, in turn, exercises its activity through an instrumental entity: a corporation, originally referred to as 'Collection', with the task of initiating the activities required to a prompt reordering of the discipline of the functions related to the national collection (Article, paragraphs 1 and 2, Decree Law 203 of 2005).

As envisaged in the public administration reform, the IRS is obliged to observe the principles of efficiency and economy (Article 1, paragraph 2, lett. C, l.n.59 of 1997); Decree No. 300 of 1999 adds to these principles those of liability - with the assignment to a single subject of the functions and related tasks - and of identifiability - on behalf a single subject also associative of the administration responsibilities (Article 3, paragraph 1, lett. e).

190. R. Nicolò, *Ibid.*
191. M.S. Giannini, *Istituz.dir.amm.*, 169.

In accordance with these principles, the tax agencies, established with d.l. no.300 of 1999, work in the exercise of the public functions entrusted to them, according to the principles of legality, impartiality and transparency, with criteria of efficiency, economy and effectiveness in the pursuit of the missions entrusted to them (Article 61, paragraph 3, d.lgs.n.300). The agencies, therefore, have the nature of *munus*: a private subject exercising public functions. This aspect appears more clearly if one considers that, unlike the agencies, the Ministry of Finance exercises the functions listed in Article 56, paragraph 1 of the same decree.

The emphasis on the private nature of the agencies has also repercussions on the nature of the financial institutions, which have preserved the unity of the content in public finance and the legal shape in administrative law, due to their economic substance. Financial law was considered a branch of administrative law, which must be considered as a separate right or a branch of public law worthy of being considered and studied separately.[192] The reason for this has to be found both in the special nature of its content, and in the fact that it shares the nature and the tasks of the social legislation and of the political and economic law. The private aspect of tax debt arose during the debate about the nature of the relationship, which has seen two positions: according to the former, *tax* obligation is not included in the code because it is *politics*, not a civil obligation (Mantellini), according to the prevailing doctrine, the tax payment has the nature of an obligatory relationship.

§2.20 TAX LAW BETWEEN OBLIGATORY RELATIONSHIP AND TAX ADMINISTRATIVE PROCEDURE

During the modernization of the traditional administrative doctrine, Ranelletti, who had previously defined the financial law as an autonomous branch of public law, establishes the character of 'legal science', which studies the financial phenomenon from the legal point of view. It means that it studies the legal rules that a certain State has established in order to regulate its own organization and financial activity as regards expenditures and revenues, i.e. the legal system of the various taxes, fees, etc., the rules related to the assessment of the incomes affected by them, those concerning collection and so on.[193]

Also tax law originates from Ranelletti's studies. Contribution is imposed on taxpayers by the public authority, according to a general rule, so as to achieve the collective goals and the public purposes.[194] Tax law stands, therefore, in the sphere of financial law, where it joins the national accounting.

Ranelletti's commitment is not limited to the reversal of the order of the financial disciplines, and to the arrangement of the financial institutions, whose legal nature, deriving from the tax of Roman law had always been accepted. Ranelletti went further, with an active presence in the commissions for the recruitment of university professors. It is significant that, in 1925, A.D. Giannini obtained the professorship with a

192. V. Tangorra, *Il dir.fin*, etc., estr. from 'Digesto it.', 10.
193. O. Ranelletti, *Dir.fin*, rist., 39.
194. O. Ranelletti, *Natura giur.*, rist., 7.

beautiful report written up by Oreste Ranelletti.[195] With this professorship and the pressures from the outside in the competition for becoming full professor, always in favour of Giannini, Ranelletti had established the criterion of equivalence of the financial law and administrative law studies[196]

It is more significant the professorship in financial law conferred, in 1931, to Giorgio Tesoro, with two economists in the Commission: A. de 'Stefani, who wrote the presentation of the collection of documents on the Italian tax system development,[197] and Marco Fanno. Giorgio Tesoro's tenure has extended the admission to the teaching of financial disciplines even to lawyers. Once the old order of financial disciplines was restored, the criterion fell into crisis, also because of the decline of public science, flown into the stream of economic and financial policy, which has made both the disciplines marginal. It must be admitted that Ranelletti's foresight has allowed the two scholars to be assigned the professorship. In the years 1937–38, they laid the foundations of tax law, albeit with different perspectives. Giannini sees the unity of the matter, but not of the disciplines where it is split up, by taking the German tax law principles to Italy. He takes into account, however, the systematic needs of the Italian tax system, which also includes taxes and contributions in the concept of tax. Being a supporter of the different nature of tax law compared to the State accounting, Giannini does not fail to warn that taxes are on a sort of ridge that separates the levies from the capital revenues, showing, in this way, the proximity of the two categories. The situation has become even more problematic with the liberalization of the local public services; even if the rates have been transformed in fees, many services have maintained in the new regulations the rules of the previous companies.

The construction proposed by Giorgio Tesoro is different. He places the taxes close to the capital revenues, as original revenues of public law, which the State collects from the individuals, as a result of the political constraint of subjection, and by virtue of tax sovereignty.[198] The relevant legal functions of the two revenues correspond with the nature of the rights of the State: property right, capital revenues, personal right, tax revenues.[199]

There are also other differences between the two scholars: Tesoro connects the tax legal theory with the tax obligation, while Giannini adopts the concept of tax relationship, in which the tax debt develops; a figure that is not only *similar*, but it is the same obligation of civil law, used by the legal system in matters of taxes (A.D. Giannini).

The approaches of the sixties and seventies of the last century are generally characterized by the criticism of the traditional doctrine, with arguments which are not always accurate, and which aim at formulas that are far from the dogmas of that doctrine. They are often conflicting judgments: on the one hand, the assessment

195. A.C. Jemolo, *Mio caro Giannini, vecchio amico da quarant'anni*, in 'Studi Giannini', then in *La simmetria imperfetta*, edited by N.d'Amati, C.Coco, A. Urichio, Bari, 2009, 135 ff.
196. A confidence by Giannini.
197. A. Buscema, N.d'Amati, *Documenti e discussioni sulla formazione*, ecc.,Padua, 1962.
198. G. Tesoro, *Princìpi di diritto tributario*, Bari, 1938, 537 ff.
199. O. Ranelletti, *Dir.fin*, 171 ff.

activity appeared to be as indissoluble and ever recurring,[200] on the other hand, the declarative theory would not have legally considered as relevant the subjective situations previous to the compliance, although regulated by law.[201] The difference is to be found in the legislative references: both the theories overlap or connect the regulations issued at different times, without notifying the discontinuity determined by the principle of the annual tax return, codified in the legislation of the fifties: the one (variable composition) flattening the plurality of the acts in the liquidation effect, the other maintaining the legislative view of the forties, no longer valid.

It is the cornerstone of the procedural theory the configuration of the power of taxation as all-embracing, from the phase of tax application to the control phase by the financial administration, even if it is not followed by any assessment act.[202] It is a 'pale' view of the *Finanzgewalt*, which makes the process a form of *Gewaltverhältnis* (authority relationship), which places not the contribution to public expenditure, but a general power of taxation as the foundation of the levy: a view that could still have a weak compatibility with the T.U. of 1958, but has none with the current system, in which the levying authority works by means of tax agencies: they are configured as legal persons of public law. They place at the heart of the tax rule implementation the recognition of the tax liability made by the taxpayer, which the State can adjust, but not change.

Differently from the alchemical formula, of the variable composition assessment, much quoted but little deepened, the procedural theory is widespread, but with different formulations; at the root of the phenomenon, there is the deviation from the legal component of the public finance theory. The school of thought created by Griziotti in the University of Pavia, very active in examining the various components, had trained an entire generation of lawyers, who have been scattered by several events. In the vacuum following the resignation of Renzo Pomini, it was introduced late Federico Maffezzoni, who noticed only the external aspect of the debate between Griziotti and Giannini, developing a concept of procedure, alternative to tax obligation as a necessary form of tax implementation (A. Fedele). The confusion arises when the same approach claims that in *Nuove riflessioni*, Allorio has produced a diversity of relationships that would have undermined the theory of obligation, without warning that the new relationship is configured as an adjustment of the previous, which it joins in the implementation of the tax service. However, it passes unnoticed the fact that Maffezzoni placed himself on the wrong side of the debate: precisely the formal nature of Allorio's *Diritto processuale tributario* was the subject of the criticisms by Griziotti. According to Griziotti, Allorio does not follow the substantial analysis of the political, economic and social (as well as legal and technical) elements.[203] A process opposed to the obligation, which makes it an empty shell, breaking the economistic conception of the school of Pavia.

200. E. Capaccioli, *supra*, 7.
201. G.A. Micheli, *Consideraz.*, 621.
202. G.A. Micheli, *supra*, 622 ff.
203. B. Griziotti, *Rcensione* al *Dir.proc.trib.*, in 'Riv.dir.fin.', 1943, I, 197 ff.

Other followers of the procedural theory bring criticism on the upper floors: up to Oreste Ranelletti's *Diritto Finanziario* (G. Falsitta). The first argumentation, on the existence of works on tax law previous to Ranelletti's *Lezioni*, falls before the very nature of things, being they writings of financial legislation, very far from tax law. It is even weaker the other argumention, based on Romano's construction, of which it is neither understood the view, in the instrumental nature of the financial activity, preordained to finance the administration, as well as the State purposes in general. The very conception of taxes considers, as a basic and characteristic element, the means by which these goals are implemented. In this way, it is missed the nature, the intrinsic element, which is the real characteristic element of these activities.[204]

Nor it is worth insisting on the contrast between Griziotti and Ranelletti. As Griziotti himself remembers, it was Ranelletti, member of the commission, to suggest him during the doctoral dissertation to integrate the economic study of the public debt with that of the legal aspect; even the jurists from the School of Pavia are, therefore, the result of a solicitation by Oreste Ranelletti. These observations do not tend to diminish the importance of the tax administrative procedure, but to bring it back to its instrumental (not alternative or substitutive) function towards tax obligation.

With Law No. 25 of 1952, the annual declaration changes the assessment, which consists in the adjustment of the declaration. It is an activity that does not assess nor represents the *ex lege* obligation fulfilled – sometimes partially – of which the finance asks for the full fulfilment.

At the same time, new cases in point are introduced in administrative law. In these cases, the law fixes combinations of procedures and contracts for the joint care of public interests and private interests;[205] as in tax law, the protection of the balanced interests is achieved with a similar combination of acts of autonomy and procedures. The legal obligation takes effect with the recognition of the debt made by the taxpayer.[206] The synthetic assessment (preventive) plays, however, a subsidiary function of the declaration – whenever it misses – also including the omitted act of autonomy in the office action.

The real problem concerns jurisdiction. In the original system, the distinction between legitimate interests and subjective rights was marked by the publication of the rolls, which made the taxpayer debtor for the tax corresponding with the income declared or assessed. The double assessment of the accuracy in the fulfilment (regularity of the declaration submission) (Article 1176, Civil Code.) and of the correspondence of the payment made by the taxpayer with the bank delegation, by implementing the creditor's interest, makes tax disputes the subject of two different jurisdictions: the ordinary jurisdiction and the tax one.

The exclusivity of the special jurisdiction – referring to the matter (taxes) rather than to the situations – does not allow to distinguish the protection of the subjective rights from that of the legitimate interests. The obstacle has been circumvented by configuring the tax process as challenging, but regulated with the ritual and the

204. O. Ranelletti, *Recensione* al *Dir.amm.* by S. Romano, in 'Riv,.it.sc.giur.', 1902, 98 ff.
205. F. Tedeschi, *supra*, 897.
206. In this sense, M.S. Giannini, *supra*.

guarantees of the civil process, so as to absorb the demand for refund of the tax wrongly paid in the formal act of the denial, and to qualify the tax process with the unnatural combinatorial formula: challenging-decisional, which subverts the fundamental principles of procedural law.

Nor the solution of making tax commissions specialized sections of the ordinary jurisdiction seems feasible, since the issues concerning the assessments are incompatible with it.[207] Allorio's proposal seems to be more realistic. It aims at maintaining the two jurisdictions within the tax process, albeit with different paths. Positive rules able to support this proposal do not miss. During the preliminary examination of the appeal, the presiding officer of the section invested with the disputes, evaluates the prevailing aspect of the main aspect of the dispute (Article 27, Legislative Decree No. 5461), assigning it to the jurisdictional sections, configurable as ordinary courts, or to the administrative sanctions, not unlike what happens in the S.C., with the tax section, which maintains the original nature of civil department, and of the criminal justice one, which decides on the violations of financial rules.

Articles 36*bis* and 36*ter*, Presidential Decree No. 600, could flow - together with Article 37 ff. of the same decree and Article 37 ff., Presidential Decree No. 602 - into the special jurisdiction, regulated in the shape of the improper hierarchical procedure. The merit of Allorio's proposal is due to the fact that it makes the tax process organic, within the differences in the paths, adapting the ritual to the nature of the single disputes.

207. E. Allorio, *Nuove, supra*.

CHAPTER 3

Tax Law and Private Law

Lerke Osterloh

Tax law regulates the State's financial interest in private income, assets and consumption. Private law determines the rules applying to the exchange of goods and services on the market between producers, merchants and consumers. Tax law considers private assets and transactions in private assets as potential sources of State income in a manner regulated by private law, and must react to this standard. The expedient, fair reaction to legal forms and tools of private law in the drafting of tax law provisions is hence one of the core problems of any expedient, fair fiscal system.

§3.01 GENERAL TRENDS IN GERMAN TAX LAW

The potential solution to this problem has been discussed at great length for many years in German tax law as a fundamental question,[1] although the outcome is doubtful.

1. Popitz, 'Die Ideale im Recht und das Steuerrecht', in *Archiv für öffentliches Recht*, 1921, p. 129 et seq.; Becker, 'Die Entwicklung des Steuerrechts durch die Rechtsprechung seit 1919', in *Steuer und Wirtschaft*, 1924, sp. 1005 et seq.; Becker, 'Von der Selbständigkeit des Steuerrechts. Klare Entwicklung seiner Grundgedanken als Lebensbedingungen des Steuerrechts. Zur wirtschaftlichen Betrachtungsweise', in *Steuer und Wirtschaft*, 1932, Sp. 481 et seq.; Becker, *Die Reichsabgabenordnung, RAO*, §4 Bem. 21 et seq., 7thedn, 1930, p. 76 et seq.; Ball, *Steuerrecht und Privatrecht (Theorie des selbständigen Steuerrechtssystems)*, Mannheim, 1924. Lion, 'Steuerrechtliche Wirtschaftsbegriffe, zugleich ein Beitrag zur Lehre von der Gesetzesauslegung und -umgehung', in *Vierteljahresschriftfür Steuer- und Finanzrecht*, 1927, p. 132 et seq.; Lion, *Gesetzlich erlaubte Steuerersparungen*, 3rd edn, Berlin, 1933; Lion, 'Gesetzlich erlaubte Steuerersparungen', in *Steuer und Wirtschaft*, 1931, Sp. 609 et seq.; Hensel, *Steuerrecht*, 3rd edn, Berlin, 1933, p. 52 et seq.; Bühler, *Lehrbuch des Steuerrechts, I, Allgemeines Steuerrecht*, Berlin, Vahlen, 1927, §§14, 15, p. 106 et seq.; Flume, 'Steuerwesen und Rechtsordnung', in *Rechtsprobleme in Staat und Kirche (Script in honour of Rudolf Smend on his 70th birthday)*, Göttingen, 1952,p. 59 et seq.; *Raupach, Der Durchgriff im Steuerrecht. Zugleich ein Beitrag zum Verhältnis des deutschen und internationalen Steuerrechts zum Zivil-, Verfassungs-, und Völkerrecht*, München, 1968, p. 46 et seq.; Tipke, 'Steuerrecht und bürgerliches Recht', in *Juristische Schulung*, 1970, p. 149 et seq.; Gassner, *Interpretation und Anwendung der Steuergesetze*, Vienna, 1972; Maaßen, *Privatrechtsbegriffe in den Tatbeständen*

Even though the case law and reference material on the relationship between tax law and private law have assumed a magnitude which is virtually incomprehensible, a very radically worded December 1991 judgment by a Chamber of the Federal Constitutional Court,[2] which explicitly rejects the 'definitive nature' of civil law for the interpretation of provisions of tax law, is evidence of the vigorous nature of the dispute on the existence, content and legislative ranking of basic rules regarding the 'correct' positions of tax law and private law with regard to one another.

This dispute about basic rules moved and continues to swing between the poles of 'priority for private law' or 'independence of tax law', and its history is at the same time the history of the emancipation[3] of 'young' tax law from 'old' private law, which

des Steuerrechts, Berlin, 1977; Walz, *Steuergerechtigkeit und Rechtsanwendung. Grundlinien einer relativ autonomen Steuerrechtsdogmatik,* Heidelberg, Hamburg, 1980, at 211 et seq.; Crezelius, *Steuerrechtliche Rechtsanwendung und allgemeine Rechtsordnung. Grund-lagenfür eine liberale Besteuerungspraxis,* Herne, Berlin, 1983; Kirchhof, in Kirchhof/Söhn/Mellinghoff, *Einkommensteuergesetz,* Heidelberg, §2, 1992, A 208 et seq.; Kirchhof, 'Verfassungsrechtliche Maßstäbe für die Auslegung von Steuergesetzen', in *75 Jahre Reichsfinanzhof- Bundesfinanzhof, Festschrift,* Bonn, 1993, p. 285 et seq.; Schulze-Osterloh, Zivilrecht und Steuerrecht', in *Archiv für die zivilistische Praxis,* 190, 1990, p. 139 et seq.; Schön, Die zivilrechtlichen Voraussetzungen steuerrechtlicher Leistungsfähigkeit, in *Steuer und Wirtschaft* 2005, p. 247 et seq.; Lang, in Tipke-Lang, *Steuerrecht,* 20th edn, Köln, 2010, §1, Rz 16 et seq., §5 Rz 65 et seq.; Kruse, *Lehrbuch des Steuerrechts I, Allgemeiner Teil,* München, 1991 p. 18 et seq., 131 et *seq.;* Drüen, in Tipke/Kruse, *Abgabenordnung, Finanzgerichtsordnung,* Köln, §4 AO Rz 320 et seq., 2006; Tipke, *Die Steuerrechtsordnung* I, 2nd edn, Köln, 2000, p. 43 et seq. Ruppe, in Herrmann-Heuer-Raupach, *Einkommensteuer- und Körperschaftsteuergesetz,* Köln, 1990, Einf. EStG Rz 450 et seq.; González Gárcia-Perez de Ayala, 'Presunciones y ficciones en materia tributaria', in *C.I,* No. 61/1992; Amatucci, 'L'interpretazione della legge tributaria', in *Trattato di Diritto Tributario,* edited by Amatucci, Annuario, Padova, 2001. For further indications on Spanish and Italian theory, see respectively the last two authors. Here and subsequently, for theory and jurisprudence a few texts useful for further study will be cited.

2. BStBl II1992,212 et seq. – Decision of the Third Chamber of the Second Senate of the Federal Constitutional Court v. 27.12 1991 – 2 BvR 72/90; critical opinions on this Meincke, *StuW* 1992,188 et seq.; Jehner, *DStR* 1992,485 et seq.
3. Kruse, *Lehrbuch des Steuerrechts I, Allgemeiner Teil,* München, 1991 p. 18 et seq.; *Urbas, Die wirtschaftliche Betrachtungsweise im Steuerrecht,* Lang, Frankfurt a.M., 1987; Schulze-Osterloh, 'Zivilrecht und Steuerrecht', in *Archiv für die zivilistische Praxis* 190 (1990), p. 139; Fischer, 'Grundlagen und Grenzen der Rechts(fort)bildung im Steuerrecht', in *Steuerliche Vierteljahresschrift,* 1991, p. 3; Weber-Grellet, 'Auf den Schultern von Larenz: Demokratisch-rechtsstaatliche Rechtsanwendung und Rechtsfortbildung im Steuerrecht', in *Deutsches Steuerrecht* 1991, p. 238; Weber-Grellet, *Steuern im modernen Verfassungsstaat. Funktionen, Prinzipien und Strukturen des Steuerstaats und des Steuerrechts,* Köln, 2001, p. 207 et seq.; Cipollina, *La legge civile e la legge fiscale,* Padova, 1992; Koller, *Privatrecht und Steuerrecht — Ein Grundlagenstudie zur Interdependenz zweier Rechtsgebiete,* Bern, 1993; Tipke, *Die Steuerrechtsordnung,* I, 2nd edn, Köln, 2000, p. 43 et seq.; Amatucci, 'L'interpret. della legge civ. e dir. civ.: prof. costituz.', in Riv. *di Dir. Trib.,* 1995, I,145; Koller, 'Privatrecht und Steuerrecht - Ein erschöpftes Thema?', in *Zeitschrift des Bernischen Juristenvereins,* 131,1995, p. 92; Ferlazzo Natoli, 'La teoria dell'interpretazione nel diritto tributario: spunti introduttivi', in *Dir. eprat. trib.,* 1996, I, p. 335; D'Amati, *Diritto tributario,* Bari, 2002, p. 30; Fischer, 'Wirtschaftliche Betrachtungsweise als gesetzliches Tatbestandsmerkmal der Grunderwerbsteuer', in *Deutsches Steuerrecht,* 1997, p. 1745; Gonzalez-Lejeune, *Derecho Tributario,* I, Salamanca, 2003, p. 138; Woerner, 'Spielraum der Rechtsanwendung im steuerlichen Eingriffsrecht', in *Gedächtnisschrift für Knobbe Keuk,* Köln, 1997, p. 544; Fantozzi, *Il Diritto tributario,* 3rd edn, Torino, 2003, p. 192; Tesauro, *Istituzioni di diritto tributario,* 8th edn, Torino, 2003, p. 32; Lang, in Tipke-Lang, *Steuerrecht,* 20th edn, Köln, 2010, §1 Rz 16 et seq., §5 Rz 77 et seq.; Amatucci (A), *L'ordinamento giuridico dellafinanza pubblica,* 7th edn, Napoli, 2004, p. 249; De

has continued with considerable discontinuity and many fluctuations, and repeatedly revives old contentious issues to the present day.

Whilst at the end of the 19th century and at the beginning of the 20th, tax law was initially conceived and interpreted, in part automatically, as a 'follow-up law' of civil law, we can already recognize in the case law of the Reich Court of Justice regarding the Reich Stamp Duty Act *(Stempelgesetz)* in the time before and especially during the First World War, a clear trend in cases of doubt to interpret the legal definitions within tax law also in derogation from their meanings under private law.[4] The vital, fundamental paradigm shift towards an independent, 'economic' view by the legislature handing down tax law itself, as well as also in the framework of the application of fiscal legislation, however took place immediately after the First World War, and is largely associated with Enno Becker, this probably being his most important contribution towards the development of German tax law, namely the Reich Tax Code *(Reichsabgabenordnung)* of 13 December 1919. §4 of this first codification of a general Administrative Procedure Act *(Verwaltungsverfahrensgesetz)*, as well as of a general part of a substantive law on tax liability, drafted by Enno Becker[5], containing a politically clear view as a vital foundation of a sustainable, uniform national taxation system lit a torch for the independence of the formation of definitions under tax law: 'When interpreting fiscal legislation, its purpose, its economic significance and developments in circumstances are to be taken into account'.

If one takes a look today at the debate taking place within legal policy and legal science on the content and scope of this declaration of belief in the so-called economic view in tax law, one will find that the basic topics under controversial discussion already clearly arose in the 1920s, a brief blossom period in tax law teaching in Germany. These are methods and interests with very tax law-specific connections – first, 'conceptual jurisprudence' and a 'positivist' interpretation of the law as opposed to 'legal realism'[6] and interpretation using as its standard the purpose pursued by fiscal legislation, second legal security and effective legal protection of taxpayers as against unvarying, effective implementation of the State's right to levy taxes as against taxpayers' inventive private autonomous shaping of the law.[7] The unique link between

Mita, *Principi di diritto tributario,* Milano, 2002, p. 8; Falsitta, *Manuale di diritto tributario,* Padova, 2003, p. 7; Ferlazzo Natoli, *Lineamenti di diritto tributario,* Milano, 2002, p. 34; Lupi, *Diritto tributario,* Milano, 2000, p. 4; Russo, *Manuale di diritto tributario,* Milano, 2002, p. 3.

4. See for more details Ball, *Steuerrecht und Privatrecht (Theorie des selbständigen Steuerrechtssystems)*, Bensheimer, Mannheim, 1924, at 33 et seq.; Lion, *Gesetzlich erlaubte Steuerersparungen*, in *Steuer und Wirtschaft,* 1931, at 140 et seq.
5. See his introduction to the RAO, at XIII et seq.
6. Against this accusation and for clear delimitation of an economic view taking account of the purpose of the statute and of interests, but energetic Becker, *Die Reichsabgabenordnung,* 7th edn, 1930, §4 Bem. 5, p. 54 et seq.
7. See on these contrasts also Knobbe-Keuk, *Das Steuerrecht — eine unerwünschte Rechtsquelle des Gesellschaftsrechts?*, Köln, 1986, p. 53 et seq.; Knobbe-Keuk, *Bilanz- undUnternehmenssteuerrecht*, 9th edn, Köln, 1993, §9II3 c, p. 390 et seq.; Knobbe-Keuk, 'Rechtsfortbildung als Aufgabe des obersten Steuergerichts; erlaubte und unerlaubte Rechtsfortbildung durch den Bundesfinanzhof', in *75 Jahre Reichsfinanzhof -Bundesfinanzhof, Festschrift,* Bonn, 1993, p. 303 et seq.; Schön, Die zivilrechtlichen Voraussetzungen steuerlicher Leistungsfähigkeit', in *Steuer und Wirtschaft 2005, p. 247* et seq.

a dispute of methods and of interests as to the legitimization and boundaries of economic or teleological interpretation of fiscal legislation, as well as with regard to legitimization and boundaries 'of legally permitted tax savings',[8] explains in the same way why the fundamental positions on the relationship between tax law and private law have always reflected a considerable element of perception as an individual and perception of capacity as the State on the part of those involved in the process of drafting the law, and hence also made a decisive contribution towards shaping constitutional trends in Germany by means of the changeable political and constitutional trends in Germany.

For instance, as a result of the terrible financial situation in the German Reich after 1918, the trend towards the instrumentalization of fiscal legislation in fiscal terms gained ground, and then with the victory of the National Socialists entered almost seamlessly[9] into their popular ideology, inimical as it was to individual rights,[10] according to which the 'unlimited interpretation'[11] was in any case already prevalent under private law. This trend found its notable expression in tax law in the shape of Section 1 of the Fiscal Adjustment Act *(Steueranpassungsgesetz)* of 16 October 1934. Subsection II of this provision included the provision from the previous §4 of the Reich Tax Code, supplemented by the 'popular view' as a guide for interpretation, but above all ordered as follows in very general terms in accordance with Subsection I: 'Fiscal legislation shall be interpreted in accordance with the National Socialist world view'. It is not surprising against this background that the pendulum has swung in the other direction since the 1950s, precisely in the case law of the Federal Finance Court,[12] so that now once more fundamental declarations of belief in the priority of private law appear with the content-related trend, in particular also in the interest of the protection of private autonomous legislation, to interpret the provisions of tax law in the interest of legal certainty and protection of individual rights, in a 'narrow' and 'positivist' sense. This line of Supreme Court rulings, initially also supported by the Federal Constitutional Court,[13] was however never unbroken, and was in particular accompanied by contrary case law principles in the particularly problematic area of the

8. See Lion, *supra* note 1.
9. See already the insightful, sarcastic criticism by Lion, 'Gesetzlich erlaubte Steuerersparungen', in *Steuer und Wirtschaft,* 1931, Sp. 609 at 634 et seq.; Lion, *Gesetzlich erlaubte Steuerersparungen,* 3rd edn, Berlin, 1933, p. *2929* et seq.
10. See for instance the entry of the zeitgeist (not until) the last pages in the closing remarks in Liebisch, *Ein Beitrag zur Förderung der Rechtseinheit,* 1934, p. 165 et seq.; in particular also Becker, 'Erläuterungen zur Rechtsprechung', in *Steuer und Wirtschaft,* 1935, p. 363 et seq.; Becker, 'Die Einheitlichkeit des deutschen Steuerrechts', in *Steuer und Wirtschaft,* 1937, p. 705 et seq.; Riewald, in Becker-Riewald, *Reichsabgabenordnung und Steueranpassungsgesetz,* Part I, 1941 (and also 8th edn, of Becker's commentary), §1 StAnpG, p. 8 et seq. with references from contemporary literature; on the role of the Reich Finance Court e.g. Kumpf, *StuW* 1994, 15 et seq.
11. On this in general terms see Rüthers, *Die unbegrenzte Auslegung. Zum Wandel der Privatrechtsordnung im Nationalsozialismus,* 6th edn, 2005.
12. BFH BStBl [Decisions of the Federal Finance Court, Federal Tax Gazette] III 1958, 97; 1959, 197; 1962, 304; 1962, 310; having said that, this case law was by no means uniform, see on this, for instance, the overview in Crezelius, *Steuerrechtliche Rechtsanwendung und allgemeine Rechtsordnung. Grundlagen für eine liberale Besteuerungspraxis,* Herne, Berlin, 1983, p. 65 et seq.
13. More details on this below at 2.

'recognition'[14] of contracts which apply between close relatives,[15] and has now given rise to a situation which can probably be referred to - considering the general trends in other fields of law - as the 'normal legal situation'. In line with the general victory of the objective and teleological interpretation of the norm,[16] a line of finance court rulings noticeably borrowing from the methodical dogma put forward by Karl Larenz[17] also leans towards the differentiating outcomes of interpretations orientated in line with the respective purpose of tax law provisions. That the opposing basic currents in the fundamental dispute over the primacy of private law or the independence of tax law remain able to release considerable forces[18] here too is shown by certain clear contrasts, for instance between the case law of the various Senates with jurisdiction for income tax law, or fundamental statements of the Fifth Senate of the Federal Finance Court[19] with jurisdiction for VAT, as well as legal science criticism.[20] In overall terms, however, the current legal status can be recognized by a turn away from the 'big' to the 'small' answers regarding the fundamental question of the relationship between tax and private law.[21] A variety of solutions are being developed on a case-by-case basis, depending on the more specific problem to be resolved and the tax law provision to be applied.

Against this general background, the portrayal below focuses in detail on the following aspects of the topic, which are particularly significant to current German tax law: After outlining the obligations of the legislature handing down tax law to the Basic Law specifically in dealing with the tension with civil law (2.a.), the illustration gives itself over to the standards of the Basic Law for the application of the law, including their implications in legal dogma, as they are presented on a model basis in a constitutional court ruling (2.b.). Next, the current state of the discussion on selected contentious matters is explained by way of an example (3.).

14. Translator's note: for the purposes of tax deductibility.
15. Details of this special complex not dealt with in the present article: Osterloh, *Gesetzesbindung und Typisierungsspielräume bei der Anwendung der Steuergesetze,* Baden-Baden, 1992, p. 335 et seq.
16. Larenz, *Methodenlehre der Rechtswissenschaft,* Berlin - Heidelberg - New York - Tokyo, 6th edn, 1991, p. 316 et seq., 333 et seq.
17. Critical: Weber-Grellet (judge of the Federal Finance Court), *Aufden Schultern von Larenz: Demokratisch- rechtsstaatliche Rechtsanwendung und Rechtsfortbildung im Steuerrecht,* in *Deutsches Steuerrecht,* 1991, p. 438 et seq.
18. Cf. e.g. Woerner, „Verfassungsrecht und Methodenlehre im Steuerrecht', in *Finanzrundschau,* 1992, p. *226* et seq.
19. In accordance with its constant line of rulings, the law on turnover tax (VAT) in principle (with exceptions) follows civil law in entitlement relationships, e.g. BFH BStBl II 1989, 677.
20. See *supra* note 7.
21. As an across-the-board fundamental requirement, the definitiveness of civil law is today probably only advanced by Crezelius, *supra* note 1, *Steuerrechtliche Rechtsanwendung und allgemeine Rechtsordnung. Grundlagen für eine liberale Besteuerungspraxis,* Herne, Berlin, 1983.

§3.02 CONSTITUTIONAL STANDARDS FOR FISCAL LEGISLATION AND APPLICATION OF THE LAW AND THEIR IMPLICATIONS IN LEGAL DOGMA

The Basic Law does not explicitly say anything about the relationship between tax law and private law. Nevertheless, the case law of the Federal Constitutional Court has always exerted considerable influence on trends in tax law in relation to this topic too, something which ceases to surprise as soon as one takes account of the fact that this always also concerns unvarying taxation, of effective legal protection (in particular also by means of legal certainty) and the boundaries of the interpretation of the law by the administration and the courts.

[A] On Obligations Incumbent on the Legislature Handing Down Tax Law to Adhere to the Basic Law

A judgment from 1962[22] applies as a major landmark judgment of the Federal Constitutional Court on the fundamental question of any obligation incumbent on the legislature enacting ordinary legislation to adhere to private law standards in drafting tax law provisions. This judgment was concerned with the constitutional admissibility of a tax-increasing 'encroachment' on an 'employer's salary' in 'private companies' under trade tax law. Whilst its practical outcome is still highly restrictive (the equality under tax law of private companies with partnerships was declared to be unconstitutional), it makes the following fundamental statement on the relationship between tax law and private law:[23]

> Given the particular nature of tax law, serving as it does primarily fiscal purposes, the legislature handing down tax law does not need to borrow from the civil legal order on an across-the-board basis. Private and tax law are however fundamentally linked where tax law connects not only to real life situations, and hence also to the civil law order, but determines the fiscal subject on principle by means of civil law legal forms. Certainly, such a qualified link does not simply rule out tax law derogations from the civil law structure in individual cases; however, a derogation is only 'factually sufficiently justified'... in a case in which fiscal legislation renounces the logic which it made for itself if it is borne by convincing reasons.

At first sight, the legislature handing down tax law is accordingly subjected to a two-fold rule-exception obligation to adhere to private law, which has multiple consequences. In the first step, namely the fundamental determination of the fiscal subject, it does not have to connect 'on an across-the-board basis' to the civil law order. If, however, it follows civil law to some degree, its obligation becomes more concrete. With the second step, consisting as it does of the more detailed differentiation of the fiscal subject in the legal provisions, it requires 'convincing reasons' if it intends to 'derogate' from its fundamental ruling.

22. BVerfGE [Decisions of the Federal Constitutional Court] 13, 331 et seq.
23. *Ibid. at 339* et seq.

If one takes a closer look, however, the wording quoted already shows what is confirmed by the subsequent trends in case law, namely that at least the 'first step' taken by the legislature handing down tax law is largely free, even as against the prescribed private law order: it is already obvious that the 'fiscal purpose' of tax law is to justify a derogation from private law. In consequence, however, there can be no question of a rule-and-exception relationship which is significant in terms of content, of a constitutionally relevant qualification of tax law as 'downstream law' in relation to private law. The way is clear to separately draft legal provisions in a manner which pursues the separate purposes of tax law.[24] It is not private law which has primacy, but constitutional law, and this places the legislature handing down tax law under a particular obligation to adhere to the principle of equality from which the Federal Constitutional Court also derives a binding 'principle of fiscal fairness' in a constant line of rulings, and in particular a fundamental principle of taxation in accordance with ability to pay.[25] At the same time, moreover, it permits Parliament a very considerable degree of freedom in pursuing economic, financial, social and fiscal policy goals.[26]

There is, by contrast, greater doubt as to the obligations to which the legislature handing down tax law is subjected in the 'second step'. If, for instance, as we know to be the case not only for German tax law, it has opted on principle for taxation depending on legal form, namely to fundamentally link the tax provisions to the distinction between natural and legal entities, and hence between partnerships and corporations, then, according to the quoted landmark ruling of the Federal Constitutional Court, a Parliament should be specifically 'self-obligated' by its 'first step'; a certain degree of 'systematic justice' is demanded of it. It must now be able to claim 'convincing reasons' for breaking the 'logic it set itself'. The question of the prerequisites placed on such convincing reasons goes far beyond the more restricted matter of the relationship between private law and tax law, and is a matter for detailed controversial discussions within the general constitutional debate[27]. The Federal Constitutional Court[28] has clearly shown itself to be generally reticent recently in making requirements as to the constitutional systematic fairness of the legislature enacting ordinary legislation. Accordingly, 'system caesuras' (at best) act as an indication of a possible violation of the principle of equality, but do not yet give rise to it. Also specifically on tax law, the court has relatively quickly withdrawn its original tendency to make binding on tax law the order-related structures of private law via the

24. D. Birk, *Steuerrecht*, 13th edn, Heidelberg, 2011, §1 Rz 46.
25. E.g. BVerfGE 43, 108 (120); in recent times, with increasingly spectacular consequences for the law as it stands, see BVerfGE 66, 214 (222 et seq.); 67, 290 (296 et seq.); 82, 60 (86 et seq.); 82, 198 (206 et seq.); 84,239 (268 et seq.); 99,280 (289 et seq.), 105,73 (110 et seq.); 107,27 (45 et seq.); 120, 125 et seq.; 122, 210 et seq.; see also BVerfGE 87, 153 (169 et seq.) on the protection of the minimum income as a basic right to freedom in accordance with Art. 2 I GG.
26. BVerfGE 81, 108 (117 et seq.); cf. Amatucci-Hemmer, *Wirtschaftliche Entwicklung und Investitionspolitik in Süditalien*, Vol. XV of the Book Series edited by Zentrum für regionale Entwicklungsforschung of the Universities of Giessen, Saarbrücken, Fort Lauderdale and Breitenbach, 1981, p. 185.
27. See on principle critical Peine, *Systemgerechtigkeit*, Baden-Baden, 1985.
28. Since BVerfGE 59, 36(49); see e.g. BVerfGE 81, 156(207); 104, 74 (87); the Second Senate even has changed his terminology prefering the term '*Folgerichtigkeit*', e.g. BVerfGE 93, 121 (136); 99, 280 (290); 122, 210 et seq.

figure of systematic fairness. As far back as in 1964,[29] it considered it necessary to 'interpret' its guiding ruling of 1962 'restrictively'. From this 'it could not be concluded that anonymous corporations and controlled corporations had to be dealt with equally in all matters related to tax law, in other words also in tax law relating to financial statements'. For this reason, according to the specific conclusion drawn in the decisive contentious case, 'in interpreting whether a reserve for pension allocations to controlling shareholders/managing directors of a corporation is to be fiscally recognized, an 'encroachment' on the persons standing behind the corporation' was compatible with the constitutional principle of fiscal fairness in accordance with Article 3 I of the Basic Law.

Therefore, it was basically made clear for future practice that neither the constitutional principle of equality in general, nor prerequisites as to a systematic structure of fiscal legislation in particular, give rise to a fundamental primacy of private law as against the legislature handing down tax law, and the opposing position is no longer being seriously put forward today almost anywhere in the reference material.

Accordingly, as has been recognized, there are no constitutional reservations against some central norms of the law as it stands, in accordance with which one should on principle derogate from civil law standards in tax law in the interest of an 'economic view'. For instance, in accordance with §39II of the Tax Code, merchandise is to be attributed to the 'economic owner', whilst in accordance with §40 of the Tax Code it is 'irrelevant to taxation whether conduct which completely or partly fulfils the provision of a fiscal statute violates a statutory principle or prohibition or good morals', and in accordance with §41 of the Tax Code, the ineffectiveness of a legal transaction 'is irrelevant for taxation where those concerned nevertheless let the economic outcome of this legal transaction occur and remain', and finally, in accordance with §42 of the Tax Code, a provision the content and area of application of which is however particularly contentious:[30] 'It is not possible to circumvent tax law by misusing ways available to shape the law.'

Despite all this, it remains remarkable that there was no need whatever for clarifying statements on the part of the Federal Constitutional Court concerning the obligation to private law of the legislature handing down tax law.

29. BVerfGE 18,224 (232 et seq.) with fundamental information on the legitimacy of the economic view by the legislature enacting tax law. See in the practical outcome, accordingly also already BVerfGE 15,313 (318 et seq.); also 24,112 (117 et seq.); 25,309 (313); 26,327 (334 et seq.) – all rulings (still) use standard wording to refer to BVerfGE 13, 331, but derogating decisions are taken in individual cases.

30. Critical (because of constitutionally insufficient certainty) in particular: Kirchhof, 'Steuerumgehung und Auslegungsmethoden', in *Steuer und Wirtschaft,* 1983, p. 173 et seq.; Kirchhof, in: Kirchhof-Söhn-Mellinghoff, *Einkommensteuergesetz,* Heidelberg, §2 Rdnr. A 225, 1992; cf. chapter by Kruse, 'Il risparmio di imposta, l'elusione fiscale e l'evasione', in *Trattato di diritto tributario,* edited by AMATUCCI, Annuario, Padova, 2001.

[B] On Obligations to Adhere to the Basic Law in Interpreting Fiscal Legislation

The fundamental ruling that the 'right' mutual attribution of tax law and private law is not bindingly specified by the Constitution, but constitutes a fundamental problem, the solution to which is entrusted to the legislature enacting ordinary legislation, in conclusion, gives us at the same time a major starting position for the contentious consequential question as to the primacy of civil law or the independence of tax law at the level of the interpretation and application of fiscal legislation.[31] For a lack of general constitutional primacy rules, it becomes a matter of the 'simple' problem of interpreting ordinary legislation in line with the prescribed method, which, depending on the specific content and the purpose of the norm to be applied, may lead to a variety of results. The fact that contentious issues which are specifically constitutional in nature also emerge in this context, and why this is so, is made clear by the order of the Chamber of the Federal Constitutional Court,[32] mentioned at the outset, which related to the constitutional admissibility of an independent interpretation of such tax law provisions, linked in a specific manner to civil law transactions (such as purchase agreements, acquisition of property), as is the case as a rule for so-called legal transaction taxes.

The basis of a potential obligation to adhere to the civil law meaning imposed by the Basic Law within tax law provisions of such terms coined within civil law is the general principle of the rule of law in accordance with Article 20 III and 28 of the Basic Law, in particular the principle of lawfulness. It is debatable here whether and to what degree the constitutional boundaries of the permissible interpretation and refinement of the law are demarcated by the courts by the (possible) civil law meaning of the legal terms used.

This question is closely linked to the further highly debated fundamental question of a constitutional prohibition of analogies serving to tighten up tax. If one concurs with the long-prevailing view[33] to prohibit analogies in such a manner, and if one furthermore determines the boundary between the interpretation and the analogy by methodically following the concept of the 'possible meaning of the word',[34] one may arrive quickly at an obligation incumbent on the courts to follow the civil law meaning of tax law terms which have been used in the past in civil law. Each independent tax law delimitation of a definition can then in fact be understood at the same time to be a new linguistic creation, that is, as an expansion of the-previously-possible meaning of the word by forming a new rule on the use of language.

Against this background, the ruling of the Third Chamber of the Second Senate of the Federal Constitutional Court on the fundamental constitutional legitimization of

31. See BVerfGE 26, 327 (335 et seq.).
32. *Supra* note 2.
33. On the state of the dispute, see Lang, in Tipke/Lang, *Steuerrecht*, 20th edn, Köln, 2010, §4 Rz 53, 64, §5 Rz 53 et seq., who reject such a prohibition of analogy.
34. E.g. Papier, 'Der Bestimmtheitsgrundsatz', in Karl Heinrich Friauf (ed.), *Steuerrecht und Verfassungsrecht*, 1989 *(Deutsche Steuerjuristische Gesellschaft)*, p. 61, 66, with differentiating consequences in individual cases at 74 et seq.

independent interpretation and refinement under tax law also of provisions of tax law with a specifically civil law orientation shows the way in a prominent manner, and has also influenced the tax law dogma over and above the constitutional question, the ruling, diction and concept of which betrays the hand of former Federal Constitutional Court judge Paul Kirchhof, contains a credo that is obliged to adhere to the rule of law in constitutional and legal dogmatic, as well as methodical terms, but at the same time an interpretation and refinement of tax law provisions that is 'free', in contradistinction to private law. The vital constitutional statements read as follows:

> The interpretation of statutes and the refining of the law belong to the recognized tasks and powers of the courts..... There is however a need to define them as against the correction of the law, which is the preserve of Parliament. The boundary drawn by constitutional law runs in general where the courts, without the existence of a loophole emerging from the system and meaning of the law alone, by calling on general legal principles which do not permit concrete legal derivations, create new rules or legal institutions on the basis of legal policy considerations....

These general statements are quite representative of the case law of the Federal Constitutional Court,[35] but actually add nothing new, and certainly do not provide a magic formula for the 'clear' rule-of-law restriction of judicial refinement of the law, but recognizably leave many questions unanswered. However, they contain considerable explosive material by means of their specific relation to tax law, measured against the general tax law discussion. The 'normal' analogy[36] is clearly shown here as being constitutionally unobjectionable even for tax law. The wording becomes completely subject to the system and the meaning of the law as legitimate guidelines of judicial refining of the law, the path towards an independent teleological refinement of tax law provisions by the courts is constitutionally released with all clarity. The 'relativity of legal terms'[37] common and recognized in the general methodical teaching can also lead to a divergence of identical civil and tax law terms, as is also frequently the case in accordance with the case law of the finance courts,[38] such as in 'letting and leasing'

35. For instance in particular the rulings referred to in the order BVerfGE 34,269 (287 et seq., 290); 49,304 (318 et seq.); 65, 182 (194); 71, 354 (362 et seq.); see also decision auf the 3rd Chamber of the Second Senate, BVerfG, *NJW [Neue Juristische Wochenschrift]* 1993, 2734 et seq., on the constitutionality of the case law on 'Separate Business Assets II'.
36. Kirchhof, 'Steuerumgehung ...', *supra* note 30, however rejects the qualification as an analogy, and speaks instead of teleological and constitutionally conforming interpretation, see *StuW* 1983,173 (175), but intends thereby to cover also in particular those cases 'in which the interpretation of the word related to the individual provision ends and the systematic, teleological interpretation commences which refers to the entirety of the statute'. This doubtlessly goes far beyond what for instance Vogel, 'Grundzüge des Finanzrechts des Grundgesetzes', in Isensee/Kirchhof, *Handbuch des Staatsrechts IV*, 2nd edn, Heidelberg, 1999, §87 Rz 73, viewed as a still permissible analogy or extensive interpretation, (also on the lack of definitiveness of the terminology used in each case). The approval of teleological refinement of the law filling loopholes remains decisive in the order of the chamber, for instance also Woerner, *supra* note 18,232.
37. Engisch, *Einführung in das juristische Denken*, 8th edn, Stuttgart, 1983, p. 78, 156 et seq.
38. On the contrary, there is more of a need to look for cases of a concurring interpretation, at least in the law on incometax, see e.g. Groh, *Die wirtschaftliche Betätigung im rechtlichen Sinne*, in *Steuer und Wirtschaft*, 1989, 227 (230 with note 24).

within the meaning of §21 of the Income Tax Act (EStG)[39] or also with 'annuities' within the meaning of §§10 I No. 1 a and 22 No. 1 third sentence 3 a) of the Income Tax Act.[40]

If, accordingly, the rule of law-prescribed boundaries imposed on judicial interpretation and refinement of the law are to be created in tax law also not by being obliged to adhere to civil law standards, but exclusively by imposing an obligation on the system, meaning and purpose of the fiscal legislation to be applied, this is conditional on an element which is energetically disputed in some of the reference material[41], namely that fiscal legislation has a content which is not created only by positive decision-making, but also by a content which can be binding by virtue of its system, meaning and purpose. Without explicitly referring to those critical voices, the ruling of the Third Chamber of the Second Senate of the Federal Constitutional Court also takes a very clear stand on this, thus providing at the same time the tax-law-dogma foundation without which the overall constitutional construction could quickly prove itself to be an element of fantasy.

Independent drafting of provisions of tax law therefore does not mean negating the civil law situation, and in particular also not negating legal relationships which are shaped in a private, autonomous manner by legal transactions through a 'freely fluctuating' economic view. It is, rather, a matter of necessary differentiation. The mandate to shape civil law is restricted to civil law consequences, but does not also cover the consequences under tax law. A careful distinction should be made between qualifying the legal transaction according to the standard set in the relevant civil law, on the one hand, and subsequent allocation to a tax law provision on the other. From the point of view of the fiscal legal provision, the drafting of civil law is described as creating a *fait accompli*. Whether the economic success brought about by this *fait accompli* fulfils a fiscal provision is then considered to determine its tax law valuation. 'The fiscal provision is fulfilled if the *fait accompli* leads to a success which justifies a burden in accordance with the tax law provision.'

One should not expect today's opponents of independent teleological interpretation and application of fiscal legislation to come to believe in the effect under the rule of law of imposing boundaries of the tax law justification for the burden which is

39. Drenseck, in Schmidt, *Einkommensteuergesetz*, 30th edn, München, 2011, §21 Rz 1.
40. Großer Senat, BFH BStBl II 1992,78 et seq.
41. E.g. Knobbe-Keuk, *supra* note 7; in this respect fundamentally on the 'positivist' nature of tax law Flume, *'Steuerwesen und Rechtsordnung '*, in *Rechtsprobleme in Staat und Kirche (Script in Honour of Rudolf Smend on his 70th birthday)*, Göttingen, 1952, at 59 et seq., 69 et seq.; Flume, 'Steuerrechtsprechung und Steuer- recht', in *Steuerberater-Jahrbuch*, 1967/68, p. 63 et seq.; Flume, 'Steuerrechtsprechung und Steuerrecht', in *Steuerberater-Jahrbuch*, 1985/86, p. 277 et seq.; with different distinctions in detail: Vogel, 'Grundzüge des Finanzrechts des Grundgesetzes', in Isensee/Kirchhof, *Handbuch des Staatsrechts IV*, 2nd edn, Heidelberg, 1999, §87 Rz 71 et seq.; Kruse, *Lehrbuch des Steuerrechts, I, Allgemeiner Teil*, München, 1991, §1 II, p. 25 et seq. with 20 et seq.; critical on this approach Osterloh, *Gesetzesbindung und Typisierungsspielräume bei der Anwendung der Steuergesetze*, Baden-Baden, 1992, p. 161 et seq.

accordingly decisive.[42] Equally, one may doubt that, here, the constitutionally, methodically and legal dogmatically enticing and consistently worded fundamental concept of the interpretation of fiscal legislation not according to civil law, but according to the rule of law, is suited in all instances to resist the dangers of 'unlimited interpretation'. As experience shows, the latter cannot be introduced, however, by any interpretative teaching, but may at best be implemented by the competent legal practitioners in cooperation with the legislature. Finally, it is also clear that this basic concept for the independence of tax law, which is also representative of a good section of the current tax law teaching and practice, does not yet provide a finished patent solution to the many legal questions which lie between tax law and private law, but only general guidelines which offer the case law fundamental assistance in orientation, but which at the same time open considerable scope for proper differentiation of the applicable tax law on the basis of independent responsibility.

If one takes a look back once more from this outcome to the beginnings of modern German tax law, it can perhaps be said that, rather than the legal policy-maker and judge Enno Becker, bound as he was by vested interests, it was the legal academic Enno Becker who ultimately won on all fronts: His notion that §4 of the 1919 Reich Tax Code had actually been superfluous on the basis of 'modern' methodical teaching has come true. In spite of the fact a general interpretation rule in accordance with the model of §4 of the Reich Tax Code has not existed in German tax law since 1977, the year in which the current Tax Code came into effect, and this for good reasons,[43] the 'purpose in the law'[44] as a dominating guideline for interpretation has also taken over tax law – but under much changed economic and constitutional conditions in comparison to the situation at the time of Enno Becker. The fact that the judiciary has been made comprehensively independent also in financial jurisdiction, in the manner in which it is obliged to adhere to the law, prohibits such favouritism, and going beyond the rule of law boundaries of legislation-bound judicial law is actionable before a Constitutional Court, which in any case is currently far from any suspicion of a fiscal orientation of interests.[45] Thus, today, the basic concept of the independence of tax law in relation to private law, and to other subsidiary legal orders, is not ultimately also an expression of confidence in the performance of an independent judiciary which in the context of its mandate of legal protection has been entrusted with the effective, even implementation of fiscal legislation by providing a balance in the meaning of the rule of law between individual interests in the protection of rights and the fiscal interest in obtaining income.

42. On this with an appeal to the legislature: Kirchhof, 'Verfassungsrechtliche Maßstäbe für die Auslegung von Steuergesetzen', in *75 Jahre Reichsfinanzhof - Bundesfinanzhof, Festschrift*, Bonn, 1993, P. *295* et seq.
43. In general terms on the problem of rules of statutory interpretation e.g. Engisch, *Einführung in das juristische Denken*, 8th edn, Stuttgart, 1983, p. 93 et seq.
44. Becker, *Die Reichsabgabenordnung*, 7th edn, 1930, §4 Bem. 1 a, p. 43: '... §4 means for tax law a victory of Jhering against his academic opponents, who were at that time almost the entire legal academia in Germany.'
45. On this only the indications of more recent rulings: *supra* note 25.

The fact that, and how, this all remains significant in the ins and outs of individual practical contentious questions is to be indicated finally by using a few examples.

§3.03 INDIVIDUAL CONTENTIOUS ISSUES ON THE 'INDEPENDENCE' OF THE INTERPRETATION AND APPLICATION OF TAX LAW

[A] Ascertaining Income

The standard problems of tax law practice, the 'teleologically' founded solution of which is particularly difficult, include the question of the attribution of an activity that is (potentially) liable to income tax to one of the seven types of income set out in §2 I of the Income Tax Act.

In addition to many relaxations or instances of relief dependent on types of income, their delimitation is particularly significant because of the different ways of ascertaining the income in accordance with §2 II of the Income Tax Act, on the one hand, in the types of profit income of §2 I Nos. 1-3 of the Income Tax Act (agriculture and forestry, trade, self-employed work) and, on the other hand, in the types of surplus contained in Nos. 4-7 (dependent work, capital assets, letting and leasing, other income). Whilst value changes in the assets used to obtain income influence profit before tax, this is on principle (with the important exception of capital assets since 2009) not the case with net income in accordance with previous German law - outside certain periods between acquisition and sale.[46] For instance, in particular value increases of land brought about through sale were, under income tax law, on principle taxed only in the context of the types of profit income. Over and above this (only) specifically trade activity is additionally taxed in accordance with the Trade Tax Act *(Gewerbesteuergesetz)*.

This background is decisive in practice for a large volume of more recent Supreme Court case law[47] to distinguish between commercial trade in land (income from trading) and 'private' asset administration (where appropriate, income from letting and leasing).

In accordance with an 'unwritten' negative provision of the tax law definition of trading from §15 II of the Income Tax Act, it is a matter for delimitation of whether an activity exists which remains within the framework of 'private' asset administration, or indeed extends beyond it. According to a general legal definition, which is however not directly relevant to the provision of §15 II of the Income Tax Act of the 'operation of a commercial business' within the meaning of §14 of the Tax Code, asset administration

46. These periods for what used to be called speculation profits (until 1998, two years for real estate, six months for securities) were made much longer from 1999 for what are now called 'private sales transactions' (on principle ten years for real estate, one year for securities). This has however merely somewhat alleviated the consequences of the general decision as to whether or not to subject 'private' proceeds of sale to taxation, but has not fundamentally addressed this question.
47. For a survey see Wacker, in Schmidt, *Einkommensteuergesetz*, 30th edn, München, 2011, §15 Rz 47 et seq.

'as a rule exists if assets are used, such as capital assets being invested in return for interest, or immovables being let or leased'.

For the context at hand, this delimitation problem is particularly interesting in the application of §15 of the Income Tax Act because at first sight here the disciples of a 'positivist' interpretation of fiscal legislation can bring on the big guns against the proponents of an independent teleological interpretation of tax law. This is why. Where can one find the reason justifying the different tax burden on proceeds of sale according to the meaning and purpose of the law?[48] In fact, the different income tax treatment of realized value increases, as well as value decreases, depend on whether it is a matter of business assets and liabilities within the meaning of the provisions on the determination of income, or private assets which are the subject of dispute not only in terms of legal policy, but also constitutionally,[49] and the same applies to other differences in burden which depend on types of income. However, those who conclude from legal policy or indeed constitutionally founded criticism of the specific burden resulting from different income qualifications that the statutory regulation has no decision-influencing meaning and purpose, and hence refer to private law 'standards', confuse two different questions, namely the question as to the binding content and purpose of the legal basis on which decisions are to be made, and the question of its evaluation under legal policy or constitutional law.

The dualism of ascertaining income, with its 'split' definition of income, contains a fundamental systematic decision contained in the Income Tax Act against the background of diverging financial science theories of the 19th century. The meaning and purpose of this systematic decision has been open for all to see since it came into effect in 1925.[50] Determination of income tax follows above all for considerations of practicability, but also of economic rationality in the principle of the commercial law determination of income, and the types of profit income cover activities which are characterized by using assets in the context of self-employed work. The business assets and liabilities are here a major tool of economic activity, the value development of which is therefore also included in the fiscal determination of success. Equally important for reasons of practicability, by contrast, 'private' assets are in principle left alone as a 'source' of possible surpluses in the types of net income. The provisions of net income cover activities where, as with income from dependent work, the focus is sharply on the deployment of the individual worker, or where assets are used to produce income, but this is at the same time only in its function as the 'labour' of the private individual managing his assets. The abovementioned provision of §14 of the Tax Code also conforms in particular with this picture.

48. Knobbe-Keuk, *Das Steuerrecht — eine unerwünschte Rechtsquelle des Gesellschaftsrechts?*, Köln, 1986, p. 53 et seq.; Knobbe-Keuk, *Bilanz- und Unternehmenssteuerrecht*, 9th edn, Köln, 1993, §9 II 3 c, p. 390 et seq.; Knobbe-Keuk, 'Rechtsfortbildung als Aufgabe des obersten Steuergerichts; erlaubte und unerlaubte Rechtsfortbildung durch den Bundesfinanzhof', in *75 Jahre Reichsfinanzhof— Bundesfinanzhof, Festschrift*, Bonn, 1993, p. 303 et seq.
49. See Lang, in Tipke/Lang, *Steuerrecht*, 20th edn, Köln, 2010, §9 Rz 185 et seq., 560 et seq.
50. On this in detail Kirchhof, in Kirchhof-Söhn, *Einkommensteuergesetz*, Heidelberg, 1992, §2 A 437 et seq., A 663 et seq., A 674 et seq.

The functional context of the deployment of merchandise with self-employed gainful work carried out by the economic owner is hence decisive for the delimitation of the types of income, and this context forms the statutory justification for the burden with regard to covering proceeds of sale.

In the light of the differing tax burdens imposed on proceeds of sale by income tax and trade tax, it cannot come as a surprise that a lot of clever legal reasoning is used in this context to show that an activity is 'private', and to avoid the context of a sale associated with commercial activity. A central example of this problematic area of the relationship between civil law and tax law is shown by the boundaries drawn between commercial trade in land and so-called private asset management. The established case law is based to some degree on whether the activities of those acquiring land and its owners are primarily aiming to make income not by means of use, but through sale, in other words by moving assets, and that this activity is to be evaluated as sufficiently 'sustained' within the meaning of §15 II of the Income Tax Act.[51] In this case, what we are talking about is not private asset management, but commercial activity, suggesting an interpretation in line with the system and the purpose of the relevant provisions on income, taking as a basis the different economic functions of the property deployed for earning purposes.

The characteristics of intention to move assets and sustainability that are accordingly vital in this instance to determine commercial trade in land are applied in the case law in a roughly illustrative manner. The Federal Finance Court has for a long time been operating with an approximate model and quantifying rule of thumb, namely with the so-called three-object limit: a 'sustained' activity aimed at 'moving assets', and hence a commercial activity within the meaning of §15 II of the Income Tax Act, exists in accordance with this formula if more than three objects are acquired and re-sold in a close chronological and factual context, in particular in each case within five years.[52]

It was against this background that the idea arose of a tax savings construction which has been rather made fun of in the reference material,[53] the legal evaluation of which however necessitated a ruling by the Great Senate of the Federal Finance Court.[54] The idea consisted simply of factually overcoming the three-object limit by using partnerships as intermediaries (typically companies between close persons). Participation in several partnerships active on the market in each case as (legally independent) acquirers and sellers of real estate, whilst in each instance for themselves not exceeding the three-object limit, would, according to this idea, remain within the sphere of private asset management, and hence not incur trade tax and income tax on the proceeds of sale. The civil law independence of partnerships to become separate legal subjects, as well as the differentiation between income and sale of a share of the company and acquisition and sale of a (direct) share in a piece of real estate, would

51. E.g. BFH *BStBl* II 1982, 700.
52. On the problem of distinguishing between trade and production in this context BFH GrS *BStBl II* 2002, 291.
53. Schmidt, *Finanzrundschau*, 1991,16 (17).
54. BFH GrS *BStBl* II 1995, 617 (622).

hence also be relevant to the tax law evaluation. As a result convincing the Great Senate of the Federal Finance Court did not follow such an assumption proposal based on civil law forms and in particular orientated in line with the modern civil law partnership dogma for tax law, but clearly recognized an independent tax law evaluation. The concept of the unity of the partnership must take a back seat to the concept of the large number of shareholders 'if otherwise a factually correct taxation of the shareholder' would not be possible. Here, as also in other cases, the independent tax law evaluations of the economic content of the activities call for an 'encroachment solution'. Trade in real estate does not lose its commercial character by spreading these activities among several partnerships.

All this may not be misunderstood as a constitutional or indeed a legal policy justification of the legal situation currently relevant in Germany (in 2011). On the contrary, there is much to suggest that the different treatment under tax law, in particular of the proceeds of sale, needs further correction.[55] For one thing, the legitimate goals of practicability of ascertaining income are probably unlikely to plausibly justify the largely perceived lack of individual fairness. For another, however, the practicability of the current state of the law has also been called into question for some time by the countless 'thrift constructions' provoked by this situation. However, it remains decisive that such objections to be considered by the legislature against the fundamental system of the dualism of the ascertainment of income do not provide a justification for cancelling loyalty to an applicable statutory decision-making programme by refusing to interpret and apply it in line with the system and purpose in enforcing the law. Legal policy corrections are the preserve of Parliament, and constitutional rejection that of the Federal Constitutional Court.

This must also be the point of departure for the income tax evaluation of private law situations to be described by the example below. It is not the sequence of laws determined in private autonomy which is decisive, but their evaluation by meaning and purpose of the relevant fiscal provision.

[B] Independence of Tax Law

A number of equally notable rulings of the Federal Constitutional Court[56] on the problem of the tax law 'recognition' of civil law contracts only seemingly contradicts the postulate of the independence of tax law evaluations. This is related to the long-contentious question of whether 'wage' or 'salary' payments on the basis of 'employment' between spouses are also to be recognized (as deductible operational expenses) under tax law, even if the payments in question are effected to an account to which both the employee and the employer spouse have equal and unrestricted access.

55. See Lang, in Tipke/Lang, *Steuerrecht*, 20th edn, Köln 2010, §9 Rz 560 et seq.; Birk, *Einkommen, Einkunftsarten und Einkünfteermittlung*, in Hey (ed.), *Einkünfteermittlung, Köln, 2011 (Deutsche Steuerjuristische Gesellschaft)*, p. 1 (20 et seq.).
56. BVerfG (Chamber) *BStBl* II 1996, 34; similar decisions of 9.1.1996 and 15.8.1996 published in JURIS.

The Great Senate of the Federal Finance Court[57] denied this in 1989 with carefully phrased reasons. In the interest of clear ascertain ability and controllability of the relevant structures between close relatives, strict separation of assets was to be demanded for the recognition of employment.[58] One may not presume serious wage payments, and hence deductible operational expenditure, if such payments remain at the disposal of the employer spouse (and subject to access by his/her creditors). The Federal Constitutional Court contradicted this and found that the relevant case law of the Federal Finance Court was arbitrary, with the consequence that, since then, employment between spouses is to be recognized even where there is no strict separation of the respective assets.

At first sight, however, the Federal Finance Court had refused to 'recognize' civil law structures between spouses with independent tax law considerations here, whilst the Federal Constitutional Court gives a genuine civil law argument as to the need for recognition. The payment of the salary to an account beyond the employer spouse's disposal is alleged to not be a separate precondition for the effectiveness of employment, and may hence also not be raised by the finance courts to become a constitutive provision if otherwise employment was seriously intended to be created, and had indeed been implemented. Taking a closer look, the Federal Constitutional Court is also not concerned with a civil law obligation, but with a rule-of-law obligation of the application of fiscal legislation, namely of evidentiary requirements covering more than one area that discriminate against the spouses, where it is a matter of proving 'serious' civil law structures. One could therefore argue as to whether the mistrust of the previous finance court case law towards 'wage payments' being effected into a joint account of the spouses was realistic, and hence also justifiable from a rule-of-law point of view, or whether the constitutional court's confidence in the effectiveness of the employment contract under civil law claimed by taxpayers is really constitutionally necessary – the legitimacy and necessity of independent tax law evaluations in comparison with the civil law situation is in any case also not questioned by these more recent constitutional court rulings.

The recognition of the independence of tax law as against civil law is, finally, also impressively confirmed (in this case as against labour law) by the legislation on the definition of 'employee' in connection with the problem of so-called pretend self-employment. On this, the Federal Finance Court[59] – in agreement with its previous case law – has explicitly stressed once more that, for the evaluation of an activity as self-employed or employed under tax law, the category allocated under social law and under labour law could be significant as an indication, but was not binding. For this reason, in particular also the definition under labour law of a 'person similar to an employee' had no impact on the tax law delimitation.

57. BFH GrS *BStBl* II 1990, 160.
58. Translator's note: for the purposes of tax deductibility.
59. BFH BStBl II 1999, 534.

[C] Partnerships and Corporations

As a final example of the problems which can occur in the relationship between civil and tax law, I would like to mention the distinction that is made between partnerships and corporations. In the light of the large proportion of partnerships in Germany, the differences between the taxation of the income of partnerships and the corporation tax that is levied on corporations lead to problems which are as specific as they are explosive – not only in relation to other Member States of the European Union, but also in general terms within international competition. Here, we can still consider the necessary distinction between partnerships and corporations to be a reserved area in which civil law is definitive for tax law, something which has only rarely been called into question despite all the instances in which the two types have been mixed under company law.[60] The lack of neutrality as to legal form has for a long time been one of the unsolved problems of German tax law, and has intensified since 2001 as a result of the *'Halbeinkünfteverfahren'*[61] (since 2009: *'Teileinkünfteverfahren'*).

For a long time, however, the definitive nature basically recognized in this context of civil law legal forms had already been put into perspective for a major sub-area, namely as far as the basic freedoms contained in European Community law on cross-border transactions are concerned.[62] Although in accordance with previous German company law, when foreign corporations sought access to domestic territory, these companies had been refused the status of domestic legal entities under German law on the basis of the so-called residence theory for lack of a corresponding act of establishment, the Federal Finance Court[63] already counted such companies among subjects under corporation tax, even if with uncertainties as to the interpretation of the statutes in detail. Now that the European Court of Justice in the case of *Überseering*[64] had rejected the restrictions imposed by national law on companies' access to domestic territory, this also led to a correction of taxation of foreign corporations which have a base in Germany. In order to avoid discriminatory restrictions, these companies also have to be regarded as corporations in accordance with §1 Subsection 1 No. 1 of the Corporation Tax Act (KStG), with all its consequences for instance for the special tax unit and under the law governing the taxation of conversions. This should however not be viewed as a direct consequence of the effect of Community law on German company law via the 'definitive nature' of civil law for tax law. For tax law too, the equal treatment of domestic and foreign corporations is not a consequence of civil law, but of the higher-priority protection of the basic freedoms of supranational Community law, a consequence which is quite independent of national civil law.

60. Schmidt, *Gesellschaftsrecht*, 4th edn, Köln, 2002, §5 II 4, III, p. 106 et seq.
61. Half of the dividend which has been paid out, on which 25% corporation tax has been levied, was included in shareholder's income tax assessment basis.
62. For more details see Laule, *Auswirkungen der EuGH-Rechtsprechung auf deutsche Steuervorschriften, Institut 'Finanzen und Steuern'*, Bonn, 2003, p. 22 et seq.; Krutthoffer-Röwekamp *(ed.), Die Rechtsprechung des EuGH in ihrer Bedeutung für das nationale und internationale Recht der direkten Steuern*, Baden-Baden, 2010.
63. BFH *BStBl II* 1992, 972; 1998, 650; 1999, 437.
64. Case C-208/00, *IStR* 2002, 809.

CHAPTER 4

Administrative Provisions in Taxation Law*

Christoph Trzaskalik and Marion Petri

§4.01 TAX STATUTES SUBJECT TO FURTHER CONCRETION

It is common practice that in all modern democratic systems only Parliament has the power to levy taxes. In this respect it is true that taxation law rests on the *Dictum* given by the legislator. Due to such primacy of Parliament in the field of taxation law the Executive is authorized by Parliament to enact certain acts of legal force, these acts being variously described as *Rechtsverordnungen* (in Germany), *legislative decrees* (Italy), *statutory instruments* (in Great Britain), and *decrets-lois, règlements* (in France).

Here the main problem is to what extent Parliament is allowed to delegate its powers. Given that competences always imply obligations as well, it becomes apparent that the essential decisions must in any event be taken by way of parliamentary legislation (see below 5.b.ii.).

Therefore, the strong belief that taxation procedures were regulated exclusively by way of statutes and decree-laws is one which only lies on loose grounds. After all legislative provisions do not only need interpretative criteria to rely on but, to some extent, can also prove to be inapplicable in the absence of further provisions. The need to provide concrete, substantial meaning to legislative norms *(Konkretisierungsbedarf)* becomes more urgent given the tax legislators tendency to act at short notice and rather selectively. In addition, the tax legislator deals with imaginative taxpayers who constantly make efforts for their own relationships to be handled in a way that will

* This chapter, which is identical to the one published in the first edition, has been updated by the annex written by Henning Tappe, which follows immediately after this. This chapter was based on the article 'Verwaltungsvorschriften im Steuerrecht' by Christoph Trzaskalik, published e.g. as 'Las disposiciones administrativas en el derecho tributario' in Andrea Amatucci (ed.) (2001) *Tratado de Derecho Tributario*, Bogotá-Colombia: Temis, 684–701, revised and supplemented by Marion Petri.

trigger the lowest possible tax being charged on them. Therefore, it should always be examined whether and to what extent any new situation is already covered by the existing provisions.

There are many entities (each in its own capacity) actively involved in determining tax statutes more closely as well as in judge-made laws *(Rechtsfortbildung)*: taxation authorities called on to apply tax statutes; citizens frequently interpret the law differently from the tax authorities; the courts whose task it is to take decisions in the field of tax law; legal scientists committed to construing and thinking out the different regulations.

This context of providing substantial, concrete meaning to ordinary legislation becomes essential in connection with the need to make an analysis of administrative provisions *(Verwaltungsvorschriften)* within the framework of taxation law.

§4.02 THE CONCEPT OF ADMINISTRATIVE PROVISION

To begin with, it is not easy to identify a uniform terminology in this context. The use of the term 'administrative provision' in public law literature is combined with other terms and definitions such as 'directive' *(Richtlinie)*, 'decree' *(Erlass)*, 'provision' *(Verfügung)*. It should be taken into account that taxation law is a system applicable to everyone. Given the aim of procedural economy set by tax authorities, it would be illogical for each tax authority officer to autonomously interpret the relevant statutes in every single matter arising. This is the reason why financial authorities are called on to enact provisions which are designed for their officers to use and which also define the proper methods for tax statutes to apply. In this way, it is possible to ensure that legislation is uniformly implemented. The difference that lies between the law, or law decrees, and administrative provisions, can be understood as follows: statutes and law decrees, on the one hand, are intended to regulate the legal relationships between the State being regarded as the body in charge of levying tax, and the citizens being regarded as potential taxpayers. Administrative provisions, on the other hand, are used by financial authorities to arrange for the application of tax statutes. These provisions are addressed to the financial authorities officers, not to the citizens.

§4.03 THE CONTENT OF ADMINISTRATIVE PROVISIONS

The function of administrative provisions is, generally speaking, to arrange for the necessary application of the law. Therefore, the scope and meaning of administrative provisions can vary a lot. Partly, they are designed to regulate such things as the structure, the internal organizational system and the various procedures financial authorities apply. This is necessary if the law itself does not contain the relevant information (so-called organizational administrative provisions, *organisatorische Verwaltungsvorschriften)*.

The content of administrative provisions may also include useful guidelines as to the interpretation of tax statutes (so-called interpreting administrative provisions, *nor-minterpretierende Verwaltungsvorschriften)*. The content of administrative provisions ranges from explaining the criteria identified in taxation jurisprudence to explanatory calculations, as well as detailed guidelines relating to the fiscal treatment of complex economic issues. Together with the administrative provisions about the exercise of discretion *(ermessenslenkende Verwaltungsvorschriften)*, the interpreting provisions are qualified to have a conduct-directing character. Both guide the administration's decision-making process. Administrative provisions of a further type are meant to fill in the 'blanks' a legal regulation has left (law-concretizing administrative provisions, *normkonkretisierende Verwaltungsvorschriften)*. They are used in technical contexts mainly, e.g. in environmental law, and they have been attributed the weight of an anticipated expert's report *(antizipierte Sachverständigengutachen)*. Another function of administrative provisions is to simplify the levy of taxes (so-called simplifying administrative provisions, *Vereinfachungsvorschriften)* by way of flat rates, minimum value thresholds and estimated tax assessment criteria.

The gamut of the administrative provisions corresponding with single tax statute depends essentially on two elements: the economic relevance of the tax being imposed and the quality of the relevant tax statute itself. General, the scope of individual administrative provisions is seen to be much wider than the scope of individual tax statutes. Even if a mere count of regulations does not allow any conclusion about their material quality, the proportion between laws and administrative provisions can illustrate this issue: currently, in tax law, there exist about 120 laws, 90 'executive decree-laws' *(Rechtsverordnungen)*, and 40,000 administrative provisions – with 2,000 new ones added annually. Concerning the tax payers, 120 million administrative decisions are taken every year.

§4.04 THE ENACTMENT PROCEDURE

The competence of authorizing the enactment of administrative provisions has to be clearly distinguished from the legislative competence *(Gesetzgebungskompetenz)*. This distinction is a direct consequence of the vital principle upon which the separation of powers *(Gewaltenteilungsprinzip)* is actually based. The competence of authorizing the enactment of administrative provisions forms a necessary part of every administrative competence. If a Constitution is based on the principle of the separation of powers and the executive power is assigned the task of applying the statutes, it will then be the responsibility of administrative tax authorities to make arrangements as to how these statutes should be executed also. This automatically comes with the enactment of administrative provisions. Therefore, the competence to enact administrative provisions does not have to be assigned by a certain statutory provision, hence, the laws governing the enactment of administrative provisions whose significance normally is only declaratory.

Thus, the principle holds true that each taxation authority may issue administrative provisions within the ambit of organizational and managerial power they are vested in. Given that administrative provisions 'only' contain guidelines designed for the use by tax authorities' officers, this concept still meets the requirements of the fundamental principle of legal reservation *(Gesetzesvorbehalt)*.

§4.05 THE LEGAL MEANING OF ADMINISTRATIVE PROVISIONS

[A] Binding Effects on Tax Authorities' Officers

Administrative provisions are binding directives for public servants. They connect legal consequences to a matter of fact and demand obedience from the addressees. In this respect, they are legal norms. Considering that administrative provisions merely organize the internal affairs of public authorities, their qualification as legal norms is unambiguous. They are not the product of the legislative power which is occupied by Parliament. Thus it becomes apparent that administrative provisions should be clearly distinguished from the legal rules regulating the relationship between State and citizens. Only by taking this difference into account is it understandable that civil servants have to obey the administrative provisions even if they are proven to contradict the law. To illustrate this point: under the German law system of employment in the public sector the fundamental rule has been established whereby civil servants must immediately and hierarchically raise questions affecting the legitimacy and validity of the provisions governing their work. However, if the provision in question is deemed to be legitimate and valid by any of their superiors, the civil servants have to apply it. There is just one exception: civil servants do not have to offend against criminal law or against human dignity. All this may be convincing, seen from a practical point of view, but it is difficult to understand if administrative provisions are placed on the same level as statues and decrees.

Because administrative provisions are binding for the tax authorities' officers, any failure to observe them can result in disciplinary measures. It is rather peculiar that, for example, under the court practice in Germany the State can be obliged to give compensation for citizens' damages *(Schadensersatz)*, if it is proved that a civil servant has failed to observe the relevant administrative provisions (liability of public authorities, *Amtshaftung)*. As the relationships between citizens and the State are exclusively regulated by the legislation and not by administrative provisions, only the infringement of law can justify liability for damages. This jurisdiction is even more surprising because citizens are not protected by the obedience of civil servants to administrative provisions. If a taxpayer cannot invoke administrative provisions as to taxes levied upon him/her, he/she should not be entitled to claim compensation for damages if the act to levy tax is found to violate a given administrative provision.

[B] Binding Effects on Citizens and Jurisdictional Authorities

[1] Are Administrative Provisions to be Ranked as Legislative Acts?

If taxation is to be regulated by an act of Parliament or by decree-law, administrative provisions must not conflict with these higher ranking specimen of law. This is a consequence of the primacy of the statutory law. Since legislative power also bears an obligation, issues which have to be regulated by the law cannot be so by administrative provisions. Therefore, the important question is: which matters can be regulated by the statutory law only (question of legal reservation)? While it is generally accepted that an obligation to pay tax can only be created by an act of Parliament, it is, for example, less certain whether the competence of fiscal authorities needs to be regulated by the law. The one who denies that – underestimating the importance of organizational rules for the implementation of substantive law – may vote for competences of tax authorities being regulated by administrative provisions. The fact that certain questions may be settled by administrative provisions and not by the statues does not justify the conclusion that administrative provisions have the same binding force as an act of Parliament. The binding force *(Bindungswirkung)* of an administrative provision has to be determined independently.

The scope of provision of legality plays an important role in the debate on the binding effects of administrative provisions, as it is generally accepted that the legislative bodies in all countries are hopelessly overburdened with work and should therefore concentrate on the fundamental issues. The obvious conclusion seems to be that questions of less importance can be solved by administrative provisions. If this argument is accepted, the fiscal authorities would obtain the power to close the gaps left by legislation.

The above reflections resulting in a joint competence of Parliament and tax authorities have to be rejected for various reasons. The boundary between the essential matters which have to be decided by Parliament and those which are less important and may be handled by administrative provisions depends on which points of view are taken into account. If the principle of legal reservation is one which must retain its own meaning, the problem of definition can only be solved by Parliament and not by the administration. If Parliament is requested to define the fundamentals which have to be regulated by Parliament itself, it is a reasonable solution that the Parliament delegates the legislative power to regulate the details to the administration by a specific act of authorization. If an explicit authorization to enact decrees limited in content is waived and if tax authorities are allowed to complete and amend parliamentary legislation as they think best, the tax authorities obtain the original power of legislation. This is what the constitution wants to avoid. Additionally, the power of legislation would require succinct rules of competence, because the legislative power cannot be considered a part of every administrative competence.

This argumentation received support by the European Court of Justice's case law on the issue, whether the Member States can transform EU Directives into their national legal systems using administrative provisions. European legislation does not dictate any particular way of transformation. Thus, each Member State transforms the EU Directives according to its own rules. The European Court of Justice is not competent to control the national transformation laws. But it has to decide whether a Member State fulfils its transformation obligations by the instruments it employs. As a result, administrative provisions must not be used.

The principles of legal reservation and of legal clarity and definiteness do not inhibit the usage of general principles *(Generalklauseln)* and indeterminate legal concepts *(unbestimmte Rechtsbegriffe)*. These legal instruments are concretized by administrative provisions. The undoubted competence to apply law implies the competence to concretize law. Therefore, it is necessary to answer the main question: is the competence to concretize a law a part of the legislation *(Rechtsetzung)* or of the application of the law *(Rechtsanwendung)?* Considering the differences between legislation and application of law the answer is quite clear. If the administration were vested with power of legislation, the administrative provisions would be binding for citizens and for the jurisdictional bodies. Both, administration and jurisdiction have the function to interpret law and, therefore, to concretize law. A primacy of the administration to interpret law would not only change the meaning of law for the legal position of the citizens but restrict the function of jurisdiction significantly.

[2] Administrative Provisions and their Function as Acts to Implement the Law

Therefore, administrative provisions are not a part of binding legislation, but of application of law. As a consequence, the German Supreme Court of Taxation does not use the word 'binding' as far as administrative provisions issued by tax authorities are concerned but distinguishes between 'substantial' *(beachtlich)* **and 'insubstantial'** *(unbeachtlich)*.

As administrative provisions do not create any legally binding system but apply binding law, they can be used only if the binding law leaves spaces for rules of application. Hence, administrative provisions can fill unscheduled legislative gaps by analogy.

Independent of their legal qualification, it has to be emphasized that their effective impact is enormous. For tax accountants, it is more important to know the relevant administrative provisions than to have a good command of the legal methods concerning the application of laws.

Although the promulgation of administrative provisions is intended to clarify the legal point of view of tax authorities, these provisions just give information about general, interpretative and doubtful issues, not about how to handle a concrete tax matter. Therefore, the function of administrative provisions is not to help inform individual taxpayers about their personal tax situation or to give them binding information about the treatment of their tax matters.

Given that tax authorities are bound by legislation, the objection individual taxpayers can raise is that a particular administrative provision does not rely on a correct interpretation of a statute. The real difficulty is that some statutes can be interpreted in several different ways. The thesis of 'one single fair decision' to be taken in the interpretative process is not convincing. When considering this aspect, one has to raise the issue as to whether the interpretation of statues by the tax authorities should be accepted by the jurisdictional bodies as far as it is a justifiable interpretation.

The above point is about jurisdictional competence. Should the jurisdictional body find a decision according to its own interpretation of law? That means, the interpretation by the tax authorities can only be either correct or incorrect. Or should the jurisdictional body consider different interpretations and restrict the control to the question whether the interpretation of the tax authorities is possible or not?

The question of jurisdictional competence is one that has to be asked in every single administrative case in which a statute has to be applied whether there is a relevant administrative provision or not. If we give a positive answer to the question of jurisdictional competence, the question is even more important, because the jurisdictional bodies have to come to a decision in the knowledge that the provisions have been applied to numerous cases. If a uniform application of a statute is required and if a similar uniformity is ensured by the administrative provisions, the question then is whether the jurisdictional bodies considering the uniformity have to accept the interpretation by the tax authorities to the extent that it is justifiable.

The key to the question above is one which usually depends on how the relationship between the executive and judicial powers in a given national legal system is actually understood. For example in Germany it is often argued as follows: due to the constitutional law concerning the relationship between tax authorities and jurisdictional bodies, the latter have the power to give the final and ultimate decision. This means, administrative provisions that interpret a statute are considered by the jurisdictional bodies to be like an opinion stated by a reputable legal scholar. However, the ranking of jurisdictional bodies and tax authorities can be contested. The jurisdictional bodies have the competence to come to a final decision in a legal case. This competence is necessary to finish the legal proceeding, which is the main function of jurisdictional bodies. But it is not their general function to interpret the statutes. Therefore, legal decisions are binding, even if the underlying reasoning is not entirely correct.

Due to possible errors of jurisdictional bodies, tax authorities do not have to follow their interpretation of statutes in other cases. The concrete tax matter and the process of interpretation of law have to be distinguished. The concrete fiscal case has to be solved in reasonable time, if necessary by the final binding decision of a tax court. The interpretation of law is a steady process, which follows the 'trial and error' model. Each interpretation of law can be changed due to a new insight. The regulation of this procedure is not desirable. Therefore, there is no primacy of either tax authorities or jurisdictional bodies with regard to this procedure. The uniformity of legal application is even more irrelevant. Tax authorities and jurisdictional bodies may have a consistent legal opinion. But the uniform interpretation of the statutes may be incorrect. The purpose of legal interpretation is the correct application of law.

Different legal opinions of tax authorities and jurisdictional bodies are necessary to find the correct interpretation of law. This is the common purpose of tax authorities and jurisdictional bodies. Such purpose is more difficult to attain, if one opinion is generally binding. Tax authorities must respect that jurisdictional bodies take their function seriously and vice versa. That means that jurisdictional bodies must examine the arguments pointed out by tax authorities carefully and not to reject them without reason. They must not misuse their power to come to a final decision in the concrete tax case. Jurisdiction does not mean condescending. Tax authorities should not be reluctant to change their point of view in the wake of substantial arguments. The success of this procedure depends more on the human quality of the people who are involved than on the rules of the procedure.

How difficult the relationship between administration, courts and legislator happen to be can be seen from the evolution in practice of the so-called non-application decrees *(Nichtanwendungserlasse)*. In these cases, the Ministry of Finance instructs tax authorities not to apply a certain judgment to any other than the individual case. The intention is to let this kind of issue be judged again by the Supreme Court of Taxation – with a different result, hopefully. This instruction lasts until Parliament enacts the corresponding 'non-application law'. That way it happened, for example, with a Supreme Court of Taxation's judgment from September 2003. It said that if the entire sum of interests for building lease *(Erbbauzinsen)* was paid in advance, the interests could remove the taxable income in the same year. Until now, this judgment has not been published in the Federal Tax Review *(Bundessteuerblatt)* – this would have been the precondition for its application by the tax authorities. Instead, the Income Tax Law *(Einkommensteuergesetz, EStG)* was modified. Now, the payment can be deducted in small portions only, according to the period agreed for the use of the building lease. It stands to reason that mainly fiscal motives were decisive for this regulation.

It has been stated that non-application decrees were against the principle of legality binding the administration *(Gesetzmäßigkeitsprinzip)*. This opinion is not convincing as judgments are not of the same quality as laws. According to the Separation of Powers in the German Constitution *(Grundgesetz, GG)*, the Executive Branch may decide not to apply a certain judgment it considers dogmatically unconvincing. However, a legal basis for non-application decrees out of fiscal motives does not exist. The Ministry of Finance has come to use this instrument so frequently that it may undermine the courts' task of controlling the acts of the administration. Thus, administration and legislation are likely to get an actual surplus weight. The fact that even the European Court of Justice's judgments are no longer exempt from this evolution aggravates the alarming impression.

[3] Particular Meaning of Administrative Provisions in the Ambit of the Discretionary Powers Recognized for Tax Authorities within the Relevant Legislation

Despite the principle, which has constantly been upheld, that administrative provisions in the form of internal instructions to be applied by the members of tax authorities do not carry any binding effect either on citizens or on jurisdictional bodies, several groups of similar cases have emerged in German tax judicature whereby administrative provisions must be 'respected by' the citizens and by the jurisdictional bodies themselves in exceptional circumstances. The concept of 'abidance' by administrative provisions because of their being 'substantial' is twofold. On the one hand, there is the need for administrative provisions and statutes to be vigorously distinguished. In contrast with administrative provisions, only the statutes have got a binding character. On the other hand, a certain degree of flexibility should be ensured in that jurisdictional bodies should be allowed to depart from administrative provisions in exceptional cases. The reason behind the observance of certain administrative provisions is usually identified in the particular capacities vested in the tax authorities by ordinary legislation. This is how the objection whereby a general power to make rules may be granted in a hidden way to tax authorities is disproved.

The feature found to be in common with ordinary legislative provisions – at least according to their wording – lies in the discretionary power granted to tax authorities to make their own decisions. Tax authorities are sometimes said to be empowered to act 'in accordance with their own best judgment'. The same meaning is given to other provisions under which tax authorities may be allowed to take particular measures, prior to authorization. According to prevailing opinion, to provide tax authorities with certain discretionary powers *(Erme ssen)* also marks their ambit of responsibility and at the same time free decision. Discretionary powers are attached to several constitutional and legislative constraints. However, within the free decision-making powers, it is understood that a variety of attitudes and behaviours may be regarded as in compliance with the legislation.

The reference to the above legal constraints by the granting of discretionary powers is one which has effects on the judicial scrutiny. Discretionary measures can only be controlled if boundaries – for the purpose of exercising discretionary powers – have been fully respected. Despite some contention among legal scholars, these discretionary measures traditionally have to be distinguished from indeterminate legal terms defined in order to bridge the gap between dynamic or complicated facts and abstract legal norms. In contrast to provisions providing discretionary powers, these indeterminate legal terms do not grant any ambit of free decision to tax authorities. For the purpose of legal protection, this means that the interpretation of indeterminate legal terms is subject to thorough judicial scrutiny. A similar distinction between discretionary powers and indeterminate legal terms is only rarely found in other European legal systems. Nevertheless, in every common law system discretionary powers are attributed to the respective tax authorities; only their limits vary according to different criteria. The ambit within which tax authorities are given discretionary powers to make their own decisions acquires a certain meaning for the binding effects of administrative regulations according to German judicial custom: the principle of equal treatment *(Gleichbehandlungsgebot)* – in Article 3 of the German Fundamental Law – obliges tax authorities to exercise their discretionary powers in a uniform way. If these authorities always appear to exercise their ambit of free and discretionary decisions in a certain way so that it is possible to speak of an established practice, the principal of equal treatment imposes a binding effect on the previous practice which then becomes mandatory with the consequence that diverging decisions are not allowed unless sufficiently justified. Given the assumption that tax authorities follow their own administrative provisions, these administrative provisions represent the self-imposed standards for decision-making. A diverging decision therefore implies an infringement of the fundamental principle of equal treatment. The binding effect of an administrative provision does not have its reason in the regulation itself but rather derives from an obligation based on the principle of equal treatment not to arbitrarily depart from one's own established criteria and standards *(Willkürverbot)*.

This theory about the binding effect of administrative provisions caused by the principle of equal treatment originates from the general constitutional doctrine. It turns out to be problematic because the principle of equal treatment is applicable for the interpretation of indeterminate legal terms as well. Nevertheless, administrative provisions providing concrete, substantial meaning to indeterminate legal terms must always have a non-binding character. The crucial problem lies in the question of whether and to what extent the legislator may grant discretionary powers to tax authorities through ordinary legislation while depriving jurisdictional bodies of their competence to decide on the legal admissibility of the exercise of such powers.

[4] Types of Administrative Provisions Requiring Abidance

[a] Interim Decrees

The so-called *interim decrees (Übergangserlasse)* constitute a significant category of administrative provisions requiring observance. They are based on the plausible consideration that citizens cannot get sufficient legal orientation from the rather 'abstract' statutes but only from their more tangible and detailed definition by tax authorities and jurisdictional bodies. For example, if a taxpayer has made certain arrangements in line with the criteria identified in the Supreme Court case law, his confidence as to how the law used to be interpreted by the Court previously deserves protection whenever his arrangements turn out to be irreversible in relation to tax matters. An example may illustrate this point: in German taxation law one-family houses and two-family houses used to be treated in a considerably different way for a very long time. If a taxpayer built a house which, following the criteria established by the court practice at that time, was to be recognized to fall under the two-family house category and could therefore benefit from fiscal incentives, his/her investments were necessarily protected in the event that he/she would have been denied tax advantages according to a change in the established court practice. This kind of protection is reached by a particular administrative provision which states that a building project carried out prior to a change in the criteria established by the court practice has still to be decided upon according to the previous criteria. The legal basis for such an interim decree requiring abidance by the jurisdictional bodies can be found in the regulations governing taxation procedural law. These provisions state that the tax levy may be abstained from either entirely or partially if the levy seems inequitable in the particular case.

The main concern of the court practice, i.e. to protect the financial decisions and dispositions of the taxpayers, has to be approved of. In fact, the above purpose is not entirely convincing. On the one hand, administrative provisions that interpret and clarify other statutes are held to be completely irrelevant. On the other hand, any erroneous interpretation of the statute by an administrative provision is regarded as a valid reason for tax authorities to correct the consequences of their judicially 'irrelevant' actions according to their discretionary powers. The circumstances are not seen to differ a lot if the financial actions of a taxpayer lapse due to a change of court practice. Generally, a change in the criteria established by the court practice or differences in the interpretation of a statute between tax authorities and jurisdictional bodies result in an atypical state of emergency in which equitable decrees are the suitable instrument to provide remedies. This is an old and enduring problem. Only the legislator may replace this vacuum of norms. In Germany, just a small part of this issue has been regulated so far. In Sec. 176 of the general Taxation Procedure Code *(Abgabenordnung, AO)*, it is stated that no tax assessment notice may be repealed or modified to the disadvantage of a taxpayer on the basis of a change in the criteria of Supreme Court practice. The same applies to the content of a general administrative provision enacted by the Federal Government or a supreme federal or Land authority or by one of the federal Supreme Courts that turns out not to be consistent with the legislation in force. Sec. 176 AO only applies to a tax assessment notice that has to be modified for different reasons anyway, for example when tax authorities explicitly reserve their power for modifications at a later date or if it becomes necessary because of taxpayers providing incorrect information in their income tax returns. This regulation gives rise to the assumption that tax authorities would have made a decision based on the former court practice or on their own administrative provisions respectively if the tax assessment notice was to be issued directly with final effect. But additionally, it is important to note that Sec. 176 AO only states that a modified court practice and conclusions about the unlawfulness of an administrative provision after a tax assessment notice has been issued do not constitute a reason for the repeal of the original notice. The regulation does not contain information on the question as to whether the taxpayer deserves protection simply because he/she took his/her financial decisions in reliance on the continuity of a certain administrative provision or court practice. It appears to be fairly unbalanced that the legislator regulated the rather secondary question of the consequences of a modification in the jurisdictional practice and of an administrative provision respectively being declared incompatible with another rule of higher normative status – whereas the legislator leaves the crucial problem of the protection of a taxpayer's confidence with the tax authorities. Article 80 L 80 of the French Taxation Procedure Code *(Livre des procédures fiscales)* includes a far more extensive solution to this problem. Under particular circumstances the taxpayer receives the formal right that the administrative provision – meanwhile recognized to be unlawful – must be applied to his case. However, this solution is not ideal either because it forces tax authorities to persist with a conduct known to be unlawful. In Italy, the legislation governing administrative procedure (No. 241 of 7 August 1990) does not include any provision of a similar content as the German law. However, following the Constitutional Court declaring Article 5 of the Procedural Code to be partially unlawful, other articles, such as Article 8 of Law No. 516 of 7 August 1982, which is a special application of taxation law in Article 47, paragraph 3, of the Procedural Code, and Article 8 of the legislative decree No. 546 of 31 December 1992 in the field of case-load tax cases, should also be interpreted in such a way as to provide effective mitigation to all those circumstances in which a proper interpretation of the statute is difficult to achieve for the average citizen.

[b] Rules to Typify and Simplify Taxable Amount Procedures

The second area with most significance for the practice in which the German jurisdiction accepts administrative provisions to have a compulsory character basically relates to simplified implementation of legislation (the so-called *simplifying decrees, Typisierungs—oder Vereinfachungserlasse)*. For example, there are administrative provisions which state that the gift of material assets and items (i.e. flowers, books, CDs) made by the employer to his employees or their relatives upon occurrence of a special personal event, up to the value of 40 Euro, is not included in the amount of revenue liable to income tax. A considerable tendency has grown to translate indeterminate legal terms through administrative provisions into precise figures in order to simplify the application of laws. There are even more administrative provisions relating to the investigation of the state of facts in the taxation procedure. Indirectly, they cause a deformation of the substantive law. It is interesting to give some examples from the German case law: the procedure to identify the amount of taxable income requires taking into account the expenses incurred in order to make a profit (business expenses, *Betriebsausgaben,* income-related expenses, *Werbungskosten)*. The taxpayer has to provide the tax authorities with relevant information regarding the kind and amount of these costs. Since it is difficult for several occupational groups (e.g. acrobats, conjurers, ventriloquists, journalists and disc jockeys) to provide such information, they are allowed by tax authorities to declare lump sums *(Pauschalbeträge)*. Up to these lump sums there is no need for taxpayers to provide any documentary proof. If taxpayers wish to obtain a higher amount of deduction, they will be required to prove their costs individually. The method of lump sums is furthermore used with expenses incurred on specific occasions and it is very difficult to keep a detailed record. In this context, mention should be made of lump sums which need to be stated and settled when it comes to increased subsistence costs, to costs caused by the use of cars, hotel accommodation, travel expenditures or relocation expenses, among others. In the business field, for example, scales on the ordinary useful life *(betriebsgewöhnliche Nutzungsdauer)* of economic assets are of significant importance. Such scales influence the extent and duration of the permissible tax depreciation. Tax authorities formulate these scales for the individual economic assets, often diversified according to the different economic sectors. As a result, any entrepreneur who, in his balance sheet, states a useful life shorter than the average useful life displayed in the respective scale, is required to account for and to prove this divergence especially. These lump sum scales are not always reasonable. For example, if we analyse the figures relating to the ordinary useful life of cars, the impression will be that – unlike the statements given in advertising campaigns – they do not have a solid constitution at all. Therefore, doubt is raised as to whether exceedingly short average useful life scales are meant to indirectly increase the car industry turnover.

Such simplifying decrees are based on the tax authorities' competence to appraise the taxation basis. It is argued that tax authorities should be given the opportunity to establish certain lump sums as general appraisals by way of administrative provisions because in many similar cases a precise determination or calculation of the relevant taxation basis is not possible. These lump sums partly are based on particular observations of the tax authorities, on their general experience or even on a common experience of life. Jurisdictional bodies are required to observe appraised standards unless their application may lead to an evidently inequitable taxation in an individual case. Then their application would be unlawful.

There are several advantages gained by the use of typifying and simplifying decrees: they exempt taxpayers from the obligation to procure complicated documentation of the particulars. Tax authorities are relieved of their mass processing duties considerably. The administrative tax regulations, however, cannot be traced back to the administrations' authority to appraise as provided by law. After all, tax appraisals are only permitted in cases where it is not possible to determine or calculate the taxation basis. Thus, administrative tax regulations evoke the situation where investigation of the precise taxation basis is not even tried. The purpose of administrative provisions to relieve taxation authorities of their work load is not a sufficient reason for taxation according to the notion of past experience in singular cases. The evolution in practice shows the disadvantage of such a system because taxpayers request the application of administrative provisions only if the results are seen to be favourable for them. It would an overstatement to say that a taxpayer requests the application of an administrative provision in order to obtain advantages which are not otherwise transferred to them by law. The reservation made by jurisdictional bodies that an administrative provision cannot be applied if this will lead to an evidently inequitable taxation only amounts to a severability clause. If a taxpayer is satisfied with the lump sum specified in a given administrative provision, the particular circumstances of his/her case will not be checked. The argument raises doubt that, without similar typification and simplification mechanisms, the law could not be applied given the human resource requirements. The legislator is responsible for enacting legislation ready to be implemented and applied *per se*. It is against the dignity of the law if it then has to be made manageable and applicable by means of administrative provisions.

[c] General Instructions to Ascertain the Facts of the Precise Tax Case

Administrative provisions that influence the general obligations of the tax authorities to ascertain the facts of the case on a rather abstract level are even more dangerous for the implementation of substantive law – although their distance from the real decision about a tax charge seems to be larger. German examples of this kind of provisions are the so-called banking decree *(Bankenerlass)* as well as the administrative provision about the reorganization of tax authorities and taxation procedures *(Grundsätze zur Neuordnung der Finanzämter und zur Neuordnung des Besteuerungsverfahrens, GNOFÄ)*.

The banking decree, which was made into a legislative provision in 1988, was designed to regulate the conduct of taxation on capital gains. In substantive law, these gains do not pertain to any privileged status except for certain minimum values of savers' income being exempt from taxation by law. However, taxation of savers' income constitutes a rather controversial issue in legal policy. By means of administrative provisions it was stated that account should be taken of the confidential relations between banking institutions and their clients when auditing capital gains in particular. In average cases it had to be assumed that the information provided in income tax returns was complete and precise. In audits of banking institutions, it was not allowed to use bank documents in order to check whether the institutions' clients had paid their tax on capital gains correctly. By these instructions on taxation procedures, the essential control instrument to comprise capital gains that were not taxed was removed. The payment of tax on capital gains therefore depends essentially on each taxpayer's abidance by the law. The total amount of tax lost because taxpayers had omitted to submit their capital gain tax returns was estimated to be 5–7.5 billion Euro. All attempts to justify the banking decree and the regulation replacing it (Sec. 30a AO) are not reasonable. The motivation of this legal regime is ultimately reflected in the capital market system. It aims at avoiding all measures which result in capital amounts disappearing abroad. Nevertheless, the real reasons for the alleged disturbance of the capital market system are all hidden in the area of substantive taxation law. Therefore, this is where modifications should begin. The function of procedural law is to ensure the enforcement of substantive law. If procedural statutes are formulated in a way that substantive law may not be enforced, the whole system is deficient, however reasonable the intentions may have been in creating the given system.

The most ambitious attempt by means of administrative provisions to make sure that the reduced in-house staff of tax authorities is deployed as effectively as possible, can be found in the decree concerning the reorganization of revenue boards and taxation procedures. Administrative provisions divide taxpayers into two groups by characteristics which appear to be rather general in nature (company size, types of taxable income). The division intends to adjust the extent and intensity of an audit to the degree of relevance of the individual tax case. In nearly 80% of cases, auditing of taxpayers is not required. They are assessed on the basis of their income tax return only as to their conclusiveness and their plausibility, without further documentation being checked. If no errors or apparent contradictions are seen to emerge from the tax return, a final tax assessment notice is issued on the basis of the information provided by the taxpayer. By this regulation the tax authorities' auditing capacities are concentrated on 'interesting' cases. Those taxpayers belonging to the group of cases which require a careful, detailed auditing procedure do not hold any defence measures. For under the relevant law, every taxpayer has the duty to tolerate that the data of his/her income tax return are subject to further checking and inspection. Still it happens that taxpayers feel discriminated against because other taxpayers receive a far more cursory treatment. As the relevant decree is published and known, those who belong to the 'featherweight' group of cases are likely to avoid further inquiry by tax authorities by the way they provide their information in the income tax return.

To justify this kind of regulation it was argued that the facts of the case must be ascertained ex officio, with tax authorities having the power to establish the method and the extent of the audit in accordance with their own best judgment. Part of this discretionary ambit consists in the decision as to which tax cases have to be examined and audited in an especially detailed way. According to this argumentation, the grouping of cases in administrative provisions only contributes to the auditing system being carried out uniformly by the tax authorities. Furthermore, tax authorities should ensure legality and uniformity of taxation. If this is correct, they are responsible for the entire enforcement procedures, and for such a responsibility to be taken on, it would be necessary to consider how the staff of tax authorities should be used as well as possible to ensure productivity. The notion of productivity would also justify the application of simplification techniques especially in 'smaller' cases without special circumstances when special efforts do not appear to be worthwhile because they would not produce more than minimal public revenue. If all tax cases were treated according to the same rules, given the absence of a sufficient number of administrative staff, the resulting situation would definitely be even more against constitutional principles and ordinary legislation alike.

There is no doubt that the main problem lies in the fact that human resources employed to ascertain the facts of tax cases are insufficient. Nevertheless, even increased staff numbers would not be able to alter this result. It is also appropriate that financial considerations may have their rightful place within the problems affecting the application and implementation of the law. However, it has to be doubted whether the administrative provisions referred to above will be beneficial. The taxation statutes themselves cause implementation problems, being complex, unsystematic and subject to continuous changes. This does not mean that tax authorities are being faced with a crisis – it means a crisis is being mainly faced by tax legislation itself. Administrative provisions as described above only contribute to perpetuate this crisis. Imperfect tax statutes cannot favour the willingness of the taxpayers to accept and observe them. The less willing taxpayers are to accept the statute, the less willing they will be to present complete and authentic information about the relevant facts for taxation purposes. Thus, tax authorities have to play a role they are not supposed to, one which makes them feel uncomfortable. If auditing and inspection become the main basis for a correct taxation, imposition and collection, then the auditor rather than the statute will determine who eventually has to pay taxes and to what extent. Here, too, the fact that tax authorities have taken on the role as substitute legislators – whether willingly or not – adds to the evidence of malfunction.

§4.06 FINAL COMMENTS

The interest which essentially lies behind taxation, i.e. to allow citizens to participate in financing the public duties by virtue of their contributory financial capacity, can be fulfilled by Parliament only. Whoever does not appreciate the call for the parliamentary legislator, thinking him to be overcharged both qualitatively and quantitatively, should take into account the following aspects: it is not convincing to believe, on the one hand, that the legislator is capable of taking great and important decisions; and on the other, to deny him/her the capability of issuing a statute appropriate to fit the current needs. Normally, those who are regarded as being incapable are deprived of the essential rather than the secondary tasks.

In the discussion about the legal meaning of administrative provisions, tax authorities' experience and expert knowledge play a decisive role. This does not argue in favour of the importance of parliamentary laws. Furthermore, it is not taken seriously enough into account that the various situations regulated by taxation legislators are subject to continuous change over the years. At the beginning of the 20th century, it was important to elaborate the basic structures and principles of the main taxation sectors, whereas the real task today is to restructure the individual taxation statutes in order to remove discriminatory taxation by unequal treatment as well as to simplify the existing regulations.

The need for simple and uniform taxation cannot only be satisfied when laws are applied by administrative provisions. To put it differently, if the complaints about the actual taxation system are basically justified, they all cover fundamental matters upon which Parliament has do decide.

If the decision to levy taxes is one which increasingly depends less and less on the content and substance of administrative provisions, it is an illusion to expect the courts to accomplish their task in a satisfying way in the long run. The system of legal protection by the courts is only prepared to examine administrative provisions to a limited extent. Their main purpose is to prevent citizens from tax surcharges without foundation in the relevant statute. Citizens can therefore raise objections – although the act of levying tax is regulated by administrative provisions – because these provisions do not accord with the respective statutes. Any judgment which holds the levying act to be unlawful is only valid to the extent that tax authorities use administrative provisions to reach their decision. Given that jurisdictional bodies are geared towards the exclusion of tax surcharge where it is not provided by the statute, this control will entirely fail when a given administrative provision, through inobservance of the statute itself, provides taxpayers with a privileged position. The gravamen for a taxpayer to be treated as prescribed by the statute is not enforced in the same way towards another taxpayer, has no foundation in the traditional system for the jurisdictional protection of individuals. A typical feature behind this dilemma used to lie in the unsuccessful result of the judicial proceedings concerning the so-called banking decree. In these proceedings, the argument was not accepted that the payment of tax could not be claimed until taxation on capital gains was levied to all taxpayers equally. According to the judges, those who paid tax in the amount provided by the law were not damaged in their own right merely because other taxpayers behaved in a way that was against the law. This problem is only seen from a different angle since the German Federal Constitutional Court *(Bundesverfassungsgericht)* declared laws concerning the taxation of security sales unconstitutional in 2004 due to structural deficiencies in their imposition.

Although the current tendency is to attribute administrative provisions the character of statutes, this provides evidence of a crisis in legislation. It is the wrong way to attempt compensating the deficiencies by making tax authorities to substitute for Parliament.

Tax statutes should instead be phrased in such a way as to imply sufficiently certain provisions that tax authorities can rely on. When taxation statutes are elaborated, attention should be paid to the need to ensure an imposition in as simple and as economic way as possible for their application.

Annex to Chapter 4: Administrative Provisions in Taxation Law: Current Developments*

Henning Tappe

I THE CONCEPT OF ADMINISTRATIVE PROVISIONS

In complex, globally interlinked economies, there are increasing demands on taxation law, which has to appropriately deal with a wide variety of economic activities and ensure a State's competitiveness and its tax revenue. This gives rise to a need – both on the part of the State and on that of the taxpayer – for concretizing provisions facilitating the practical manageability of tax bills passed by Parliament and making taxation foreseeable. In their original contribution, *Trzaskalik* and *Petri* already pointed to a number of these possibilities.[1]

A comparatively new, case-related form of concretization is an 'authoritative information' (*verbindliche Auskunft*, section 89 [2] Fiscal Code, *Abgabenordnung, AO*)[2] introduced in the year 2006, based on which the individual taxpayer can apply for an advance ruling on the treatment for tax purposes of precisely defined, as yet unrealized circumstances where this is of special interest in light of the significant tax implications.

As regards mass cases, administrative provisions are still the most important means of concretization. The often mentioned number of 40,000[3] (2,000 new administrative provisions per year) can hardly be verified. The codified 'directives'

* This annex updates the previous chapter by Christoph Trzaskalik and Marion Petri.

1. Cf. C. Trzaskalik and M. Petri, *Administrative Provisions*, Chapter 4. See also D. Birk, *Steuerrecht*, §1, paras 60 et seq.
2. The Fiscal Code of Germany in the version published on 1 October 2002 (Federal Law Gazette [*BGBl.*] Part I p. 3866; 2003 I p. 61), as amended by statute of 22 December 2011, BGBl. I p. 3044.
3. Cf. C. Trzaskalik and M. Petri, §4.03 'The Content of Administrative Provisions'; J. Lang, in K. Tipke and J. Lang, *Steuerrecht*, §5, para. 24 (same figures since the 12th edn of 1989).

(*Richtlinien*) referring to the respective tax statutes (such as the directives on income tax or on turnover tax [*EStR, UStR*] etc.) are complemented by numerous measures on the different levels of a federal State. However, it has been realized that a too large number of administrative provisions can have the effect of counteracting their very purpose of simplifying the application of the law. In the context of its program 'Staunching the Flood of Provisions in Taxation Law', the Federal Ministry of Finance seeks to permanently reduce the number of fiscal administrative provisions. Based on four rulings or 'Letters' issued thus far by the German Federal Ministry of Finance (*BMF-Schreiben*) on 7 June 2005, 29 March 2007, 23 April 2010 and 4 April 2011, approx. 1,000, approx. 2,500, 473 and 115 rulings, respectively, as previously issued by the Federal Ministry of Finance were revoked to the extent not listed in the so-called 'positive lists' attached to the rulings issued by the Federal Ministry of Finance. There are plans to publish one positive list of the applicable rulings issued by the Federal Ministry of Finance and one list of such rulings that are no longer included in the respective update of the positive list once a year, from 2011 onwards. The current positive list 2012 (only) contains 1,484 applicable rulings issued by the Federal Ministry of Finance.[4] Compared to the list of April 2011[5], another 94 rulings, which are no longer relevant due to statutory changes or lapse of time, have been revoked.

II TYPES AND FUNCTIONS OF ADMINISTRATIVE PROVISIONS

As set out in the main chapter, the labelling 'Administrative Provisions' embraces numerous measures under merely different designations (provisions, regulations, guidelines, directives, instructions, decrees, letters).

All of these measures have in common, that they are derived from the hierarchy or 'command structure' of public administration. Basically, they are general instructions of senior authorities issued on subordinated administrative agencies or public servants. Therefore, they normally only have binding effects on tax authorities' officers (internally) and are usually not ranked as legislative acts.[6] Administrative provisions aim at standardizing both the organization and the proceedings of the civil service.[7] They ensure a uniform implementation of tax law, but their (external) effects on taxpayers are executed only indirectly.

Generally, in the field of tax law, there are three different functions of administrative provisions: (1) Provisions dealing with the organization of administrative processes, (2) directives on the exercise of discretion (concerning the legal consequences of a rule), and (3) guidelines as to the interpretation of tax statutes (on the elements of a rule).[8] Where there is scope for administrative evaluation regarding the

4. See Letter of 27 March 2012, Federal Tax Review (*BStBl.*) Part I, 2012 p. 370.
5. BStBl. I 2011 p. 356.
6. C. Trzaskalik and M. Petri, §4.04 'The Enactment Procedure'; for exceptions and further details see 4. *infra*.
7. F. Ossenbühl, in J. Isensee and P. Kirchhof, *Handbuch des Staatsrechts*, Vol. 5, §104, para. 4.
8. Cf. K.-D. Drüen, in K. Tipke and H. Kruse, *AO/FGO*, s. 4 AO para. 80; R. Wernsmann, in W. Hübschmann, E. Hepp and A. Spitaler, *AO/FGO*, s. 4 AO para. 86.

elements of a rule (*Beurteilungsspielraum*[9]), interpreting administration provisions may mutate into law-concretizing administrative provisions. These have traditionally been classified as anticipated experts' reports[10], but are nowadays often regarded as legal rules with an external effect due to the functional aspect of the separation of powers.[11] Administrative bodies may thus be granted a right not only to apply but also to set law in a special field of reference, where they are presumed to have more expert knowledge.[12] But this 'grant' of law-setting powers has at all times to be derived from a parliamentary act, which states or at least implies such conferment. However, unlike in other more 'technical' fields, there is no such act in tax law.[13]

For a long time, the legitimacy of so-called non-application decrees (*Nichtanwendungserlasse*) has been a controversial issue among commentators. By means of these decrees, mostly issued as *BMF*-Letters[14], the tax administration responds to unwanted decisions by the Federal Fiscal Court (*Bundesfinanzhof*) and declares the *ratio decidendi* for non-applicable in general cases - beyond just the individual case adjudicated upon.

Though a court's judgment is legally binding upon the parties only (section 110 Tax Court Code, *Finanzgerichtsordnung, FGO*), a number of authors suggest that this refusal to render the courts *ratio* a general administrative concept is a kind of 'contempt of court', given that the main function of jurisdiction is to dispense justice, and precedents set by the highest court have to be followed by the administration.[15]

But the tax administration may have good reasons for issuing a non-application decree, as fiscal authorities must keep an eye on a great variety of tax cases. However, those reasons have to be disclosed in a transparent manner in order to achieve the decree's objective of reconsidering and shaping the tax law.[16] An increasing number of scholars share the view that the enactment of non-application decrees is not contrary to the principle of legality.[17] Given that most non-application decrees are reversed in

---

9. See S. Müller-Franken, *Maßvolles Verwalten*, p. 367 et seq.; M. Jestaedt, in H.-U. Erichsen and D. Ehlers, *Allgemeines Verwaltungsrecht*, §11 para. 44.
10. Cf. C. Trzaskalik and M. Petri, §4.03 'The Content of Administrative Provisions'.
11. Federal Administrative Court, 19 Dec 1985, BVerwGE 72, p. 300 (320 f.) - *Wyhl*; S. Müller-Franken, *Maßvolles Verwalten*, p. 367 et seq.; K. Vogel, StuW 1991, p. 254 (257); A. Baars, *Rechtsfolgen fehlerhafter Verwaltungsvorschriften*, pp. 52 et seq.
12. Law-concretising administrative provisions can particularly be found in the field of environmental law to substantiate the 'state of technology', cf. F. Ossenbühl, "Autonome Rechtsetzung der Verwaltung", in J. Isensee and P. Kirchhof, *Handbuch des Staatsrechts*, Vol. 5, §104, paras. 71 et seq.
13. K.-D. Drüen, in K. Tipke and H. Kruse, *AO/FGO*, s. 4 AO paras. 92 et seq.; for details see 4. *infra*.
14. See 3. *infra*.
15. E.g. W. Spindler, Vol. 45 *Deutsches Steuerrecht (DStR)* issue 25 (2007), p. 1061 (1064); W. Leisner, *Die allgemeine Bindung der Finanzverwaltung an die Rechtsprechung*, Wiesbaden: KBI, 1980.
16. See M. Desens, *Bindung der Finanzverwaltung an die Rechtsprechung*, pp. 33 et seq.; R. Wernsmann, in W. Hübschmann, E. Hepp and A. Spitaler, *AO/FGO*, s. 4 AO para. 342.
17. Cf. C. Trzaskalik and M. Petri, §4.05[B][2] 'Administrative Provisions and their Function as Acts to Implement the Law'; M. Desens, *Bindung der Finanzverwaltung an die Rechtsprechung*, pp. 216 et seq.; K.-D. Drüen, in K. Tipke and H. Kruse, *AO/FGO*, s. 4 AO para. 119; J. Lang, in K. Tipke and J. Lang, §5, para. 28; R. Wernsmann, in W. Hübschmann, E. Hepp and A. Spitaler, *AO/FGO*, s. 4 paras 86, 341.

case of a second confirmative decision on the highest judicial level[18], those decrees may well be seen as a reasonable and legitimate form of legal discourse.

III ENACTMENT OF ADMINISTRATIVE PROVISIONS IN A FEDERAL STATE

In Germany, the most important taxes (such as income tax, corporation income tax and VAT) are federally regulated but administered by the States' fiscal authorities (*Länderfinanzbehörden*).[19] In order to arrive at a homogeneous imposition of these taxes, the Federal Government has passed comprehensive administrative provisions (*Richtlinien*) concerning the most important (mostly joint) taxes e.g. regulations on income tax (*EStR*), corporation tax (*KStR*), turnover tax (*UStR*) and inheritance tax (*ErbStR*) according to Art. 108 (7) Basic Law (*Grundgesetz, GG*). These 'directives' require the consent of the Federal Council (*Bundesrat*). The Federal Ministry of Finance also has the right to issue instructions and to exercise supervision in more individual cases according to Art. 108 (3), 85 (3) GG. These powers aim at safeguarding both the uniform application of tax law and the financial interests of the federation. Unlike in a 'unitary' hierarchy, where there is no need for a certain statutory provision[20], the 'encroachment' from the federation to the States needs a constitutional basis.

In addition, the Federal Ministry of Finance frequently issues rulings *(BMF-Schreiben)* dealing with the interpretation of statutes and clearing up borderline cases. These 'letters' (rulings) are neither directives as defined by Art. 108 (7) GG nor general instructions according to Art. 85 (3) GG.[21] They have binding force according to a trade-off-agreement of 1970 concluded between the Federal Ministry of Finance and the highest tax authorities of the States[22] for purposes of resolving a controversy about the federal influence on State level.[23] This agreement has now been affirmed by a new section 21a Fiscal Administration Act (*Finanzverwaltungsgesetz, FVG*) introduced in 2006[24]. A 'Letter' from the Federal Ministry has binding force only for the administrative authorities (they do not bind taxpayers or fiscal courts) and comes into force only upon being transformed into 'own' instructions by the States' highest tax authorities.[25]

18. Cf. Federal Fiscal Court, 18 March 2010, BStBl. II 2010 p. 627.
19. See J. Englisch and H. Tappe, in G. Bizioli and C. Sacchetto, *Tax Aspects of Fiscal Federalism*, pp. 302 et seq.
20. Cf. C. Trzaskalik and M. Petri, §4.04 'The Enactment Procedure'.
21. The Federal Government takes a different view and argues that *BMF-Schreiben* do fall under Art. 108 (3), 85 (3) GG as 'general instructions', see Bundestag printed paper (*BT-Drs.*) No. 14/6716, p. 2. This conception runs the risk of bypassing the consent of the Federal Council and is therefore not shared by the States, cf. C. Starck, Vol. 56 *Juristenzeitung (JZ)*, issue 3 (2001), p. 132 (133); B. Pieroth, in H. D. Jarass and B. Pieroth, *Grundgesetz*, Art. 85, para. 6; R. Seer, in R. Dolzer, *Bonner Kommentar zum Grundgesetz*, Art. 108 GG, paras. 121, 180.
22. Cf. P. Flockermann, "Umsetzung von Steuergesetzen im Bund-Länder-Verhältnis", in W. Bühler, *Steuervereinfachung – Festschrift für Dietrich Meyding*, p. 111.
23. K.-D. Drüen, in K. Tipke and H. Kruse, *AO/FGO*, s. 4 AO para. 80.
24. Accompanying Law to the 'First Reform of Federalism' of 5 September 2006 (BGBl. I p. 2098), as amended by statute of 10 August 2009 (BGBl. I p. 2702). Cf. M. Desens, *Bindung der Finanzverwaltung an die Rechtsprechung*, p. 47 et seq.
25. R. Seer, in R. Dolzer, *Bonner Kommentar zum Grundgesetz*, Art. 108 GG, paras. 121, 180.

On State level, both the highest authorities (i.e. State ministries) and the intermediate authorities (i.e. regional finance offices, *Oberfinanzdirektionen, Landeszentralämter*) may issue administrative provisions (decrees, provisions) that are binding for local tax authorities only, but may well have a practical influence on other authorities. In many cases, however, those provisions will be coordinated between the different States.

IV THE LEGAL MEANING OF ADMINISTRATIVE PROVISIONS

Organizational administrative provisions deal with the set-up, the internal order as well as the competencies and procedures of agencies in the context of the genuine executive organizational power of the administrative authority. They have an external impact to the extent that the administrative provisions regulate intra-agency competencies (e.g. section 14 BpO, section 195 AO[26]).

Discretion guidelines offer decision-making standards and decision-making patterns for an appropriate and equality-consistent exercise of discretion. By reason of the standard of equality, the administrative authority considers itself to be bound to a previous decision when exercising discretion in similar cases (*Selbstbindung*). This aspect bears comparatively little relevance to tax law, where cases of discretion only play a minor role in the law of procedure. There is no margin of discretion in the field of substantive tax law due to the principle of legality.

Law-interpreting administrative provisions relate to the elements of a rule: They serve to resolve issues of doubt relating to the interpretation of statutes and lay down, in a binding manner, the administrative opinion for statute interpretation to be applied within the administration. Law-interpreting provisions are binding to the administration for the time of such practice, and they have external impact to such extent; they are, however, entirely subject to judicial review.

Law-interpreting administrative provisions differ from so-called law-concretizing administrative provisions, which complete the meaning of terms that are particularly wide, thus, requiring a particularly high degree of interpretation (e.g. ordinary useful life, section 7 paragraph 1 [2] Income Tax Code, *Einkommensteuergesetz, EStG*). Law-concretizing administrative provisions may have a 'real' binding effect on taxpayers and on courts comparable to statutory instruments.[27]

Depreciation tables (*Afa-Tabellen*) define the ordinary useful lives of numerous economic assets and form an important as well as typical example that draws near to law-concretizing provisions. According to legal practice, depreciation tables are not considered legally binding, but they are presumed to be 'correct' (*Vermutung der Richtigkeit*).[28] The tax court has to give detailed reasons if it wants to deviate from the

26. Federal Constitutional Court, 31 May 1988, BVerfGE 78, p. 214 (277).
27. Some scholars have therefore suggested to abandon the concept of law-concretising provisions and to enact (more straightforward) statutory instruments instead, see H.-U. Erichsen and C. Klüsche, Vol. 22 *Juristische Ausbildung (Jura)* issue 10 (2000), p. 540 (548).
28. Federal Fiscal Court, 9 December 1999, BStBl. II 2001, p. 311; E. Kulosa, in L. Schmidt, *EStG*, s. 7, para. 105.

findings of the tax administration as laid down in such provisions. However, depreciation tables are considered to be insubstantial if they do not rely on practical experience and lead to an apparently unfounded imposition of taxes.[29]

This view is reminiscent of the former 'anticipated expert's reports', but since the tables lack a clear parliamentary act indicating their legally binding effect, the depreciation tables may – as well as other simplifying or stereotyping administrative provisions – not be seen as law-concretizing provisions in terms of the 'modern' concept.[30]

In all of these cases of interpreting and channelling the law with a view to ensuring an equal and consistent imposition of taxes, the question of whether or not these provisions have binding effects on citizens and courts is not an easy one to answer. Depreciation tables, valuation guidelines, standard rates or lump sums defined by administrative provisions help to achieve a simple and fair taxation law. The Federal Fiscal Court has upheld simplifying and stereotyping provisions as a 'justifiable construction of the law giving no cause for concern'.[31] Accordingly, such provisions gain nearly legally binding effects due to the demand for equality in taxation law.[32]

However, the Federal Constitutional Court has recently affirmed its view that administrative provisions concerning the elements of a rule, unlike discretion guidelines, cannot bind the judiciary. Indeterminate legal terms have to be finally clarified by the courts themselves.[33] If the court erroneously assumes to be bound by administrative provisions, this might be regarded as a violation of the principle of effective legal remedies as guaranteed in Art. 19 (4) GG (similar to Art. 47 [1] CFREU).[34]

The Court of Justice of the European Union does not believe in the binding force of administrative provisions either. It has been subject to dispute whether European directives according to Art. 288 (3) TFEU may be transposed into national law by administrative provisions.[35] However, the Court of Justice has considered administrative provisions to be insufficient unless expressly stated otherwise in the European directive.[36]

29. Federal Fiscal Court, 26 July 1991, BStBl. II 1992, p. 1000; E. Kulosa, in L. Schmidt, *EStG*, s. 7, para. 105; recently: Federal Fiscal Court, 14 April 2011, BStBl. II 2011, pp. 696 et seq. – 'wind farm'.
30. K.-D. Drüen, in K. Tipke and H. Kruse, *AO/FGO*, s. 4 AO paras 87–92.
31. Federal Fiscal Court, 30 August 1963, BStBl. III 1963, p. 582, K.-D. Drüen, in K. Tipke and H. Kruse, *AO/FGO*, s. 4 AO paras 84, 87.
32. Cf. Federal Fiscal Court, 20 March 1980, BStBl. II 1980, p. 455; 26 January 1994, BStBl. II 1994, p. 529 (531); R. Wernsmann, in W. Hübschmann, E. Hepp and A. Spitaler, *AO/FGO*, s. 5 AO para. 198; critically: K.-D. Drüen, in K. Tipke and H. Kruse, *AO/FGO*, s. 4 AO para. 87 and recently Federal Fiscal Court, 15 March 2011, BFH/NV 2011, p. 983; Federal Constitutional Court, 31 May 2011, http://www.bverfg.de (headnote 4).
33. Federal Constitutional Court, 31 May 2011, http://www.bverfg.de.
34. Federal Constitutional Court, 31 May 2011, http://www.bverfg.de, paras 68–72.
35. Cf. K.-D. Drüen, in K. Tipke and H. Kruse, *AO/FGO*, s. 4 AO para. 95.
36. See e.g. ECJ, 30 May 1991, C-361/88, OJ C 166, 1991, p. 10 (paras 15 et seq.); ECJ, 24 June 2004, C-212/02, OJ C 201, 2004, p. 3 (para. 26); cf. R. Wernsmann, in W. Hübschmann, E. Hepp and A. Spitaler, *AO/FGO*, s. 4 AO para. 111.

V FINAL COMMENTS

To take up the wording of *Trzaskalik* in the last sentence of his original contribution: Of course tax statutes should 'be phrased in such a way as to imply sufficiently certain provisions that tax authorities can rely on'.[37] However, this call for more specific acts of Parliament is slightly ambiguous. It is, on the one hand, most legitimate as statutes have to avoid being imprecise, but, on the other hand, more detailed provisions are also problematic, since statutes have to be abstract, universal and concentrated on the essentials.

Given that there has always been a need for commentaries and explanatory notes to legal provisions, there is no reason why those notes may not be issued by the tax authorities themselves. Unlike discretion guidelines, law-interpreting administrative provisions, which play the most prominent role in taxation law, generally do not bind courts and taxpayers - but they may still be helpful. Where the construction of a legal rule as set out in an administrative provision is 'wrong' (and has thus been adjudged 'wrong' in highest judicial rulings), this leaves hardly any room for the 'established practice' to give rise to an obligation based on the principle of equal treatment according to Art. 3 (1) GG[38] - unless there is an exceptional need for protection of confidence in 'old cases'.[39]

Otherwise, if the construction of a legal rule is 'correct' (or better: justifiable) there is no need to take recourse to 'equal treatment' either, because the legal consequences may be traced back to the tax statute itself.[40]

37. C. Trzaskalik and M. Petri, §4.06 'Final Comments'.
38. C. Trzaskalik and M. Petri, §4.05B[3] 'Particular Meaning of Administrative Provisions in the Ambit of the Discretionary Powers Recognized for Tax Authorities within the Relevant Legislation'.
39. Changes in jurisdiction might then lead to a mandatory interim decree governing old cases for constitutional reasons, cf. C. Trzaskalik and M. Petri, §4.05B[4][i] 'Interim Decrees'; J. Hey, Vol. 42 *Deutsches Steuerrecht (DStR)* issue 45 (2004), p. 1897 (1901).
40. Cf. R. Wernsmann, in W. Hübschmann, E. Hepp and A. Spitaler, *AO/FGO*, s. 5 AO para. 191.

CHAPTER 5

The Administrative Procedure for Determining Tax Liability*

Eusebio González

§5.01 SYSTEMS FOR DETERMINING THE BASIS ON WHICH TAX IS APPLIED

The procedure for determining tax liability (or settlement procedure), whether this operation takes place through the tax authorities or initially through the taxpayers, constitutes a regulated administrative procedure, at least when it is applied to the stages concerned with the assessment and definitive establishment of the tax liability. This procedure relies on two basic stages. The first one, which is complex, controversial and difficult in character, consists in the conversion of the wealth taxed (taxable income) into a unit of measurement (taxable amount), i.e. into an amount on which it is feasible to subsequently apply a percentage. The second one, much simpler compared to the first one, consists in the application of this percentage (of taxation) to the basis for measurement determined previously. In this chapter, we shall deal with the first operation.

It is essential to take the Model of the Tax Code for Latin America (MCTAL) as a point of reference in a work of this type, since this model has long been the source of inspiration for most of the tax codes in force in South America.

Before analysing the systems leading to the determination of the basis on which tax is generally applied, we should clarify the concepts and the methodology associated with the different terms generally used in legislation.[1]

* This chapter, which is identical to the one published in the first edition, has been updated by the annex written by Antonio Vázquez del Rey, which follows immediately after this.

1. See Sainz de Bujanda, *Los métodos de las bases imponibles y su proyección sobre la estructura del sistema tributario*, Madrid, 1970, p. 25 *et seq.*; Perez de Ayala, *Explicación de la técnica de*

The theory behind the 'methods of determination', which became widespread in Italy after the approval of the Consolidated Text on Direct Taxation (1958), relies on a solid basis regarding the various means used in the different cases, i.e. financial statements on the one hand and indexes and estimates on the other.

In the Spanish General Tax Law (LGT), mention is made of the 'means and methods' for determining the basis on which tax is applied, in the context of 'systems' which are mentioned subsequently in the legislative text. These systems are denominated 'estimate' types and the different procedures in this regard are then discussed. The MCTAL refers to 'elements of judgment' (Article 137) in the first case, and 'forms and systems of determination' (Article 136) in the second. We shall now attempt to bring some order to this rather varied terminology.

In the first place, there are numerous means conceivable for determining the basis on which tax is applied. Therefore, legislators list these means in the law corresponding to each tax. In this case 'means' refers to instruments or mechanisms, or something equivalent to 'that which can serve for a given end'. In this sense, means can be considered as: accounting documents, value indexes, indications of income, etc.

Undoubtedly, there are basically two methods known in tax law to determine the basis on which tax is applied: the direct method and the indirect method, which the MCTAL calls on a 'certain basis' and on a 'presumptive basis' (Article 136). Of these two, only the former can be said to determine the basis on which tax is applied with any certainty, so that it is considered to be a method or system of determination. The second method is actually designed to quantify the most simple or accessible basis on which tax is applied, though only on an approximate or 'presumptive basis', and so must be called a method or system for estimation. In the context of these methods, different systems can be established in the various types of tax legislation. For example, in Spain, up until 1980, these systems were the three stated in Article 47 of the LGT, so that after this date the system of estimation was replaced by the indirect estimation system. Of course, this neither reduced nor increased the number of existing methods.

Finally, the term 'procedure' refers to the path or formal proceedings followed to determine or estimate the basis on which tax is applied in any system in force. In this sense, there should obviously be sufficient harmony between the system established in order to determine or estimate definite bases and the corresponding procedure. Otherwise, the system could be distorted by the procedure.[2]

This having been said, we should make a general survey of the forms or systems for determining the basis on which tax is applied contained in the MCTAL.

Article 136 of the MCTAL states:

> The determination through the Administration shall take place by applying the following systems:

---

los impuestos, Madrid, 1981, p. 55 *etseq.;* Fantozzi, *IlDiritto Tributario,* 3rd edn, Torino, 2003, p. 315–327; Gonzalez and Lejeune, *Derecho Tributario,* Vol. II, Salamanca, 2001; Lago Montero, 'Accertamento e liquidazione', in *Trattato Diritto Tributario,* edited by Amatucci, Annuario, Padova, 2001, p. 969.

2. See Fantozzi, Il *Diritto tributario,* 3rd ed., Turin, 2003, p. 271–276; Tesauro, *Istituzioni di diritto tributario,* Turin, 2003, vol. 1, Chap. 9; Schick, 'Il procedimento nel Diritto Tributario', in *Trattato di Diritto Tributario,* edited by Amatucci, Annuario, Padua, 2001, p. 929.

1. On a certain basis, taking into account the elements for obtaining direct knowledge about the facts causing the tax to arise.
2. On a presumptive basis, with regard to the facts and circumstances which, being binding on or normally related with the fact generating the obligation, enable the identification by an inductive process of the existence and the value of the obligation'.

Article 149 of the MCTAL allows for all the legal means of proof in the context of the administrative procedures for determination, although it would be more logical for the law on each tax to establish the means and methods for determining the basis on which tax is applied within the systems involved. Both in the Italian Consolidated Text on Direct Tax and in the MCTAL, the two systems are the ones already mentioned, although in both cases there is a clear preference for the former. Undoubtedly, in the framework of the LGT, the systems for direct and objective estimation (forfeit amount) are immediately applicable,[3] as long as the system of indirect estimation, which always derives from the unlawful behaviour of taxpayers, is applied on a subordinate basis. Therefore, in principle, it seems we can conclude that there is a significant tendency in modern tax systems to consider the direct determination system as the very backbone of the systems for assessing the basis on which tax is applied. Nevertheless, in the following analysis, the systems of direct determination and objective estimation, on the one hand, and the system of indirect estimation on the other, appear to be grouped by purely system-related factors.[4]

Objective estimation may involve problems, in the first place regarding the contradictions of this system, and in the second place, because of its own dual characteristic. On the one hand, it involves the individual and internal character of the direct determination system, and on the other it introduces objective elements not declared by the taxpayer, closer to systems that are presumptive and based on indirect evidence. The purpose is to enable the tax authorities to rely not so much on the elements used in a given type of evaluation, but rather to rely on something that can provide a definitive path with respect to the procedure of a given type of assessment system in the context of direct or indirect methods for the evaluation of the basis on which tax is applied.

3. Currently it is not easy to draw conclusions on the character of the system of objective estimation, so that except for income tax on real persons, when both systems are the same, objective estimation has a clearly subsidiary character. Naturally, the fact that it is not easy to draw a conclusion now does not mean that it was easier in the past. See Palao, 'La estimación objetiva singular', in *Rev. Esp. Der. Fin, 197 4;* Banacloche, 'Estimación objetiva singular', in *Cron. TribTrib,* 1979.
4. There is no objection to the thesis which, instead of concentrating on the immediate or direct application of the corresponding evaluation system, considers the involvement of the certain or presumed character of the basis on which tax is applied, thus grouping objective and indirect estimation together. This seems to be the position of Albiñana, who considers the systems of evaluation cited above to be exceptional, in relation to the system of direct determination *(Sistema tributario español y comparado,* Madrid, pp. 57–58).

[A] The Systems of Direct Determination and Objective Estimation

In examining the systems of immediate application, the following points must be analysed:

(1) concept and function;
(2) basic differences to assess between the systems.

[1] *Concept and Function*

Although tax legal systems do not usually provide a sufficient technical concept of the systems of direct determination and objective estimation, a set of aspects must be inferred from them to enable us to differentiate between them for evaluating the basis on which tax is applied. The differentiating aspects are those arising from the various means and techniques used in any system.

Legal theorists have developed technical categories that may be a useful introduction to the analysis of this topic. In the first place, there is a distinction between the methods of evaluation of the basis on which tax is applied and the application procedures themselves, which are necessary in order to arrive at the evaluation according to one of the methods indicated previously.

The methods of evaluation of the basis on which tax is applied can, in turn, be classified as direct methods and indirect methods. Direct methods are those based on the returns, documents submitted by the taxpayer or the data recorded in books and registers, confirmed by the tax authorities (cf. Article 130 and 135 of the MCTAL). The indirect method is based to a greater or lesser degree on assumption or indexes.[5]

The applicable procedures are those which are based on individual collaboration by taxpayers.

As pointed out by Albiñana, there is a certain correlation between the various methods and procedures we have just mentioned. In this sense, the direct method must necessarily follow the procedure based on the individual collaboration of the taxpayer (ordinary procedure for tax management), while the indirect method can, depending on the case, utilize an ordinary procedure, based on the individual collaboration of the taxpayer, or a special procedure, derived from the principle of social collaboration of taxpayers, generally through trade unions or professional bodies.

In order to provide a more complete analysis and to identify the technical categories for a detailed study of the topic, it must be pointed out that in either procedure referred to (ordinary and special), evaluation techniques are applied, and

5. On the different ways of applying assumptions, see Sainz de Bujanda, *Los métodos de las bases imponibles y su proyección sobre la estructura del sistema tributario,* Madrid, 1970, p. 31–35; Tesauro, 'Le presunzioni nel processo tributario', in *Riv. Dir. Fin. Sc.fin.*, 1986, p. 188; Trimeloni, 'Le presunzioni tributarie', in *Trattato Diritto Tributario,* edited by Amatucci, Annuario, Padova, 2001, p. 691.

must be recalled. These techniques may include: a) indexes; b) checked returns; c) forfeiting.[6]

[a] *Indexes*

This term, used in the broad sense,[7] can be defined as objective evidence. The other terms, such as forms, indexes and parameters, used in the strict sense, have the following basic characteristics:

(1) They always refer to facts occurring externally and which can be freely and easily perceived by third parties.
(2) They are assumed to be related to the economic capacity of the taxpayer, of which they form indirect evidence, and are mediated, so that they are referred to as evidence or external signals.[8]

The evidence-based system, as mentioned, is one which provides above all convenience and simplicity of evaluation, while on the other hand considerably reducing the accuracy.[9]

[b] *Checked returns*

This system is what is referred to as 'determination' in Article 132 of MCTAL, corresponding to determination on a 'certain basis' in Article 136. Actually, this technique is the one used in the ordinary procedure for determination, when it is normally started through returns, and develops through a series of stages: start, provisional settlement, checking and definitive settlement.

Theorists unanimously agree on the fact that in an ideal system, this is an excellent technique. Theoretically, this is the only one enabling us to know about and evaluate the real taxpaying capacity of the taxpayer.

---

6. See for example, the clear explanation by Trotabas and Cereze, *L'imposition forfataire des benefices industriels et commerciaux*, Paris, 1958; p. 16 seq.
7. The concept of index can be used in a narrow sense and in a broad sense. It is used in the narrow sense in Spanish legislation, for example, when it refers to forms applied to global assessment.
8. As we can see, the text uses the words indexes, evidence and external signs in a broad sense and without identifying them with the ones existing in global assessment, or with the former 'external signs' of income tax. These are all variations of a single method: that of indexes or external signs in a broad sense, mentioned in the text.
9. See Trotabas and Cereze, *L'imposition forfaitaire des bénefices industriels et commerciaux*, Paris, 1958, p. 17; Sainz de Bujanda, *Los métodos de las bases imponibles y su proyección sobre la estructura del sistema tributario*, Madrid, 1970, p. 35 and following.

[c] *Forfeiting*

Finally, the forfeiting system is an intermediate technique between indexes and checked returns. At the start, the authorities can and must use the data which the taxpayers have to supply, and are found in their documents, registers, accounts etc. On the other hand, however, external elements, parameters, indexes, assumptions etc. can be used concurrently. This type of technique is typical of the objective estimation system.[10]

[2] Differences to be Established between Systems of Direct Determination and Objective Estimation

Whether we consider the system of objective estimation as a system where the basis on which tax is applied is partly assessed on the direct and indirect system (Palao), or if we opt for the position held by Albinana, who includes this system of estimation among the indirect ones that can be applied by any procedure adjusted to the individual, the basic difference between the systems involves the means or techniques utilized (procedures) and the objectives pursued. In this context, and in relation to the widespread paralysis of the process of extending the objective estimation system, there must be no doubt on the general inclination to apply objective estimation, as the system for assessing tax liability. The differences between this and the system of direct determination, as we developed with Sainz de Bujanda and Ramallo,[11] are qualitative and not only quantitative. The objective is not to try to find the true basis on which tax is applied to the taxpayer, as an accurate and certain determination of economic capacity involved in tax liability, but with a ('another' according to Sainz de Bujanda) criterion as similar as possible to the true one, and only presumptive, at least in all the elements not deriving directly from some data, such as net income, personnel expenditure, purchases and similar items, which require accurate quantification.

With regard to the procedure followed in both systems, there is a point deriving from the difference regarding objective indicating a substantial difference between the two. In the system of direct determination, since all the figures declared must be certain, administrative checking can and must be conducted on any aspect. In the system of objective estimation, only the values indicated have this quality. With respect to all the others, the normal situation is that the tax authorities can utilize, based on the information provided by the taxpayer and that already held by the authorities, either the indexes, signs and forms established by the Ministry of the Treasury and Finance, or income or values different from those shown in the returns submitted by the taxpayer.

---

10. See Palao, 'La estimación objetiva singular', in *Riv. Dir. Fin.*, 1974; C. Albiñana, *Sistema tributario español y comparado*, Madrid, p. 52; Lopez Geta, 'La estimación objetiva singular', in *Riv. Dir. Fin*, 1979.
11. Ramallo, 'Hecho imponible y cuantificación de la prestación tributaria', in *Rev. Esp. Der. Fin*, 1978.

[B] The System of Indirect Estimation

This system of estimation relies on all those circumstances stated in Article 135 of MCTAL as its basis of application (determination for lack of compliance), i.e. substantially incorrect behaviour by the taxpayers in their relationship with the tax authorities. Starting from this assumption, and according to the information induced by incorrect taxpayer behaviour, Article 136 of MCTAL provides the tax authorities with two paths: determination on either a certain or a presumed basis. Thus the 'determination on a presumed basis', which is not really 'determination', is what Italian tax legal theorists call 'inductive assessment', and 'indirect estimation' in Spanish theory. The general characteristics of indirect estimation are as follows:

(a) subordinate application with respect to systems of direct determination and objective estimation;
(b) the hypotheses of application are based on legally incorrect behaviour by the taxpayer;
(c) the presumptive character of the estimated basis for tax liability;
(d) the decisions or agreements adopted regarding the estimation of the basis on which tax is applied under the corresponding studies are taken in accordance with the ordinary laws governing the development of the administrative procedure;
(e) finally, as the logical conclusion of the aforesaid, the corresponding administrative acts shall be liable to appeal (cf. Article 137 MCTAL).

§5.02 CHARACTERISTICS OF THE ADMINISTRATIVE ESTIMATE PROCEDURE

Starting from the fact that the acts forming the procedure are legal acts, and consequently, must produce legal effects, and assuming that all the theory on the procedure for determination must identify the effects produced by each of these acts, the formal concept of the procedure of determination requires rigorous examination of the link between the effects of the legal acts both in form and substance, which is however impossible to achieve. We should accept that the determination procedure - if only for recognizing whether the tax liability arises or not - exists in any case to provide a clear effect from the substantial point of view as to whether the subjective right of the authorities to demand the corresponding amount should be fully recognized.[12]

12. See Capaccioli, 'L'accertamento tributario', in *Riv. Dir. Fin. Sc. Fin.*, 1966; Falsitta, 'Struttura della fattispecie dell'accertamento nelle imposte riscosse mediante ruoli', in *Studi Proc. Amm. Trib.*, Milano, 1971; Micheli, 'Il procedimento tributario di liquidazione' and Perez de Ayala, 'Función tributaria y procedure de gestion', both in *Rev. Der. Fin*, 1974; Bollo, 'L'accertamento: natura e funzioni', in *Trattato Diritto Tributario*, Padova, 1994, vol. III, p. 89. The text closely follows the explanation given by Perez de Ayala.

Since the effects of the determination procedure are not discussed here when dealing with the origin of the obligations, it seems preferable to focus our attention on the characteristics of the procedure mentioned above.

[A] First Characteristic

The first characteristic to point out is the procedure of determination, although it originally belongs to the class of formal administrative procedures for implementing an administrative function, the tax function, and has certain particular characteristics.

The theory of administrative procedures as acts of the tax authorities is usually interpreted as a group of acts that neither declare nor form the rights of the taxpayer, but only have a simple character or internal instrumental effect for achieving or conducting the entire procedure, and which culminate in an act, sometime declarative and sometimes setting forth the rights or obligations of the taxpayer (final act of settlement).

As is well known, the technical consideration of the administrative procedures structured in this way developed in modern theory as follows.

Initially, and as a consequence of the fact that the concept of 'administrative act' originated historically with tax authorities being subject to the law, classical authors reserve the concept only for those which, while being issued from an organ of the tax authorities, contain a declaration of rights and obligations or form a right or obligation concerning the sphere of the taxpayers (in this sense we can include the classical definition of the administrative act, for example, in Spain, those of Gascon y Marin, Fernandez de Velasco, etc.).

Starting from this traditional definition of administrative act, the technical consideration of the administrative procedure leads to the following conclusion: the procedure culminates in a true administrative act, which concludes a series of acts by the tax authorities, which, in order not to be subject to appeal or to declare or form rights and obligations, do not have the typical characteristics of administrative acts (they would merely be acts by the tax authorities).

In modern theory, the extension of the concept of administrative act not only includes the acts of the tax authorities that are declarations of willingness to promote an immediate legal effect, but also any act issued by a branch of the administration, forming a declaration of willingness, desire, knowledge or judgment and achieved in the exercise of administrative power (Zanobini), by which the traditional narrow concept of the administrative act is overcome. Most of what traditional theory calls mere acts by the tax authorities, are converted into 'administrative acts', and in a broader concept, from mere 'intermediate' administrative acts.

In line with this tendency, the ordinary administrative procedure is integrated by a series of mere 'intermediate' administrative acts and culminates in a principal or definitive act.

Having summarized the characteristics of administrative procedures, we can now understand the characteristics of the administrative procedures for the determination of tax liability. Although it amounts to a kind of administrative procedure, the procedure for tax determination has the peculiarity of being integrated not only by a series 'intermediate' administrative acts, but also by 'intermediate' acts which, additionally and with certain effects, are considered to be definitive acts, without losing the condition of acts with an instrumental character within the procedure of determination. We shall explain this more clearly.

In various legislation, e.g. Spanish, French or Italian, until relatively recently, the only truly definitive act of the procedure for tax determination was the act of final settlement, this being considered to be declarative of rights and obligations and to be subject to appeal in court. The remaining acts of the settlement procedure, referring to the economic or legal sphere of the taxpayers (e.g., provisional settlement or acts of checking) were not generally considered, with a few exceptions, to be administrative acts open to appeal, and could not be considered as administrative acts, but characterized as mere 'intermediate' or instrumental administrative acts.

Given that no single solution existed to the problem of challenging acts by the tax authorities, the MCTAL opted for two alternative texts in Chapter VII (Resources). The first one states: 'The acts of the tax authorities with regard to those determining taxes or applying sanctions can be challenged ....' (Article 171), while the second text states: 'The acts of the tax authorities in tax matters contrary to law can be challenged ...'(Article 171).

Undoubtedly, this characteristic is fully recognized by the tax jurisprudence of the countries allowing provisional settlements, where the following theory is often advanced: provisional settlement is not a definitive administrative act, and consequently, provisional and definitive settlements do not mean having two different settlements, but rather two stages of a single settlement, which extends over two administrative acts, of which only the second one has a definitive character (Spanish STS of 1 June 1951).

In Spain, since the promulgation of the LTG (1963) and the development of the principles it lays down, this concept has changed radically, and today we can say that:

(1) Not only definitive settlements, but also provisional settlements and acts of checking the basis of tax liability amount to administrative acts, unilateral acts of settlement and, for the challenging purposes, definitive acts.
(2) The procedures for tax determination culminate in an administrative act, unilateral acts of settlement and final settlement. However, they are not simply integrated by 'intermediate' or non-definitive administrative acts, but during the procedure a series of acts is produced having instrumental and subordinate efficacy within the procedure to produce the final act, since they establish or declare rights and obligations of the taxpayer and are open to administrative appeal, and thus have the character of definitive administrative acts.[13]

13. We are aware that, from the theoretical point of view, the solution adopted in the text is insufficient, that different acts of the procedure of determination have an instrumental function subordinate to the achieving of the final act and, for certain effects, are subject to appeal and

[B] Second Characteristic

The second characteristic which may affect the procedure for tax determination, is an immediate consequence of the first one. It refers to the types of acts that integrate the administrative procedure of determination.

These acts can be classified, according to their legal and administrative nature and content and their effects, into three major groups:

(a) Acts that are exclusively unilateral and definitive legal settlements (the final settlement).
(b) Acts that are, according to the effects being considered, unilateral and definitive legal settlements and instrumental acts of the procedure (voluntary payments, provisional settlements, acts that embody the result of the checking of the basis for tax liability or determining the tax system applicable to the taxpayer).
(c) Mere 'intermediate' or instrumental administrative acts.

The analysis of such triple classification enables us to observe that the most interesting aspect is the group of acts mentioned in (b). These acts, which are the most interesting legal category in this study, are special because they have a double legal effect:

In the first place, since they establish or make the rights of the tax authorities applicable to the taxpayer or lead to immediate obligations for the latter, effects occur outside the administrative procedure, producing a relationship between the two spheres.

Moreover, the acts we are referring to also produce secondary legal effects. Since they are an element of the administrative procedure or integrate a necessary phase of it, they form the basis for a further creation of acts within the same procedure. The legal efficacy of these acts is purely instrumental and procedural, and they do not produce a relationship of external obligation with respect to the procedure between tax authorities and taxpayers.

For example, voluntary payments, provisional acts of settlement or acts for verifying the basis for determining liability, have a double legal function. On the one hand, they involve legal effects immediately affecting the tax authorities and the taxpayers. On the other, they are an obligatory stage in the administrative determination procedure. Their effects, in this second level, are separable in the conceptual sense from others which are declarative of obligations and rights, since as procedural acts

---

require the character of definitive acts. However, whether we like it or not, this is the solution adopted by positive Spanish law.

Rationally, Palao points out that this formulation is not theoretically accurate ('Estudio Preliminar' in the Spanish translation of Vol. III of *Principi di Diritto Tributario,* by Berliri), though we believe that Spanish tax legislation, on this point, cannot be provided with a technically pure explanation, otherwise it would be forcibly reduced to theoretical frameworks developed for other laws.

In this sense, we can see the sensible and pragmatic explanation of Albiñana, in his *Studio Preliminare* on the book by Romani Biescas, *Procedimiento Economico-Administrativo,* Madrid, Inst. Est.

they are limited to preparing the implementation of the subsequent act, which will declare the rights and obligations of the taxpayer (the final settlement).[14]

[C] Third Characteristic

In the procedure of tax determination there are acts subject to appeal by the taxpayers who, however, can only limit the legal effect of the act as a legal settlement, and not its effects as an act of the procedure.

Once the two levels on which the legal effects of the provisional settlement exist, together with the acts of checking the values and determining the taxation system applicable to a taxpayer, such as specific acts of the settlement procedure, an important consequence must be pointed out.

Insofar as these acts constitute administrative acts considered similar to definitive ones, i.e. as producing rights and obligations, the taxpayer can obviously challenge them. However, what effects does this produce? To answer this question, two aspects surrounding these acts must be taken into account as unilateral acts of settlement and as mere procedural acts. Taxpayers obviously reserve the right to appeal just to impugn the legal effects of the act regarding them in an immediate sense, i.e. to impugn the obligations that the act declares them to be subject to. However, they cannot limit the purely instrumental effects of the act, unless the latter coincide with those declaring or forming the act, as a final settlement with regard to the taxpayer.

§5.03 CONTROL FUNCTIONS OF THE TAX AUTHORITIES

It is virtually impossible to understand the procedures for the application of taxes without taking into account the role of the competent body vested with assessing what is declared by taxpayers and discovering what is not declared by them. These functions are usually mandated to the tax authorities, or in a specific form to a particular branch, called 'tax inspectors' in some countries.

A systematic interpretation of Articles 130 and 139 of the MCTAL enables us to classify the functions and jurisdiction of the tax authorities into a preliminary inquiry phase of the determination or assessment procedure as follows:

- legal assessment and investigation;
- evaluation;

14. These characteristics are perfectly clear, for example, in voluntary payments and provisional settlements. Provisional settlement, which is usually preceded by a limited check, basically serves for collection purposes. In this sense, the provisional settlement implies an obligation for the taxpayer to pay and the corresponding right of coverage to benefit the tax authorities. Since it is subject to appeal, it stands as an administrative act with procedural efficacy identical to that of definitive acts. Moreover, provisional settlement is, occasionally, a procedural basis in the procedure of determination so that an in-depth checking of the facts and the basis for tax liability can take place; in other cases, the provisional settlement is a necessary procedural stage so that, upon expiry of the corresponding deadline for appeal on the basis of liability or the tax rates, the act of final settlement can be allowed.

- settlement;
- obtaining of information.

[A] Procedures of Legal Qualification, Assessment and Investigation

These are procedures designed to assess the facts declared by the taxpayers. For discovering facts not declared by the taxpayer, the procedure is called investigation. With respect to both, the tax authorities exercise functions of legal qualification. These procedures may regard:

- Qualification, assessment and investigation of facts involving tax liability.
- Qualification, assessment and investigation of the basis for determining tax liability.
- Qualification and assessment of the settlements made in declarations of taxpayer returns.

The last-mentioned function has led some countries, including Spain, to introduce the so-called compulsory provisional settlement, that is an administrative measure requiring settlement based on a specific technique and legality, which is surrounded by controversy. It is processed by the tax authorities a few months after presentation of taxpayer returns, after an ascertainment of limited scope, similar to the 'formal check' of Article *36bis* enshrined in the Italian Presidential Decree 600/1973.[15]

Compulsory provisional settlements are calculated by computer at the payment offices. They were conceived to correct material, mathematical errors of the payments made by the taxpayers. However, in practice, the offices also make corrections implying a legal character, which do not correspond to the nature of these settlements, above all when they lack any possibility of motivation as to the changes being made because of their merely numerical format. They are criticized in legal theory, and some jurisprudence has declared them to be void if they extend to legal modifications which, as we said, correspond to different administrative requirements.[16]

Besides the above-mentioned procedures of legal qualification, assessment and investigation of chargeable events, the tax authorities also have the task of dealing with the tax benefits, subsidies, relief and so on that they grant to the taxpayers.

Finally, the function of qualification of the tax authorities with respect to the extremes mentioned here, is not limited to verifying whether the taxpayer has correctly complied with the tax regulations. It is also extended to define whether there has been a willingness to violate, in the event of a failure to fulfil requirements, and to propose

15. Cf. Juan, *La Inspección de la Hacienda ante la Constitución*, Madrid, 1993; Magraner, *La comprobación tributaria de los órganos de gestión*, Aranzadi, 1995; Fernandez, *La comprobación de los hechos por la Inspección de los Tributos*, Madrid, 1998; Gaffuri, *Lezioni di Diritto Tributario*, Padova, 2002, p.74 seq.; Lupi, *Lezioni di Diritto Tributario*, Milano, 2000, p. 161 seq.
16. Perrone, 'Evoluzione e prospettive dell'accertamento tributario', in *Riv. dir.fin. sc.fin.*, 1982; Fantozzi, 'I rapporti tra fisco e contribuente nella nuova prospettiva dell'accertamento tributario', in *Riv. dir.fin. sc.fin.*, 1984; De la Peña, 'La liquidación provisional de oficio y la comprobación abreviada', in *Impuestos*, 1996.

the corresponding penalties. In this regard, the tax authorities also have the task of making an initial assessment of a possible existence of a tax crime, in this case by granting permission to the corresponding prosecutor's department or to the Ministry of Finance for a possible trial to proceed.

[B] Procedures of Evaluation

Frequently, tax regulations define *iuris et de iure* presumptions (and sometimes 'legal inventions') regarding the values applicable to the facts which are liable to tax. For example, when company shares are sold, the possible profit to be ascribed to the seller is logically given by the difference between the sales prices and the purchase price. Therefore, for tax on this income to arise, income tax and corporate tax laws establish that the sales price cannot be less than the economic value of the shares as shown in the company books.

In this case – and in many others – the tax authorities have no role in making an evaluation. They limit themselves to applying the concept of value as stated in the law. However, except in these cases, tax officials also have the duty to assess the value of the taxable items.

In order to undertake the function of evaluation, it is not sufficient to have legal and accounting training in taxation matters. More and more often, technical training (in architecture, for evaluating buildings; in engineering for industrial plant; in farming for rural property etc.) is required. This requirement is not always legally requested, although it is, unfortunately, by jurisprudence, which has repeatedly annulled evaluations when these are made by officials without a specific professional qualification suited to the technical or economic character of the goods to be assessed.

[C] Settlement Functions

When the document (in which the administrative procedures are stated) is signed for acceptance by the taxpayer, it becomes a settlement document. Thus the proposal for tax settlement drawn up by an official produces the legal effects of a mere settlement.

When this is not the case, i.e. in cases of settlement proposals not duly signed by the taxpayer, the settlement produced by the official is just a proposal of settlement, that can be impugned by the taxpayer by the proper annexes.

In both cases, the function of settlement (or proposal) of the tax authorities is extended not only to the quantification of the tax to be paid, but also to other elements of tax liability, such as late payment interest, pecuniary penalties and other increases which may be applied to the base amount (except for the amount of a fine, which is normally applied by the tax collection personnel).

[D] The Function of Obtaining Tax-related Information

Article 31 of the MCTAL expressly provides for the tax authorities to collect data and documents, both from the taxpayer on whom the inspection is undertaken, and from third parties. The supply of this information is obligatory, except in the case of professionals who are informed by way of their professional duties and are expressly authorized to keep this information confidential.

In relation to this point, is should be recalled that not all professionals or entrepreneurs approached for information can refuse to provide it by claiming the confidentiality or secrecy of their customers' data and documents. There must be an express rule allowing them this option, and if this does not exist, they are obliged to provide the information or documents being requested, otherwise they may be deemed to have resisted inspection with consequences and implications to be examined later.

Furthermore, there are some officials such as public notaries, court chancery officials, currency and stock exchange brokers, commercial agents and banks which the law requires to periodically assist the tax authorities with information on the economic contents of the transactions involved. These data are processed by computer and classified by the taxpayers *a priori*, i.e. before and independently of the possible occurrence of inspection.

In any case, these computerized databases are always made available to the tax authorities, before inspection is started. Therefore, the taxpayer cannot refuse to provide them.

Save for the limit imposed on inspection concerning the right of certain professionals to invoke confidentiality, the powers conferred upon the tax authorities for the collection of tax-related data, information and documents are in practice almost unlimited.[17]

From what we have seen it is easy to conclude that the powers granted to the tax authorities are extraordinarily extensive. Among these there is the requirement of access to all the rooms and premises where elements are container or activities subject to taxation take place, without no other limitations than the ones provided by the constitutional principle of the inviolability of domicile, a principle that the Constitutional Courts in various countries have also extended to the registered offices of commercial companies (in Spain by judgment of 17 October 1985). This power of providing free access is probably the most obvious one with the most practical impact accorded to the tax authorities. In any case, when dealing with administrative powers that limit fundamental rights, they must be established by law, since merely regulatory coverage is to say the least dubious.

Undoubtedly, the various legal systems are rather miserly in listing the duties of tax officials, just mentioning the duty to behave objectively and with courtesy, and to maintain professional secrecy.

17. See Palao, 'La potestad de obtención de información de la Administración tributaria y sus límites', in *Gac. Fisc*, 1987; Fedele, 'I principi costituzionali e l'accertamento tributario', in *Riv. Dir.Fin.Sc.fin.Dir. Fin. Sc.fin.*, 1992; Garcia Añoveros, 'Los poderes de comprobación, la actividad de liquidación y la discrecionalidad de la Adminstración financiera', in *Rev. Esp. Der. Fin*, 1992; Eseverri, 'Potestades de la Administración y derechos del contribuyente', in *Cron. Trib*, 1994.

§5.04 THE SETTLEMENT PROCEDURE IN THE DIRECT ESTIMATION SYSTEM

The procedure followed in the system of direct determination or of 'certain basis' has two basic phases: submission of returns and checking. Due to various circumstances,[18] basic phases have over time been extended and become needlessly complicated, producing different phases in the various systems involving:

(1) the returns, which, accompanied by a proposal of settlement and payment, receive the name of voluntary settlement;
(2) abbreviated checking, which is something more than a merely formal check and less than a full verification; the administrative branches of the tax authorities are generally involved;
(3) the compulsory provisional settlement, issued by the administrative branch of the tax authorities and involving abbreviated checking procedures;
(4) the 'traditional' provisional settlement, practised by the authorities before a full in-depth verification takes place;
(5) full verification, undertaken by specialized branches of the tax authorities;
(6) final settlement undertaken by the tax authorities after the legally allowed checking procedures have been conducted.

From this brief summary of the procedures, from a conceptual point of view, i.e. aside from the conflicts implied between various administrative branches, we can clearly see that a problem lies in distinguishing the types of checking as described in points 2) and 5) and the settlements as described in points 3) and 4). In particular, tracing the definitive aspects of provisional settlements 3) and 4) can be a highly intellectual exercise.

[A] Legal Nature of 'Voluntary Payment'

Much can be said about the legal nature of voluntary payments since an act by the taxpayer is involved, producing important legal effects (returns, proposal of settlement and income) and a habitual and ordinary basis for producing the final effects in the management of taxes where this system is provided.[19] There are currently two contrasting theories in this regard, both having solid technical arguments for and against.

The first theory says that 'voluntary payments' are a system, with some peculiarities (basically procedural), similar to provisional settlements. It is true that they are

18. See in greater detail our study *Medios de defensa del contribuyente frente a la crecientepresiónfiscal indirecta* in *Derecho tributario* (Argentina) and Quinc Fiscal (Spain), 1996.
19. See Bollo *Análisis jurídico de la liquidación provisional,* Madrid, 1983; Basciu, 'Autoliquidazione del tributo', in *Riv. Dir. Fin. Sc.fin.*, 1986; Clavijo, 'La autoliquidación tributaria', in *Est. der. Hda,* Madrid, 1987, vol. II; Ruiz, *La liquidación en el ordenamiento tributario,* Madrid, 1987; Fernandez Paves, *La autoliquidación tributaria,Madrid,* 1995.

not initiated by the tax authorities but by the taxpayer, so that they are not the result of the exercise of power by the tax authorities to exact payment (exercised in the context of an administrative function). However, because of their content and their actual effect under tax law, since they determine on a provisional basis the amount forming the material tax liability, they are not distinguished from other classes of provisional settlement. This is the opinion of some theorists, previously expressed by Gutierrez del Alamo in 1971, the most objective author, together with the excellent study by M.C. Bollo Arocena entitled 'Legal Analysis Provisional Settlement'.[20]

According to the second theory, 'voluntary payments' are not easy to include with 'advance payments' within provisional settlements, despite the fact that this is what they are called in some national legislation. The main argument against this option lies in the fact that provisional settlement amounts to an administrative act that is part of the procedure of tax determination, integrating one of its phases. Therefore, there is no longer an administrative act by which administrative power is exercised within the corresponding administrative function, and 'voluntary payments' do not presuppose the exercise of the power of checking by the tax authorities within their tax collection functions. These 'voluntary payments' are simply one of the so-called 'acts of the taxpayer', and administrative law theorists generally hold that these 'acts of the taxpayer', insofar as the taxpayers undertake 'public functions', neither convert the taxpayer into a de facto tax officer, nor are the acts being undertaken administrative acts in the technical and legal sense.[21] Undoubtedly, from a substantive point of view, voluntary payment by the taxpayer constitutes a true settlement, since it determines, qualifies and settles the tax liability on a provisional basis.[22]

By way of the theories on the different effects surrounding the acts of the taxpayer, there is sufficient basis for us to affirm that the qualification of 'voluntary payment' as for the categories of the 'acts of the taxpayer' with legal and administrative effects, is not only possible, but also acceptable from a theoretical point of view, provided we adopt the theory according to which these acts are part of the taxpayer's activity, being presumed by the administrative act. In this case, which must be established by law (in accordance with the requirements of the principle of legality),

20. See Gutierrez del Alamo, 'Naturaleza juriídica de the autoliquidación', in *Rev. Der. Fin,* 1971. Authors, whether or not expressing uniform opinion on this, are: Benitez de Lugo, *El recurso de reposición previo al economico-administrativo,* Madrid, 1980, p. 58 seq.; Mantero, *Procedura en the inspección tributaria,* Madrid, 1990, p. 127 seq. An accessible summary of the problem can be found in Eseverri, *Sobre la naturalezzajurídica de las autoliquidaciones tributarias,* in *Rev. Esp. Der. Fin,* 1983. On the consequences deriving from the innovations introduced in the settlement procedure, see 'Prologos' to the studies by Bollo and Lejeune (the latter in *La anticipación de ingresos).* See the interesting study by Ferreiro, 'La privatización de la gestión tributaria y las nuevas competencias de los Tribunales Economico Administrativos', in *Rev. Esp. Der. FinFin,* 1983; Ruiz, cit., p. 269 seq.; Salvini, *La partecipazione delprivato all'accertamento,* Padova, 1991.

21. Interested readers can see a wide panorama of theories in this regard in Garrido Falla Item, 'Actos del administrado', in *Nueva Enc. Jur. Seix,* vol. II.

22. On this point, besides the cited basic works by Bollo and Ruiz, we can see in a similar vein: Ferreiro, *Curso de Derecho Financiero,* Madrid, 1998, p. 554–555; Lejeune, cit., p. 198 seq.; Martinez Lafuente, 'La nueva legalidad en la via economico administrativa', in *Cron. TribTrib,* 1981; Mazorra, 'La exigibilidad de los tributos', in *Rev. Esp. Der. Fin,* 1981.

these 'acts of the taxpayer' are part of the administrative procedure, but are not administrative acts. Voluntary payments would come under this category, with the final consequence that they would not be provisional settlements, and not be administrative acts, therefore provisional settlements would be administrative acts.

Legal theory often rejects the first of the two theories stated above, while not expressly adopting the second one.[23] Generally, it just points out that voluntary payments are not administrative acts, but 'duties of tax collaboration' required of taxpayers, and of which the obligation on private citizens to undertake the tax settlement operations pursuant to Article 132 MCTAL is an express manifestation.

To summarize the above points, we believe that the latter idea can be harmonized with the second theory stated above. Voluntary payments do amount to 'acts of the taxpayer', which the taxpayer is legally obliged to undertake in the context of the procedure of tax determination with the effects attributed to it by law. From the point of view of substantive tax law, its contents and effects can be deemed to be similar to those that the law attributes to provisional settlements. However, from the court hearing point of view, and from the point of view of administrative tax law, they are neither administrative nor provisional settlements. Moreover, also from the court trial point of view, it is normal that that direct appeal to the courts cannot be made against voluntary payment, unlike provisional settlements; they can only be corrected through the specific administrative procedure established for this purpose, since the express or tacit use of this procedure allows for appeal to be made before the courts.[24]

[B] Provisional Settlement: Concept, Characteristics and Legal Nature

[1] Concept

In the Spanish positive law, Article 120 of the LGT divides the administrative acts of determination into two basic categories: provisional settlements and definitive settlements. This classification in any case corresponds to the regulation introduced by Article 1 of Italian Presidential Decree 309/1973, with partial settlements being allowed as exceptions to the principle of the unity and global nature of the act of determination, since these settlements have in common with provisional settlements the origin of their data in the tax office database, their anticipated character and the inability to judge

23. SeeGota,See Gota, *Tratado del Impuesto sobre la Renta,* Madrid, 1972, vol. IV, pp. 448–449; Albiñana *Derecho Financiero y Tributario,* Madrid, 1982, p. 537 seq.; Clavijo, *La autoliquidación tributaria,* in *Est. der. Hda,* Madrid, 1987, vol. II, p. 754 seq.; Eseverri, 'Sobre la naturalezza juridica de las autoliquidaciones tributarias', in *Rev. Esp. Der. FinFin,* 1983. p. 102 seq.; Rodriguez Ferreiro, 'Las denominadas autoliquidaciones en el ITPAJD', in *Gazz. Fisc,* 1984.
24. Spanish jurisprudence on this topic is extraordinarily rich. See, among other judgments, the STS of 1 October 1984 (comment by Falcon in *Rev. Esp. Der. Fin,* 1984); Res. TEAP Jaen of 30 September 1986 (comment by Manteroin *Carta Trib.,* 1986); SAT Valenciade 123 December 1987 (comment by Albiñanain 'Tapia', October 1988) and the SSTS of 13 May and 19 October 1988, and 6 February 1989 (comment by Castillo in *Carta Trib.,* n 101).

prematurely the issue of a subsequent final settlement.[25] We could also think, though in this case with fewer results, of non-definitive settlements, which lead to provisional acts collection.[26]

Undoubtedly, Spanish law distinguishes provisional from definitive settlements, focusing attention on the role they occupy within the procedure of determination, in relation to the phase of verification or regular reporting of facts and the basis of tax liability.

In accordance with this precept, we can define provisional settlements as those issued on a basis which has not been verified definitively or in-depth, as long as the deadline for verification has not elapsed. Therefore, if this deadline has elapsed, the settlement issued on a non-verified basis would be definitive and not provisional.

The recent amendment of the LGT (Article 123) has added the so-called compulsory provisional settlements to the above traditional concept of provisional settlement. They are distinguished from the previous ones: 1) by the department of origin (the tax authorities in general); 2) by the need to be preceded by a short checking.

[2] Characteristics

The basic characteristics of provisional settlements are as follows:

(1) They are settlements that are normally issued on data supplied by the taxpayer. Undoubtedly, the tax authorities are not obliged to limit themselves to these, however if they refer to data other than that declared by the taxpayer, they must notify the taxpayer before settlement of any elements the taxpayer has not provided and that are taken into consideration (Article 121 LGT).

(2) If the settlement is issued correctly on data declared by the taxpayer, it is completely legal (assuming that all the laws have been respected in providing this data) and it seems that it can only be impugned on the basis of mistakes of fact made by the taxpayer. Since varying opinions exist on this, there is considerable jurisprudence affirming that corrections to returns must be proposed in the checking and not in a hypothetical appeal against the provisional settlement.[27]

(3) Mistakes of fact made in returns can and must be solved during the checking phase. The same can be said of mistakes of fact or omissions occurring in the

25. See Basilavecchia, *L'accertamento parziale,* Milano, 1988; Fantozzi, *Il Diritto tributario,* 3rd edn, Torino, 2003, p. 339; Tesauro, 'Le presunzioni nel processo tributario', in *Riv. Dir. Fin. Sc.fin.*, 1986, p. 175.

26. See De Mita, *Lafunzione e gli atti della riscossione* in *Trattato di Diritto Tributario. Annuario,* 2001, Padova, p. 1101; Gaffuri, *Lezioni di diritto tributario,* Padova, 2002, p. 183; Tesauro, 'Le presunzioni nel processo tributario', in *Riv. Dir.Fin.Sc.fin.,Dir. Fin. Sc.fin.*, 1986, p. 187.

27. The topic is open to discussion either in administrative or in general legal theory. Regarding the latter, special consideration should be given to the contrary opinion of Bollo, who cites three resolutions of the T.E.A.C. to support his theory (cit., pp. 202–207). In agreement with the text, considering the S.T.S. of 16 June 1977 and 24 June 1978, Res. T.E.A.C. of 29 November 1979 and Cano, 'La devolución de ingresos tributarios indebidos. Especial consideración de las autoliquidaciones', in *Riv. Amm. Pub*, 1980.

provisional settlement, whether they derive from the taxpayer's return or from administrative activities of checking. There is a different criterion for mistakes in law made by the tax authorities in issuing the provisional settlement. If it is clear that in the case of traditional provisional settlement the requirement of advance declaration of damage must prevail in order to amend the act,[28] this is not so much the case of the compulsory provisional settlements.

(4) This leads to the important conclusion according to which the provisional settlement, like the Italian partial settlement, is issued before being completely determined and the settlement of the tax liability that is the one defined on a firm basis in the final settlement. Furthermore, the provisional settlement can be either increased or decreased as a consequence of the modifications made in the checking phase and in the subsequent final settlement. In the second case (of the tax liability being lower with respect to the amount collected in the provisional settlement), the taxpayer will be entitled to the return of the amount unduly paid. If the liability in the final settlement is higher than the amount paid on a provisional basis, the balance must be paid.

(5) This leads to the conclusion that the provisional settlement is part of a further process of checking and final settlement. In other words, the provisional settlement is issued on facts and a basis for tax liability that are only presumed, since the declaration can be amended by proof to the contrary (Article 141 of MCTAL). This affirmation is connected with the concept of traditional provisional settlement, but is not easy to relate to compulsory provisional settlement, which Article 123 of LGT seems to state as being subject to checking twice, once in an abbreviated form prior to the provisional settlement, and the other in a complete or in-depth form before the final settlement.

(6) With regard to the points made above, jurisprudence has repeatedly stated that provisional settlement has a pure and simple fiscal character of collection, using, in our view, a vague and dubious expression so that its character and aims are different from those of definitive settlement.

(7) In the end, it is formally an administrative act, whose legal nature, for the effects of its immunity from appeal, is that of a 'definitive' administrative act (Article 171 of MCTAL).

[3] What Is the Legal and Administrative Nature of Provisional Settlements?

To respond to this question we must begin with the following ideas:

28. Nevertheless, there is well-founded theory to the contrary; see, for example, Res. T.E.A.C. of 24 February, 5 July, 16 September and 3 November 1983, 6 November 1984 and 26 June 1985, commented favourably by Mantero and Albiñana in *Carta Tributaria*, nums. 28 and 59, respectively.

(1) Provisional settlements, in ordinary tax management procedure, are based (if it is not correct to say that they are adapted to this) on the taxpayer returns, and when the returns contain a positive element according to which a chargeable event occurs, the taxpayer has to prove the contrary. Starting from this admission, the existence of the chargeable event should be deemed to be proved. In our view, there is no objection in theory to admitting that tax liability arises from the combination of both factors, i.e. the chargeable event (being proved by the returns) and the administrative act of provisional settlement.

(2) The fact that there may subsequently be a negative final settlement is not sufficient to invalidate this conclusion. Let us suppose that this negative settlement is due to the fact that in the verification of the returns and subsequent provisional settlement, the taxpayer proves to have made a factual mistake in the returns, considering a non-existent chargeable event as being dubiously confirmed. Undoubtedly, in this case, the taxpayer has the right to ask for the return of the amount unduly paid in the provisional settlement. However, this simply means that only the provisional settlement (and proved *a posteriori* that the taxpayer's returns are erroneous) cannot produce a tax obligation. The previous occurrence of the chargeable event is also required; and proving that this does not exist means that the basis for the tax obligation never existed.

Paradoxically, however, the reconstruction backwards in time shows the proven existence of the chargeable event, and the administrative act of provisional settlement is sufficient to cause the tax obligation to arise.

In this regard, the administrative act of provisional settlement enjoys the presumption of legitimacy, applicability and requirement of execution typical of administrative acts, which are the premises for rights and obligations. It is precisely that presumption of legitimacy that is made void when it is shown *a posteriori* and within the procedure of determination that the returns are in error with regard to the existence of the chargeable event.

In general, the same applies to all administrative acts which have such characteristics. The fact that the presumption of legitimacy is legally voided *a posteriori* is not sufficient to deny to the administrative act of provisional settlement its character as a tax obligation. Under the opposing theory, it would not be possible to affirm the character of the presumption of obligations of any administrative act, since this could be subject to review. In this regard, the only peculiarity of provisional settlement is that it can be revised, regarding the correction of the facts on which it is based in the context of a procedure of determination, without the need to use a special procedure or an actual appeal.

(3) From what has been stated above, we can conclude that is not possible to consider the procedure of tax determination as a procedure that has as its necessary final effect the production of a tax obligation. This is due to various reasons. In the first place, this effect can arise before the end of the procedure of determination, with the administrative act of provisional settlement. In the second place, including those cases in which the tax obligation is produced as

> the final effect of the procedure (with the act of final settlement, e.g. in relation with chargeable events not declared by the taxpayer) this effect would not derive only from the undertaking of the procedure of determination, but also and necessarily, from the existence of the chargeable event. In any case, the production of the tax obligation is determined by two elements: the chargeable event and the procedure of tax determination. And this applies not only to the latter, which, isolated and alone, and without considering the chargeable event, would not be sufficient to create a basis for that obligation.[29]

Some arguments contrary to the above conclusions could be cited, since not only provisional, but also definitive settlements are subject to revision for material or factual errors, or items included to appear as new elements regarding chargeable events. However, in any case, these are special procedures for revision outside the ordinary tax management procedures and operate after these have concluded with the act of final settlement. While it has the same nature of the provisional settlement, it can be modified, since the correction of the facts on which it is based in the settlement procedure has the same nature as the final settlement in closing the procedure for tax determination, and it is not modifiable within this procedure, but in any case outside of it.

[C] Verification of the Existence and Evaluation of the Chargeable Event

[1] Concept and Classes

In the procedure of tax determination, the phase of verification has the aim of assessing the chargeable events and the taxable amounts.[30] Starting from this fundamental idea, the study of the administrative activity of checking must begin with analysis of the various classes of checking which are already known. We should take into account the fact that within the work done by tax authorities, the administrative activity of checking is sometimes entrusted to the administrative branch and in others, in a specific form, to the specialized branches. The latter case applies whether the checking is conducted in the system of direct determination, on the basis of taxpayer returns (Article 134 MCTAL) or in the system of objective estimation or checking on a 'certain basis' (Article 136 MCTAL).

29. In this paragraph we substantially follow Perez de Ayala, in his *Dinámica de la relación jurídica tributaria*, Madrid, 1997, in line with the thought of Micheli, Maffezzoni, Fantozzi, Fedele, Gallo etc.
30. For theory see: Sanchez Serrano, 'Comentario a los artículos 109 y ss. de la L.G.T.', in *Comentarios*, Madrid, 1982; Martinez Lafuente, 'La comprobación de valores', in *Hda. Púb. Esp*, 1983; Nuñez, 'La actividad administrativa de comprobación tributaria', in *Rev. Esp. Der. Fin*, 1987; La Rosa, 'Caratteristiche e funzioni dell'accertamento', inDir. *Prat. Trib*, 1990; Magraner, *La comprobación tributaria de los órganos de gestión*, Aranzadi, 1995; Falsitta, *Manuale Diritto Tributario*, Padova, 2003, p. 375; Lupi, *Diritto Tributario*, Milano, 2000, p. 51.

Leaving aside option of abbreviated checking by the management offices, we can, according to the objective, distinguish between two classes of checking:

- a direct class designed to ascertain the real existence and structure of the chargeable events declared;
- another class designed to determine the accuracy of the evaluation of the various elements of the chargeable event provided by the taxpayer (checking values or taxable amount).

[2] Legal Effects of the Checking Activity

The two checking activities included here have both common and different legal effects:

(1) Common legal effects. Given that they constitute a phase within the procedure, both the activities can be considered as consisting of a series of 'intermediate' administrative acts, with an internal and instrumental legal efficacy for continuing the procedure. In general, the final settlement is considered to be only the one practised after the checking phase or once the deadline provided by regulations has elapsed without the checking being undertaken.
(2) Different legal effects. More than its legal and administrative quality as an act or series of acts, 'intermediate' or instrumental for the continuation of the procedure, the checking of values, unlike the checking of facts, must conclude with an act of approval, which is in principle challengeable.

The act of ascertainment of values must be notified to taxpayers so that they can know the means used by the tax authorities in the checking and appeal if they do not consider them to be suitable. Presentation of an appeal does not suspend the settlement procedure, and the checking of values and the settlement can be notified jointly.

[3] Function and Structure of the Checking Procedure

The procedure for checking the chargeable event and taxable amount has a 'close' and a 'remote' function; the 'close' function can, in turn, be classified as an immediate or intermediate function.

The immediate 'close' function of the checking procedure consists in assessing the economic size of the chargeable event giving rise to the basis for tax liability which is basically the element quantifying the contributory capacity to be subjected to tax.

The intermediate 'close' function consists in determining a proportional amount that can provide support to the further settlement of the tax amount. This tax amount forms the basic, though not the sole, element of the tax liability.

The 'remote' or final function of the checking procedure aims to ensure that all taxpayers are taxed on the basis of their real contributory capacity, since the checking technique seeks to assess the chargeable event and to allow the settlement of the amount owed. It should not be forgotten that: a) the chargeable event must involve some manifestation of contributory capacity; and b) the tax amount represents the part of contributory capacity taken by the tax.

Once the 'close' and 'remote' functions assigned to the checking procedure have been determined, we can see their internal logical structure. In this regard, we can point out two objectives of the checking procedure.

In the first place, the identification, case by case, of the elements forming the chargeable event and the necessity of revising the basis for tax liability. From this point of view, the tax authorities must strictly comply with the legal definitions of the chargeable event and basis for tax liability contained in the tax law.

The second objective consists in the mediation and evaluation of the basis for tax liability as the quantitative aspect of the chargeable event. This work of case by case evaluation of the basis on which tax is applied to any taxpayer, starting from the general definition in the law, must be conducted by the tax authorities following the procedures established in the law, and using the elements and means set forth therein.

[4] Possible Discretionary Action by the Tax Authorities in the Checking Procedure

In principle, as we have said, both for the basic function of the checking procedure in the application of tax, and for the conclusions reached through analysis of the logical structure, the checking procedure is obviously an example of the regular activity of the tax authorities.

Therefore, there are cases where the law, instead of using a single characteristic to choose only one means of estimation of the basis for tax liability or checking, has a number of these available without however establishing priority among them. In this case, the basic issue is whether the tax authorities have discretionary powers to choose or apply any means established by the law.[31]

It seems clear, in our view, that in this case there are absolute and total discretionary powers. The legislator takes into account a wide variety of possible factual situations to which the checking procedure is applied, and it is therefore inevitable also to have a range of means, though not with the idea that the tax authorities can freely choose these means with absolute discretion, but with the clear aim of enabling the tax authorities to make a clear and concrete choice of the most suitable and adequate means provided by the regulations.

31. See Perrone, *Discrezionalità e norma interna nell' imposizione tributaria*, Milano, 1969; Gallo, 'Ladiscrezi-onalità nel Diritto Tributario', in *Trattato Diritto Tributario*, edited by Amatucci, Annuario, Padova, 2001, p. 951.

§5.05 SUMMARY

(1) The administrative activities of proving (prior to, and on the basis of facts) and providing counter-proof (subsequently and combining facts with regulations) have, as we know, numerous aspects, admirably summarized in theory, in the sense of sustaining that the action of the tax authorities during assessment must be a reasoned and analytical process, in other words motivated. This is because in the contrary case, taxpayers would not be protected, the public would not be guaranteed and it would be impossible to fulfil the checking function of the judiciary.

(2) The administrative activities of proof and counter-proof are also essentially aimed at establishing the size of the chargeable event and quantifying the basis for determining tax liability, utilizing the means and procedures provided for in the legal system. Among these procedures, the one of direct determination or on 'certain basis' is the most accurate, and is thus normally preferred.

(3) The presumption of the legality of administrative acts acquires full significance when the tax authorities habitually act according to the law. However, this prerogative does not assume that administrative acts are exempt from the need for proof, with the taxpayers having to prove their illegality, and simply means that they have the onus of appealing against acts in the courts. The presumption of legality of administrative operation cannot be extended to the facts taken into consideration for the acts, and does not guarantee the administrative activities that result, if any concrete administrative act simply becomes a matter of legal technique, in determining which acts are legally valid and which are not. The tax authorities must prove the fact underlying the presumption and the taxpayer can eliminate the presumed fact by bringing suitable proof to the contrary.

(4) The power to check is a public power, aimed at ensuring that contributory capacity is correctly taxed, in order to favour the fair distribution of the tax burden. This power has no limit other than that derived from application in compliance with the law, since the law determines the chargeable event, the size of the basis for tax liability and the procedure established for its determination.

(5) Once we accept that tax law tends to eliminate unlimited checking systems by the tax authorities, ensuring the regular exercise of their powers, we can easily conclude that the range of means of assessment provided by regulations is aimed at demonstrating to the tax authorities the setting and evaluation of what should be considered as the truth or reality of the facts and the basis on which tax is applied. Consequently, the tax authorities must in any case use the most suitable means for setting the chargeable event and assessing the basis for tax liability.

Annex to Chapter 5: Recent Developments on Administrative Determination of Tax Liability*

Antonio Vázquez del Rey

The contribution that Professor González made to the first edition of this *International Tax Law* addressed a great variety of topics. References were made not only to the administrative procedure but also to the different methods for the determination of the tax base, the evidences in the tax procedures, the obtention of tax-related information, the nature of voluntary compliance, etc. This appendix focuses on some of the issues that were then raised - specifically those regarding the administrative assessment - while addressing some new implications. An update of the legal references is also made with regards the 2006 MCTAL and the Spanish 2003 General Act on Taxation (GAT). This necessarily brief commentary is made as a personal token of respect and admiration for both the academic and the person that wrote the original piece.

I ADMINISTRATIVE PROCEDURE AND DETERMINATION OF TAX LIABILITY

In modern tax systems, tax assessment is primarily conferred to individuals and corporations regarding the most relevant taxes - e.g. individual income tax, corporate tax, VAT, excises, etc. Not only does the taxpayer submit the tax return, which is the primary source of information for tax assessment[1], but he/she also estimates the amount to be paid - self-assessment or 'voluntary compliance' according to the 2006 Tax Model Code for Latin America (MCTAL). Besides, third parties, who are related to the taxpayer as a result of the economic activity, usually perform as de facto tax

* This annex updates the previous chapter by Eusebio González.

1. In general, the determination of the tax liability relies on the tax returns filed by the taxpayer and third parties which content is assumed to be true, subject to verification by the tax authorities (Article 43(2) MCTAL).

collectors – e.g. withholding agents, undertakings for VAT purposes[2]. The main role of tax authorities in this context is no longer that of tax assessment but verification and examination of the compliance of fiscal duties by both taxpayers and third parties[3].

Leaving aside the indisputable relevance of procedural aspects related to tax application[4], not every single administrative action has necessarily to be framed within an administrative procedure[5]. An administrative procedure is usually regarded as a formal way of making administrative declarations of will, knowledge, opinion, etc., in other words, a way of exercising formalized administrative activities.[6] Strictly speaking, a tax assessment procedure involves a series of related acts which are directed to a formal administrative decision. However, the taxpayer usually files a tax return and pays the tax while the administration verifies the taxpayer has properly completed his fiscal duties, with no further decision to be made unless an improper compliance is observed. Therefore, any action carried out by both the taxpayer and the tax administration who agrees to the proposed self-assessment cannot be regarded as part of an administrative procedure.

Regarding the Spanish tax system some scholars have stated that the tax assessment procedure concludes with the administrative act of final assessment, which is issued at the conclusion of an inspection procedure in which the tax authorities have verified all the elements of the tax liability[7]. Leaving this rather extraordinary situation aside, in most cases no administrative act is issued where the tax authorities accept the self-assessment proposed by the taxpayer. Moreover, where the taxpayer incorrectly

2. Calvo Ortega, R.: *Las actividades de colaboración de los privados con la Administración Tributaria: en torno a un nuevo ordenamiento*, Real Academia de Jurisprudencia y Legislación, Madrid, 2006, *passim*.
3. As a matter of fact, with regards to the initial determination of the tax liability, tax authorities 'have passed the buck' to the taxpayer (see Fantozzi, A.: *Corso di Diritto Tributario*, UTET, Torino, 2004, p. 264). According to Pérez de Ayala, J.L. and González, E.: *Curso de Derecho Tributario*, t. II, 4ª ed., Edersa, 1984, p. 12, assessment by the tax authorities involve a set of powers similar to those which can be found in the administrative police (no matter they can be formally and materially distinguishable).
4. Schick, W.: "Il procedimento nel Diritto Tributario", in Amatucci (dir.), *Trattato di Diritto Tributario*, vol. III, 1, Cedam, Padova, 1994, pp. 69 ff.
5. Due to their simplicity, certain proceedings do not require a formal procedure, but just a simple administrative action. This assumption is implicit in the Spanish 2003 GAT which distinguishes between assessment 'actions' and 'procedures' (Menéndez Moreno, A.: "Las actuaciones y procedimientos de gestión tributaria: una aproximación a su significado" in Arrieta Martínez de Pisón et al (dir.): *Tratado sobre la Ley General Tributaria*, t. II, Thomson Reuters, 2010, p. 485).
6. Sánchez Morón, M.: Derecho Administrativo, Parte General, 6ª ed. Tecnos, Madrid, 2010, pp. 479 f. See also Boquera Oliver, J. Mª.: *Estudios sobre el acto administrativo*, Civitas, Madrid, 1982, p. 473.
7. The use of the information technologies may, however, challenge the aforementioned model. The tax authorities can be in a position to determinate the tax amount, particularly from the data provided by withholding agents, non-profit entities, financial institutions, etc. This has led in Spain to the so-called tax return drafts in the context of the individual income tax. An administrative draft can be sent to those taxpayers with a rather simple tax return – only specific items of income such as labour, interests, dividends, capital gains subject to withholding, etc. Where the taxpayer agrees to the administrative determination, the situation is similar to the traditional provisional assessment, with the difference that no tax return has been previously submitted by the taxpayer. However, where the draft does not reflect the taxpayer's economic situation, he/she will have to file an ordinary tax return.

determinates the tax, the tax authorities may issue an act of provisional assessment which, however, does not imply that an inspection procedure is to be initiated later on. And vice versa, no administrative provisional assessment is required for the administration to issue a final assessment act at the conclusion of the examination process[8]. Thus, it remains unclear how this complex reality can be framed within the classical concept of administrative procedure. The idea of a single administrative procedure which encompasses every action that takes place with regards tax application could be only embraced figuratively, as a mere abstraction.

The administrative procedure usually rises as a formal reaction against an unduly behaviour of the taxpayer. Actually, Article 83 MCTAL states that the procedure for the administrative determination of the tax liability starts with an administrative act signed by the competent officer who states the relevant facts and omissions which have been observed and involve an infringement of the tax law by the taxpayer or a third person liable, making reference to the allegations or charges presented to him/her.[9] Similarly, the Spanish 2003 GAT states a number of administrative procedures, however, none of them includes the self-assessment stage except where the taxpayer claims for a refund[10].

II DETERMINATION OF THE TAX BASE. SOME ISSUES REGARDING PRESUMPTIVE TAXATION

Leaving aside those taxes in which the amount to be paid derives directly from the law, the tax base is usually determined by either a direct method - taxation 'on an actual base' according to Article 43(3) MCTAL, or an indirect method - taxation 'on a presumptive base' or presumptive taxation[11]. While taxation on an actual base implies that the tax base is determined with regard to actual receipts, expenses, asset values,

8. The final tax assessment act may not be issued by the tax authorities, however, a number of administrative actions - e.g. provisional assessments, verification of values - may take place in the meantime which obviously affect the taxpayers' rights. From this derives the need to extend the right to challenge these actions.
9. Article 83 MCTAL establishes the following structure of the tax determination procedure: a) The interested party is entitled to submit his allegations and present any evidences within a certain period of time; b) At the conclusion of this period, the tax authorities issue a decision which specifies the omitted taxes, accessories and penalties; c) the decision is notified to the interested party. No decision is needed, however, where the taxpayer or the third party agrees to the allegations and charges presented. That agreement shall produce the effects of a return for the liable person and a final assessment for the tax authorities.
10. The Spanish GAT states administrative procedures with regards to: 1) taxes which are still governed by the traditional tax assessment model, according to which the taxpayer files a return and the administration estimates the amount to be paid from the data provided by the taxpayer and any other relevant sources of information; and 2) taxes which are self-assessed, where the taxpayer claims for a tax refund or the tax authorities (i) require the taxpayer to clarify any aspect of the tax return; (ii) intend to verify the values or (iii) initiate an inspection procedure, limited or complete.
11. Some scholars consider, however, that the indirect method must not be regarded as a method for the determination of the tax base but as a method for the verification of tax compliance (García Novoa, C.: "Elementos de cuantificación de la obligación tributaria", in Calvo Ortega (dir.), *La nueva Ley General Tributaria*, Thomson Civitas, 2004, p. 231).

etc., of the taxpayer, presumptive taxation relies on indexes, parameters, statistical reports, etc. Theoretically the direct method reflects income, wealth, etc., more accurately while indirect estimation is a more imprecise technique. From this derives that those countries which are in a position to apply the direct method rely, if any, on presumptive taxation only to a limited extent.

The MCTAL regards both methods in the context of the determination of the tax by the authorities, although self-assessment may obviously involve also taxation on an actual or on a presumptive base. Under the provisions set forth in Article 44 MCTAL, taxation on an actual base derives from those elements which allow a direct knowledge of the taxable events. Regarding presumptive taxation, MCTAL states that tax authorities are only entitled to this method in a limited number of situations which basically reveal an incorrect behaviour by the taxpayer – e.g. the taxpayer refuses or obstaculizes the verification proceedings, provides no indication with regard to the compliance of fiscal duties, relevant records are missing, etc. (Article 45 MCTAL). In order to indirectly estimate the base the tax authorities can: (i) apply any relevant data and precedents; (ii) use those elements which indirectly prove the existence of assets, income, receipts, turnover, expenditures, etc., average in that economic sector, considering the size of the units to be compared; and (iii) measure those parameters, indexes, etc. the taxpayer meets, according to the data and precedents which are available in similar or analogous situations.

Presumptive taxation can be implemented either as an exclusive method or as a minimum tax[12]. In the first case the actual income, turnover, etc. is irrelevant as taxation only derives from those specific parameters or indexes. Presumptive taxation is regarded as a minimum tax where the tax liability is no less than that determined under the presumptive rules. Article 45 (2) MCTAL promotes this latter as it states that the determination of tax on a presumptive base does not release the taxpayer from tax liability with regards to any positive differences that may derive from a later determination of the tax on an actual base. The tax that derives from parameters, indexes, etc., is, therefore, regarded as a provisional statement in order to guarantee taxation.

Presumptive taxation is mostly used as a subsidiary tool where the tax base cannot be estimated on an ordinary basis[13]. Some countries, however, rely on presumptive taxation also as a primary method for determining the tax base (forfeit amount) with regard to those taxpayers who cannot be relied on to estimate their receipts or sales on proper accounting – e.g. small enterprises and agriculture[14]. This

12. For further references, Thuronyi, V.: "Presumptive Taxation", in *Tax Law Design and Drafting*, Kluwer Law International, 2000, p. 494 f.
13. Initially the tax authorities are compelled to determinate the tax base from the information that derives from the taxpayer's accounting, however, where books are not available or they are not reliable, the tax authorities are entitled to an indirect method. According to the Supreme Court, the indirect estimation requires a physical impossibility to know the necessary data in order to estimate the tax base according to direct estimation (STS 16 July 1988).
14. For a general view, Thuronyi, V.: "Presumptive taxation" in Cordes et al. (eds), *Enciclopedia of Taxation and Tax Policy*, 2nd ed., 2005, Urban Institute, p. 302. The GAT regards direct estimation method as the general rule, while the so-called objective estimation arises as a special rule that applies voluntarily to certain taxpayers in the context of the individual income tax and VAT. Subsidiarily, where the tax authorities cannot access to the necessary data in

technique, however, have risen some criticism in those countries where ability to pay is regarded as a constitutional principle which binds the action of the public powers[15]. According to some commentators, this method leads to situations in which taxpayers with the same ability to pay are taxed differently while taxpayers with different ability to pay would be taxed equally. Other authors argue that a forfeit estimation lead to a tax base which is not consistent with the taxable event so the result is the statement of an alternative tax. None of these arguments justify a full rejection of the method. First of all, not only does presumptive taxation introduce simplicity and efficiency but it is also a convenient tool in order to guarantee an effective taxation on those 'hard-to-tax', thus promoting a fair tax distribution among the taxpayers. Furthermore, according to some interpretations (STC 37/1987, 26 March), the ability to pay principle does not prevent taxation on a potential income. In our view, this statement allows the existence of a presumptive taxation, particularly where indexes and parameters are used to determine only some specific elements of the tax base – e.g. receipts, expenses[16]. Finally, in order to avoid any further criticism from the ability to pay and equality principles, this method should only apply voluntarily, e.g. as far as the taxpayer does not resign to its application.

III TAX AUTHORITIES GUIDANCE AND ADVANCE INSTRUMENTS REGARDING THE DETERMINATION OF TAX

Self-assessment has brought an unprecedented development of the instruments by which the tax authorities assist the taxpayers on the fulfilment of their tax obligations. Tax authorities usually provide with informal guidance through information letters, pamphlets, websites, etc. Bearing in mind the complexities and technicalities of tax law, not only do these instruments promote transparency and certainty but they also help to prevent tax litigation. Some countries (UK, Italy, USA and Spain) have even formally stated the taxpayer's right to be informed and assisted by the tax authorities with regard the exercise of his/her rights and the fulfilment of the tax obligations. According to the MCTAL, not only does the taxpayer have the right to be assisted by the tax authorities but to formulate queries. Those replies are not binding on the tax authorities (Article 96 MCTAL, except for a limited number of situations); however, no penalty may be imposed on those taxpayers who fulfilled their fiscal duties accordingly.

---

order to a complete determination of the tax base, they are entitled to an indirect estimation insofar as that situation derives from some specific causes, mostly related to an unduly behaviour of the taxpayer (Articles 50 to 53 GAT).

15. Not only is the ability to pay regarded as the necessary basis for the enactment of taxes but as the main parameter of equality in order to distribute the public expenditures among taxpayers.
16. Furthermore, the Constitutional Court specifically legitimates the use of forfeit methods to estimate the amount of deductible expenses (STC 214/1994, 14 July). A more recent decision (Auto 71/2008, 26 February) even states that the ability to pay must be regarded only as a requirement of the tax system as a whole so that no every single tax needs to be informed by this principle. See Orón Moratal, G.: "La determinación de la base imponible", in Arrieta Martínez de Pisón et al (dir.): *Tratado sobre la Ley General Tributaria*, t. I, Thomson Reuters, 2010, pp. 1154 ff.

Informal opinions differ from advance tax rulings whose nature and characterization vary in each country[17]. According to IFA, advance rulings are 'a more or less binding statement from the Revenue authorities upon the voluntary request of a private person, concerning the treatment and consequences of one or a series of contemplated future actions or transactions'[18]. As a matter of fact, advance tax rulings usually have a binding effect on tax authorities[19]. Therefore, not only do they provide guidance and legal certainty in the interpretation and application of tax law provisions but they also have an indirect effect on the tax amount[20]. Many countries - e.g. Italy, the Netherlands, Spain and United States - have lately moved from a closed system in which rulings were only issued in a limited number of situations to an open system.

The value of assets, which is primarily estimated by the taxpayer for the purposes to of the tax return, can be later modified by the tax authorities bringing uncertainty into the application of taxes. Advance pricing agreements are binding agreements between the taxpayer and the tax authorities in order to settle the value of transactions between associated enterprises. From this derives two of the most relevant differences from advance tax rulings. Under paragraph 3 of the OECD Guidelines on Transfer Pricing, 'an APA differs from and advance ruling principally because it deals with factual matters more than it deals with the interpretation and application of the law (...)'[21]. Besides, APAs are usually binding on both tax authorities and taxpayers and, therefore, regarded as an alternative dispute resolution method[22].

Article 91 GAT states a generic advance valuation agreement, according to which taxpayers may submit an advance proposal on the value of receipts, products, assets, expenses and other elements related to the tax. The tax authorities may then verify the facts and the circumstances and once an agreement is reached it is binding for the next three years unless there is a legislative modification or a substantial alteration of the economic circumstances. Where the administrative decision is not

17. For a comparative approach with regards the USA, the Netherlands and Italy, Romano, C.: *Advance Tax Rulings and Principles of Law. Towards a European Tax Rulings System?*, IBFD, 2002, *passim*. As for specifically the Spanish tax system, Villaverde Gómez, Mª B.: *Las consultas a la Administración tributaria*, Marcial Pons, 2002, *passim*.
18. Ellis, M.: "General Report", in *Advance Rulings*, IFA Cahiers de Droit Fiscal International, Vol. LXXXIVb, 1999, p. 22.
19. In some countries, including Spain, tax authorities are bound not only with regard to the requesting taxpayer but to any other who is in the same position. Furthermore, those taxpayers who are not in the same but in a similar position may benefit from an existing ruling as no penalties can be imposed on them insofar as they fulfilled their duties relying on a sound interpretation.
20. Advance tax rulings are rarely binding on taxpayers and tax courts. From this derives, as a further implication, that they cannot be directly appealed.
21. These agreements usually have a direct effect on the tax base of associated enterprises located in other tax jurisdictions.
22. A further difference derives from their different legal nature, as 'APAs are generally regarded as agreements between (one or more) tax authorities and taxpayers, whereas advance rulings should be considered as one-sided statements by the tax administrations. Although also in an APA the taxpayer is not always seen as a party of the procedure, his agreement is a requisite. No APA may be implemented without the approval of the taxpayer, whereas advance rulings are valid regardless of the consent of the applicant'.

issued within the legal period, those values the taxpayer originally proposed shall be accepted[23]. As another sample of these instruments, taxpayers may require information from tax authorities as to the value of immovable property to be immediately transferred or acquired (Article 90 GAT). This decision is binding on the tax authorities for the next three months. In contrast with the aforementioned advance valuation agreements, no acceptance of the values initially proposed by the taxpayer occurs where the decision is not issued within the legal period.

IV CHECK COMPLIANCE AND ADMINISTRATIVE DETERMINATION OF THE TAX LIABILITY

As already mentioned, the most relevant taxes in modern tax systems are self-assessed whereas the tax authorities display a number of check compliance procedures which range from a formal verification of the self-assessment returns, particularly assisted by the information technologies, to an in-depth investigation of the taxpayer compliance status over a period of years. The administrative findings may obviously affect the determination of the tax liability.

Where the taxpayer does not submit the return within the legal period, the tax authorities may require him to do so as soon as the unduly behaviour is observed. Under the provisions set forth in Article 85 MCTAL, where tax returns, communications and other documents are not submitted within the legal period, the tax authorities normally require the taxpayer to submit the document, while imposing a penalty on him/her. However, in order to encourage a voluntary regularization, some countries allow a voluntary compliance out of the legal period which either involves a substantial reduction of penalties – e.g. the *ravvedimento operoso* in Italy - or no penalties at all – e.g. the Spanish *recargos por declaración extemporánea sin requerimiento previo*, regardless of the payment of interests, surcharges, etc.

Where the taxpayer insists on not filing the tax return, the tax authorities normally issue an administrative act of assessment in which the tax base either derives from the fiscal information available from other sources – e.g. withholding agents, financial institutions, public officers, etc. – or is estimated according to an indirect method[24]. The MCTAL provides with a further guarantee with regards to periodic tax returns. Under the provisions set forth in Article 85 MCTAL, the tax authorities may require the taxpayer to pay a sum equivalent to the amount paid according to the last tax return submitted. This payment does not release the taxpayer from submitting the tax return and paying the appropriate amount. Where the tax return is submitted after the provisional payment has been made, that sum will be charged against the amount that derives from the tax return. However, where the taxpayer files the return before the payment has being made, he/she will be released from the provisionally assessed payment.

23. In practice, however, these agreements have only been implemented under the form of the usual advance pricing agreements for the purposes of Corporate Tax.
24. However, as mentioned, for this latter to apply, it is usually required that the tax authorities do not have all the necessary data in order to a complete estimation of the tax base.

A further issue arises as to the extent to which administrative assessment acts may be later modified by the tax authorities. As mentioned, some countries consider that a final assessment act is only issued at the conclusion of a complete investigation procedure, while those administrative acts which may have been previously issued are only provisional. This does not imply, however, that those acts can be freely modified. Actually, under Article 84 MCTAL, those administrative decisions can only be modified against the taxpayer or a third party when the decision makes a specific reference to the partial scope of that determination while defining the aspects which have been examined. Accordingly, only those aspects which have not been previously addressed can be later modified. Similarly, the Spanish tax system does not allow modifying those administrative acts of provisional assessment but only to a limited extent, in the context of some specific verification procedures[25].

Some countries have stated tax settlements or tax deals between the tax authorities and the taxpayer - e.g. the US closing agreements[26] in the context of verification or inspection procedures. In Italy the *accertamento con adesione* (also known as *concordato fiscale*) leads to a modification of the tax base deriving from an agreement between the tax authorities and the taxpayer. From this derives that the taxpayer cannot appeal the decision, while the tax authorities cannot modify the situation within the legal period, except under certain circumstances - e.g. where the verification had a limited scope. Those taxpayers who enter into these agreements may benefit from a reduction of penalties. Although there has been some debate with regards the legal nature of these agreements, most of the scholars agree to this formula[27].

Another sample can be found in the Spanish *actas con acuerdo* which may only be agreed where an inspection procedure is carried out (Article 155 GAT)[28]. Actually, the tax authorities are entitled to issue these certificates only in particularly troublesome situations - i.e. where the regularization relies on indefinite legal concepts, or an appropriate appreciation of the reality is required in order to a correct application of the law or, finally, where valuations, estimations or measurements of data, elements or other relevant features cannot be established with certainty, as an alternative dispute resolution mechanism. Interestingly enough, however, not only does the taxpayer agree to the aforementioned aspects but to the certificate in its integrity, including any aspects and legal consequences that may derive. The taxpayer cannot appeal the

25. See Articles 133 and 140 GAT. For further references, Bertrán Girón, M.: *La liquidación tributaria*, IAAP, Sevilla, 2009, pp. 119 ff.
26. Usually under the form of 'Agreements as to Final Determination of Tax Liability' or 'Closing Agreements on Final Determination Covering Specific Matters' (both in IRC 7121).
27. Tesauro, F.: *Compendio di Diritto Tributario*, 2° ed., UTET, Torino, 2005, p. 133, Fantozzi, *op. cit.* pp. 214 ff.
28. The GAT states a number of administrative procedures which range from a formal verification of the tax return to an exhaustive examination of the status of tax compliance. See Fernández Junquera, M.: "Procedimientos tributarios: aspectos comunes y procedimientos de gestión", in Calvo Ortega (dir.), *La nueva Ley General Tributaria*, Thomson Civitas, 2004, pp. 377 ff. Regarding specifically inspection certificates, García Ovies Sarandeses, I.: "Procedimiento de inspección" in Calvo Ortega (dir.), *La nueva Ley General Tributaria*, Thomson Civitas, 2004, pp. 566 ff.

decision – neither the tax assessment nor the penalty imposed – unless through a void administrative procedure or an administrative litigation process before the Court. Similar to its Italian precedent, the taxpayer that agrees benefits from a reduction of tax penalties (50%, according to Article 188 GAT).

V SUMMARY

(1) On an ordinary basis, regular tax assessment does not require of an administrative procedure. The taxpayer files the return and pays the tax while the activity of the tax authorities focuses on checking the compliance of fiscal duties. Only where an incorrect behaviour is observed a formal administrative procedure initiates.

(2) The tax base can be determined through direct and indirect methods. Although indirect methods usually apply subsidiarily, some countries rely on them on an ordinary basis. This may raise some objections particularly from the ability to pay principle, however, none of them seem conclusive.

(3) Beyond informal guidance on tax compliance, there are a number of advance instruments (tax rulings, agreements related to transfer pricing, etc.) which are intended for the tax authorities to provide taxpayers with legal certainty before they actually enter into a taxable transaction. These agreements are usually binding on tax authorities and where taxpayers are also bound they are usually regarded as alternative dispute resolution mechanisms.

(4) The administrative determination of the tax liability usually arises where an unduly behaviour of the taxpayer is observed as a result of a check compliance procedure. However, there are situations in which the tax liability derives to a certain extent from an agreement between the tax authorities and the taxpayer.

CHAPTER 6

Double Taxation Conventions

Victor Uckmar

§6.01 INTRODUCTION

Tax treaties are international agreements entered into by countries and hence subject to general international law on treaties as codified in the Vienna Convention on the Law of Treaties.[1] Actually they can be seen as having a dual nature. On the one hand, double taxation conventions are international agreements entered into between governments for the allocation of fiscal jurisdiction. On the other hand, they become part of the tax law of each Contracting State, whether by direct incorporation into the domestic law or by enactment into that law.

Most tax treaties are bilateral, that is, involve two countries only, and cover income and capital taxes, though there are some examples of multilateral tax treaties.[2]

The number of bilateral tax treaties currently in force exceeds 2,500, and the number is growing. In fact, the importance of tax treaties has increased significantly in recent years as a consequence of the globalization of the economy and the liberalization of cross-border trade and business.

1. Cf. the Vienna Convention on the Law of Treaties of 23 May 1969. As provided in Art. 84 thereof, this Convention came into effect on 27 January 1980 with the ratification and accession of the thirty-fifth State. It is noteworthy that the Convention to a great extent merely codifies existing norms of customary international law.
2. Cf. the Nordic Convention on income and capital entered into by Denmark, Finland, Iceland, Norway and Sweden and concluded in 1983 and replaced in 1987, 1989 and 1996. See also the Convention on Mutual Administrative Assistance in Tax Matters, which was drawn up within the Council of Europe on the basis of a first draft prepared by the Committee on Fiscal Affairs and entered into force on 1 April 1995.

The majority of these treaties are based on the Model Convention drafted by the Organization for Economic Cooperation and Development (OECD),[3] which is now revised on a regular basis.

§6.02 THE HISTORY OF TAX TREATIES AND MODEL CONVENTIONS

Since the end of the 19th century, individual States have entered into bilateral conventions for the avoidance of double taxation. At first only federally related or closely allied States were involved, e.g. conventions were concluded between Prussia and Saxony regarding direct taxes on 16 April 1869, between Austria and Hungary concerning the taxation of business profits on 18 December 1869, and between Austria and Prussia regarding avoidance of double taxation on 21 June 1899.

After the First World War a number of tax treaties were concluded, and an extensive treaty network developed in Europe.

Today's tax treaties between industrialized countries, and the structure of those treaties, are to a large extent influenced by the work of the Financial Committee and the Fiscal Committee of the League of Nations, which was later continued by the Fiscal Committee of the Organization for European Economic Cooperation (OEEC) and the Fiscal Committee of the OECD. Indeed the first structured study of the economic consequences of double taxation and the principles of international competence in taxation was conducted by a group of four economists and contained in the *Report on Double Taxation* which was presented to the Financial Committee of the League of Nations in 1923.[4]

To encourage further progress, the Council of the League of Nations appointed a standing committee on taxation in 1928, which in the following year drafted two competing model treaties. A subcommittee, which due to the advent of the Second World War was composed primarily of representatives from Latin American countries, drafted the Model Treaty of Mexico in 1943; this was followed in 1946 by the London Model Treaty in the drafting of which industrialized States were able to participate and to bring their views to bear.[5] Both draft conventions cover taxpayers of the Contracting States, but in fact restrict their application to persons having their fiscal domicile in one of the Contracting States.

The efforts of the OEEC and its successor, the OECD, picked up where the preparatory research of the League of Nations had left off, to develop a system for the avoidance of double taxation.

The Committee on Fiscal Affairs (which was formed in 1956) submitted a series of model treaty articles in four interim reports between 1956 and 1961 and a summary report in 1963 to which the complete model treaty (the so-called 'OECD Model

3. OECD, *Model Tax Convention on Income and on Capital,* Paris, looseleaf ed. Last amendments in July 2010.
4. *Report on Double Taxation submitted to the Financial Committee by Professor Bruins, Einaudi, Seligman and Sir Josiah Stamp,* League of Nations Doc. E.F.S.73.F. 19 (Geneva 1923), p. 36.
5. London and Mexico Model Tax Convention, Commentary and Text, League of Nations Doc. C.. 88. M. 1946 II.A. (Geneva 1946), Art. I of the Protocol.

Convention') and an official commentary (hereinafter referred to as the 'OECD Commentaries') were appended. To the extent the OECD Member States did not wish to follow particular recommendations in the Model Convention, they entered their reservations in the Commentaries. Aside from the reservations, a number of Member States include observations; these observations do not express any disagreement with the text of the Conventions, but furnish a useful indication of the way in which those countries will apply the provisions of the Article in question.

The 1963 Model Convention was revised in 1977, and recently updated in 1992, and subsequently in 1994, 1995, 1997, 2000, 2003, 2005, 2008 and 2010.

It must be borne in mind that the Model Convention is only a recommended format with no legal biding force either at the international or national level. It is simply a document concluded by an international organization, and its use is discretionary, not mandatory. However, the members of the OECD largely use the OECD Model as a basis for negotiating their double taxation conventions.

It is noteworthy that certain countries have developed their own models for negotiation; these models are based largely on the OECD Model. The Netherlands, for example, has published its Model.[6] The United States Treasury published a Model in 1977 and a revised version in 1981 (the so-called 'US Model').[7] These were withdrawn in 1992 as part of a review of treaty policy.[8] A new US Model was issued on 20 September 1996, together with a Technical Explanation.[9]

Another Model was published by the United Nations in 1980. This treaty is the result of more than ten years of preparation by a group of experts appointed by the United Nations Economic and Social Council (ECOSOC). Its structure corresponds to the OECD Model Convention; however, it explores ways of facilitating the conclusion of double taxation conventions between developed and developing countries.[10] The 1980 UN Model consists, in essence, of the OECD Model with some 27 specific adaptations that take into account the interests of the developing countries. The 1980 UN Model was also accompanied by Commentaries. During the 1990s, the UN carried out work on updating the 1980 UN Model. In May 1999 an amended Model was

6. The Netherlands' Model was published in 1988. The Model may been found in *Bullet.*, 1988, p. 396. For an analysis of the Model, cf. Van Raad, 'The Netherlands Model Income Tax Treaty', in *Int.*, 1988, 241, and Lyons & Van Waardenburg, 'Some Aspects of International Tax Treaty Strategy of the Netherlands', in *Bullet.*, 1988, p. 374.
7. The US Model of 1981 can be found in Van Raad (ed.), *Model Income Tax Treaties*, Deventer, 1983.
8. For an overview of US treaty policy cf. Mogle, *United States Treaty Policy*, F.T. World Tax Report, 1983, p. 222.
9. For the text of the 1996 US Model, cf. Doernberg and Van Raad, *The 1996 United States Model Income Tax Convention*, The Hague, 1997.
10. The UN Model has been published by the UN as Document ST/ESA/102 (UN, New York, 1980). For a commentary on the UN Model cf. IFA, *UN Draft Model Tax Convention*, Deventer, 1979. Cf. also Wijnen and Magenta, 'The U.N. Model in Practice', in *Bulletin*, 1997, p. 574. and Owens, 'The Main Differences between the OECD and the United Nations Model Conventions', in Vann (ed.), *OECD Proceedings: Tax Treaties — Linkeages Between OECD Member Countries and Dynamic Non-Member Economies*, OECD, Paris, 1996.

adopted, subject to certain editorial changes. These revisions were adopted in April 2000.[11]

It is noteworthy that in recent years the importance of the UN Model has been waning, with the OECD Model becoming the most important.

Another Model, shaped according to the special interests of developing countries, was adopted in 1971 by the Member States of the Andean group, an alliance between Bolivia, Chile, Ecuador, Colombia, Peru and Venezuela. The Andean Model was drafted as an alternative to the OECD Model and it emphasizes the traditional concerns of Latin American countries, especially the source principle.[12]

§6.03 PURPOSE OF DOUBLE TAXATION CONVENTIONS

The purpose of bilateral tax treaties is typically expressed in their preamble[13] to be 'the avoidance of double taxation and the prevention of fiscal evasion'.[14] And indeed most substantive provisions of the typical bilateral tax treaty are directed at the achievement of this goal. For example, tax treaties contain tie-breaker rules to make a taxpayer who is otherwise resident in both countries a resident in only one of the countries. They also limit or eliminate the source country tax on certain types of income and require residence countries to provide relief for source country taxes either by way of a foreign tax credit or an exemption for foreign-source income.

In reality a treaty is more correctly described as an instrument which refines and improves existing provisions in domestic legislation which are designated to eliminate international juridical double taxation, i.e. most countries have in their own tax law provisions which are designated to alleviate double taxation and the treaty serves to assist in that process and better integrate it with the corresponding provisions in the treaty partner's law.

11. In the 2000 UN Model, there are fundamental changes and specifications, such as a new arm's length condition with respect to 'independent agents with one principal' in Art. 5(7), an exception to corresponding adjustment in case of fraud in Art. 9(3), and new definitions concerning capital gains on 'real estate shares' in Art. 13(4). Moreover, the possibility for source taxation on income from independent personal services in case a certain amount is exceeded, was removed from the UN Model. Cf. Van Den Bruggen, 'Preliminary Look at the New UN Model Tax Convention', in *British Tax Rev.*, 2002, p. 119.
12. The Andean Model is published in Supplement D, *Bullet.*, 1974, p. 309.
13. The OECD and the UN Models leave the contents of the preamble to be dealt with in accordance with the constitutional procedure of negotiating States.
14. It must be borne in mind that generally tax treaties are utilized for the avoidance of international juridical double taxation and not against international economic double taxation. The definition of juridical double taxation may be found in the *Introduction* to the OECD Model Tax Convention on Income and on Capital, *viz.*: '1. International juridical double taxation can be generally defined as the imposition of comparable taxes in two (or more) States on the same taxpayer in respect of the same subject matter and for identical periods.'. On the other hand, double taxation is 'economic' if more than one person is taxed on the same item; for instance, in the international context, where one country, for tax purposes, makes a downward adjustment of transfer prices paid by a subsidiary company in its transactions with a non-resident parent company, and the country of residence of the parent does not make a corresponding adjustment for tax purposes to the receipts of that company.

Moreover tax treaties do not just indicate international sourcing rules that determine in which Contracting States certain income originates or capital assets are located. These rules must be read together with other rules establishing under what conditions and in relation to which Contracting State the income or assets concerned may be justifiably taxed. Therefore, tax treaties create an independent device to avoid double taxation, through restriction of Contracting States' tax claims, where there could be an overlapping of these claims. In this way, States waive tax claims, and they bind themselves not to levy taxes, or to tax only to a limited extent, in cases when the treaty gives the taxing right to the other Contracting State either entirely or in part. It could be said that tax treaties in a way establish boundaries on domestic taxation. In contrast, a tax treaty neither generates a tax claim that does not otherwise exist under domestic law nor expands the scope or alters the type of an existing claim.

Moreover, it must be borne in mind that the extent to which a State levies taxes within the limits posed by a tax treaty, can only be made in accordance with its domestic law: indeed a tax treaty cannot create nor extend the taxing rights of a country.

For what it has been said so far, the avoidance of double taxation is achieved by employing a set of common definitions in the treaty, by assigning the right to tax items of income to one State or the other, or partly to both of them, and finally by providing for an exemption or credit mechanism to effectuate the avoidance of double taxation.

The emphasis on the elimination of double taxation should not obscure the fact that most tax treaties have another equally important operational objective: i.e. the prevention of fiscal evasion[15]. This objective counterbalances the elimination of double taxation. The prevention of fiscal evasion primarily refers to cases where taxpayers fraudulently conceal income in an international setting and rely on the inability of tax administrations to obtain information abroad. Over the last decades, globalization and the diffusion of multinational enterprises dealing on the international market have contributed to a dramatic spread of international tax avoidance and evasion to the extent that countries have felt the need to overcome the strict rule of territoriality and to cooperate with each other. By far the most important form of cooperation is now represented by the exchange of information between revenue authorities of different countries. The exchange of information article (Article 26 of the OECD Model) in tax treaties is the major device utilized for this scope (see below).[16]

In addition to the two principal operational objectives of tax treaties, there are several ancillary objectives. One ancillary objective is the elimination of discrimination against foreign nationals and non-residents. A non-discrimination article which is based on the OECD Model Convention (i.e. Article 25, see further below) furthermore contain specific provisions relating to non-discriminatory taxation in respect of permanent establishments, to deductibility of certain payments, including royalty and

15. For a particularly good analysis of the governmental objectives of the tax treaties, cf. Gravelle, 'Tax Treaties: Concepts, Objectives and Types', in *Bullet.*, 1988, p. 522.
16. It has been suggested that whereas the prevention of tax evasion is an explicit objective of tax treaties which are based on an OECD Model Convention, such explicit objective does not extend to the prevention of tax avoidance, including the improper use of the treaty. Cf. Van Weeghel, *The Improper Use of Tax Treaties*, Deventer, 1998, p. 35.

interest payments, and, finally, this article contains a provision safeguarding non-discriminatory treatment of non-resident-controlled enterprises (see below). Moreover, most Contracting States provide a mechanism in their treaties for resolving disputes arising from the interaction of their tax system (the so- called 'mutual agreement procedure', provided for by Article 25 of the OECD Model, see below).

Another reason for having double taxation conventions is that they provide for the reduction of the withholding tax rates on investment income. In fact, it must be borne in mind that withholding tax on investment income (e.g. interest and dividend) is being imposed at a flat rate on the gross amount of income. Therefore the reduction of withholding tax rates is very important for taxpayers. Moreover, countries that apply an exemption system as a method for the relief of double taxation will usually apply the tax credit method with respect to investment income.[17]

§6.04 RELATIONSHIP OF TAX TREATIES AND DOMESTIC LAW[18]

Double taxation conventions are international agreements and their creation and their consequences are determined according to the rules contained in the above-mentioned Vienna Convention on the Law of Treaties.

By signing the treaty, the Contracting States commit themselves to initiating the procedures necessary under the domestic law to conclude a treaty, but there is no commitment to conclude it. A treaty cannot be applied until it is concluded or comes

17. See para. 47 of the OECD Commentaries on Art. 23 of the OECD Model. Note that Art. 23A (Exemption), para. 2, of the OECD Model, provides for the switch to the tax credit method for the interest and dividends flows of income.
18. It must be borne in mind that there is another relevant perspective to be considered, which is the relationship between the double taxation conventions and the European Union law. It is true that the EU fundamental freedoms allow Member States to determine the structural elements of their own tax systems and they are free to allocate the taxation powers between each other, as well as to choose the methods to abolish international double taxation; however the ECJ's case law points out the EU's main concern within the internal market is the avoidance of double taxation, also after the repeal of Art. 293 EC under the Lisbon Treaty. This objective can be clearly found in *Gilly*, in which the ECJ ruled 'the abolition of double taxation within the Community is [...] included among the objectives of the Treaty [...] (Case C-336/96, para. 16). *Kerckhaert-Morres* and *Columbus Container Services*, confirm this position by arguing 'that conventions preventing double taxation [...] are designed to eliminate or mitigate the negative effects on the functioning of the internal market resulting from the coexistence of national tax systems' (Cases C-513/04, *Kerckhaert-Morres*, para. 21 and C-298/05, *Columbus Container Services*, para. 44). As regards further ECJ's relevant case law on the issue, *Avoir Fiscal* (Case C-270/83), *Wielockx* (Case C-80/94), *RBS* (311/97), *Saint-Gobain* (Case C-307/97), the *D.* case (Case C-376/03), *Bouanich* (Case C-265/04), *FII GLO* (Case C-446/04), *ACT IV GLO* (Case C-374/04), *Denkavit International* (Case C-170/05), *Amurta* (Case C-379/05), *Aberdeen Property* (Case C-303/07) and *Damseaux* (Case C-128/08). For a perspective following the entryinto force of the Treaty of Lisbon, see Kemmeren, 'After repeal of Article 293 EC Treaty under the Lisbon Treaty: the EU objective of eliminating double taxation can be applied more widely', in *EC Tax Review*, 2008, 4, pp. 156–158; Hinnekens, 'The Uneasy Case and Fate of Article 293 Second Indent EC', in *Intertax*, 2009, 11, pp. 602–609.

into force. It comes into force only after the Contracting States declare their consent or ratify through an exchange of instruments under their respective constitutional laws.[19]

Each State follows its own rules for the inclusion of the treaty under its law. Some countries follow the monistic principle where the domestic law is linked and subordinated to the international law under the so-called 'doctrine of incorporation'. Other countries follow the dualistic doctrine where the international and domestic law are treated separately and require a specific domestic legislation under the 'doctrine of transformation'. Each State is free to decide its approach under its own laws to comply with its international obligations. Thus, there are two groups of countries:

(i) Direct effect: international treaties are self-executing and automatically become a part of the domestic law when they are ratified.[20] In some countries, the treaty may require parliamentary approval;[21]
(ii) Indirect effect: treaty provisions must be enacted into domestic law and require special legislative steps.[22] The Courts cannot enforce the treaty provisions until they are 'transformed' into domestic law, normally by a legislative act or delegated legislation. Under the dualistic doctrine, it is usually the related statute, and not the treaty, which has legal authority under the domestic law.

The provisions of tax treaties are intended to have precedence over any inconsistent provisions of domestic tax law. Again, how this is effected is a matter for the constitutional law of the countries concerned. A common practice is to insert such a provision either into the law giving effect to the treaty or into the domestic tax law itself. The usual result of such a provision under the law of most countries is that, apart from the administrative treaty provisions on the mutual agreement procedure and the exchange of information, a treaty sets limits on the operation of domestic law but does not expand its operation.

Thus, if a country wishes to tax business profits arising from sales to residents of the country by a resident of another country without reference to a permanent establishment in the country, the business profits article of a tax treaty will usually prohibit such taxation, unless those profits are attributable to a permanent establishment in the country. The outcome is the same if the domestic law uses a permanent establishment concept, but the concept is wider than that used in a relevant treaty. Similarly, if the tax applied under domestic law to dividends and interest paid to a resident of the other treaty country exceeds the maximum rates permitted in the treaty, the source State is obliged to reduce its taxation accordingly.

On the other hand, if a country levies no tax on dividends or interest paid to non-residents, then the fact that a treaty allows such taxation up to a specified limit

19. As far as the relationships between tax treaty and domestic law is concerned, see, *amplius*, OECD, *Tax Treaty Override*, 1989; Edwards-Ker, *Tax Treaty Interpretations*, London, Ch. 33; Rezek, — Lüthi, *Tax Treaties and Domestic Legislation*, 43rd IFA Congree, Rio de Janeiro, 1989; Vogel, *On Double Taxation Conventions*, Deventer, 1997, p. 67 et seq.
20. E.g.: France, Japan, Netherlands, USA.
21. E.g.: Germany, Italy, Ireland.
22. E.g.: Canada, India, United Kingdom.

does not mean that such dividends and interest are taxable. It is possible, however, for domestic law to provide that if a treaty permits taxation that does not otherwise occur under domestic law, then the treaty rule will become the domestic rule for this case. This is the position in France[23] (and many Francophone African countries under their tax legislation) where unique provisions in its domestic law enable taxing income provisions in its domestic law enable taxing income attributed to it by a tax treaty even when no tax liability would normally arise under general domestic law.

A convincing lecture of the relationship between domestic law and tax treaties can be found in the so-called 'three steps approach' of M. Edwardes-Ker.[24] According to this author, the application of a tax treaty should be divided into three steps: step one must be for the domestic law of the relevant State to be applied to determine if this State's domestic law does, potentially, impose tax. Thus, in step one, domestic law must be applied without regard to tax treaties. If no tax arises under that State, the tax treaty is never applied, since, as already stated, a treaty cannot impose/create tax.

On the other hand, if tax does arise under that State law, then, in step two, the tax treaty is applied to see how it allocates the right to tax the income or the capital in question.

If the tax treaty precludes this State from taxing at all, the tax treaty will override this State's domestic law, and this is the end of the matter. However, the treaty could pose a limit up to which the State can tax (e.g. 10% for interest). Step three is to determine a State's actual right to tax within treaty-defined limits. Therefore, according to this approach, in step three, domestic law applies except to the extent that its application is precluded by a tax treaty.

§6.05 TAX TREATY INTERPRETATION

[A] The Vienna Convention on the Laws of Treaties

Tax treaties are international agreements entered into between States. The interpretation of international treaties[25] is governed by public international law, and more

23. FRA CGI §§165 *bis*, 209I.
24. Edwards-Ker, *Tax Treaty Interpretations*, London, Ch. 33.
25. The literature on tax treaty interpretation is particularly extensive, see, *ex multis*, Avery Jones et al., *The Interpretation of Tax Treaties with particular reference to Art. 3(2) of the OECD Model*, in *British Tax Rev.*, 1984, Nos. 1 and 2; Vogel, *On Double Taxation Convention*, Deventer, 1997, p. 33; Vogel, 'The Influence of the OECD Commentaries on Treaty Interpretation', in *Bullet.*, 2000, p. 612; Ellis, 'The Influence of the OECD Commentaries on Treaty Interpretation - Response to Prof. Dr. Klaus Vogel', in *Bullet.*, 2000, p. 618; Avery Jones, *The 'one true meaning' of a Tax Treaty*, in *Bullet.*, 2001, p. 221; Avery Jones, 'The Effect of Changes in the OECD Commentaries after a Treaty is Concluded', in *Bullet.*, 2002, p. 102; Lang, 'How Significant are the Amendments of the OECD Commentary Adopted after the Conclusion of a Tax Treaty?', in *Dir. prat. trib. internaz.*, 2002, p. 2; Van Raad, 'International Coordination of Tax Treaty Interpretation and Application', in *Int.*, 2001, p. 212; Van Raad, 'Interpretation and

specifically by customary international law, as embodied in the Vienna Convention on the Law of Treaties.[26]

According to Article 31, paragraph 1, of the Vienna Convention, 'a treaty shall be interpreted in good faith in accordance with the ordinary meaning to be given to the terms of the treaty in their context and in light of its object and purpose'.

Thus, Article 31 of the Vienna Convention is based on the view that the text must be presumed to be the authentic expression of the intentions of the parties, and that, in consequence, the point of interpretation is the elucidation of the meaning of the text (so- called 'textual approach'), and not an investigation *ab initio* into the intentions of the parties.

The 'ordinary meaning' of the terms is not necessarily that of everyday usage. To the extent that an internationally uniform legal usage or to the extent that a specific technical language – such as tax law – has developed, the 'ordinary' usage is within the meaning of Article 31, paragraph 1 of the Vienna Convention.

The 'context' under Article 31, paragraph 2, includes the text of the treaty and any agreements between the parties made in connection with the conclusion of the treaty and any instrument made by one of the parties and accepted by the other party. With reference to tax treaties, this includes notes or letters exchanged during the signing of the treaty. However, unilateral explanations by one party that have not been expressly confirmed by the other party cannot be included.[27]

In addition, under Article 31, paragraph 3, subsequent agreements between the parties and subsequent practice with respect to the interpretation of the treaty and any applicable rules of international law must be taken into account together with the context. Moreover, according to Article 31, paragraph 4, a special meaning must be given to a term if it is established that the parties so intended.

It must be borne in mind that the application of paragraphs 1, 2 and 3 of Article 31 is a single combined operation, since such article has to be considered as a single, closely integrated rule.

Application of Tax Treaties by Tax Courts', in *Eur. Tax.*, 1996, p. 3; Wattel and Marres, 'The Legal Status of the OECD Commentary and Static or Ambulatory Interpretation of Tax Treaties', in *Eur. Tax.*, 2003, p. 223.

For a comparative analysis of tax treaty interpretation in different countries, cf. Lang (ed.), *Tax Treaty Interpretation*, Vienna, 2001.

26. The Vienna Convention rules have been referred to in a growing number of decisions around the world involving the interpretation of double taxation conventions. Cf., *inter alia*, the Australian case *Thiel v. F.C.T.* (1990) 90 Australian Tax Cases 4,717 (High Court of Australia); the Canadian case *Hunter-Douglas v. R.*. (1979) 79 Dominion Tax Cases, 5,340 (Federal Court) and the well-known *R. v. Crown Forest Industries Ltd.* (1995) 95 Dominion Tax Cases 5,389 (Supreme Court of Canada); the U.K. case *I.R.C. v. Commerzbank A.G.* (1990) Simon's Tax Cases 285 (High Court). For other cases where the Vienna Convention has been cited in the context of the interpretation of a double taxation convention, cf. Edwards-Ker, *Tax Treaty Interpretations*, London, Ch. 33, paras 3.03–3.16.

27. For instance, the US Department of the Treasury usually publish technical explanation in connection with the publication of treaty text. According to Vogel, *On Double Taxation Conventions*, Deventer, 1997, p. 38, these kinds of documentation are neither part of the context of the treaty nor materials, and neither Art. 31, paras. 1 and 2, nor Art. 32 grant their use in treaty interpretation.

Under Article 32 of the Vienna Convention, other material, referred to as supplementary means of interpretation, which include the *travaux préparatoires* (preparatory work) of the treaty, are only to be considered to confirm the meaning established pursuant to Article 31, or to establish the meaning if Article 31 produces an ambiguous, obscure, absurd or unreasonable result.

Article 33 of the Vienna Convention provides that in respect of treaties authenticated in two or more languages, each language is equally binding. According to Article 33, paragraph 4, in the case of discrepancy in the meaning between two (or more) linguistic versions, the interpretation adopted should be the one that best reconciles the different versions.

[B] Reference to the OECD Commentaries

Although the OECD Model Treaty and Commentaries are very important for the interpretation of tax treaties, their legal status under the provision of the Vienna Convention is unclear. However, in current case law on interpretation of double taxation conventions reference has been made and is increasingly made to the OECD Model Convention.[28]

Scholars disagree on whether the use of the OECD Commentaries is in accordance with the rules set out in the Vienna Convention. Nevertheless, the Commentaries have been viewed either as an 'ordinary meaning' in the sense of Article 31 of the Vienna Convention,[29] or a 'special meaning' in the sense of Article 31, paragraph 4,[30] or as a supplementary means of interpretation in the sense of Article 32 of the Vienna Convention.[31]

At first glance, they could appear to be supplementary means of interpretation under Article 32. However, if so, they are relevant only to confirm the meaning otherwise established by the application of the principles of interpretation in Article 31

28. Cf., for instance, the *Philip Morris* decision of the Italian Supreme Court (Decision No. 7682 of 25 May 2002, published in *Dir. prat. trib. inter.*, 2002, No. 3), where constant reference to the OECD Commentaries is made by the Court.
Cf. OECD, *Commentaries*, Introduction, para. 29.3, *viz.* 'The courts are increasingly using the Commentaries in reaching their decision. Information collected by the Committee on Fiscal Affairs shows that the Commentaries have been cited in the published decisions of the courts of the great majority of Member countries. In many decisions, the Commentaries have been extensively quoted and analysed, and have frequently played a key role in the judge's deliberations ...'.
29. Professors Vogel and Prokisch *(General Report*, in Cahiers, vol. LXXVIIIa, 1993,63) believe that the OECD Commentaries fall within the *instruments made in connection with the conclusion of the treaty* ex art, 31, para. 2, lett. b) of the Vienna Convention, since they represent the result of discussions among OECD Member countries, which could make reservations to the Commentaries.
30. Ault, 'The Role of the OECD Commentaries in the Interpretation of Tax Treaties', in Alpert and Van Raad, *Essays on International Taxation, To Sidney I. Roberts*, 1993, p. 61; Avery Jones, 'Tax Treaty Interpretation in the United Kingdom', in Lang (ed.), *Tax Treaty interpretation*, Vienna, 2001, p. 364.
31. Mössner, 'Zur Auslegung von Doppelbesteuerungsabkommen', in *Liber Amicorum I. Seidl-Hohenveldern*, 1988, p. 403; Steichen, 'Tax Treaty Interpretation in Luxembourg', in Lang (ed.), *Tax Treaty Interpretation*, Vienna, 2001, p. 234.

or to establish the meaning if the meaning under Article 31 is ambiguous, obscure, absurd, or unreasonable.

On the other hand, the OECD does not intend for the Commentaries to have such a limited role.[32] In our opinion, as far as the interpretation of tax treaties between OECD countries is concerned, the OECD Model Convention and the Commentaries should be considered as primarily part of the 'context' and not simply 'preliminary materials' in the sense of Article 32 of the Vienna Convention.[33] The OECD Commentaries will be less significant for treaties between an OECD member and non-member and between two non-member countries. However, insofar as the OECD Model Convention served as a basis for the negotiations of the last-mentioned treaties, it should be considered as part of the 'context' as well.

It is difficult, however, to justify including the Commentaries as part of the context of a treaty under Article 31 of the Vienna Convention, especially if the treaty being interpreted was entered into before the Commentaries were revised or if one of the Contracting States is not a member of the OECD and therefore had no part in the preparation of the Commentaries.

It is even harder to find a justification in the Vienna Convention for applying a later version of the Commentaries to the interpretation of an existing treaty. The OECD Commentaries, at paragraph 35 of the introduction, address the issue in a very elegant way.[34] In any case, the Commentaries are, after all, a mere aid to the interpretation of the tax treaty text, and subsequent amendments to the Commentaries should not override the text of an existing Convention, especially now that there are more and more frequent versions of the OECD Commentaries (1992, 1994, 1995, 1997, 2000, 2003, 2005, 2008 and 2010).[35]

---

32. Cf. OECD, Commentaries fall within the *instruments made in connection with the conclusion of the treaty* ex art, 31, para. 2, lett. b) Introduction, para. 15.
33. In the *Thiel case [Thiel v. F.C.T.* (1990) 90 Australian Tax Cases 4,717], the Australian High Court held that the OECD Model Convention and Commentaries should be regarded as part of the context under Art. 31 of the Vienna Convention.
34. Cf. OECD, Commentaries fall within the *instruments made in connection with the conclusion of the treaty* ex art, 31, para. 2, lett. b) Introduction, para. 35: 'Needless to say, amendments to the Articles of the Model Convention and changes to the Commentaries that are a direct result of these amendments are not relevant to the interpretation or application of previously concluded conventions where the provisions of those conventions are different in substance from the amended articles. However, other changes or additions to the Commentaries are normally applicable to the interpretation and application of conventions concluded before their adoption, because they reflect the consensus of the OECD Member countries as to the proper interpretation of existing provisions and their application to specific situations'.
35. Actually, there is a debate among the scholars on the significance that must be attributed to the amendments of the OECD Commentaries after the conclusion of a tax treaty: see Vogel, 'The Influence of the OECD Commentaries on Treaty Interpretation', in *Bullet.*, 2000, p. 612; Ellis, 'The Influence of the OECD Commentaries on Treaty Interpretation - Response to Prof. Dr. Klaus Vogel', in *Bullet.*, 2000, p. 618; Van Raad, 'Interpretation and Application of Tax Treaties by Tax Courts', in *Eur. Tax.*, 1996, p. 4; Avery Jones, 'The Effect of Changes in the OECD Commentaries after a Treaty is Concluded', in *Bullet.*,, 2002, p. 102; Lang, 'How Significant are the Amendments of the OECD Commentary Adopted after the Conclusion of a Tax Treaty?', in *Dir. prat. trib. inter.*, 2002, p. 6 and Wattel and Marres, 'The Legal Status of the OECD Commentary and Static or Ambulatory Interpretation of Tax Treaties', in *Eur. Tax.*, 2003, p. 225 *et seq.*

[C] The Interpretation Rule of Article 3(2) of the OECD Tax Model Convention

In addition to the provisions of the Vienna Convention, tax treaties based on the OECD Model Convention contain an internal rule of interpretation. In fact, Article 3, paragraph 2, of the OECD Model Convention provides that undefined terms used in the treaty have the meaning that they have under the domestic law of the country applying the treaty, unless the context otherwise requires.[36] Article 3, paragraph 2, is considered as being a general provision with respect to the special rules of interpretation of double taxation conventions, and namely the convention definitions such as those found under Article 3, paragraph 1, or under Article 4 (resident), Article 5 (permanent establishment), Article 6, paragraph 2 (immovable property), Article 10, paragraph 3 (dividends), Article 11, paragraph 3 (interest) and Article 12, paragraph 2 (royalties). Each of these definitions has priority over the *general revoi clause* contained in Article 3, paragraph 2.[37]

The rule under Article 3, paragraph 2, has several practical advantages: first of all it prevents excessive length in drafting double taxation conventions that would render the application of treaties difficult. Moreover, fiscal authorities, national courts and taxpayers can keep to the meaning of a term that they know from their domestic law.

On the other hand, the rule could often lead to a different application of the treaty in the two Contracting States.

Article 3, paragraph 2, was amended in 1995 to provide that an undefined term should have 'the meaning that it has ..... under the law of that State for the purposes of the taxes to which the Convention applies, any meaning given to the term under other laws of that State'. It clearly states that it is the tax law definition that is to be applied, though this may import a definition from the general law. Moreover, it is clear that if a term used in the treaty has a meaning in a branch of domestic law other than that of taxes, its meaning under tax law shall prevail.

The article at stake says that the domestic law meaning shall apply 'unless the context otherwise requires'. This raises the further issue of what constitutes 'the context'[38] and what matters may be taken into account before resolving reference to the domestic law meaning.[39] Article 31, paragraph 2, of the Vienna Convention defines the context for the purposes of the treaty interpretation as including any preamble or

36. As far as Art. 3, para. 2, of the OECD Model Convention is concerned, see Avery Jones et al., 'The Interpretation of Tax Treaties with particular reference to Art. 3(2) of the OECD Model', in *British Tax Review*, 1984 *passim;* Vogel, *On Double Taxation Convention*, Deventer, 1997, p. 42; Baker, *Double Taxation Conventions*, London, looseleaf ed., E-19.
37. Cf. Vogel, *On Double Taxation Convention*, Deventer, 1997, p. 209.
38. The OECD Commentaries (OECD, *Commentaries*, C(3)-12) states that: 'The context is determined in particular by the intention of the Contracting States when signing the Convention as well as the meaning given to the term in question in the legislation of the other Contracting State (an implicit reference to the principle of reciprocity on which the Convention is based). The wording of the Article therefore allows the competent authorities some leeway.'
39. This point is widely discussed in Avery Jones et al., 'The Interpretation of Tax Treaties with particular reference to Art. 3(2) of the OECD Model', in *British Tax Rev.*, 1984, p. 90 et seq.

annex to the treaty, any agreement reached between the parties and any instrument accepted by the parties as relating to the treaty.

Commentators have pointed out how this notion of 'context' seems to be too narrow. In fact, the 'context' concept should be interpreted as broadly as possible:[40] context should encompass the relevant provisions of the two national legal systems and also the Model Convention and the Commentaries.

Therefore, the departure from interpretation by reference to domestic law will be admissible to the extent that the context, in this broad sense, reveals arguments in favour of such a departure.

Another important and controversial issue of interpretation in connection with Article 3, paragraph 2, of the OECD Model Treaty is whether a term has its meaning under domestic law at the time that the treaty was entered into (the so-called *static approach)* or the meaning at the time the treaty is applied (the so-called *ambulatory approach)*. The OECD Commentaries make clear that the ambulatory approach should, in principle, be applied.[41] In fact, with relevant changes in a Contracting State's domestic tax law, it might be impossible for that State to continue to apply the Convention.

Most countries appear to apply the ambulatory approach,[42] and some have even incorporated it into treaties explicitly. The ambulatory approach allows treaties to accommodate changes in domestic law without the need to renegotiate the treaty. However, although the ambulatory approach seems correct, radical amendments to domestic law should be excluded from Article 3, paragraph 2.

[D] Conflicts of Qualification

The attribution of a certain payment to one of the tax treaty classes of income is particularly difficult where the treaty does not define the term in question. In such cases, the Contracting States often favour a classification based on their own law, regardless of whether or not Article 3, paragraph 2, of the OECD Model is applicable. As a result, the Contracting States will often apply the treaty differently if their classifications under domestic laws differ. For instance, if a severance payment is characterized as deferred compensation, it would appear that Article 15 of the OECD Model Treaty would apply, and the payment could be subject-to-tax in the country where the services were rendered. If characterized as a pension payment, Article 18 of

40. Cf. Vogel, *On Double Taxation Convention*, Deventer, 1997, p. 214.
41. Cf. OECD, Commentaries, C(3)- 11, 'the question arises which legislation must be referred to in order to determine the meaning of terms not defined in the Convention, the choice being between the legislation in force when the Convention was signed or that in force when the Convention is being applied, i.e. when the tax is imposed. The Committee on Fiscal Affairs concluded that the latter interpretation should prevail, and in 1995 amended the Model to make this point explicitly'.
42. Cf. Edwards-Ker, *Tax Treaty Interpretations*, London, Chs 9 and 10.

the OECD Model Treaty provides that it is the country of residence that has exclusive tax jurisdiction.[43]

It is clear that, resulting from conflicts of qualification in the countries of source and residence, double taxation or double non-taxation may occur.[44] Moreover the interplay of the tax credit method and the exemption method of relief from international double taxation introduce a further dimension of complexity.

There has been a big debate among scholars[45] for many years on whether the residence State, i.e. the State where the taxpayer is a resident, is required to categorize income when giving relief under a tax treaty for the tax paid in the source State. The debate should now have an end after the amendments to the OECD Commentaries made in 2000, following the OECD Partnership Report.[46]

The clarification added to the OECD Commentaries states that the residence State should accept the source State's qualification of the income and give relief accordingly, even if the residence State would have classified the income differently.[47] Thus the residence State has to exempt, or to give credit for the tax in the source State on income 'which, in accordance with the provisions of the Convention, may be taxed [in the source State]'.[48]

Therefore if the source State, applying the treaty and referring to its domestic law *ex* Article 3, paragraph 2, regards a severance payment (back to our previous example) as not falling within Article 18 since in its domestic law the term 'pension' does not encompass such remuneration, but as falling under Article 15, then the residence State has to grant an exemption or credit notwithstanding its own qualification. The residence State must refrain from inserting its own categorization of the income, which leads to all the problems we pointed out before. It must only check whether the source State has taxed the income in accordance with the treaty, which merely involves the residence State reading and not applying the treaty.

---

43. Another example of double taxation arising from differences in domestic law meanings is the well-known *Boulez* case (Decision of the U.S. Tax Court in (1984) 83 Tax Court Reports (U.S.) 584), discussed in *Eur.* Tax., 1985, p. 154.
44. See *infra* the new approach proposed by the 2000 version of the OECD Commentary.
45. There is a summary of this debate in Rotondaro, 'The Application of Art. 3, para. 2, in Case of Differences between Domestic Definitions of 'Associated Enterprises'', in *Internat. Transf. Pric. Journ.*, 2000, p. 172.
46. OECD, 'The Application of the OECD Model Tax Convention to Partnership, Issues', in *Internat. Tax.*, no. 6, Paris, 1999.
47. Cf. C(23)-32.1 et seq. in the version of the OECD Model Tax Convention on Income and Capital of April 2000 states: '32.2 The interpretation of the phrase 'in accordance with the provisions of this Convention, may be taxed', which is used in both articles, is particularly important when dealing with cases where the State of residence and the State of source classify the same item of income or capital differently for purposes of the provisions of the Convention.
    32.3 Different situations need to be considered in that respect. Where, due to differences in the domestic law between the State of source and the State of residence, the former applies, with respect to a particular item of income or capital, provisions of the Convention that are different from those that the State of residence would have applied to the same item of income or capital, the income is still being taxed in accordance with the provisions of the Convention, as interpreted and applied by the State of source. In such a case, therefore, the two articles require that relief from double taxation be granted by the State of residence notwithstanding the conflict of qualification resulting from these differences in domestic law'.
48. Arts 23 A(1) and 23B(1) of the OECD Model Convention.

Part of the doctrine has supported the view[49] that the divergence in interpretation of treaty terms arising from differences in domestic law which both Contracting States apply pursuant to the *general renvoi clause* (Article 3, paragraph 2), rather than be solved by the obligation of the residence State to follow the source State's qualification, should be removed through the set up of a *lingua franca,* a sort of 'international fiscal language'.[50] According to the these writers, such a development would be possible through a comparison of the legal system of the States and by looking at the decisions made so far by the Courts[51] and tax authorities. In creating this international fiscal language a key role would be played by the OECD Committee on Fiscal Affairs, which should establish a specific meaning for every tax treaty term.[52]

§6.06 BASIC CONTENTS OF THE MODEL TAX TREATY

The tax treaty under the Model Conventions contains the classification and assignments rules (so-called 'distributive rules'[53]) for avoiding double taxation. These 'distributive rules' classify the various items of income by type and source and then assign the taxing rights to the Contracting States. For each State, they specify the three alternatives by source of income, namely (i) full taxing rights, (ii) limited or shared taxing rights, or (iii) no taxing rights for one of the Contracting States.

Generally, the source country has the taxing rights limited to the income derived from sources within its territorial jurisdiction. On the other hand, the residence State has full taxing rights on the worldwide income. Therefore, except as provided under the treaty, the residence State retains the rights to tax all income and capital. However, it is required to give relief for double taxation to the taxpayer if the same taxing rights are given to the source State. In the OECD Model Treaty, relief from double taxation is

49. Vogel-Prokisch, 'General Report', in Cahiers, vol. LXXVIIIa, 1993, p. 63, and Van Raad, 'International Coordination of Tax Treaty Interpretation and Application', in *Int.*, 2001, at 215.
50. Another possible solution is for a State to determine unilaterally what a term means for treaty purposes. For instance, in respect of pension and annuities, Canada, in its Income Tax Conventions Interpretation Act (section 5.1), gives its own definition of the terms (see *Canada amends Income Tax Conventions Interpretation Act,* in *Tax Notes International,* February 1999, at 540 *etseq.).* Although such definition does not solve any possible qualification problems, it may surely contribute to their avoidance since it is easier for the other Contracting State to forsee how Canada will apply Art. 18 of the Tax Convention.
51. Professors Vogel and Prokisch *(Ibid.)* report a case of a South Africa Court *(SIR v. Downing)* where there is an express acknowledgment of the existence of 'an international fiscal language', a reference of the *Bundesfinanzhof (BFH* BStBl. II1986,4.5, concerning the term 'employer' in Art. 15(2)(b) of the German- Swiss Tax Treaty) to the proper language of double taxation conventions that should be taken into account in interpreting tax treaties and a *Hoge Raad's* decision which considered the term 'capital gain' used in Treaties as being unambiguously determined, thus excluding a *renvoi* to domestic law *(BNB,* 1991/248).
52. Professor van Raad *(ibidem)* also endorses a creation of a panel of independent tax treaty experts to which submit upon the request of Courts and competent authorities, opinions on the interpretation of a specific tax treaty clause, and its application to the case under consideration.
53. The distributive rules are contained in Arts 6 to 22 of the OECD Model Convention.

provided either by Article 23A (Exemption Method) or by Article 23B (Credit Method).[54]

[A] Coverage and Scope

Under Article 1 of the OECD Model, the provisions of the treaty apply to persons who are 'residents on one or both of the Contracting States'. A 'person' is defined in Article 3, paragraph 1, to include 'an individual, a company and any other body of persons'. Any legal entity that is recognized under the laws of a Contracting State is likely to be treated as a 'person' for tax treaty purposes.[55] Although a partnership is probably a person for purposes of a typical treaty, it may not be a resident of one of the Contracting States if the partners rather than the partnership are liable to tax there.[56]

Article 4 of the OECD Model defines what is to be understood by 'resident of a Contracting State' for the purposes of the Convention.[57] It refers to criteria, such as 'domicile, residence, place of management or any other criterion of a similar nature', which, under the domestic law of one or both of the Contracting States, establish the worldwide tax liability of a person. Residence of a person in one or both of the Contracting States generates such person's treaty entitlement, namely the authority to claim rights under the double taxation convention.

Article 4, paragraph 2, contains the so-called 'tie-breaker rule': this paragraph relates to the case where, under the provisions of paragraph 1, an individual is a resident of both Contracting States. It determines the individual's treaty residence by connecting factors, which have to be applied in a specific order.[58]

In the event a person, other than an individual (such as a company), is a resident of both Contracting States, Article 4, paragraph 3, determines the treaty residence to be the State in where the 'place of effective management' is located. The place of effective management is the place where key management and commercial decisions that are necessary for the conduct of the entity's business are in substance made. This will ordinarily be the place where the most senior person or group of persons (e.g. board of

54. In respect to Art. 23A and Art. 23B of the OECD Model Tax Convention, see Avery Jones et al., 'Credit and Exemption under Tax Treaties in cases of differing income characterization', in *Eur. Tax.*, 1996, p. 118.

55. The 2010 OECD Model Tax Convention extends the granting of benefits of tax treaties with respect to the income of collective investment vehicles, see *Commentary on Article 1*, par. 6.8 *et seq.*

56. As far as the application of the Convention to partnerships, cf. OECD, *Commentaries,* C(1)-2 et seq. OECD, *The Application of the OECD Model Tax Convention to Partnership,* cit. In literature, see Schaffner, 'The OECD Report on the Application of Tax Treaties to Partnerships', in *Bullet.*, 2000, p. 218 et seq., Doernberg- Van Raad, 'Hybrid Entities and the U.S. Model Income Tax Treaty', in *Tax Notes Internat.*, 1999, p. 745 et seq.

57. For the notion of residence for treaty purposes, see Ward et al, 'A Resident of a Contracting State for Tax Treaty Purposes: A Case Comment on *Crown Forest Industries*', in *Canad. Tax Journ.*, 1996, p. 408 et seq., Vogel, *On Double Taxation Conventions,* Deventer, 1997, p. 229 et seq.

58. The allocation of treaty residence to one country is achieved through a hierarchy of tests involving the individual's permanent's home, centre of personal and economic relations, habitual abode, and nationality. Cf. OECD, *Commentaries,* C(4)-9 *e tseq.*

directors) makes its decisions. No definitive rule can however be given and all relevant facts and circumstances should be examined.[59]

Article 2 (taxes covered) of the OECD Model specifies the taxes that are covered by the treaty. It provides that the treaty is to apply 'to taxes on income and on capital imposed on behalf of a Contracting State or of its political subdivisions or local authorities', e.g. provincial taxes, municipal or communal taxes. Article 2, paragraph 3, extends the treaty to the new taxes introduced after the treaty has been signed, provided they are identical or substantially similar to the existing taxes to which the treaty applies. The competent authorities in the Contracting States must notify each other of any significant changes in their taxation laws.

[B] Income from Immovable Property

Article 6 (income from immovable property) of the OECD Model gives the right to tax the income derived by a resident of a Contracting State from immovable property or real property situated in the other Contracting State to that State. The right is not exclusive. Although both Contracting States may tax the income from immovable or real property, the State of source or *situs* of the asset or right has the primary taxing right. The article does not apply to income from immovable property located in the State of residence or in a third State; the provisions of Article 21 apply to such income.[60]

Under Article 6, paragraph 2, the definition of the term 'immovable property' is based on the domestic law of the State, where the property is situated. Immovable property expressly includes 'property accessory to immovable property, livestock and equipment used in agriculture and forestry, rights under domestic law attached to landed property, usufruct of immovable property, and rights to variable or fixed royalty payments for the working of, or the right to work, mineral deposits, sources and other natural resources'.

The *situs* principle under this article takes precedence over the rules, contained in Article 7 of the OECD Model, governing the business profits (see further Article 6, paragraph 4).

[C] Business Income

The taxation of business income is governed by Articles 5 and 7 of the OECD Model Convention. In particular, Article 7 provides the rule regulating the taxation of business profits, and since the 2000 revision of OECD Model, it also regulates income from

59. Cf. OECD, *Commentaries*, C(4)-21 et seq. See also Romano, 'The Evolving Concept of 'Place of Effective Management' as a Tie Breaker Rule under the OECD Model Convention and Italian Law', in *Eur. Tax.*, 2001, p. 339 et seq.
For a discussion on the triangular cases arising in presence of dual resident companies, cf. Van Raad, 'Dual Residence', in *Eur. Tax.*, p. 241 et seq. and Avery Jones and Bobbett, 'Triangular-Treaty Problems: A Summary of the Discussion in Seminar E at the IFA Congress in London', in *Bullet.*, 1999, p. 19.
60. Cf. OECD, *Commentaries*, C(6)-1.

professional services and other activities of an independent character, previously dealt with under Article 14.[61]

According to Article 7, paragraph 1, the profits of an enterprise[62] carried on by a resident of a Contracting State *shall be taxable only* in that State, unless the enterprise carries on business in the other Contracting State through a permanent establishment situated therein. If an enterprise of a Contracting State has a permanent establishment in the other Contracting State, then it is taxable in the source State only on the taxable income attributable to the permanent establishment.

The definition of the term 'permanent establishment' is provided in Article 5 of the OECD Model Convention.[63] The permanent establishment concept (hereinafter also 'PE') is a threshold for source State taxation of business profits; it is a criterion reflecting the involvement of a non-resident person in the economy of the source State to a significant degree.

The first paragraph contains the general definition of 'physical PE'. The second paragraph contains non-exhaustive list of facilities that may *prima facie* constitute a PE (such as a place of management, a branch, an office, a factory, etc.). The third paragraph specifies the concept of PE in relation to building sites or construction or installation projects. The fourth paragraph contains a list of places of business that, by way of exception, do not constitute PE.[64] The fifth and sixth paragraphs define the concept of 'agency PE' and the seventh paragraph contains a rule on associated enterprises.[65]

---

61. The OECD *Commentaries* [C(7) -2.1] makes now clear that 'The elimination of Article 14 on 2000 reflected the fact that there were no intended differences between the concepts of permanent establishment, as used in Article 7, and fixed base, as used in Article 14, or between how profits were computed and tax calculated according to which of Article 7 or 14 applied ...'.
62. For an analysis of the notion of the term 'enterprise' in the context of the Model Convention, see Van Raad, 'The Term 'Enterprise' in the Model Double Taxation Conventions - Seventy Years of Confusion', in *Int.*, 1994, p. 491 *etseq.*
63. For a deeper discussion on the notion of permanent establishment, see Vogel, *On Double Taxation Conven tions,* Deventer, 1997, p. *271–356; Skaar, Permanent Establishment,* Deventer, 199 1;Ifa, 'The Development in Different Countries of the Concept of a Permanent Establishment', in *Cahiers,* vol. 52, Deventer, 1987; Baldwin, 'Fixed, Business and Permanent Establishments', *The Tax Journal,* April 1997, p. 13–16; Avery Jones and Ward, 'Agents as Permanent Establishments under the OECD Model Tax Convention', in *Eur. Tax.*, 1993, p. 154 et seq. Roberts, 'The Agency Element of Permanent Establishment. The OECD Commentaries from the Civil Law View', in *Int.*, 1993, p. 396 and Pleijsier, 'The Agency Permanent Establishment: the Current Definition', in *Int.*, 2001, p. 167 and Uckmar, *La tassazione degli stranieri in Italia,* Padova, 1955.
64. The fourth paragraph enumerates preparatory or auxiliary activities, such as (a) the use of facilities solely for the purpose of storage (e.g. warehouse), display (e.g. showroom), or delivery, of goods or merchandise belonging to the enterprise; (b) the maintenance of a stock of goods or merchandise belonging to the enterprise solely for purpose of storage, display or delivery; (c) the maintenance of a stock of goods or merchandise belonging to the enterprise solely for the purpose of processing by another enterprise; (d) the maintenance of a fixed place of business solely for the purpose of purchasing goods or merchandise and (e) the maintenance of a fixed place of business solely for any combination of any of the activities mentioned, provided that the overall activity is still of a preparatory or auxiliary character.
65. According to Art. 5, para. 7, the control of a company, or control by a company does not of itself constitute a PE for the other company. Therefore a subsidiary owned or controlled by its parent does not of itself create a PE for the parent in the source State. The 'anti-single entity' clause respects the separate legal identity of a subsidiary.

The definition of a 'physical PE' is made up of a number of elements, namely it must be a 'fixed place of business through which the business of an enterprise is wholly or partly carried on':

(1) 'fixed': both geographically (to a distinct place in the Source State), and in time, i.e. permanently;
(2) 'place': there must be a physical space, premises, machinery or equipment; this must be at the disposal of the non-resident (including owned, leased, or shared premises);
(3) 'of business': it is necessary to carry on a commercial activity, not necessarily 'productive' (i.e. profitable);
(4) 'through which business of an enterprise': it is not necessarily 'in', so long as the place makes possible the carrying on of business in the source State; the PE should be the tool through which the business of an enterprise is carried on;
(5) 'carried on': it is now clear that human intervention is not required, and automation is sufficient.

The PE exists as soon as business itself starts; it ceases when all activities end or are abandoned, or when the PE business is alienated to a third party.[66]

Article 5, paragraph 3, specifies a special type of PE which does not have to fulfil the requirements of the first paragraph: the so-called 'Project PE'. It consists of a building site, or construction or installation project - including the construction of roads, bridges, canals, the laying of pipelines, excavating, dredging, and demolishing - only if it lasts more than 12 months. The minimum period is calculated separately for each site and the aggregation is possible only for those sites forming a coherent geographical and commercial whole.[67]

Where no physical or project PE subsists, a non-resident can still have a PE through an agent, pursuant to Article 5, paragraph 5 (Agency PE). This is because, through its agent, the non-resident is nonetheless involved to a significant extent in the economy of the Source State. According to the last-mentioned paragraph, where a person is acting on behalf of a person and has, and habitually exercises, an authority in a country to conclude contracts in the name of the person, that person shall be deemed to have a permanent establishment in that country in respect to any activities which that other person undertakes for the person.

The agent's authorization is a question of fact, and not of a formal grant of agency status. Again, whether the agent binds the principal is a question of fact, and finding an agency PE is not precluded by the fact that the contract was signed by the principal, if the negotiations leading to that contract were determined by the agent.[68]

Whether or not the agent acts 'in the name of', depends on whether the authority is granted by a common or civil law jurisdiction. What is required is an authority to

66. These elements can easily be inferred from the *Commentaries* to Art. 5, para. 1.
67. Cf. OECD, *Commentaries*, C(5)-16 et seq.
68. Cf. OECD, *Commentaries*, C(5)-32.

bind the principal: in civil law countries this necessitates direct representation, not indirect representation with an undisclosed principal who is not bound. On the other hand, in common law countries, a principal is still bound even if he/she is not named/disclosed by the agent.[69]

The fifth paragraph does not apply - and no agency PE subsists - to an independent agent acting in the ordinary course of business (see further Article 5, paragraph 6 of the OECD Model).

Thus, if an enterprise has a permanent establishment, as defined in Article 5 of the Model Convention, in the other Contracting State, that State (i.e. the State where the PE is situated) may tax the income attributable to that PE.[70] Hence, the source State cannot tax business profits of a non-resident arising within its territory, unless such profits can be attributed to a PE of the non-resident.

The 2010 update to the OECD Model includes a renewed version of Article 7 which requires the use of the arm's length principle to determine the attributable business profits: i.e. the PE's income must be computed as 'the profits it might be expected to make, in particular in its dealings with other parts of the enterprise, if it were a separate and independent enterprise engaged in the same or similar activities under the same or similar conditions, taking into account the functions performed, assets used and risks assumed by the enterprise through the permanent establishment and through the other parts of the enterprise'. It is equivalent to the profits that a PE might be expected to earn as an independent entity. Article 7, as it read before 2010, required at paragraph 3 the PE's taxable profits be computed after the deduction of all expenses incurred for the purposes of the PE, such as a share of executive and general administration expenses which were expressly mentioned in the Article.[71] As now worded, however, Article 7 requires the recognition and arm's length pricing of the dealings through which one part of the enterprise performs functions for the benefit of the PE (e.g. through the provision of assistance in day-to-day management). The deduction of an arm's length charge for these dealings, as opposed to a deduction limited to the amount of the expenses, is required by paragraph 2. The previous paragraph 3 has therefore been deleted to prevent it from being misconstrued as limiting the deduction to the amount of the expenses themselves[72]. In particular,

69. See, *amplius*, Avery Jones and Ward, 'Agents as Permanent Establishments under the OECD Model Tax Convention', in *Eur. Tax.*, 1993, p. 160; Roberts, 'The Agency Element of Permanent Establishment. The OECD Commentaries from the Civil Law View', in *Int.*, 1993, p. 402 and Pleijsier, 'The Agency Permanent Establishment: the Current Definition', in *Int.*, 2001.
70. Cf. Art. 7, para. 1, of the Model Convention.
71. Cf. OECD, *Commentaries*, C(7)-16 et seq. As far as the allocation of income and expenses to the PE is concerned, see Van Raad, 'Deemed Expenses of a Permanent Establishment under Article 7 of the OECD Model', in *Int.*, 2000, p. 253 *et seq.;* Becker, 'The Determination of Income of a Permanent Establishment or Branch', in *Int.*, 1989, p. 73 et seq.
72. As it has been pointed out in the *Commentary on Article 7*, the deletion of paragraph 3 'does not affect the requirement, under paragraph 2, that in determining the profits attributable to a permanent establishment, all relevant expenses of the enterprise, wherever incurred, be taken into account. Depending on the circumstances, this will be done through the deduction of all or part of the expenses or through the deduction of an arm's length charge in the case of a dealing between the permanent establishment and another part of the enterprise' (para. 40).

according to the 2010 Report,[73] the OECD approach for the profit allocation, which confirms a separate entity approach, contains two steps, (i) the attribution of assets, risks, and capital to the PE based on a functional analysis, and (ii) the attribution of the PE's profits based on the functional analysis and application of the arm's length principle.

[D] Dividends, Interest and Royalties

As already stated, a major objective of most tax treaties is to provide for reduced rates of withholding tax levied by the source State on dividends, interest and royalties paid to residents of the other Contracting State. This objective is being addressed in Articles 10 (dividends), 11 (interest) and 12 (royalties) of the Model Convention. And indeed, the amount of tax imposed by the State of source is restricted, while the recipient's State of residence gives credit for the levied by the State of source, and does so even where the treaty otherwise employs the exemption method (see further Article 23A, paragraph 2, of the OECD Model).

The Model specifically defines the term dividends (Article 10, paragraph 3) interest (Article 11, paragraph 3) and royalties (Article 12, paragraph 2), so as to make the definitions contained in the domestic law of the Contracting States uniform.[74]

Article 10, paragraph 1, stipulates dividends taxation by the State where the shareholder resides. Moreover, the second paragraph of Article 10 authorizes source State taxation of the dividends albeit only at a limited rate. The Model provides for different maximum tax rates, depending on whether intercompany dividends (direct investments) or dividends from portfolio investments are involved. As per portfolio dividends, the maximum rate applicable is 15% of the gross amount, whereas it is of

---

Moreover,. Article 7, as it read before 2010, also included a provision that allowed the attribution of profits to a PE to be done on the basis of an apportionment of the total profits of the enterprise to its various parts. That method, however, was only to be applied to the extent that its application had been customary in a Contracting State and that the result was in accordance with the principles of Article 7. For the Committee, methods other than an apportionment of total profits of an enterprise can be applied even in the most difficult cases. The Committee therefore decided to delete that provision because its application had become very exceptional and because of concerns that it was extremely difficult to ensure that the result of its application would be in accordance with the arm's length principle.
At the same time, the Committee also decided to eliminate two other provisions that were found in the previous version of the article, that is to say (i) the profits to be attributed to the PE were to be 'determined by the same method year by year unless there is good and sufficient reason to the contrary', and (ii) '[n]o profits shall be attributed to a permanent establishment by reason of the mere purchase by that permanent establishment of goods or merchandise for the enterprise'. See *Commentaries*, paras 41–43.

73. Cf. OECD, *Report on the Attribution of Profits to Permanent Establishments, Commentary on Article 7 concerning the taxation of business profits*, paras. 21–22.

74. Whereas the definitions of 'interest' and 'royalties' do not rely on domestic definition, the definition of 'dividends' does. This can lead to the consequence that one country regards a payment as a dividend whereas another country regards it as something else: for instance, one country may treat a payment on the liquidation of a company to its shareholders, in whole or in part, as a dividend, whereas another country may treat it as a disposal of the shares, and so cover it by the capital gain article in the treaty. See Helminen, *The Dividend concept in International Tax Law*, The Hague, 1999, p. 81 et seq.

5% in the case of intercompany dividends when the parent holds at least 25% of the capital of the distributing company.

Article 11, paragraph 1, authorizes unlimited taxation by the residence State of the recipient. However, the State of source may tax the interest, but only at a limited rate: the maximum rate applicable amounts to 10% of the gross income (Article 11, paragraph 2).

Contrary to Articles 10 and 11, which provides for a tax sharing between the two Contracting States, Article 12 (royalties) assigns exclusive tax rights to the residence State of the investor. The reasoning that lies behind this policy choice is to enable the residence State to recapture the revenue foregone by allowing deductions for the expenses incurred by resident taxpayers for the development of the right in respect of which royalties are being paid.

Articles 10, 11 and 12 stipulate that the treaty benefits – i.e. the reduction of the withholding taxes for dividends and interest and tax exemption for royalties in the State of source – shall be available only if the *beneficial owner* of such payment is resident in the other Contracting State.[75] The term beneficial owner, which is not defined in the Model Convention,[76] is not to be construed by reference to domestic laws of the State applying the treaty. The term is instead to derive its meaning with reference to the context of the treaty, with a view to the purpose pursued by the restriction. In particular, the clause is aimed at denying treaty benefits whenever an intermediary (such as an agent or a nominee) is interposed between the beneficial owner and the company paying out the dividends merely to enable the beneficial owner to get access to treaty protection whenever the beneficial owner is not entitled to it, since he/she is not a resident of the other Contracting State.[77]

75. For the notion of *beneficial owner* in the context of Model Convention, see Oliver-Libin-Van Weeghel-Du Toit, 'Beneficial Ownership', in *Bullet.*, 2000, p. 310 *et seq.;* Du Toit, *Beneficial Ownership of Royalties in Bilateral Tax Treaties,* Amsterdam, 1999; Van Weeghel, *The Improper Use of Tax Treaties,* London-The Hague-Boston, 1998, p. 54–91; Vogel, *On Double Taxation Conventions,* Deventer, 1997, p. 561–564; Born, 'Beneficial Ownership-Decision of the Netherlands Supreme Court of 6 April 1994, n. 28638', in *Eur. Tax.*, 1994, p. 469 *etseq.;* Ward, 'Abuse of Tax Treaties', in Albert and Van Raad (eds.), *Essays on International Taxation,* London-The Hague-Boston, 1993 *(Series on International Taxation,* no. 15) and Killius, 'The Concept of 'Beneficial Owner' of Items of Income under German Tax Treaties', in *Int.*, 1989, p. 340 et seq.

76. Only few tax treaties support the term. For example, under the Germany-Italy treaty a person is a beneficial owner if he/she owns the asset and the rights over them, and the related income is attributed to him/her.
The US Model Convention 1996 regard a person as a beneficial owner if the income is attributable to him/her for tax purposes as a resident. However, the domestic law may still exclude a person if he/she receives the income but in substance does not have the control or the rights over it.

77. See OECD, *Commentaries*, cit., C(10)-12.1, where it is stated: 'Where an item of income is received by a resident of a Contracting State acting in the capacity of agent or nominee it would be inconsistent with the object and purpose of the Convention for the State of source to grant relief or exemption merely on account of the status of the immediate recipient of the income as a resident of the other Contracting State.
The immediate recipient of the income in this situation qualifies as a resident but no potential double taxation arises as a consequence of that status since the recipient is not treated as the owner of the income for tax purposes in the State of residence. It would be equally inconsistent with the object and purpose of the Convention for the State of source to grant relief or exemption where a resident of a Contracting State, otherwise than through an agency or

The distributive rules on dividends, interest and royalties generally take precedence over the provisions of business profits contained in Article 7. However, Article 10, paragraph 4, Article 11, paragraph 4 and Article 12, paragraph 3, provide an exception for cases where the holdings, debt claims and usable assets, are effectively connected to a permanent establishment maintained by the enterprise in the State of source. In this case, the source State encounters no restriction for what concerns the level of the rate of tax applied to these items of income. For instance, the source State is allowed to tax interest income earned by a bank through a PE at the tax rates generally applicable to business income, not at the special rate generally applicable to interest income.

[E] Employment and Pension Income

Article 15 governs the taxing rights on income from employment and it is a *lex generalis* in relation to the other articles on employment income, i.e. Article 16 (director's fee), Article 17 (artistes and sportsmen), Article 18 (pensions) and Article 19 (government service), which take precedence as *leges speciales*. Thus, whenever an item of income should fall outside the provisions of the aforementioned articles, Article 15 will display its *umbrella function*[78]

Under Article 15, the State of residence has the exclusive right to tax the salaries, wages and other similar remuneration derived by a resident of that Contracting State, unless the employment is exercised in the other Contracting State (see further Article 15, paragraph 1). In the latter case, the State of activity may taxes the remuneration derived by the activity performed in its territory, only if one of these conditions is met:

(i) the physical stay of the employee in the State of activity exceeds 183 days in any 12-month period that begins or ends in the tax year concerned;[79]

nominee relationship, simply acts as a conduit for another person who in fact receives the benefit of the income concerned. For these reasons, the report from the Committee on Fiscal Affairs entitled 'Double Taxation Conventions and the Use of Conduit Companies' concludes that a conduit company cannot normally be regarded as the beneficial owner if, though the formal owner, it has, as a practical matter, very narrow powers which render it, in relation to the income concerned, a mere fiduciary or administrator acting on account of the interested parties.'

78. For a dissertation of the umbrella function of Art. 15 vis-à-vis Arts 16, 17, 18 and 19, see Potgens, 'The 'Closed System' of the Provisions on Income from employment in the OECD Model', in *Eur., Tax.*, 2001.

79. In reference to the calculation of the 183-day period, see OECD, *The 183 day rule: some problems of application and interpretation,* in *OECD Model Tax Convention: four related studies,* Issues in international taxation, n. 4. It is now clear that reference must be made to the days of physical presence [cf. OECD, *Commentaries,* cit., C(15)-5], therefore the following days are included in the calculation: part of a day, day of arrival in the work State, day of departure from the work State, all days spent in the State of activity such as Saturdays, Sundays and other holidays, day of sickness, etc.

(ii) the remuneration is paid by, or on behalf of, an employer who is a resident in the State of activity;[80] or

(iii) the remuneration is borne by a PE that the employer has in the State of activity.[81]

The reasoning behind conditions (ii) and (iii) is to guarantee the source taxation of employment income to the extent that such income is allowed as a deductible expense in the activity State, either because the employer is taxable as a resident there, or because he/she maintains a PE in the State of work, to which the remuneration of the employee is attributed.

Article 16 provides that directors' fees and other similar payment derived by a resident of a Contracting State (whether an individual or a legal person), in the capacity of a member of board of directors of a company which is a resident of the other Contracting State, may be taxed in that other State. This only applies to payments received by members of the board of directors only in such capacity (thus excluding other income earned from the same company). The Model contains no special provision for the situation where the company has a permanent establishment in the other Contracting State to which a director is assigned and for which his/her work is primarily carried out. It has been suggested[82] that in this case the directors' fees should be taxable in the State of the permanent establishment.

Income derived by artistes and sportsmen is governed by Article 17: according to this article income may be taxed in the State where their personal activities are exercised. Therefore, the primary taxing rights are given to the State of performance (source) and the justification is that the State of residence can very likely be a tax haven or may otherwise have difficulties in keeping track of the artistes and sportsmen because of their high mobility.[83] No specific rules for the State of residence are

80. For an analysis of the expression 'paid by, or on behalf of, an employer', see De Broe, et al., 'Interpretation of Article 15(2)(b) of the OECD Model Convention: 'remuneration paid by, or on behalf of, an employer who is not a resident of the other State'', in *Bullet.*, 2000, p. 503 et seq.

81. The third condition has been clarified by the addition provided to the OECD *Commentaries* in 2000 [C(15)-7]: 'The phrase 'borne by' must be interpreted in the light of the underlying purpose of subparagraph c) of the article, which is to ensure that the exception provided for in paragraph 2 does not apply to remuneration that is deductible, having regard to the principles of Article 7, in computing the profits of a permanent establishment situated in the State in which the employment is exercised. In this regard, it must be noted that the fact that the employer has, or has not, actually deducted the remuneration in computing the profits attributable to the permanent establishment is not necessarily conclusive since the proper test is whether the remuneration would be allowed as a deduction for tax purposes; that test would be met, for instance, even if no amount were actually deducted as a result of the permanent establishment being exempt from tax in the source country or of the employer simply deciding not to claim a deduction to which he was entitled'. Thus, as a consequence of what stated in the *Commentaries*, the accounting proceeds are not relevant for this purposes.

82. Baker, *Double Taxation Conventions and International Tax Law*, 2nd edn, London, 1994, p. 314.

83. See, *amplius*, OECD, 'Taxation of Entertainers, Artistes and Sportsmen', in *Issues* in *Internat., Taxat.*, No. 2, 1987; Sandler, *The Taxation of International Entertainers and Athletes. All the World's stage*, The Hague, 1995; Grams, 'Artist Taxation: Art. 17 of the OECD Model Treaty - a Relic of Primeval Tax Times?', in *Int.*, 1995, p. 193 *etseq.*

indicated in Article 17, though the Commentaries suggest subject-to-tax clauses and tax credit method also to exemption countries, so as to avoid double non-taxation.[84]

The second paragraph of Article 17 is primarily aimed at a particular form of tax avoidance where a performer contracts with another person that this other person will have the right to provide the performer's services. As long as that other person does not have a permanent establishment in the country where the services are performed, the profits received by the other person in consideration for supplying the services would be not subject to taxation in the State where the services were performed under Article 7 Model Convention. The paragraph at stake counters this by providing that income in respect of personal activities exercised by an entertainer and sportsman which accrues to another person may be taxed where the activities are exercised.[85]

Pensions and other similar remuneration are taxable, under Article 18, only in the State of residence of the recipient. Thus the place where the employment was effectively exercised and the residence of the pay or are insignificant. In fact, the provision does not establish any link between the right to tax and the type of work in connection with which the pension was built up.[86]

Article 18 overrides the general rule contained in Article 15 for remuneration in respect of dependant personal services, and it has to be read in conjunction with Article 19, paragraph 2, dealing with income from government services including pensions. If a pension is paid for work performed as employee of a State or political subdivisions or local authority thereof, the taxing right is assigned to the country paying the pensions only, unless the recipient is not only a resident but also a national of the country of residence. Article 18 consequently does not apply to pensions paid in consideration of past employment with the State authorities of a Contracting State. On the other hand, Article 18 will be applicable to private pensions paid in consideration of a past employment, including cases where the Contracting States themselves carry on a business and employ people in this respect.[87]

With certain exceptions, individuals performing services on behalf of a Contracting State are taxable only by that State, pursuant to Article 19, paragraph 1, of Model

---

See Molenaar, 'Obstacles for International Performing Artists', in *Eur., Tax.*, 2002, p. 149 and Nitikman, 'Article 17 of the OECD Model Treaty - An Anachronism?', in *Int.*, 2001, p. 268 et seq. for analysis of the 'side-effects' of provisions contained in Art. 17 of the Model Convention.

84. Cf. OECD, *Commentaries*, C(17)-12.
85. See Molenaar and Grams, 'Rent-A-Star - The Purpose of Art. 17(2) of the OECD Model', in *Bullet.*, 2002, p. 500 and Betten and Lombardi, 'Article 17(2) of the OECD Model in Triangular Situations - Does Article 17(2) Apply if the Artiste or Sportsman is Resident in a Third State?', in *Bullet.*, 1997, p. 560 et seq.
86. It is uncertain whether severance payment and lump-sum compensation upon termination of employment fall under Art. 18, the alternatives being Arts 15 and 21. However payments compensating loss of office should not fall under Art. 18 insofar as they replace income that could have been earned by the employee. Moreover severance pay designed to ease the burden on an employee moving to another job or paid on premature dismissal and designed to bridge a waiting period should come under Art. 15, because it was based on the previous employment relationship. See Ballancin, 'Art. 18 of the OECD Model Tax Convention', in *Dir., prat. trib., intern.*, 2002, p. 128.
87. See Art. 19, para. 3. Cf. OECD *Commentaries*, C(18)-1: 'It also applies to pensions in respect of services rendered to a State or a political subdivision or local authority thereof which are not covered by the provisions of paragraph 2 of Article 19'.

Convention. Students and certain business apprentices or trainees who visit a Contracting State for educational or training purposes are generally not taxable in that Contracting State on the foreign payments they receive for maintenance, education, or training under Article 20 of the Model Convention. Some tax treaties also provide reciprocal exemptions for visiting professors and teachers.

[F] Capital Gains and the 'Other Income' Article

Article 13, paragraph 1, makes it clear that gains from the disposition of immovable property are also taxable in the source country *(situs* principle). According to the *Commentaries*, the gains arising from the alienation of immovable property situated in the Contracting State in which the alienator is a resident in the meaning of Article 4 of the Model Convention, or in a third State, shall be covered by Article 21, paragraph 1.[88]

Several countries specifically provide in their tax treaties that the right to tax gains from the disposition of shares of a company is reserved to the source country when the assets of the company consist primarily of immovable property. It is noteworthy that in the 2003 version of the OECD Model, it has been added a paragraph to Article 13, where it is provided that 'gains derived by a resident of a Contracting State from the alienation of shares deriving more than 50% of their value directly or indirectly from immovable property situated in the other Contracting State may be taxed in that other State'. The provision brings an exception to the general rule of taxation of gains deriving from shares (taxation in the State of residence of the alienator), to counteract all those avoidance-aiming manoeuvres that exploit Article 13, paragraph 4, to avoid the taxation in the State of *situs* as set forth by Article 13, paragraph 1.

The gains from the alienation of movable property forming part of the business property of a permanent establishment may be taxed in the Contracting State where the permanent establishment is situated, even if the property is located in the other Contracting State. It must be borne in mind that, in such case, the movable property must be attributable to the permanent establishment (cf. Article 13, paragraph 2).

Gains from the alienation of any property other than those referred in the first three paragraphs of Article 13, are taxable only in the alienator's State of residence, as provided for by paragraph 4 of the mentioned article. Article 13, paragraph 4, is a catch all clause, and encompasses gains from the alienation of shares in a company or of securities, bond debentures and the like.[89]

88. Cf. OECDOECD *Commentaries*, C(13)-22.
89. It should be noted that, in special circumstances, the gains deriving by the sale of shares may not fall under Art. 13, para. 4 of the Model Convention. Cf. OECD *Commentaries*, cit., C(13)-31: 'If shares are sold by a shareholder to the issuing company in connection with the liquidation of such company or the reduction of its paid-up capital, the difference between the selling price and the par value of the shares may be treated in the State of which the company is a resident as a distribution of accumulated profits and not as a capital gain. The Article does not prevent the State of residence of the company from taxing such distributions at the rates provided for in Article 10.... The same interpretation may apply if bonds or debentures are redeemed by the debtor at a price which is higher than the par value or the value at which the bonds or

Finally, Article 21 of the Model Convention gives exclusive taxing rights to the State of residence, if the income of a resident of a Contracting State, wherever arising, is *not dealt with* under the distributive rules contained in Articles 6 to 22.[90] The article also covers sources of income that are not covered in the specific articles. In fact, most distributive rules (e.g. Articles 6, 10, 11, 12 etc.) deal with taxing rights over income that has a source in one Contracting State and is paid to a resident of the other Contracting State. This article covers income with source in one Contracting State when paid to a resident of the same State and income sourced in a third State that is paid to a resident of one of the two Contracting State.

An exception is contained in the second paragraph of Article 21 when the income *not dealt with* is received by a resident of a Contracting State from an activity, which is effectively connected with its permanent establishment on the other Contracting State. The taxing rights are then given to the State where the permanent establishment is located (hence Article 7 applies). This exception does not apply to income from immovable property as the State of *situs* always has the primary right to tax.[91]

[G] Non-discrimination

The non-discrimination article (Article 24) of tax treaties is designated to ensure that foreign investors in a country are not discriminated against by the tax system compared with domestic investors.[92]

The first paragraph of Article 24 lays down the non-discrimination principle based on nationality. It follows that only a national of either of the two Contracting States irrespective of the State of which he/she is resident may invoke the non-discrimination provision. In particular, it prevents nationals of one Contracting State from being subjected to any taxation (or any requirements connected therewith) that is *other or more burdensome* than that imposed on nationals of the other Contracting State *in the same circumstances, in particular with respect to residence.* Therefore a non-resident alien is not in the same circumstances as a resident national: the provision does not prohibit discrimination against non-residents, but only discrimination on the grounds of nationality alone. Because most countries do not tax individuals on the basis of nationality, this provision is primarily important with respect to legal entities.

debentures have been issued; in such a case, the difference may represent interest and, therefore, be subjected to a limited tax in the State of source of the interest in accordance with Article 11'.

As far as the characterization of income from the purchase of shares by the issuing company, see Betten, 'Tax Treaty Interpretation: Income from the Purchase of Shares by the Issuing Company: Dividend and Capital Gain?', in *Eur. Tax.*, 1993, p. 424 and Huiskes, 'Capital Gains on a Company's Repurchase of Shares', in *Eur. Tax.*, 1994, p. 472.

As for the application of tax treaties to emigration taxes, see, *amplius*, Betten, *Income Tax Aspects of Emigration and Immigration of Individuals*, Amsterdam, 1998, p. 112 et seq.

90. E.g. winnings from gambling, financial derivatives, punitive damages, etc. See Ward et al., 'The Other Income Article of Income Tax Treaties', in *Bullet.*, 1990, p. 409 et seq.
91. See Rust, '*Situs* Principle v. Permanent Establishment Principle in International Tax Law', in *Bullet.*, 2002, p. 15 et seq.
92. See the comprehensive work of Van Raad, *Non-Discrimination in International Tax Law*, The Hague, 1986, *passim;* Amatucci (F), *Ilprincipio di non discriminazione fiscale*, Padova, 1998.

It must be borne in mind that Article 24 applies to taxation of person and not to income; thus the discrimination in taxing foreign income compared to domestic income is not covered: e.g. if a taxpayer has a choice between straight-line depreciation and declining balance method in determining income from domestic business activities, a taxpayer with foreign business income cannot rely on Article 24 in computing his/her foreign profits for purposes of double taxation relief, to have the same choice.[93]

Article 24, paragraph 3, provides that permanent establishments of enterprises of one Contracting State should be subject to no less favourable taxation than the taxation of enterprises of the other State carrying on the same activities. The OECD Commentaries discuss at length six aspects of equal treatment of permanent establishment, viz. the assessment of tax, the special treatment of dividends received in respect to holdings owned by permanent establishments, the structure and rate of tax, the withholding tax on dividends, interest and royalties received by a permanent establishment, the credit for foreign taxes and the extension to permanent establishments of the benefit of double taxation conventions concluded with third State.[94]

Considering the last-mentioned aspect, it is noteworthy that Article 24, paragraph 3 does not imply that the permanent establishment located in a Contracting State of an enterprise resident of the other Contracting State may take advantage of the first-mentioned State's treaty with a third State. In the case that the permanent establishment 'receives' dividends, interest or royalties that are effectively connected to that PE from a third State, the Commentaries recommend (paragraphs 51–52), to the extent that double taxation of the permanent establishment's profits cannot be avoided by the unilateral tax credit relief of the domestic law of the PE State, the inclusion of a provision in the treaty between the PE State and the resident State of the enterprise, that obligates the PE State to credit the tax paid by the permanent establishment in the third State. However, the maximum credit should be the level of tax provided for in the tax treaty between the resident State of the enterprise and the third State.

Article 24, paragraph 4, provides that, subject to the position where a special relationship exists between the enterprise and the recipient pursuant to Article 9, paragraph 1, Article 11, paragraph 6 and Article 12, paragraph 4, interest, royalties and other disbursements paid to a resident of the other Contracting State must be deductible to the same extent that they would be deductible if paid to a resident of the same State. This provision does not prohibit the thin capitalization rules in force in the Contracting States, as long as they are compatible with Article 9, paragraph 1 and Article 11, paragraph 6.[95] However, the Commentaries[96] add that if thin capitalization

93. Cf. Avery Jones et al., 'The Non-Discrimination Article in Tax Treaties', in *British Tax Rev.*, 1991/1, p. 359.
94. Cf. OECD, *Commentaries*, C(24)-24 et seq.
95. See OECD, 'Thin Capitalization, Taxation of Entertainers, Artistes and Sportsmen - Issues', in *Internat. Taxat.*, No. 2, Paris, 1987. As for the relationship between thin capitalization rues and tax treaties, see F.C. De Hosson and Michielse, 'Treaty Aspects of the 'Thin Capitalization' Issue - A Review of the OECD Report', in *Int.*, 1989, p. 476 *et seq.;* Luthi, 'Thin Capitalization of companies in International Tax Law', in *Int.*, 1991, p. 446 *et seq.;* ICC - Commission on Taxation (Working Party on Thin Capitalization), *Thin Capitalization*, (ICC, 18 March 1998).
96. Cf. OECD, *Commentaries*, C(24)-56.

rules apply only in respect to non-residents creditors, excluding resident creditors, then such treatment is prohibited by paragraph 4.

Article 24, paragraph 5, ensures that corporations, partnerships and other entities resident in a country, whose capital is owned or controlled by residents of the treaty partner, must be treated no less favourably than domestically owned or controlled enterprises. The Commentaries[97] clarify that this provision is aimed at prohibiting discriminatory taxation on enterprises, not on the persons owning or controlling their capital. Therefore the provision does not extend to shareholders of the other Contracting State: namely Article 24, paragraph 5, does not prevent income stemming from such shareholdings and accruing to non-resident shareholders to be taxed differently from the income accruing to shareholders who are resident of the same State of the enterprise.

It must be borne in mind that the non-discrimination article does not prevent a country from discriminating in favour of non-residents, as with tax holidays or other incentives that apply only to foreign investors nor does the article prohibit provisions in the domestic law that favour the location of investment in the country.

[H] Mutual Agreement Procedure, Exchange of Information and Assistance in the Collection of Taxes

The OECD Model Convention provides a mutual agreement procedure (Article 25) for resolving disputes that arise under a tax treaty. In particular, this article performs three functions: it provides a dispute resolution mechanism in relation to the application of the provisions of tax treaties to specific cases; it allows the countries to settle common interpretations and applications of their tax treaty; and it allows them to resolve cases of double taxation not otherwise dealt with.

The taxpayer has three years to invoke the procedure from the first notification of the act complained of. The States are obliged under the article to consult on the problem raised by the taxpayer if the State with which the problem is raised is unable or unwilling to resolve it unilaterally, but they are not obliged to resolve the case. However, any agreement reached by them can be carried out despite any time limits under the domestic law of the Contracting State.

The 2008 OECD Model update added the new paragraph 5 to Article 25 which provides that a case shall be submitted to arbitration when the competent authorities are unable to reach an agreement within two years from presentation of its case to the competent authority of the other Contracting State. The Commentary clarifies that the arbitration process is an integral part of the mutual agreement procedure and it does not constitute an alternative procedure to solve the disputes arising from the application of the Convention.

Generally, the mutual agreements are binding on the on the tax authorities to the extent that the treaty, the domestic law or judicial decisions permit them. However,

97. Cf. *Ibid.* C(24)-57.

they do not bind the Courts and, therefore, the taxpayers.[98] Under the Vienna Convention on the Law of Treaties, they must be considered as subsequent agreements or practice when interpreting the treaty (Article 31, paragraph 3).

Taxpayer dissatisfaction with the mutual agreement procedure has led some countries to adopt arbitration procedures in their tax treaties for cases where it is not possible for the competent authorities to resolve disputes. The main purpose of such provisions is to put pressure on the tax administration to resolve international disputes rather than to actually engage in arbitrations.[99]

As already mentioned, Article 26 of the OECD Model provides for an exchange of information between tax authorities of the Contracting States.[100] Before 2000, Article 26 of the OECD Model was worded so as to restrict exchange of information only to taxes covered by the Convention (i.e. taxes on income and capital) although exchange of information could always take place when necessary to carry out both the provision of the Convention and the domestic laws of the Contracting States. The 2000 version of the OECD Model Tax Convention expressly provides that 'the exchange of information is not restricted by Art. 1 and Art. 2', hence allowing countries to exchange information concerning any kind of taxes, not also covered by the Convention. This revision is very considerable, although one has to bear in mind that most tax treaties still contain the limitation to exchange information concerning taxes on income and capital only.[101]

---

98. Vogel, *On Double Taxation Conventions,* Deventer, 1997, footnote 105.
99. For a discussion of these issues, see Tillinghast, 'Issues Arising in the Implementation of the Arbitration of Disputes Arising Under Income Tax Treaties', in *Bullet.*, 2002, p. 90; *Ibid.* 'The Choice of Issues to be Submitted to Arbitration under Income Tax Conventions', in *Essays on International Taxation,* 1993, p. 349 *et seq.;* Van Der Bruggen, 'The Compulsory Jurisdiction of the ICJ in Tax Cases', in *Intertax,* 2001, p. 250 *et seq.* Bricker, 'Arbitration Procedures in Tax Treaties', in *Internat. Tax Rev.*, 1998, p. 97 *et seq.* and Zueger, 'ICC Proposes Arbitration in International Tax Matters', in *Bullet.*, 2001, p. 221 et seq.
    The EU has implemented an arbitration procedure in transfer pricing cases, Convention of 23 July 1990, on the Elimination of Double Taxation in connection with the Adjustment of Profits of Associated Enterprises, 90/436/EEC, O.J.No. C304 of 21 December 1976,4.
100. In reference to Art. 26 of the OECD Model cf. *inter alia,* Vogel, *On Double Taxation Conventions,* Deventer, 1997, p. 1402; Ruchelman and Shapiro, 'Exchange of Information', in *Int.,*, 2002, p. 408; Vegh, 'Towards a Better Exchange of Information', in *Eur., Tax.*, 2002, p. 394; Oberson, 'The OECD Model Agreement on Exchange of Information - a Shift to the Applicant State', in *Bullet.*, 2003, p. 14.
101. On the other hand, the Council of Europe/OECD Multilateral Convention on Mutual Administrative Assistance in Tax Matters has been very broad in scope from the beginning regarding all kinds of taxes, present and future.
    The EC Directive (the Mutual Assistance Directive) of 19 December 1977 (77/799/EEC) was originally applied only to direct taxes (of whatever description), but was later extended also to VAT by the EC Directive of 27 December 1979 (79/1070/EEC) and to excise duties by the EC Directive of 25 February 1992 (92/12/EEC).
    Recently, the European Commission issued a Communication on *Good Governance in Tax Matters* [COM(2009) 201 final] with the intention to launch a debate about concrete actions that could be taken in order to improve synergies between tax and development. Moreover, due to the tremendous development of the mobility of taxpayers, of the number of cross-border transactions and of the globalization of the economy, the recent Council Directive 2011/16/EU of 15 February 2011 (2011/16/EU) has pointed out that the Council Directive 77/799/ECC no longer provides for appropriate measures to fulfil the EU objectives and should therefore be repealed and replace by the new 2011 Directive.

The OECD Commentaries on Article 26 have also been modified in 2000: a new paragraph has also been added (paragraph 9.1) where it is stated that the three methods of exchange (on request, automatic and spontaneous[102]) may also be combined. Paragraph 9.1 stresses the fact that the article does not restrict the possibilities of exchanging information to these methods and that the Contracting State may use other techniques to obtain information which may be relevant to both Contracting States such as simultaneous examinations, tax examinations abroad and industry-wide exchange of information.

The current edition of the OECD Model Tax Convention eliminates all reservations and positions contrary to the international tax standard on exchange of information that is incorporated in Article 26. Consequently, that standard is now universally endorsed and it represents an important achievement, especially for what is concerning bank secrecy, after the four OECD countries that had formerly opposed Article 26, that is to say Austria, Belgium, Luxembourg and Switzerland, have lifted their reservations to it.

Information obtained by the tax department of a Contracting State under an exchange of information article must be kept confidential, although release of the information in court proceedings is allowed. Moreover, a Contracting State is not obliged under the exchange of information article to carry out administrative procedures on behalf of its treaty partner that are contrary to its own laws or practices, or that would result in the disclosure of trade secrets or similar information.

Until 2002, the OECD Model Convention was silent on the question of mutual assistance in the collection of taxes.[103] In the 2003 version of the OECD Model, a new Article 27 on Assistance in the Collection of Taxes has been implemented. The Article is aimed at ensuring mutual assistance in the collection of revenue claims. As it stands, it provides for comprehensive collection assistance, but the Contracting States may agree on a more limited form of assistance. In particular, the new article specifies two forms of assistance: (i) assistance in enforcing collection (Article 27, paragraph 3) and (ii) assistance in taking measures of conservancy (Article 27, paragraph 4). In any case, when negotiating a treaty, each Contracting State needs to decide for itself whether and to what extent assistance should be given to the other State.[104]

102. From a general point of view, it is possible to say that an international exchange of information can be carried out in different forms, namely: (1) upon request; (2) automatically; (3) spontaneously; (4) simultaneous examination. Cf. Vogel, *On Double Taxation Conventions*, Deventer, 1997, p. 1407.

103. It is noteworthy, however, that the OECD Committee on Fiscal Affaire prepared a 'Model Convention for Administrative Assistance in the Recovery of Tax Claims' (OECD, Paris, 1981). Moreover in 1988, the OECD and Council of Europe opened for signature a Convention on Mutual Administrative Assistance in Tax Matters (at present, ratified by 8 countries: Denmark, Finland, Iceland, the Netherlands, Norway, Poland, Sweden, United States). This multilateral convention contains provisions on exchange of information, assistance in the recovery of tax, and the service for documents for taxation purposes. It entered into force on 1 April 1995.

104. Cf. OECD, *Commentaries*, C(27)-1 and 2.

§6.07 TREATY SHOPPING

Treaty shopping has come under scrutiny in recent years. It is defined as the routing of income arising in one country to a person in another country through an intermediary country to obtain the tax advantage of tax treaties. It usually involves the 'flow-through' of income through conduit companies in treaty havens. Other examples include triangular structures where a low or zero taxed branch of a company in a treaty country receives income from a third country. A third example of treaty shopping may involve the use of hybrid entities that are characterized differently in two Contracting States.[105]

Generally the use of tax treaties by third country residents to obtain treaty benefits not available directly to them is lawful, as long as it is not prohibited by treaty provisions or general international law. However, many countries regard treaty shopping as unacceptable and improper. Therefore, several jurisdictions have enacted specific anti-treaty shopping provisions. The main categories of anti-treaty shopping measures are:

(i) Specific measures that deny benefits to entities, which are not subject to tax in their State of residence. That is the case of Luxembourg 1929 holding companies which are generally excluded from Luxembourg tax treaties.
(ii) Comprehensive measures imposed under the domestic legislation or treaties.

Germany has enacted a general provision in the German Tax Code under the Anti-abuse and Technical Amendment Act to curb treaty shopping by third country residents. According to this disposition the tax authorities can now disallow the treaty and EU Directive benefits to entities that are set up as conduit companies, primarily to take advantage of treaty benefits not otherwise available to them. In Switzerland, the 1962 Abuse Decree excludes fiduciary or collecting agents of non-resident principals from treaty benefits.[106] Many US treaties contain a Limitation on Benefits Article to exclude certain residents from treaty benefits.[107] Article 22 on the Limitation on benefits under the 1996 US Model Treaty is substantially more detailed than the 1981 US Model. It includes various restrictive clauses but it also provides objective safe harbour provisions in case of *bona fide* business activities.[108] Despite the detailed

105. For more detailed studies on this subject see Van Weeghel, *The Improper Use of Tax Treaties*, Deventer, 1998; Ward, 'Abuse of Tax Treaties', in *Int.*, 1995, p. 178 *et seq.* David, Oliver, 'Access to Tax Treaties', in Int., 1989, p. *330 et seq.*
106. See Reinarz, 'Revised Swiss Anti-Treaty Shopping Rules', in *Bullet.*, March 1999; Hull, Teuscher, 'Treaty Relief in Switzerland on Outbound Investment', in *Bullet.*, February 2001.
107. See Van Herksen, 'Limitation on Benefits and the Competent Authority Determination', in *Bullet.*, January 1996.
108. Under the US-Netherlands treaty, the taxpayer must have a business purpose for residing in the Netherlands and holding their US investments through a Dutch entity. In addition to other objective safe harbours, it provides for additional qualifying provisions to extend derivative treaty benefits to other European Union residents, as well as a headquarters-company test. Furthermore, it includes six subjective or 'intent' factors to assist the competent authority in applying the principal purpose test.

provisions and explanations, it contains several subjective rules that may be difficult to apply.[109]

Since 1987[110] the OECD considered that treaty shopping was undesirable since it frustrated the spirit of the treaty, if not the provisions. The recommendations of the 1987 Report have been included in the Commentaries to Article 1 of the OECD Model Convention. The OECD Model Convention itself expresses concern over treaty shopping but provides only a rudimentary solution to the problem. It contains few provisions limiting its use. For instance, the treaty benefits are denied if a person is not liable to worldwide tax in his/her country of residence. Indeed, a treaty shopper must qualify as a resident under Article 4, paragraph 1, of the OECD Model Convention, i.e. he/she must be liable to comprehensive taxation (full liability to tax on world income) under the domestic law.[111] And again, Articles 10 (dividends), 11 (interest) and 12 (royalties) mention that only a 'beneficial owner' is entitled to treaty benefits. As already analysed, the Model Convention excludes the concessional withholding tax benefit from the legal owner if he/she is not the beneficial owner and the beneficial owner is not a resident in the same Contracting State. The legal owner, like an intermediary with very narrow powers, such as a nominee or agent or a conduit company, cannot take advantage of the benefit above-mentioned unless the beneficial owner is also a resident of that State. The 2003 amendments to the OECD Model Commentaries contain important novelties in the subject, proposing the introduction of new provisions on possible anti-abuse measures, new provisions on possible measures against harmful tax competition and clarifications regarding the requirement of beneficial ownership.[112]

---

109. As evidenced by Ellis, 'Limitation on Benefits - a Netherlands Perspective', in *Int.*, 1989,8/9.
110. See OECD (Committee on Fiscal Affairs), *Double Taxation Conventions and the Use of Base and Conduit Companies*, Paris, 1987. The 1998 OECD Report [OECD (Committee on Fiscal Affairs), *Harmful Tax Com petition*, 1998, pp. 46–50] refers to treaty shopping and mentions that it encourages harmful tax competition. It, therefore, advocates more extensive use of tax treaties to counter such competition.
111. The Commentaries specifically refers to the exclusion of conduit companies in treaty havens that tax-exempt offshore income of residents. See OECD, *Commentaries*, C(4)-8.
Although concerning the air transport sector, there have to be mentioned the so-called 'open skies' cases of the European Court of Justice, of 5 November 2002, C-466/98, C-467/98, C-468/98, C-469/98, C-471/98, C-472/98, C-475/98, C-476/98, see MASON, *U.S. Tax Treaty Policy and the European Court of Justice*, in *Dir. prat. trib. int.*, 2007, I, 57. Moreover, the ECJ has considered compatible with EU law the LOB clause of the Double Taxation Convention between the Netherlands and the UK (see European Court of Justice, 12 December 2006, C-374/04, *Test Claimants in the IV ACT Litigation Group*; O'SHEA, *Netherlands-U.S. Air Transport Agreement Won't Fly, Says ECJ*, in *Tax Notes Int'l*, 2007, 790).
112. For a description of these measures see IBFD, *OECD Model Tax Convention on Income and on Capital 2003(Condensed version) and Key Features of Tax Systems & Treaties of OECD Member Countries*, Amsterdam, 2003; Végh, 'The 2003 OECD Model', in *Eur. Tax.*, 2003, p. 244 et seq.

CHAPTER 7

Tax Treaties in the Americas: The United States Experience*

Charles H. Gustafson

§7.01 INTRODUCTION

[A] In General

The United States is party to more than 60 bilateral income tax treaties and 17 bilateral estate tax treaties. The US Treasury Department is constantly engaged in the revision or replacement of existing tax treaties and the negotiation of new ones. One might reasonably expect that the list of treaty partners would include a substantial number of countries in the Americas. However reasonable, that expectation has not been realized.

The United States has in force only a limited number of income tax treaties with her neighbours in the Americas. The treaties in force can be divided into some useful categories for purposes of comparison and analysis. The United States and Canada have been income tax treaty partners for many years. An income tax treaty was concluded between the United States and Mexico only in 1993 to supplement the North American Free Trade Agreement (NAFTA). Attempts to establish income tax treaties in Central and South America have had almost no success. The income tax treaty concluded in 1999 between the United States and Venezuela is the sole product of these efforts. In addition, there are in force income treaties with the relatively small Caribbean countries of Barbados, Jamaica and Trinidad and Tobago. A treaty dealing with a limited number of tax issues relating to insurance was concluded between the United States and Bermuda in 1988. There are no estate tax treaties in force between the United States and her neighbours in the Western Hemisphere. An earlier estate tax

* This chapter, which is identical to the one published in the first edition, has been updated by the annex written by Roberta Scarpato, which follows immediately after this.

treaty with Canada was terminated when Canada repealed its estate tax. However, in addition to the seven income tax treaties, there are a number of treaties in force between the United States and Western Hemisphere countries providing for cooperation in the administration and enforcement of tax laws although not affecting the substantive tax rules of the treaty countries.

[B] Impact of Income Tax Treaties

Bilateral income tax treaties tend to advance the same well-known objectives. A primary objective is to allocate jurisdictional authority to tax between the treaty countries. Under principles of customary international law, every nation is empowered to exercise legal authority over individuals, entities and events within its territory. However, nations are also empowered by these principles to exercise legal authority over their citizens and residents, even with respect to activities beyond territorial borders. This means that international transactions are susceptible to taxation by more than one nation, both or all of which are acting within permissible limits under customary international law. However, the resulting risk of double taxation is not mitigated by customary international law principles. The income tax treaties effectively allocate primary taxing jurisdiction between the treaty partners, either favouring the taxing power of the country of source or the country of residence. Source countries are favoured by the establishment of an obligation on the country of residence to mitigate double taxation. Residence countries are favoured by the reduction or elimination of withholding taxes generally imposed by source countries on certain forms of investment income and by narrowing the range of business profits that will be taxed in the source country.

Another function of most income tax treaties is to clarify issues of tax administration. One way is to define more specifically circumstances in which a foreign taxpayer will be deemed to be generating business income through permanent establishments. Another is to commit the treaty partners to cooperate in the administration of their respective taxes.

[C] Outline of This Chapter

This chapter will compare the income tax treaty arrangements in effect between the United States and her Western Hemisphere treaty partners. To provide a context for analysing the impact of tax treaties, the chapter begins with a brief description of the process of treaty making in the United States and the posture of treaties within the US legal system. It continues with a brief outline of the principal elements of US income tax law first generally and then with respect to international transactions. It then analyses the impact of income tax treaties in force between the United States and her neighbours in the hemisphere, including both provisions for allocating taxing jurisdiction and areas of cooperation in tax administration and enforcement. The chapter will conclude with a very brief reflection on the way in which other treaties between the United States and Western Hemisphere countries advance cooperation in tax administration and enforcement.

§7.02 THE JURISPRUDENCE OF TREATIES IN UNITED STATES LAW AND PRACTICE

[A] Establishing a Treaty

The US Constitution includes treaties as a part of the 'supreme law of the land'.[1] The Constitution also prescribes the procedure for establishing treaty relationships. Once negotiated and signed by the President or his delegate, a treaty must be submitted to the Senate for approval. Such approval requires a vote of two-thirds of the Senate, which consists of two members from each state, or 100 Senators.[2] The House of Representatives has no formal role in the establishment of treaty relations.

While not explicitly prescribed by the Constitution, the United States has entered into other binding international agreements even though the constitutionally designated pathway has not been followed in their establishment. Such agreements are commonly referred to as 'executive agreements'. There are several sources of legal authority for the conclusion of executive agreements. A treaty approved by the constitutionally designated process may contemplate the conclusion of more specific agreements to implement the treaty arrangement. Legislation may be passed through the normal processes (which include approval by the House of Representatives) that authorize, explicitly or by inference, the conclusion of executive agreements. In some instances executive agreements concluded by a President have been justified by the inherent right of the President under the Constitution to conduct foreign relations for the United States. In many cases a combination of the foregoing rationales has been asserted to support the legality of an executive agreement. However authorized, an executive agreement is treated as a treaty commitment by the United States under international law.[3]

Treaty arrangements have also been effected through the adoption of legislation by the Congress that effectively establishes treaty commitments. This technique, often called 'fast track legislation' because the usual rules allowing for amendment during the legislative process are suspended, has been used in particular for international trade agreements, such as the World Trade Organization agreements and NAFTA.[4]

Executive agreements and 'legislative agreements' are considered to be binding treaty commitments of the United States even though not deriving from the process described in the Constitution.

Income tax treaties and estate tax treaties have been established through the normal treaty-making process, meaning that the Senate has approved the terms of the treaty negotiated by the executive branch. In some instances, however, the Senate has

1. US Constitution, Art. VI.
2. US Constitution, Art. II, Sec. 2.
3. Restatement (Third) of the Foreign Relations Law of the United States, §303.
4. Folsom, *NAFTA in a Nutshell* (West 1999), p. 67.

rejected a portion of the treaty under consideration, thereby approving the treaty with a 'reservation' with respect to certain portions of it. In such instances, US negotiators must return to the potential treaty partner to determine whether the treaty, absent the unapproved language, is acceptable. Needless to say, such a result places US negotiators and the US government in a rather uncomfortable position with respect to the potential treaty partner. To reduce the probability that such a reservation will be taken by the Senate, representatives of the executive branch responsible for negotiating treaty arrangements will generally advise key Senators of negotiations that are being undertaken and seek to identify potential problem areas before the text of the treaty is signed.

Tax Information Exchange Agreements, which do not modify the tax liability established by the traditional sources of tax law, are executive agreements authorized by various legislative acts. On the other hand, Mutual Legal Assistance Treaties, used to enhance cooperation in criminal law enforcement including tax crimes, are approved by the process explicitly prescribed in the Constitution.

Once a treaty has come into force, the President is responsible for its administration. In fact, the President can terminate a treaty without the approval of the Congress even though the Senate participated in its establishment.[5]

[B] Posture of Treaties in US Practice

While treaties are defined to constitute a part of the 'supreme law of the land', the United States follows a practice referred to as the 'later-in-time' doctrine. Under this practice, a US court will apply the terms of a treaty when it supersedes a prior existing statute. However, should Congress adopt legislation subsequent to the establishment of a treaty that is inconsistent with the treaty, a US court will apply the legislation even though the result constitutes a violation of the treaty commitment. While occurring only rarely, so-called 'treaty overrides' with respect to tax matters have been enacted by Congress on a number of occasions.[6]

The United States has not acceded to the Vienna Convention on Treaties. However, in a number of instances involving treaty interpretation and administration, the United States has cited the Vienna Convention as evidence of customary international law with respect to matters addressed in it.

§7.03 BASIC PROVISIONS OF US INCOME TAX LAW AND PRACTICE

[A] General Rules

Income tax treaties will generally either clarify or modify the effect of the usual sources of tax law with a country. Before undertaking any analysis of the effect of income tax treaties, therefore, it is useful to review the basic principles of domestic tax law that

5. *Goldwater v. Carter*, 617 F. 2d 697 (D.C. Cir. 1979).
6. Restatement (Third) of the Foreign Relations Law of the United States, §115.

apply in the absence of a treaty. There follows a brief summary of the principal elements of US federal income tax law relevant to the issues addressed in this chapter.[7]

The United States taxes the income of individuals, corporations, trusts and estates. As in most economically developed countries, income tax is not in fact a tax on income as such. Rather, the tax liability depends upon the application of a formula involving exemptions and exclusions of certain income, business and (in the case of individuals) personal deductions, personal exemptions for individuals and credits. The principal source of US tax law is the Internal Revenue Code (referred to herein as 'Code'; all references in this chapter to section numbers are references to the Code unless otherwise indicated).

The federal income tax has since its inception included a progressive rate structure. Under present law, the highest nominal tax rate for individuals and corporations is 35%.[8] The highest rate currently applies to individual incomes in excess of USD 250,000 per year. Because of certain complex recalculations, the actual maximum marginal rate is somewhat higher than the maximum nominal rate.

Gross income is defined as 'all income from whatever source derived'.[9] In practice, however, the determination of gross income is somewhat complicated. There is a range of technical issues of definition which are based upon financial, accounting and economic considerations. For example, the rule of 'realization' applies, so that appreciation in the value of property is not normally taxed until it has been 'realized' by the taxpayer in a taxable transaction.

Further, a substantial number of exclusions and exemptions have been created over time. As a result, certain items that would normally be considered to be income under economic or financial definitions are not subject to tax. They include a range of employee fringe benefits, such as medical care and insurance, certain educational opportunities, and work-related fringe benefits.[10] Interest on bonds issued by state and local government authorities is also exempt from federal income tax.[11]

The character of income is important. Taxpayers have traditionally been taxed at lower rates for long-term capital gains. Under current law, the maximum tax on most capital gains will be 15% (compared to the maximum rate of about 35% that will continue to apply to ordinary income).[12] As a result of legislation adopted in 2003, dividends paid to individual shareholders will in most instances be subject to a maximum tax rate of 15%.[13]

7. Most state governments and some local governments in the United States also impose taxes on income. Such taxes are not affected by treaty arrangements and are beyond the purview of this chapter.
8. Code§§1, 11.
9. Code §61.
10. See, e.g. Code §§104–106, 132.
11. Code §103.
12. Capital gains on certain assets will be taxed at a 28% rate. For some lower income taxpayers the capital gains rate will be 5%.
13. Code §1(h).

Business and investment deductions are essentially the cost of producing income and are justified by economic or financial considerations that are generally consistent with accounting concepts of income determination.[14]

There are a number of personal deductions available to individual taxpayers that are not justified by reference to accurate income calculation. Some were created to assist taxpayers who incur extraordinary costs or losses. Accordingly, taxpayers with high medical expenses and casualty losses compared to their income are entitled to deduct an amount in excess of a specified minimum.[15] Other personal deductions are intended to encourage taxpayer activity and support organizations or segments of the economy. They include a deduction within limits for charitable contributions and interest paid to finance the acquisition of a principal residence.[16] Still other deductions reflect an element of political accommodation. For example, certain taxes paid to State and local governments are deductible.[17]

Individual taxpayers are also entitled to deduct a 'personal exemption' for themselves and each dependent member of his/her family. The personal exemption for tax year 2004 was approximately USD 3,100. The amount of the personal exemption is indexed to inflation, however, and increases each year.[18]

Some tax credits are intended to encourage income productivity, such as the credit for certain research and development.[19] Some are intended to provide personal benefit, such as the child care credit for single parents or children of two-worker families.[20] Others are designed to encourage low-income taxpayers to work rather than to rely on government payments.[21] The foreign tax credit, which is discussed in more detail later in this chapter, is intended to mitigate double taxation of the income of international trade and investment.[22]

Corporations and individual shareholders are generally subject to double taxation; there is no 'integration' of corporate and individual shareholder taxation as has been adopted in some countries. The taxable income of a corporation is taxed. Dividends paid to individual shareholders are also taxed. Dividends are not deductible to the corporation making the payment. There is, however, relief when dividends are paid by a US corporation to a US corporate shareholder. If the US corporate shareholder owns 80% of the US corporation paying the dividend, it will not be subject to tax. If the US corporate shareholder owns between 20% and 80% of the US corporation paying the dividend, only 20% of the intercorporate dividend will be effectively taxed. If the corporate shareholder owns less than 20% of the stock, only 30% of dividends paid will be taxed.[23]

14. Code §§162,212.
15. Code §§213, 165(h).
16. Code §§163,170.
17. Code §164.
18. Code §151.
19. Code §174.
20. Code §24.
21. Code §32.
22. Code §§901 *etseq.*
23. Code §243.

In the calculation of its tax liability, business deductions and credits are available to corporate taxpayers. Corporations have no personal deductions or exemptions, although charitable contributions are allowed within specified limits. Depreciation and amortization of capital assets are not necessarily restricted to traditional accounting techniques.[24] The principal purpose for such provisions is to encourage investment in various segments of the economy.

While cost depletion of mineral resources is the normal accounting approach, US tax law allows taxpayers to take a 'percentage depletion allowance'. The effect is to create a deduction calculated by the application of a statutory percentage to the gross income resulting from the exploitation of the minerals. This deduction is not tied to or limited by the actual cost of the mineral rights.[25]

Corporate reorganization provisions allow for certain corporate transactions to be effected without subjecting either the corporations or their shareholders to tax, even though gain may have been realized in the transaction. Examples include mergers, consolidations, split-ups, spinoffs and recapitalizations. These provisions become a very important part of the planning for major corporate transactions involving changes of stock ownership, either of joining or dividing businesses.[26]

Partnerships are the other principal form of business association used in the United States. They may include limited partners, but a partnership must always have at least one general partner that is subject to potential liability for all partnership debts and liabilities. If there is more than one general partner, each is 'jointly and severally' liable for partnership debts, meaning that any could be sued for the entire debt.

Partnerships are not taxpayers. Results of a partnership operation are allocated to partners usually according to the partnership agreement or to provisions of partnership law or special tax rules. Each partner must include income or may deduct losses allocated thereto. Partnerships file information returns showing the allocation. Limited liability companies (LLCs) are generally taxed as partnerships under current law even though they do not generally require a member who has personal liability for the LLCs obligations.[27]

'Small business corporations' are corporations held by no more than 75 individual US shareholders that may elect to have income and losses allocated to shareholders according to their equity interests under Subchapter S of the Code. The result is somewhat similar to that of a partnership because the entity pays no taxes, and the owners pay tax whether or not a dividend is in fact distributed during the tax year. A number of eligibility limits apply. The corporation may have no corporate shareholders. No shareholder may be a non-resident alien of the United States.

24. Code §§167–168.
25. Code §§611 *etseq.*
26. *See generally* Code §§351 *etseq.*
27. *See generally* Code Subchapter K.

[B] Tax Administration

Federal taxes are administered by the Internal Revenue Service (IRS), which is a part of the US Treasury Department. Tax treaties are normally negotiated by officials of the US Treasury Department. Federal tax cases can be tried in three different federal courts: the United States Tax Court (which has jurisdiction over federal tax cases); the United States District Courts (which are courts of general civil and criminal jurisdiction); and the US Court of Federal Claims (which has jurisdiction in cases brought against the US Government). Either the taxpayer or the IRS may appeal from any of the trial courts to a US Circuit Court of Appeals. Either the taxpayer or the IRS may seek permission of the Supreme Court for a further appeal, but there is no appeal to the Supreme Court as a matter of right.

§7.04 TAXATION OF INBOUND TRANSACTIONS: US TAXATION OF US INCOME OF FOREIGN TAXPAYERS

[A] Definition of Foreign Taxpayer

The taxation of international transactions under US law, as in most countries, depends initially upon determining whether the taxpayer is foreign or domestic. Foreign taxpayers are (with a few limited exceptions) only taxed upon income earned from United States sources. Foreign taxpayers consist primarily of foreign corporations and non-resident aliens. All resident aliens (as determined by immigration laws) will be treated as tax residents. However, some non-residents (as determined by immigration laws) will also be treated as resident aliens for tax purposes under a 'substantial presence test'.[28] Foreign corporations are corporations organized under the laws of any country other than the United States, regardless of the location of its residence, management or investors.[29]

[B] Source Rules

The taxation of foreign taxpayers usually depends upon whether income has been derived from US sources. The source rules for most (but not all) forms of income have been prescribed statutorily and generally yield unsurprising results, although differing in some respects from rules adopted in other countries and from OECD formulations.

The source of income for the performance of services is the place where the services are performed.[30] However, there is a *de minimis* exception for compensation not in excess of USD 3,000 earned by a non-resident alien present in the United States for a period not exceeding ninety days while working for a foreign principal not engaged in a US trade or business.

28. Code §770 1(b).
29. Code§7701(a)(4)and(5).
30. Code §861(a)(3).

Dividends from US corporations are generally treated as US-source income.[31] Dividends from foreign corporations will not be treated as US-source income unless more than 25% of the corporation's gross income during a base period (three years ending with the year preceding the dividend declaration) is attributable to the conduct of a US trade or business. In such case a percentage determined by a comparison of gross income will be treated as US-source income.

Interest payments from residents of the US and domestic corporations are generally characterized as US-source income.[32] There are exceptions for interest paid by US residents which may be attributable to a foreign trade or business. Interest paid by the US trade or business of a foreign corporation will be treated as US-source income.[33]

The source of rental and royalty income is determined by the place where the property is located or used. The source of rental income for tangible property will depend upon the location of the property. The source of royalty income for intellectual property rights will depend upon where the rights are to be used.[34]

The source of income realized from the sale or other disposition of real property (primarily land, buildings and mineral interests) is determined by the location of the property.[35]

The source of income realized from the purchase and sale or other disposition of personal property is generally the residence of the taxpayer.[36] There are, however, several exceptions to the rule of residence. The most important applies to inventory. The source of income from the purchase and sale of inventory depends upon the location of the property when title passes from the buyer to the seller. This so-called 'passage-of-title' test permits a substantial degree of flexibility for taxpayers who, as is usually the case, wish to have income characterized as foreign sourced to minimize US tax liability. The IRS has challenged the application of the test where formal title passage is not accompanied by the transfer of the normal risks of property ownership.[37] Income from the manufacture and sale of property is generally divided between United States and foreign sources when the manufacture and the sale take place in different countries.[38]

When forms of income are realized by foreign taxpayers with respect to which there is no statutory source rule, courts have been required to develop an appropriate interpretation of the sourcing principles. For example, alimony (which is taxed to the recipient under US law) is sourced at the residence of the payer because the obligation to make periodic payments is deemed to be analogous to a debtor's obligation to pay interest.[39]

31. Code §861(a)(2).
32. Code §861(a)(1).
33. Code§884(f)(1).
34. Code §861(a)(4).
35. Code §§861(a)(5), 862(a)(5).
36. Code §865.
37. See *Balanovski v. United States*, 236 F.2d 298 (2d Cir. 1956), *cert. denied*, 352 US 968.
38. Code §863(b)(2) and (3).
39. Rev. Rul. 69–108,1969-1 C.B. 192.

[C] US Trade or Business Income

The net income 'effectively connected' with the operation of a US trade or business by a foreign taxpayer (e.g., the US branch of a foreign corporation) will be subject to normal US income tax rates.[40] Appropriate deductions and credits attributable to the operation of the US trade or business may be taken by the foreign taxpayer in determining US tax liability. As indicated previously, the maximum nominal rate under current law is 35% for both individuals and corporations. Although foreign taxpayers are generally taxed only on US source income, in certain limited circumstances, foreign-source income may be deemed to be effectively connected with the US trade or business and, therefore, will be subject to tax.

There is no general definition of a 'US trade or business' in the Code. Only two rules are statutorily prescribed. The performance of personal services within the US is deemed to constitute a US trade or business unless the *de minimis* exception applies.[41] The use of a stock or commodities broker in the United States will not be treated as a US trade or business even if the broker has discretionary authority to act on behalf of the foreign principal.[42] In all other instances, the existence of a US trade or business will be determined by an examination of all of the relevant facts and circumstances.[43] The term 'trade or business' is used in various parts of the Code and has, therefore, been addressed in many cases. The principal distinction is between doing something to produce income (operating a trade or business) and merely owning something to produce income (passive investor). In general, a taxpayer would not be found to be conducting a US trade or business without a systematic operation involving the production and/or sale of goods and/or services within the US The ownership and rental of real property in the US does not necessarily constitute a US trade or business.[44] Occasional transactions in the US would not normally be treated as a US trade or business.

Under the Code, a US trade or business can exist in certain situations even though the foreign taxpayer does not operate through a permanent establishment. Moreover, the activities of an agent in the US may result in finding that the principal is operating a US trade or business.[45]

Only income 'effectively connected' with the US trade or business will be taxed under this regime. A foreign taxpayer may have other US source income that is not so connected. Such income will either be taxed under the other taxing regime (withholding tax on gross income) or not at all. Whether the effective connection exists will

40. Code§§.871(b)(1),882(a)(1).
41. Code §864(b).
42. Code §864(b)(2).
43. Treasury Regulations (hereinafter referred to as 'Regs'.) §1.864-2(e).
44. *Lewenhaupt v. Commissioner.*, 20 T.C. 151 (1955). Because of the substantial deductions available to investors in real property, foreign taxpayers may prefer to have their real estate investments treated as a US trade or business. The Code authorizes taxpayers to elect such treatment. Code §§871(d); 882(d).
45. *See Handfield v. Commissioner.*, 23 T.C. 633 (1955).

depend upon a nexus between the transaction giving rise to the income and the US trade or business.

Appropriate deductions and credits (those effectively connected with the US trade or business) are generally available to the foreign taxpayer.[46] Substantial controversy, however, attends many situations in which costs are allocated between the US operation and foreign operations of the foreign taxpayer.

Because loan proceeds in effect help to finance all of the assets of a company, special rules were adopted to allocate interest payments. Code §864(e)(2) provides that all 'allocations and apportionments of interest expense shall be made on the basis of assets rather than gross income'. Thus, the amount of interest attributable to the US trade or business will be determined by a comparison of asset values (US trade or business/worldwide).

In order to narrow the difference in tax burdens for foreign corporations that operate in the United States as a branch (rather than through a subsidiary, as discussed in the next segment of this chapter), Section 884 imposes a withholding tax (called a 'branch profits tax') on the repatriation of earnings from a US branch of a foreign corporation.

[D] Withholding Tax on Non-Trade or Business Income

Foreign taxpayers are subject to a 30% tax on the 'amount received from sources within the United States ... as ... interest ...., dividends, rents, wages, premiums, annuities, compensations, remunerations, emoluments, and other fixed or determinable annual or periodical gains, profits, and income ...' if such amounts are not effectively connected with a US trade or business.[47] Such items of income are often referred to by practitioners - and in this chapter - as 'FDAP income' (i.e. fixed, determinable, annual, periodical). The tax is imposed upon the gross amount of the payment. No deductions are allowed. A single, lump-sum royalty payment was held to be 'annual or periodical' and, therefore, subject to the tax.[48] A foreign taxpayer that conducts a US trade or business and also receives FDAP income not effectively connected therewith will be subject to US income taxes under both of the regimes.

To encourage foreign taxpayers to use US banks and savings institutions, payments of interest earned on certain deposits are exempt from tax even though constituting US source interest income.[49] Interest on 'portfolio debt investments' is also exempt from tax.[50] As a result, most interest payments to foreign taxpayers on publicly traded debt securities issued by US companies will not be taxed. However, debt held by a corporation to a lender that owns 10% of the voting power of the borrower will not qualify as portfolio debt regardless of the form in which it is represented. As indicated previously, interest paid on bonds issued by state and local governments is generally

46. Code §882(c)(1).
47. Code§§871(a),881(a).
48. *Wodehouse v. Commissioner*, 337 US 369 (1949).
49. Code§§871(i), 881(d).
50. Code§§871(h), 881(c).

exempt from federal income tax as a political accommodation to reduce the effective cost of borrowing to such governments. As such, payments are not treated as 'income' and the 30% withholding tax does not apply.

If a US corporation earns 80% or more of its gross income from foreign sources as a result of the conduct of a foreign trade or business, a portion of its dividend will not be subject to the withholding tax.[51] The untaxed portion will be determined by the percentage of gross income, for a base period, that derived from such foreign sources.

Gains realized from the sale of property are not treated as FDAP income and have historically not been subject to either taxing regime even though derived from US sources unless effectively connected to a US trade or business.[52]

The 30% tax, although imposed on the foreign taxpayer, is usually collected from the 'withholding agent'.[53] This includes 'all persons, in whatever capacity acting... having the control, receipt, custody, disposal or payment of any of the items of income specified ...' in Sections 1441(b) (for non-resident aliens) and 1442(a) (for foreign corporations). A foreign corporation or non-resident alien could make a payment deemed to be from US sources under applicable statutory provisions. In such cases, the US withholding tax would apply even though the payer is a foreign taxpayer. The withholding obligation applies even if the withholding agent mistakenly pays the entire amount to the foreign taxpayer.

The items of income are those defined by FDAP. Withholding is generally not required if the item of income is effectively connected with a US trade or business. However, the 30% withholding requirement may apply to compensation income earned in the US even though the performance of services constitutes the conduct of a US trade or business. In such cases, the amount withheld is unlikely to be exactly equal to the tax liability. The foreign taxpayer will either be required to pay additional taxes or be entitled to a refund. Also, a US partnership is required to withhold in respect of US trade or business income allocated to a foreign partner whether or not an actual distribution of profits is made. The withholding rate is the highest rate that would apply to the foreign taxpayer.[54]

Under prior law, many foreign taxpayers were able to invest in US real property without incurring any material income tax burdens on their gains. The principal reason was that the mere ownership of income producing real property in the United States did not necessarily constitute the conduct of a US trade or business. When the real property was eventually sold for gain, no tax would apply because the gain, though deemed to be from US sources, was not effectively connected with a US trade or business and did not constitute FDAP income. A number of complicated transactions and/or treaty provisions further assisted in the achievement of such tax avoidance.

Concerned that such arrangements created an unfair and unintended competitive advantage for foreign taxpayers, Congress adopted section 897 of the Code, which provides that gain or loss realized by foreign taxpayers on the disposition of US real

51. Code §§871(i)(2)(B), 881(d).
52. Regs§1.1441-2(a)(3).
53. Code §§1441, 1442.
54. Code §1446.

property interests will be treated generally as if such gain or loss were effectively connected with a US trade or business. In some instances gains realized on the sale of stock in US corporations that hold a substantial percentage of assets in the form of US real property will also be taxed.

The result can spring an unpleasant surprise on foreign investors. For example, gain on the sale of stock in a US corporation by a foreign investor would usually be characterized as foreign source income and, therefore, not subject to US tax. However, if the US corporation qualifies as a 'US real property interest', the gain will be treated as if it were US source income effectively connected with a US trade or business and taxed accordingly. A US corporation will be treated as a US real property interest if at any time during the five years preceding the transaction the fair market value of its US real property interests is 50% of the sum of the fair market value of:

- its US real property interests;
- its interest in real property located outside the United States;
- any other of its assets that are used or held for use in a trade or business.

Note that the test is based upon market valuations and not book value. Accordingly, a corporation could become subject to the tax even though its managers sought to arrange investments in a way to avoid it.[55]

§7.05 OUTBOUND TRANSACTIONS: US TAXATION OF FOREIGN INCOME OF US TAXPAYERS

[A] Worldwide Taxability

US taxpayers include primarily US citizens, resident aliens (as defined for tax purposes) and US corporations. A partnership is not a taxpayer. The results of a partnership operation are allocated to the various partners usually according to the terms of the partnership agreement. Whether a foreign entity is a corporation or a partnership will be determined for US tax purposes by US law.

US taxpayers are generally subject to US tax on income earned from any place in the world, regardless of the currency in which it is paid and regardless of the place where it is deposited. The operation of a foreign branch by a US corporation will result in an immediate US tax liability because of the rule of worldwide taxability.

The apparent harshness of this approach, however, is mitigated by two factors. A foreign subsidiary of a US corporation is not a US taxpayer. US taxes may, therefore, generally be deferred through the use of a foreign corporation. In that event, no US income tax liability will generally arise until profits are repatriated from the foreign corporation. Further, the rule of worldwide taxability is accompanied by a generous provision allowing US taxpayers to credit foreign income taxes paid on foreign earnings against their US income tax liability.

55. Code §897(c)(2).

[B] Entity Classification

Whether a foreign entity is a corporation or partnership for US tax purposes affects the availability of deferral. If a foreign entity is regarded as a partnership, the income accruing to a US participant will be immediately taxable in the United States even if no profits are repatriated. If the foreign entity is regarded as a corporation, US taxes are generally deferred until repatriation.

Forms of business association used in other legal cultures must generally be characterized as either a corporation or a partnership for US tax purposes. In earlier times, the result was sometimes difficult for US joint venturers in foreign operations who could not repatriate earnings because of local legal restrictions or for some other reason, but who were treated under US tax law as partners in a foreign partnership. Under current regulations, however, US investors abroad have rather broad latitude to elect whether to characterize the foreign enterprise as a corporation or a partnership. Except in the case of certain foreign entities that are required to be treated as corporations, the so-called 'check-the-box regulations' allow taxpayers in many instances to choose whether to treat an entity as a corporation or as a pass-through entity, such as a partnership.[56] The result of the choice provides dramatic opportunities for tax planning. For example, a US investor in a limited liability company organized in another country can normally choose whether the company will be treated as a corporation or as a partnership.

[C] The Foreign Tax Credit

The rule of worldwide taxability makes it very likely that income realized by US taxpayers abroad will be subject to double taxation because the country in which the activity or transaction occurs is also entitled to exercise its taxing jurisdiction. To avoid the imposition of additional tax burdens on international transactions, the US taxpayer is entitled to a foreign tax credit in respect of income taxes paid abroad on foreign source income.[57] Although other foreign taxes may be deducted as a business expense by the US taxpayer operating abroad, no credit is available except in the case of income taxes or taxes paid in lieu of an income tax.

The foreign tax credit is available to US taxpayers under the Code. While tax treaties reaffirm the obligation of the United States to take steps to mitigate double taxation, it should be noted that the foreign tax credit provisions are available whether or not a foreign taxpayer is resident of a treaty partner country.

The foreign tax credit can best be demonstrated through a simple example. Suppose that USCo is a US corporation that is allowed under local law to operate through a branch in Argentina, that the US corporate tax rate is 35% and that the Argentine corporate tax rate is 20%. The Argentine branch earns the equivalent of USD 100,000 and pays a tax of USD 20,000 in Argentina. The US tax on the income of USD

56. Regs. §§301.7701-1 to -3.
57. Code §§901 *etseq.*

100,000 is USD 35,000, but USCo is entitled to a credit of USD 20,000. It must pay only USD 15,000 to the US Treasury.

In order to remove an unintended incentive to use foreign branches, a US corporation may enjoy a credit for taxes paid by a foreign corporation in which it owns at least a 10% interest. This 'indirect' credit may also be explained by a simple example. Suppose that USCo decided to organize a subsidiary in Argentina (SubCo) to operate there. When SubCo earns USD 100,000, it pays a tax of USD 20,000 to Argentina. It then declares a dividend of the remaining USD 80,000 to USCo. USCo will report income of USD 100,000 for US tax purposes (the actual dividend of USD 80,000 'grossed up' by the taxes paid in Argentina in respect thereto), but will receive a credit for the USD 20,000 in fact paid by SubCo. Note in this instance that the advantage of deferral may be coupled with the availability of the foreign tax credit.

The foreign tax credit is not intended to serve as a device for reducing the US tax on US-source income. Accordingly, the foreign tax credit, whether direct or indirect, is limited to the US tax on foreign-source income. If the Argentine tax were 40% in the foregoing example, so that taxes of USD 40,000 were paid by the Argentine branch or subsidiary, the maximum foreign tax credit would be limited to USD 35,000 (the US tax on the foreign-source income). The excess credit of USD 5,000 could be carried back to the prior year and, to the extent not fully used, forward for the following 15 years.[58]

The overall limitation is calculated on a worldwide basis. This provides an opportunity for tax avoidance by a US taxpayer with excess foreign tax credits through so-called 'cross-crediting'. In the foregoing example, USCo might use the excess credits paid to Argentina if it also realized other foreign source income that was subject to a lower or no foreign tax. For example, if USCo also earned USD 100,000 in Peru but paid no income tax there, its total foreign source income would be USD 200,000 and its maximum credit would be USD 70,000. As a result, the entire USD 40,000 paid to Argentina would be available as a credit.

Concerned that the overall limitation was not sufficient to deter excessive tax avoidance, Congress has established a number of additional limitations on the availability of the credit. As a result, in 1986 separate limitations (each of which operates in the manner described above) were created for nine different categories of income, separating transactions which could be most easily arranged to soak up excess credits. The complexity generated by so many calculations was the immediate target of criticism, particularly by multinational corporations. In 2004, Congress limited the baskets to two: a general limitation basket and a basket for passive income.[59]

Individual US taxpayers who reside overseas or remain outside of the US for 330 days during a twelve-month period may exclude up to USD 80,000 of their earned income plus a housing cost allowance.[60] The exclusion applies in lieu of the foreign tax credit that might otherwise be available. It does not apply to investment income.

58. Code §904(c).
59. Code §904(d).
60. Code §911.

[D] Anti-Deferral Regimes

[1] Foreign Personal Holding Companies

The basic rules for taxing foreign income earned by US investors provide an opportunity to defer US taxes by using foreign corporations as the vehicle for investment. During the past several decades, some legislators have sought to end this deferral benefit. Although there has been no general limitation on this deferral opportunity, a number of mechanisms have been established to mitigate deferral benefits in circumstances deemed to be abusive. The foreign personal holding company (FPHC) provisions were adopted in the late 1930s to respond to arrangements wherein US investors simply established companies in tax haven jurisdictions to serve as vehicles for their investments.[61]

United States shareholders of foreign personal holding companies were taxed on the undistributed foreign personal holding company income even though no dividend payment had been made. The adjusted basis of the taxpayer's shares in the foreign corporation was increased to reflect the fact that income had been taxed even though no dividend had in fact been paid. The net result was the same as if a dividend were paid and then contributed as capital back to the foreign corporation.

A foreign corporation was to be treated as an FPHC if two criteria were satisfied:

- more than 50% of the value or of the total combined voting power of all classes of the stock of the foreign corporation is owned, directly or indirectly, by five or fewer individuals who are US citizens or residents (the ownership test); and
- at least 60% of its gross income for the taxable year is FPHC income (the income test).

Rules of attribution and constructive ownership applied in connection with the ownership test so that an individual may be treated as owning stock in fact held by certain relatives or entities.

FPHC income included dividends, interest, royalties, gains from the sale or exchange of securities, certain income from trusts and estates, gains from futures transactions and, in certain cases, rents, amounts received for the use of personal property and amounts received under certain personal service contracts.[62]

If a corporation was properly characterized as an FPHC in a taxable year, it was treated as an FPHC until ownership no longer satisfied the ownership test or until FPHC income was less than 50% of the gross income of the foreign corporation for three consecutive years.

61. Code §§551 *etseq.*
62. Code §§543,553.

The foreign personal holding company provisions were repealed at the end of 2004 because it was believed that the Subpart F regime, described below, provides a sufficient defence to income deferral.[63]

[2] Subpart F

During the early 1960s the mechanism of the FHPC provisions was applied to a broader array of corporations and transactions by the adoption of Subpart F of the Code.[64] As a result, Subpart F income earned by controlled foreign corporations (CFCs) and certain other amounts are taxed to US shareholders even though no dividend has been paid. Again, the adjusted basis of the US shareholders is be increased by the amount of the constructive dividend. With the repeal of the FPHC provisions in 2004, Subpart F now stands as the principal defence against unacceptable forms of deferral through the use of foreign corporations.

A foreign corporation is a CFC if 'US shareholders' own more than 50% of the combined voting power of all classes of stock entitled to vote or of the total value of the stock of the corporation.[65] A US shareholder is a US person that owns 10% or more of the total combined voting power of the foreign corporation. A 'US person' includes US citizens, residents, corporations and partnerships.[66] Rules of attribution and constructive ownership apply so that shares held by one person or entity may be deemed held by others.

Code Sec. 954(a) defines Subpart F income to include:

- FPHC income.
- Foreign base company sales income.
- Foreign base company services income.
- Foreign base company oil-related income.

The definitions of each form of Subpart F income are rather complicated. FPHC income is generally the same as for FPHC purposes, but a number of differences exist.[67] Foreign base company sales income arises where a foreign corporation buys from or sells to a related corporation a product that is not to be used in the country where the CFC has been organized.[68] Foreign base company services income arises where a CFC performs services for a related entity in a place other than the place where the CFC was organized.[69]

63. American Jobs Creation Act of 2004 (JOBS Act), §413.
64. Code §§951 *etseq.*
65. Code §957(a).
66. Code §7701(a)(30).
67. Code §954(c).
68. Code §954(d).
69. Code §954(e).

Subpart F income also includes certain insurance income, certain bribes and kickbacks, income derived from participation with certain foreign boycotts and income from certain countries with respect to which economic sanctions have been imposed.[70]

Subpart F will also treat as a constructive dividend amounts invested in US property by CFCs.[71]

[3] Passive Foreign Investment Companies

Section 1291 effectively imposes an interest charge on deferred income created when US shareholders invest in a passive foreign investment company (PFIC). A PFIC is any foreign corporation in which 75% or more of gross income is passive income or the average percentage of the value of assets of the corporation producing passive income is at least 50% of all assets. The interest charge is imposed when the US taxpayer either receives distributions or when the shares are sold or exchanged. The interest is charged on the taxes that were effectively deferred from prior taxable years through the use of the foreign investment vehicle.

§7.06 US TAX TREATY RELATIONS IN THE AMERICAS

[A] The NAFTA Countries

While NAFTA establishes extensive trade and other economic relationships among Canada, Mexico and the United States, there is no tax treaty to which all three countries are party. The United States and Canada have been parties to income tax treaties for many years. The current treaty[72] came into force in 1984 when it replaced a treaty concluded in 1942. The income tax treaty between Mexico and the United States[73] was only concluded in 1993 as part of the process of negotiating the NAFTA arrangements. Because Canada and Mexico are very important trading and investment partners with the United States, the existence of tax treaty relationships is not surprising. However, the relative recentness of the US-Mexico treaty and the fact that the terms of the two treaties are not congruent provide an interesting basis for comparison.

[B] South and Central America

Over time, a series of United States administrations have expressed the desire to establish income tax treaties with countries in South and Central America and have endeavoured to do so. Particular importance has been placed on the development of

70. Code §952.
71. Code §§951(a)(1)(A)(iii), 958.
72. Convention Between the United States of America and Canada with Respect to Taxes on Income and on Capital (US-Canada Treaty).
73. Convention Between the Government of the United States of America and the Government of the United Mexican States for the Avoidance of Double Taxation and the Prevention of Fiscal Evasion with Respect to Taxes on Income (US-Mexico Treaty).

treaties with the large countries to the south having the largest economies: Argentina, Brazil, Chile and Venezuela. The results have, however, been very underwhelming. Although negotiations have been undertaken with different countries over the years, the only income tax treaty in force between the United States and a South American country is with Venezuela.[74] While some hoped that the establishment of this treaty in 1999 was the harbinger of a wave of new treaties between the United States and Latin America and negotiations with a number of countries have occurred, no treaty has since been concluded between the United States and other countries in the region.

[C] The Caribbean

The United States is party to income tax treaties with three Caribbean island nations: Barbados; Jamaica; and Trinidad and Tobago.[75] Obviously, the flow of investment is primarily from the United States to those countries. As a result, the flow of investment earnings is primarily from the island nations to the United States. One reasonably might expect, therefore, that treaty terms would be materially different from those with the NAFTA partners and the oil-producing country of Venezuela.

[D] Bermuda: A Special Case

There is an income tax treaty in force between the United States and Bermuda.[76] Because Bermuda has in the past been used as at least a partial tax haven by US companies and investors and because it is the *situs* of many insurance companies, including 'captive insurance companies' that insure risks for their US affiliates, the terms of the US-Bermuda Treaty are very restricted compared to other income tax treaties. The treaty, established in 1988, exempts Bermuda insurance enterprises from certain US income and excise taxes on premiums earned from insuring risks in the United States. Because of its limited scope, the US-Bermuda Tax Treaty is not discussed further in this chapter.

---

74. Convention Between the Government of the United States of America and the Government of the Republic of Venezuela for the Avoidance of Double Taxation and the Prevention of Fiscal Evasion with Respect to Taxes on Income and Capital (US-Venezuela Treaty).
75. Convention Between Barbados and the United States of America for the Avoidance of Double Taxation and the Prevention of Fiscal Evasion with Respect to Taxes on Income (US-Barbados Treaty).
Convention Between the Government of the United States of America and the Government of Jamaica for the Avoidance of Double Taxation and the Prevention of Fiscal Evasion with Respect to Taxes on Income (US-Jamaica Treaty).
Convention Between the Government of the United States of America and the Government of Trinidad and Tobago for the Avoidance of Double Taxation, the Prevention of Fiscal Evasion with Respect to taxes on Income, and the Encouragement of International Trade and Investment (US-Trinidad and Tobago Treaty).
76. Convention Between the Government of the United States of America and the Government of the United Kingdom of Great Britain and Northern Ireland (on Behalf of the Government of Bermuda) Relating to the Taxation of Insurance Enterprises and Mutual Assistance in Tax Matters (US-Bermuda Treaty).

§7.07 PROVISIONS FAVOURING COUNTRY OF RESIDENCE

[A] Withholding Tax Provisions

[1] In General

Most countries impose withholding taxes on at least some forms of passive investment income realized by foreign taxpayers. Income tax treaties commonly provide for reduced rates on withholding taxes or the complete exemption of certain categories of income from any withholding tax obligation, thus effectively establishing primary tax jurisdiction in the country of residence rather than source.

All of the treaties in force between the United States and countries in the Western Hemisphere provide either for reduced withholding rates or in some instances for total exemption from withholding tax regimes. The principal rationale for lesser rates and/or exemption is to simplify the process of taxing income from international investment. It must be noted, however, that the revenue effects on the two treaty partners are not necessarily equal. The flow of investment from the wealthier to the less wealthy country is likely to exceed the flow in the other direction. As a result, the flow of investment income from the less to the more wealthy country is likely to exceed the flow in the other direction. The likely result is that the treasury of the less wealthy country will lose more potential tax revenues than the treasury of the more wealthy country. One might expect this disparity to be reflected in different treaty provisions. As the following discussion indicates, however, the treaties effected between the United States and her Western Hemisphere neighbours do not reflect the substantial differences in the size and wealth of the various economies or the relative flows of investment and investment income.

[2] Repatriation of Corporate Profits

[a] Dividends

Most of the bilateral income tax treaties to which the United States is a party reduce the permissible withholding tax on dividends not effectively connected with the conduct of a trade or business. Such treaties usually also establish a lower permissible withholding rate for 'direct investment', as distinguished from 'portfolio investment' when made by corporations. A number of recent treaty negotiations have resulted in the total exemption of at least some dividend payments from withholding taxes. Although the treaties between the United States and her NAFTA partners are not identical, both provide for reduced withholding rates and distinguish between direct investors and portfolio investors.

The US-Canada Treaty provides that the maximum withholding rate for dividends will be 15% generally, but only 5% if the payee is a corporation owning at least

10% of the company paying the dividend.[77] The US-Mexico Treaty, when it was originally concluded, provided for a general withholding rate of only 10% with the lesser rate of 5% for dividends paid to a shareholder that is a corporation owning at least 10% of the voting stock of the company paying the dividends.[78] However, an amendment to the US-Mexico Treaty concluded in 2003 provides for a complete exemption from the withholding tax on dividends if the shareholder is a company owning at least 80% of the voting stock of the dividend-paying company for a year prior to the payment of the dividend. This modification implemented an understanding that the rates would be adjusted to lower levels if other treaties establishing such lower rates were brought into force.

The treaty with Venezuela provides for a general withholding rate of 15% and a 5% rate for corporate shareholders owning at least 10% of the voting stock of the corporation paying the dividend.[79]

The treaties between the United States and her three Caribbean treaty partners also provide for reduced withholding rates on a reciprocal basis, although the provisions are somewhat different in each treaty. The treaty with Barbados reduces the rate to 15% generally and 5% for direct corporate investors.[80] The treaty with Jamaica reduces the general withholding tax rate to 15% and 10% for direct corporate investors.[81] The treaty with Trinidad and Tobago provides for a withholding rate of 25% generally and 10% for direct investors. The 10% rate is only available, however, if the payee corporation has owned at least 10% of the pay or company for the entire taxable year preceding the year in which the dividend is paid. Further, the 10% rate is not available if more than 25% of the distributing corporation's gross income consisted of interest and dividends during the prior taxable year that did not derive from certain banking, insurance or financing businesses.[82]

[b] Branch Profits Taxes

The branch profits tax, as indicated previously, is a tax imposed on the repatriation of profits by a foreign corporation from its US branch operation. The rationale for the tax is to equate the overall US income tax burdens upon foreign corporations that operate directly in the United States with the tax burden that results when a foreign corporation establishes a US subsidiary to implement its business interests. If a subsidiary were established, a withholding tax would apply on dividend distributions. The branch profits tax is considered to be the effective equivalent of such a withholding tax, even though the repatriation of earnings from a branch operation is not normally considered to be an event of income realization. The statutory rate of the branch profits tax is 30%. However, because of the rationale for its adoption, the Code provides that the branch

77. US-Canada Treaty, Art. X.
78. US-Mexico Treaty, Art. 10.
79. US-Venezuela Treaty, Art. 10.
80. US-Barbados Treaty, Art. 10.
81. US-Jamaica Treaty, Art. 10.
82. US-Trinidad and Tobago Treaty, Art. 12.

profits tax rate be the same as the rate that would apply under a treaty with the taxpayer's country of residence if it were receiving a dividend distribution from a wholly owned US subsidiary.[83]

The US-Canada Treaty provides express authority for the imposition of a branch profits tax not exceeding 5%. The tax may be applied against after-tax profits in excess of operating losses of the permanent establishment not reinvested in the taxing country in excess of CAD 500,000 or the US equivalent.[84] The US-Mexico Treaty expressly authorizes the imposition of a branch profits tax at the same rates that would apply if dividends were paid to a parent corporation from a corporation organized within the taxing country.[85] However, the 2003 amendment also provides for the exemption from the branch profits tax, which is consistent with the rationale for the tax since the protocol would exempt dividends from paid by a wholly owned subsidiary in the other country.

The US-Venezuela Treaty also expressly authorizes a branch profits tax.[86] The treaties with Barbados and Jamaica do not explicitly authorize a branch profits tax. However, the US-Trinidad and Tobago Treaty authorizes the countries to impose a 10% withholding tax on branch profits.[87]

[3] Interest

Many of the bilateral income tax treaties to which the United States is party exempt interest payments from the imposition of a withholding tax. One of the policy justifications for the exemption is that the domestic borrower is likely to bear the cost of any such withholding tax because international lenders often require an after-tax interest rate.

The treaties with Canada and Mexico do not, however, provide a general exemption. The US-Canada Treaty provides that interest payments are subject to withholding tax in the source country, but at a maximum rate of 10%.[88] Interest paid by or to governmental entities is wholly exempt. Moreover, no withholding tax is imposed if the debt arises from the sale on credit by the taxpayer of any equipment, merchandise of services except where such sale or debt is between related persons.

The US-Mexico Treaty provides for a general withholding tax rate of 15%, but there are several exceptions. The withholding tax rate shall not exceed 4.9% for interest derived from certain obligations. These include loans granted by banks, including investment banks and savings banks, and insurance companies and bonds or securities that are regularly and substantially traded on a recognized securities market. A 10% rate applies if the interest is paid by banks, including investment and savings banks, or paid by the purchaser of machinery and equipment to the seller of the

83. Code §884(e).
84. US-Canada Treaty, Art. X(6).
85. US-Mexico Treaty, Art 11 A.
86. US-Venezuela Treaty, Art. 11 A.
87. US-Trinidad and Tobago Treaty, Art. 12.
88. US-Canada Treaty, Art. XI.

machinery and equipment in connection with a sale on credit.[89] The US-Venezuela treaty provides for a general withholding tax rate on interest of 10%. However, interest is subject to a withholding tax rate of 4.95% in the source country if the payee is any financial institution including an insurance company.[90]

The US-Barbados Treaty provides for a withholding tax rate on interest of 5%.[91] The US-Jamaica Treaty provides for a withholding rate of 12.5%.[92] The US-Trinidad and Tobago Treaty authorizes a withholding rate of 15%.[93]

[4] Royalties

Many of the treaties concluded in recent years by the United States provide for an exemption from withholding taxes for royalty payments. However, the treaties with NAFTA partners authorize a withholding tax of 10% on royalties.[94] Nevertheless, the US-Canada Treaty provides an exemption for certain royalty payments: copyright royalties regarding literary, dramatic, musical or artistic work (other than payments in respect of motion pictures and works on film videotape or other means of reproduction for use in connection with television); royalties pertaining to computer software; royalties for patents and information concerning industrial, commercial or scientific experience; and royalties with respect to broadcasting as may be agreed between the parties. A 5% withholding tax is authorized in respect of royalties for the use of industrial, commercial or scientific equipment.[95]

The US-Venezuela Treaty also distinguishes among different intellectual property interests giving rise to royalty payments. A 5% withholding rate is authorized for royalties for the use of industrial, commercial or scientific equipment. A 10% withholding tax rate is authorized on royalties for the use of any copyright of literary, dramatic, musical, artistic, or scientific work including cinematographic films, tapes and other means of image or sound reproduction, any patent, trademark, design or model, plan, secret formula or process.[96]

The US-Barbados Treaty authorizes a withholding rate on royalties of 5%.[97] The US-Jamaica Treaty authorizes a withholding rate on royalties of 10%.[98] The US-Trinidad and Tobago Income Tax Treaty authorizes a withholding rate on royalties of 15%, except for royalties derived from copyrights or rights to produce or reproduce any literary, dramatic, musical, or artistic work which are exempt from a withholding tax.[99]

89. US-Mexico Treaty, Art. 11.
90. US-Venezuela Treaty, Art. 11.
91. US-Barbados Treaty, Art 11.
92. US-Jamaica Treaty, Art. 11.
93. US-Trinidad and Tobago Treaty, Art. 13.
94. US-Canada Treaty, Art XI; US-Mexico Treaty, Art 11.
95. US-Canada Treaty, Art. XII.
96. US-Venezuela Treaty, Art. 12.
97. US-Barbados Treaty, Art. 12.
98. US-Jamaica Treaty, Art. 12.
99. US-Trinidad and Tobago Treaty, Art. 14.

[B] Trade or Business Income

[1] The Permanent Establishment Requirement

As indicated previously, the United States (unlike some other countries) taxes the net income derived from the conduct of a US trade or business by a foreign taxpayer (such as a non-resident alien or a foreign corporation) whether or not the trade or business is conducted through a permanent establishment. The income tax treaties, however, establish an important exception to the statutory rules. Virtually all income tax treaties to which the United States is a party, provide that trade or business income will only be taxed if the foreign taxpayer is conducting the trade or business through a permanent establishment. Virtually all treaties also include definitional provisions setting forth criteria for recognizing a permanent establishment and also a list of situations that will not be so treated.

The US-Canada Treaty defines a permanent establishment as a fixed place of business through which the business of a resident is wholly or partly implemented. It expressly includes a branch, an office, a factory, a workshop, a mine, an oil or gas well, a quarry or any other place of extracting natural resources. A permanent establishment is also created by a person who habitually exercises authority to conclude contracts in the taxing country on behalf of the taxpayer resident in the other country. As is often the case, the use of certain independent agents, such as a broker or general commission agent acting in the normal course of its business will not result in the existence of a permanent establishment.[100]

There are certain activities that will not of themselves be deemed to constitute a permanent establishment. These include a fixed place of business used solely for certain activities such as the use of facilities for the purpose of storage, display or delivery of goods or merchandise. A building site or construction project will only become a permanent establishment if it continues for more than a year. The use of an installation or drilling rig or ship to explore for or exploit natural resources will constitute a permanent establishment only if such use continues for more than three months in any twleve-month period. Under the US-Canada Treaty, no business profits will be attributed to the permanent establishment 'by reason of [its] use ..... for either the mere purchase of goods or merchandise or the mere provision of executive, managerial or administrative facilities or services'.[101]

The US-Mexico Treaty reflects a few differences in detail. For example, a building site, construction project or drilling rig or ship used for natural resource exploration and exploitation will be treated as a permanent establishment only if the activity lasts more than six months. Under the US-Mexico Treaty, a permanent establishment will be found where a person habitually processes goods or merchandise on behalf of the taxpayer even if that person has no habitual contracting authority. The US-Mexico Treaty also provides that a permanent establishment exists if a taxpayer constituting an

100. US-Canada Treaty, Arts V and VII.
101. US-Canada, Art. VII(4).

insurance enterprise collects premiums or insures risks through a representative other than an independent agent.[102]

The US-Venezuela Treaty provides a number of modest variations. A permanent establishment will include the provision of services, including consultancy services, by an enterprise through employees or other personnel where such activities continue for more than 183 days in any twelve-month period. A building or construction site or drilling rig or ship will be considered a permanent establishment if it continues for more than 183 days during any twelve-month period. The US-Venezuela Treaty explicitly provides that time spent by a subcontractor must be considered as time spent by a general contractor. The safe harbour for the storage, display or delivery of goods or merchandise is unavailable if the taxpayer maintains sales personnel within the country.[103]

The treaties with the Caribbean countries all contain permanent establishment provisions that are similar to those reflected in the treaties discussed above.[104]

[2] Provision of Services by Individuals

As indicated previously, the provision of services within the United States by a resident alien, with a modest *de minimis* exception, is treated as a US trade or business. However, most of the treaties provide limitations on the taxation of compensation earned by residents of the treaty party that are conceptually analogous to the permanent establishment provisions applicable to trade or business income. The applicable standards depend upon whether the individual taxpayer is regarded as an 'employee' or as an 'independent contractor'. It should be noted in this connection that the international labour flow in the Americas presents a rather different situation than that presented by international trade and investment.

The US-Canada Treaty provides that no tax may be imposed upon an independent contractor unless the individual has a fixed base regularly available to him within the country.[105] The US-Mexico Treaty contains a similar provision, but also allows a tax on the income of an independent contractor who is present for at least 183 days within a twelve-month period regardless of the availability of a fixed base.[106] The US-Venezuela Treaty contains provisions similar to those in the US-Canada Treaty.[107]

All three of the treaties cited above also restrict the power to tax employees who reside in the other country but who are working in the taxing country. The US-Canada treaty provides that income up to USD 10,000 will be taxable only in the country of residence (and not the country of source) if the individual is present in the source country for not more than 183 days. These limitations apply only if the employer is not a resident of the taxing nation or a permanent establishment or fixed base of such

102. US-Mexico Treaty, Arts 5 and 7.
103. US-Venezuela Treat, Arts 5 and 7.
104. US-Barbados Treaty, Arts 5 and 7; US-Jamaica Treaty, Arts 5 and 7; US-Trinidad and Tobago Treaty, Arts 8 and 9.
105. US-Canada Treaty, Art. XIV.
106. US-Mexico Treaty, Art. 14.
107. US-Venezuela Treaty, Art. 14.

employer in the source country. Remuneration from employment exercised in both nations on a ship, aircraft, motor vehicle or train will be taxable only the country of residence.[108] The provisions of the US-Mexico Treaty are very similar.[109] However, there is no monetary limitation on the exemption and no specific provision dealing with employees in international transport. The US-Venezuela Treaty is similar to the treaty with Canada and includes a provision dealing with employees who work on ships or aircraft in international traffic.[110]

The Caribbean treaties are somewhat different. The US-Barbados Treaty provides that income of an independent contractor will only be taxed if the individual has a fixed base regularly available for performing activities, if the individual is present in the country for ninety days or more in a taxable year or if the net income attributable to the services performed exceeds USD 5,000.[111] The US-Barbados Treaty provides that employment income will be taxed only if the employee from the other country is in the United States for 183 days or less and receives income not exceeding USD 5,000.1[112]The US-Jamaica Treaty includes the same provisions.[113]

The US-Trinidad and Tobago Treaty does not distinguish between employees and independent contractors. Income from the performance of services in the other country will not be taxed unless the individual was present for more than 183 days during the year and one of two conditions is satisfied: the income cannot be deducted in calculating the profits of a permanent establishment, and the individual earned less than USD 3,000 during the year.[114]

§7.08 LIMITATIONS ON TREATY BENEFITS

[A] Problem of 'Treaty Shopping'

Tax administrators in many countries are concerned about the practice of 'treaty shopping' in which individuals and entities are able to exploit treaty benefits in ways not contemplated by the parties at the time the treaties were negotiated. Historically, corporations organized under the laws of a treaty country were entitled to the benefits of the treaty. Thus, by establishing a corporate entity in a treaty country, investors residing in a third country without treaty advantages could effectively reduce taxes on their income. Of course, the device would not reduce tax burdens to the extent that the country of incorporation would impose its own taxes on the newly created corporation.

A well-known example of treaty shopping is the use of a financing subsidiary to borrow funds. Suppose, for example, that a US corporation wishes to borrow from a foreign lender in a non-treaty country. The 30% withholding tax would apply to interest payments, and in many situations the lender would insist that the borrower

108. US-Canada Treaty, Art. XV.
109. US-Mexico Treaty, Art. 15.
110. US-Venezuela Treaty, Art. 15.
111. US-Barbados Treaty, Art. 14
112. US-Barbados Treaty, Art. 15.
113. US-Jamaica Treaty, Arts 14 and 15.
114. US-Trinidad and Tobago Treaty, Art. 17.

effectively bear the burden of the additional expense. If the US borrower would establish a subsidiary corporation in a treaty country where interest payments were exempt from the withholding tax, interest payments from the US parent to the foreign subsidiary would not be subject to the withholding tax. Thus, the foreign subsidiary could borrow from the foreign lender and in turn loan the amount borrowed to the US parent corporation. If the treaty exempted interest payments and if the country in which the financing subsidiary had been created imposed no withholding tax, the withholding tax would be effectively avoided.

A similar advantage might be sought by a foreign investor from a non-treaty country contemplating an equity investment in the United States that would produce dividends or the owner of intellectual property to be licensed for use in the United States.

The greatest concern about treaty shopping obviously arises in situations when tax havens are treaty partners or when the domestic laws of treaty partners, although not generally regarded as tax havens, provide for little or no tax on the intermediary entity.

[B] Termination of Treaties

A treaty in force between the Netherlands Antilles and the United States (albeit an old treaty initially established between the Netherlands and the United States prior to independence of the Netherlands Antilles) was at one time a prime vehicle for treaty shopping because interest payments under the treaty were exempt from the withholding tax and the Netherlands Antilles was regarded as a tax haven. The treaty was terminated by the United States in 1987, and US officials indicated that they would take similar action if other treaties were widely used as vehicles for shopping their benefits to taxpayers not intended to be covered by the treaty.

[C] Treaty Limitations

During the past several decades, US negotiators have insisted upon the inclusion of specific provisions limiting the treaty benefits to classes of taxpayers having a substantive connection with the treaty partner. Such concerns have led to the inclusion of limitation provisions in virtually all of the treaties concluded by the United States during this period. However, the separate negotiations have produced different formulations in the various treaties. Many are very long and very detailed.

A provision limiting benefits under the US-Canada Treaty was added by a Protocol signed in 1995.1[115] The point of the limitation is to endeavour to maintain treaty benefits for Canadian residents, entities owned and controlled by Canadian residents, and entities traded on Canadian stock exchanges. Somewhat different provisions are found in the US-Mexico Treaty, which applies separate criteria in the

115. US-Canada Treaty, Art. XXIXA.

case of dividends, branch profits taxes, interest and royalties.[116] US-Venezuela Treaty also includes provisions limiting its application.[117] The US-Trinidad and Tobago Treaty contains no provision defining the limit on treaty benefits. The treaties with Barbados and Jamaica include limitation provisions that are less complex than those set forth in the other Western Hemisphere treaties, which is often the case with older treaties.[118] Concerns with the exploitation of the US-Barbados Treaty led to the conclusion of an amendment in 2004 which substituted a lengthy and complex 'modern' limitation article for the version contained in the original treaty.[119]

[D] Domestic Law Limitations

[1] Judicial Decisions

Even in circumstances in which the treaty does not itself limit the availability of its benefits, the IRS has taken the position that treaty benefits should not be recognized. In a number of cases, for example, the IRS has argued that intermediary entities established for the purpose of exploiting treaty benefits should be disregarded when analysing the tax consequences of transactions. In such a case, for example, the financing subsidiary described previously would be disregarded. The loan described previously would be treated as a loan directly from the foreign lender to the US borrower. Interest payments would in turn be treated as if made from the US borrower to the foreign lender. Since the treaty would not apply to the foreign lender, the statutory withholding tax of 30% would apply to interest payments. The IRS position was most likely to succeed when the intermediary corporation had no other assets, no business activities and was required to pay over the proceeds of its borrowing immediately to the 'true' borrower.[120]

[2] Anti-Conduit Regulations

In 1993, Congress authorized the IRS to promulgate regulations to defend against unacceptable degrees of treaty shopping.[121] The regulations authorize rules allowing for the 'recharacterisation' of multiple-party financing transactions as a transaction directly among any two or more of the parties to it if such characterization 'is appropriate to prevent avoidance of any tax'. Acting on this authority, the IRS promulgated the so-called 'anti-conduit' regulations.[122] The effect of these regulations, when applied, will be to deny treaty benefits in situations in which the text of the treaty

116. US-Mexico Treaty, Art 17.
117. US-Venezuela Treaty, Art. 17.
118. US-Barbados Treaty, Art. 22; US-Jamaica Treaty, Art. 17.
119. Second Protocol Amending the US-Barbados Treaty, 14 July 2004.
120. *See*, e.g. *Aiken Industries, Inc. v. Commissioner*, 56 T.C. 925 (1971).
121. Code §7701(l).
122. Reg. §§1.881-3,-4.

does not so limit the treaty's application and to situations in which benefits would not have been disregarded under the judicial decisions cited in the previous section.

As indicated previously, the United States applies the 'later in time' doctrine when there is a conflict between the provisions of a treaty and a statute. It is possible that the anti-conduit regulations will conflict with existing treaty provisions. It is not clear whether US courts would apply the regulations if they conflict with existing treaty commitments.

§7.09 PROVISIONS FAVOURING SOURCE COUNTRY

[A] In General

Income tax treaties normally include a commitment by the parties to take steps to mitigate double taxation. The reduction or elimination of withholding taxes, discussed in the prior section of this chapter, favours the country of residence. The alternative is for the residence country to take steps to mitigate taxes on income deriving from the source country.

All of the income tax treaties in force between the United States and her Western Hemisphere neighbours include a provision committing the parties to take steps to mitigate double taxation.[123] As described in part V.C. of this chapter, the United States provides such mitigation statutorily through the foreign tax credit. It is not necessary, therefore, for a taxpayer to realize income in a treaty country to benefit from the foreign tax credit provisions.

[B] Tax Sparing

Among the requirements for a foreign tax credit is that foreign taxes must actually have been paid by the taxpayer. Thus, if the US taxpayer pays no foreign income tax, no US credit is available. This rather unsurprising conclusion has been the subject of some discussion and debate. Countries, particularly a number of developing countries, that proffer tax holidays to attract foreign investment recognize that the operation of the foreign tax credit mechanism under US law effectively negates at least a portion of the tax incentive that they have chosen to grant to US investors. In fact, the granting of a tax holiday in such circumstances can have the effect of increasing revenues to the United States by reducing foreign tax credits otherwise available.

There are treaties in force between various countries that provide for 'tax sparing'. Under a regime of tax sparing, a taxpayer would receive a credit, not only for taxes actually paid, but for taxes that would have been paid but for the provision of a

123. *See*, e.g. Art 24 of the US-Mexico Treaty, which provides for a direct foreign tax credit and an indirect foreign tax credit for corporate shareholders owning at least 10% of a company paying dividends. Both provisions effectively reiterate provisions statutorily available in the United States in any event. *See also* US-Canada Treaty, Art. 24; US-Venezuela Treaty, Art. 24; US-Barbados Treaty, Art. 23; US-Jamaica Treaty, Art. 24; US-Trinidad and Tobago Treaty, Art. 4.

tax holiday by the country in which an investment is being made. No treaty to which the United States is a party provides for such tax sparing. The treaty negotiated between the United States and Trinidad and Tobago included such a provision. However, the Senate approved the treaty with a reservation with respect to the provision. The treaty now in force contains no provision for tax sparing.

§7.10 COOPERATION IN TAX ADMINISTRATION

[A] Bilateral Income Tax Treaties

Bilateral income tax treaties commonly provide for cooperation in the administration of the tax laws of the treaty partners. Such cooperation may take many forms, including the exchange of relevant information and efforts to deal with issues that may arise with a view to preventing double taxation.

The treaties in force between the United States and her hemispheric partners all include commitments to advance such cooperation. Article 26 of the US-Canada Treaty provides that a person may present a case to the competent authority in the treaty nation in which the person is a resident if the person is subject to taxation that is inconsistent with treaty provisions. If the person is not a resident of either treaty country, he/she may present his/her case in the country of which he/she is a national.

The US-Canada Treaty provides that the competent authority of a treaty nation that cannot arrive at a satisfactory resolution of a case shall endeavour to resolve the matter by mutual agreement. The competent authority of the treaty nation in which the case is presented must receive notice of such case within six years from the end of the taxable year to which the case relates. Agreements must be implemented notwithstanding any time or other procedural limits in the domestic law of either country.

The treaty, moreover, enumerates a series of areas in which the treaty partners are committed to apply the mutual agreement procedures:

(a) To the same attribution of profits to a resident of one country and its permanent establishment in the other.
(b) To the same allocation of income, deductions, credits or allowances.
(c) To the same determination of the source and same characterization, of particular items of income.
(d) To a common meaning of any term used in the treaty.
(e) To the elimination of double taxation with respect to income distributed by an estate or trust.
(f) To the elimination of taxation with respect to a partnership.
(g) To eliminate double estate taxation.
(h) To increases in any dollar amounts referred to in the treaty to reflect monetary or economic developments.

The treaty also commits the parties to endeavour to collect for the other amounts necessary to ensure that relief is not provided to persons not entitled thereto.

Collecting taxes owing from a person or entity in another country is a major problem of tax administration. The so-called 'revenue rule' holds that comity under international law and practice does not extend to allowing litigation by a foreign government to enforce its tax laws. Designed to increase the likelihood of successful tax collection, the US-Canada Treaty also contains a very unusual provision in which the parties undertake to assist each other in the collection of taxes covered by the treaty.[124] Both treaty parties agree thereunder to assist in the collection of income taxes owed in the other State. The mechanism is triggered by the submission of a request for assistance in collection of a revenue claim certified to be finally determined. If the request is accepted, the requested State treats the revenue claim as a tax liability subject to the usual collection powers in that State. Such provisions exist in only five treaties to which the United States is a party, but none are included in other treaties with countries in the Western Hemisphere. Even when such provisions are included in a treaty, in practice they are very seldom invoked.

Finally, the US-Canada Treaty includes an agreement by the parties to exchange information and, in certain cases, to seek information requested by the other party.[125] This commitment is, however, subject to several limitations. A party is not required to carry out administrative measures at variance with the laws and administrative practice of that country, to supply information which is not obtainable under the laws of the country, or to supply information that would disclose information relating to trade, business, industrial, commercial or professional secret or trade processes, or information the disclosure of which would be contrary to public policy.

The US-Mexico treaty provides that a person may present a case to the competent authority in the country in which he is a resident or national.[126] The commitment to use the mutual agreement procedure is, however, more broadly stated to include 'any difficulties or doubts arising as to the interpretation or application' of the treaty. As with many treaties concluded in recent years, the US-Mexico treaty also contemplates the reference of unresolved disputes to arbitration, but does not commit the parties to submit such disputes to binding arbitration. No arbitration cases have been reported.

The US-Venezuela Treaty provides that a person may present a case to the competent authority of either treaty nation and that they are committed to endeavour to reach agreement on issues of allocation, characterization, source rules, definitions, the application of fines, penalties and interest and 'any increase in specific amounts ..... to reflect economic or monetary developments'.[127] It also provides for the exchange of information, and includes limitations similar to those described in the US-Canada Treaty.

The treaties in force with the three Caribbean countries also provide for mutual agreement procedures and the exchange of information.[128]

124. US-Canada Treaty, Art. XXVIA.
125. US-Canada Treaty, Art. XXVII.
126. US-Mexico Treaty, Art 26.
127. US-Venezuela Treaty, Art 16.
128. US-Barbados Treaty, Arts 25 and 26; US-Jamaica Treaty, Arts 26 and 27; US-Trinidad and Tobago Treaty, Arts 23 and 24.

More recent treaties include an undertaking by the treaty partners to consider the use of binding arbitration in situations when the mutual agreement procedures fail to produce a mutual agreement. Article 26(5) of the US-Mexico Treaty provides, for example:

> If any difficulty or doubt arising as to the interpretation or application of this Convention cannot be resolved by the competent authorities pursuant to the previous paragraphs of this Article, the case may, if both competent authorities and the taxpayer(s) agree, be submitted for arbitration, provided that the taxpayer agrees in writing to be bound by the decision of the arbitration board. The decision of the arbitration board in a particular case shall be binding on both States with respect to that case. The procedures shall be established between the States by notes to be exchanged through diplomatic channels. The provisions of this paragraph shall have effect after the States have so agreed through the exchange of diplomatic notes.

A protocol to the US-Mexico treaty, moreover, sets forth a rather elaborate procedure for invoking the arbitration provision.[129] However, the treaty does not obligate the two countries to submit to arbitration, and no arbitration proceedings have yet taken place.

129. With reference to paragraph 5 of Art. 26 (mutual agreement procedure)
(a)After a period of three years after the entry into force of this Convention, the competent authorities shall consult in order to determine whether it is appropriate to make the exchange of diplomatic notes referred to in paragraph 5 of Article 26 (mutual agreement procedure).
(b)If the competent authorities of both States agree to submit a disagreement regarding the interpretation or application of this Convention in a specific case to arbitration according to paragraph 5 of Article 26, the following procedures will apply:
(i) If, in applying paragraphs 1 to 4 of Article 26, the competent authorities fail to reach an agreement within two years of the date on which the case was submitted to one of the competent authorities, they may agree to invoke arbitration in a specific case, but only after fully exhausting the procedures available for paragraphs 1 to 4 of Article 26. The competent authorities will not accede to arbitration with respect to matters concerning the tax policy or domestic law of either State, (ii) The competent authorities shall establish an arbitration board for each specific case in the following manner:
A. An arbitration board shall consist of not fewer than three members. Each competent authority shall appoint the same number of members, and these members shall agree on the appointment of the other member(s). The competent authorities may issue further instructions regarding the criteria for selecting the other member(s) of the arbitration board.
B. Arbitration board member(s) (and their staffs) upon their appointment must agree in writing to abide by and be subject to the applicable confidentiality and disclosure provisions of both States and the Convention. In case those provisions conflict, the most restrictive condition will apply.
(iii) The competent authorities may agree on and instruct the arbitration board regarding specific rules of procedure, such as appointment of a chairman, procedures for reaching a decision, establishment of time limits, etc. Otherwise, the arbitration board shall establish its own rules of procedure consistent with generally accepted principles of equity.
(iv) Taxpayers and/or their representatives shall be afforded the opportunity to present their views to the arbitration board.
(v) The arbitration board shall decide each specific case on the basis of the Convention, giving due consideration to the domestic laws of the States and the principles of international law. The arbitration board will provide to the competent authorities an explanation of its decision. The decision of the arbitration board shall be binding on both States and the taxpayer(s) with respect to that case. While the decision of the arbitration board shall not have precedential effect, it is expected that such decisions ordinarily will be taken into account in subsequent

[B] Tax Information Exchange Agreements

The United States is a party to many tax information exchange agreements (TIEAs) with her neighbours in the Western Hemisphere. TIEAs are executive agreements authorized by statute that have not been approved as such by the Senate. Nevertheless, as indicated previously, they represent treaty commitments by the United States.

TIEAs do not modify the substantive rules of taxation in either country. Rather, they provide for rather extensive cooperation in the eliciting of information and other assistance for each country in the enforcement of its tax laws. The United States has been particularly concerned about the use of Caribbean island nations for purposes of tax evasion and money laundering. As a result, substantial energy has been devoted to the negotiation of TIEAs with such countries. At the end of 2004, there were TIEAs between the United States and:

- Antigua and Barbuda
- Aruba
- Barbados
- Bermuda
- Costa Rica
- Dominica
- Dominican Republic
- Grenada
- Guyana
- Honduras
- Jamaica
- Mexico
- Netherlands Antilles
- Peru
- St Lucia
- Trinidad and Tobago.

One of the most recent TIEAs was concluded by the United States with Antigua and Barbuda. It is representative of the kind of arrangements commonly found in TIEAs.

---

competent authority cases involving the same taxpayer(s), the same issue(s), and substantially similar facts, and may also be taken into account in other cases where appropriate.
(vi) Costs for the arbitration procedure will be borne in the following manner:
A.each State shall bear the cost of remuneration for the member(s) appointed by it, as well as for its representation in the proceedings before the arbitration board;
B.the cost of remuneration for the other member(s) and all other costs of the arbitration board shall be shared equally between the States; and
C.the arbitration board may decide on a different allocation of costs.
However, if it deems appropriate in a specific case, in view of the nature of the case and the roles of the parties, the competent authority of one of the States may require the taxpayer(s) to agree to bear that State's share of the costs as a prerequisite for arbitration.
(vii) The competent authorities may agree to modify or supplement these procedures; however, they shall continue to be bound by the general principles established herein.

The heart of the commitment is found in Article 4 of the treaty. It commits the competent authorities of the two countries to:

> [E]xchange information to administer and enforce the domestic laws of [both countries] concerning taxes ..., including information to effect the determination, assessment, and collection of tax, the recovery and enforcement of tax claims, or the investigation or prosecution of tax crimes or crimes involving the contravention of tax administration.[130]

The commitment is obviously rather broad. It applies without regard to the person to whom the information relates or whether the information is held by a resident or national of one of the countries. Moreover, if the requested information available in the tax files of the requested country is not sufficient to enable compliance with the request, the authorities are committed to 'take all relevant measures to provide the information requested'.[131] The requested State must endeavour to provide the requested information regardless of whether it needs such information for purposes of its own tax.[132]

The forms of information subject to the agreement are also very broad. They include 'depositions of witnesses and authenticated copes of unedited original documents (including books, papers, statements, records, accounts and writing), to the same extent such depositions and documents can be obtained under the laws and administrative practices of the requested State with respect to its own taxes'.

There are certain limits on the obligations established under the TIEAs. A State is not required to carry out administrative measures at variance with the laws and administrative practices of either State. It is not obligated to supply particular items of information which are not obtainable under the laws or in the normal course of the administration of that State or the other. There is no obligation to supply information that would disclose trade, business, industrial, commercial or professional secrets or trade processes or to supply information the disclosure of which would be contrary to public policy.[133]

The agreement explicitly provides to 'information held by financial institutions, nominees, or persons acting in agency or fiduciary capacity or information respecting ownership interests in a person'. The agreement commits both countries to use 'all legal means and its best efforts to execute a request'.[134] Moreover, the countries agree to 'allow representatives of the applicant State to enter the requested State to interview individuals and examine books and records with the consent of the individuals contacted'.[135]

130. Tax Information Exchange Agreement between the Government of the United States of America and the Government of Antigua and Barbuda (US-Antigua TIEA), Art. 4(1).
131. US-Antigua TIEA, Art. 4(2).
132. US-Antigua TIEA, Art. 4(3).
133. US-Antigua TIEA, Art. 4(4).
134. US-Antigua TIEA, Art. 4(5).
135. US-Antigua TIEA, Art. 4(6).

[C] Mutual Legal Assistance Treaties

The United States is also a party to a number of mutual legal assistance treaties (MLATs) with her Western Hemisphere neighbours. These treaties provide for cooperation in criminal prosecutions and have been used in support of prosecutions for crimes under US tax laws.

At the end of 2004, there were in force MLATs between the United States and the following Western Hemisphere countries:

- Anguilla
- Antigua/Barbuda
- Argentina
- Bahamas
- Barbados
- Belize
- Brazil
- British Virgin Islands
- Canada
- Cayman Islands
- Dominica
- Grenada
- Jamaica
- Mexico
- Montserrat
- Panama
- St Kitts and Nevis
- St Lucia
- St Pierre and Miquelon
- St Vincent/The Grenadines
- Trinidad and Tobago
- Turks and Caicos.

Further, the United States is party to a multilateral convention for such legal assistance sponsored by the Organization of American States.

A detailed examination of these various treaties is beyond the scope of this undertaking. However, the treaties tend to commit the partners to provide mutual assistance in connection with the prevention, investigation and prosecution of offences, and in criminal proceedings. The MLAT between the United States and Argentina provides a good example of the scope of the commitment. The forms of assistance include:

(a) taking testimony or statement of persons;
(b) providing documents, records and articles of evidence;
(c) serving documents;
(d) locating or identifying persons;

(e) transferring persons in custody for testimony or other purposes;
(f) executing requests for searches and seizures;
(g) immobilizing assets;
(h) assisting in proceedings related to forfeiture, restitution and collection of fines;
(i) any other form of assistance not prohibited by the laws of the requested State.

§7.11 CONCLUSION

The number of bilateral income tax treaties that have been established between the United States and other countries in the Americas is very limited. While the treaties deal with the same agenda of issues, the results of the various independent negotiations have produced somewhat different results.

Changes in the taxing laws and policies of some Latin American countries may in particular suggest that treaty negotiations may be more successful.[136] During the 1990s, there seemed to be a trend toward freer trade arrangements. At the same time, enthusiasm for providing tax holidays diminished, thereby reducing the conflicts attributable to the refusal of the United States to provide tax sparing. Some have noted a trend away from territorial approach to taxation, which had been traditional in many Latin American countries. Also, withholding rates were being reduced in some Latin American countries, facilitating treaty relief on withholding tax rates.

It is obviously very difficult to predict the course that future treaty negotiations is likely to take. Moreover, economic challenges have effected policy shifts in a number of Latin American countries during the past several years. However, as approaches to tax policy and administration among the countries of the Western Hemisphere become less disparate, it is almost certain that tax treaty relations will be extended substantially.

136. See generally Byrne, 'Foreign Tax Problems of US Companies Doing Business in Latin America', 50 *U. Mia. L.R.* 483 (1996).

Annex to Chapter 7: US Tax Reforms*

Roberta Scarpato

During recent years, there have been few reforms affecting US tax law. In this chapter we analyse the most important acts. In particular, we briefly describe the characteristics of the *Housing and Economic Recovery Act*[1], the *Emergency Economic Stabilization Act*[2] and the *Patient Protection and Affordable Care Act*[3].

The *Housing and Economic Recovery Act* and the *Emergency Economic Stabilization Act* were enacted as a response to the recent economic crises. Through a series of tax breaks, these acts attempted to stimulate economic growth and preserve home-ownership.

The *Patient Protection and Affordable Care Act* significantly affected the US Health Care System. The main purpose of this Act is to expand health insurance-coverage, to provide coverage for patients with preexisting conditions, to help small business to afford their employees' coverage costs, and to make insurance more affordable for people at the poverty line.

I HOUSING AND ECONOMIC RECOVERY ACT

The Housing and Economic Recovery Act (HERA) was enacted on 30 July 2008, to help solve the subprime mortgage crisis. This act includes numerous revisions of the low-income housing tax credit, housing and mortgage revenue bonds, and a reform of the rules regarding real estate investment trusts. We shall describe the main provisions and their effects on U.S. legislation. Some of these provisions aim to support home-owners in order to reduce foreclosures, whereas others try to discourage homeowners from selling their property in order to stabilize home prices.

First, this law enables the Federal Housing Administration, a government agency, to guarantee up to USD 300 billion in refinanced mortgages for borrowers who are at

* This annex updates the previous chapter by Charles H. Gustafson.

1. *Housing and Economic Recovery Act* Pub. L. 110- 289, 122 Stat. 2654.
2. *Emergency Economic Stabilization Act* Pub. L. 110–343, 122 Stat. 3765.
3. *Patient Protection and Affordable Care Act* Pub. L. 111–148, 124 Stat. 119.

risk of losing their homes. This allowed the Federal Housing Administration to reduce the risk of foreclosure.

In the same spirit, the HERA provides a temporary increase in mortgage revenue bonds. Before, there was a national limit on the annual amount of tax-exempt housing bonds that each state could issue. Many States had reached their limits, but this law increased this national limit in 2008 to allow for the issuance of an additional USD 11 billion in tax-exempt bonds in order to provide loans to first-time home buyers and to finance the construction of low-income rental housing. The bill also temporarily allows qualified mortgage revenue bonds (a form of tax-exempt bond issued by states to help provide financing to first-time home buyers) to be used to refinance certain subprime loans.

At the same time, Congress has tried to reduce the tax burden on homeowners who were experiencing difficulties in paying their mortgages. For instance, the HERA includes a refundable tax credit for the first-time purchase of a home. The granted amount is 10% of the purchase price of a principal residence up to USD 7,500. Specifically, a first-time home buyer credit is being presented as a refundable tax credit that is equivalent to an interest-free loan for home purchases made between 9 April 2008 and 1 July 2009. This is a somewhat new type of hybrid credit because it is only temporary and must be repaid in equal installments over a period of fifteen years beginning two years after the credit is taken. It could be considered an interest-free loan from the government.

Furthermore, an additional deduction, valid for the 2008 tax year only, has been introduced. This deduction, between USD 500 and USD 1,000, is intended for taxpayers who do not itemize and claim as an additional amount on top of their standard deduction.

Another innovation concerns the percentage of profits resulting from the sale of a house that can be excluded. In order to discourage the selling of properties during this time, the excludable amount is now based on the percentage of time during which the house was used as a primary residence. Previously, if you sold a property that had been your personal residence for at least two of the past five years, you might exclude from your taxable income up to USD 250,000 of the capital gains (USD 500,000 for a married couple). Now, the amount of gain available for exclusion depends on a ratio between the amount of 'qualified' and 'nonqualified' use of the property. Qualified use is defined as any use of the property as a primary residence. Nonqualified use is defined as any use of the property other than as a primary residence, including use as a second home, a vacation property, a rental or investment property or use in a trade or business. The ratio-period is based on the length of ownership of the property. Only the qualified use portion is available for exclusion from taxable gain.

The HERA also eliminates costs imposed on housing programs by the alternative minimum tax (AMT)[4]. The alternative minimum tax (AMT) can increase the cost to State and local governments of issuing tax-exempt private activity bonds. In general,

4. The AMT is a parallel tax system, which was originally enacted to make sure that wealthy Americans did not escape paying taxes. Several deductions, such as state, local and property taxes are not permitted under the ATM system. Taxpayers who may be subject to the AMT

interest on tax-exempt private activity bonds is usually subject to the AMT. This limits the marketability of these bonds and, therefore, forces state and local governments to issue these bonds at higher interest rates. The HERA excluded private activity bonds from the AMT if the bond was issued in 2009 or 2010. Additionally, it allows the low income housing tax credit and the rehabilitation tax credit to be used to offset the AMT and ensures that interest on tax-exempt housing bonds is not subject to the AMT.

Finally, the Congress also appealed to state and local governments to obtain financing for necessary projects (e.g., constructing roads, repairing bridges, building and renovating schools and hospitals, funding college loans, etc.) at a lower cost, with the objective of decreasing unemployment. In order to do so, municipal bonds guaranteed by Federal home loan banks eligible for treatment as tax exempt bonds were also changed. The new municipal bonds, guaranteed by Federal home loan banks, could not qualify as tax-exempt bonds unless the bonds were used to finance housing programs. During the last few years, state and local government have faced significant costs when issuing tax-exempt municipal bonds to finance state and local projects. This Act helps these municipalities by temporarily allowing bonds that are guaranteed by Federal home loan banks to be eligible for treatment as tax-exempt bonds regardless of whether the bonds are used to finance housing programs.

II EMERGENCY ECONOMIC STABILIZATION ACT

The Emergency Economic Stabilization Act (EESA) was enacted on 3 October 2008, in response to the subprime mortgage crisis and is commonly regarded as a bailout of the U.S. financial system. It authorized the United States Secretary of the Treasury to spend up to USD 700 billion with the purpose of purchasing distressed assets, especially mortgage-backed securities, in order to make capital injections into the banks. Both foreign and domestic banks were included in the program.

The original purpose of the EESA was to reduce the uncertainty regarding the worth of the assets the banks had on their balance sheets, and to restore confidence in the interbank lending market. However, the Act was broadened during the legislative process to include extensive tax, energy, and disaster relief provisions. It provides for an estimated USD 150 billion in business and individual tax incentives and approximately USD 44 billion in revenue-raising offsets over the next ten years.

To encourage a broad spectrum of energy conservation and production-related activities, the Act extends and establishes tax incentives for wind energy, biodiesel, and other clean energy sources, while promoting additional oil production through a refinery expensing provision. The Act also includes disaster tax relief for the Midwest and other federally-declared disaster areas. We shall discuss the main provisions and their implications in all the mentioned sectors.

must calculate their tax liability under the regular federal tax system and under the AMT system and are accountable for the greatest amount.

[A] Tax Exemptions for Homeowners

First, the EESA provides additional relief for homeowners on different issues not covered by the HATA. In particular, to help more homeowners stay on their financial feet in the ongoing economic crisis, it modifies the previous legislation which entailed that when homeowners have parts of their mortgages forgiven, they immediately owe income taxes on the amount of indebtedness forgiven. In fact, to keep struggling homeowners from facing higher tax bills, the EESA allowed homeowners caught up in the mortgage crisis to avoid paying tax on forgiven mortgage debts through 2009. Moreover, it has been recently extended, with the exclusion of home equity loans, through 2012.

To allow homeowners who are already in a tight financial position due to the decline in the real estate market to avoid a significant current year tax bill due to a mortgage write-off act provides individuals with several areas of relief from AMT liability.

In particular, the EESA increased individual AMT exemption amounts. The 2008 exemption amounts are increased from:

- USD 45,000 to USD 69,950 for married couples filing jointly and surviving spouses;
- USD 33,750 to USD 46,200 for other unmarried individuals; and
- USD 22,500 to USD 34,975 for married individuals filing separate returns.[5]

These increases in the exemption amounts for 2008 are the latest in a series of annual increases. As in past years, this increase is effective for only one year and under the current law, the exemption is phased out at higher levels of alternative minimum taxable income (AMTI). In fact, the exemptions are fully phased out at USD 429,800 of AMTI for married couples filing jointly.

Finally, the act also extends the ability of individuals to offset their entire regular tax with personal non-refundable tax credits to tax years beginning in 2008[6]. Eligible non-refundable personal tax credits include the dependent care credit, the credit for the elderly and disabled, the adoption credit, the child credit, the credit for interest on certain home mortgages, the Hope scholarship and lifetime learning credits, the credit for savers, the credit for certain non-business energy property, the credit for residential energy-efficient property, and the DC first-time homebuyer credit.

[B] Energy Incentives

Among the provisions included in the EESA, there are tax credits intended to spur investment in alternative energy properties by making their use economically viable for a wider range of taxpayers.

5. I.R.C. §55(d)(1).
6. I.R.C. §26(a).

For instance, it entails a tax credit for the purchase of energy-efficient improvements to existing homes for two years through 2009 and includes energy efficient biomass fuel stoves as a new class of energy-efficient property eligible for a consumer tax credit of USD 300.[7]

The act also provides an eight-year extension of the credit for residential energy efficient solar property[8]. In addition, the act eliminates the current USD 2,000 cap on the credit for solar electric investments. The legislation also creates tax credits for residential small wind energy property (USD 4,000 cap) and geothermal heat pumps (USD 2,000 cap).

[C] Disaster Relief

The act liberalizes the casualty loss rules for individuals who are victims of a federally declared disaster that occurred after 31 December 2007, and before 1 January 2010. The act waives the rule[9] that a casualty loss is deductible only to the extent it exceeds 10% of the taxpayer's adjusted gross income. However, the act also raises the USD 100 per-casualty threshold under to USD 500[10]. The act also allows non-itemizers to claim casualty losses as a standard deduction.

In addition to revising the casualty loss rules, the act extends the time period when taxpayers can carry back net operating losses attributable to a casualty loss incurred in a federally declared disaster from two to five years.

Furthermore, the act provides tax relief for those affected by the floods, severe storms, and tornadoes in Midwest states such as: Arkansas, Illinois, Indiana, Iowa, Kansas, Michigan, Minnesota, Missouri, Nebraska, and Wisconsin and declared as disaster areas by Federal emergency Management Agency on or after 20 May 2008, and before 1 August 2008.

III PATIENT PROTECTION AND AFFORDABLE CARE ACT

President Barack Obama, as part of his health care reform agenda, signed into law the Patient Protection and Affordable Care Act (PPACA) on 23 March 2010.

This reform, by helping more children get health coverage, ending lifetime and most annual limits on care, and giving patients access to recommended preventive services without cost, has given Americans new rights and benefits. The PPACA aims to reduce premium costs for millions of families and small business owners, who are priced out of coverage today, affecting as many as 32 million Americans who currently have no health care. Moreover, few other new benefits of the law have taken effect, including 50% discounts on brand-name drugs for seniors and tax credits for small businesses that provide insurance to employees.

7. I.R.C. §25C.
8. I.R.C. §25D.
9. I.R.C. §165(h)(2).
10. I.R.C. §165(h)(1).

To improve coverage for those with pre-existing conditions, to expand access to care for over 30 million Americans, and to reduce the long term costs of the United States health care system, the PPACA significantly affected the private health insurance industry and the public health insurance programs.

To lower the costs of the U.S. health care system the PPACA:

(1) Launched – through state Exchanges – a new, competitive, private, health insurance market giving millions of Americans and small businesses access to affordable coverage. It will provide in this way the same choices of insurance that members of Congress have. Furthermore, Americans who earn less than 133% of the poverty level (people with an approximately income of USD 14,000 for an individual and USD 29,000 for a family of four) will be eligible to enroll in Medicaid. To support this expanded coverage, States will receive 100% federal funding for the first three years, phasing to 90% federal funding in subsequent years.

(2) To end discrimination against Americans with pre-existing conditions, it made the insurance companies accountable by keeping premiums down and preventing many types of insurance industry abuses and denials of care. Moreover, guaranteed issue and community rating will be implemented nationally so that insurers must offer the same premium to all applicants of the same age, sex, and geographical location regardless of pre-existing conditions. A Pre-Existing Condition Insurance Plan (PCIP) will provide new coverage options to individuals who have been uninsured for at least six months because of a pre-existing condition and serves as a bridge to 2014, when all discrimination against pre-existing conditions will be prohibited. States have the option of running this new program in their State, but if a state chooses not to do so, a plan will be established by the Department of Health and Human Services in that State.

(3) By cutting government overspending and reining in waste, fraud and abuse, it is expected to reduce the deficit by more than USD 100 billion over the next ten years – and by more than USD 1 trillion over the second decade.

(4) In order to make insurance more affordable, it gave a tax credit to small businesses to provide coverage. In particular, to offset the cost of insurance, businesses with fewer than twenty-five employees are qualified for a small business tax credit of up to 35% (up to 25% for non-profits). In 2014, tax credits to those who need help in buying insurance will be established. In fact, tax credits will be available for those with income between 100% and 400% of the poverty line who are not eligible for other affordable coverage.

Moreover, another interesting feature of these tax credits is that they are paid in advance, so it can lower the premium payments each month, rather than making taxpayers wait for tax time. It's also refundable, so even moderate income families can receive the full benefit of the credit.

CHAPTER 8

The Commentary of the OECD Model Tax Convention as Two-Tiers Soft Law: Rule of Conduct for Tax Authorities and Living Law for Taxpayers

Konosuke Kimura*

§8.01 DEFINING THE ISSUES

The Japanese Supreme Court indicated its willingness to consider the OECD Commentary to be an aid to interpretation by stating that the Commentary 'can be referred to as "material"[1] and as a mere "supplementary means of interpretation"' within the meaning of Article 32 of the Vienna Convention on the Law of Treaties (VCLT).[2,3] This is the first judgment in which the Supreme Court expressly referred to the OECD-argument and recognized that the provisions of double tax treaties (DTT), as far as they are based on the Model Tax Convention, should respect the OECD Commentary;

* The author wishes to thank Dr. Thomas Dubut for prudential review.

1. Lang, Michael, The Application of the OECD Model Tax Convention to Partnerships: A Critical Analysis of the Report Prepared by the OECD Committee on Fiscal Affairs, Schriftenreihe zum Internationalen Steuerrecht, No.11, Linde Verlag, 2000,20 and footnote 26 (where tax treaty negotiators followed the OECD Model Tax Convention, one might conclude that they wanted to create a provision having the same meaning which the Commentary gives to the corresponding provisions of the OECD Model Tax Convention. It is clear that the Commentary is part of the material which can be taken into account when interpreting the provision of the bilateral tax treaty.)
2. United Nations Treaty Series, vol. 1155, p.331. The Convention entered into force on 27 January 1980. Corten, Olivier & Pierre Klein, The Vienna Conventions on the Law of Treaties: A commentary, Vol. I Oxford University Press 2011, 841 ff. (Yves le Bouthillier).
3. Asatsuma, Akiyuki, 'Supreme Court Judgment: Anti-Tax Haven (CFC) Legislation does not Infringe Japan-Singapore Tax Treaty', 64(10) Bulletin for International Fiscal Documentation, 518 (2010).

domestic CFC legislation should also not infringe the Commentary.[4,5] In this respect, the Court appeared to confirm the soft law function of the OECD Commentary since it follows it.

It is not doubtable that the National Tax Administration of Japan (NTA) takes the position that 'the Commentary provides important guidance for the interpretation and application of the OECD Model and in practice will often need to be taken into account for the interpretation of DTTs, at least where the wording is not clear, which is inherently more likely in treaties than in relevant domestic legislation.' In practice, the NTA considers it appropriate to take into account, at least the most recently adopted/ published OECD Commentary as well as other materials that may have been available at the time of negotiation, unless the Commentary makes it clear that a former interpretation has been substantively altered, rather than merely elaborated, or unless it is obviously that the substance of the OECD Model has itself changed since the DTT concerned was negotiated or if the DTT does not follow the OECD Model.[6]

Frank Engelen successfully points out the reasons why the tax administrators of OECD member countries follow the OECD Commentary. They can constitute Estoppel, acquiescence and the protection of legitimate expectations based on the principle of good faith.[7,8] However, this does not mean that the OECD Commentary is hard law. International treaties negotiated by the government or by delegates become binding on

4. Cf. Gutmann, Daniel, Robert J. Danon and Hugues Salome, French-Swiss Point of View on the Societe Schneider Electric Case: Some Thoughts on the Personal Attribution of Income Requirement in International Tax Law, 31(49 Intertax, 156(2003); Bourtourault, Pierre-Yves and Marcellin N. Mbwa-Mboma, French High Tax Court Confirms that The Former France-Switzerland Tax Treaty Overrides the French CFC Legislation, 30(12) Intertax, 493(2002). See also Murray Clayson, The Impact of European Law and Treaty Relies on the UK Controlled foreign companies Rules, 26(11) Intertax, 326(1998)
5. Körner, Andreas, German Reference to the ECJ for a Preliminary Ruling: Unilateral Switch-over Clause and CFC Rules, 34(1) Intertax, 32(2004); Helminen, Marjaana, Is There a Future for CFC-regimes in the EU?, 33(3) Intertax, 117(2005)..
6. Cf. the Australian Taxation Office (ATO) TR 2001/13, paras 104 and 108.
7. Engelen, Frank Antonius, Interpretation of Tax Treaties under International Law: A study of Articles 31, 32 and 33 of the Vienna Convention on the Law of Treaties and their application to tax treaties, IBFD Amsterdam, 2004, 128–130, 552 (the acquiescence of both parties can also operate as estoppel. In any event, international law protects the legitimate expectations of each party that considered in good faith that the provisions of treaty that are identical to those of the OECD Model Tax Convention should be interpreted in accordance with the Commentaries thereon. Moreover, the compelling in inter-State relations demand that the parties inform each other within a reasonable period of time if and when they consider that the identical provision of the treaty must be interpreted and applied differently than set out in the Commentaries thereon. Otherwise, the presumption necessarily arises that the parties have acquiesced in the interpretation agreed on in the Commentaries.); Sinclair, Ian, Estoppel and acquiescence, in: Vaughan Lowe and Malgosia Fitzmaurice (eds), Fifty years of the International Court of Justice: Essays in honour of Sir Robert Jennings, Cambridge University Press, Cambridge, 1996, 104,120('Estoppel and acquiescence will continue to play a significant part in the decision-making process of the Court; but the Court will likewise continue to exercise considerable caution in admitting too decisive a role for either of these concepts [of estoppel and acquiescence] in the final determination of inter-state disputes.').
8. Engelen (*supra* note 7), 122–125,549f.; Bruggen, Edwin van der, 'Good Faith' in the application and Interpretation of Double Taxation Convention, (1) British Tax Review, 25(2003), 43; O' Connor, J.F., Good Faith in International Law, Dartmouth Publishing Company Limited, England, 1991,119(definition of the principle of good faith in international law).

citizens and courts only after approval by the competent-parliamentary- or executive authorities. The OECD Commentary can bind only the competent tax authorities, unless provided otherwise. If the adoption of the OECD Commentary by the Committee on Fiscal Affairs (CFA) could be considered to be a multilateral treaty, the same would apply.[9]

Article 32 VCLT allows 'supplementary means of interpretation',[10] such as 'preparatory work of the treaty' or 'the circumstances of its conclusion' to be taken into account. However, recourse to such material may only be made to confirm an interpretation based on Article 31 VCLT or to determine the meaning of terms when an interpretation according to Article 31 VCLT 'leaves the meaning ambiguous or obscure' or 'leads to a result which is manifestly absurd or unreasonable'.[11,12]

The OECD Model Convention and the OECD Commentary could qualify as 'supplementary means of interpretation' under Article 32 VCLT. The preparatory work of the treaty and the circumstances of its conclusion figure in Article 32 VCLT as examples of such material, but the use of supplementary means of interpretation is not limited to material expressly mentioned in Article 32 VCLT. Recourse may be had to any evidence establishing the common intention of the Contracting States. If a tax treaty is negotiated on the basis of the OECD Model, the OECD Model Convention and the Commentary thereon may provide guidance in establishing the meaning of DTT provisions. It follows that the OECD Model Convention and the OECD Commentary can be characterized as supplementary means of interpretation under Article 32 VCLT, provided that the treaty provision in question is based on the OECD Model Convention.[13] So the OECD Model Convention and the OECD Commentary carry more relevant weight in the interpretation process if the Contracting States chose to follow the wording of the OECD Model Convention in negotiating and drafting a particular provision. It is then reasonable to assume that they intend such a provision to inherit the meaning it has in the OECD Model.[14]

9. Vogel, Klaus, The Influence of the OECD Commentaries on Treaty Interpretation, 54(12) BIFD 613(2000).
10. Cf. Engelen (*supra* note 7), 542f.
11. Ault, Hugh J., The Role of the OECD Commentaries in the Interpretation of Tax Treaties,22(4) Intertax 146(1994)(Commentaries as 'confirming' the Presence of a Special Meaning).
12. Lang, Michael and Florian Brugger, The role of the OECD Commentary in tax treaty interpretation, 23 Australian tax forum, 98(2008); Ward, David A., The Role of the Commentaries on the OECD Model in the Tax Treaty Interpretation Process, 60(3) BIFD at 98 and footnote 7 and 8(2006)(The commentary on the Vienna Convention makes it perfectly clear the International Law Commission, in drafting Arts 31 and 32, did not attempt to codify all of the principles and maxims that have been adopted by international tribunals in their jurisprudence in dealing with treaty interpretation. Arts 31 and 32 of the Vienna Convention have a limited role to play in the application of the OECD Commentaries in the interpretive process.).
13. John F. Avery Jones, Are Tax Treaties Necessary?, 53 Tax L. Rev. 23(1999); Lang/Brugger (*supra* note 12), 23 Australian tax forum, 98(2008); Ault (*supra* note 11),.22(4) Intertax 145(1994)(fitting the Commentaries into the Vienna Convention Pattern).
14. Lang/Brugger (*supra* note 12), 23 Australian tax forum, 100(2008)(this does not necessarily apply if the wording of a provision of the existing tax treaty is different from the OECD Model). See also, Dubut, Thomas, 'Les Commentaires du Modèle de Convention fiscale de l'OCDE et l'interprétation des conventions bilatérales contre la double imposition. Contribution à l'étude

If the use of the Commentary is admitted, a further question then arises as to which version should be used. This issue became relevant after the publication of the 1977 OECD Model Tax Convention (MTC) which updated the OECD's 1963 Draft Double Taxation Convention (DDTC) in respect with tax treaties concluded on the basis of the 1963 DDTC. In addition, the issue has become even more important as further updates of the MTC are being published on an ongoing basis since 1992.[15]

In other words, can a paragraph of the Commentary be taken into account in interpreting a treaty which was concluded before the Commentary concerned was formally adopted by the Council of the OECD?[16] If it can, should it be taken into account also for taxable periods prior to the formal adoption of the Commentary or only for subsequent periods? [17,18]

The OECD CFA takes the following position on this issue:

> [A]mendments to the Articles of the Model Convention and changes to the Commentaries that are a direct result of these amendments are not relevant to the interpretation or application of previously concluded Conventions where the provisions of those conventions are different **in substance** from the amended Articles. However, other changes or additions to the Commentaries are normally applicable to the interpretation and application of Conventions concluded before their adoption, because they reflect the consensus of the OECD member countries as to the proper interpretation of existing provisions and their application to specific situations. (emphasis added)[19]

The CFA asserts that the Commentary is of relevance not only for the interpretation of future tax treaties, but also for the interpretation of the previously concluded treaties. In this respect, the CFA takes position on the relevance of its own statements.[20]

However, reference has to be made to Articles 31 and 32 VCLT to determine if the position taken by the OECD CFA is indeed in accordance with the rules on interpretation contained in the VCLT. Later Commentary amendments are emitting no light on the intentions of the Contracting States upon conclusion of the treaty.[21] Later Commentary amendments are not part of the context as defined in Article 31 (2) VCLT, since such amendments are not made 'in connection with the conclusion of the treaty'.

---

de la normativité sans efficacité en droit international public', *Revue de la recherche juridique – Droit prospectif*, vol. 34, 2009, n° 3, pp. 1449–1472.

15. See OECD Commentary 2005, Introduction paras 9–11; also Lang/Brugger (*supra* note 12), 23 Australian tax forum, 101 f.(2008).
16. Waters, Mike,'The relevance of the OECD Commentaries in the interpretation of Tax Treaties', in: Lang, Michael and Heinz Jirousek (eds), Praxis des Internationalen Steuerrechts, Festschrift für Helmut Loukota,Linde Verlag Wien, 2005, 679 and footnote 17.
17. Waters (*supra* note 16), in: Lang/Jirousek (eds), Praxis des Internationalen Steuerrechts, 679.
18. The courts in Japan have not expressly considered this point. However, I endorsed the use of subsequent commentary material, with referring to the OECD Commentaries on the MTC (so Kimura, Konosuke, The International Tax Law of Japan, Seibun-do, Tokyo1998, at 757, 759(in Japanese).
19. OECD Commentary 2005, Introduction para 35.
20. Lang (*supra* note 1), 15.
21. Wassermeyer, F, in Debatin H/Wassermeyer, F (eds), Dopperbesteuerung Kommentar, Vor Art. 1 MA MN 60;Vogel (*supra* note 9), 54(12) BIFD, 615(2000); Avery Jones, J., The Effect of Changes in the OECD Commentaries after a Treaty is Concluded, 56(3)BIFD 103(2002), 109('There is certainly no clear answer to when later

They might, however, fall within Article 31 (3) VCLT, which refers to 'any subsequent agreement between the parties regarding the interpretation of the treaty or the application of its provisions' (Article 31 (3) (a) VCLT) and 'any subsequent practice in the application of the treaty which establishes the agreement of the parties regarding its interpretation' (Article 31 (3) (b) VCLT).

Recourse to subsequent practice under Article 31 (3) (b) VCLT may only be had to clarify an otherwise ambiguous interpretation result.[22] An amendment to the OECD Commentary does not constitute an agreement under international law[23] and thus falls outside the scope of Article 31 (3) (a) VCLT.[24]

To sum up, if a bilateral tax treaty is typically based on the OECD Model Convention and the particular provisions follow the wording of the OECD Model, it can clearly be presumed that the Contracting States intended such provisions to have the meaning they have in the OECD Model, and the OECD Commentary thereon that existed at the time the particular bilateral treaty was concluded. Especially if both are members of the OECD and represented in the CFA and neither party has formulated a contrary observation.[25,26] In contrast, under the OECD Model convention, a change in the Commentary can never in a technical sense overrule an existing double taxation convention. If the interpretation of a convention inevitably leads to a result which deviates from the Commentary, this interpretation should legally prevail.[27]

Commentaries are useful in interpreting an earlier treaty. None of the members of the panel argued that a court should not even look at later Commentaries.'); Lang/Brugger (*supra* note 12), 23 Australian tax forum, 98(2008). However, Wattel, Petter J. and Marres, Otto, The Legal Status of the OECD Commentary and Static or Ambulatory Interpretation of Tax Treaties, 43(7/8) European Taxation, 222(2003), 228 ('We have no doubt that the Commentary at the time of treaty conclusion can at the very least function as a supplementary means of interpretation, provided the two conditions in Art. 32 are fulfilled.'... 'We therefore believe that a later Commentary can in fact be a 'supplementary means of interpretation' [qualified under Article 32 VSLT].' 'In our opinion, a Commentary can even be a 'supplementary means of interpretation' if the treaty was concluded on the basis of a model other than the OECD Model (e.g., the United Nations Model Double Taxation Convention between developed and developing countries), provided the treaty does not deviate from the OECD Model on the relevant point.').

22. Lang/Brugger (*supra* note 12), 23 Australian tax forum, 104(2008)
23. See, e.g. Reuven S. Avi-Yonah, International Tax as International Law: An Analysis of the International Tax Regime, Cambridge University Press, New York,1(2007)(an international tax regime forms a significant part of international law.). Exceptionally see Ishiguro Kazunori, Legal Light to Borderless Economy, 53(9) Boueki to Kanzei (i.e.Trade and Customs), 57(conflict of laws in a broad sense govern international tax law) (in Japanese. The author is full professor of private international law (conflicts law) at the Tokyo University.); Yamauchi, Koresuke, The concept of international tax law, 13 International Taxation, 259(7) (the author assert that the international law belongs to the private international law.)(in Japanese. He is full professor of private international law at Chuo University).
24. Lang/Brugger (*supra* note 12), 23 Australian tax forum, 105(2008).
25. Ward (*supra* note 12), 60(3) BIFD, 101 (2006).
26. See the 1995 OECD Commentary, para 30 at Introduction ('Observations on the Commentaries have sometimes been inserted at the request of Member countries that are unable to concur in the interpretation given in the Commentary on the Article concerned. These observations thus do no express any disagreement with the text of the Convention, but usefully indicate the way in which those countries will apply the provisions of the Article in question.').
27. So Vogel (*supra* note 9), 54(12) BIFD, 614(2000).

Amendments to the OECD Model Convention and to the OECD Commentary made after the conclusion of a bilateral tax treaty do not form part of 'context' of the existing treaty. Subsequent Commentary amendments cannot therefore establish the intention of the Contracting States at the time of negotiation and conclusion of the bilateral tax treaty.[28] That, however, is not to say that subsequent Commentary has no value at all.[29]

May such amendments play any role in the interpretation of previously concluded tax treaties if recourse to other means of interpretation remains inconclusive. Changes to the OECD Model Convention and the OECD Commentary are made frequently than until 1992. Are such amendments simply not relevant for the interpretation of bilateral tax treaties concluded afterwards? Does an ongoing revision of the OECD Models and the OECD Commentary undermine the authority of the OECD Commentary for the purpose of interpretation?[30]

David Ward points out that the OECD Commentary that existed at the time of the conclusion of a bilateral treaty is a part of the context of the particular treaty and, on that basis, plays an important role in the interpretive process. The OECD Commentary is much more than a vanilla commentary. Its influence in harmonizing the interpretation of treaties is enormous. At the same time, the Commentary is not directly binding in international law at all.[31]

Why is it possible that the OECD has such low expectations for the Commentary when it spends so much effort on updating it?[32]

Arguments about whether to apply a new Commentary to a prior treaty is influenced by whether the new Commentary:

- records what States have already been doing in practice;
- fills a gap in the existing Commentary by covering matters not previously mentioned at all;
- amplifies existing Commentary by adding new examples or arguments to what is already there or[33]
- contradicts the existing Commentary.[34,35]

28. Lang/Brugger (*supra* note 12), 23 Australian tax forum, 107(2008).
29. Ward (*supra* note 12), 60(3) BIFD, 100 and footnote 22 (2006).
30. Cf. Lang (*supra* note 1), 15ff.(20) (The OECD Report is of importance insofar as its court decisions and scholarly writing. They give an indication of the position that the tax authorities might take in a certain situation. This helps the taxpayer prepare his arguments to challenge his position in court if he does not find it appropriate.); Lang/Brugger (*supra* note 12), 23 Australian tax forum, 108(2008).
31. Ward (*supra* note 12), 60(3) BIFD, at 99 and footnote 10 (2006). See also, Dubut,Thomas, 'Modélisation des normes et normativité des modèles. Le caractère normatif ambivalent du Modèle de Convention fiscale concernant le revenu et la fortune de l'OCDE en droit international public', *Revue belge de droit international – Belgisch Tijdschrift voor Internationaal Recht*, 2009, n° 1, pp. 212–239.
32. Avery Jones (*supra* note 13), 53 Tax L. Rev. 19(1999).
33. Vogel (*supra* note 9), 54(12) BIFD,612(2000); Ward (*supra* note 12), 60(3) BIFD, 101(2006).
34. Waters (*supra* note 16), in: Lang/Jirousek (eds), Praxis des Internationalen Steuerrechts, 680; Ward (*supra* note 12), 60(3) BIFD, 102(2006)(the new Commentary has no legitimate role to play in the interpretation of bilateral tax treaties made between the OECD countries or even non-OECD countries and concluded before the reversal of the prior Commentary, as is the case

(i) Some Commentary changes are made to bring it into line with what is already the practice. Examples are:

- taking residence into account when interpreting the phrase 'in the same circumstances' in Article 24(1) (added in 1992);[36]
- the amendment of Article 3(2) in 1995;[37]
- the treatment of Governments as residents (added in 1995);[38]
- treating benefits in kind as 'salaries, wages and other similar remuneration' under Article 15 (added in 1997);[39]
- the reference to six months in relation to permanent establishments in paragraph 6 of the Commentary on Article 5 (added in 2003).

In the case the new Commentary records what of the OECD Member States have been doing in practice as regards the interpretation and application of their treaties, the new Commentary should be analysed to determine whether it is a genuinely interpretive Commentary or whether it is gap-filling and treated accordingly.[40]

(ii) Where the new Commentary fills a gap in the existing Commentary and thereby indirectly fills a gap in the existing Model, the new Commentary may be viewed as an attempt to fill a gap in the Model while avoiding a direct amendment of the Model which would require amendment of most bilateral treaties based on the Model made prior to the amendment.[41] For instance, it seems obvious that the DDTC 1963 and the MTC 1977 did not contain any reference as to the treatment of payments for computer software under Articles 7 and 12, or that new Commentary on them was not added to the MTC until 1992 (it was then amended in 2000 to refine the analysis).[42] Moreover, the bilateral tax treaties had not kept up with information technology and could not cope with that when not physical but intangible property was at stake.[43]

for the changing Commentary on Art. 1 in respect of anti-abuse and the Commentary on Art. 17(2) in respect of corporations providing entertainment, sporting and artistic performances.). Also see Ault, Hugh J., The role of the OECD commentaries in the interpretation of tax treaties, in: Herbert H. Alpert and Kees van Raad (eds), Essays on International Taxation, Kluwer Law and Taxation Publishers, Deventer/Boston, 1993, 67.

35. See Avery Jones (*supra* note 21), 56(3) BIFD, 102(2002); Avery Jones (*supra* note 13), 53 Tax L. Rev. 21(1999).
36. Paragraph 3 of the commentary on Article 24; Article 24(2) was similarly amended in 1997.
37. Paragraph 13.1 of the Commentary on Article 3.
38. Paragraph 8.1 of the Commentary on Article 4.
39. Paragraph 2.1 of the Commentary on Article 15. Cf. paragraph 1.1 of the Commentary on Article 16 and paragraph 2.2 of the Commentary on Article 19.
40. Ward (*supra* note 12), 60(3) BIFD, 102(2006).
41. Ward (*supra* note 12), 60(3) BIFD, 101(2006).
42. Waters (*supra* note 16), in: Lang/Jirousek (eds), Praxis des Internationalen Steuerrechts, 680.
43. Kingson, Charles I., Taxing the Future, 51 Tax L. Rev. 641(1977); Avery Jones (*supra* note 13), 53 Tax L. Rev. 11(1999).

According to Mike Waters's view, the new Commentary should be taken into account under Article 31(1) or (3) or Article 32 VCLT when interpreting pre-1992 treaties.[44] David Ward suggests that such gap-filling Commentary should be taken into account by treaty interpreters, particularly by domestic courts, to determine whether it has any legitimate role in the interpretative process.[45] However, he does not indicate the legal reasons supporting his views.

It might be difficult for Mike Waters to justify the use of later Commentary text under Article 31(4) VCLT since the wording of this provision implies that one has to respect the intention of the parties as it existed when the treaty was concluded.[46]

So Mike Waters points out four dimensions of the issue above. The last recommendations of the Council of the OECD recommended prospectively that the tax administrations of the Member States follow the Commentary as modified from time to time when interpreting and applying the provisions of their bilateral tax treaties, which are based on the articles of the Model. The Council has only 'adopted' the periodic updates to the Model and the Commentary since 1997, except of the 2000 update, which was adopted only by the CFA and seems not to have been adopted by the Council. Therefore, the prospective 1997 recommendations of Council may apply to the periodic updates continuously.[47] The new wording is ambulatory and applies to the present as well as to further amendments. [48]

I am going to analyse points (i) and (ii) in the light of soft law[49] and living law considerations[50],[51] in order to solve the issue.[52,53,54] Maarten J. Ellis has compared the

44. Vogel, Klaus, Double Tax Treaties and Their Interpretation, 4(1) International Tax & Business Lawyer, 1(1986)39f.(the OECD Model Treaty and its Commentaries), 41('At least some form of a 'soft' obligation must therefore be derived from the recommendation regarding the OECD Model.'... 'The recommendation, in other word, generates "a loose legal duty, but a legal duty nonetheless" '), 41 footnote 214.
45. Ward (*supra* note 12), 60(3) BIFD, 101(2006).
46. Waters (*supra* note 16), in: Lang/Jirousek (eds), Praxis des Internationalen Steuerrechts, 680 footnote 19.
47. Ward (*supra* note 12), 60(3) BIFD, at 97 and footnote 3(2006).
48. Vogel (*supra* note 9), 54(12) BIFD, 613(2000).
49. Hard law refers to binding rules of a given legal order, soft law refers to non-binding rules however enjoying a certain judicial effectiveness (i.e. applied by the organ of a legal order) and, no law refers non-binding rules without normative effect. See Cl. Jabloner and W. Okresek, Theoretische und praktische anmerkungen zu Phänomenen des Soft law, ÖzöRV 1983, 217–241; R. Walter, Soft Law aus rechtstheoretischer und verfassungsrechtlicher Sicht, in: M. Lang, J.Schuch and C. Staringer (eds), Soft Law in der Praxis, Wien, Linde, 2005,21–28. Cf. Ward (*supra* note 12), 60(3) BIFD, 99 (2006) (the concept of soft law is not binding in international law. The soft law thesis (that is to say, that soft law is not binding) is not supportable as there are no varying degrees of legality or bindingness in international law, only hard law which is binding.); also Klabbers, Jan, The Concept of Treaty in International Law, Kluwer, Hague/London/Boston, 1996,157f..;Klabbers, Jan, The undesirability of Soft Law, 67(4)Nordic journal of international law, 381–391 (1998).
50. Kimura, Konosuke, The Revenue Law of Japan, Seibun-do,Tokyo,129,143–147(1998)(in Japanese), I explained the living law and soft law concerning the roles of circular notes (Verwaltungsvorschrift) for taxpayers as well.
51. Ehrlich, Eugen, Die Erforschung des lebenden Recht (Aus: Schmollers Jahrsbuch für Gesetgebung, Verwaltung und Volkswirtschaft im Deutschen Reich 35[1911],S.129–147)),in: E. Ehrlich, Recht und Leben. Gesammelte Schriften zur Rechtsttatsachenforschung und zur Freirechtslehre, Duncker & Humblot, Berlin 1967,19('Das ist also das lebende Recht im Gegensatze zu dem bloß vor Gericht und den Behörden *geltenden*.' ...'Das lebende Recht ist

concept of 'soft law' with the concept used in other areas of law of 'an obligation based on morality and decency'. According to his report, one of the few examples in inheritance tax law is where the Dutch Succession Duties Act accepts that an obligation based on morality and decency may be deducted from the value of a decedent's estate.[55]

This paper focuses on the legal base on which the Courts take into account the OECD Model Conventions and their Commentary for the justification of their judgments.

§8.02 INSTRUMENTS TO ANALYSE THE ISSUES

Since the mid-1980s, the question of the legal basis of the practice of tax administrations and Courts around the world to conform to the Commentary when interpreting and applying bilateral tax treaties based on the OECD Model has been the subject of ongoing academic debates.

In determining the status of the Commentary of the OECD Model Tax convention, we should distinguish between the question of whether, under international law, the

das noch nicht in Satzungen festgelegte Recht, das aber doch das Leben beherrscht. Die Quellen seiner Erkenntnis sind vor allem die moderne Urkunde [namely das gerichtliche Urteil here], aber auch die unmittelbare Beobachtung des Lebens, des Handels und Wandels, der Gewohntheiten und Gebräuche, dann aber aller Organisationen[namely Organisation des staatlichen, gesellschaftlichen wirtschaftlichen Lebens here. See Ehrlich (*supra* note 51, 1911), 39], sowohl der rechtlich anerkannten als auch der von dem Rechte ignorierten, ja sogar der rechtlich mißbilligten.'); Ehrlich, Eugen, Ein Institut für lebendes Recht (Aus:Juristische Blätter 1911, S.229–231, 241–244), in: in: Ehrlich (*supra* note 51, 1967), 37('aber lebendes Recht is er (i.e. der Inhalt der Urkunde) doch nur so weit, als sich die Parteien daran regelmäßig halten, auch wenn sie es nicht auf einen Prozeß ankommen lassen wollen.'); Ehrlich, Eugen, Gesetz und Lebendes Recht, 38(12)Hougaku-Kyoukai-Zasshi, 9f.(1920) ('Die Regeln, die die Menschen selbst in ihrem Zusammenleben als für sich verbindlich beobachten, sind das lebend Recht: sie bilden ebenso gut eine Rechtsordnung, wie die in den Gesetzbüchern enthaltenen. Der Unterschied besteht darin, dass die ersten in freiwilligen Handeln der Parteien zur Geltung kommen, die zweiten zum groβsen Teil durch Gerichte und andere Behörden erzwungen werden müssen. Da jedoch Gerichte und andre Behörden doch shlieβslich nur verhältnismäβsig selten angerufen werden, so dringen die Normen des lebenden Rechts oft genug selbst gegen das Gesetz durch.'), and 11('Das lebende Recht füllt also einen ungeheuren Raum aus, den ihm das Gesetz freilässt, und es ist Aufgabe des Juristen, es in diesem Raums aufzusuchen.'). See also, Ehrlich, Eugen,Gesetz und lebendes Recht. Vermische kleinere Schriften, Dunker und Humblot, Berlin 1986, 228–240.

52. Cf. Lang/Brugger (*supra* note 12), 23 Australian tax forum, 95ff.(2008)(the authors discusses how the OECD Commentary and related publications of the OECD Committee on fiscal Affairs fit within the rules on treaty interpretation contained in the VCLT. Based on these rules, the relevance of amendments to the OECD Commentary for the interpretation of previously concluded tax treaties is analysed.)
53. Ward (*supra* note 12), 60(3) BIFD, 102(2006)(subsequent gap-filling and reversing Commentaries should be applied in interpreting earlier treaties.).
54. Raad, C.van, Interpretation and Application of Tax Treaties by Tax courts, 36(1) European Taxation, 3 (1996), 6(the author proposes 'Advisory body on interpretation' to solve the issues in a different way.)
55. Maarten J. Ellis, The Role of the Commentaries on the OECD Model in the Tax Treaty Interpretation Process – Response to David A. Ward, 60(3) BIFD 103f. (2006).

States party to a tax treaty are legally bound by posterior Commentary for the purpose of the interpretation and application of the provisions of the treaty that are identical to those of the OECD Model Tax Convention on the one hand and, the question of whether, under the Contracting States' internal law, taxpayers and tax authorities follow the Commentary in practice to apply them to the tax matters on the other hand.[56]

This chapter addresses the second question. As far as the second question is concerned, a clear distinction should be made between, on the one hand, the question of whether the tax courts and tax authorities are equally bound to apply the Commentary if and when the Contracting States themselves are bound by them under international law and, on the other hand, the question of whether the taxpayers follow the Commentary in practice to apply them to the tax matters.

As known, there are two types of legal norms: the rules of conduct (or norms of conduct),[57] and the norms for decision (Entscheidungsnormen, norms for decision).[58,59]

56. Cf. 'Conference Position Paper: The quest for the holy grail in international tax law – The legal status of the Commentaries on the OECD Model Tax Convention on Income and on Capital', in: The Legal Status of the OECD Commentaries, Sjoerd Douma and Frank Engelen (ed.) Amsterdam 2008, at 261.

57. See Ehrlich, Eugen, Grundlegung der Soziologie des Recht, Duncker & Humblot, München und Leipzig,1913,65,365(Regel des Handelns); Ehrlich, Eugen and Walter L. Moll (translated), Fundamental Principles of the Sociology of Law, Cambridge Mass., Harvard University Press, 1936, 81, 453f.(rules of conduct). Also Ehrlich, Eugen, Die Soziologie und des Rechts, 40(1)Hougaku-Kyoukai-Zasshi,10(1922)('Staatliches Recht bestheht zum gröβsten Teil aus Verwaltungsnormen,Weisungen, die an die Verwaltungsbeamten gereichet sind).doch sind darunter auch Entscheidungsnormen (Weisungen an den Richter, wie er in Rechtsstreitigkeiten vorgehen und entscheiden solle. '). See also, Ehrlich, Eugen,Gesetz und lebendes Recht. Vermische kleinere Schriften, Berlin, Dunker und Humblot, 1986, S.241–253. However, Verwaltungsnormen are slightly different from the rule of conduct which address both to civil servants and the public.

58. See Ehrlich (*supra* note 57, 1913), 65(Entscheidungsnormen sind ein Recht nur für die Gerichten und staatliche Behörden, nicht eine Regel des Handelns.'), 98('Die Entscheidungsnorm ist wie alle gesellschaftlichen Normen eine Regal des Handelns, aber doch nur für die Gerichte, sie ist, wenigstens in erster Lie nicht eine Regel für die Menschen, die im Leben wirken, sondern für die Menschen, die über diese Menschen, zu Gericht sitzen. Insoweit die Entscheidungsnorm eine Rechtsnorm ist, erscheint sie daher als Rechtsnorm besonderer Art, verschieden von den Rechtsnormen, die allgemeine Regel des Handelns enthalten.'), 140f. ('Jede Entscheidungsnorm enthält schon den Keim eines Rechtssatzes. Auf das in ihr enthaltene Grundsätzliche zurückgeführt, in Worte gefaßt, mit dem Anspruch auf Allgemeingültigkeit autoritativ verkündet, wird die Entscheidungsnorm zum Rechtssatz'... '... , sind diese[i.e. Rechtssätze] gewiß mit sehr seltenen Ausnahmen aus Entscheidungsnormen entstanden, die zum ersten Male von einem Juristen aus Anlaß eines ihm zur Entscheidung vorliegenden Streitfalles ausgesprochen wurden.'), 365(Entscheidungsnormen); Ehrlich (*supra* note 57, 1936), 81(norms for decision are addressed to the authorities and not to the people.), 122f.('The norm for decision, like all social norms, is primarily a rule of conduct, but only for the courts. It is not, primarily at least, a rule for the men who are the doers in life, but for men who sit in judgment upon the doers. In so far as the norm for decision is a legal norm, it appears to be a legal norm of a special kind, different from the legal norms that contain general rules of conduct.'), 174f.('Every norm for decision contains the germ of a legal proposition. Reduced to that part of its content that is basic principle, couched in words, proclaimed authoritatively with a claim to universal validity, the norm for decision becomes a legal proposition.'... '..., these[i.e. legal proposition], with rare exceptions, undoubtedly have had their origin in norms for decision which were first enunciated by a jurist when a dispute was submitted to him for decision.'); Ehrlich (*supra* note 51, 1920), 38(12) Hougaku-Kyoukai-Zasshi, 7 (1920) (Entscheidungsnormen).

We must identify the binding rules of conduct, which are independent of the norms for decision of the Courts. Even if a certain rule is not included in Article 38 of the ICJ Statute, this rule may be binding among States as a rule of conduct. In fact, when we discuss the binding force of the rules and principles of national or international law, we assume that we are dealing with the whole range of national or international legal norms regulating its subjects. The binding force of international law as related to the norms to be applied by the Japanese Courts constitutes a part of this whole range of national or international legal norms.

We may understand under the binding rule of conduct (1) the legislative law made by the parliament, and (2) the circular notices (like official notices, circulars, Verwaltungsvorschriften) made by the administration.

As far as (3) the living law in the *Ehrlich* meaning concerned, Eugen Ehrlich distinguishes the law and the living law, and points out the features as follows:

> The standard therefore according to which the Sociological school of jurisprudence must test, not only the legal propositions, but also the legal document, is actual life, Here too it must observe the distinction between the law that is enforced by the courts and the living law. The entire valid content of the document is law that is enforced by the courts (i.e. **norm for decision**) for, in case the parties resort to litigation, the decision will hinge upon it; but **it is living law only in so far as the parties habitually insist upon it even if they not wish to risk litigation.**'... 'But the contrast is of the utmost importance for the administration of justice and for legislation as well. It is questionable whether the latter should lend themselves to permitting those things to be taken seriously which were never intended to be taken seriously. (emphasis added)[60]

Ehrlich suggests that the significance of the living law may exercise an influence on the norms for decision and it constitutes the foundation of the legal order of human society as follows:

> But the scientific significance of the living law is not confined to its influence upon the norms for decision which the courts apply or upon the content of statures. The knowledge of the living law has an independent value, and this consists in the fact that it constitutes the foundation of the legal order of human society. In order to acquire a knowledge of this order we must know the usages, relations of domination, legal relations, contracts, articles of association, declarations by last will and testament, quite independently of the question whether they have already

59. See Hans Kelsen, General Theory of Law and State, Cambridge Mass., Harvard University Press, 1945, at 113(it is distinguished among hard law, soft law and no law.).

60. Ehrlich (*supra* note 57, 1936), 498; Ehrlich (*supra* note 57, 1913), 402('Die soziologishche Rechtsbetrachtung wir daher nicht bloß die Rechtssätze, sondern auch die Urkunde am Leben zu messen haben, sie wird auch hier zwischen geltendem und lebenndem Rechte untersc-heiden. Geltendes Recht (Entscheidungsnorm) ist wohl der ganze gültige Inhalt der Urkunde; denn im Prozesse wird es darauf ankommen; aber **lebendes Recht ist er doch nur so weit, als sich die Parateien daran regelmäßig halten, auch wenn sie es nicht auf einen Prozeß ankommen lassen wollen.** ' ...'Aber auch für Rechtspflege und Gesetzgebung ist der Gegensatz selbstverständlich von größter Wichtigkeit. Es ist gewiß fraglich, ob sie sich unbedingt dazu hergeben sollen, das ernst zu nehmen, was gar nicht bestimmt war, ernst genommen zu werden.') (emphasis added).

> found expression in a judicial decision or in a statute or whether they will ever find it.[61]

The living law does not bind the courts typically:

> The living law is not the part of the content of the document that the courts recognize as binding when they decide a legal controversy, but only that part which the parties actually observe in life.[62]

The living law is recognized in the ways as follows:

> This then is the *living* law in contradistinction to that which is being enforced in the courts and other tribunals. The living law is the law which dominates life itself even through it has not been posited in legal propositions. The source of our knowledge of this law is, first, the modern legal document; secondly, direct observations, not only of those that the law has recognized but also of those that it has overlooked and passed by, indeed even of those that it has disapproved. In our day, doubtless, the most important source of knowledge of the living law is the modern legal document.[63]

Commentary can be characterized as modern legal document. The living law is created by the following sources:

> '*Bona fides, Treu und Glauben* [good faith], and business usage accordingly become not only sources of the living social law, but also sources of norms for decision and finally of legal propositions.'[64] In addition, '[t]he living law, even where it is created by the state, preponderantly, as to its content, limited to an association.'[65]

61. Ehrlich (*supra* note 57, 1936), 502; Ehrlich (*supra* note 57, 1913), 406('Aber die wissenschaftliche Bedeutung des lebenden Rechts beginnt nicht erst da, wo es für die Entschedunsnormender Gerichte oder für den Inhalt der Gesetze bestimmend wird. Es hat seinen eigenen Erkenntniswert, und dieser liegt darin, daß es die Grundlage der rechtlichen Ordnung der menschlichen Gesellschaft ist. Um diese kennen zu lernen, müssen wir die Übung, Herrschafts-und Rechtsverhältnisse, Verträge, Satzungen, letzwilligen Erklärungen feststellen, ganz unabhängig davon, ob sie in einer Entscheidung order in einem Gesetze bereits Ausdruck gefunden haben order je darin Eingang finden würden.')
62. Ehrlich (*supra* note 57, 1936), 497; Ehrlich (*supra* note 57, 1913), 401('Lebendes Rech is vom Urkendeninhalte nicht das, was etwa die Gerichte bei der Entscheidung eines Rechtsstreites als verbindlich anerkennen, sondern nur das, woran sich die Parteien im Leben halten.').
63. Ehrlich (*supra* note 57, 1936), 493; Ehrlich (*supra* note 57, 1913), 399 ('Das ist also das *lebende* Recht im Gegensatze zu dem bloß vor Gericht und den Behörden geltenden. Das lebende Recht ist das nicht in Rechtssätzen festgelegte Recht, das aber doch das Leben beherrscht. Die Quellen seiner Erkenntnis sind vor allem die moderne Urkunde, aber auch die unmittelbare Beobachtung des Lebens, des Handels und Wandels, der Gewohnheiten und Gebräuche, dann aber aller Verbände sowohl der rechtlich anerkannten als auch der von dem Rechte übersehenen und übergangenen, ja sogar der rechtlich mißbilligten. Die wichtigste Quelle für Erkenntnis des lebenden Rechts ist in unserer Zeit zweifellos die moderne Rechtsurkende.').
64. Ehrlich (*supra* note 57, 1936), 401; Ehrlich (*supra* note 57, 1913), 324. ('So wird die bona fides, Treu und Glauben, Verkehrsgebrauch und Usance nicht bloß zu einer Quelle des lebenden gesellschaftlichen Rechts, sondern auch zu einer neuen Quelle von Entschedungsnormen und schließlich sogar von Rechtssätzen.')
65. Ehrlich (*supra* note 57, 1936), 81; Ehrlich (*supra* note 57, 1913), 65('Das lebende Recht dagegen ist meist schon seinem Inhalte nach, selbst wenn es staatlichen Ursprungs ist, auf einen Verband beschränkt.')

The living law is neither 'no-law' nor 'customary law'. The civil servants should legally obey the circular notices and the tax practitioners should follow the circular notices as the living law in practice.

The circular notices reflect the rules of conducts for the civil servants. We can call these circular notices as primary soft law for these circular notices and the living law as the rule of conduct.

We do not understand typically under the binding norms for decision by the Courts (1) the circular notices (like official notices, circulars) and (2) the living law. However, the Courts of Japan refer exceptionally to the circular notices as norms for decision since the Courts and the administrative Agents should apply equally the circular notices to every administrative matter under the same or similar circumstance. It follows that the Courts employ the circular notices and the living law only to solve the issues with equity. We can call these circular notices as two tier soft law and the living law as the norms for decision.

We may ignore the other types[66] of soft law,[67] as well as, customary law approach[68] and hard law approach[69] here.

66. Cf. Baxter, Richard R., The Indus Basin, in; A.H. Garretson, R.D. Hayton and C.J. Olmstead (eds), The Law of International Drainage Basins, New York University School of Law, Oceana Publications, Dobbs Ferry, New York, 1967, 443 (476)(the author suggests concepts of hard law and soft law); Frank, Thomas M., The power of legitimacy among nations, Oxford University Press, Oxford, etc. 1990, 29; Kenneth W. Abbott and Duncan Snidal, Hard and Soft Law in International Governance, 54(3) International Organization, 421(2000); Steven R. Ratner and anne-Marie Slaghter, Appraising the Methods of International law: A Prospectus for Readers,93(2) The American Journal of International Law, 291(1994); Kingsbury, Benedict, The Concept of Compliance as a Function of Competing Conceptions of International Law, 19(2) Michigan Journal og Internationall Law,(1998);Clwmwna Jabloner und Wolf Okresek, Theoretische und praktische Anmerkungen zu Phäomenen des 'soft law', in: Ösrerr. Z. öffentl. Recht und Völkerrech 34,217ß241(1983); Grigory I. Tunkin, International law and other social norms function within the international system, in: Bin Cheng and E.D. Brown, Contemporary Problems of International Law: essays in honor of Georg Schwarzenberger on his eightieth birthday, London, Stevens & Sons Limited,1988, 282–300; Christoph Schreuer, Recommendations and the Traditional sources of International Law, German Yearbook of International Law: Jahrbuch für Internationales Recht, 20 (1977) 103–118; Onuma, Yasuyuki, International Law and with International Politics: The Functions of International Law in International Society, 14(1) EJIL, 105 (2003), 134('Whether the framework [of communication and mediation] can by enforced is of secondary importance. Therefore, the 'soft law', common policies of nations concerned and the 'rules of the game' can play a similar role.').
67. Thurer, Daniel, 'Soft Law', in: Bernhard (ed.), Encyclopedia of International Law, vol. 4, 452–469 (1998), 459f.; Kenneth W. and Duncan Snidal, Hard and Soft Law in International governance, 54(3) Legalization and World Politics, 421(2000). Cf. Daniel E. Ho, Compliance and International Soft Law: Why do Countries Implement the Basel Accord?, 5(3) Journal of International Economic Law,647(2002).
68. See Allison Christians, Hard Law, Soft Law, and International Taxation, 25(2) Wisconsin International Law Journal, 325 footnote 2(2008), also 329f. (the author criticizes on the customary law approach.).
69. Christians (*supra* note 68), 25(2) Wisconsin International Law Journal, 325 footnote 4)(2008).

§8.03 THE STATUS OF THE OECD MODEL TAX CONVENTION

As Thomas Dubut points out:

> it makes no doubt that the Model Tax Conventions *in genuine mean* are neither international treaties nor international customary law as reflected in VCLT in light of international public law: they are not 'international agreements concluded between States in written form and governed by international law', Therefore, the Commentaries on these Models cannot be characterized as an 'agreement relating to treaty which was made between all the parties in connection with the conclusion of the treaty' according to Article 32 (2) a) VCLT.[70]

On the other hand, within the OECD legal order, the Organization may take decisions which are legally binding for member countries, provided that they do not abstain at the time they are adopted. However, neither the Model Tax Convention nor its Commentary that refer to them have taken the legal form of decision or an agreement, but constitute the scope and content of mere recommendations.[71]

The OECD Model tax treaties have been all accompanied by Commentary. This Commentary has also support frequent changes with amendments approximately every two years. The OECD is run by its Council, which is composed of the 30 Member States and the European Commission. The OECD Council makes decision under Article 5 of the Convention on the Organization for Economic Co-operation and Development (signed in Paris on 14 December 1960 (the OECD Convention)). The OECD Model Tax Convention is not International law in the genuine mean. However, the OECD Model and its Commentary is also the subject of a recommendation of the OECD Council to its Member States. Moreover, according to the OECD Convention this recommendation results in a legal obligation of the Member States. This obligation is known as a 'soft obligation'.[72]

The Council also makes recommendations by mutual agreement. The 1963 OECD draft Model, the 1977 OECD Model and the current looseleaf Model Conventions on Income and on Capital and their respective Commentary are all supported by recommendations of the Council rather than by a decision.[73]

The Model Tax Convention is significant not only for the text of the Model Treaty Articles but also for the explanatory Commentary which follows each article. In the recommendations of the Council made in 1997, the Council recommended prospectively that the tax administrations of the Member States follow the Commentary on the

70. See also Dubut, Thomas, 'The Court of Justice and the OECD Model Tax Conventions or the Uncertainties of the Distinction Hard Law , Soft Law , and No Law in the European Case Law', 40(1) Intertax 3(2012)(the Model Tax Conventions stricto sensu are not international treaties according to international customary law as reflected in VCLT.).Obviously international treaties should be distinguished from international customary law.
71. Dubut(*supra* note 70),40(1)Intertax 4,footnote 4(2012).
72. Lehner, Moris, Interpretation of Tax Treaties according to German Theory and Practice, in:Klaus Vogel (ed.) Interpretation of Tax Law and Treaties and Transfer Pricing in Japan and Germany, The Hague et set., Kluwer Law International, 1998, 85 (91); also Ward (*supra* note 12), 60(3) BIFD,97(2006)(these decisions have binding force to all members when the various members have complied with their constitutional procedures, except as otherwise provided.)
73. Ward (*supra* note 12), 60(3) BIFD,97 and footnote 3 (2006).

articles of the Model as modified from time to time when applying and interpreting the corresponding provisions of their bilateral tax treaties. The actual treaties are negotiated on the basis of the Model Convention.[74]

Moreover, the Council has only 'adopted' the periodic updates to the Model and the Commentary since 1997. In addition, the CFA adopted the 2000 update and the Council seems not to have adopted it. The prospective 1997 recommendations of Council therefore continue to apply to the periodic updates.[75] It seems to exist a general agreement that the Commentary is an important source of tax authority in determining the scope and content of the treaty articles[76] but much less agreement on exactly how the Commentary fit into the treaty interpretative process.[77] The Introduction to the Model Tax Convention describes the status and function of the Commentary as follows:

> As the Commentaries have been drafted and agreed by the experts appointed to the Committee of Fiscal Affairs by the governments of Member states, they are of special importance in the development of international fiscal law. Although the Commentaries are not designed to be annexed in any manner to the conventions to be signed by Member states, which alone constitute legally binding international instruments, they can nevertheless be of great assistance in the application and interpretation of the conventions and, in particular, in the settlement of any disputes.[78]

Unfortunately, the Introduction and the Commentary themselves do not give an answer as to how the 'special importance' which the Commentary is expected to have in the application and the interpretation of treaties based on the Model Tax Convention can be achieved, given the generally applicable principles and rules of treaty interpretation.

I agree with the following comment by Sidney Robert and Hugh J. Ault:

> [U]nder limited circumstances, later OECD commentaries may also be relevant to interpretation of an earlier treaty by a court where the relevant language in each treaty is the same.[79]

We see the Commentary as the norm rather than the exception.[80]

---

74. Ward (*supra* note 12), 60(3) BIFD,97 and footnote 3 (2006).
75. Ward (*supra* note 12), 60(3) BIFD,97 (2006).
76. See, Vogel, Klaus, On Double Taxation Conventions,Kluwer, 1991, 33 (The Commentary is very important for the interpretation of tax treaties in that it provides a source from which the courts of different States can seek a common interpretation.).
77. Ault (*supra* note 34), in: Herbert H. Alpert and Kees van Raad (ed.), Essays on International Taxation.
78. Intro, para. 29.
79. Robert and Glicklich, U.S. Interprets Netherlands-U.S. Treaty by Reference to Later Treaties with Other Nations, 34 Can. Tax J. 228(1986). Also, Ault (*supra* note 34), in: Herbert H. Alpert and Kees van Raad (ed.), Essays on International Taxation, 67. See, Ward (*supra* note 12), 60(3) BIFD, 99 (2006) ('The OECD Commentaries that existed at the time of the conclusion of a bilateral treaty form part of the context of the particular treaty form part of the context of the particular treaty or, ..., form part of the 'legal context' of the treaty and, on that basis, play an important role in the interpretive process.').
80. Ward (*supra* note 12), 60(3) BIFD, 98 (2006).

The Commentary is characterized as a rule of conduct, since the tax administrations of the OECD Member States, like the NTA of Japan, follow the Commentary as modified from time to time when applying and interpreting the provisions of their bilateral tax treaties. I point out two issues: first, should the tax administration follow the Commentary if the articles of the bilateral tax treaties are different from the articles of the Model as modified from time to time when applying and interpreting the provisions of bilateral tax treaties?

First of all, the intention of the treaty parties is referred to in Articles 31 and 32 of VCLT.[81] The Commentary on VCLT, however, underlines the extreme significance of the role of the intention of the parties in the treaty interpretive process in international law. On determining the intentions of the parties in the treaty, we seek not a subjective determination but rather an objective determination[82] derived from the text of the existing treaty itself, the application of the general rule of interpretation (Article 31) and the supplementary means of interpretation (Article 32) of VCLT as well as the application of the other interpretive principles of logic and linguistic sense. We presume that the parties have the intention to use the terms with their ordinary meaning.[83] The parties, to a bilateral treaty who are both members of the OECD, are presumed to have the intention that the provisions of the tax treaty negotiated by them should be interpreted on the same basis as set out in the relevant provision of the current Commentary rather than the earlier Commentary that existed at the time they were negotiating the particular treaty.[84]

Second, should the tax payer follow the Commentary on the articles of the Model as modified from time to time when applying and interpreting the provisions of their bilateral tax treaties?

§8.04 THE STATUS OF THE COMMENTARY THEREON

Similarly, the Commentary cannot be considered as an 'agreement relating to the treaty which was made between all the parties in connection with the conclusion of the treaty', so that they can become part of the context in the meaning of Article 31 (2) b) VCLT.[85]

However, the OECD Council has, in a series of instruments adopted in accordance with Article 5(b) of the OECD Convention, recommended that the member

81. 1155 UNTS 332.
82. Cf. Canaris, Claus-Wilhelm, Systemdenken und Systembegriff in der Jurisprudenz: entwickelt am Beispiel des deutschen Privatrechts,2. Aufl., Duncker und Humblot, Berlin, 1983, 88–95.
83. Ward (*supra* note 12), 60(3) BIFD, 99 and footnote 13 (2006).
84. Schaumburg, Harald, Internationales Steuerrecht, 3.Aufl. Dr. Otto Schmidt Köln, 2011, Rz. 16.59f., S.641(Dynamic Interpretation).
85. An opposite position is defended by Frank Engelen, Some Observations on the Legal Status of the Commentaries on the OECD Model, 60(3) BIFD 106 (2006) (109) (the author argues that states can bind themselves to the Commentaries as a matter of (hard) international law.). His argumentation suggests that careful scrutiny must be made with respect to other OECD guidance, as well as guidance from other organizations concerned with international tax matters, such as the United Nations. So Christians (*supra* note 68), 25(2) Wisconsin International Law Journal, 325 footnote 3) (2008).

countries and their tax administration 'conform to the Model Tax Convention, as interpreted by the Commentary thereon' and 'follow the Commentaries on the Articles of the Model Tax Convention, as modified from time to time, when applying and interpreting the provisions of their bilateral tax conventions that are based on these Articles'. These recommendations are obviously not intended to be legally binding.[86] These recommendations may appropriately be referred to as 'soft law'.[87]

Every OECD member country understands that the OECD Commentary are not intended to have any normative effect in law, whether or not international law, or domestic or commune law.[88,89] It cannot therefore be assumed that the member country or any other treaty negotiating State ought to follow the Commentary in interpreting and applying the particular bilateral treaty.

The Commentary existing at the time a particular bilateral tax treaty was concluded should be treated as part of legal context in respect of that treaty to the extent that the articles in the treaty follow the articles of the OECD Model, particularly in respect with treaties concluded between OECD Members states. As part of the legal context, the existing Commentary can be indicative of the intention of the contracting parties and therefore of the interpretation of the treaty provisions on a non-binding basis.[90]

In summary, it is clear that the Commentary as such is not legally binding and that there is no legal obligation in international law to follow the Commentary.[91,92]

Nevertheless, tax administrations of Member States (like Japan) follow the Commentary[93] in practice.

86. So Engelen (*supra* note 85), 60(3) BIFD, 106(2006).
87. Engelen (*supra* note 85), 60(3) BIFD, 106(2006).
88. Davis A. Ward,'Is there an obligation in international law of OECD Member states to follow the Commentaries on the Model?', in: Sjoerd Douma and Frank Engelen (eds)The Legal Status of the OECD Commentaries, Amsterdam 2008, 92.
89. I do not mention to the questions concerning the binding force of the Model Tax Convention within the European Union legal order as well as the irrelevance of the OECD Model Tax Convention for the interpretation of secondary EU law.
90. Ward, in:Douma/ Engelen (*supra* note 88), 93.
91. So, Ward, in: Douma/ Engelen (*supra* note 88), 93.
92. Engelen (*supra* note 85), 60(3) BIFD, 109(2006)(insofar as the OECD Member countries have not entered an observation on the interpretation of the articles of the OECD Model and the Commentaries thereto and, when concluding or revising their bilateral tax treaties, conformed to those provisions, as recommended by the Council in accordance with Art. 5(b) of the OECD Convention, it is clear that the circumstances of the negotiations were such as called for some reaction if the parties wished to disagree with or had any serious question to raise regarding that interpretation. If the parties failed to do so, they must be held to have acquiesced in that interpretation so as to become legally bound by it.). This is not my position.
93. Ellis, Maarten J., The Influence of the OECD Commentaries on Treaty Interpretation – Response to Prof. Dr. Klaus Vogel, 54(12) BIFD,618(2000) (very often the Commentaries do not provide a clear interpretation. They are written to explain the background, why this provision was considered necessary. They give some insight in the thinking of the administrations, letting every administrator put in his thoughts.).

[A] Rule of Conduct for Tax Administration

We should clearly distinct between, on the one hand, the question of whether the Contracting States follow (or should follow) the Commentary under principles of international law, and on the other hand, the question of whether taxpayers and tax courts follow (or should follow) the Commentary. In this respect, a distinction is usually made between monism and dualism. Taxpayers of states adhering to the monistic theory usually follow the Commentary if the state is so followed under principles of international law. However, taxpayers of states adhering to the dualistic theory do not usually follow the Commentary even if the state is so followed under principles of international law.[94] So, the question of the status of the Commentary according to a State's internal law can only be answered on a country-by country basis.[95] In my view, the Japanese government has adopted the monistic theory,[96] because tax treaties are part of internal tax law affecting taxpayers and subject to interpretation by courts in that country (Japan).[97] Tax treaties are not restricted to regulating the relations between and among States but are primarily focused on the private actors who will be applying the treaty rules in the first instanced to determine their tax planning.[98]

In light of statements in the Introduction of the Model Tax Concention that existing conventions should, as far as possible, be interpreted in the spirit of revised Commentary,[99] the tax authorities may consider that they cannot appropriately argue against the interpretation contained in the Commentary, but made later than the treaty in question has entered into force.[100]

The competent tax authorities then issue the circular notices (like official notices, circulars) in which they normally follow the paragraphs of the Commentary on the particular provision of OECD Model Tax Convention. The civil servants in the tax administrations should obey these circular notices employing Commentary on the ground of Article 14 (2) the National Administrative Organization Act of Japan. When we observe the circumstance in the tax practice, we may call such circular notices as rules of conduct that are not legally binding for taxpayers and tax courts.

---

94. Cf. Engelen (*supra* note 85), 60(3) BIFD, 105(2006) (Taxpayers of states adhering to the monistic theory are usually bounded by the Commentaries if the state is so bound under principles of international law. However, taxpayers of states adhering to the dualistic theory are normally bounded by the Commentaries even if the state is so follow under principles of international law.).
95. Engelen (*supra* note 85), 60(3) BIFD, 105(2006).
96. Engelen (*supra* note 7), 553(in the Netherlands, international law also has direct internal effect pursuant to an unwritten rule of constitutional law and is an integral part of the law of the Netherlands.)
97. See Avery Jones (*supra* note 13), 53 Tax L. Rev. 22(1999).
98. See Ault (*supra* note 34), in: Alpert/Raad (eds), Essays on International Taxation, 64.
99. The 1995 OECD Commentary, paras 33–36 at Introduction. para 35 at Introduction ('other changes or additions to the Commentaries are normally applicable to the interpretation and application of conventions concluded before their adoption, because they reflect the consensus of the OECD Member countries as to the proper interpretation of existing provisions and their application to specific situations.').
100. Avery Jones (*supra* note 13), 53 Tax L. Rev. 21f.(1999); Vogel (*supra* note 9), 54(12) BIFD, 612(2000).

[B] Living Law for Tax Payers and Tax Practitioners

Neither taxpayer nor tax practitioner (certified tax accountant, Steuerberater as well) is bound by the circular notices which the NTA issues. generally, the circulars have not any binding force on the public.

However, most of taxpayers and tax practitioners normally follow these circular notices since the tax practitioners try to avoid disputes with the tax offices and the taxpayers, all the more so that they have not enough knowledge of tax treaties and interpretation thereon.[101] The Commentary reflects still the opinion of high-ranking experts, although their interpretation is not binding on taxpayer and tax practitioner.

In this context, we may characterize such circular notices as living law for taxpayers and tax practitioners in the field of taxation.

Moreover, it may happen that the tax lawyers and tax practitioners assert the application of the circular notice following the Commentary to their own tax matters, or apply directly the Commentary in the absence of the relevant provision of circulars, because taxpayers and tax practitioners probably consider that the administration is likely to apply them. Needless to say, taxpayers and their advisers are not bound by the Commentary.[102]

Then, taxpayers follow indirectly the Commentary through the circular notices in practice, or, directly the Commentary to their own tax matters in the case of lack of the law and circular corresponding with the particular paragraph of the Commentary.

In this context, we may also characterize the Commentary as the living law for taxpayers and tax practitioners and call them as secondary soft law.

[C] The Equal Application of the Rule of Conduct to Tax Cases

Needless to say, the courts are not bounded by the recommendations of the OECD. The courts should observe the law exclusively, to which international treaties belong, but not mere resolutions/recommendations of international bodies.[103]

The tax administrations should apply the circular notices to the same or similar tax matters equally. Exceptionally, in case that the tax office did unequally applied the specific provision of the circular notice to the same tax matters, the High Court of Osaka held that the tax office should equally apply that provision of the circular notice to the same tax matters in a case when a tax office in a province did not apply the favourable provision to the plaintiff, but other tax offices in the other provinces had applied the same provision to all of the taxpayers. This means that the circular notices should be characterized as a rule of conduct for the tax administration and the equally application of such circular notices can also play a role as a norm for decision before the courts substantially.

101. See Ault (*supra* note 11), 22(4) Intertax 145(1994)(fitting the Commentaries into the Vienna Convention Pattern).
102. Vogel (*supra* note 9), 54(12) BIFD, 614(2000).
103. Vogel (*supra* note 9), 54(12) BIFD, 614(2000).

Consequently, the circulars which follow the Commentary should be characterized as a rule of conduct for the tax administration and in equal application such circular notices can also play a role as norms for decision before the courts substantially.

[D] The Tentative Conclusion: The Commentary as Soft Law

The Commentary is not binding for the Member States, but tax administration normally follows it. Moreover, the competent authority usually issues the circular notices which follow the paragraphs of the Commentary. Such circular can be characterized as the rule of conduct for the tax administration substantially.

Moreover, taxpayers and tax practitioners normally follow the circular notices in the field of taxation.

In practice, they apply directly the Commentary to their own tax matters in the case of lack of the law and circular corresponding to the particular paragraph of the Commentary. Such circulars and the Commentary itself can be characterized as the living law for taxpayers and tax practitioners..

To sum up, the Commentary can be characterized as a 'primary' soft law when the competent tax authority issues the circular notices corresponding to the Commentary and the tax administration should obey the circulars which should be considered to be rules of conduct.

Taxpayers and tax practitioners normally follow the fiscal circular notices/ the Commentary which constitute the living law. Theses can be called as a 'secondary' soft law.

The Council has never recommended that the tax payers follow the Commentary on the articles of the Model. However, the majority of tax payers and their practitioners prospectively follow the Commentary in practice. In this context, the Commentary belongs to the secondary soft law as the living law typically.

A part of taxpayers and their practitioners does not follow the Commentary when applying and interpreting the provisions of their bilateral tax treaties. Instead of ignoring them, one may use the Commentary as secondary soft law through the circulars following them, since everyone should comply with the law, but someone does not follow that law.

Moreover, the courts should apply the Commentary equally to the same or similar tax matters in the case of lack of the circular corresponding with the particular paragraph of the Commentary. This Commentary can be characterized as a ' two-tier' soft law. Finally, the tax courts should equally apply the circulars corresponding to the Commentary when the tax offices apply these circulars to the majority of taxpayers.[104]

Should the Court of Justice employ the Commentary on the articles of the Model as modified from time to time when applying and interpreting the provisions of the bilateral tax treaties, in case that the tax payers or the tax administrators did violate the Commentary? The Commentary is not intended by the CFA or the Council to be binding

104. So the Judgments of Osaka High Court dated 12.05 1969, Gyousyu vol. 20, no. 5=6, 675; Utsunomiya Direct Court dated 24.11.1955,Gyousyu vol. 21,no.12,2817.

on the Courts either in international law or domestic law.[105] The Commentary is not designed to be annexed in any manner to treaties signed by the Member States and which only belong to the legally binding international instruments.[106] This is because the Commentary is not law. However, the tax administration of the States that apply the tax treaty follow the Commentary, which is a rule of conduct like the circular notices (Verwaltungsvorshriften), but not a norm for decision. The tax administrations usually follow the Commentary without their Reservation in the paragraph of the Commentary concerned.

The Commentary does not bind the Court of Justice typically in the same way as the circular notice (Verwaltungsvorschriften). However, the Court exceptionally refers to the Commentary when applying and interpreting the provisions of the bilateral tax treaties or applying them in case that the Courts and the administrative Agents should apply equally the Commentary to every tax payer under the same or similar circumstances. In this context, the Commentary belongs to the two-tier soft law as a norm for decision. It is surely that later Commentary is at least taken into account by courts in interpreting treaties, also by making reference to the possibility of their existence.[107]

Similarly, the Transfer Pricing Guidelines for Multinational Enterprises and Tax Administrations approved by the OECD Council is not the International law in the genuine mean, but may be characterized as the two-tier soft law like the Commentary on the OECD Model Tax Convention.

§8.05 THE INFLUENCE OF THE COMMENTARY ON INTERNATIONAL TAX CASES OF JAPAN

The Model Tax Conventions appear in few Japanese judgments on the provisions of domestic law concerning direct taxation. In fact, even though Member States (like Japan) hold an exclusive competence in the field of taxation, the Japanese Judge examines whether the exercise of this competence has infringed the fundamental freedoms of self-decision and transaction. In this context, the next question is whether compliance with the OECD Model Tax Conventions' rule and Commentary' interpretation can establish a justification for the tax matter and dispute.

(i) *Toyota Motor Corporation* case about Californian unitary taxation affecting the local taxation: Judgment of the Yokohama District Court.
(ii) *Imabari Shipbuilding Company* case concerning transfer pricing transaction: Judgment of the Supreme Court dated 14 April 2008.
(iii) *Glaxo* case concerning no infringement of the JPN-Singapore tax treaty: Judgment of the Supreme Court dated 29 October 2009 (the Japanese

105. Cf. Waters (*supra* note 16), in: Lang & Jirousek (eds), Praxis des Internationalen Steuerrechts, 674; Ward (*supra* note 12), 60(3) BIFD, 99(2006). Waters and Ward do not distinguish the norms for decision from the rule of conducts.
106. Ward (*supra* note 12), 60(3) BIFD,99 and footnote 15 (2006).
107. Avery Jones (*supra* note 13), 53 Tax L. Rev. 37f.(1999).

anti-tax haven legislation does not infringe the Article 7(1) of the Japan-Singapore tax treaty about business profits).[108]

The Japanese Supreme Court indicated its willingness to consider the Commentary as an aid to interpretation. The Supreme Court held that the OECD Commentary 'can be referred to as material'[109] and as a mere 'supplementary means of interpretation' within the meaning of Article 32 in the VCLT.[110,111]

This is the first judgment of the Supreme Court in which the Court expressly recognized that the provisions of double tax treaties, as far as they are based on the Model Tax Convention, should respect the OECD Commentary and not be infringed by the domestic CFC legislation.[112,113] In this respect, the Court appeared to confirm the soft law of the OECD Commentary since it follows the Commentary.

The tax lawyers and tax practitioners tend to apply directly the Commentary under the monism in the absence of any relevant provision of circulars which can follows the Commentary, because taxpayers as well may consider that the tax administrator is likely to apply them. Needless to say, taxpayers and their advisers are not bound by the Commentary. The Court is not bound by the interpretation of the Commentary. However, the Commentary may play a role as the two-tier soft law there.

§8.06 CONCLUSION

In assessing the value of the subsequent Commentary, it should be pointed out that the Commentary is the product of the work of Working Party I and the CFA, all of whose members are experienced representatives of the tax administrations of the member countries. As a consequence of the membership, the Commentary has been perceived by some to have a bias in favour of the fisc. On the other hand, taxpayers and

108. Asatsuma (*supra* note 3), 64(10) BIFD, 517–525 (2010).
109. Lang (*supra* note 1), 20 and footnote 26(where tax treaty negotiators followed the OECD Model Tax Convention, one might conclude that they wanted to create a provision having the same meaning which the Commentary gives to the corresponding provisions of the OECD Model Tax Convention. It is clear that the Commentary is part of the material which can be taken into account when interpreting the provision of the bilateral tax treaty.)
110. United Nations Treaty Series, vol. 1155, p.331. The Convention entered into force on 27 January 1980. Corten/Klein (supra *note* 2), 8411 ff. (Yves le Bouthillier).
111. Asatsuma (*supra* note 3), 64(10) BIFD, 518 (2010).
112. Cf. Gutmann, Daniel, Robert J. Danon and Hugues Salome,French-Swiss Point of View on the Societe Schneider Electric Case: Some Thoughts on the Personal Attribution of Income Requirement in International Tax Law, 31(49 Intertax, 156(2003); Bourtourault, Pierre-Yves and Marcellin N. Mbwa-Mboma, French High Tax Court Confirms that The Former France-Switzerland Tax Treaty Overrides the French CFC Legislation, 30(12) Intertax, 493(2002). See also Clayson, Murray, The Impact of Europeann Law and Treaty Relies on the UK Controlled foreign companies Rules, 26(11) Intertax, 326(1998)
113. Körner, Andreas, German Reference to the ECJ for a Preliminary Ruling: Unilateral Switch-over Clause and CFC Rules, 34(1) Intertax, 32(2004); Helminen, Marjaana, Is There a Future for CFC-regimes in the EU?, 33(3) Intertax, 117(2005)..

organizations representing taxpayers whose treaty rights may be affected by the Commentary have no such opportunity.[114]

We look at the similar phenomena in the circular notes issued by the tax authority. Taxpayers and their tax practitioners whose treaty rights may be affected by the circular have no such opportunity. Neither the Commentary nor the circular notes have typically binding force.

It appears so far that, the Commentary of the OECD Model Conventions provides with soft law for the interpretation of double tax treaties which follow the Models. Soft law here can be characterized as the rule of conduct for tax administration, as the living law for taxpayers and tax practitioners and, as a norm for decision in equally applying the tax treaties in problem before the courts. This is the two-tier soft law.

The OECD-argument seems relevant for the interpretation of DTT provisions, in other words, as 'soft law' before the courts. Even if this conclusion is not automatically valid for the Commentary, which is applied by the organs of a legal order and by Courts with a certain judicial effectiveness: to paraphrase Thomas Dubut,[115] between 'no law' (the Models in a narrow sense) and 'hard law' (the tax treaties), a small room is left for two-tier soft law considerations. The OECD-argument can provide a rule of conduct and living law for the interpretation of double tax convention and domestic tax law provisions through the Commentary. It does not follow that the courts have the obligation to conform to an interpretation set out in the Commentary although, under principles of international law, the OECD member countries adhering to the monistic theory (like the Nederland), are legally bound by that interpretation.[116] OECD Commentary is "none binding soft law" which has typically "a certain interpretive value". However, the two-tier soft law approach may be useful in identifying and defining the principles we use to explain what role players in international tax field can do, and ought to play in the formation of tax law.[117]

114. Ward (*supra* note 12), 60(3) BIFD, 101(2006)

115. Dubut(supra note 70), 40(1)*Intertax* 12(2012)(one thing seems clear in the case law of the ECJ: between 'no law' (the Models *stricto sensu*) and potential 'hard law' (the Commentaries), no place is left for genuine soft law considerations. Dubut recharacterizes the Commentaries as potential hard law. His analyse might be not convincing. The Model and its Commentary can be the legal documents in the context of living law, when tax payers and their tax practitioners follow them without law and circulars as reflected in the Model and its Commentary.

116. Cf. Engelen (*supra* note 7), 554.

117. Cf. Christians (*supra* note 68), 25(2) Wisconsin International Law Journal, 333(2008). See Court of Appeals of Antwerp, 21 June 2011 Decision, TFR 2011/62(OECD Commentary: "none binding soft law" which has "a certain interpretive value".); also Danish High Court, December 2011, NO. SKM20012.121OLR (Term "beneficial owner" must be interpreted in the light of the guidelines laid down in the Commentary.); Czech Supreme Administrative Court, 13 January 2011,No.9 Afs 66/2010-189(In the decision regarding the interpretation of Art.5in the treaty between at/cz concluded in 1979, which does not explicitly comprise separate time threshold and separate provision for service PE , the court has used OECD Commentary as the interpretative tool.).Quelle: Tax Treaty Case Law around the Globe, June 14-16, 2012, Tilburg University.

CHAPTER 9

A European Legal Tax Order Based on Ability to Pay*

Joachim Lang & Joachim Englisch

§9.01 THE NEED FOR A EUROPEAN TAX ORDER

Europe has come a long way in overcoming political and economic barriers ever since the end of World War II. A first decisive step was certainly the foundation of the so-called European Coal and Steel Community in 1952, when six European States transferred a part of their sovereign powers to a supranational institution. A few years later, the Treaty of Rome established the European Community (EC)[1] as a customs and economic unity consisting of those six countries. Seven other European countries which preferred to confine themselves to the creation of a mere customs union created the European Free Trade Association (EFTA) as an alternative organization. By virtue of the Single European Act in 1986 the idea of an internal market without any obstacles for the trade between EC Member States was explicitly included as a Community objective. The political integration so far culminated in the ratification of the Treaty of Maastricht in 1992, which integrated the existing European Communities into a European Union (EU) supplemented by a common foreign and security policy as well as cooperation in the fields of justice and home affairs. One will see whether the Treaties will eventually be merged into the European Constitution adopted at the Brussels Summit on 18 June 2004[2] and still to be ratified by the Member States. At present, the European Monetary Union (EMU) is the latest milestone on the road to an

* This chapter, which is identical to the one published in the first edition, has been updated by the annex written by Werner C. Haslehner, which follows immediately after this.

1. Initially established as European Economic Community (EEC) but renamed European Community in the Treaty of Maastricht in 1992.
2. Treaty Establishing a Consitution for Europe, adopted by consensus by the European Convention on 13 June and 10 July 2003 (2003/C 169/01), and adopted by the Conference of

internal market without trade barriers. It allows the purchase and sale of goods and services anywhere in the participating Member States without currency risks and conversion costs, thus enhancing intra-community trade. Parallel to the deepening of the political and economic union, the EU has also considerably enlarged its territorial extension through the accession of new Member States. In May 2004, in its fifth and biggest enlargement exercise, the organization welcomed a total of ten new European Member States. Furthermore, the scope of the Common Market concept was extended to all EFTA Member States except Switzerland as a consequence of the agreement on a European Economic Area (EEA) between them and the EU. This means that from mid-2004 on, twenty-eight European countries form a single market characterized by the free movement of goods, services, persons and capital.

Logically, the more obstacles for free trade within Europe that have been removed, the more obvious the remaining ones have become, and this counts especially for those raised by taxation.[3] Here, three ways in which national tax provisions cause distortions of the Common Market can be identified: First, various national tax provisions still restrict the free movement of goods, persons, services and capital between Member States as provided in Article 3(1) (c)[4] by regulations which specifically discriminate or burden cross-border activities. However, the European Court of Justice (ECJ) increasingly challenges these tax obstacles by qualifying them as a breach of the four basic freedoms or of Article 90, both representing cornerstones of the EC Treaty. The Member States are therefore forced to react and to adapt their tax systems towards a non-restrictive, especially non-discriminatory set of rules. Secondly, the legal and factual conditions for doing business in the Member States are converging more and more as a result of Community integration. Thus, unharmonized national tax systems have turned into a major factor in the location of capital and enterprises.[5] The importance of tax arbitration increases to the very same extent as existing tax discrimination of cross-border activities is abolished by the ECJ's rulings. This is why tax competition among Member States has become an increasingly sensitive issue in recent years. In addition, the monetary union which was perfected in 1999 has undoubtedly fostered the temptation to attract foreign investment via tax policy, as monetary and fiscal policy-making powers have been shifted to the European level and are no longer available to improve a single State's competitive position. Correspondingly, Member States which lag behind in offering an attractive tax environment are punished by the market agents, which will move their activities abroad. The two main aspects of this development towards a European tax competition are the creation of special tax privileges for certain investments of non-residents, and a significant reduction in the taxation of internationally fluctuating capital and business

Representatives of the Governments of the Member States on 18 June 2004 with modifications as specified in document CIG 85/04.

3. Lindencrona/Lodin/Wiman/Lodin, *Liber Amicorum LeifMutén*, p. 199 (218); Wathelet, *EC Tax Review* 2004, p. 2.
4. Articles without further specification refer to the EC Treaty.
5. Cf. Report of the Ruding Committee, p. 102; Chown, *Intertax* 2000, p. 102; Wathelet, *EC Tax Review* 2004, p. 2; Klaver/Timmermans, *EC Tax Review* 1999, p. 185; Stevens/van der Beek/Sommerhalder, *EC Tax Review* 1998, p. 80(81).

investments.[6] With the latest enlargement of the European Union by, among others, eight former Communist planned economies with a great revenue emphasis on indirect taxation and, consequently, low taxes on personal and corporate income, the competition has become even more intense. Finally, the lack of harmonization results in significant compliance costs for 'free movers' confronted with twenty-five different tax systems and, not to be forgotten, administrative procedures. This alone may impede small businesses from engaging in cross-border activities, an effect clearly not in line with the idea of an internal market.

Why does all this call for a European Legal Tax Order? A first aspect is that currently, there does exist a high degree of uncertainty among Member States on just how to reform the unharmonized parts of their national tax systems to cope with the requirements of a single market as defined in the EC Treaty. As a consequence, tax planning of those entities and individuals involved in transnational economic activities is greatly hampered by the apparent unpredictability of possible breaches of EC law and Member States' reactions to eventual judgments of the ECJ.[7] In almost every Member State large lists of national tax rules suspected of infringing primary Community law are circulating which call for a major tax reform and the abandonment of traditional structures accepted as a part of international tax law.[8] However, Member States are reluctant to change those provisions and usually claim their EC conformity until one of them is hit directly by an ECJ ruling. This is mostly due to the fact that the Court's interpretation of the relevant treaty provisions, especially the four basic freedoms, has still not been transformed into generally accepted principles of a non-restriction test for national tax law. This uphill task is not simplified by the fact that the ECJ has interpreted those quasi-constitutional requirements which are not specifically related to tax in an evolutionary, rather undogmatic and sometimes inconsistent manner. This state of affairs is not only a present danger to budgetary planning of the Member States. It is also contrary to the principle of legal certainty underlying both the Community legal order as well as those of the Member States[9] and hence impairs taxpayers' right to a foreseeable and reliable tax framework when engaging in transnational activities. Thus, the groundwork in establishing a European Legal Tax Order needs to be dedicated to the constitutional principles governing taxation of intra-community business and labour as derived from primary Community law. While these principles are specifically important in those fields of taxation not yet subject to Community harmonization, they nevertheless also apply to harmonized areas of direct and indirect taxation.[10] This study is an attempt to give some orientation on the main principles and their impact on national tax laws.

6. Cf. Ruding, *EC Tax Review* 1998,72.
7. Cf. Wathelet, *EC Tax Review* 2004, p. 2 (3); Hinnekens, *ET*1996, p. 286 (289).
8. Cf. Vanistendael, ET 2000, p. 3 (4): 'If all provisions listed in this survey [contained in ET 1/2000] have to be rewritten in the light of the non-discrimination principle, this will amount to the biggest tax reform ever in all the Member States... Therefore, the term 'tax revolution'... is not an overstatement.'
9. Cf. Tridimas, *The General Principles of EC Law*, 1999, p. 163 et seq.
10. As concerns direct taxes see, for example, ECJ, 18.9.2003, C-168/01 (Bosal),DB 2003,p. 2097 et seq. and commentary by *Snel*, ET 2003, p. 420 et seq.; for indirect taxes ECJ, 23.1.1986, case 39/85 (Bergeres-Becque), ECR 1986, 259. It is important to note, though, that in its recent case

Of course, 'negative integration' through constitutional principles which prohibit specific tax burdens only to be borne by cross-border activities does not by itself guarantee the undistorted functioning of the internal market as it leaves disparities between national tax jurisdictions untouched.[11] Rather, tax competition among Member States and compliance costs incurred by a diversified tax landscape raise the question of which, if any, 'positive' coordination or even harmonization measures should be agreed upon within the Community.[12] Various implications arise. As a first step, the fields of taxation which require a coordinated approach by all Member States must be identified. This is not merely a political issue because the EC Treaty establishes some elementary legal prerequisites for harmonization or coordination on Community level. As taxation is frequently an expression of historical developments, cultural peculiarities and the overall socio-economic policy of each Member State, special attention must be paid to the principle of subsidiarity laid down in Article 5 (2). If Community action can be deemed necessary and justified, the instruments available for a coordinated approach must be evaluated. There is a wide range starting from non-binding 'soft law' up to detailed Community directives leaving little space for national diversification. Again, it is also a legal question as to which kinds of measures are appropriate in which cases.[13] Furthermore, the rules concerning the 'genuine' harmonization procedure deserve critical attention, as legally binding measures generally require the unanimous vote of the Council. In a Union of twenty-five Member States this kind of decision-making process is hardly adequate to deal with the challenges that tax systems face in today's globally acting, technically advanced business environment. Moreover, its democratic legitimation can be seriously doubted. Finally, a European Tax Order must deal with the question of what principles the harmonization of certain fields of taxation should be based on and how they can be developed in a consistent manner. However, these questions will have to be left unconsidered here, meriting as they do an analysis of their own.

§9.02 THE CONSTITUTIONAL CORE OF A EUROPEAN TAX ORDER: CROSS-BORDER ABILITY TO PAY

[A] Foundation in Member States' Constitutions

Any European Tax Order will essentially rely on the basic common values of the European constitutions. Not only does Article 6 (2) of the EU treaty state that the Union shall respect fundamental rights as they result from the constitutional traditions

law the ECJ demanded a separate action of judicial review of Secondary EC Law if it cannot be adapted to the exigencies of Primary EC Law by way of interpretation, ECJ, 5.10.2004, case 475/01 *(Commission v. Greece)*, paras 17 et seq. with further references.

11. Hinnekens, *ET* 1996, p. 286 (300).
12. Cf. Farmer/Lyal, *EC Tax Law*, 1994, p. 10: 'Taxes affect the conditions of competition between business in different countries, and the degree of harmonization necessary in order to ensure equality is much greater than that necessary for the elimination of tax frontiers.' See also Vanistendael, *ET* 2000, p. 3 (6).
13. For further details, see Grau/Herrera, *EC Tax Review* 2003, p. 28 et seq.

common to the Member States, as *general principles of Community law*,[14] but the tax-relevant provisions of the founding treaties, especially the fundamental freedoms of the EC Treaty, are themselves a reflection of beliefs and convictions shared throughout Europe. Consequently, they should be applied in a manner which respects the aforementioned constitutional values, notwithstanding their unique character as supranational law. Any interpretation which disregards their common roots would meet such considerable resistance in the long run that it could not be upheld if the Union was not to be endangered as a whole.

In this respect it can first be observed that almost all Member States fully recognize the fundamental idea of *tax equity* in their constitutional law, the only exception being the United Kingdom.[15] In Europe's modern, democratic States governed by the rule of law, tax equity is inseparably intertwined with tax equality. Its concept is embedded in the general principle of equality before the law which is upheld in all European constitutions.[16] Tax equity thus calls for equal taxation of taxpayers in objectively similar situations and different taxation of taxpayers in objectively different circumstances. The importance of tax equality for a European Legal Tax Order is further enhanced by Article 14 and Article 1(1) of the Protocol No. 1 to the European Convention for the Protection of Human Rights and Fundamental Freedoms. According to the European Court of Human Rights, those two provisions prohibit discriminatory treatment in the duty to pay taxes.[17] Although the Court has done little to develop a consistent concept of contributory discrimination, it is nonetheless evident that tax equality is in principle a basic right enforceable in all the contracting European States.

Tax equality, in its turn, requires a criterion which is both just and appropriate in determining the similarities and differences relevant for the distribution of the tax burden. In developed countries worldwide, the ability-to-pay principle is perceived to be most appropriate to meet these requirements[18]. Article 13 of the 1789 *Déclaration des Droits de l'Homme et du Citoyen,* which represents the common origin of the basic rights enshrined in today's continental constitutions, already established that taxes should be levied in accordance with the respective capacity of contribution.[19] Other

14. A similar provision can be found in Art. 7 para. 3 of the 'Draft Constitution for Europe' as adopted by the European Convention on 13 June and 10 July 2003 (2003/C 169/01).
15. Peters/Snellaars, *EC Tax Review 2001, p.* 13.
16. Cf. Wouters, *EC Tax Review* 1999, p. 98.
17. Cf. Judgment, 23.10.1990, Application No. 11581/85 *(Darby v. Sweden),* paras 30 et seq. For further details see Baker, *European Taxation* 2000, p. 298 (317 et seq.).
18. Tipke in: *Direito Tributário,* p. 361 (362); *ibid.,* StRO I, 2. Aufl., p. 482 et seq.*; ibid* in: Kirchhof/Lehner/ Raupach/Rodi (editors), *Staaten undSteuern,* 2000, p. 561 (567); Niessen in: Verburg/Vries/Ydema (editors), *Liberale Gifte,* p. 273 et seq.*;* Lindencrona/Lodin/Wiman/ Gunnarsson, *Liber Amicorum LeifMutén,* p. 141 (147);Trotabas/Cotteret, *Droitfiscal,* 8thedn,p. 80 eííe¢.;Herrera Molina, *Capacidad Económica y Sistema Fiscal,* 1998, p. 74 et seq.; van Houtte, *Beginselen van het Belgisch Belastingrecht,* 1979, p. 144; Doralt/Ruppe, Steuerrecht I,7th edn, p. 17; Reich, *Archivfür Schweizerisches Abgabenrecht* 53, p. 5 (6); Steichen, *Manuel de Droit Fiscal,* vol. 1,1996, p. 259 et seq.*;* Musgrave/Musgrave, *Public Finance in Theory and Practice,* 3rd edn, 1980, p. 242 et seq. A general overview is given by Birk in: Kirchhof/Lehner/ Raupach/Rodi (editors), *Staaten undSteuern,* 2000, p. 157 (161 et seq.).
19. 'Pour l'entretien de la force publique, et pour les dépenses de l'administration, une contribution commune est indispensable; elle doit être également répartie entre tous les citoyens, en raison de leur facultés'.

European constitutions also contain an explicit reference to the ability-to-pay principle, such as Article 53 (1) of the Italian Constitution, Article 31 of the Spanish Constitution and Article 4 (5) of the Greek Constitution.[20] Those constitutions that do not mention ability to pay *expressis verbis* nevertheless need it for the application of the equality principle in the field of tax law. In Germany, for example, the Constitutional Court has frequently employed ability to pay as *tertium comparationis* in testing the compatibility of tax law provisions with the fundamental right of equality before the law established in Article 3 (1) of the German Constitution (Basic Law).[21] In other countries a similar approach is undertaken.[22] Even in Great Britain the ability-to-pay principle forms part of customary law, albeit without constitutional rank.[23] The benefit principle, which is the main theoretical alternative, usually lacks practicability, because in most cases neither the benefit of public services financed by taxes nor the public spending provoked by individual behaviour can be quantified and attributed to single taxpayers.[24] It may serve to justify the levy of a tax together with the ability-to-pay principle, especially when a group benefit can be attributed to the (ultimate) taxpayers, but it will hardly ever be operational in determining the tax base.[25]

To summarize, tax equity specified as taxation according to individual ability to pay is the common denominator of European tax law which must form the constitutional core of a European Legal Tax Order. As the constitutional framework of European law is predominantly enshrined in the EC and EU treaties, their application in the field of cross-border taxation will have to realize this as a starting point.

Therefore, the ability-to-pay principle as the relevant specification of tax equality cannot merely be regarded as a rule of prudence for legislators in the design of the tax system,[26] but rather it is a genuine and binding limit to governmental taxing powers. Taxes which do not respect the taxpayers' ability to pay violate tax equality unless justified by conflicting reasons of common interest. Those few scholars who still argue against the ability-to-pay principle[27] cannot offer an acceptable alternative; they rather advocate the fundamental absence of principles. However, a Tax Order must not be

20. For a general overview cf. *Tipke*, StRO vol. II,2ndedn,p.488II, 2nd edn, p. 488 et seq. Art. 134 of the German Constitution of 1919 (Weimarer Reichsverfassung) also did mention the ability-to-pay principle explicitly; however, the present German Constitution does no longer make any specific allegations to principles of tax justice.
21. BVerfG, 9.3.2004, case 2 BvL 17/02, paragraph 72 (not yet published); BVerfG, 22.2.1984, case 1 BvL 10/80, BVerfGE 66, 214 (223) with further references.
22. Cf. the Austrian Constitutional Court on 12.12.1991, case G 290/91.
23. Cf. Davies, *Principles of Tax Law*, 3rd edn, p. 6. See also Gammie, *Bulletin I.F.D.* 2003, p. 86 (88): 'ability to pay tax'.
24. There are some exceptions; a tax on mineral oils for example can be justified on the grounds of the benefit principle insofar as it internalizes the costs which their consumption causes to the environment and, in ultimate consequence, the public welfare, or the costs of road building. See Andel, *Finanzwissenschaft*, 4th edn, p. 364; Haller, *Die Steuern*, 3rd edn, p. 363 et seq.; Musgrave/Musgrave, *Public Finance*, 3rd edn, p. 241. Alternatively: Tipke, StRO, vol. II, 2nd edn, p. 1093: Mere behaviour control.
25. A notable exception may be 'green taxes', e.g. the tax on mineral oils. Here, a rough correlation between the external costs caused to society by pollution and the amount of energy carriers consumed can be made out.
26. Cf. Vanistendael in: Thuronyi (ed.), *Tax Law Design and Drafting*, Vol. 1,1996, p. 22.
27. For example Gassner/Lang, *ÖStZ* 2000, p. 643 (644); *ibid.*, 14. ÖJT Band III/1, p. 64.

built on the shifting sands of arbitrary distinctions; it relies on a firm foundation which specifies constitutional requirements of equal treatment for the tax sector.

The ability-to-pay principle is fundamental and therefore no specific contents can be directly attributed to it; on the other hand, it is not indefinable. Basically, it requires that any two taxpayers with equal ability to pay in terms of the relevant tax base should be taxed equally, whereas taxpayers in different conditions of ability to pay should be taxed to a greater or lesser extent corresponding to their higher or lower capacity. The former rule is referred to as horizontal and the latter as vertical equity.[28] As tax equality is a material rather than a formal rule of law, the ability-to-pay principle is aimed at equality in the effective tax burden; a legally intended or presumed tax shift and the accumulation of different taxes on the same taxable activity must therefore be taken into account in an overall comparison. A European Legal Tax Order will essentially have to clarify what implications arise from the requirement of equal tax burdens according to individual ability to pay from the supranational internal market viewpoint inherent to the founding treaties.

The individual ability to pay can further be divided into an objective and a subjective one. Objective ability to pay can be defined as being determined by objective criteria of the tax base; on the contrary, subjective ability to pay contemplates the deductions and relief granted for personal and family circumstances. Of course, the specific expression of both concepts varies from tax to tax and from country to country. Social and cultural diversities among European countries are of special importance in this area, which would be neglected by establishing precise figures and requirements. However, all European tax systems acknowledge the general necessity to consider basic personal needs in direct as well as in indirect taxation, i.e. a subjective element in calculating the taxable base and/or the tax rate. In fact, complete ignorance in this respect would risk depriving the individual tax payer of his/her means to satisfy his/her basic human needs and leave him/her at the mercy of the welfare state; a result certainly not in line with the idea of a free, self-responsible and dignified individual underlying all European constitutions. A European Legal Tax Order must formulate the impact of these requirements in a pan-European context.

Ability to pay is traditionally associated with the taxation of individuals. The application of this concept on the taxation of legal persons and other associations (hereinafter 'legal entities') is highly disputed. The academic discussion sharply contrasts with the existing reality of corporation and business taxation worldwide. In our opinion, the scientific dispute is misled in large parts by terminological and teleological confusion. On the one hand, it is evident that subjective ability to pay cannot be attributed to legal entities as they have neither basic personal needs nor a family life. On the other hand, as far as they are vested with the capacity to hold property under the respective civil law, it cannot be seriously doubted that they also dispose of an original taxpaying capability. Since taxes can only be paid out of one's

28. Holmes, *The Concept of Income*, p. 19; Birk in: Tipke/Bozza (editors), *Besteuerung von Einkommen*, p. 103 (104); Musgrave/Musgrave, *Public Finance in Theory and Practice*, 3rd edn, 1980, p. 242 et seq.

property,[29] the holder of such property is potentially subject to tax. If he/she further fulfils the elements of a tax rule, e.g. the accumulation or possession of property, he/she can be made liable for the tax himself/herself. If the tax base is to be comprehensive, this must hold true independently of his/her natural or legal personality.

Under these premises, the taxation of legal entities can undoubtedly be justified. In order to not distort competition, at least among themselves – and in some countries also for constitutional requirements[30] – these entities will have to be taxed equally. So again a *tertium comparationis* to determine similarity or relative differences for taxation purposes has to be applied. The benefit principle will usually have to be ruled out to structure the tax base, because also for legal entities it is hardly possible to calculate the public services they receive. Hence, one is left with the ability-to-pay principle in its objective impress, i.e. without consideration of personal circumstances. This is the adequate measure of each legal entity's individual capacity to contribute to public spending. The aversion to applying ability to pay to legal entities has its roots in a historical understanding as an equal-sacrifice prescription[31] which is restricted to individuals, since legal entities do not feel any personal sacrifice when paying taxes. However, this concept of ability to pay is not only largely overcome by modern economic and legal research, it also fails to offer an operational alternative to guarantee equal taxation of legal entities and therefore should, if not given up, at least be applied in a modified sense, taken back to its objective element of the loss in money which is immanent to a financial sacrifice. Consequently, a European Legal Tax Order will have to deal with the question as to how the ability to pay of legal entities is to be treated in intra-Community affairs.

To be distinguished from these considerations is the also highly controversial relationship between the ability to pay of legal entities, especially companies, and that of their associates or shareholders. Here we encounter a century-old debate between the conduit view, which calls for full (or at least partial) integration of the corporate and shareholder taxation of company profits, and the so-called classical model which treats both levels of taxation independently.[32] Member States have adopted a large range of positions in this matter, and even though we incline towards an integrationist viewpoint, this can hardly be claimed to be the only one acceptable under every Member State's constitution. Thus, the challenge a European Legal Tax Order must meet here on a constitutional level is how to reconcile unharmonized national concepts of integration or non-integration in cross-border investments and dividend flows.

The ability-to-pay principle does not stand alone. In a democratic, open society any legal order will not be monistic, i.e. based on just one single principle, but will rather recognize various ethical principles which may well be in conflict with each other. A European Legal Tax Order must state to what extent a breach of ability to pay

29. Tipke, StRO, vol. I. 2nd edn, p. 326 and 501.
30. In Germany this is a consequence of the conferral of basic rights to (domestic) entities, see Art. 19 (3) Grundgesetz. As regards Spain, consult Goméz Montoro, *Cuestiones Constitucionales* 2000, p. 23 et seq.
31. Cf. Musgrave/Musgrave, *Public Finance in Theory and Practice*, 3rd edn, 1980, p. 250.
32. Cf. Schlunk, *Tax Law Review* 2003, p. 329 et seq.

is admissible for the sake of other constitutional principles or public interests in a European context.

Three key factors to be taken into consideration can be derived from the Member States' constitutional traditions. First, any public interests or constitutional values conflicting with a taxation based on ability to pay must be brought in a *proportional* balance with this fundamental requirement. The principle of proportionality, well established in German constitutional and administrative law,[33] has by now been incorporated in all the European legal systems.[34] It has even found reception in the EC Treaty in the course of the Maastricht revision, as it is now expressively mentioned in Article 5 (3) as guideline for all Community actions. Moreover, it has long before been established by the ECJ as a general rule of Community law.[35] It must therefore form an integral part of a European Legal Tax Order, and particularly of a European concept of public interests compromising a cross-border concept of ability to pay. Basically, tax rules infringing a transnational notion of ability to pay must serve a legitimate public interest, they must be suitable to achieve this objective, shall not go beyond what is necessary for this purpose and finally must be adequately balanced with the loss of tax equality incurred. The specifics of a European proportionality test in tax matters, especially its tripartite structure, will therefore have to be considered.

Second, a possible loss in revenue may by itself never constitute a legitimate public interest capable of justifying a deviation from taxation according to ability to pay. This is so because the ability-to-pay principle aims at an *equal* distribution of the entire tax burden among all persons subjected to a State's tax jurisdiction. In the eventual case of an increase in public spending or a loss of other revenue sources the additional fiscal need may not be satisfied by overcharging individual taxpayers, but must rather be met by all taxpayers in compliance with ability to pay. As the fiscal need of today's modern welfare state with a market economy is the *spiritus rector* of the ability-to-pay principle, this very fact may not be used in order to justify a breach of its own consequences.

Third, the ability-to-pay principle in theory demands distribution of the tax burden exactly according to the individual capacity of contribution taking into account the peculiarities of every single case. However, tax law is a law of mass assessment dealing with millions of tax subjects and billions of taxable transactions. In order to secure the equal application of the law, simplifications and generalizations must be introduced into the tax system. Certainly, in every Member State there is potential for structural simplifications which would not conflict with individual ability to pay but rather promote it by eliminating tax privileges and special tax regimes, thus creating a

33. Cf. Grabitz, AöR 98 (1973), p. 568 et seq.; BVerfG, 5.3.1968, case 1 BvR 579/67, BVerfGE 23, 127 (133) with further references.
34. Cf. von Danwitz, EWS 2003, p. 393; Emiliou, *The Principle of Proportionality in European Law;* Kutscher in: *Der Grundsatz der Verhältnismäßigkeit,* p. 89 et seq.
35. Cf. rulings of the ECJ dating from 11.7.1989, case 265/87 (Schräder), ECR 1989,2237, para. 21; 13.11.1990, case C-331/88 (Fedesa),ECR 1990, I-4023, para. 13; 16.12.1992, case 210/91 (Commission / Greece), ECR 1992, I-6735, para. 19. Confirmed by Schweitzer/Hummer, *Europarecht,* 5th edn, paras 790 et seq.; García Prats, *Imposición directa,* p. 165; Tridimas, *The General Principles of EC Law,* p. 89.

transparent, broad tax base. Despite this caveat, in today's complex economy, tax law will never be simple. Even systematic tax law would grow overly complicated when any possible particularity would be contemplated in the tax acts. Hence every national tax system relies to a certain extent on classification, standardization and lump sum taxation.[36] In reality, this is a precondition for an effective equality in taxation: if a tax system is too complex to ensure sufficient verification and investigation of taxable facts, it will set incentives for tax fraud and undermine public taxpaying morals. Tax audits could only be effectuated on a small scale, because too many administrative resources would be bound in everyday assessment business. An exaggerated emphasis on individual equity would thus create a climate of tax evasion in which honest taxpayers would bear the tax burden of their less scrupulous fellow citizens. Nevertheless, dogmatically we are confronted with a breach of the ability-to-pay principle. The limits of administrative capacities to which generalizations pay tribute are not inalterable facts more or less immanent to the ability-to-pay concept. In fact, they warrant effective and high-yielding revenue raising. In some cases standardization may also serve to respect taxpayers' privacy or to lower compliance costs. The respective objectives must be weighed against the loss of individual tax equality. To strike the right balance in a pan-European context is a task to be mastered by a European Legal Tax Order.

[B] The Cross-border Aspect Enhanced by the EC Treaty's Provisions on Free Movement

[1] The Constitutional Quality of the Provisions on Free Movement in an Internal Market

The supranational embodiment of a European concept of tax equality can be found in the provisions of the EC Treaty on free movement in an internal market. In accordance with the ECJ, the Treaty makes up 'the constitutional charter of a Community based on the rule of law'.[37] The implementation of the European Union has not changed its constitutional quality, as the Union, according to Article 1 EU Treaty, is founded on the European Communities.[38] It is further illustrated by the fact that its main provisions, including the above-mentioned so-called fundamental freedoms, are incorporated in the recently adopted Treaty establishing a Constitution for Europe. These basic economic rights guaranteed by the EC Treaty consist of the free movement of goods, persons, services and capital between Member States without obstacles related to internal frontiers.

36. Cf. Peters/Snellaars, *EC Tax Review 2001*, p. 13 et seq.
37. ECJ, Opinion 1/91, ECR 1991, I-6079, para. 1. See also van Thiel, *Free Movement of Persons and Income Tax Law*, 2002, p. 1; *ibid.*, *EC Tax Review 2003*, p. 4(5); Vanistendael, *ECTaxReview* 1996, p. 114.
38. Zuleeg, BB 1994, p. 581.

Even though they do not make any explicit reference to the area of tax law, they nevertheless deliver the quasi-constitutional yardstick for all national tax rules pertinent to pan-European economic activities. This is due to the direct effect and supremacy of all Community law imposing clear and unconditional obligations on the Member States, foremost the Treaty articles on free movement.[39] Therefore, any provisions of Member States' legislation incompatible with those basic rights may not be applied by national courts and administrations. Any other actions attributable to a Member State's sovereign power, such as administrative or judicial rulings and decisions, must also comply with the basic freedoms.[40] The constitutional scrutiny of national law does not depend on its previous harmonization.[41] As the ECJ established in a series of rulings, these principles hold true also for national tax laws.[42] There is no sovereignty exception for taxation, not even for direct taxes.[43] This would be contrary to the Community objective of an internal market without obstacles caused by national borders, as taxes may certainly provoke such obstacles.[44] Hence, although Member States remain in great part competent to exercise their sovereign powers in the area of taxation, especially direct taxation, they must do so in consistence with Community law.[45]

[2] Personal and Territorial Scope

The personal and territorial scope of the basic freedoms are closely related and shall therefore be discussed together. The basic rights constituting the internal market concept can be roughly divided into two groups.

Only citizens of the Union, as defined in Article 17 (1) 2, are in principle beneficiaries of the free movement of persons, i.e. the freedom of movement for workers and the right of establishment, as well as of the freedom to provide services. Moreover, the latter freedom and the so-called secondary freedom of establishment provided for in Article 43 (1)2 additionally require that the entrepreneur is established in one of the Member States. Except for, naturally, the freedom for workers, the

39. Freedom of goods: ECJ, 3.7.1974, case 192/73 *(Van Zuylen)*, ECR 1974,731, para. 2/5; freedom of movement for workers: ECJ, 4.12.1974, case 41/74 *(van Duyn)*, ECR 1974,1337, para. 5/7; freedom of establishment: ECJ, 21.06.1974, case *2/74(Reyners)*, ECR 1974,631, para. 24/28 etseq.; freedom of services: ECJ, 3.12.1974, case 33/74 *(van Binsbergen)*, ECR 1974,1299, para. 27; freedom of capital: ECJ, 23.2.1995, case C-358/93 et al. *(Bordessa etal.)*, ECR 1995, I-361, para. 35 (concerning the directive on the freedom of captial together with Art. 67 (1) of the Treaty before the Maastricht revision, cf. Grabitz/Hilf *Ress/Ukrow*, EU-Kommentar, EGV Art. 73b, para. 24) and ECJ, 14.12.1995, case C-163/94 et al. *(Sanz de Lera etal.)*, ECR 1995, I-4821, para. 48.
40. Cf. Streinz/Müller-Graff, EUV/EGV, Art. 43 EGV, para. 35.
41. See landmark case ECJ, 15.7.1964, case 6/64 *(Costa/E.N.E.L.)*, ECR 1964, 1251.
42. ECJ, 28.1.1986, case 270/83 *(Avoir fiscal)*, ECR 1986, 273, para. 24; ECJ, 26.10.1999, case C-294/97 *(Eurowings)*, ECR 1999, I-7447, paras 28 and 32.
43. de Koort, *Weekblad voor Fiscaal Recht* 1996, p. 1594 et seq.
44. See also van Thiel, *Free Movement of Persons and Income Tax Law*, p. 22 et seq.
45. EuGH *v.* 14.2.1995, Rs. C-279/93 *(Schumacker)*, Slg. 1995, I-225, para. 21; EuGH *v.* 14.12.2000, Rs. C-141/99 *(AMID)*, Slg. 2000, I-11619, para. 19; EuGH *v.* 8.3.2001, Rs. C-397/98etal.(C-397/98 et al. *(Metallgesellschaft et* al.), Slg. 2001, I-1727, para. 37.

aforementioned freedoms can also be enjoyed by companies and firms which have been incorporated in one of the Member State and are also seated in one of them, as stipulated by Article 48.[46] The personal scope of the freedoms has been further widened by a convincing case law development of the ECJ. As distorting discriminations and restrictions might just as well address the recipients of the products and production factors protected by the free movement provisions, they too must be able to claim their violation.[47] Thus, the freedoms do have an 'active' and a 'passive' personal element. For the latter one, it should be sufficient if the recipient is a resident of a Member State, even if he/she is not a citizen of the Union.[48]

The provisions on goods and capital warrant the free movement between Member States as such without further specifications of the respective beneficiaries. It is therefore generally accepted that anybody affected by possible restrictions of intra-Community movement can rely on them. Individuals and companies are included in their personal scope independent of their nationality or place of residence. As far as the free movement of capital is concerned, there is not even a pan-European element required, since the movement of capital between Member States and third countries is protected, too.

Finally, by virtue of Article 31 EEA Treaty, all fundamental freedoms also apply to nationals of the EFTA Member States except Switzerland and for companies seated there.

From the above it follows that the taxation of both companies and individuals must comply with the basic freedoms. Regarding the nationality requirement, the judicial approach must be distinguished from the legislative approach. A court decides only the case presented to it and therefore will have to bear in mind the special requirements exposed above. The legislator, though, must establish general regulations which should only allow for exceptions on a broad base, if at all. Hence, all economic activities that fall under the substantial scope of the basic freedoms should be taxed in a way that does not incriminate or restrict cross-border transactions and movements, independently of the respective agent's nationality. A branch exception may be established for activities from or to third countries, if national constitutional law so permits, but *prima facie* not as far as capital transfers or yields are taxed.

[3] Principles of Equal Treatment

Despite their denomination, the basic 'freedoms' of movement constitute specific elements of a cross-border equality principle. This statement merits scrupulous explanation, as there exists a wide range of opinions regarding the substantive scope of the respective treaty provisions.

46. Explicitly specified in Art. 48 for the freedom of establishment; as regards the freedom to provide services Art. 55 contains a reference to Art. 48. For further details, see *van Thiel,* Free movement of persons and income tax law, p. 209 et seq.; *ibid., EC Tax Review* 2003, p. 4 (8).
47. Cf. ECJ, 8.3.2001, case C-397/98 et al. *(Metallgesellschaft),* ECR 2001, I-1727, paras 4242 et seq.; ECJ, 31.1.1984, cases 286/82 and 26/83 *(Luisi* and *Carbone),* ECR 1984,377, para. 16.
48. Cf. Bater, ET 2000, p. 8 (11). For a detailed discussion from a German perspective see Streinz/Müller-Graff, EUV/EGV, Art. 49, paras 53 et seq.

A closer examination has to take into consideration two opposite findings. On the one hand, the integration process initiated by the ratification of the Communities' founding treaties is a dynamic and open one.[49] Since the fundamental freedoms are, according to Article 14 EC Treaty, essentially dedicated to promoting the process of economic integration, it comes as no surprise that they themselves have undergone legal evolution as well. This process by no means terminated at the end of the transitional period in 1992, because the internal market is in reality still far from being fully completed.[50] Consequently, historical intentions of the Community's founding fathers do not play a significant role in the interpretation of EC law.[51]

On the other hand, the ECJ, which is, according to Article 220 EC Treaty, the Community organ competent to interpret the Treaty provisions, is not authorized to do so in a free floating manner. Just as the competencies of the Community are limited by the objectives laid down in Articles 2, 3 and 4 EC Treaty, the primary law must be interpreted in the light of those objectives, too. Here already, it is important to note that they adhere to an *internal* rather than a *neoliberal* market rationale, as can be derived from Article 3 (1) (c). Furthermore, it must be borne in mind that any approximation of the laws of Member States via Community harmonization is subjected to a political agreement requiring qualified majorities specified in various Treaty provisions.[52] The Treaty thereby respects the different social, cultural and economic traditions and beliefs of the Member States. It implicitly accepts national disparities also in areas affecting the internal market or other Community objectives, as long as an agreement cannot be reached. An interpretation of the EC Treaty should be mindful of these persisting disparities and their legitimacy, because otherwise it will undermine the elaborate harmonization requirements and overly curb remaining regulatory powers of the Member States.

Finally, it can be observed that the common ground of all the provisions on freedom of movement, i.e. the establishment of an internal market as provided in Article 3(1) (c), 14 (2) EC Treaty, must lead to a high degree of convergence in their dogmatic structure. Since their interpretation has to be inspired by this objective, any differentiation in their substantive scope would have to be rooted in special requirements of the respective market factor. While such exceptions should not be ruled out *a priori,* in general all four freedoms should follow the same principles as regards the key questions of applicability, substantive scope, and possible justifications of their infringements. A trend in that direction can already be made out in the case law of the ECJ.[53]

---

49. Van Thiel, *Free Movement of Persons and Income Tax Law,* p. 79 and 154.
50. Behrens, EuR 1992, p. 145 (147).
51. Cf. Vanistendael, *EC Tax Review* 1996, p. 114(117). Concerning secondary Community law cf. Schön, *Die Auslegung europäischen Steuerrechts,* p. 56 et seq.
52. In the area of taxation, Art. 93, 94 and 95 (2) EC Treaty are most often relevant. For 'eco-taxes', see also Art. 175 (2) (a).
53. The most prominent example is the decision of the ECJ on 30.11.1995, case C-55/94 *(Gebhard),* ECR 1995, I-4165, para. 37. See also van Thiel, *Free Movement of Persons and Income Tax Law,* p. 79; differentiated Oliver/Roth, CMLR 2004, p. 407 (439 et seq.).

[a] De Jure and De Facto Discrimination

Under these premises, discrimination on grounds of nationality, understood as a legal differentiation based on this criterion, is certainly not in line with the constitutional principle of free movement enshrined in the fundamental freedoms. In the case of the freedom of movement for workers, Article 39 (2), and the freedom of establishment, Article 43 (2), this can already be deducted from the wording of these provisions. Furthermore, Article 12 states that within the scope of application of the EC Treaty, any discrimination on grounds of nationality shall be prohibited, without prejudice to special provisions. It can be assumed that the special provisions on free movement do not fall behind that basic standard. Finally, any discrimination based on nationality would certainly be an eminent obstacle to an internal market as pursued by the Community according to Article 3 (1) (c). The prohibition of such discrimination can therefore be considered to form an essential part of all fundamental freedoms.[54]

However, to narrow the forbidden differentiation criterion down to nationality would fall short of the mandate expressed in Article 3(1) (c), 14 (2), to realize an internal market without internal frontiers. The objectives exposed in those articles are legally binding,[55] and thus the fundamental freedoms mentioned there must be interpreted in such a way as to allow their effective implementation.[56] Forbidden obstacles obstructing the free movement between the Member States can undoubtedly emanate not only from the State of destination, but just as well from the State of origin. This is explicitly admitted by Article 29 concerning the free movement of goods, implicitly by Article 58 (1) (a) regarding the free movement of capital, and is proven to be true for the other freedoms by abundant case law. In that case, the affected subjects will usually be nationals rather than foreigners, so a mere prohibition of discrimination on grounds of nationality would be ineffective. Hence, this criterion must be complemented by one related to the cross-border or pan-European character of the economic transaction in question.[57] Neither the State of origin nor the State of destination may discriminate cross-border activities as compared to purely internal ones.[58] For the sake of *effet util*, it cannot make any difference whether discrimination is explicitly based on such grounds or if it is a covert one hidden behind other criteria which, however, do have the same effect. Article 90 (1), which expressly prohibits indirect discrimination

54. ECJ, 12.2.1987,case 221/85 *(Commission v.Belgium)*,ECR 1987, 719, para. 5; ECJ, 7.2.1979, case 136/78 *(Auer)*, ECR 1979, 437, paras 16 and 2316 and 23 et seq.; Farmer, *EC Tax Review* 2003, p. 75; Jacobs, *Internationale Unternehmensbesteuerung*, 5th edn, p. 200; Cordewener, *Grundfreiheiten*, p. 245; Oppermann, *Europarecht*, 2nd edn, para. 1588;Wouters, 1588; Wouters, *EC Tax Review* 1999, p. 98 (99); Dourado, *EC Tax Review* 1994, p. 176 (180).
55. ECJ on 21.2.1973, case 6/72 *(Europemballage)*, ECR 1973, 215, para. 23; *Knobbe-Keuk*, DB 1990, p. 2573 (2574).
56. This kind of teleological interpretation is circumscribed in EC law as giving *effet util* to the respective treaty provisions, cf. ECJ on 25.2.1988, case 299/86 *(Drexl)*, ECR 1988, 1213, para. 24; Cordewener, *Grundfreiheiten*, p. 203; Nuñez Sanz, *Impuestos* 2001, p. 1143 (1146).
57. Cf.ECJ, 12.9.2002, case C-431/01 *(Mertens)*, ECR 2000, I-7073, paras 32 etseq.; Ilhi/Malmer/ Schonewille/ Tuominen, CDFI LXXXVIIIa, p. 71 (83); Farmer, *EC Tax Review* 2003, p. 75 (77); Sanz Gadea, *Impuestos* 2001, p. 161 (180); van Thiel, TFO 2001/78, p. 3; Lechner/Staringer/ Tumpel, *Kapitalverkehrsfreiheit*, p. 93 (103); Schuch, *EC Tax Review* 1996, p. 161.
58. Cordewener, ET 2003, p. 294 (299).

in the area of indirect taxation, is a specific coinage of this basic principle. The ECJ accepts the aforementioned reasoning when contemplating discriminations for which the home State is responsible; however, it still tends to declare this kind of discrimination an unspecified 'restriction'.[59] When the host State discriminates on grounds of the cross-border criterion, however, it assumes a covert discrimination on grounds of nationality.[60] This different orientation and denomination of the discrimination test according to the addressee of the free movement provisions is neither necessary nor convincing and should be abandoned. In all cases, discrimination on grounds of a cross-border element in the relevant transaction is at issue.

Of course, even when applying this extended understanding of forbidden discrimination, the latter can only be assumed when the cross-border and the internal situation are similar and comparable.[61] This must be determined according to the underlying principles of the respective field of law.

As the ECJ has stressed on various occasions, 'discrimination' can also occur when one and the same national rule is applied without any distinction to different situations.[62] Atypical example for this would be constellations where the undifferentiated application of national rules to both cross-border and internal activities may lead to *factual extra burdens* on the former, which frequently face similar regulations to comply within the home and the host state. Such 'double burden' effects are contrary to an internal market without obstacles to the free movement as between Member States.[63] Even though the ECJ is not always clear in its dogmatic formulations here, it nevertheless has supported such an understanding of forbidden restrictions in a number of cases.[64] To avoid terminological confusion it would certainly be preferable to not call this kind of infringement 'discrimination' since we defined this concept as 'legal differentiation'.[65] Rather, it is a form of non-discriminatory violation of the equal treatment requirement inherent to the fundamental freedoms. However, to assure conformity with international custom we shall address these constellations for the purpose of this article as one kind of ' de facto discrimination'.[66]

59. See, for example, ECJ, 7.9.2004, case C-319/02 *(Manninen)*, not yet published, paras 20 et seq.: Here, a detrimental tax treatment is identified as 'restriction' rather than 'discrimination'.
60. Cf. ECJ, 12.6.2003, case C-234/01 *(Gerritse)*, ECR 2003, I-5933, para. 28.
61. Cf. ECJ, 17.7.1963, case 13/63 *(Italy v. Commission)*, ECR 1963,359,384; *Gammie*, Bulletin I.F.D. 2003, p. 86 (88); *Jacobs*, Internationale Unternehmensbesteuerung, 5th ed., p. 194; Lehner/Reimer, Grundfreiheiten, p. 39 (45–50); *Steichen* in: Festschrift Debatin, p. 417 (421).
62. ECJ, 27.6.1996, case C-107/94 *(Asscher)*, ECR 1996, I-3089, para. 40; ECJ, 11.8.1995, case C-80/94 *(Wielockx)*, ECR 1995, I-2493, para. 17; ECJ, 14.2.1995, case C-279/93 *(Schumacker)*, ECR 1995, I-225, para. 30. See also *Hinnekens*, ET 1996, p. 286 (288).
63. Cf. Roth in: GS Knobbe-Keuk, p. 729 (737 et seq.).
64. For an in-depth analysis consult Lyal, *EC Tax Review* 2003, p. 68 (70 et seq.).
65. Like here Peters/Snellaars, *EC Tax Review* 2001, p. 13. See also Wouters, *EC Tax Review* 1999, p. 98 (104), who distinguishes between 'formal' and 'substantive' discrimination.
66. Cf. Lyal, *EC Tax Review* 2003, p. 68 (74).

[b] A Step Too Far: A Second Constitutional Layer of Liberal Freedom Rights

A fundamental question is whether the concept of forbidden restrictions actually requires the existence of an extra burden on cross-border activities, or in another words, if a restriction can only be assumed if the national rule under scrutiny *specifically* disadvantages intra-Community as compared to purely internal activities. The Court's answer here is negative. It increasingly interprets the free movement provisions as true freedom rights which prohibit any restriction on the free movement of goods, persons, services and capital.[67] The only limits to this far-reaching approach are a partial exception for so-called 'sales modalities'[68] which are too 'uncertain' in their restrictive effects,[69] and, seemingly, the need for a cross-border element in the case presented. Such an extensive interpretation can no longer rely on an internal market rationale; rather, it is an expression of a liberal market rationale which is in principle adverse to any kind of regulation.[70] As a consequence, the fundamental freedoms convert into a second layer of liberal constitutional scrutiny of any kind of national market regulation. At least prior to the ratification of the European Constitution, we cannot join the ECJ on this road, neither in general terms nor from a tax law perspective. It leads to results beyond the scope of the Treaty provisions, it is inconsistent, and it cannot reasonably be applied on direct taxation issues.[71]

The key argument of the ECJ is that in an internal market the basic freedoms must assure market access.[72] In the Court's opinion, national legal provisions must therefore not render the use of freedoms less attractive or 'illusory'[73] by influencing the decision to engage in the activity in question. Indeed, it is true that an internal market as defined in Article 3 (1) (c), 14 (2), aims at the abolition of restrictions to market access. As becomes evident from the wording of those provisions as well as of the particular articles governing each freedom, such restrictions must however result from internal frontiers to fall under their scope. Only obstacles to market access *as between Member States* are prohibited, not any obstacles resulting from the general economic order of a particular Member State affecting equally internal and external economic activities. Such an understanding of unrestricted market access can also still be based on a comparative assessment of domestic and cross-border activities, since the former already have full and unrestricted access to their targeted market resulting in a disadvantageous position of the latter. This kind of discrimination can be de jure, as

67. For a detailed analysis, consult Spaventa, CMLR 2004, p. 743 et seq.
68. ECJ, 24.11.1993, case C-267 et al. *(Keck)*, ECR 1993, I-6097, para. 16.
69. ECJ, 20.6.1996, case 418/93 et al. *(Semeraro Casa Uno* et al.), ECR 1996, I-2975, para. 32.
70. Cf. Spaventa, CMLR 2004, p. 743 (764 et seq.).
71. Cf. Haferkamp, *Kapitalverkehrsfreiheit,* p. 100 et seq.; Hinnekens, *EC Tax Review* 2002, p. 112 (117): 'Saying that there are no intra-Community tax borders or that there should not be any under the Single Market concept, is going a bridge too far.' A careful approach to applying an 'obstacle approach' to the field of tax law is also advised by Lyal, *EC Tax Review* 2003, p. 68 (74). For a dissenting opinion see Lehner in: FS Offerhaus, p. 117 (131); *ibid., EC Tax Review* 2002, p. 5 (7).
72. ECJ, 13.5.2003, case C-463/00 *(Commission v.* Spain), ECR 2003, I-4581, paras 60 et seq.; ECJ, 13.5.2003, case C-98/01 *(Commission v. United Kingdom),* ECR 2003, I-4641, paras 46 et seq.
73. ECJ on 4.6.2002, case C-367/98 *(Commission v. Portugal),* ECR 2002, I-4731, para. 44; ECJ on 4.6.2002, case C-483/99 *(Commission v. France),* ECR 2002, I-4781, para. 41.

would for instance be the case in tariffs on the import or export of certain goods,[74] or de facto, as in the case of restrictions on the number of branch establishments effectively privileging local competitors. In any case, the specificity of the detriment to the cross-border movement is upheld.

The vision underlying the internal market provisions of the EC Treaty is to establish in the end a kind of European domestic market for all market participants. This is not the vision of a deregulated market, where market forces rule, in principle, without limits.[75] This seems to be exactly the vision of the ECJ, though, when it holds that national regulations may neither render market activities 'less attractive' nor influence the way they are conducted. Of course, a completely deregulated market would at the same time be one variant of a perfect domestic market, as any 'restricting' disparities would be swept away in a judicial race to the bottom. Notwithstanding this, to decide on the extent of deregulation and of approximation of national laws necessary for the fulfilment of the Community tasks set out in Article 2 falls to the political responsibility of the Council and, ultimately, to that of the Member States. An internal market, whose completion is the very purpose of the basic freedoms, does not imply a legally enforceable statement in that respect. This is without prejudice to the mandate of the Community and the Member States to coordinate the national economic policies in accordance with the principle of an open market economy with free competition as expressed in Articles 4(1) and 98. On the contrary, Article 4(1) clearly distinguishes between the aforementioned guideline for economic policy coordination on the one hand, and the internal market, on which these policies are based, on the other hand. Moreover, the inconsistency of the economic policy of a Member State with this guideline can only be sanctioned, according to Article 99 (4), by way of an eventual non-binding recommendation of the Council. It is therefore not legally enforceable; an interpretation of the fundamental freedoms as adopted by the ECJ would indeed render this concept 'illusory'.

Besides this fundamental objection, it is also inconsistent to exclude a determined kind of restriction, namely sales modifications, from the scope of a presumed freedom right. The assumption of the ECJ that such restrictions do not hamper market access are rather speculative and not based on empirical data. To suggest that there may be 'uncertain' and 'certain' restrictions must lead to arbitrary judgments certainly not based on professional expertise.[76] It is furthermore inconsistent to claim the necessity of a cross-border element if a national regulation of market activities is as such subject of judicial scrutiny, independently of any specific discriminatory or disadvantaging

---

74. Cf. Heiskanen, *Journal of World Trade* 2004, p. 1 (2).
75. Cf. Roth in: GS Knobbe-Keuk, p. 729 (737 et seq.), regarding the freedom of establishment. It should be noted that the draft Treaty establishing a Constitution for Europe indeed shows close affiliation to such an ideal, as can be deducted from its Art. 3 (2): 'The Union shall offer its citizens ...*a single market where competition is free and undistorted*' [italics added]. Also, Art. 4 (1) no longer links the free movement of persons, goods, services and capital to the internal market objective or cross-border aspects. Since the Constitution still faces an uncertain ratification procedure in 25 Member States, it can however not yet be taken into account when interpreting the scope of the fundamental freedoms.
76. Sceptical also Hinnekens, ET 1996, p. 286 (299).

effects on intra-Community transactions.[77] Finally, the application of the Court's doctrine in the area of tax law would lead to the bewildering result that taxes on cross-border activities would *prima facie* be inadmissible, as they certainly tend to render less attractive any taxable economic activity.[78] A justification for this supposed infringement of fundamental freedoms would be hard to find as it is generally prone to be proven unnecessary. Even if in this special case the raising of revenue would exceptionally be held to be a legitimate aim, an increase of taxes only on purely domestic activities would be considered equally suitable for that purpose, while less restrictive on cross-border activities. Not surprisingly, the ECJ itself admitted, albeit in an obiter dictum and without further explanation, that differences in national tax systems encountered by free movers do not infringe the basic freedoms.[79]

From the above it is clear that the fundamental treaty provisions on the free movement of goods, persons, services and capital guarantee equal treatment of foreigners and nationals as well as equal treatment of cross-border economic activities and internal ones. They prohibit open and covert de jure discrimination, in the sense of legal differentiation based on these criteria, as well as de facto discrimination which cause a particular detriment to cross-border movements. Discrimination can only be assumed if the situations to be compared are similar according to the underlying principles of the national rule to be examined.

[4] Tax Implications: A Cross-border Concept of Ability to Pay

In tax law, this underlying principle by which similarity has to be measured is, in general, ability to pay. Thus, the consequences of the aforementioned concept of the fundamental freedoms for national tax systems become obvious. If the results or circumstances of a determined economic activity are presumed by the national legislator to create or diminish ability to pay, he/she must, in principle, not distinguish any further between the cross-border or internal character of this activity. Rather, he/she must impose an equal tax burden in both cases.[80] There is no degree of permissible discrimination; any restriction must be eliminated even if of limited scope or minor importance.[81] The national legislator must furthermore take into account that from a supranational point of view, even equal taxation might lead to an extra tax

77. Cf. Kingreen, *Struktur der Grundfreiheiten,* p. 116.
78. Cf. Farmer, *EC Tax Review* 1998, p. 13 (27).
79. ECJ, 14.7.1994, case C-379/92 (Peralta), ECR 1994, I-3453, para. 34; see also Peters/Snellaars, *EC Tax Review* 2001, p. 13 (17). Schön, EWS 2000, p. 281 (289) tries to explain the Court's statement by qualifying differences in the national tax law systems as 'too uncertain and too indirect' for constituting a restriction to market access. Apart from our fundamental scepticism towards this arbitrary criterion, differences in tax systems such as, for example, the spread in corporate tax burdens between Germany and Ireland of almost 30 per cent can hardly be regarded too uncertain for assessing an effect on market access in the sense of rendering it less attractive.
80. Cf. Schuchin: Multilateral Tax Treaties, p. 35(41): '... the tax burden as such is the sole decisive element.' See also van Thiel, Free movement of persons, p. 599 et seq.; *Valat,* ET 2002, p. 446; *Tumpel,* SWI2002, p. 454 (456).
81. ECJ, 11.3.2004, case C-9/02 *(Hughes de Lasteyrie du Saillant),* not yet published, para. 43; ECJ, 15.2.2000, case C-34/98 *(Commission v. France),* ECR 2000, I-995, para. 49). Hinnekens, *EC*

burden which specifically disadvantages cross-border activities, most prominently in the case of international double taxation. Since, in dealing with the fundamental freedoms' implications in tax law, the ECJ is basically and necessarily guided by the concept of an internal market, frictions with common traditions of national and international tax law are inevitable. Each national concept of ability to pay must be reconsidered from a cross-border perspective; this is the revolutionary challenge presented by EC Treaty law to a European Legal Tax Order.[82] Nevertheless, we reject the general idea that unfolding EC law in the area of taxation must lead to conflicts with fundamental principles carrying the national tax system.[83] On the contrary, as far as taxpayer's basic rights are concerned, it enhances those principles in a single market environment. Rather, conflicts will arise in the issue of allocating taxing rights; the basic freedoms do indeed require a fundamental reform of a Member State's set of double taxation conventions.

The ECJ has not yet taken a comprehensive approach to similarity in direct taxation and prefers to use narrower criteria to examine if there is an 'objectively comparable situation', such as the similarity in modalities of taxation and the likeness of rules determining the taxable base[84]. However, if consistently applied, the Court's way of proceeding may lead to deficits in judicial protection, because Member States might easily set up different methods in computing the taxable base. On the contrary, if concentrating on ability to pay one will not adhere to such superficialities but rather advance to the underlying object of the tax, thereby eliminating any room for manipulation. Notably, the ECJ itself does not always restrict its similarity test to the specific criteria mentioned before when it would risk miss a discrimination by doing so. In a recent case, the Court relied on the fact that the 'business expenses in question [were] directly linked to the activity that generated the taxable income'.[85] Putting emphasis on the economic activity that is liable to tax points the right way; it hints at the ability to pay which is derived from this activity and which is the underlying reason for the tax liability. The ECJ might soon be bold enough to address ability to pay directly.

Comparability of situations can, of course, not be determined by this key factor when discriminating administrative procedures are to be assessed. Here, objectively comparable situations should be assumed generously on the basis of a similar obligation to pay taxes, in order to clear the way for a proportionality test. In principle,

---

Tax Review 2002, p. 112 (117) proposes that such a strict approach should not be taken as regards non-discriminatory restrictions.

82. Cf. Raventós, ET 1998, p. 336 (339). See also van Thiel, *EC Tax Review* 2003, p. 4 (13): '... in a cross-border Community-relevant situation, the taxpayer's ability to pay tax is no longer a purely national issue.'
83. Lehner, *EC Tax Review* 2002, p. 5 (12); *ibid.*, DStJG 2000, p. 263 (278 et seq.); Jacobs, *Internationale Unternehmensbesteuerung*, 5th edn, p. 198; Williams, *EC Tax Review* 1997, p. 4; Vermeend, *EC Tax Review* 1996, p. 54 et seq.
84. Cf. ECJ, 28.1.1986, case 270/83 (Avoirfiscal), ECR 1986, 273, paras 19 etseq.; ECJ, 29.4.1999, case311/97 *(Royal Scotland)*, ECR 1999, I-2651, para. 28.
85. ECJ, 12.6.2003, case 234/01 *(Gerritse)*, ECR 2003, I-5933, para. 27.

taxpayers are not only entitled to the same tax burden but also to the same tax compliance burden.[86]

Finally, ECJ rulings on tax affairs concerning international transactions usually reverberate on the entire national tax subsystem under scrutiny. Consequently, the European Legal Tax Order surely has its impact on taxing purely internal constellations as well. A good example for this is the recent decision on German thin capitalization rules,[87] which has influenced governments throughout Europe to modify their respective concepts and in a second step to extend their scope to financing schemes in domestic constellations as well.

[5] Complementation by the Basic Provisions on Non-discrimination and Free Movement

The provisions on free movement for the sake of conducting economic activities in the Community internal market are complemented by the general right to free movement of persons enshrined in Article 18. Every citizen of the Union can, without prejudice to the limitations and conditions laid down in the Treaty, move and reside freely in the territory of the Member States. The freedom of movement comprises the prohibition of discrimination on grounds of nationality.[88] However, as far as economic activities protected by the special provisions of Articles 39, 43 and 49 are concerned, Article 18 must not be taken into consideration.[89] In tax law matters, Article 18 will therefore gain importance only in a small number of cases regarding non-economic, though nevertheless taxable activities. An example for this is the former and now abolished Sec. 21 (2) of the German Income Tax Act (EStG) which taxed fictitious income presumably derived from the use of self-owned real property for dwelling purposes.[90] Hence, we shall not discuss here whether, in contrast to the basic economic freedoms, Article 18 goes beyond an equality principle and grants a true freedom right.

Finally, Article 12 stipulates a general prohibition of discrimination on grounds of nationality within the scope of application of the EC Treaty. The ECJ has interpreted the latter requirement widely; it deems the provision applicable if the discriminatory national rule has any effect, albeit indirectly, on the intra-Community exchange of goods and services.[91] Moreover, in conformity with the basic freedoms, Article 12 is seen to address both overt and covert discrimination.[92] This is reasonable because the prohibition could otherwise be easily circumvented by national legislation. Particularly, any differentiation based on residence must usually be considered a covert

86. Van Thiel, *EC Tax Review* 2003, p. 4 (11).
87. ECJ, 12.12.2002, case C-234/88 *(Lankhorst-Hohorst)*, ECR 2002, I-11779.
88. Cf. ECJ, 11.4.2000, case C-356/98 *(Kaba)*, ECR 2000, I-2623, paras 30 et seq.
89. ECJ, 29.2.1996, case C-193/94 *(Skanavi and Chryssanthakopoulos)*, ECR 1996, I-929, para. 22; ECJ, 19.1.1999, case C-348/96 *(Calfa)*, ECR 1999, I-11, paras 29 et seq.
90. Such a case has now come up before the ECJ (case C-152/03, *Ritter*). For further details see Cordewener, ET2003, p. 294 et seq.
91. ECJ, 20.3.1997, case C-323/95 *(Hayes)*, ECR 1997, I-1711, para. 17.
92. ECJ, 23.1.1997, case C-29/95 (Pastoors), ECR 1997, I-285, para. 16, with further references.

discrimination.[93] Article 12 only applies to situations, though, not covered by specific rules prohibiting discrimination[94] and is therefore subsidiary to the basic freedoms. As a consequence, and similar to Article 18, it has little impact on national tax law. Article 12 may come into play especially in the taxation of foreign non-profit institutions which, according to Article 48 (2), do not enjoy the protection of the basic freedoms but nevertheless provide goods or services within the Common Market.[95]

§9.03 CROSS-BORDER ABILITY TO PAY IN DIRECT TAXATION

[A] Non-discrimination of Non-residents

The most far-reaching implications of a cross-border concept of ability to pay as demanded by the basic freedoms can certainly be found in the direct taxation of non-residents. 'In the European legal order the distinction between residents and non-residents of different Member States is by hypothesis irrelevant for the implementation of the European legal tax order.'[96] This means a radical break with a century-old tradition accepted in international tax law and usually not questioned by national courts. Instead, at least the objective ability to pay resulting from activities subject to tax must bear an equal tax burden independent of the taxpayer's place of residence[97]. Objective ability to pay is usually related to some source of income and its proper consideration does not depend on an overall assessment of the entire personal income, which is a characteristic feature only of resident taxation.[98] This leads to the conclusion that as far as the taxable base, the tax rates and the assessment procedures are concerned, residents and non-residents will usually have to be assumed to be in objectively comparable situation.[99] Any distinction directly or indirectly based on the criterion of residence infringes the basic freedoms and must be objectively justified. If a Member State deems a certain economic transaction or condition as an indicator of taxable ability to pay, the legal implementation of this view must affect residents and non-residents equally as regards liability to and amount of tax. If, on the other hand, a Member States exempts certain transactions or conditions from tax because it does not

93. ECJ, 23.1.1997, case C-29/95 *(Pastoors)*, ECR 1997, I-285, para. 17.
94. ECJ, 26.6.2003, case C-422/01 *(Skandia)*, EWS 2003, p. 379, para. 61 with further references; *Farmer, EC Tax Review* 2003, p. 75.
95. Opposed to the application of Art. 12 in these cases are *Isensee*, DStJG 2003, p. 93 (109) and Jachmann/Igl/ Eichenhöfer, *Ehrenamt und bürgerschaftliches Engagement im Recht*, 2002, p. 91; they do not consider the possibility of covert discrimination, though, which makes their reasoning hardly convincing.
96. Vanistendael, *EC Tax Review* 1996, p. 114(121). Dissenting Hinnekens, ET 1996, p. 286 (290); Avery Jones, ET 1996, p. 46.
97. Englisch, *Dividendenbesteuerung in Deutschland und Spanien*, unedited doctoral thesis, 2003, p. 242; van Thiel, *EC Tax Review* 2003, p. 4 (12); Cordewener, *Grundfreiheiten*, p. 894. Some what more narrow Hinnekens, ET 1996, p. 286 (292); Wattel, ET 1996, p. 159.
98. Cf. Wattel, ET 1995, p. 347 (349).
99. Cf. van Thiel, *EC Tax Review* 2003, p. 4 (10 et seq.); Jacobs, *Internationale Unternehmensbesteuerung*, 5th edn, p. 196. See also Bater, ET 2000, p. 8 (13): 'In can also be predicted ... that more attention will be paid to alleged infringements by the Member States that take the form of procedural, rather than substantive, discrimination.'

consider them to indicate ability to pay, or if it imposes a relatively lower tax burden because of a presumed lesser manifestation of ability to pay, this estimation must not be ignored in case of non-residents. Especially tax relief must be granted without any such distinction.

Finally, it will usually make no difference whether the purpose of this relief is to respect a diminished ability to pay, or whether the national government wishes to influence individual behaviour to promote economically or socially desired effects. The incentives set by this kind of rule serving government's economic and social control must, in principle, not be limited to residents.[100] Hence, a discrimination can only be ruled out if the tax concession is necessarily linked to the overall ability to pay which will, in general, only be considered in the State of residence.[101] Otherwise, the motivation of the different treatment can only be taken into account as a possible justification for a discriminatory treatment.[102]

The only exception to the above rule stems from the limitations in national tax sovereignty drawn by a narrowly defined *territoriality principle:* taxation without any point of contact, for example the taxpayer's nationality or residence, or the location of his/her economic activities, is inadmissible under international law.[103] Hence, foreign income of non-residents may not be taxed as there is no objective link to the host State. Consequently, negative foreign income, i.e. losses resulting from activities abroad, need not to be taken into account either.[104] Discrimination cannot be claimed since resident and non-resident taxpayers are not comparable due to coercive requirements of international public law.[105] Even in that regard, though, Member States must act consistently: if they do choose to install a saving clause as to progression when determining the tax rate for non-residents, positive and negative foreign income will have to be considered.

Indeed, this broad concept of similarity is also the posture adopted by the ECJ in a variety of rulings, concerning the taxation of both individuals and companies.[106] It is therefore wrong to insist that according to the Court's judgment, only a 'virtual' resident who is not domiciled in the host State but derives the bulk of its income from activities located there could be compared to a 'real' resident. This figure created in the

100. Cf. the request for a preliminary ruling of the ECJ by the German Bundesfinanzhof, 14.7.2004, C-386/04 *(Centro di Musicologia Walter Stauffer).*
101. This seems reasonable, for instance, in the case of an income tax relief to stimulate the acquisition of immobile property for dwelling purposes, common in many Member States. Here, there is no visible connection to any income schedule (provided that such property does not create fictitious rental income) but a close link to the taxpayer's overall economic condition and his/her personal circumstances which will generally be taken into account only in the State of residence. See also ECJ, 12.6.2003, case C-234/01 *(Gerritse),* EWS 2003, p. 330, paras 44 et seq.
102. See below in 6 (d).
103. Zuber, *Reichweite der internationalen Besteuerung,* p. 37; Wassermeyer, DStJG 8, p. 49 (53).
104. ECJ, 15.5.1997, case C-250/95 *(Futura),* ECR 1997, I-2471, paras 21 et seq.; see also see also *KokottAG,* Opinion, 18.3.2004, case C-319/02 *(Manninen),* para. 42.
105. See also Weber, *EC Tax Review* 2003, p. 220 (228).
106. ECJ, 29.4.1999, case C-311/97 *(Royal Bank of Scotland),* ECR 1999, I-2651, paras 27 and 29; ECJ, 21.9.1999, case C-307/97 *(Saint-Gobain),* ECR 1999, I-6181, para. 48; ECJ, 27.6.1996, case C-107/94 *(Asscher),* ECR 1996, I-3089, para. 42.

Schumacker case[107] actually still matters only where tax laws take into consideration personal circumstances for allowances, deductions or lower tax rates. Here, the ECJ persists in that it is, in general, the duty of the home State to allow for such personal relief, so that in the field of subjective ability to pay an equal treatment with the host state's residents cannot be claimed.[108] At first sight, this seems reasonable, because personal circumstances affect the entire ability to pay, not only those parts resulting from domestic activities. Thus, the home State might be held responsible for granting relief depending on the taxpayer's personal status, as only the home State purports to tax worldwide income. And an exception would only have to be made when, due to treaty law, most of that income can only effectively be taxed in the host State.[109]

Taking a closer view, one can however doubt the soundness of the Court's arguments. Of course, it is a traditional principle of international tax law that the host State does not offer the same personal allowances for residents and non-residents, see Article 24 (3) 2 OECD-MC. But it is not a generally accepted principle of international law which would *a priori* have to be respected in the interpretation of the basic freedoms.[110] Furthermore, personal allowances are not inseparably tied to the country pretending to tax worldwide income. One might also take the stand that if the global income is split up and taxed in several jurisdictions, each one of them puts the taxpayer in a *proportionally* comparable situation to a resident who has only domestic income.[111] Consequently, he/she would be entitled to a fraction of the personal and family allowances or relief, the numerator of the fraction being his/her income definitely taxable in the host State and the denominator being his/her total taxable income.[112] In his/her home State he/she would be in a situation comparable to other

107. ECJ, 14.2.1995, case C-279/93 *(Schumacker)*, ECR 1995, I-225, paras 31–36; approved by van Thiel, *EC Tax Review* 2003, p. 4 (12); *Hinnekens*, ET 1996, p. 286 (292).
108. ECJ, 1.7.2004, *C-169/03 (Wallentin)*, not yet published, paras 15 et seq.
109. In this regard it does not, in principle, matter whether the home State employs the exemption or the credit method to avoid double taxation: under the exemption method, the income may not be taxed, so no personal allowances can be deducted. The credit method, on the other hand, permits the deduction as all income may be included in the taxable base. However, in general only an ordinary credit is granted to offsetforeign taxes, limiting the credit to the domestic tax resting on foreign source income. As this tax burden is diminished by personal allowances, so is the maximum credit. Depending on the respective levels of taxation, the progression of the tax system, and the relation between foreign and domestic income, it may well be that in the overall perspective the personal deductions in the credit state do not have any effect. For some examples see Avery Jones, ET 1996, p. 46 (47 et seq.); Farmer, *EC Tax Review* 1998, p. 13 (15 et seq.).
110. Customary international law and generally accepted principles of international law form part of the Com munity legal order and must be respected by all Community institutions in the exercise of their power, cf. ECJ, 16.6.1998, case C-162/96 *(Racke)*, ECR 1998, I-3655, paras 45 et seq.; Streinz/*Schroeder*, EUV/EGV, Art. 249 EGV, para. 19. Thus, the ECJ must interpret the basic freedoms in conformity with these sources of law.
111. Cf. Cordewener, *Grundfreiheiten*, p. 922. Too remote is the approach of Toifl, SWI 1995, p. 149 (154 et seq.), who believes all Member States involved in an individual's taxation must concede 100 per cent of the personal relief granted to residents with domestic income, similar Vanistendael, ET 2000, p. 3 (4).
112. Such has been the solution of the Commission proposal for a Council Directive concerning the harmonization of income taxation provisions with respect to freedom of movement for workers within the Community, COM/79/737 final; and subsequently of Wattel, ET 1995, p. 347 (350), Saß, BB 1995, p. 69 (70); Kaefer, BB 1995, p. 1615 (1621); Van Raad, *Taxation ofCross-Border*

residents only to the extent that his/her total income can be taxed there, which means personal allowances could be cut on the same *pro rata* basis without constituting a discrimination.[113] Such an understanding does not only take into account that the principle of worldwide taxation is in reality to a great extent undermined by the exemption method to avoid international double taxation, which leads to isolated assessments of parts of the overall ability to pay both in the home and the host State(s). It is also better in line with the intention of the basic freedoms to ensure that cross-border activities are not specifically hampered as compared to domestic ones. The 'virtual-resident' concept falls short of this objective at least when the bulk of income is earned abroad, but in more than one Member State, because then personal allowances would not be granted anywhere.

A proportional similarity should also be assumed when the home State applies the credit method rather than the exemption method. It cannot be assumed that any concession of personal relief benefits only the treasury of the credit country.[114] If the State of source grants higher or different deductions than the State of residence, the taxpayer may eventually benefit from them even if the latter avoids double taxation by crediting foreign tax.[115] But even if the amount of deductions is more or less the same in both countries, it can be beneficial for the 'free mover' to have his/her personal circumstances considered in the host State, given that most credit countries reduce their credit for foreign tax by an amount equivalent to their own personal allowances.

Recent ECJ case law gives rise to the affirmation that a discriminatory tax regulation of the host State must be judged on its consistency with the basic freedoms independently of home State regulations.[116] When deciding the *de Groot* case, the ECJ stated that Member States could allocate the obligation to consider personal and family circumstances among themselves and that even in the absence of such an agreement, a discrimination could only be assumed if the aggregation of reliefs granted in all Member States involved would not make up for 'all' circumstances concerned.[117] A similar reasoning has very recently surfaced in the context of a dividend relief granted by the home State only to residents.[118] We cannot follow the Court in this reasoning, because the basic freedoms do oblige each single Member State to abolish any discrimination emanating from *its own* legal order.[119] It is indeed established case law that discriminating tax burdens in the Member State of destination cannot be compensate by a more favourable treatment in the Member State of origin, and vice versa.[120]

Income, p. 43 (45), among others. A positive evaluation is also given to this concept by Farmer, *EC Tax Review* 1998, p. 13 (19), who also gives an overview over other possible solutions.

113. Cf. Cordewener, *Grundfreiheiten*, p. 924 et seq.; Wattel, ET 2000, p. 210 (222 et seq.).
114. See also Wattel, ET 1996, p. 159 (160).
115. Cf. Toifl, *EC Tax Review* 1996, p. 165 (167). As has been specified before, this effect depends also on the level of taxation in both the source and the residence country.
116. Cf. Cordewener, ET 2003, p. 294 (300); Wattel, ET 1996, p. 159 (160); Toifl, *EC Tax Review* 1996, p. 165 (166 et seq.).
117. ECJ, 12.12.2002, case C-385/00 (de Groot), ECR 2002, I-11819, para. 101.
118. Cf. ECJ, 7.9.2004, case C-319/02 *(Manninen)*, not yet published, para. 34.
119. See also Jacobs, *Internationale Unternehmensbesteuerung*, 5th edn, p. 204 et seq.; Schuch, *EC Tax Review* 1998, p. 29 (31 et seq.).
120. Cf. ECJ, 26.10.1999, case C-294/97 *(Eurowings)*, ECR 1999, I-7447, paras 43 et seq.; ECJ, 26.6.2003, case C-422/01 *(Skandia)*, ECR 2003, I-6817, para. 52.

To create an interdependency of home and host State taxation is also harmful because it provokes constant uncertainty,[121] as each State may at any time change its rules unilaterally, letting the other slip into discrimination. Moreover, the aggregate perspective taken by the ECJ ignores the disparities persisting in national tax laws and admissible under EC law. The Member States' tax systems do contemplate objective and subjective ability to pay, e.g. personal and family allowances, to quite a different extent. In particular, deductions can therefore not be added up to examine whether, in total, they reach the level enjoyed by residents with equivalent domestic income in one of the Member States. Rather, each state has to assure that the taxation of non-residents is equal to the tax treatment experienced by its own residents with domestic income, insofar as they are objectively comparable. In this sense, there does not exist one single cross-border concept of ability-to- pay valid for all Member States – this could only be installed by way of legal harmonization.[122] Instead, the principle of ability to pay rooted in each one of the Member States' constitutional and taxing traditions must open its respective window towards a cross-border outlook.

[B] Non-discrimination of Foreign Source Income

In taxing residents on a worldwide basis, national income tax laws frequently distinguish between domestic and foreign source income, and in general to the detriment of the latter one. Within the single market, though, cross-border activities may not be discriminated against in regard to their purely internal counterparts. Therefore, a preferential taxation of ability to pay rooted in domestic transactions as compared to ability to pay gained outside the home State's boundaries, but within the Community,[123] is no longer admissible. The similarity of both sources of ability to pay is usually recognized by Member States themselves, because as home States, they claim to tax gains of ability to pay worldwide and, in principle, independent of their place of origin. The ECJ has until recently indeed always assumed that domestic and offshore income are comparable without further reasoning.[124] Thus, the very idea that income gained outside a particular Member State, but within the Community, is 'foreign income' conflicts with the single market concept.[125] Rather, it must be considered as domestic income, bearing in mind, of course, that it can straddle two or more tax jurisdictions.[126] Even though Community law, as it stands at present, does not

121. Notably, this is also the position taken by the EFTA Court in deciding the issue of cross-border dividend relief in the reverse situation of outbound dividends, cf. judgment of 23.11.2004, case E-1/04 *(Fokus Bank)*, para. 37.
122. Birk, DStJG 1996, p. 63 (76 et seq.). As far as national tax law is harmonized and thus a true common market environment is, albeit partially, created, the EJC's supranational approach might indeed be appropriate, as disparities no longer exist.
123. Understood in a wide sense, i.e. including all EEA Member States.
124. Cf. ECJ, 6.6.2000, case C-35/98 (Verkooijen), ECR 2000, I-4071, paras 33 et seq.; ECJ, 14.12.2000, case C-141/99 (AMID), ECR 2000, I-11619, para. 23.
125. Cf. Gammie, *Bulletin I.F.D.* 2003, p. 86 (88).
126. As regards this aspect, see the Treaty implications for international double taxation discussed below.

prohibit 'reverse discrimination' of internal situations,[127] in most Member States such discrimination would not be tolerable under their constitutional principle of tax equality. Hence, when taxing residents, the cross-border concept of ability to pay planted in their common constitutional traditions, and enhanced by the basic freedoms, calls for equal taxation of all income originated within the EEA. As far as capital investments are concerned, this even applies on a global scale, because the freedom of capital is not limited to Member States but also protects transactions involving third countries.

In two recent judgments on dividend taxation, the ECJ has taken a somewhat modified approach in determining similarity of foreign source income as compared to domestic source income. Similarity was assumed if the aims of the tax rule in question, i.e. of the shareholder relief, required its cross-border application.[128] Methodologically, there is a striking parallel to the 'aims and effects' test adopted by some GATT and WTO panels in their appreciation of de facto discrimination caused by differentiated excise duties in the context of Article III GATT and Article XVII GATS. They, too, determined similarity of foreign and domestic goods or services according to the regulatory purpose of the rule suspected to discriminate against cross-border trade.[129] However, the 'aims and effects' test in world trade law has also drawn considerable criticism by prominent scholars,[130] and has in the meantime been expressly rejected by the WTO Appellate Body as a criterion to establish similarity.[131] The 'aims and effects' approach is indeed inadequate both in the WTO and in the EC internal market environment. The GATT and GATS national treatment provisions, as well as the EC fundamental freedoms, are aimed at warranting undistorted competition between local and cross-border market agents, albeit to a different extent.[132] Given this objective, discrimination on grounds of the cross-border character of a transaction must *prima facie* be prohibited independent of the Member State's regulatory purposes.[133] Such policy goals may only be invoked to justify a breach of the fundamental freedoms, thereby opening the way to a thorough proportionality test including a weighing and balancing of the conflicting interests. Hence, it is clearly preferable to determine similarity of foreign and domestic income for tax purposes on the basis of a broadly construed ability-to-pay criterion, which is closely related to competitive neutrality, and leave specific legislative aims to be discussed as possible justifications for unequal taxation.

127. Cf. von der *Groeben/Schwarze/Tiedje/Troberg*, EUV/EGV, 6th edn, Art. 43 EG, paras 109–111 with further references.
128. ECJ, 7.9.2004, case C-319/02 *(Manninen)*, not yet published, paras 33 to 36; ECJ, 15.7.2004, case C-315/02 *(Lenz)*, not yet published, para. 30.
129. See the landmark case US – Malt Beverages, Panel Report adopted 16.3.1992, DS23/R, para. 5.25. Supportive: Hudec, *International Lawyer* 1998, 619 (634 et seq.); Regan, *J. World Trade* 2003,737 (752).
130. Cf. Choi, *Like Products' in International Trade Law*, 2003, p. 82 et seq.; Verhoosel, *National Treatment and WTO Dispute Settlement*, 2002, p. 53 et seq.; Charnowitz, *Am. J. International Law* 2004, p. 610 (614).
131. Appellate Body Report, 12.3.2001, *EC -Asbestos*, WT/DS135/AB/R, para. 99; 9.9.1997, *EC - Bananas III*, WT/DS27/AB/R, para. 241.
132. As regards the EC Treaty fundamental freedoms, cf. Oliver/Roth, CMLR 2004, p. 407 (413).
133. Cf. Cordewener, ET 2003,294 (299).

However, the generous assumption of comparability of foreign source and domestic source income is not undisputed in legal science. Some argue that unfolding the fundamental freedoms when judging the tax system of the home State would not guarantee equal treatment but instead lead to a distorting 'equalization' of cases which are *per se* not comparable. As a consequence, the systematic foundations of resident taxation, namely the differences in taxation of domestic and foreign source income according to their different enjoyment of public infrastructure, would be shattered. It is further advanced that the subsidiarity principle stipulated in Article 5 (3) is also binding for the ECJ, and the Court should therefore refrain from demanding equal taxation of domestic income and income rooted in another Member State.[134] We shall not engage in the discussion as to whether the ECJ is bound at all by the subsidiarity principle.[135] Here, it is sufficient to indicate that the above objections do have an inappropriate starting point, as they are based on the exception instead of being based on the principle itself.

The general principle to start out from is the taxation of worldwide income which itself negates any differences between domestic and foreign income. The basic freedoms only enhance this fundamental evaluation. The compromises introduced in national tax laws in form of, for example, limitations in offsetting foreign losses, are not 'systematic foundations' based on considerations of ability to pay, but rather exceptions motivated by principles governing the allocation of taxing rights and the desire to prevent abusive tax schemes. However, the former allocation principles are, ultimately, budgetary criteria irrelevant for the discrimination test, if the basic freedoms are not to be deprived of their effectiveness. The prevention of tax abuse, in its turn, is not a fundamental principle of tax law but only an assisting one, aimed at effectively protecting the principle of tax equality. Thus, it can be taken into account as a justification for what is seemingly discrimination, but not to rule out similarity of conditions in the first place. It is undeniable that a cross-border concept of ability-to-pay challenges Member State's tax systems; this challenge should not be defied as unsystematic, though. *Reasonable* interests of Member States conflicting with this concept can be balanced against it by considering them as possible justifications for a deviation.

Finally, a forbidden discrimination also occurs when the State of residence levies an 'exit tax' on the transfer of shares or moveable assets to another Member State, which cuts the link that allows the home State to recoup tax deferrals or excessively granted deductions. The detrimental treatment is caused by the conversion of domestic source income into foreign source income, thus providing for the necessary cross-border nexus to activate the fundamental freedoms. While it is true that the underlying tax obligation would also materialize in case of a domestic transfer which leads to taxable capital gains, there can be no doubt that a 'premature' taxation upon crossing the border is more burdensome for the taxpayer in terms of liquidity and interest. The

134. Lehner, DStJG 2000, p. 263 (278 et seq.).
135. An idea firmly rejected by the majority of scholars, cf. van Thiel, Free movement of persons, p. 222 et seq.; *Streinz/Streinz*, EUV/EGV, Art. 5 EGV, para. 34; Groeben/Schwarze/Zuleeg, EUV/EGV, 6th edn, Art. 5 EG, para. 34.

same holds true when such 'hidden reserves' are taxed upon the taxpayer's decision to move abroad, either in exercising his/her economic activities,[136] or for private reasons in virtue of Article 18. If the taxpayer or the taxable property move within the Member State, no such obligation arises, hence discrimination is evident. The comparability does not depend on the treatment of capital gains in the state of immigration,[137] since discrimination must always be determined regardless of tax advantages enjoyed abroad. It is the tax claim of the home State which is at issue, not that of the host State. Indeed, exit taxes are a fine example of the need to readjust double taxation conventions, permitting the affected Member State to pursue his/her tax claim upon the realization of a capital gain abroad.

[C] Equal Treatment of Different Alternatives to Realize a Freedom?

Some experts in the field of European tax law believe that the basic provisions on free movement, especially the freedom of establishment, also guarantee tax neutrality as between different alternatives of realizing the freedom; most notably, the host State should tax a branch and a subsidiary, i.e. different ways to make use of the right to secondary establishment, equally and independently of legal form.[138] Some further propose that the decision in financing the establishment by equity or by debt must not be influenced by differences in tax treatment.[139] Even the ECJ has seemingly inclined in favour of such a wide interpretation in two of its rulings.[140] Indeed, tax neutrality, especially neutrality as regards legal form and financing, is not merely an economic aspect irrelevant for tax equity. Of course, any tax except a capitation tax like Margaret Thatcher's poll tax will influence an individual's economic preferences, e.g. on the choice between work and leisure or saving and spending.[141] Nevertheless, within these limits tax neutrality is a good indicator for equal taxation according to ability to pay.[142] Hence, we support the idea that tax neutrality should play a major role in a European Legal Tax Order.

However, we respectfully submit that it would overstretch the fundamental freedoms to read such a concept into their substantial scope. The free movement provisions enhance only one aspect of the respective national coinage of tax equality: the cross-border aspect, according to their purpose to establish an internal market without frontiers, as *between* Member States. As has already been pointed out, it is not their objective to abolish all obstacles to the efficient allocation of resources *within* a

136. ECJ, 11.3.2004, case C-9/02 *(Lasteyrie du Saillant)*, not yet published; van Thiel, *EC Tax Review* 2003, p. 4(9).
137. Different opinion van Thiel, *EC Tax Review* 2003, p. 4 (9).
138. Wattel, *EC Tax Review* 2003, p. 194 (197); Zoll, *Verlustberücksichtigung*, p. 296; Dautzenberg, EWS 2001, p. 270 (276 f.); Schön, EWS 2000, p. 281 (288 et seq.); Herzig in: GS Knobbe-Keuk, p. 627 (634).
139. Dautzenberg, *Unternehmensbesteuerung im EG-Binnenmarkt*, p. 65; see also Herzig in: GS Knobbe-Keuk, p. 627 (635 et seq.).
140. ECJ, 28.1.1986, case 270/83 *(Avoirfiscal)*, ECR 1986,285, para. 22; ECJ, 21.9.1999, case C-307/97 *(Saint Gobain)*, ECR 1999, I-6181, paras 35 and 43.
141. Blankart, *Öffentliche Finanzen*, 3rd edn, p. 210; Elschen, StuW 1991, p. 99 (104).
142. *Cf. Vogt, Neutralitätund Leistungsfähigkeit, p.* 121 et seq.

particular Member State. If inequalities in national tax law do not specifically distort cross-border business but rather influence internal and pan-European economic behaviour alike, they cannot be challenged under the fundamental freedoms[143]. The suggestion of a specific need for an unbiased choice between different legal forms to allow different degrees of market integration[144] does not convince as the respective consequences are equally faced by domestic competitors. This interpretation is, besides, also perfectly consistent with the wording of Article 43 (2). Tax neutrality between substitutable alternatives of realizing a freedom will therefore have to be introduced into the European Legal Tax Order by way of harmonization; it cannot be enforced by the ECJ prior to the required political agreement.[145]

[D] Abolition of International Double Taxation

The ECJ has so far not handed down a decision on how the basic freedoms relate to international double taxation.[146] Hinnekens comments that this question 'is one of today's trickiest issues concerning the scope of the prohibition of national tax practices based on the fundamental freedoms ...'.[147] Obviously, Article 293, second indent, which calls upon the Member States to enter into negotiations to avoid international double taxation, does not have any direct effect.[148] Taking the supranational roots of a cross-border concept of ability-to-pay in a single market as a starting point, however, there can be no doubt that any international double taxation within the EEA is an infringement of the relevant basic freedom(s).[149] This is so because, naturally, only cross-border activities may suffer double taxation resulting from competing tax

143. See also Jacobs, *Internationale Unternehmensbesteuerung,p.* 196 and 202; *Tumpel,DStJG* 2000,321 (362); Jaeger, *Die Körperschaftsteuerysteme in Europa,* p. 110 et seq.
144. Schön,EWS 2000, p. 281(289).
145. Of course, insofar as a different treatment of legal forms can at the same time be understood as a discrimination of cross-border establishment, it will have to stand up to the discrimination test of Art. 43. Such is the case in the taxation of domestic branches and subsidiaries of a foreign corporation: the taxation of the subsidiary can be considered as an internal tax treatment due to its legal form which makes it national of the state of destination, whereas the taxation of the branch is, legally speaking, the taxation of the foreign company because the branch does not constitute a legal entity of its own. Hence, a branch may not be taxed higher (but may be taxed lower!) than a subsidiary, not because of a presumed freedom of choice between different legal forms, but because of the prohibition of discriminating cross-border activities.
146. The ECJ has only stated that Member States are free to allocate taxing rights among themselves in order to avoid international double taxation and may do so depending on the nationality of the taxable subject, cf. ECJ, 12.12.2002, case 385/00 *(de Groot),* ECR 2002, I-11819, para. 93; ECJ, 12.5.1998, case C-336/96 *(Gilly),* ECR 1998, I-2793, para. 30. However, this does not give any clue as to what rules apply in a constellation where double taxation is not avoided.
147. Hinnekens, ET 2001, p. 206 (208).
148. ECJ, 12.5.1998, case C-336/96 (Gilly), ECR 1998, I-2793, para. 14–17; Wattel,EC *Tax Review* 2003, p. 194 (199); van den Hurk, *EC Tax Review* 1999, p. 211 (213).
149. See also Hosson, *Intertax* 2003, p. 482 (483); van Thiel, *EC Tax Review* 2003, p. 4 (10); Schön, EWS 2000, p. 281 (290); Jacobs, *Internationale Unternehmensbesteuerung,* p. 204. ScepticalWattel,Sceptical Wattel, *EC Tax Review* 2003, p. 194 (198 et seq.): *'ultra vires* interpretation'. An intermediate position is taken by Hinnekens, *EC Tax Review* 2002, p. 112(118): 'Also not *every* case of international double taxation is by itself a prohibited tax restriction of cross-border trade and investment' [the italics are ours].

jurisdictions, whereas purely domestic activities do not run any such risk. Thus, international double taxation specifically disadvantages pan-European economic activities, putting a higher tax burden on them than would be the case if they were realized internally in any one of the Member States involved.

The issue of double taxation is nevertheless not one of overt or covert de jure discrimination. The State of origin and the host State may each perfectly comply with their respective obligation to tax equally domestic and offshore income or resident and non-resident income, without any legal distinction, and still international double taxation takes place. Consequently, this disparate, more burdensome impact of apparently unbiased rules qualifies as a de facto discrimination of the cross-border movement of, depending on the activity affected, persons, services or capital.[150] In a broad sense, it constitutes a two- or even multifold 'regulation' of one single internal market activity, and therefore it treats equally a situation which, on the grounds of the coincidence of more than one tax jurisdiction, is not comparable with a purely domestic one. The dogmatic approach of tackling double taxation therefore differs from a discrimination test: the latter takes as a starting point the tax rules in only one particular Member State irrespective of taxpayer's treatment in other jurisdictions, whereas the restriction caused by double taxation results from the interaction of two or more Member States.

Even so, an excessive tax burden arising from double taxation is not sufficient to accuse any of the Member States involved in violating their Treaty obligations. Additionally, it must be resolved which one of them is responsible for avoiding this kind of non-discriminatory restriction which arises from the interaction of more than one jurisdiction, and, consequently, has to waive or at least limit its sovereign taxing powers. EC law itself provides clear guidelines only in those exceptional cases governed by secondary law, especially the parent/subsidiary directive and the directive on interest and royalty payments.[151] Apart from those partial regulations, the issue indeed gets tricky. One might retreat to the position that the avoidance of international double taxation amounts to a 'joint obligation' of home State and host State, and in the absence of harmonization none of them could be held responsible.[152] We do not agree with that opinion, because it renders the basic freedoms ineffective. It can therefore be no acceptable interpretation in the light of the legally binding Community objective of establishing an internal market without discriminatory obstacles, as between Member States, to the free flow of products and productions factors.

Thus, a criterion for determining the responsibility must be named, and in this context, the ECJ's reference to the generally accepted rules of international tax law[153]

150. In general terms, see also Ehring, *Journal of World Trade* 2002, p. 921 (925); Spaventa, CMLR 2004, p. 743 (746 et seq.). The free movement of goods is usually not affected by international double taxation in the field of direct taxes, because direct taxes burden the economic outcome of personal activities and investments rather than the flow of goods, cf. Schön, RIW 2004, p. 50 (51).
151. Directive 2003/49/EC, 3.6.2003, OJ L157/49.
152. Cf. van der Linde, *EC Tax Review* 2004, p. 10 (14); Lehner, IStR 2001, p. 329 (336); Schön, EWS 2000, p. 281 (290); *Lehner/Reimer*, Grundfreiheiten, p. 39 (58); Ståhl, *EC Tax Review* 1997, p. 227 (228 et seq.). See also Farmer, *EC Tax Review* 1998, p. 13 (27).
153. ECJ, 12.5.1998, case C-336/96 *(Gilly)*, ECR 1998, I-2793, para. 31.

points in the right direction. At present, the Member States have already knit a comprehensive net of bilateral conventions on double taxation, which serve two closely intertwined purposes: to allocate the taxing rights between the contracting parties and in doing so, avoid double taxation of the taxpayers which fall into their scope of application. Of course, the conventions do not create any obligation *directly* enforceable under EC law, as they do not form part of the Community legal order. But even when acting within its remaining sovereign powers, each Member State must respect the rights and interests of other Member States and their citizens protected by the Community.[154] Especially when an agreement has been reached between two or more Member States in an area relevant for the establishment of an internal market, the principle of Community loyalty stipulated in Article 10 requires that such treaties be interpreted and applied in a way that is consistent with Community law.[155] The responsibilities negotiated in an agreement binding according to the principles of international law are thereby transformed into responsibilities which the contracting parties can be held accountable for under EC law as well. This must also hold true for bilateral conventions between Member States aiming at the avoidance of double taxation. These conventions, too, form part of Member States' efforts to promote the single market, as becomes evident from Article 293, even if not explicitly agreed upon for this purpose. Hence, if there exists such a treaty between two Member States, both are obliged under Community law to apply and interpret its stipulations in a way that conforms with the basic freedoms, i.e. in a way that avoids double taxation. Consequently, when one national jurisdiction fails to correctly implement the treaty provisions, it can be identified as the one that is responsible for the infringement of the basic freedoms caused by international double taxation.

In those rare cases not governed by a bilateral convention, it will usually be the home State that will have to surrender its tax claims. All Member States grant a unilateral credit for foreign taxes to their residents with outbound activities or investments. On the contrary, a similar source country provision for taxes non-residents have to pay in their home country is generally unknown in the legal order of international tax law. From that it can be deducted that there exists a silent consensus, at least within the Community, about the home State's rather than the host State's responsibility to avoid double taxation. This unilateral recognition expressed in the respective Tax Act's provisions may not be denied by Member States in the context of the fundamental freedoms, as this would be contrary to the idea of a *bonafide* conduct.

From the above, the different approach in addressing de jure and 'double burden' de facto discriminatory restrictions of the fundamental freedoms as well as their complementary function in tax law becomes obvious. First, it must be assured that all the Member States adopt a 'domestic outlook'[156] to any internal market activity which is subjected to their tax jurisdiction, free of discrimination on grounds of nationality,

154. ECJ, 10.7.1980, case 32/79 *(Commission v. United Kingdom)*, ECR 1980, 2403, para. 46. See also: Groe- ben/Schwarze/Zuleeg, EUV/EGV, 6th edn, Art. 10 EGV, para. 12.
155. ECJ, 27.9.1988, case 235/87 *(Mateucci)*, ECR 1988, 5589, para. 19; Calliess/Ruffert/Kahl EUV/EGV, 2nd edn, Art. 10 EGV, para. 53.
156. Gammie, *Bulletin I.F.D.* 2003, p. 86 (87).

residence or source of income. In judging the consistency of their tax legislation, tax administration and tax judiciary with those premises, only their measures should be taken into account, independent of the taxation in other Member States. This respects the remaining disparities in national tax laws tolerated by the fundamental freedoms while at the same time guaranteeing that in neither of the tax jurisdictions involved, are pan-European economic activities hampered by discriminating tax rules. It is true that in so proceeding, only equality within the respective 'national box' can be achieved;[157] however, this is the logical consequence of a single market concept that, in principle, permits different national systems of direct taxation.[158] In a second step, nevertheless, the concept of 'double burden' de facto discrimination allows for a truly supranational perspective and prohibits the accumulation of national taxes which are, each viewed from a national stance, levied in apparently equal conditions. Hence, specific disadvantages of cross-border activities originating in their transnational character rather than in national tax laws are abolished as well, provided they do not merely result from national disparities. Member States are forced to restrain their tax claim to the extent that they are responsible for avoiding international double taxation. Due to the lack of harmonization, the respective responsibility can be agreed upon by the Member States by means of bilateral or multilateral conventions.

Altogether, tax equality based on the supranational, cross-border concept of ability-to-pay as exposed so far requires equal taxation within any national box and in setting the ceiling for the overall tax burden of all national boxes, but not between any two such boxes. In the words of the ECJ, Member States are free to allocate taxing rights among themselves according to residence and source concepts without thereby infringing the fundamental freedoms; they must however not exercise their respective rights in a way that treats cross-border activities less favourably than domestic ones,[159] and, we may add, they must exercise them in a way that truly avoids international double taxation. From a pan-European taxpayer's perspective, his/her accumulated tax burden must be no higher than that of domestic activities in either the host or the home State.[160] He/she may also demand to be treated equally in the exercise of the taxing powers remaining with each tax jurisdiction. He/she cannot complain, though, that he/she suffers a higher tax burden than domestic activities in the Member State with the more favourable tax system as a result of the allocation of taxing rights[161]. Consequently, Member States are free to choose between the exemption and the credit method to avoid double taxation[162].

157. Birk, DStJG 1996, p. 63 (77); Lehner/Reimer, *Grundfreiheiten*, p. 39 (50).
158. Cf. Tumpel, DStJG 2000, p. 321 (328 et seq.); Schuch, *EC Tax Review* 1996, p. 161 (162).
159. ECJ, 12.12.2002, case 385/00 *(de Groot)*, ECR 2002, I-11819, para. 94. See also Kofler, IStR 2003, p. 184 (186 et seq.); van Thiel, *EC Tax Review* 2003, p. 4(15); Calderón Carrero, *Convenios de doble imposición*, p. 40.
160. Cf. Lehner/Reimer, *Grundfreiheiten*, p. 39 (57 et seq.).
161. Gammie, *Bulletin I.F.D.* 2003, p. 86 (89); Jacobs; *Internationale Unternehmensbesteuerung*, 5th edn, p. 248; Hinnekens, *EC Tax Review* 2002, p. 112 (115); Tumpel, DStJG 2000, p. 321 (348); Avery Jones, *EC Tax Review* 1998, p. 96; Schön in: GS Knobbe-Keuk, p. 743 (762).
162. Kostense, *EC Tax Review* 2000, p. 220 (229 et seq.); Jacobs, *Internationale Unternehmensbesteuerung*, 5th edn, p. 247; Bernhard, IStR 2001, p. 366 (367); Tumpel, DStJG 2000, p. 321 (348); Lehner, DStJG 2000, p. 263 (283); Avery Jones, *EC Tax Review* 1998, p. 95 (96); Hey,

[E] Most Favoured Nation Clause?

Finally, a highly disputed issue related to the basic freedoms' impact on international tax law is the existence of a most favoured nation (MFN) treatment obligation. The supporters of such a concept argue that any Member State must extend double taxation treaty advantages granted to at least one other particular Member State or a third State unilaterally to all other Member States. As a consequence, a taxpayer being taxed in a Member State as the State of source may invoke the most favourable rule contained in any of the tax treaties which this State has concluded.[163]

The ECJ has not yet handed down a decision concerning the possibility to derive such a concept from the Treaty's free movement provisions. However, in his Opinion on the pending *D* case, Advocate General Colomer has made an 'auxiliary comment' concerning the obligation of Member States to grant most favoured nation treatment in tax treaty concessions. He/she wants to distinguish between provisions regarding the allocation of taxing rights and provisions stipulating national treatment in the exercise of these rights and sees a need for MFN treatment only in case of the latter.[164] Even though the reasoning upon which these suggestions are based is not fully convincing, they nevertheless point the right direction. In our opinion, a general MFN interpretation would go clearly beyond the scope of the basic freedoms and lead to completely unacceptable results.[165] As their defenders admit, a MFN clause can only be construed by comparing a Member State's treatment of two non-resident taxpayers domiciled in different home jurisdictions, at least one of which is another Member State.[166] The basic freedoms, though, must be interpreted according to the purpose intended for them by the internal market objective stipulated in Article 3 (1) (c) and Article 14 (2) and its underlying principles. On the one hand, they are to assure that no discrimination obstructs the free movement of goods, persons, services and capital between Member States. On the other hand, they cannot be used as an instrument to overcome disparities in national tax systems. As has been outlined already, such disparities are admitted by EC primary law and can only be removed via harmonization measures adopted by the Council or the Member States.

Harmonisierung der Unternehmensbesteuerung, p. 152. Dissenting Schönfeld, ET 2004, p. 441 (445); Wattel, ET 1996, p. 159 (161 et seq.). Left undecided by Hinnekens, ET 1996, p. 286 (294).

163. Schuch, *EC Tax Review* 1996, p. 161 (165); Rädler, *EC Tax Review* 1995, p. 66 (67); Farmer, *EC Tax Journal* 1995/96, p. 91 (101).
164. Opinion of AG Colomer, 26.10.2004, case C-376/03 (D), paras 82 and 96; somewhat incoherent in para. 101. A similar stand is taken by the Commission, cf. COM(2001) final, 23.10.2001, Company Taxation in the Internal Market, pp. 286–289 and 316; see also Weber/Spierts, ET 2004, p. 65 (68); *van der Linde, EC Tax Review* 2004, p. 10 (14 et seq.).
165. See also Hinnekens, ET 1996, p. 286 (297).
166. Schuch, *EC Tax Review* 1996, p. 161 (162). This difference in comparative standard (usually, residents and non-residents will be compared) is overlooked by AG Colomer in his reasoning in the D case, paras 91 et seq. In cases of taxing capital income, none of the two taxpayers compared must reside in a Member State, because the freedom of capital may be invoked by third country residents as well.

From the above follows that relevant discrimination can only occur in relation of a cross-border activity as compared to a domestic one.[167] Here, the affected taxpayer faces disadvantages on the grounds of acting outside its home jurisdiction and he/she might therefore be deterred from doing so. On the contrary, a tax treaty 'discrimination' in the source State as compared to a national or resident of a third country, be it a Member State or not, will not influence the competitive situation of the 'free mover' *specifically* because of his/her activities' cross-border character. This becomes evident if one would hypothetically place him/her in the situation of a resident taxpayer: his/her tax burden in the source State would not be any lower, it might possibly even be higher.[168] Any possible disadvantage will instead arise only from the allocation of taxing rights.[169] Only exceptionally will a triangular 'detrimental' treatment stem from factors other than tax system disparities, especially if the tax treaty with a third country grants a tax deduction or privilege reserved for residents of the source State also to the third country residents. These 'national treatment concessions' are the constellations AG Colomer is concerned with; in these cases, however, the discrimination of other Member States' residents can be challenged already by claiming discrimination as compared to resident taxpayers; there is no need to make intricate reference to special tax treaty provisions applying to third country residents.

From the hosting Member State's perspective, the higher tax burden imposed on the non-resident 'discriminated' against by less favourable treaty provisions is thus usually not rooted in the cross-border character of his/her activities. From an overall perspective, accumulating the tax burden in the host State and the respective State of residence, cross-border activities may indeed be taxed differently, also within the Community, depending on where the entrepreneur or worker is domiciled. However, these variations ultimately stem from differences in the levels of taxation in the tax jurisdictions involved who claim their share of the tax object. Usually the tax burden of the home State will be decisive, as restrictions on withholding taxes agreed upon by the source State will most often be overcompensated by the taxation in the State of residence. In any case, differences must therefore be considered as disparities accepted under primary EC law. Hence, it would not be appropriate to rely on the prohibition of covert discrimination on grounds of nationality to claim MFN treatment,[170] since in fact the core issue is not a discriminatory tax *treatment* but rather the allocation of disparate taxing *rights*. This can also be derived from the *Gilly* case, where the ECJ expressly admitted the allocation of taxing rights according to taxpayers' nationality even if this resulted in disparate tax burdens.[171]

We find our position further strengthened by the fact that an MFN clause might easily have been incorporated into the EC Treaty, taking similar GATT and GATS provisions as examples. But even though various Treaty revisions have been inspired by these treaties, the Member States evidently preferred not to include any such

167. See also Martín Jiménez/García Prats/Calderón Carrero, *Bulletin I.F.D.* 2001, p. 241 (250).
168. Presuming the usual case that the tax treaty provision in question stipulates the abolition of double taxation by way of restricting the source country's taxing rights.
169. Cf. van den Hurk, *EC Tax Review* 1999, p. 211 (217).
170. Cf. Weber/Spierts, ET 2004, p. 65 (68 et seq.).
171. ECJ, 12.5.1998, case C-336/96 *(Gilly)*, ECR 1998, I-2793, para. 30.

stipulation.[172] Finally, to assume the existence of an MFN clause might show absurd consequences undermining the source State's revenue base: the renunciation of withholding taxes on a particular type of income such as, for example, dividends in relation to just one minor third country would implicate the loss of all taxing rights on dividends as regards non-resident shareholders domiciled within the EEA. Even a multilateral tax treaty concluded between all Member States would not provide any relief here, as it could not override exigencies of primary EC law.[173]

[F] Possible Justifications for Unequal Taxation

Discrimination or a non-discriminative restriction in national tax law can nevertheless be upheld if it is based on a justification acceptable under EC law and if it is enacted proportionally. It is important to realize that only such national objectives that can be considered legitimate from the viewpoint of EC primary and secondary law may be put forward by national governments; they will not always coincide with the constitutional limits to equal taxation accepted in the Member State affected. The same holds true for the principle of proportionality to be respected when infringing the basic freedoms. This yardstick is a genuinely European one and its interpretation by the ECJ will most often be much stricter than its applications by Member States' constitutional or supreme courts, as we shall discover later on.

Some grounds of justification are expressly formulated in the Treaty articles. Most of them, such as the public order clause in Articles 30, 39 (3), 46 (1) and 58 (1) lit. b, are usually irrelevant in tax matters and can therefore be neglected in this study. Only Article 58 (1) (a), added by the Treaty of Maastricht, allows for seemingly far-reaching exceptions from the prohibition of restricting the free movement of capital in the tax law area. The provisions of this freedom shall be 'without prejudice to the right of Member States to apply the relevant provisions of their tax law which distinguish between taxpayers who are not in the same situation with regard of their place of residence or with regard to the place where their capital is invested'. However, according to Article 58 (3) this is with the reservation that such a distinction may not constitute a means of arbitrary discrimination or a disguised restriction. In the *Verkooijen* case, the EJC has decided, and rightly so, that the exceptions are therefore to be understood as a reference to its rulings on legitimate and proportional justifications prior to the introduction of this proviso.[174] Hence, the heated dispute over the implications of Article 58 (1) (a)[175] can be seen as settled in the sense that it is only a

172. Cf. Schön, RIW 2004, p. 50 (51).
173. An aspect not taken into account by Raventós, ET 1998, p. 336 (340).
174. ECJ, 6.6.2000, case C-35/98 *(Verkooijen)*, ECR 2000, I-4071, paras 43 et seq.; confirmed by ECJ, 15.7.2004, case C-315/02 *(Lenz)*, not yet published, paras 26 et seq.; ECJ, 7.9.2004, case C-319/02 *(Manninen)*, not yet published, paras 28 et seq.
175. For an overview see Haferkamp, *Kapitalverkehrsfreiheit*, p. 141 et seq.; Schön in: GS Knobbe-Keuk, p. 743 (765); Tumpel, DStJG 2000, p. 321 (327, footnote 30); Sedlaczek, ET 2000, p. 14 (22).

declaratory provision.[176] This is convincing, among other considerations,[177] because the systematically comparable reservation of Article 30 has always been similarly interpreted before the incorporation of Article 58 into the Treaty.[178]

From the above it follows that the relevant grounds of justification in the area of national tax law are not the ones stipulated in the Treaty, but the unwritten ones developed in the jurisprudence of the ECJ – without prejudice to critical questioning of the Court's reasoning in detail. In the landmark case *Cassis de Dijon*[179] the ECJ formulated for the first time the so-called 'rule of reason' which was subsequently applied to all basic freedoms. Non-discriminatory[180] restrictions may be justified by 'imperial reasons of general interest', if they are suitable and necessary to pursue such objectives. The Court has not come up with a dogmatic foundation of this essential conclusion so far. It merits an in-depth analysis, though, to solidify, clarify and specify the rule of reason as developed by the ECJ.

The basic freedoms primarily serve the internal market objective, i.e. an economic goal of the EC. However, this is not the only activity pursued by the Community or by the EU. The EC has other tasks laid down in Article 2, such as the promotion of a high level of social protection, the protection of the environment and social cohesion, which must be considered to be equally important as its economic objectives. Conflicts between these principle aims of the European project will have to be resolved by balancing them out proportionally.[181] The ECJ itself has repeatedly stated that all Community institutions, when pursuing the objectives laid down in Article 2, must constantly assure a balance required by possible contradictions between these objectives.[182] No absolute priority must be given to any of them, rather each one of them must be optimized by way of reciprocal counterbalancing.[183] What applies for Community institutions also holds true for the Member States when they implement the non-economic goals in areas of shared or even exclusive competence, and in doing so

176. Consenting are Liede/Hintsanen, ET 2003, p. 31 (34); Toifl, SWI2003, p. 458 (462); Witzel, IStR 2002, p. 758 (761); van Thiel, TFO 2001/78, p. 13; Sedlaczek, ET 2000, p. 14 (23 and 27); Lechner/Staringer/Tumpel/ Ruppe, Kapitalverkehrsfreiheit, p. 9 (26).

177. For a more detailed discussion see the references in the footnote above and Englisch, *Dividendenbesteuerung*, 2005, p. 280 et seq.

178. See ECJ, 14.7.1983, case 174/82 *(Sandoz)*, ECR 1983,2445, para. 18;ECJ, 10.12.1985,case247/ 84(Motte), ECR 1985,3887, para. 23; ECJ, 6.5.1986, case 304/84 *(Muller)*, ECR 1986,1511, para. 23; ECJ, 12.3.1987, case 178/84 *(Reinheitsgebot)*, ECR 1987, 1227, para. 44; ECJ, 4.6.1992, case C-13/91 et al. *(Debus)*, ECR 1992, I-3617, para. 16.

179. ECJ, 20.2.1979, case 120/78 *(Cassis de Dijon)*, ECR 1979, 649, para. 8.

180. Cf. ECJ, 30.11.1995, caseC-55/94(Gebhard), ECR 1995, I-4165, para.37; ECJ, 15.12.1995, caseC-415/93 *(Bosman), ECR* 1995, I-4921, para.104;ECJ, *15.5.1997, para.C-250/ 95(FuturaParticipations), ECR* 1997, I-2471, para. 26.

181. Heselhaus, EuZW 2001, p. 645 (648); Calliess/Ruffert/Ukrow, EUV/EGV, 2nd edn, Art. 2 EGV, para. 30; Schwarze/Stumpf, *EU-Kommentar*, Art. 2 EUV, para. 23.

182. ECJ, 24.10.1973, case5/73 *(Balkan-Import-Export), ECR* 1973, 1091, para.24; ECJ, 20.10.1977, case 29/77 *(Roquette)*, ECR 1977, 1835, para. 29/31; ECJ, 17.10.1995, case C-44/94 *(Fishermen's Organizations)*, ECR 1995, I-3115, para. 37.

183. Cf. Opinion of AG Lagrange in case 13/57 *(Wirtschaftsvereinigung Eisen- und Stahlindustrie)*, ECR 1958, 271 (372); Schwarze/Hatje, *EU-Kommentar*, Art. 2 EGV, para. 23; Calliess/Ruffert/ Ukrow, EUV/EGV, 2nd edn, Art. 2 EGV, para. 30.

conflict with the basic freedoms. Thus, these objectives are *per se* legitimate reasons of general interest which can justify an infringement of the freedom provisions.

However, a proportional balance will have to be struck not only in case of non-discriminatory restrictions on these grounds, but also when the measure aimed at promoting them constitutes discrimination. Otherwise, one would have to assume a general predominance of the economic policies here, contrary to the obligation of seeking reconciliation of all basic principles promoted by the Community.[184] We see no reasonable argument why such supremacy of one and the same objective should – only – be acceptable in case of its eventual infringement through discrimination, but not when it is affected by way of restriction.[185] The ECJ has indeed acknowledged the undesirable effects of such differentiation and now extends the rule of reason to cases of indirect discrimination according to residence rather than nationality.[186] This is not entirely convincing, though, since such distinction, if strictly applied, would still rule out any justification for discriminatory taxation of companies, as their 'nationality' is determined according to their seat[187], hence any discrimination on grounds of residence is equivalent to an 'overt' discrimination on grounds of nationality[188].

Moreover, it would be too short-sighted to limit the circle of legitimate grounds of justification to the non-economic policy goals pursued by the Community. After all, the Member States have only conferred parts of their sovereign powers to the EC. Some areas still fall, in principle, within their exclusive competence, and there is a large field of activities where competencies are shared between the Community and the Member States, leaving the latter room for maintaining and developing national peculiarities as long as the former has not taken legislative action. It cannot be assumed that these competencies remaining with the Member States are *per se* of inferior rank[189]. The European Union is based on the national identities of their Member States (Article 6 (3) EU Treaty), and the EC as a part of it is governed by the principle of Community loyalty (Article 10). From these two fundamental stipulations a principle of 'sincere consideration' can be deducted[190] which, *inter alia,* obliges the Community to take into consideration all elementary interests which Member States remain competent to define on a national level.[191] Neither Community objectives nor national interests

184. Cf. Poiares Maduro, *We the Court,* 1998, p. 166 et seq.
185. Like here Roth/Oliver, CMLR 2004, p. 407 (436).
186. ECJ, 14.7.1998, case C-389/96 *(Aher Waggon), ECR* 1998, I-4473, para. 19; ECJ, 23.5.1996, case C-237/94 *(O'Flynn), ECR* 1996, I-2617, paras 18 etseq.; ECJ, 2.8.1993, case C-259/91 etal. *(Alluéetal.), ECR* 1993, I-4309, paras 14 et seq. See also Hinnekens, *EC Tax Review* 2002, p. 112 (114).
187. ECJ, 19.9.2000, case C-156/98 *(Peralta),* ECR 2000, I-6857, para. 83; Meussen, *EC Tax Review* 2003, 144 (145).
188. Cf. Gammie, *Bulletin I.F.D.* 2003, p. 86 (88 and 92).
189. Steindorff, ZHR 148 (1984), p. 338 (344).
190. ECJ, 22.10.1998, cases C-36/97 and C-37/97 *(Kellinghusen* and *Ketelsen),* ECR 1998, I-6337, para. 30; ECJ, 14.7.1998, case 431/95 *(Bettati),* ECR 1998, I-4355, para. 77; ECJ, 28.11.1991, cases C-213/88 and C-39/89 *(Luxemburg v. Parliament),* ECR 1991, I-5643, para. 29; ECJ, 13.7.1990, case C-2/88 *(Zwartveld),* ECR 1990, I-3365, para. 17; Streinz/Pechstein, EUV/EGV, Art. 6 EUV, para. 26; Streinz/Streinz, EUV/EGV, Art. 10 EGV, para. 47; Calliess/Ruffert/Kahl, EUV/EGV, Art. 10 EGV, para. 50.
191. Streinz/Streinz, EUV/EGV, Art. 10 EGV, para. 50.

prevail over their respective counterpart under any circumstances. As a consequence, the concept of Community law supremacy is indeed a relative one coming into effect only after weighing conflicting national concerns. Both levels of policy-making must be seen as to complement each other and hence their objectives must be optimized by counterbalancing each other.[192] As far as the legal system of the Member States is concerned, this is a task of the national legislator, subject to revision by the ECJ. When the ECJ rules on an infringement of the basic freedoms, it must therefore take into account conflicting imperial reasons of general interest *as defined by the Member State*. This notwithstanding, the Court may still judge on the proportionality of the solution that has been adopted by the Member State, and it may also rule on the consistency of the interest pursued with other provisions of primary or secondary EC law.

It should be noted that the ECJ applies a two-fold and rather strict concept of proportionality when ruling on national measures which infringe the basic freedoms. In its understanding, such rules or practices must be suitable to achieve the legitimate national interest, and furthermore necessary for that purpose. The latter criterion is not met when there exist measures equally suitable to serve the national interest in question which nevertheless interfere to a lesser degree with the fundamental freedoms.[193] Here, the Court feels competent to investigate scrupulously into possible alternatives and leaves hardly any discretion to Member States. This position deserves support since the basic freedoms could otherwise easily be rendered ineffective. Notwithstanding this, it contrasts sharply with the lax supervision of Community acts which are already deemed justified if they cannot be considered arbitrary.[194] One must additionally be aware that the proportionality test essentially is a threefold one, the third element being proportionality *strictu sensu* between the objectives pursued by the national legislator or administration and the restrictions of intra-Community business.[195] The latter ones must not be so grave and evident as to outweigh the formerly mentioned. The ECJ acknowledges this requirement, but usually does not highlight its dogmatic structure.[196]

In the area of direct taxation, the Court has developed a set of special grounds of justification usually tested in its case law. Before entering into closer examination, it is useful to categorize possible 'imperial reasons' according to their underlying objective.

192. Cf. Bater, ET 2000, p. 8.

193. ECJ, 30.11.1995, case C-55/94 *(Gebhard)*, ECR 1995, I-4165, para. 37. See also ECJ, 15.5.1997, case C-250/95 *(Futura Participations)*, ECR 1997, I-2471, para. 26; ECJ, 31.3.1993, case C-19/92 *(Kraus)*, ECR 1993, I-1663, para. 32; ECJ, 20.5.1992, case C-106/91 *(Ramrath)*, ECR 1992, I-3351, para. 31.

194. Instructive ECJ, 5.10.1994, case C-289/93 *(Germany v. Council)*, ECR 1994, I-4973, paras 88–97; for further details, see von Danwitz, EWS 2003, p. 393 (395 et seq.). There is no sound argument which could support such a double standard. Instead the ECJ should elevate its criteria to those applied when deciding the consistency of national measures with primary EC law to warrant a high level of protection for the basic rights of the citizens of the Union.

195. Cf. Hinnekens, *EC Tax Review* 2002, p. 112 (114); Cordewener/Dahlberg/Pistone/Reimer/Romano, ET 2004, p. 218 (223).

196. ECJ, 14.7.1998, case C-389/96 *(Aher Waggon)*, ECR 1998, I-4473, para. 20; ECJ, 23.10.1997, case C-189/95 *(Franzén)*, ECR 1997, I-5909, Rz 75; ECJ, 9.7.1997, case C-34/95 et al. *(de Agostini)*, ECR 1997, I-3843, para.45; ECJ, 13.11.1990, case C-331/88 (Fedesa), ECR 1990, I-4023, para. 13; ECJ, 23.2.1983, case 66/82 *(Framançais)*, ECR 1983, 395, para. 8.

They can roughly be divided into fiscal and extra-fiscal reasons, and the fiscal reasons further into budgetary reasons on the one hand, reasons of international equity and principles aiming at *effective* taxation according to ability to pay on the other hand.

[1] Budgetary Reasons

It is settled case law of the ECJ that a loss or diminution of revenue cannot constitute an overriding reason in the general interest justifying a restriction of a fundamental freedom.[197] And rightly so, because the fundamental freedoms would be deprived of their effectiveness if budgetary reasons alone could justify their disregard. Member States have mutually agreed upon the installation of an internal market without obstacles and must bear the costs incurred by the subsequent abolition of tax barriers.[198]

[2] Reasons of International Equity

Member States may, in principle, not claim a lack of reciprocity in granting a certain tax relief aimed at the implementation of a Member State's particular understanding of ability to pay.[199] This is a logical consequence of their remaining sovereignty and the lack of harmonization in the field of direct taxes. Just as the citizens of the Union must accept the enduring disparities between twenty-five national tax systems, so must Member States themselves. They are obliged to treat equally all taxpayers subjected to their jurisdiction regardless of their place of residence or the source of their income, i.e. within their 'national box'. The demand that other Member States would have to accept the specific, national understanding of ability to pay, too, would come close to a harmonization reserve. However, such a proviso does not exist for the enforcement of primary EC law.

Likewise, the fact that a national tax rule is in accordance with a double taxation convention cannot serve as a valid justification for a breach of the fundamental freedoms.[200] Here, one must bear in mind that such conventions become valid in the

197. ECJ, 8.3.2001, case C-397/98 et al. *(Metallgesellschaft et al.)*, ECR 2001, I-1727, para. 59; ECJ, 6.6.2000, case C-35/98 *(Verkooijen)*, ECR 2000, I-4071, para. 48; ECJ, 21.9.1999, case C-307/97 *(Saint Gobain), ECR* 1999, I-6181, para. 51; ECJ, 16.7.1998, case C-264/96 *(ICI)*, ECR 1998, I-4695, para. 28; ECJ, 28.4.1998, case C-120/95 *(Decker)*, ECR 1998, I-1831, para. 39; ECJ, 28.4.1998, case C-158/96 *(Kohll)*, ECR 1998, I-1931, para. 41.
198. Different opinion Baker, ET 2004, p. 453 (455).
199. ECJ, 28.1.1986, case 270/83 *(Avoirfiscal)*, ECR 1986, 273, para. 26; Liede/Hintsanen, ET 2003, p. 31 (35); Cordewener, *Grundfreiheiten*, p. 399; Dautzenberg, BB 2001, p. 2137 (2139); van Thiel, TFO 2001/78, p. 11; García Prats, *Imposición directa*, p. 186. See also the decisions not related to tax matters: ECJ, 2.2.1989, case 186/87 *(Cowan)*, ECR 1989, 195, para. 12 et seq.; ECJ, 25.10.1979, case 159/78 *(Commission v. Italy)*, ECR 1979, 3247, paras 21; ECJ, 22.6.1972, case 1/72 *(Frilli)*, ECR 1972, 457, para. 19.
200. ECJ, 28.1.1986, case 270/83 *(Avoirfiscal)*, ECR 1986, 273, para. 26. See also the opinion of Mischo AG in case C-324/00 *(Lankhorst-Hohorst GmbH)*, ECR 2002, I-11779, paras 80 et seq.; Dourado, *EC Tax Review* 2002, p. 147 (153 et seq.); Calderón Carrero, *Convenios de doble imposición*, p. 5 u. 14; van den Hurk, *EC Tax Review* 1999, p. 211 (216); Takacs, *Das Steuerrecht*

national legal order only by adoption or transformation.[201] Hence, they form part of this national order which is, in its turn, subject to the requirements of the directly enforceable EC Treaty provisions. Consequently, stipulations of an international convention cannot override the binding orders and prohibitions of the fundamental freedoms. This is confirmed by Article 307 which exempts only those bilateral agreements which were concluded before the EC Treaty entered into force from conformity with its provisions. Furthermore, if double taxation conventions cannot be relied upon to justify a breach of the fundamental freedoms, the revenue distribution effects intended by their provision cannot be invoked either. If an equal taxation of cross-border activities would lead to distortions in the distributive balance between the two contracting parties, the Member State affected must try change the convention rather than go on discriminating.[202]

The above conclusions may have to be modified, nevertheless, when equal taxation might disturb the balance and reciprocity of a bilateral international convention concluded between a Member State and a non-member country. The ECJ itself has conceded that such circumstances can constitute an objective justification for discriminating tax rules. It has only contemplated them, though, in the case that the fundamental freedoms would oblige a Member State party to that convention to extend to nationals of other Member States the advantages which its own nationals derive from it.[203] Here, the Court ruled that rights of the non-Member party would not be affected and therefore the balance of the treaty would not be endangered. This reasoning is somewhat obscure because the imperative interest claimed by the Member State is, in general, not a disturbance of the treaty equilibrium at the cost of the non-Member State, but rather at its own revenue cost. In spite of this, in the constellation envisaged by the ECJ we agree with the final result, because the balance between the contracting parties is indeed not touched upon by the unilateral extension of tax concessions. The loss in revenue by the Member State is not offset by a respective gain in the other jurisdiction; rather, it is an irrelevant budgetary loss merely due to the equal treatment of residents and non-residents domiciled within the Community.

However, the balance in revenue distribution underlying a double taxation convention may be seriously affected in the case that the fundamental freedoms require advantageous tax rules of a Member State to apply to residents domiciled in or income derived from non-Member States. This may especially happen in the substantial scope of the freedom of capital, since this freedom is not limited to citizens of the Union or residents of the Member States. If, for example, a Member State is obliged to extend a credit for underlying corporation tax to residents of a third country, the source country entitlement governing the dividend article of an eventual double taxation

der Europäischen Union, p. 496; Lang in: Gassner, *Doppelbesteuerungsabkommen*, p. 25 (30); Scherer, *Doppelbesteuerung*, p. 110; García Prats, *Imposición directa*, p. 184; Farmer, *EC Tax Review* 1998, p. 13 (23).

201. Seidl-Hohenveldern/Stein, *Völkerrecht*, 10th edn, para. 564 et seq.
202. Cf. Gammie, *Bulletin I.F.D.* 2003, p. 86 (89); see also ECJ, 11.3.2004, case C-9/02 *(Lasteyrie du Saillant)*, not yet published, para. 68.
203. ECJ, 15.1.2002, case C-55/00 *(Gottardo)*, ECR 2002, I-413, para. 36; ECJ, 21.9.1999, case 307/97 *(Saint- Gobain)*, ECR 1999, I-6161, para. 60.

convention with that country would be violated. The balance of revenue distribution would also be upset in the reverse situation of granting a credit for corporation tax underlying foreign dividends, as this would be contrary to the principle that foreign taxes are not refunded. Here, it must be possible for Member States to deny equal treatment unless the balance is restored by comparable concessions on part of the non-Member State.[204] The reason why such justification is (only) admissible in relation to third countries is, on the one hand, the lack of structural reciprocity, because third countries are not obliged to tax equally the residents of the Member State as well. Hence, there will be little incentive for them to renegotiate the conventions or harmonies tax systems, which is why Member States can have an imperial interest in safeguarding their fair share of cross-border revenue by limiting tax 'benefits' to residents of the Community. On the other hand, the internal market objective guiding the application of the fundamental freedoms would not be seriously impaired by denying unilateral concession of such benefits to third country residents, since third countries do not form part of the internal market.[205]

[3] Reasons Aiming at Taxation According to Ability to Pay

There are two kinds of reasons acceptable as objective justifications which aim at an effective taxation according to the Member States' concept of equal distribution of the tax burden. On the one hand, Member States may wish to install procedural rules which guarantee that the tax is assessed and levied in formal compliance with the law. On the other hand, they may claim the need for a deeper or broader view of cross-border activities to warrant equal taxation according to ability to pay in substance.[206]

[a] Prevention of Tax Fraud

As regards the former group, Member States have an imperial interest in preventing tax fraud.[207] The treaty allows for an objective justification on these grounds in the context of the freedom of capital, Article 58 (1) (b);[208] within the scope of the other freedoms, it is a concern evidently to be considered as an expression of national tax sovereignty. Therefore, the ECJ has recognized the right of Member States to implement effective fiscal controls.[209] However, the Court has decided that such controls may not lead to

204. A similar position is taken by Ståhl, *EC Tax Review* 2004, p. 47 (54 f.).
205. Rust, *Europäisches Wirtschafts- und Steuerrecht* 2004, p. 450 (45 1f.).
206. See also van Thiel, *EC Tax Review* 2003, p. 4 (15 et seq.).
207. The ECJ frequently talks about tax evasion, too; we prefer the term tax fraud, though, so as to not confuse illegal behaviour with tax avoidance, which is legal in form but nevertheless not recognized for tax purposes. Like here van Thiel, Free movement, p. 601.
208. ECJ, 26.9.2000, case C-478/98 *(Eurobonds)*, ECR 2000, -7587, paras 37 et seq.; ECJ, 14.12.1995, case C-163/94 et al. *(Sanz de Lera et al.)*, ECR 1995, -4821, para. 22; ECJ, 23.2.1995, case C-358/93 et al. *(Bordessa et al.), ECR* 1995, I-361, paras 21 et seq.
209. ECJ, 26.6.2003, case C-422/01 *(Skandia)*, ECR 2003, I-6187, paras 42 et seq.; ECJ, 3.10.2002, case C-136/00 *(Danner)*, ECR 2002, I-8147, paras 44 et seq.; ECJ; 26.9.2000, case C-478/98

unconditional exclusion of the cross-border activity from tax concessions or preferential tax regimes as this would be disproportionate. Instead, Member States can rely on Directive 77/799 on information exchange to satisfy their need for verification of the information put forward or detection of facts held back by the taxpayer.[210] Furthermore, the Court points at the possibility to require the taxpayer to provide such proof as they may consider necessary in order to determine whether the conditions for a preferential tax rule have been met.[211] In general, we agree with the Court's posture on this issue. The alternative measures exposed by the Court do indeed restrict the fundamental freedoms to a lesser degree than provisions which substantially rule out the application of a favourable tax rule on pan-European economic activities. While it is true that the information exchange based on the aforementioned Directive may be inapplicable,[212] insufficient or unreasonably complicated and costly in some cases, effective controls can then still be upheld by stipulating *rebuttable* presumptions or specific proof requirements for cross-border affairs.[213]

[b] Effective Tax Collection

If the right of effective controls must be conceded to Member States, the same will *a fortiori* hold true for the right to effectively enforce collection of the tax due. After all, as a general rule of international law, no State can be obliged to assist in the enforcement of foreign tax claims. The ECJ has also admitted such reasoning in the *Bachmann* case.[214] It can be seriously doubted, though, if this argument can still be put forward in a case of intra-Community taxation. Directive 2001/44/EC of 15 June 2001 extended the substantial scope of the pre-existing Directive on mutual assistance for the recovery of tax claims[215] to direct taxes as well. From then on, Member States could rely on secondary EC law to enforce their tax claims throughout the Community. It would therefore be unnecessary and hence disproportionate to achieve this objective

(Eurobonds), ECR 2000, I-7587, para. 38; ECJ, 28.10.1999, case C-55/98 *(Vestergaard)*, ECR 1999, I-7641, para. 25; ECJ; 8.7.1999, case C-254/97 *(Baxter)*, ECR 1999, I-4809, para. 18; ECJ, 15.5.1997, case C-250/95 *(Futura Participations)*, ECR 1997, I-2471, para.31; ECJ, 28.1.1992, case C-204/90 (Bachmann), ECR 1992, I-249, paras 18 et seq.; ECJ, 20.2.1979, case 120/78 *(Cassis de Dijon)*, ECR 1979, 649, para. 8.

210. ECJ, 26.6.2003, case C-422/01 *(Skandia)*, ECR 2003, I-6187, paras 42 et seq.; ECJ, 3.10.2002, case C-136/00 *(Danner)*, ECR 2002, I-8147, paras 49 et seq.; ECJ, 15.5.1997, case C-250/95 *(Futura Participations)*, ECR 1997, I-2471, paras 40 et seq.
211. Instructive: ECJ, 26.10.1995, case C-151/94 *(Commission v. Luxembourg)*, ECR 1995, I-3685, para. 21.
212. Especially in respect to third country nationals who nevertheless enjoy the freedom of capital.
213. Therefore, we do not share the critical viewpoint of *García Prats*, Imposición directa, p. 188 et seq. and Vermeend, *EC Tax Review* 1996, p. 54 (55). See also van Thiel, *Free Movement*, p. 562 et seq.
214. ECJ, 28.1.1992, case C-204/90 *(Bachmann)*, ECR 1992, I-249, para. 24.
215. Directive 76/308/EEC on mutual assistance for the recovery of claims resulting from operations forming part of the system of financing the European Agricultural Guidance and Guarantee Fund, and of agricultural levies and customs duties and in respect of value added tax and certain excise duties.

by discriminatory procedural rules.[216] Such precaution is admissible only in relation to residents of third countries not bound by the Directive.

[c] *Anti-avoidance Rules*

As regards rules that warrant equal taxation in substance, the interest of the Member States to combat tax avoidance[217] must be recognized under Treaty law. Member States vary greatly in their approach to this issue; the measures intended to tackle tax avoidance range from the application of a general case law principle of substance over form to specific provisions targeted at particular tax avoidance schemes, such as CFC legislation.[218] After an initial denial,[219] the ECJ has by now accepted the need to prevent the circumvention of national tax laws.[220] It takes a very critical view on national standardization of abusive constructions, though, and allows only for legislation which aims at the prevention of 'wholly artificial arrangements' determined according to the specific facts of the case presented. In fact, this jurisprudence leaves little room for anything else but general anti-abuse clauses like for instance §42 of the German *Abgabenordnung*, the application of which can only be decided upon in a case-by-case analysis.[221] This is in line with the Court's decision on Member States' implementation of anti-abuse provisos in EC directives, where general presumptions of tax evasion or tax fraud are ruled out as inappropriate.[222] Furthermore, the ECJ has consistently held that the mere use of the right to free movement granted by the basic freedoms does not, of itself, necessarily entail tax avoidance, since that company would in any event be subject to the tax legislation of the State of destination.[223]

Even though the position of the ECJ seems at first sight to affect Member States' sovereignty in defining tax avoidance gravely, we do approve of its basic findings. First, it should be noted that every State is still free to make use of its preferred method to describe and counter tax avoidance as long as it is applied in a non-discriminatory

216. In this regard, we respectfully submit that the opposite view of Hinnekens, *EC Tax Review* 2003, p. 207 (213), does not consider less restrictive measures than, for instance, final withholding taxes, such as an option for later assessment enjoyed also by domestic taxpayers.
217. The ECJ sometimes employs the term 'tax evasion' when it talks about the circumvention of tax laws by modifications in the taxable incident. However, this expression should be reserved for illegal behaviour liable to criminal prosecution, i.e. tax fraud. In any case, a clear terminology helps to avoid confusion in this issue.
218. For a general overview see Mössner, ET 1999, p. 92 et seq.
219. Cf. ECJ, 28.1.1986, case 270/83 *(Avoirfiscal)*, ECR 1986, 273, para. 25.
220. ECJ, 11.3.2004, case C-9/02 *(Lasteyrie du Saillant)*, not yet published, paras 50 et seq.; ECJ, 12.12.2002, case C-324/00 *(Lankhorst-Hohorst)*, ECR 2002, I-11779, para. 37; ECJ, 8.3.2001, case C 397/98 et al. *(Metallgesellschaft)*, ECR 2001, I-1727, para. 57; ECJ, 26.9.2000, case C-478/98 *(Eurobonds)*, ECR 2000, I-7587, paras 37 et seq.; ECJ, 16.7.1998, case C-264/96 *(ICI)*, ECR 1998, I-4695, para. 26.
221. ECJ, 12.12.2002, case C-324/00 *(Lankhorst-Hohorst)*, ECR 2002, I-11779, para. 37; ECJ, 16.7.1998, case C-264/96 *(ICI)*, ECR 1998, I-4695, para. 26.
222. ECJ, 17.7.1997, case C-28/95 *(Leur-Bloem)*, ECR 1997, I-4161, para. 44.
223. ECJ, 11.3.2004, case C-9/02 *(Lasteyrie du Saillant)*, not yet published, para. 51; ECJ, 12.12.2002, case C-324/00 *(Lankhorst-Hohorst)*, ECR 2002, I-11779, para. 37; ECJ, 8.3.2001, case C 397/98 et al. *(Metall- gesellschaft)*, ECR 2001, I-1727, para. 57; ECJ, 16.7.1998, case C-264/96 (ICI), ECR 1998, I-4695, para. 26.

manner. Hence, only such anti-abuse clauses which are limited in scope to cross-border situations must allow for a specific analysis of every single case. This is, in principle, justified by the fact that the basic freedoms prohibit 'any' discrimination within their field of application. Correspondingly, a justification must be sought for each individual case of substantial discrimination and must not be based on general assumptions. The only kind of classification which seems permissible to us is to establish presumptions which must be reversed as a matter of law when sufficient evidence is supplied that the suspicious arrangement is not artificial, if tax authorities cannot reasonably obtain the relevant information by other means. Such an exception would be proportionate and fit well into the Court's acceptance of specific procedural arrangements for pan-European activities in general.

Second, it must indeed be conceded that within the internal market, shifting economic activity across borders cannot be deemed as a circumvention of national taxation in itself.[224] Not so much because the activity will fall under another of the Member States' tax jurisdictions,[225] but rather because the EC Treaty grants free movement in awareness of the existing disparities in the national legal orders. If a market participant deems business conditions, including the tax environment, more convenient in another jurisdiction, it is the very intention of the basic freedoms to permit the transition of all or part of his/her activities abroad. Member States which have a competitive disadvantage in the respective matters cannot invoke overriding reasons of a general interest to protect the national economy or tax revenue, because these consequences are immanent to an internal market.[226] If disparities resulting from the national legislative frameworks turn out to distort economic competition on a large scale, harmonization rather than discrimination is the right answer. Moreover, if the taxpayer is still linked to both tax jurisdictions after engaging in a cross-border scenario, it is up to them to negotiate how the revenue should be fairly divided. Indeed, most specific cross-border anti-avoidance clauses, such as thin capitalization rules, aim at preventing revenue losses due to inappropriate double tax convention (DTC) provisions. Such provisions must hence be adapted, preferably in form of a multilateral tax treaty, to the specific concept of supranational equity prevailing in the internal market. It is up to the Member States to assure that the inter-personal equity enshrined in the basic freedoms does not conflict with concepts of international equity in the field of revenue sharing.[227]

224. Cf. Gammie, *Bulletin I.F.D.* 2003, p. 86 (94). Different opinion Kube, IStR 2003, p. 325 (332).
225. This argument of the Court is, on the one hand, too general in its terms because a cross-border activity may be subjected to the tax jurisdiction of both Member States involved if none of them has completely waived its taxing rights. On the other hand, it ignores that from the national treasury's point of view, which is the relevant one in the justification test, it does make a great difference whether it can collect the taxes itself or whether they are levied abroad.
226. Cf. Schönfeld, ET 2004, p. 441 (444 and 448).
227. Member States so far have been little aware of this correlation. The finest example for this is the failure of coordination between the Parent/Subsidiary Directive and the Interest and Royalties Directive. The former effectively concedes all taxing powers for company profits, i.e. equity yields, to the source State, whereas the latter allocates taxing rights concerning interest payments, i.e. loan yields, exclusively to the home State. As equity and debt financing are to a high degree substitutable for today's modern multinationals, this kind of divergence leaves

An exception to the above rule can only be made for national anti-abuse clauses which deny recognition to cross-border arrangements seeking to benefit from measures of unfair tax competition employed by another Member State.[228] National tax policies which by virtue of EC law or of outspoken consensus among Member States are to be considered harmful and incompatible with the functioning of the internal market are contrary to the very objective pursued by the free movement provisions. Thus, national anti-avoidance rules tackling such beggar-my-neighbour policies must be seen as reactions justified in order to re-establish the level playing field also aimed at by the basic freedoms. In more dogmatic terms, one could say that in these cases, the equal treatment requirement would in fact lead to an *unfair* privilege for cross-border activities which is not in line with the general concept of taxation according to ability to pay in either of the Member States involved. Therefore it *substantially* infringes the cross-border concept of ability-to-pay supported by the fundamental freedoms as well and may be counteracted to restore taxpayer equity. Consequently, anti-abuse provisions which specifically address foreign tax measures either violating Article 87 because they have to be considered a forbidden State aid or which must be declared as unfair tax competition according to the Code of Conduct[229] are proportionate and justified.[230]

[d] *Fiscal Cohesion*

Finally, the most hotly debated reason of public interest put forward to defend breaches of the basic freedoms is the fiscal 'cohesion' or 'coherence' of the national tax system. In the established case law of the ECJ, this concept constitutes an exception to the general rule that the disadvantages incurred by discriminatory tax treatment cannot be justified by referring to advantages enjoyed by the taxpayer in other aspects or in other jurisdictions.[231] In particular, a low level of foreign taxation cannot be invoked to defend an extra tax burden as compared to purely internal situations.[232] However, if there exists a 'direct link' within the national tax system between the discriminatory tax rule and the compensating tax advantage, the former may be justified if it is proportionate as well. It has been suggested that under such circumstances, discrimination should be disregarded in the first place, rather than introducing a subsequent stage of

them with a high margin of discretion as to where they pay their taxes, which in turn provokes potentially discriminating thin capitalization rules.

228. See Kirchhof, *Einkommensteuer Gesetzbuch*, p. 329.
229. Conclusions of the ECOFIN Council Meeting on 1 December 1997 concerning taxation policy - Resolution of the Council and the Representatives of the Governments of the Member States, meeting within the Council of 1 December 1997 on a code of conduct for business taxation, *Official Journal* C 002,06/01/1998, pp. 1–6.
230. Cf. Hey in: Schön, *Tax Competition in Europe*, p. 253 (275); Paschen, *Steuerumgehung*, s. 219 f.
231. Cf. ECJ, 6.6.2000, case C-35/98 *(Verkooijen)*, ECR 2000, I-4071, para. 61; ECJ, 26.10.1999, case C-294/97 *(Eurowings)*, ECR 1999, I-7447, paras 43 et seq.; ECJ, 21.9.1999, case C-307/97 *(Saint Gobain)*, ECR 1999, I-6181, para. 54; ECJ, 28.1.1986, case 270/83 *(Avoirfiscal)*, ECR 1986, 285, para. 21.
232. ECJ, 26.6.2003, case C-422/01 *(Skandia)*, EWS 2003, p. 379, para. 52; ECJ, 26.10.1999, case C-294/97 *(Eurowings)*, ECR 1999, I-7447, paras 43 et seq.

justification reasoning.[233] While such an approach would have its merits, too, the attribution to imperial reasons of national interest fits better into the narrow similarity concept of the ECJ in matters of direct taxation and shall therefore be employed in this study as well.

The ECJ created the category of fiscal cohesion in the *Bachmann* case and has subsequently specified that a direct link could only be assumed if the compensation rules involve the same taxpayer and the same tax.[234] This aspect has been of particular significance in the context of dividend taxation, since until recently the Court ruled out the cohesion of systems providing a relief for economic double taxation arguing that corporation tax on distributed profits and income tax on dividends are 'two separate taxes levied on different taxpayers'.[235] Furthermore, the Court has repeatedly held that the internal cohesion of the tax system may be derogated by bilateral tax treaties if they offset the balance between the tax advantage and the corresponding disadvantage.[236] Only in its decision on *Manninen* did the Court finally endorse a somewhat broader concept of fiscal cohesion, allowing for a relief from underlying corporation tax at the shareholder level if it warrants *exact* compensation[237].

From the above can first be concluded that the ECJ does not accept a reasoning relying on fiscal cohesion if it is based on a criterion other than inter-personal compensation of tax burdens. In particular, treating outbound activities mirror-inverted to the respective inbound activities does not constitute sufficient cohesion[238]. Hence, the ECJ does not yet operate with an 'internal consistency test' comparable to the one developed by the US Supreme Court when judging inter-state double taxation[239]. To provide for deductions in one of the two directions (inbound or outbound) in which a cross-border business is conducted cannot compensate for the disadvantage suffered by the one still discriminated against. The same holds true for the inverted situation of unilaterally avoiding double taxation only for inbound or for outbound activities; according to the Court's understanding, this would not offset a restriction caused by possible remaining double taxation in taxing its respective counterpart.

233. Lyal, *EC Tax Review* 2003, p. 68 (73).
234. ECJ, 28.1.1992, case C-204/90 *(Bachmann)*, ECR 1992, I-249, paras 21–23; ECJ, 28.1.1992, case C-300/90 *(Commission v. Belgium)*, ECR 1992, I-305, paras 14–16; ECJ, 11.8.1995, case C-80/94 *(Wielockx)*, ECR 1995, I-2493, paras 23–25; ECJ, 14.11.1995, case C-484/93 *(Svensson)*, ECR 1995, I-3955, para. 18; ECJ, 27.6.1996, case C-107/94 *(Asscher)*, ECR 1996, I-3089, paras 55–60; ECJ, 16.7.1998, case C-264/96 (ICI), ECR 1998, I-4695, para. 29; ECJ, 26.10.1999, case C-294/97 (Eu rowings), ECR 1999, I-7447, para. 42; ECJ, 13.4.2000, case C-251/98 *(Baars)*, ECR 2000, I-2787, paras 33–40; ECJ, 6.6.2000, case C-35/98 (*Verkooijen)*, ECR 2000, I-4071, paras 56–58; ECJ, 26.9.2000, case C-478/98 *(Eurobonds)*, ECR 2000, I-7587, paras 33–35; ECJ, 8.3.2001, case C-397/98 et al. *(Metallgesellschaft et al.)*, ECR 2001, I-1727, paras 67–70.
235. ECJ, 15.7.2004, case C-315/02 *(Lenz)*, not yet published, para. 36; ECJ, 6.6.2000, case C-35/98 *(Verkooijen)*, ECR 2000, I-4071, paras 57 et seq. See also ECJ, 18.9.2003, case C-168/01 *(Bosal Holding)*, IStR 2003, p. 666, paras 30 et seq.; ECJ, 13.4.2000, case C-251/98 *(Baars)*, ECR 2000, I-2787, para. 40.
236. ECJ, 15.7.2004, case C-242/03 *(Weidert and Paulus)*, not yet published, para. 25; ECJ, 11.8.1995, case C-80/94 *(Wielockx)*, ECR 1995, I-2493, para. 24.
237. ECJ, 7.9.2004, case C-319/02 *(Manninen)*, not yet published, para. 44.
238. Cf. ECJ, 18.9.2003, case C-168/01 *(Bosal Holding)*, IStR 2003, p. 666, para. 36; see also CFE Opinion Statement, ET 2004, p. 506 (512).
239. For further details see Cordewener, p. 875 et seq.

Although from a supranational perspective, such a system would provide for an adequate consideration of deductions and avoid double taxation in all cases if identical rules were maintained by all other Member States, the ECJ does not accept this kind of coherence. Hence the above remark that the cohesion principle as defined by the ECJ is but a specific expression of a rule on tax advantage compensation.

It has been suggested that the Court should also accept the aforementioned systematic consistencies as alternative or even preferable concept of fiscal cohesion,[240] giving Member States more leeway in the design of their tax systems. On the contrary, others suggest that a 'micro coherence' test on the level of the individual taxpayer and a 'macro coherence' test warranting inter-country equity would have to be met *cumulatively* to allow for an objective justification,[241] thereby raising the hurdles for passing the justification review. We do not agree with either of these positions. In principle, the inter-personal coherence criterion elected by the ECJ fits better into the specific concept of equal tax burdens on equal ability to pay as promoted by the basic freedoms than a concept of inter-country coherence. As has been outlined before, the prohibition of discriminatory treatment demands equal taxation 'within the national box', i.e. regardless of the tax treatment the respective activity experiences in another tax jurisdiction. A Member State cannot rely on a preferential or compensating treatment in the other Member State affected by the cross-border movement in order to justify its own discriminatory taxation.[242] An 'internal consistency test' would be equivalent to such an excuse, though, because its key factor is the avoidance of extra tax burdens assuming identical tax treatment in the foreign tax jurisdiction. Moreover, as it is based on a merely hypothetical assumption, it cannot even guarantee to avoid such overburdening of pan-European business in tax reality. Rather, it would still allow for double taxation or double non-taxation (and double consideration or double non-consideration of deductions), if the two jurisdictions involved happen to discriminate complementary inbound and outbound movements.

It is therefore clear that such a test cannot be sufficient to justify discriminatory taxation; on the other hand, it is not a necessary requirement either.[243] The relevant comparison in determining or disproving discrimination must be made between the

240. Cf. Weber, *EC Tax Review* 2003, p. 220 (229); Wattel in: Lang, *Direct Taxation*, p. 153 (162).

241. Cf. Cordewener, ET 2003, p. 102 (110 et seq.); Snel, ET 2001, p. 403 (405 et seq.).

242. Cf. Toifl, SWI 2002, p. 458 (465); van Thiel, TFO 2001/78, p. 8; Martens, *Tijdschrift voorformeel belas- tingrecht* 2001, p. 2 (4); Lehner/Reimer, *Grundfreiheiten*, p. 39 (50); Schuch in: *Multilateral Tax Treaties*, p. 35 (49); García Prats, *Imposición directa*, p. 176 et seq.; Kaefer, EWS 1997, p. 288.
Non-discriminatory restrictions will usually not give rise to such questions, at least as far as taxation is concerned, as they are generally based on a double regulation of the same taxable activity in more than one tax jurisdiction. If one of the Member States provides unilateral relief here, albeit without obligation, the regulation of the other State no longer causes any restriction in the first place. As far as double taxation is concerned, for example, this means that the basic freedoms unlike some tax treaties do not prohibit virtual double taxation; if some kind of income is not taxed in the host State, the home State may tax it without infringing any free movement provision, and vice versa.

243. Like here Weber, *EC Tax Review* 2003, p. 220 (228). Different opinion Cordewener/Dahlberg/ Pistone/ Reimer/Romano, ET 2004, p. 218 (222).

affected cross-border activity and its purely internal counterpart. If due to compensatory effects a *substantial* tax disadvantage for the former can be ruled out, the discrimination in form does not imply a real obstacle to the free movement in the internal market and can therefore be justified. To further demand 'macro coherence' would mean to call for an additional comparison between the affected cross-border movement on the one hand and another fictitious cross-border movement with reverse direction on the other hand. The true intention of such an extra comparison is not to determine if the affected activity is taxed adequately, as this has already been established by the 'micro coherence test', but to judge the tax treatment which a completely different activity receives. However, such an extensive revision is not within the scope of the fundamental freedoms.

From the above it follows that the ECJ is right to judge fiscal cohesion from an inter-personal perspective. Less technically speaking, while the discrimination test zooms in on a particular legal disadvantage suffered by a specific cross-border activity, the cohesion argument allows readjustment of the focus towards a broader view including correlating elements of the same tax system. This way the objective of the free movement provisions to overcome discriminatory obstacles to pan-European economic activities is reconciled with Member States interest to prevent the 'free mover' from mutating into a 'free rider' who picks out only advantageous parts of the national tax system without being burdened by corresponding disadvantages.[244] In the end, the fiscal cohesion test provides for a concept of equal tax treatment *in substance,* in line with both EC law and national beliefs of taxpayer equity.

To be consistent, any extra tax burdens suffered or tax concessions enjoyed in a foreign tax jurisdiction should not be taken into consideration either. Since the basic freedoms do prohibit discrimination for the sake of an equal treatment within one jurisdiction, only tax burdens and tax concessions emanating from this national legal order can be taken into account to determine if their objective is effectively not impaired due to compensatory effects. Any accumulation of domestic and foreign tax burdens leaves fiscal cohesion untouched and may only constitute a double burden – de facto discrimination to be judged on its own terms. If for example a withholding tax on interest payments is fully credited against the corresponding domestic income tax only in case of domestic savings, the fiscal cohesion thus created is not disturbed by the fact that foreign interest payments have also been subjected to a withholding tax. The latter has been a foreign tax burden irrelevant for the cohesion test, and from a national perspective the 'tax advantage' of fully crediting the domestic withholding tax is perfectly justified due to its prior levy by the national treasury, whereas foreign interest payments do not suffer such a 'disadvantage' within the national jurisdiction. The overall *domestic* tax burden on interest is equal. The need to consider the foreign withholding tax can arise only in the context of international double taxation, which however is to be characterized as a forbidden 'double burden' restriction. Such a de facto discriminating restriction does not necessarily call for a full credit in the State of residence, as taxation according to the level of the State of investment would also be

244. Cordewener/Dahlberg/Pistone/Reimer/Romano, ET 2004, p. 218 (221).

consistent with the free movement of capital. Initially, the ECJ has taken the same national treatment approach in determining fiscal cohesion and examined only domestic tax burdens.[245] However, in his recent judgment of the *Manninen* case, it has extended its novel supranational viewpoint in determining 'comparability' of situations into the cohesion test: foreign tax burdens are now to be taken into account in determining full compensation of any tax relief confined to purely domestic market activities.[246] Such reasoning is consistent, as the cohesion test only widens the perspective of the discrimination test, but it also suffers from the shortcomings of this new approach discussed above.[247] In the context of the 'new' cohesion test, the break-up with the traditional prohibition of cross-border compensation of tax advantages and the ignorance towards persisting national disparities become particularly obvious.

Another important aspect of the justification on grounds of fiscal cohesion is whether it requires a full and specific compensation of disadvantages on the part of every affected 'free mover' or if an abstract concept of internal cohesion, which may eventually be imperfect in a particular case, is permissible as well. A good example for conflicting views on this issue is the taxation of cross-border losses. In the home State, losses incurred in foreign subsidiaries or permanent establishments are usually excluded from compensation in national systems of group taxation or global income taxation, respectively. On an abstract level, this discriminatory treatment is coherent because it mirrors the exemption of profits pertaining to the subsidiary or permanent establishment.[248] On the level of the individual taxpayer suffering the losses, it is not, because in his/her specific circumstances his/her tax burden will effectively be higher than the one of his/her fellow taxpayer who invested at home, without any compensation whatsoever.

An analysis of the Court's rulings that considered cohesion arguments so far points to different directions and thus leaves an ambiguous impression.[249] On the one hand, the requirement of a 'direct link' or 'strict reciprocity'[250] between a tax advantage and a corresponding disadvantage hints at the need for an abstract rather than a specific compensation. The latter could also be achieved by means of pragmatic and generous tax concessions not systematically linked to the discriminatory treatment. On the other hand, the ECJ always considers the specific tax burdens imposed on the cross-border activity to be decided upon in order to determine if there is discrimination,

245. Cf. ECJ, 28.1.1992, case C-204/90 *(Bachmann)*, ECR 1992, I-249, para. 23.
246. ECJ, 7.9.2004, case C-319/02 *(Manninen)*, not yet published, paras 46 and 54; see also Kokott AG, Opinion of 12.2.2004, case C-242/03 *(Weidert and Paulus)*.
247. At the end of III1.
248. Wattel, *EC Tax Review* 2003, p. 194 (194 and 199) categorizes this reasoning as one based on territorial 'dislocation' which rules out discrimination regardless of traditional concepts of disparity and cohesion. However, we respectfully submit that the quoted 'consistency founded on territoriality' is really a matter of interpreting the principle of fiscal cohesion as outlined above, see also Cordewener/Dahlberg/Pistone/ Reimer/Romano, ET 2004, p. 218 (220 et seq.).
249. However, the ECJ will probably have to give an opinion on this subject when deciding two pending cases where the issue of cross-border loss treatment has risen: cases Ritter, C-152/03 (commentary by Cordewener, ET 2003, p. 294 et seq.) and *Marks & Spencer,* C-446/03 (commentary by Meussen, *EC Tax Review* 2003, p. 144 et seq.).
250. ECJ, 11.8.1995, case C-80/94 *(Wielockx)*, ECR 1995, I-2493, para. 24.

demanding at least equal results as compared to a domestic activity.[251] This could lead to the conclusion that an eventual compensation would have to be specific and at least fully equivalent to the disadvantage suffered. A conclusion nevertheless doubtful since in the only case the cohesion argument was accepted by the Court, there was an evident lack of such equivalence. In the *Bachmann* ruling, the tax sparing of the pensions paid out under certain insurance contracts if the insurance company was not domiciled in Belgium by no means fully made up for the discriminatory denial of the tax deductions for premiums invested in the respective pension schemes. In fact, the tax deferral granted for contracts with local insurers which received the opposite treatment obviously led to considerable, positive interest effects. In other occasions the Court held that such effects favouring domestic investment are no *quantité negligable.*[252]

In our opinion, only a concept of fiscal cohesion which guarantees full compensation of disadvantages at least in all typical constellations can constitute an objective and proportionate justification for discriminatory treatment. Establishing parallel subsystems of taxation for cross-border business on the one hand and domestic business on the other hand is contrary to the overall goal of an internal market, even if each of these subsystems is consistent in itself. As has been demonstrated, the latter approach will not necessarily result in *substantially* equal taxation in every case, which could be defended by reasons of tax equity. Thus, it would have to be justified by another reason of general interest which will be hard to find. The need for standardization would have to be ruled out because 'coherent' subsystems do not contemplate legal consequences based on a typical case but are rooted in categories of systematic consistency. The desire to preserve this consistency is no imperative reason all by itself, though, as a consistent treatment could also be realized in treating cross-border and internal affairs alike. The underlying motive for a special regime will most often be to prevent unilateral revenue losses not made up for by corresponding revenue gains, which the Member State cannot yield due to bilateral treaties or respected customs of international tax law. However, it has already been pointed out that allocation effects of the fundamental freedoms which infringe inter-nation equity as between Member States must be corrected by changing treaty provisions rather than by discriminating against cross-border activities.[253] As an – illustrative – consequence, waiving taxing rights for certain activities on the one hand does not suffice to justify a discriminatory treatment regarding related expenses and losses on the other hand.[254]

Having discussed the two-fold essence of cohesion, a more detailed look can be taken which must inevitably lead to profound criticism of the way this concept has been developed in the case law of the ECJ. Principally, this concerns the formalistic understanding of inter-personal compensation, the exclusion of any standardization and the hazy idea of a shift of cohesion to the level of bilateral treaties.

251. See for example ECJ, 12.6.2003, case C-234/01 *(Gerritse)*, EWS 2003, p. 330, para. 54.
252. ECJ, 8.3.2001, case C-397/98 et al. *(Metallgesellschaft et al.)*, ECR 2001, I-1727, paras 43 et seq.
253. Cf. Amatucci, *EC Tax Review* 2003, p. 202 (206).
254. Like here Lehner/Schuch, *Verluste*, p. 63 (69 et seq. and 73 et seq.); Lehner/Kessler, *Verluste*, p. 83 (105 et seq.). Different opinion Wattel, *EC Tax Review* 2003, p. 194 (199 and 201); Meussen, *EC Tax Review* 2003, p. 144 (147).

In principle, the ECJ is right to demand that the discriminatory taxation and the corresponding tax advantage claimed by a national government must compensate each other in case of every taxpayer conducting a cross-border activity. A persisting discrimination of some internationally mobile taxpayers cannot be justified by the privileges enjoyed by others who engage in similar activities. Otherwise, the disadvantages experienced by the former would persist, and the internal market would be partial. It is therefore not sufficient that the 'typical' or 'average' free mover is taxed equivalent to his/her fellow taxpayer who stays at home. This is even more the case because at the beginning of a cross-border venture, the free mover will often not yet know the specific, tax-relevant economic conditions and results of his/her endeavour, e.g. the costs incurred or the profitability. If depending on such uncertain circumstances, he/she might be substantially discriminated against by lump-sum rules or crude standardization, their deterring effect being even deeper than their real impact.

However, the examination of corresponding tax burdens and relief must not be narrowed to a mere technical exercise taking into account only the formal aspect of tax liability. An intended tax shift or a reasonable understanding of tax incidence obviously underlying the national tax system must be respected and considered as well. The cohesion principle aims at equal treatment in substance, thus the economic effects rather than the technical design of taxes must be the relevant yardstick. As a consequence, different taxes may be accumulated or set against each other in their economic effects if they materially affect one and the same subject, even if not formally liable to tax. If such material affectation is disputed in scientific discussion, it must be sufficient that the national legislator sided with one defendable position and made this choice clear in the drafting of the tax system. This is so because the cohesion principle seeks to reconcile the national idea of tax equity and taxation according to ability to pay with the demands of an internal market. Therefore, the 'direct link' between a tax concession and a tax burden cannot be determined regardless of the peculiarities and fundamental evaluations of the national tax system.[255] On the contrary, it must be established on the basis of coherent assumptions by the national legislator, as long as these are not evidently erroneous or obviously intended to detriment international business. This is the only reason to still talk about a cohesion principle instead of a mere compensation principle. For example, in the light of the aforementioned considerations we support the widespread belief that indeed there may exist cohesion between the (domestic) corporate tax burden on the one hand and a tax credit granted to the shareholder upon dividend distribution on the other hand.[256] It seems that the ECJ has finally embraced this point of view, too.[257]

255. Cf. Sedemund, DStZ 2003, p. 407 (409); García Prats, *Imposición directa,* p. 194.

256. Cf. Englisch, ET 2004, p. 355 et seq.; Wattel, *EC Tax Review* 2003, p. 194 (200); Schön, FR 2001, p. 381 (389); Martín Jiménez/Calderón Carrero, *Imposición directa,* p. 186; de Pablo Varona, *La tributación del socio,* p. 457; Lechner/Staringer/Tumpel, *Kapitalverkehrsfreiheit,* p. 93 (110); Bozza-Bodden, *Körperschaftsteuersystem,* p. 312. For the first time, this has now also been accepted in the Opinion of an Advocate General, see Kokott AG, Opinion, 18.3.2004, case C-319/02 *(Manninen),* para. 61.

257. ECJ, 7.9.2004, case C-319/02 *(Manninen),* not yet published, para. 44.

Moreover, even though the fundamental freedoms leave little room for generalizations and lump-sum provisions specifically addressing cross-border activities, it cannot be concluded that any free mover must be taxed at least equally to *every* domestic taxpayer in similar conditions of ability to pay. Such an assumption would completely rule out any possibility for national governments to introduce standardized elements into their internal tax system. It is immanent to any standardization that it leads to over- or undercharging the individual taxpayer as compared to an individual assessment of the peculiarities in his/her specific case. If undercharged, the advantage enjoyed by the individual domestic taxpayer would, in a strict sense, not only discriminate his/her internally active fellow taxpayers but also the free mover who does not benefit from the standardization. However, since tax law is a field of 'mass assessment' of millions of individual tax subjects and billions of tax-relevant facts, elements of standardization are indisputably needed to warrant efficiency and effective equality of taxation. Usually, this dilemma can be resolved by subjecting cross-border activities to the same kind of lump-sum rules or characterizing as their domestic counterparts. Here it becomes obvious that the individual advantages or disadvantages stem from the generalization and not from the cross-border character of the activity. However, if a compensatory mechanism operating only for domestic activities for reasons of internal coherence involves standardized assumptions, the above solution is not accessible. Here, it must suffice that the tax burden of every free mover is not higher than the overall burden of an *average,* typical taxpayer with identical ability to pay derived from domestic activities. On the one hand, Member States' interests in employing standardization must be highly esteemed, especially since their main objective is to ensure effective tax administration as a prerequisite for equal application of tax laws in a domestic environment. Also, Member States' preferences on exact compensation promoting legal equity or simplifying rules leading to administrative efficiency and, subsequently, factual equity are to a high degree an expression of the national sense of tax justice to be respected under the EC Treaty.[258] On the other hand, the interests of the free mover and, implicitly, the requirements of the internal market are essentially safeguarded if the compensation leads to an equal tax burden for every kind of cross-border activity as compared to the one of a typical domestic taxpayer with the same ability to pay. The concept of an internal market stipulated in Article 3 (1) c) and 14 (2) aims at establishing equal conditions of market access and market competition.[259] These objectives are not impaired, though, when every free mover is taxed equally as his/her typical domestic competitor. Any discrepancies regarding particular competitors will at least not constitute a *considerable* obstacle to the internal market without frontiers for the free movement of goods, persons, services and capital. Of course, even if part of a coherent subsystem, standardization must not lead to hidden privileges for domestic activities. Its limits are constituted by empirical data supporting or disproving its underlying assumptions, and by the general feasibility of typing the facts in question. In any case, a standardization that does not meet internal

258. Kube, IStR 2003, p. 325 (332).
259. Grabitz/Hilf, *EU-Kommentar,* Art. 2 EGV, Rz. 15; Lackhoff, *Niederlassungsfreiheit,* p. 85.

requirements of constitutional or supreme law cannot be invoked in the context of the cohesion principle either.

Finally, we believe that double taxation conventions do influence the internal coherence of a national tax system to a lesser degree than the ECJ assumes. The vague statement that the cohesion of the tax system is transferred to the level of bilateral agreements if only such agreements exist, does not bear close examination.[260] The essence of the cohesion test as specified above is not an issue of inter-country equity as pursued by the distribution provisions of a DTC. Instead, it focuses on inter-personal equity, i.e. equal taxation between taxpayers moving across national borders and those staying at home. The Court is mixing two equity concepts which complement each other, but are by no means interchangeable. Therefore, double taxation conventions can only be considered in the cohesion test insofar as they influence the compensatory effects claimed by the national government to defend a discriminatory tax rule. At first glance, a DTC could affect the balance between tax concessions and coherent tax burdens not borne by the free mover in two ways. On the one hand, it could allow a domestically active taxpayer to escape the tax burden that would correspond to the tax advantage enjoyed by him/her. On the other hand, it could concede tax concessions to privileged 'free movers' who fall under its scope of application and who do not have to bear the corresponding tax burden. A closer look reveals, though, that these thoughts will hardly ever carry a denial of fiscal cohesion.

First, double taxation conventions will not usually provide an unjustified escape gateway or tax loophole for taxpayers who benefit from a tax concession for domestic activities but would like to avoid the compensatory tax burden linked to it in another part of the tax system. Obviously, their field of application is the international rather than the purely domestic taxable activity. An exception can occur only in those cases where the imposition of the corresponding tax burden is deferred – such as in cases *Bachmann* and *Wielockx*[261] – so that the taxpayer may escape it by 'moving over' into an international environment subject to the DTC regulations. The most prominent example for this is national systems of pension taxation which exempt the pension plan contributions and tax the pensions only upon payment. When the taxpayer moves abroad shortly before or after retiring, the current design of most bilateral agreements orientated according to the OECD Model Convention impedes the former home State from levying taxes on the pension payments. If such distorting effects are or can be expected to be more than marginal, they indeed undermine the cohesion of the national tax system.[262] The coherence established by the internal tax law is thus given up in an 'external' context accessible to the taxpayer. For that reason, it does not matter whether the supposed cohesion is given up in a DTC concluded with the State of residence and the free mover affected by the discriminatory exclusion from the tax

260. Interestingly enough, the ECJ has not mentioned this restriction on fiscal cohesion in its recent *Manninen* judgment of 7.9.2004, case C-319/02, even though the facts of the case would have given rise to such objection.
261. ECJ, 28.1.1992, case C-204/90 *(Bachmann)*, ECR 1992, I-249; ECJ, 11.8.1995, case C-80/94 *(Wielockx)*, ECR1995, I-2493.
262. Like here Gammie, *Bulletin I.F.D.* 2003, p. 86 (94); Farmer, *EC Tax Review* 1998, p. 13 (22).

concession. Rather, any inconsistencies between the internal regulations and a bilateral allocation of taxing rights spoil the overall cohesion of the tax system. Such constellations should not be overestimated in their practical significance, though. In our view, if the national tax system does not provide for any compensation for the deferral of the tax payment enjoyed only in a domestic context, there is no cohesion in the first place and any DTC implications can be disregarded.

Second, the inverse situation that tax relief that forms part of an integrated domestic compensation scheme is granted also in a cross-border context, but only in respect to certain Member States or third countries actually will not put in question the cohesion argument as regards the other Member States. Indeed, if such concessions are not complemented by the imposition of the corresponding tax burden, the taxation of the free movers who benefit from such a regulation is no longer coherent. However, it is not the cohesion in the taxation of other free movers that matters in the discrimination test but rather the coherent taxation of the equivalent domestic situation. As has already been pointed out in the above discussion of a most favoured nation clause, the relevant groups of comparison are the affected free mover and his/her domestic counterpart, not different free movers coming from or moving to different Member States. The privileges of some cross-border activities do not influence that comparison, they do not remove the cohesion of the compensation mechanism in a domestic setting. Hence, the Member State which seemingly discriminates a certain cross-border activity can still prove that there is no real or substantial discrimination as compared to domestic activities due to a coherent tax burden only borne by the latter. Further approximation of equal treatment also in regard to cross-border activities involving other Member States can only be required by as yet inexistent harmonization measures.

Cordewener disagrees with us on this issue; he/she concludes from the sporadic concession of a tax relief without imposing the corresponding tax disadvantage that the Member State abandons his/her supposed taxation ideals in general and thereby admits that the exclusion of cross-border activities from the advantageous component is not necessary to uphold national views on tax equity. It would be contradictory to claim the necessity of a coherent taxation in respect of some free movers while at the same time not maintaining it in relation to others.[263] However, this view ignores the fact that double taxation conventions do not primarily serve the implementation of national taxation ideals; instead they seek to allocate taxing rights in accordance with the contracting parties' beliefs on inter-country equity. Discrimination issues play a lesser role, and in this context, the two parties will often have quite different views on whether a tax concession should be extended to cross-border activities as well, and will discuss this matter in terms of their respective understanding of tax equity and tax consistency. This may lead to a compromise in which no side can fully succeed with its opinions. As a consequence, the coherence which is attained in the internal tax order cannot always be expressed and maintained in the international setting of a bilateral agreement. From this it can obviously not be deducted, though, that the Member State

263. Cordewener, *Grundfreiheiten*, pp. 526 and 970.

no longer cares about the coherent taxation of domestic activities. The pressures of bilateral negotiations should not be confused with the insights into systematic necessities as expressed by the national tax system.

[4] Extra-Fiscal Objectives

Extra-fiscal rules to be found in national tax laws aim at influencing the taxpayer's behaviour by setting incentives for desired and disincentives for undesired conduct. They do not form part of the national set of rules dedicated to taxation according to individual ability to pay. On the contrary, they are infringements of this fundamental principle and guided by intentions of economic or social policy. Provided that such tax privileges fall within the substantial scope of the basic freedoms or at least of Article 12, they must, in principle, be granted regardless of the cross-border or domestic character of the promoted activity. Otherwise, it must be determined if the exclusion or detriment of cross-border activities serves a legitimate extra-fiscal objective in a proportional way. Here, it is appropriate to distinguish between economically motivated and other tax privileges as they present different challenges in ruling on their consistency with the basic freedoms.

[a] Economic Control

Tax rules aimed at controlling economic activities must be judged upon in close coordination with the Treaty provisions on forbidden State aids as stipulated in Article 87. In this respect there still exists quite some confusion in the jurisprudence of the ECJ and in scientific literature. A clear statement can only be made about tax incentives which are incompatible with Article 87 (1) regardless of their discriminatory character. In this case, their underlying motive is expressly declared illegitimate by primary EC law itself. Consequently, they cannot serve as a valid justification for a breach of the basic freedoms if they additionally discriminate against cross-border activities by excluding them from their substantial scope.

If the tax privilege constitutes State aid in the sense of Article 87 (1) but is compatible with the common market according to Article 87 (2) or (3), such as for example the tax deductions only for the domestic production of movies in Spanish tax law,[264] the relation to the basic freedoms is less evident. The ECJ seems to incline towards the position that the basic freedoms prevail over the State aid provisions and that the economic purposes specified in Article 87 (2) and (3) cannot be cited to justify a discriminatory tax advantage.[265] This can be doubted for two reasons. First, an

264. See Art. 35 (2) 1 LIS (Spanish Corporation Tax Act).
265. ECJ, 19.9.2000, case C-156/98 *(Germanyv. Commission)*, ECR 2000, I-6857, paras 78 et seq.; ECJ, 7.5.1985, case 18/84 *(Commission v. France)*, ECR 1985, 1339, para. 13. See also ECJ, 5.6.1986, case 103/84 *(Com mission v. Italy)*, ECR 1986, 1759, para. 19. Consenting, but more differentiated Streinz/Koenig/Kühling, EUV/EGV, Art. 87 EGV, para. 21. The ECJ has thereby considerably modified its initial tenure towards the relation between State aid and the fundamental freedoms which was based on a principal supremacy of the State aid provisions

infringement of the basic freedoms is inherent to some State aid permissions of Article 87 (2) and (3) since they implicate that outbound investments may be excluded from (tax) subsidies, hence cross-border activities in a specific sector are discriminated against. If one would assume that any such infringement is not permissible by the motives specified in Article 87 (2) and (3), these provisions would be deprived of effectiveness.[266] Second, it is established practice of the ECJ that the Commission must consider every provision of the EC Treaty when it rules on the compatibility of a State aid with the common market.[267] As a consequence, a kind of 'concentration effect' must be attributed to a positive decision adopted either in the preliminary examination stipulated in Article 88 (3) or in the formal investigation procedure of Article 88 (2). It includes not only a judgment on the consistency of the tax privilege with the State aid provisions, but with all treaty provisions, especially the basic freedoms. After expiry of the period within which an action must be brought according to Article 230 (5), the decision can no longer be contested and becomes final. From then on, a breach of the basic freedoms can no longer be claimed by any Member State or competitor, as otherwise the aforementioned deadline would be averted. From the above follows that the motives for State aid as laid down in Article 87 (2) (c) and (3) (a) to (d) may justify a discrimination of outbound cross-border business if they are proportionate.[268] As they aim at promoting certain branches or regions rather than specific enterprises, they can however not be relied upon to justify discrimination against non-residents who invest in those branches or regions. Moreover, after a positive decision of the Commission in the procedure of Article 88 (2) or (3), a breach of fundamental freedoms can only be considered by the ECJ in the context of an action brought forward according to Article 230.

Finally, if the tax advantage seeks to influence economic activities without qualifying as State aid, e.g. because it aims at stimulating scientific investigation in all sectors of the economy, infringements of the basic freedoms must be viewed independently, leaving little space for justification.[269] Usually, it will be impossible to prove that the exclusion of cross-border activities from the beneficial tax scheme is necessary to achieve the desired positive economic effects. The desire to foster only the national economy or to protect it against foreign competition, in any case, is no legitimate reason of public interest,[270] as the abolition of such protective behaviour is immanent to the idea of an internal market.

---

and a reduced applicability of the freedom articles only for modalities not necessary for promoting the motives underlying the State aid. See ECJ, 22.3.1977, case 74/76 *(Iannelli)*, ECR 1977, 557, para. 9/10.

266. Cf. Calliess/Ruffert/Cremer, EUV/EGV, Art. 87 EGV, paras 47 et seq.
267. ECJ, 19.9.2000, case C-156/98 *(Germany v. Commission)*, ECR 2000, I-6857, para. 78; ECJ, 15.6.1993, case C-225/91 *(Matra)*, ECR 1993, I-3203, paras 41 et seq.; ECJ, 21.5.1980, case 73/79 *(Commission v. Italy)*, ECR 1980, 1533, para. 11.
268. See also Communication from the Commission on certain legal aspects relating to cinematographic and other audiovisual works of 26.9.2001, COM(2001) 534 final, p. 8.
269. See also Cordewener, *Grundfreiheiten*, p. 895 et seq.
270. Cf. ECJ, 13.11.2003, case C-209/01 *(Schilling)*, IStR 2004, p. 60, para. 40; ECJ, 6.6.2000, case C-35/98 *(Verkooijen)*, ECR2000, I-4071, para. 48; ECJ, 28.4.1998, case C-120/95 (Decker), ECR 1998, I-1831, para. 39; ECJ, 28.4.1998, case C-158/96 *(Kohll)*, ECR 1998, I-1931, para. 41; see also Opinion of Kokott AG, 12.2.2004, case C-242/03 *(Weidert)*, not yet published.

[b] *Social or Ecological Objectives*

Insofar as tax privileges infringing the basic freedoms serve non-economic, such as charitable or environmental, purposes, a case-by-case analysis is required. Usually the respective tax privileges can in principle be defended by reasons of national interest acceptable under EC law. The treaty itself will in many cases explicitly or implicitly recognize that these objectives are deserving promotion and, in any case, will respect the Member State's remaining competence to formulate its social objectives. The key question will be, though, whether the confinement of such tax privileges to activities with a domestic element is legitimate, necessary and proportional. If the domestic element required is immanent to the promoted activity itself, such as for example the Spanish tax deduction for the acquisition of Spanish cultural treasures,[271] the discussion will first have to centre on the question of whether such limitation of a general objective – here, protection of the cultural heritage – to a strictly national one can still be considered legitimate in the face of European integration. If the answer is affirmative, the overt or covert discrimination of cross-border activities will almost always be suitable and necessary to reach this objective. In some occasions there exist treaty provisions which allow for the conclusion that this protective definition of extra-fiscal motives is tolerable under EC law, especially in cultural affairs, for instance Article 30, 151 (4). As regards the rest of the cases, a generous approach should be taken in orientation according to the extent to which the objective under scrutiny can be affiliated to the Member State's national identity. This opens the way for balancing the conflicting interests in the third part of the proportionality test. Here, the most important factors to be weighed against will be the degree of impairment of the fundamental freedoms on the one hand and the effectiveness of the national tax privilege as well as the objective necessity to promote the privileged activity on the other hand.

If the domestic element required is connected to the beneficiary rather than to the benefiting activity, as is for example the case in the tax sparing of capital investments or letting undertaken by charitable institutions only if they are residents as provided for in German tax law,[272] the focus of examination will lie on the legitimacy and necessity of such restriction. In general, this will be difficult to assume because if the privileged activity as such can also be realized by a non-resident, the protection of the national identity can hardly be invoked to exclude him/her from the contended tax relief. And as far as administrative requirements are concerned, there will usually exist less restrictive, procedural measures to examine if all requirements for a tax concession are met. Member States will probably only be able to rely on the allegation that the circle of privileged entities is strictly confined to institutions which promote activities close to affairs of national rather than European interest; a defence likely to become obsolete as the social, political and cultural integration of Europe intensifies.

271. See Art. 35 (1) LIS (Spanish Corporation Tax Act).
272. See §5(1) No. 9, (2) No. 2 KStG (German Corporation Tax Act) in combination with Art. 14 AO (German Tax Order), now brought before the ECJ by the German Bundesfinanzhof, 14.7.2004, C-386/04 *(Centro di Musicologia Walter Stauffer)*.

§9.04 CROSS-BORDER ABILITY TO PAY IN INDIRECT TAXATION

Indirect taxes are taxes that the taxpayer is expected to shift in the price of goods or services so that the ultimate taxpayer is different from the one liable to tax. Of course, any tax may be shifted if the market so permits; however, indirect taxes are those which the legislator generally intends and assumes to be shifted. Usually, they are taxes on consumption or transactions. The most important indirect tax within the European Union is the value added tax established by the common VAT system as stipulated in various EC directives. According to Article 2 (1) of the First VAT Directive, the VAT is a general tax on consumption exactly proportional to the price of the goods and services. Due to the right only for the 'taxable person', i.e. the entrepreneur, to a deduction or refund of the VAT charged on services or goods received by him, the tax is so designed as to be finally and definitely born only by the individual consumer. This characterizes the VAT as an indirect tax as specified in Article 93, according to the established case law of the ECJ[273] and legal doctrine.[274] However, we consider that the above definition of an indirect tax is not fully consistent with the EC Treaty formulation of this concept. As can be derived from Articles 92 and 93, all excise duties are also categorized as indirect taxes, even though some of them, such as the motor vehicle excise duty, are intended to be borne by the taxpayer himself and should therefore be characterized as a direct tax on consumption.[275]

In fact, indirect taxes such as defined here seek to tax ability to pay as well, namely the ability to pay demonstrated in the transaction or consumption on which the tax is shifted. This is obvious in those countries where the constitution expressly demands an orientation of the entire tax system according to ability to pay. But also as regards other Member States, the justification for levying indirect taxes on consumption or transaction can be seen in the ability to consume which indicates taxable economic capacity.[276] Hence the fundamental freedoms' basic tax implication, i.e. the development of a cross-border concept of ability to pay, comes into play with indirect taxes as well. There are some peculiarities, however, which alter some of the above conclusions drawn for direct taxes in the field of indirect taxation.

First, with Articles 90 *et seq.* there exist explicit provisions on equality in the taxation of goods which supersede the general provisions on free movement. In this respect, we would like to point out that the exigencies established by Article 90 (1) as regards indirect taxation of Member States clearly support our view that *at least* in taxation matters, the free movement provisions must be interpreted as rights to equal treatment rather than genuine freedom rights. It is undisputed that Article 90 (1) does not impede Member States from levying indirect taxes at all, nor does it require a

---

273. ECJ, 15.10.2002, case C-427/98 *(Commission v. Germany)*, ECR 2002, I-8315, para. 29; ECJ, 24.10.1996, case 317/94 *(Elida Gibbs)*, ECR 1996, I-5339, para. 19 and 22; ECJ, 3.3.1988, case 252/86 *(Bergandi)*, ECR 1988, 1343, para. 17.
274. Cf. for example *Tumpel, Mehrwertsteuer,* p. 161 *et* seq.; Terra/Wattel, *European TaxLaw,p.* 116; Farmer/Lyal, *EC Tax Law*, p. 86.
275. Cf. ECJ, 19.9.2002, case C-101/00 *(Tulliasiamies and Siilin)*, ECR 2002, I-7487. Like here Schön, EuR 2001, p. 341(342etseq.).
276. Cf. Tipke, StRO, vol. II, 2nd edn, p. 980 et seq.

justification by Member States for doing so.[277] It only prohibits a legal or factual extra burdening of cross-border trade of goods as compared to a purely domestic activity. Moreover, it is established case law that the general provision on the free movement of goods, Article 28, is not applicable on fiscal measures as contemplated in the more specific Article 90 (1).[278] It is not perceivable why this equality concept should be replaced by a freedom right concept when it comes to direct taxation.

Second, the great extent of harmonization especially of the common VAT system creates specific responsibilities for the Member States to avoid non-discriminatory restrictions, especially indirect double taxation. On the other hand, harmonization also eliminates a great number of potential infringements of the equal treatment obligation under Article 90 and the fundamental freedoms, especially as regards national treatment of imported goods and services.

Finally, it should be noted that the ECJ puts great emphasis on competitive neutrality in matters of indirect taxation, and gives very little attention to such considerations as ability to pay.[279] In principle, both concepts do not exclude each other, but rather illuminate different aspects of the same internal market requirement. Equal taxation in accordance with a cross-border concept of ability to pay will tax the consumer as the ultimate taxpayer independently of the domestic or offshore origin of the goods and services consumed. Such a concept of tax equity in indirect taxation supports at the same time the economically relevant idea of competitive neutrality. The picture becomes somewhat more complex only because in reality, an excess levy of indirect taxes on foreign goods or services can eventually turn into a quasi-direct tax on the formal taxpayer, e.g. in the field of VAT, on the entrepreneur. If he/she does not have a significant cost advantage over his/her domestic competitors, he/she will not be able to shift the excess burden since consumers would tend not to accept a relatively higher price. When the foreign supplier enjoys a competitive advantage, a shift may be possible, but only at the price of partially or fully losing his/her original advantage. Hence, the economic effects of unequal indirect taxation depend on the specific market conditions at issue and cannot generally be predicted. As a consequence, it may afflict either consumers' ability to pay – if the turnover succeeds – or the supplier's ability to pay, in experiencing an additional tax burden, or even, in case of only a partial shift of the excess burden, both of them. Free competition is impaired in any of these cases, which seemingly makes it easier to base one's argumentation on this economic aspect.

---

277. ECJ, 4.4.1968, case 27/67 *(Fink-Frucht)*, ECR 1968, 333, 345. See also ECJ, 11.12.1990, case C-47/88 *(Commission v. Denmark)*, ECR 1990, I-4509, paras 10–13: Art. 90 does not even prohibit an extraordinary high level of indirect taxes on certain goods. In the decision handed down in the early *Stier* case, the ECJ has commented that Member States must not tax foreign goods to such an extent that the free movement of goods would come to a practical standstill; however, this could not be assumed if the respective rate of turnover tax was within the margin set by the entire national system of indirect taxation (ECJ, 4.4.1986, case 31/67, ECR 1968, 351, 360 et seq.). Hence again a comparative, relative element was introduced into the examination.
278. ECJ, 3.2.2000, case C-228/98 *(Dounias)*, ECR 2000, I-577, para. 39; ECJ, 11.3.1992, cases C-78/90 to 83/90 *(Compagnie commerciale del'Ouest et al.)*, ECR 1992, I-1847, para. 20; ECJ, 3.3.1988, case 252/86 *(Bergandi)*, ECR 1988, 1343, para. 33.
279. Cf. ECJ, 29.4.2004, case C-387/01 (Weigel), not yet published, para. 66; ECJ, 15.7.1982, case 216/81 (COGIS), *ECR* 1982, 2701, para. 6; see also Schön, *Umsatzsteuer-Kongreß-Bericht* 2001/2002, p. 62.

However, a European Legal Tax Order founded on the idea of tax equity and tax equality cannot elevate an impersonal policy goal such as free competition to the exclusive yardstick of the tax system, albeit only for indirect taxes. It must rather focus predominantly on the treatment of physical or legal persons because tax equity or tax justice is necessarily a concept calling for a personalized reference point. This is not to say that economic knowledge should be ignored; rather, it must be incorporated into a concept of equal taxation which will eventually have the effect to serve also exigencies of economic efficiency, as has been outlined above. Thus, from a legal scholarly perspective the deeper reason for demanding equal conditions of indirect taxation for foreign and domestic products is to warrant equal tax burdens on consumers' ability to pay. As this can only be achieved by taxing equally the 'taxable subject', e.g. the entrepreneur, the following exposition will focus on forbidden discriminations or restrictions of the foreign competitor. As we will see, even in the area of harmonized VAT taxation there does not exist one single concept of equal taxation. Instead, and as we know from the field of direct taxation, equality of tax conditions can only be demanded within a national 'box' and in a comprehensive view of the taxes accumulated over two national boxes, but not as between any two national boxes. Disparities caused by different national levels of indirect taxation could only be reduced by further harmonization.[280]

[A] Non-discrimination of Foreign Competitors in the Domestic Market

First of all, the EC Treaty requires that goods and services offered by foreign suppliers in the domestic market are taxed equally to comparable products of their local competitors. To that effect, Article 90 (1) stipulates that no Member State shall impose, directly or indirectly, on the products of other Member States any internal taxation in excess of that imposed on similar domestic products. If no similar products exist, any taxation indirectly protecting domestic production is forbidden (Article 90 (2)). This provision has been inspired by Article III (2) GATT 1947 which prohibits excess tax burdens on like or competing foreign products.[281] The ECJ has considered it to be a fundamental principle of the Common Market;[282] and rightfully so, as it specifies the free movement of goods as one of the four fundamental freedoms in the area of taxation.[283] Its main field of application are indirect taxes; in the terminology of the Treaty, it is even its exclusive scope, as may be concluded from Article 92.[284] However, Article 90 does not cover all kinds of indirect taxes, because the taxation of services is

280. ECJ, 27.2.1980, case 171/78 *(Commission v. Denmark)*, ECR 1980, 465, para. 20; ECJ, 13.3.1979, case 86/78 *(Peureux)*, ECR 1979, 897, para. 39/40; *Schön*, EuR 2001, p. 216 (220).
281. Cf. *Schön*, RIW 2004, p. 50; Schwarze/Stumpf, *EU-Kommentar*, Art. 90 EGV, para. 4.
282. ECJ, 8.1.1980, case 21/79 *(Commission v. Italy)*, ECR 1980,1, para. 15.
283. Cf. Streinz/Kamann, EGV/EUV, Art. 90 EGV, para. 2.
284. Cf. Streinz/Kamann, EGV/EUV, Art. 90 EGV, para. 14, but see also Schön, EuR 2001, p. 341 (342 et seq.). Moreover, Art. 90 covers not only genuine taxes, which can be characterized as charges levied without an intended spending purpose, but also para-fiscal charges which, however, are not subject of this article.

excluded from its substantial scope.[285] An exception can only be made for taxes on auxiliary services such as transportation which are rendered in the cross-border trade of goods and therefore can be attributed to those goods as a relevant cost factor.[286] Here, the free movement of goods across borders is indirectly discriminated if no corresponding tax is charged on similar services rendered in a domestic context. In the rest of cases, when the services constitute the primary product purchased by the consumer, one will have resort to the general prohibition of restrictions on the freedom of services. As has been outlined above, this fundamental freedom also includes a prohibition of discriminatory taxes and, as may be added now, this prohibition is certainly not limited to direct taxes.[287] The imposition of comparatively higher indirect taxes will in any case lead to a legal disadvantage for the cross-border supply of services. If the excess tax cannot be shifted, this is evidently so. But even if the excess burden can be shifted as intended, the consumer recipient of pan-European services will have to bear a higher tax burden as a consequence of his/her choice to contract a foreign supplier, hence the rights of the 'passive' beneficiary of this fundamental freedom are impaired.

As regards the discrimination test to be conducted in the field of indirect taxation, the first and also one of the most crucial steps is to determine if there exists similarity as compared to domestic products and eventually, to which ones. Any two products will hardly ever be identical in all aspects, so the concept of similarity obviously goes beyond mere identity and requires mapping out the relevant factors of comparison.[288] Even though such an evaluation is required in the field of direct taxation as well, it merits special attention in the revision of indirect taxes. Within the European Union, direct taxes on income still tend to be global ones taxing all income regardless of its source. Given this global approach, any discrimination of cross-border activities will usually be rapidly identified as such, as it constitutes an exception to the general rule of taxation according to a generic ability to pay. On the contrary, and despite Community harmonization, a conglomerate of national turnover taxes and excise duties affecting different product categories differently still prevails in most Member States. For that reason, a discrimination of cross-border trade can be hidden more easily, and similarity must be determined carefully. Should the trend toward schedular

285. Schwarze/Stumpf, *EU-Kommentar*, Art. 90 EGV, para. 9. We do not agree with this author that Art. 90 should be applied to all indirect taxes by way of extensive interpretation or analogy. On the one hand, an extensive interpretation must be ruled out regarding the clear wording of the provision. For an application by analogy, on the other hand, there is no need since the freedom of services stipulated in Art. 49 (1) already fills any potential gap, see above. Like here von der Groeben/Schwarze/Eilers/Bahns/Sedlaczek, EUV/EGV, Art. 90 EGV, para. 31.
286. ECJ, 17.7.1997, case C-90/94 *(Haahr Petroleum)*, ECR 1997, I-4085, para. 40; ECJ, 16.2.1977, case 20/76 *(Schöttle)*, ECR 1977, 247, paras 1414 et seq.
287. Like here Haferkamp, *Kapitalverkehrsfreiheit*, p. 101 (footnote 526); Balke, *Steuerliche Gestaltungsfreiheit*, p. 25.
288. ECJ, 27.2.2002, case C-302/00 *(Commission v. France)*, ECR 2002, I-3055, para. 23; ECJ, 11.8.1995, joint cases C-367/93 to C-377/93 *(Roders etal.)*, ECR 1995, I-2229, para. 27; ECJ, 4.3.1986, case 106/84 *(Com mission v. Denmark)*, ECR 1986, 833, para. 12; ECJ, 15.7.1982, case 216/81 *(COGIS)*, ECR 1982, 2701, para. 7; ECJ, 27.2.1980, case 168/78 *(Commission v. France)*, ECR 1980, 347, para. 5; ECJ, 27.2.1980, case 169/78 *(Commission v. Italy)*, ECR 1980, 385, para. 5. See also Berlin, *Droit fiscal communautaire*, 1988, p. 133.

taxation already visible in Member State's income tax systems continue, this aspect will certainly gain importance in direct taxation of income as well. In some cases of direct taxation such as progressive vehicle tax it has been present all along, as the ample case law of the Court shows.

It is now established practice of the ECJ to determine similarity of any two products by considering whether they have similar characteristics and meet the same needs from the point of view of consumers.[289] In the face of the aforementioned chaos of indirect taxation in most Member States, the Court often conducts a detailed survey taking into account various sub-criteria.[290] In this context, the criterion of similarity in objective features, such as the nature of the raw materials used or the production processes employed, has experienced a development in the jurisdiction of the Court. Early decisions allowed the conclusion that it was employed only as an auxiliary criterion to determine the suitability of two products for one and the same use in the eyes of the consumer.[291] However, in recent times objective product characteristics have gained significance on their own in the jurisprudence of the ECJ. The Court has permitted different tax burdens on 'similar' products when a tax design based on such criteria seeks to influence desirable social, ecological or economic behaviour.[292] It has held that different objective characteristics may justify a higher or lower tax burden even though the two products compared serve similar consumer needs, e.g. electricity which is produced in different ways. According to the ECJ, Article 90 is not affected by such distinctions if the relevant criteria are applied objectively, i.e. regardless of where the affected products originate from, if they pursue objectives which are themselves compatible with the requirements of the Treaty and secondary EC legislation, and if it does not show any discriminative or protective effects.[293] The ECJ has specified that this requirement is not met if the 'objective' distinction is not suitable to promote the

289. ECJ, 19.9.2002, case C-101/00 *(Tulliasiamies andSiilin)*, ECR 2002, I-7487, para. 56; ECJ, 27.2.2002, case C-302/00 *(Commission v. France)*, ECR 2002, I-3055, para. 23; ECJ, 11.8.1995, joint cases C-367/93 to C-377/93 *(Roders etal.)*, ECR 1995, I-2229, para. 27; ECJ, 4.3.1986, case 106/84 *(Commission v. Denmark)*, ECR 1986,833, para. 12; ECJ, 15.7.1982, case 216/81 *(COGIS)*, ECR 1982, 2701, para. 7; ECJ, 17.2.1976, case 45/75 *(REWE)*, ECR 1976, 181, para. 13.

290. Instructive for example ECJ, 27.2.2002, case C-302/00 *(Commission v. France)*, ECR 2002, I-3055, paras 24 et seq. [dark- and light-tobacco cigarettes] ECJ, 11.8.1995, joint cases C-367/93 to C-377/93 *(Roders et al.)*, ECR 1995, I-2229, para. 30 [different kinds of wine]; ECJ, 7.5.1987, case 184/85 *(Commission v. Italy)*, ECR 1987, 2013, para. 10 [bananas and Italian dessert fruit].

291. ECJ, 17.2.1976, case 45/75 (REWE), ECR 1976, 181, para. 15; ECJ, 15.7.1982, case 216/81 *(COGIS), ECR* 1982, 2701, para. 7: The comparison must be made between products which have the same characteristics *in the eyes of the consumer.* This is quite different from the position taken later on, which could be circumscribed as similarity *in the eyes of the national legislator,* see above.

292. ECJ, 30.10.1980, case 26/80 *(Schneider-Import)*, ECR 1980, 3469, para. 9. Consenting Terra/Wattel, *European Tax Law*, 3rd edn, p. 12.

293. ECJ, 2.4.1998, case C-213/96 *(Outokumpu)*, ECR 1998, I-1777, para. 30; ECJ, case C-375/95 *(Commission v. Greece)*, ECR 1997, I-5981, paras 28 etseq.; ECJ, 17.7.1997, case *C-90/94(Haahr Petroleum)*, ECR 1997, I-4085, para. 29; ECJ, 3.3.1988, case 252/86 *(Bergandi)*, ECR 1988, 1343, para. 29; ECJ, 14.1.1981, case 140/79 *(ChemialFarmaceutici), ECR* 1981, 1, para. 14; ECJ, 14.1.1981, case 46/80 *(Vinal)*, ECR 1981,77, para. 13. See also Streinz/Kamann, EUV/EGV, Art. 90 EGV, para. 23.

supposed objectives[294] or leads to an abrupt increase of the tax burden which does not fit into a system of harmonic progressive taxation.[295] Altogether, this approach resembles the 'aims and effects' doctrine still fiercely disputed in world trade law.[296]

We agree only partially with the Court's approach to determine product similarity, and, subsequently, the applicability of Article 90 (1). The initial, teleological interpretation of this concept founded on equal suitability to meet consumers' needs is certainly adequate. As can be derived from a systematic analysis in the context of Article 90 (2), both paragraphs are concerned with protective tax systems favouring domestic over foreign products. Whereas the second paragraph obviously permits a higher taxation to the detriment of foreign products to a certain extent – to be specified further on – Article 90 (1) calls for exactly equal taxation of similar products. Higher taxes for similar foreign products would amount to 'direct' protection, in contrast to the 'indirect' protection addressed in Article 90 (2). The stricter approach of the first paragraph can only be explained by the closer competitive relationship between 'similar' products, resulting from their high degree of substitutability from the average consumer's point of view. To properly discern the scope of the first paragraph from that of the second, a rather narrow understanding of similarity as regards the exact extent to which foreign and domestic products must be interchangeable seems preferable. Hence, equal suitability to meet consumers' needs is an adequate choice.

Otherwise, Article 90 (1) would exert a strong pressure towards internal harmonization.[297] As the range of products traded worldwide gets constantly denser due to increasing product differentiation and invention of new goods,[298] a broad concept of similarity would almost certainly lead to the assumption that product classes of differentiated excise duties and turnover taxes distinguish between 'similar' products. Such distinction would lead to generally impermissible de facto or *indirect* discrimination if the group of imported products[299] would be predominantly or asymmetrically

294. ECJ, 17.9.1987, case 433/85 *(Feldain)*, ECR 1987, 3521, para. 16.
295. ECJ,9.5.1985,case 112/84 *(Humblot)*,ECR 1985, 1375, paras 14et seq.
296. Supportive Panel Report, 16.3.1992, *US-Malt Beverages*, DS23/R, para. 5.25.; Hudec, *International Lawyer* 1998, p. 619 (634 et seq.); *Regan*, J. World Trade 2003, p. 737 (752); Porges/Trachtman, *J. World Trade* 2003, p. 783 (796); opposed Appellate Body (AB) Report, 12.3.2001, *EC -Asbestos*, WT/DS135/AB/R, para. 99; AB Report, 9.9.1997, *EC - Bananas III*, WT/DS27/AB/R, para. 241; Choi, 'Like Products' in *International Trade Law*, 2003, p. 82 et seq.; Verhoosel, *National Treatment and WTO Dispute Settlement*, 2002, p. 53 et seq.; Charnowitz, *Am. J. International Law* 2004, p. 610 (614).
297. While such harmonization may seem desirable from an internal point of view, given its oftentimes scarce foundation in objective reasons, esp. in considerations of ability to pay, it nevertheless cannot be forced upon Member States by EC law prior to a political agreement, since considerations of internal consistency do not specifically affect cross-border trade and hence do not fall into the scope of Art. 90 or the fundamental freedoms.
298. See Ehring, *J. World Trade* 2002, p. 921 (954).
299. The ECJ has constantly interpreted Art. 90 as to require a comparison between *all* imported goods and the similar or competing domestic production, rather than imports from a certain Member State as compared to domestic goods, cf. ECJ, case 32/80 *(Kortmann)*, ECR 1981,251, para. 20; ECJ, 30.11.1995, case C-113/94 *(Casarin)*, ECR 1995, I-4203, paras 21 et seq.; ECJ, 27.2.2002, case C-302/00 *(Commission v. France)*, ECR 2002, I-2055, paras 29 et seq. We agree, since Art. 90 aims at eliminating protective effects in favour of domestic production rather than

affected by the higher tax brackets.[300] Consequently, a Member State would be faced with the difficult task of justifying such distinctions, curbing his/her national sovereignty to a considerable extent. This seems inappropriate if one recalls that equality in competitive conditions is also a precondition for equal taxation of the final tax subject, i.e. the consumer, according to its ability to pay. A consumer's ability to pay expressed in his/her purchase of goods or services may, in the view of the national legislator, vary depending on the characteristics of the respective product. A good example of this is the common distinction between 'luxury goods', normal products and products which satisfy basic human needs.[301] Given the objective of Article 90 to avoid competitive distortions only insofar as they specifically affect cross-border trade and thus secure also taxation according to ability to pay,[302] Article 90 should not be interpreted so as to demand the levy of just one unitary indirect tax on all kinds of goods and services. Only if a purchase of goods or services must be held to express similar equality to pay, due to full substitutability on the part of the consumer, the tax burden must indeed be equal for all transactions affected, justifying the application of Article 90 (1). Hence, we support the Court's scrupulous investigation into product characteristics and consumer preferences to determine the applicability of this strict national treatment provision. Unfortunately, the ECJ left the path of teleological interpretation when it gave 'objective product characteristics' a weight of their own and independently of their influence on consumers' preferences. This has led to some uncertainty and inaccuracy in the Court's reasoning. First, its argumentation is circular when it rules out discrimination on grounds of a lack of similarity due to objectively different product characteristics, but only provided that such differentiation does not show discriminating effects. Second, following the Court's line it seems no longer possible to discern properly between paragraphs 1 and 2 of Article 90. As no two products from different suppliers are identical in all possible aspects, Article 90 (1) is deprived of its effectiveness if the national legislator can avoid similarity by naming the relevant 'objective characteristics' according to which he/she wishes to differentiate the tax burden. One would always have to resort to Article 90 (2) which only requires that there exist competing, albeit not similar domestic goods. Not surprisingly, the Court is increasingly reluctant to name the respective paragraph on which it bases its examination of a national tax rule[303]. Third, the Court introduces some elements of proportionality in the discrimination test to correct the effects of its *a priori* recognition of any objective

levelling all distinctions in national taxation, which would however be inevitable if a protective effect would be determined dependant of the individual flow of goods from each of twenty-four other Member States.

300. As regards the detection of detrimental effects of apparently origin-neutral tax systems, see below.

301. Cf. ECJ, 15.3.1983, case 319/81 *(Commission v. Italy)*, ECR 1983, 601, paras 9 and 14.

302. Like the basic freedoms, the provision does not conflict with Member State's believes of fair taxation but rather enhances them. Cf. Vanistendael, *EC Tax Review* 2003, p. 136: '[The] prohibition of a heavier tax burden for foreign products in comparison with similar domestic products ... is a specific application of the principle of equality that is also enshrined in the constitutions of many Member States.'

303. See, for example, ECJ, 23.4.2002, case C-234/99 *(Nygård)*, ECR 2002, I-3657; ECJ, 2.4.1998, case C-213/96 *(Outokumpu)*, *ECR* 1998, I-1777; ECJ, 17.6.1998, case C-68/96 (Grundig Italiana), ECR 1998, I-3775. Like here Schwarze/Stumpf, *EU-Kommentar*, Art. 90 EGV, para. 13.

differences in product characteristics, but without clearly indicating their dogmatic foundation.

The underlying idea of this jurisprudence is to respect the Member States' desire to exercise economic, social or ecological control by creating incentives or disincentives for certain behaviour, for example in case of 'green' taxes. At the same time, the ECJ seeks to prevent such objectives from being abused as an excuse for hidden discrimination of foreign and protection of domestic products. Indeed, within the remaining national sovereignty regarding indirect taxation, i.e. within the limits drawn by EC harmonization measures, the national legislator is free to introduce extra-fiscal elements into his/her tax system. Consequently, such objectives claimed to be pursued by the national legislator must not be disregarded by the Court[304]. If products that equally suit consumers' needs are taxed differently, the Member State may explain this by citing *legitimate* objectives of behaviour control. However, such explanation may only serve as a justification for a generally forbidden higher taxation of foreign products; it will thus have to withstand a proportionality test which includes a weighing and balancing of the conflicting EC and national interests. Consequently, the ECJ should introduce a (generous) 'rule of reason' also for indirect taxes in the setting of Article 90, rather than trying to mould its discrimination test according to national policies not inherent in the competitive and internal market objectives pursued by Chapter 2 of Title 4 EC Treaty. Even though the Court is trying to come up with a proportionality element in this approach, too, it is neither theoretically founded nor sufficient. Since the Court's way of proceeding denies a conflict of principles, it seems odd to require proportionality; even worse, it must be confined to necessity considerations and cannot reflect the need to balance the Community and national policy goals at stake. Furthermore, the alternative examination pattern suggested here offers the advantage of corresponding to that employed when examining discriminating effects of direct taxes under the scope of the fundamental freedoms. Here, too, motives of social or economic control usually do not determine similarity, but may only justify unequal treatment.

Tackling similarity in the way described above, any objective product characteristics named relevant by the national legislator do not influence the similarity requirement. They may however be considered in a second step, to determine if the justification brought forward for an eventual unequal taxation of similar products is implemented in a proportional manner. For example, energy is a product which is equally suitable to meet consumers' electric power demands independently of product processes. When a Member State favours certain forms of energy in its system of energy taxation with the supposed objective of fostering the exploration of regenerative energy carriers while at the same time reducing CO2 emissions, there occurs unequal taxation of products which, by the yardstick of Article 90 (1), have to be considered similar. If this differentiation disadvantages imported energy due to an asymmetric impact of the apparently origin-neutral regulation,[305] it needs to be justified. Such

304. In this regard, see also Danusso/Denton, *Legal Issues of European Integration*, 1990, p. 67 (86 et seq.).
305. For a detailed discussion of the concept of hidden discrimination see below.

justification may be possible on grounds of protection of the environment, a legitimate national objective already according to the EC Treaty (cf. Article 2). However, this supposed objective would require design of the tax system in a way that contemplates all forms of 'clean' (and possibly also 'safe') energy, e.g. solar energy supplied predominantly by energy traders of other Member States would have to qualify for similar tax breaks as wind or water energy produced domestically. If the 'objective characteristics' employed by the Member State to implement its goals of environmental policy do not reflect this equivalence and limit tax concessions to the two last-mentioned forms of energy, the objective weight of national environmental concerns will have to be deemed to be rather low, or maybe even put in question the very claim of pursuing such objectives. In any case, a justification will fail, and the supposed extra-fiscal motivation cannot make up for the violation of the national treatment requirement of Article 90 (1). As can be seen, this provision will not categorically rule out any possibility for Member States to 'export' their national policies via taxation,[306] but calls for *cross-border* consistency in their implementation.

Once similarity has been determined, the discrimination test follows the same pattern as for direct taxation. Discrimination can be affirmed if the foreign product suffers a higher tax burden than its domestic equivalent. It does not matter whether such an additional burden results from a higher tax rate[307] or from differences in the relevant tax base.[308] Just as with direct taxes, different modalities in the levy of the tax may also lead to discrimination for the foreign supplier.[309] Another parallel lies in the absence of any *de minimis* rule; the Court does not accept any extra burdens on similar foreign products however small they may be.[310] Finally, a breach of Article 90 (1) or, in case of services, Article 49 (1) lies in any – overt – discrimination that occurs in the specific case brought before the ECJ. The Member State may not claim an overall even-handed tax impact on similar foreign and domestic products, but must exclude the possibility of disadvantages for foreign competitors in every single case. Thus, as with direct taxes, the discriminative *potential* of a national rule determines its incompatibility with EC law, even if in some cases it leads to equal treatment or even privileges for foreign competitors.[311]

---

306. Farmer/Lyal, EC Tax Law, p. 75 etseq.; Schön, EuR 2001, p. 341 (350).
307. ECJ, 17.11.1992, case C-105/91 *(Commission v. Greece)*, ECR 1992, I-5871, paras 16 et seq.
308. ECJ, 3.2.2000, case C-228/98 *(Dounias)*, ECR 2000, I-577, para. 47; ECJ, 17.6.1998, case C-68/96 *(Grundig Italiana)*, ECR 1998, I-3775, para. 13; ECJ, 23.10.1997, case C-375/95 *(Commission v. Greece)*, ECR 1997, I-5981, paras 19 et seq.; ECJ, 9.3.1995, case C-345/95 *(Nunes Tadeu)*, ECR 1995, I-479, para. 12; ECJ, 12.5.1992, case C-327/90 *(Commission v. Greece)*, ECR 1992, I-3033, para. 11; ECJ, 11.12.1990, case C-47/88 *(Commission v. Denmark)*, ECR 1990, I-4509, para. 18; ECJ, 5.5.1982, case 15/81 *(Schul)*, ECR 1982, 1409, para. 27.
309. ECJ, 17.6.1998, case C-68/96 *(Grundig Italiana)*, ECR 1998, I-3775, paras 22 et seq.; ECJ, 10.7.1984, case 42/83 *(DanskDenkavit), ECR* 1984, 2649, paras 29 et seq.; ECJ, 27.2.1980, case 55/79 *(Commission v. Ireland)*, ECR 1980,481, para. 8; ECJ, 16.2.1977, case 20/76 *(Schöttle)*, ECR 1977, 247, para. 21; Vanistendael, *EC Tax Review* 1996, p. 114(118).
310. ECJ, 3.7.1985, case 277/83 *(Commission v. Italy)*, ECR 1985, 2049, para. 17; Balke, *Steuerliche Gestal- tungsfreiheit*, p. 42; Vanistendael, *EC Tax Review* 1996, p. 114 (118).
311. ECJ, 15.3.2001, case C-265/99 *(Commission v. France)*, ECR 2001, I-2305, para. 40; ECJ, 22.2.2001, case C-393/98 *(Gomes Valente)*, ECR 2001, I-1327, para. 26; ECJ, 3.2.2000, case C-228/98 *(Dounias)*, ECR 2000, I-577, para. 41; ECJ, 17.6.1998, case C-68/96 *(Grundig Italiana)*, ECR 1998, I-3775, para. 12; ECJ, 23.10.1997, case C-375/95 *(Commission v. Greece)*,

This last statement must be modified, though, when a national tax system does not discriminate products that originate from another Member State de jure, but only de facto using apparently origin-neutral criteria which lead, in fact, to detrimental treatment as well. De jure discrimination occurs when national tax relief is accessible only to domestically produced goods or depends on certain requirements which foreign products cannot possibly fulfil, such as the subjecting of the supplier to continuous controls of the Member State's supervising authorities.[312] De facto discrimination is more subtle and employs criteria which could theoretically be met by foreign products as well, but tend to give preferential tax treatment to domestic products. The cross-border impact of the legal distinction can only be assessed when the higher taxation predominantly affects foreign products.[313] Otherwise, unequal taxation will not specifically affect cross-border competition and, as a consequence, the cross-border concept of ability-to-pay enhanced by Article 90 (1), but rather qualify as an internal inconsistency of the national tax system to be judged by national standards only. Therefore, it would not be sufficient to prove that some imported goods are taxed less favourably than some privileged goods produced domestically. Rather, it is necessary to conduct an 'asymmetric impact' test, which requires examination of how foreign and domestic products are spread across the favoured and disfavoured tax categories.[314] The ECJ is however not always aware of the full dimension of the comparison to be undertaken; sometimes it only surveys the distribution of national production across the disputed tax segments.[315] The correct approach in detecting asymmetric effects, especially of complex progressive excise duties, must rely on the weighted average of the tax imposed on the group of imported goods as compared to that borne by the group of similar domestic products.[316] It should be noted, though, that in its general case law, the ECJ does not request empirical data to determine a typical detriment of cross-border activities, and assumes de facto discrimination already if the rule in question is 'intrinsically liable' to have such effects.[317] In our view, this is a step too far because a de facto discrimination is characterized by the fact that it cannot be

ECR 1997, I-5981, para. 20; ECJ, 17.7.1997, case C-90/94 *(Haahr Petroleum)*, ECR 1997, I-4085, para. 34; ECJ, 26.6.1991, case C-152/89 *(Commission v. Luxembourg)*, ECR 1991, I-3141, para. 21. See also Schön, EuR 2001, p. 341 (345).

312. Cf. ECJ, 27.5.1981, joint cases 142 and 143/80 *(Essevi and Salengo)*, ECR 1981, 1413, para. 22. See also ECJ, 7.5.1981, case 153/80 *(Rumhaus Hansen)*, ECR 1981, 1165, paras 10 et seq.
313. Such a higher taxation can result from formally different subsystems of taxation which are advantageous for locally produced goods, from criteria that determine the progression of a tax system in favour of domestic products, from tax incentives that predominantly benefit domestic products, or from tax disincentives that predominantly affect foreign products.
314. Cf. ECJ, 27.2.2002, case C-302/00 *(Commission v. France)*, ECR 2002, I-2055, paras 29 et seq.; ECJ, 17.9.1987, case 433/85 *(Feldain)*, ECR 1987, 3521, paras 14 et seq.; ECJ, 16.12.1986, case 200/85 *(Com mission v. Italy)*, ECR 1986, 3953, paras 12 et seq.; ECJ, 15.3.1983, case 319/81 *(Commission v. Italy)*, ECR 1983,601, para. 18. See also Easson, *Taxation in the European Community*, 1993, p. 61 et seq.; Schön, *Europarecht* 2001, p. 341 (351); ambivalent Stumpf, EuZW 1991, p. 713 (715).
315. Cf. ECJ, 4.3.1986, case 243/84 *(Walker)*, ECR 1986, 875, para. 23.
316. Ehring, *J. World Trade* 2002, p. 921 (965).
317. ECJ, 23.5.1996, case C-237/94 *(O'Flynn)*, ECR 1996, I-2617, paras 20 et seq.; see also Farmer, *EC Tax Review* 2003, p. 75 (76).

concluded simply by studying the suspective rule, but only by examining its real-life effects.[318]

[B] Proportional Taxation of Foreign Competitors in the Domestic Market

If a certain imported product cannot be considered to be similar to any domestic product in the sense discussed above, it falls under the substantial scope of Article 90 (2). Hence, the indirect taxes imposed on these products may not afford indirect protection to other (domestic) products. This implies that there exists some form of competition between the foreign product and other, domestically produced goods. The ECJ has interpreted this competitive relationship extensively, favouring a wide scope of application of Article 90 (2). According to its settled case law, it is sufficient that the foreign and domestic products can be substituted from a consumer's point of view, albeit only indirectly, partially and potentially.[319] The ECJ does not demand that a consumer would choose between the two products in every situation and for every possible use, but only on some occasions.[320] Moreover, the Court has rejected the argument that due to consumer traditions competition between two theoretically substitutable products, e.g. beer and wine, would in fact not occur. To determine a relationship of competition, such traditions may not be seen as inalterable, given the possibilities for a future change of consumer preferences in the Common Market where goods move freely.[321] Consequently, the Court has examined product competition on basis of a Community-wide survey, setting aside national peculiarities.[322]

We support this generous approach in affirming a competitive relationship and, subsequently, the possibility of indirect protection via indirect taxation. First, a teleological interpretation of indirect competition, taking the substitutability in the consumer's eyes as point of reference, is consistent with the Court's initial and adequate understanding of the similarity concept embedded in Article 90 (1). It warrants an effective protection of free competition and of taxation according to cross-border ability to pay. These normative values are affected if a consumer has to bear heavily increased, protective taxes on foreign goods that serve, at least to some extent, the same needs as domestic ones. The ECJ is also right to not demand competition in every possible aspect, since such a close relationship is immanent only

318. Cf. Wouters, *EC Tax Review* 1999, p. 98 (103).
319. ECJ, 17.6.1999, case 166/98 *(Socridis)*, ECR 1999, I-3791, para. 17; ECJ, 11.8.1995, joint cases C-367/93 to C-377/93 *(Roders et al.)*, ECR 1995, I-2229, para. 38; ECJ, 18.4.1991, case C-230/89 *(Commission v. Greece)*, ECR 1991, I-1909, para. 8; ECJ, 9.7.1987, case 356/85 *(Commission v. Belgium)*, ECR 1987, 3299, paras 6 et seq.; ECJ, 7.5.1987, case 184/85 *(Commissionv. Italy)*, ECR 1987, 2013, para. 11; ECJ, 15.7.1982, case216/81 *(COGIS), ECR* 1982, 2701, para. 9; ECJ, 27.2.1980, case 168/78 *(Commission v. France)*, ECR 1980, 347, para. 12.
320. ECJ, 11.7.1989, case 323/87 *(Commission v. Italy)*, ECR 1989, 2275, para. 8; ECJ, 27.2.1980, case 169/78 *(Commission v. Italy)*, ECR 1980,385, paras 32 et seq.; ECJ, 27.2.1980, case 171/78 *(Commission v. Denmark)*, ECR 1980,447, para. 35.
321. ECJ, 27.2.1980, case 170/78 *(Commission v. United Kingdom)*, ECR 1980,417, para. 6.
322. ECJ, 18.4.1991, case C-230/89 *(Commission v. Greece)*, ECR 1991, I-1909, para. 9; ECJ, 27.2.1980, case 168/78 *(Commission v. France)*, ECR 1980, 347, para. 37.

to similar products treated in Article 90 (1).[323] Finally, it is appropriate to focus on potential rather than actual competition; otherwise, the very taxes that by their protective effects possibly cement consumer habits could not be scrutinized.[324]

While it is true that early decisions handed down by the ECJ attributed protective effects to any difference in taxation of competing products,[325] these rulings have by now become obsolete. The Court has readjusted its line of reasoning and has constructed a two-fold test on indirect protection. Once a preferential tax treatment of competing domestic goods has been determined, one must consider in a second step if it has the potential to afford protection to the respective domestic production.[326] Such reasoning is indeed more in line with the systematics of Article 90, which expressly prohibits any tax differences for similar products, but does not stipulate an equally strict consequence for taxation of competing dissimilar goods. On the other hand, it seems appropriate to screen the national tax system for *potential* effects on competition, since Article 90 (2) prohibits taxation *suitable* to afford protection. Of course, the concept of potential indirect protection established by the Court's case law is somewhat vague and certainly leaves the Member States with some discretion as to differences in the respective tax burden.[327] However, the Court's decisions on various systems of vehicle and alcoholic beverage taxes provide a guideline to the limits of this discretion.

First, a detrimental effect of the taxes levied on the partially competing goods or services must be affirmed. Since dissimilar foreign products will most often be faced with real or presumed disadvantages rising from apparently origin-neutral tax systems, the adequate approach to uncover preferential tax treatment of domestic production is the asymmetric impact test described above. Second, the protective effect of a potentially higher taxation of foreign products will have to be proven. In general, the closer a foreign product comes to being similar to a lower taxed group of products, i.e. the closer competitive relationship between the two is, the lesser must be the relative tax difference. In determining permissible tax steps, an evaluation of tax differences in relation to the product price rather than in relation to other factors such as taxable units is decisive.[328] Insofar as progressive tax systems or disparate taxes amount to disproportionate distortions between dissimilar yet competing products, they may nevertheless still be considered to be non-protective if they serve reasons of general interest

323. Cf. Balke, *Steuerliche Gestaltungsfreiheit*, p. 46.
324. See also ECJ, 18.4.1991, case C-230/89 *(Commission v. Greece)*, ECR 1991, I-1909, para. 9; ECJ, case 170/78 *(Commission v. United Kingdom)*, ECR 1980, 417, para. 14.
325. ECJ, 11.7.1989, case 323/87 *(Commission v. Italy), ECR* 1989, 2275, para. 12; ECJ, 15.7.1982, case 216/81 *(COGIS), ECR* 1982, 2701, para. 11; ECJ, 27.2.1980, case 168/78 *(Commissionv. France)*, ECR 1980, 347, para. 41.
326. ECJ, 27.2.1980, case 170/78 *(Commission v. United Kingdom)*, ECR 1980, 417, para. 10; ECJ, 9.7.1987, case 356/85 *(Commission v. Belgium)*, ECR 1987, 3299, paras 14 et seq. Sometimes the first step is even ignored, cf. ECJ, 30.11.1995, case C-113/94 *(Casarin)*, I-4203, paras 24 et seq.
327. Balke, *Steuerliche Gestaltungsfreiheit*, p. 141 et seq.; Schön, EuR 2001, p. 341 (347).
328. See also ECJ, 11.8.1995, joint cases C-367/93 to C-377/93 *(Roders etal.)*, ECR 1995, I-2229, para. 39; ECJ, 9.7.1987, case 356/85 *(Commission v. Belgium)*, ECR 1987,3299, paras 16 et seq. In earlier times, the Court was less certain on this issue, mainly due to inaccuracies in naming

such as environmental concerns. However, the presumption of protective effects founded on their influence of competitive positions can only be rebutted if those extra-fiscal objectives are pursued in a proportionate way. Chiefly, it is mandatory that any system based on such criteria follows a smooth line of progression coherent to the underlying objectives of taxation.[329] In fact, since Article 90 (2) takes expressly into account the - objectively - intended effects of national legislation, reasons which would otherwise be considered a legitimate justification are already blended into the infringement test.

The question has been raised if Article 90 (2) can also be applied when a foreign product is similar to a domestic one but also competes with other, dissimilar domestic products.[330] To put it differently, it can be asked if the relationship between Article 90 (1) and Article 90 (2) is necessarily one of exclusivity, or if the two provisions may be considered cumulatively if there exist different groups of competing products. The ECJ has not taken a clear position on this issue. On the one hand, some decisions indicate that the Court sees no need for enforcing Article 90 (2) if there exists a substantial domestic production of similar goods. Article 90 (2) was never expressly considered once the substantial scope of Article 90 (1) was held to be relevant.[331] If the domestic competition could be considered *quantité negligible,* it was ignored entirely by the ECJ, and in this quasi-absence of similar products Article 90 (2) could be applied without further reasoning.[332] On the other hand, it has already been stated that the Court frequently applies Article 90 as such without further differentiation and examines if the system of indirect taxation has any discriminative *or* protective effects. This comprehensive approach hints at the cumulative application of both concepts.

Some scholars believe that a relationship of strict exclusivity would be the appropriate one, but do not give a detailed explanation for this.[333] We respectfully submit that Article 90 (1) and (2) should be seen as complementing each other, so that the latter provision is not rendered inapplicable only because a tax rule has been confirmed not to be discriminating.[334] This solution avoids all-or-nothing results and counterbalances the wide margin of appreciation immanent to the concept of similarity. Indeed, from a substantial rather than formal approach, the principle of proportional differentiation inherent to Article 90 (2) can be seen as a notion of non-discrimination as well.[335] Oftentimes, the boundaries between Article 90 (1) and (2)

---

the relative group of comparison, cf. ECJ, 27.2.1980, case 170/78 *(Commission v. United Kingdom), ECR* 1980, 417, paras 18 et seq.

329. Cf.ECJ, 7.5.1987, case 184/85 *(Commission v. Italy),* ECR 1987, 2013, para. 13; ECJ, 9.5.1985, case 112/84 (Humblot), ECR 1985, 1375, paras 14 et seq. See also Lyal, *EC Tax Review* 2003, p. 68 (74).
330. Balke, *Steuerliche Gestaltungsfreiheit,* p. 142 et seq.
331. Cf. for example ECJ, 4.3.1986, case 243/84 *(John Walker),* ECR 1986, 875, paras 21 et seq. For a detailed analysis consult Balke, *Gestaltungsfreiheit,* p. 145 et seq.
332. ECJ, ECR 1987, 2013; ECJ, ECR 1987, 3299. Less clear ECJ, 18.4.1991, case C-230/89 *(Commission v. Greece),* ECR 1991, I-1909, para. 15.
333. Balke, *Steuerliche Gestaltungsfreiheit,* p. 146 et seq.; Schön, EuR 2001, p. 341 (348); Wyatt/ Dashwood, *European Community Law,* 3rdedn, p. 199 et seq. See also *Everling,* Stbg 1988, p. 281 (286).
334. Like here Terra/Wattel, *European Tax Law,* p. 8.
335. Lyal, *EC Tax Review* 2003, p. 68.

will be blurred,[336] depending on the details taken into consideration to ascertain if two products serve similar consumer needs. If the affirmation of Article 90 (1) rules out any further analysis of indirect taxes on other competing goods, the results may be arbitrary. If for example a national system of turnover taxation of fruit distinguishes between bananas and other fruit, these two products may or may not be considered similar depending on how narrowly consumer needs and product characteristics are defined. If there exists any domestic production of bananas, albeit a small one, a foreign supplier of bananas might have to content himself with a tax system that provides for an equal indirect tax on bananas regardless of their origin. The taxation of other fruit could only be scrutinized if they were deemed similar to bananas. Otherwise, even great differences in the level of taxation could not be rebuked before the Court. Such differences may have a protective potential, though, and cannot be categorized as mere internal inconsistencies, if the main competitor of imported bananas is locally produced dessert fruit rather than domestic bananas. The Court resolves constellations like this one by requiring a substantial domestic production for the application of Article 90 (1).[337] However, there is no sound reason for setting aside the discrimination test if the quantity of similar goods produced in the domestic market can be 'neglected'. Indeed, if strictly applied, this theory will lead to unsatisfactory results if the national tax system favours the domestic production by making tax concessions. If this production is to be ignored because of its small amount, a clear breach of competitive neutrality and cross-border ability to pay could not be rebutted by invoking Article 90. Moreover, the concept of a *quantité negligible* is again prone to arbitrary results.

A cumulative analysis based on Article 90 (1) and (2) avoids the described uncertainties, dogmatic weaknesses and unconvincing results. It is also consistent with the wording of Article 90 which does not give any clue for a restrictive interpretation in the sense of exclusivity between discriminative and protective effects. Finally, an extended application of Article 90 (2) should not lead to an excessive loss of national tax sovereignty: As the essence of this provision is proportional rather than equal taxation, there remains sufficient leeway for Member States in designing their tax system.

Altogether, Article 90 (2) provides a flexible instrument to judge a Member State's entire system of indirect taxation, complementing Article 90 (1) and balancing the exigencies of the internal market and Member States' remaining competence to design their tax system. Notwithstanding the different legal consequences of the respective paragraphs, one can therefore claim a harmonious standard of protection for free competition comprised of Article 90 (1) and (2).[338]

336. Cf. Schwarze/Stumpf, *EU-Kommentar,* Art. 90 EGV, para. 26; Farmer/Lyal, *EC Tax Law,* p. 56.
337. ECJ, case 184/85 *(Commission v. Italy),* ECR 1987, 2013, para. 8.
338. Too far-reaching Easson, CMLR 1981, p. 521 (535 et seq.); Danusso/Denton, LIEI1990, p. 67 (69): 'Single' standard. See also Stumpf, EuZW 1991, p. 713 (714).

[C] Non-discrimination of Domestic Competitors in the Foreign Market

EC law does not yet prevent a national legislator from discriminating domestic goods against competing foreign products in the domestic market.[339] This kind of 'reverse' discrimination lacks the pan-European component required by Article 90 and Article 49 (1). Even though it is not a purely internal situation, given that the fiscal detriment is determined in comparison to products imported from other Member States, the aforementioned provisions prohibit only discrimination of cross-border trade and services. The inverted situation is not covered by them, and may only be subject to revision once a general provision of equal treatment before the law will be expressly incorporated into the EC Treaty or a future European Constitution. Until then, it is up to the national constitutional law and the national legislator to tackle reverse discrimination. [340]

To be distinguished from the above constellation is the imposition of different tax burdens on domestic products depending on their local or foreign point of sale. If higher taxes are imposed on exported goods than on those domestically consumed, a discrimination of cross-border trade occurs. Article 90 does not explicitly prohibit such discrimination, as it regulates only the taxation of imported goods. It cannot be qualified as a forbidden charge having an effect equivalent to a customs duty in the sense of Article 25, either. The essential feature of such a charge is that it is levied on the product solely because it crosses the border as such, and must be borne only by exported goods.[341] If the export tax forms part of the internal system of taxation, but is raised in a discriminatory way, Article 25 is not relevant.

The ECJ has filled this gap by interpreting Article 90 in such a way that it covers also discrimination caused by the levy of a comparatively higher indirect tax upon exportation. The Court has founded this reasoning on a systematic analysis of the tax-relevant provisions of the EC Treaty. It has stated that a discrimination of exported goods would be inconsistent with the objective of tax neutrality towards cross-border trade immanent to Articles 91 to 93.[342] In fact, the necessity to protect outbound cross-border trade just as well as inbound can be deducted even more clearly from the general Treaty objective of free movement within an internal market, laid down in Articles 3(1) (c), 14 (2).[343] All fundamental freedoms are by now applied on inbound and outbound situations alike, prohibiting discrimination of cross-border activities as such, and only residually of foreign nationals or goods. Since Article 90 is only a

339. Cf. ECJ, 13.3.1979, case 86/78 *(Peureux)*, ECR 1979, 897, para. 38; ECJ, 22.6.1976, case 127/75 (38; ECJ, 22.6.1976, case 127/75 *(Bobie)*, ECR 1976, 1079, para. 3; Schwarze/Stumpf, *EU-Kommentar*, Art. 90 EGV, para. 20.
340. Cf. Wouters, *EC Tax Review* 1999, p. 98 (105 et seq.).
341. ECJ, 22.5.2003, case C-355/00 *(Freskot)*, ECR 2003, I-5363, para. 42; ECJ, 21.9.2000, joined cases C-441/98 and C-442/98 *(Michaïlidis)*, ECR 2000, I-7145, para. 22.
342. ECJ, 22.5.2003, case C-355/00 *(Freskot)*, ECR 2003, I-5363, para. 45; ECJ, 23.4.2002, case C-234/99 *(Nygård)*, ECR 2002, I-3657, para. 41; ECJ, 29.6.1978, case 142/77 *(Statens Control)*, ECR 1978, 1543, para. 21/27. Supported by Schön, EuR 2001, p. 341 (354); Schwarze/Stumpf, *EU-Kommentar*, Art. 90 EGV, para. 28; Balke, *Steuerliche Gestaltungsfreiheit*, p. 27 et seq.
343. Similar reasoning by von der Groeben/Schwarze/Eilers/Bahns/Sedlaczek, EUV/EGV, 6th edn, Art. 90 EGV, para. 14.

tax-specific expression of the general provision on the free movement of goods, it should be applied in line with these dogmatic developments. In fact, the ECJ practices an application by analogy, without expressly stating it, because it fills a legal gap by referring to Article 90 which regulates the comparable issue of taxing imported goods.[344]

As to the forbidden discrimination, reference can be made to the above exposition regarding imported foreign goods. It should be noted, however, that in an export situation, only Article 90 (1) is of relevance for the examination. Since exported and domestically consumed goods all stem from domestic production, a surtax or higher tax on exported goods is never suitable to afford indirect protection to the local industry in the sense of Article 90 (2).

[D] Abolition of International Double Taxation

On various occasions, the ECJ has expressed its firm conviction that Community law does not contain any provision designed to prohibit the effects of double taxation in the field of indirect taxation. The elimination of such effects could only be accomplished by harmonization efforts.[345] An exception has only been made in the area of harmonized VAT. Here, the Court has stated that the importing Member State may levy VAT only to the extent to which the imported good is still free of a VAT burden resulting from its taxation in the Member State of origin. It has substantiated its findings by making reference to the fundamental Treaty objective of a Common Market, in which all obstacles to free trade between Member States are abolished. In the light of this objective, a double taxation both in the State of origin and the State of destination is considered to be an *indirect* levy of a higher tax forbidden by Article 90 (1). The importing Member State may not ignore the amount of VAT that is still borne by a foreign product at the moment of its importation.[346]

The findings of the ECJ are somewhat surprising, if not contradictory. To judge upon the permissibility of double taxation, the Court is certainly right to resort to the basic provisions on the internal market as a guideline for interpretation. There can be no doubt that double taxation causes a specific tax burden sustained only by goods that are moved from one Member State to another. Just as in the case of direct taxes, this effect disadvantages cross-border commerce and is therefore incompatible with an internal market without obstacles, as between Member States, to the free movement of goods, Article 3(1) (c). But from this basic point on, we can no longer follow the Court's reasoning.

344. Schön, EuR 2001, p. 341 (354).
345. ECJ, 23.4.2002, case C-234/99 *(Nygård)*, ECR 2002, I-3657, para. 41; ECJ, 27.10.1993, case C-72/92 *(Scharbatke)*, *ECR* 1993, I-5509, para. 15; ECJ, 29.6.1978, case 142/77 *(StatensControl)*, ECR 1978, 1543, para. 33/36.
346. ECJ, 26.2.1991, case C-119/89 *(Commission v. Spain)*, ECR 1991, I-641, para. 6; ECJ, 26.2.1991, case C-120/88 *(Commission v. Italy)*, *ECR* 1991, I-621, para. 6; ECJ, 25.2.1988, case 299/86 *(Drexl)*, *ECR* 1988, 1213, paras 10–12; ECJ, 23.1.1986, case 39/85 *(Bergeres-Becque)*, ECR 1986, 259, paras 8 et seq.; ECJ, 21.5.1985, case 47/84 *(Schul II)*, ECR 1985, 1491, paras 16 et seq. and 21–23; ECJ, 5.5.1982, case 15/81 *(Schull)*, ECR 1982,1409, paras 31–34.

First, the aforementioned conclusion must certainly hold true not only for VAT taxation, but for all genuine indirect taxes which are supposed to be shifted to the final consumer. Any international accumulation of such indirect tax in the State of origin and the State of destination will lead to an extra burden either for the foreign supplier or, if all taxes can be shifted due to initial competitive advantages, for the domestic consumer. In both cases, the concept of equal taxation of equal cross-border ability to pay is impaired. Of course, it is easier to determine the amount of foreign indirect tax still resting on an imported good if the assessable tax base is alike in both Member States, as is the case in harmonized VAT matters. However, the ECJ has never accepted administrative difficulties as an excuse for maintaining substantial disadvantages for cross-border trade. In the field of indirect taxation, it has even stated that Member States must abolish a progressive tax system that might cause higher tax burdens for cross-border trade if it means that it is impossible to determine the respective tax class for foreign products due to administrative difficulties.[347]

Thus, international double taxation is prohibited by the EC Treaty for all kinds of indirect taxes. It seems inadequate, though, to implement this finding by a wide interpretation of forbidden indirect discrimination as stipulated in Article 90 (1). As has already been pointed out, such national treatment obligations are characterized by the fact that one single national legislator is responsible for a higher taxation of cross-border trade by levying higher taxes, regardless of the tax treatment in the other Member State involved. On the contrary, international double taxation stems from the simultaneous taxation in two tax jurisdiction, each of which does not discriminate from a national point of view. The essential issue in these constellations is which Member State can be held responsible for the extra tax burden that becomes obvious from the supranational perspective required by Articles 3(1) (c), 14 (2). Thus, one should either apply Article 90 only by analogy, or preferably discuss the issue in the context of the general provision of free movement of goods.

Second, the aforementioned administrative difficulties will in fact not arise or will at least be manageable if one attributes the responsibility for the abolition of double taxation in consistency with the underlying principles of indirect taxation. Indirect taxes are characterized by the fact that they are intended to be borne by the ultimate consumer of goods or services rather than by their supplier.[348] For that reason, it is accepted international practice that they shall be levied in the State of destination where the product is consumed. It is obvious that the country-of-destination principle is the underlying motive both of Article III.2 GATT and of Article 90 (1) in combination with Article 91 EC Treaty.[349] Furthermore, this principle has, with only few exceptions, been implemented in all relevant EC directives which aim at the harmonization of indirect taxes. It can be deducted from Articles 8 *et seq.* of the Sixth VAT directive,[350]

347. ECJ, 17.2.1976, case 45/75 (REWE), ECR 1976, 181, para. 15; see also ECJ, 8.1.1980, case 21/79 (Commission *v. Italy)*, ECR 1980, 1, para. 16.
348. Cf. Schön, RIW 2004, p. 50 (58).
349. Cf. Scharze/Stumpf, *EU-Kommentar*, Art. 90 EG-Vertrag, para. 4.
350. Sixth Council Directive of 17 May 1977 on the harmonization of the laws of the Member States relating to turnover taxes – Common system of value added tax: uniform basis of assessment

as well as from the preamble and Article 7 of the General Directive on excise duties.[351] Even those who favour VAT taxation in the state of origin as a long-term objective, such as the European Commission[352] and some scholars,[353] agree that the VAT rate would have to be a uniform one or that of the country of destination, and that the revenue should be transferred to the treasury of the latter. Therefore, it can be assumed that the 'destination-country entitlement' is a general principle of inter-nation equity as regards indirect taxes[354], at least in the European Union.

Consequently, the responsibility for removing international double taxation lies with the Member State of origin, unless otherwise agreed between Member States. The authorization of Member States to refund indirect taxes upon exportation of goods stipulated in Article 91 thus turns into an obligation, insofar as the importing Member State levies turnover taxes on the same good. The Member State of origin should also be sufficiently informed to determine to what extent a certain good is burdened with indirect taxes when it leaves its jurisdiction. The opposite approach of the ECJ, quoting an obligation of the Member State of destination, is misled by the inappropriate application of Article 90 (1). Furthermore, it is inconsistent to rule that Article 90 (1) applies on outbound as well as on inbound trade, but only take into account the latter to establish a supposed responsibility to abolish double taxation.

[E] Possible Justifications for Unequal Taxation

It has been stated that, unlike the fundamental freedoms, Article 90 (1) does not permit any kind of justification for discriminative taxation.[355] We would like to question that statement. After all, it would be quite surprising if imperative reasons of national interest should be suitable to defend discrimination in the field of direct taxation, whereas in indirect taxation the freedom of competition should prevail over all other Community or national objectives. Especially national provisions which warrant an effective, substantial equality in the levy of indirect taxes should not be disregarded *a priori,* since both direct as well as indirect taxation must comply with the principle of

(77/388/EEC), see also Cnossen, Bulletin I.F.D. 2003, p. 434 (442). Even though on cross-border services, the country-of-destination principle is applied to a more limited extent, it still is the general rule of VAT taxation, cf. Kogels, *EC Tax Review* 1999, p. 117 (118). Moreover, the Commission is planning to gear taxation of services even more towards a taxation in the country of consumption, see the follow-up report on its strategic programme that it adopted in 2000 (see IP/00/615) for the improvement of the VAT system (IP/03/1447, dating from 24.10.2003).

351. Council Directive 92/12/EEC of 25 February 1992 on the general arrangements for products subject to excise duty and on the holding, movement and monitoring of such products.
352. See Communication from the Commission to the Council and the European Parliament - A strategy to improve the operation of the VAT system within the context of the internal market, COM/2000/0348 final, para. 12 with further references.
353. Cf. Vanistendael, *EC Tax Review* 1995, p. 45 et seq.; Gutachten der Ursprungslandkommission, BMF (editor), Vol. 52, p. 13 et seq. For further references, consult Cnossen, Bulletin I.F.D. 2003, p. 434 (439 et seq.).
354. The term taxes is used in a strict sense here, excluding para-fiscal charges and tolls.
355. Schön, EuR 2001, p. 341 (342); Danusso/Denton, *Legal Issues of European Integration,* 1990, p. 67 (75).

equality in effective burdens on similar ability to pay. Not surprisingly, an in-depth analysis of the case law on indirect taxes uncovers some parallels in the Court's handling of justifications put forward by national governments in the area of direct taxation.

From early on, the ECJ has indicated that the prohibition of any discrimination or indirect protection laid down in Article 90 is directly applicable and does not require prior Community harmonization of the tax in question[356]. Implicitly, the Court has also rejected budgetary reasons as a valid justification for discriminative taxation[357]. As regards these aspects, the Court does not differ from its jurisprudence regarding direct taxes.

The same holds true when Member States claimed the need for effective fiscal controls. Substantial discrimination, i.e. discrimination that potentially leads to a higher tax burden, has been turned down by the ECJ regardless of any simplification purposes which the Member States put forward in its defence. In particular, irrebuttable legal presumptions or lump-sum rules which were applied only to imported goods have been held to be incompatible with Article 90 (1) if they could, albeit only in some cases, lead to higher charges on foreign products.[358] However, Member States may establish specific procedural requirements that only affect imported goods, if this is necessary to ascertain the prerequisites for a tax concession.[359] In this context, refutable presumptions have been admitted by the Court as one possibility to facilitate tax assessment of imported goods.[360] The ECJ does not dedicate any dogmatic reasoning to its findings. However, there can be no doubt that discrimination or indirect protection may lie also in a different procedural treatment, especially since the concept of a higher tax burden put down in Article 90 (1) has been interpreted widely by the Court. Hence, the aforementioned disadvantageous procedural requirements constitute a breach of Article 90 which can only be justified by *proportionate* reasons of effective fiscal administration and control. Just as with direct taxes, the ECJ only deems proportional procedural rather than a material discrimination.

Furthermore, as has already been indicated above, motives of social, environmental or economic control should be considered as legitimate justifications for unequal tax treatment of similar products. The alternative solution of the ECJ to exchange the similarity standard on the grounds of such national policy objectives ignores the underlying conflict of diverging Community and national interests, fails to

356. ECJ, 27.2.1980, case 171/78 *(Commission v. Denmark)*, ECR 1980, 465, para. 20.
357. ECJ, 21.5.1985, case 47/84 *(Schul II)*, ECR 1985, 1491, paras 13 and 16: In this case the Commission had put forward that a restriction of taxation rights on part of the state of destination in order to avoid double taxation would result in undesirable revenue losses for this country's treasury. The ECJ has ignored this objection, making remission to the need of implementing the principles of Art. 90 EC Treaty.
358. ECJ, 2.4.1998, case C-213/96 *(Outokumpu)*, ECR 1998, I-1777, paras 37–40; ECJ, 23.10.1997, case C-375/95 *(Commission v.* Greece), ECR 1997, I-5981, para. 47; ECJ, 17.2.1976, case 45/75 (REWE), ECR 1976, 181, para. 15.
359. ECJ, 5.5.1982, case 15/81 *(Schul)*, ECR 1982,1409, paras 36 and 39.
360. ECJ, 19.9.2002, case C-101/00 *(TulliasiamiesandSiliin)*, ECR 2002, I-7487, paras 88 et seq.; ECJ, 22.2.2001, case C-393/98 *(Gomes Valente)*, ECR 2001, I-1327, paras 31 et seq.

bring them into a proportional balance and leads to dogmatically unsatisfactory test patterns in the application of Article 90 (1).

Finally, one might ask if there even exists some kind of coherence principle in the area of indirect taxation as well. The essence of such a principle would lie in a compensation of indirect taxes borne by domestic goods, but at earlier stages of production or sale at which the product is not yet similar to the imported one which is charged with an offsetting tax once it crosses the border. An early decision of the ECJ3[361] which seemingly contradicts this thesis is in fact irrelevant, because it concerned fees rather than a genuine indirect tax in the sense employed in this study. Fees are charges which compensate a direct consideration, thus it is evident that they must be raised in accordance with the costs incurred or benefits obtained. Consequently, such a fee cannot be levied upon importation to counterbalance fees paid for services on domestically produced goods. As regards indirect taxes, the issue is different, since they are supposed to be shifted in the price of a certain good and to be borne by its respective consumer. Consequently, the ECJ has stated that the comparison of tax burdens must take into account any turnover taxes levied on the product at any stage of production or distribution.[362] Based on such considerations, the Court has indeed already accepted a higher taxation of imported products when the similar domestic product carried a tax burden resulting from its taxation at a time when it was not yet similar: In the *Schul* case and in subsequent cases, it has conceded Member States the right to tax a used cars imported by its private owner even when the corresponding domestic sale of a used car did not trigger such taxation.[363] The ECJ reasoned that a domestically sold used car was still partially burdened with VAT charged on the sale of new cars and shifted in the resale price, whereas a privately imported car had never before been taxed in the respective Member State. Even though this case is atypical insofar as a private vendor was charged a turnover tax, the essential finding can be generalized. If an imported good is taxed higher than a similar locally produced one, this may be justified by the fact that the latter carries a turnover tax imposed at an earlier production or retail stage.[364] This way, the consumer is effectively taxed according to his/her ability to pay expressed in his/her purchase of products and independently of the product origin. However, as Article 90 (1) expressly mentions taxes imposed directly *and indirectly* on domestic products, such reasoning need not be invoked as justification. The focus of Article 90 (1) is obviously wider than the one employed in the context of the fundamental freedoms as interpreted by the ECJ in the field of direct taxation. Therefore, compensating tax burdens already eliminate the supposed discrimination of the foreign product.

361. ECJ, 20.3.1984 *(Commission v. Belgium)*, ECR 1984, paras 22 et seq.
362. ECJ, 10.7.1984, case 42/83 *(Dansk Denkavit)*, ECR 1984, 2649, para. 29.
363. ECJ, 5.5.1982, case 15/81 *(Schull)*, ECR 1982, 1409, paras 29 etseq.; ECJ, 23.1.1986, case 39/85 *(Bergeres- Becque)*, ECR 1986, 259, paras 8 et seq. The disputed taxation rule was only held to be incompatible with Art. 90 (1) because it led to an international double taxation. See also ECJ, 29.4.2004, case C-387/01 *(Weigel)*, not yet published, para. 68.
364. See also Schön, EuR 2001, p. 341 (345).

§9.05 OTHER CONSTITUTIONAL PRINCIPLES

There are some other constitutional principles inherent to the European Tax Order but not derived from the EC Treaty itself. Mainly, they can be developed on grounds of the European Convention on Human Rights. The adopted, but still to be ratified Constitution for Europe seeks to incorporate the fundamental rights laid down there directly into the legal order of the EU by declaring them general principles of the Union's law and orientating its Charter of Fundamental Rights according to them. Since the present Article 6 (2) EU Treaty makes remission to them, and all Member States have sought accession to the Convention, it is nevertheless obvious that its tax-relevant provisions already form part of the European Legal Tax Order.[365] The only difference to their possible future status in Community law is that a violation of these principles by national tax laws may not as yet be subjected to a preliminary ruling of the ECJ, because Article 234 EC Treaty limits this action to questions concerning 'the interpretation of this treaty'. This might change once Article III-274 of the Constitution enters into force which widens the scope of preliminary rulings to issues concerning the interpretation of the Constitution, including its Charter on Fundamental Rights.

As regards principles of tax justice, the three most important ones established by the European Commission of Human Rights (ECn) and the European Court of Human Rights (ECt) are legality of taxation, legal certainty and the prohibition of confiscatory or excessive taxation.[366] These are fundamental principles which can also be found in Member States' constitutional law. It is noteworthy, though, that neither the ECn nor the ECt have ever held any legal provision brought under their scrutiny incompatible with these requirements; the only successful complaints concerned singular measures in the enforcement of a tax claim which evidently were excessive.[367] Hence, it can be stated that the limits of taxation imposed by the Convention have not yet been fully explored by the competent organs.

Notwithstanding this conclusion, the approach which they take in elaborating the above-mentioned tax principles can be considered as guiding the way to future effectuation of freedom rights in the area of taxation. Apart from procedural aspects, the key provision for the jurisprudence of ECn and ECt has been the protection of property as stipulated in Article 1(1) of the Convention. At first sight, this seems odd because its Article 1 (2) expressly provides that the 'peaceful enjoyment of possessions' protected by the first paragraph shall not in any way 'impair the right of a State to enforce such laws as it deems necessary to ... secure the payment of taxes'. However, from the beginning the ECn has interpreted the second paragraph not as a partial

365. See also Tridimas, *The General Principles of EC Law*, p. 237: 'Although the Community is not formally bound by [the Convention]... the Community is bound to respect, as a minimum, the standards of the Convention which forms an integral part of Community law.'

366. ECt, 21.5.2002, Application No. 28856/95 *(Jokela)*, para. 48; ECn, 15.5.1996, Application No. 27109/95 *(Kaira)*, para. 1; ECn, 16.1.1995, Application No. 15117/89 *(Travers)*, para. 4; ECn, 14.12.1988, Application No. 13013/87 *(Wasa)*. For further references see Baker, ET 2000, p. 299 (302 et seq.).

367. ECn, 2.7.1997, Application No. 26242/95 *(Lemoine)*; ECn, 5.12.1991, Application No. 13616/88 *(Hen- trich)*.

exception to the substantial scope of the right to property, but as a special justification which must fulfil certain unwritten principles underlying the Convention. As such, the ECn and the ECt have named the need for a legitimate aim[368] and the principle of proportionality.[369] In subsequent decisions the ECt has also demanded a 'qualitative' legality of taxation rules affecting the right to property.[370] The latter has been specified as to include foresee ability and publicity of the law. The principle of proportionality has practically been reduced to a prohibition of excessive taxation, since ECn and ECt have conceded to the contracting states a 'wide margin of appreciation' as to the levy and design of national taxes.

This approach clearly reflects the constitutional traditions and beliefs of the majority of the Member States. Most of them actually do understand taxation as a *prima facie* interference with the right of possessions;[371] the controversial German debate about this issue is a national peculiarity and, moreover, largely overcome.[372] At the same time, it becomes apparent that the proportionality principle is generally a paper tiger in the constitutional limitation of taxing powers by way of invoking freedom rights. Since the levy of a tax will in general be suitable, necessary and adequate in the light of its objective to finance public spending, proportionality condenses to non-confiscation. Only when tax laws are used to control economic or social behaviour, may it play a greater role, since these goals may be balanced against the tax-induced impairment of the right to property. The essential task of the freedom rights on a European level lies in another aspect: they open the door for the consideration of other constitutional principles which must be respected if the infringement of the right to property or of other basic rights is to be held legitimate.[373] Such principles would be, for example, the aforementioned fundamental elements of any national or supranational jurisdiction governed by the rule of law such as legality, legal certainty, and protection of taxpayers' legitimate expectations.[374] Here again, the requirements of a European Tax Order do not substitute or derogate national constitutional prerequisites, but rather enhance and eventually further develop them in a process of mutual fructification.

368. ECn, 14.12.1988, Application No. 13013/87 *(Wasa Liv)*.
369. ECt, 23.2.1995, 23.2.1995, Application No. 15375/89 *(Gasus)*, para. 62; ECn, 14.12.1988, Application No. 13013/87 *(Wasa Liv)*. The parallels to the interpretation of the seeming exceptions to the free movement of capital laid down in Art. 58 EC Treaty in the consistent practice of the ECJ are striking. It is evident that supranational institutions tend to interpret their competencies widely and exceptions to them narrowly for sake of their efficiency.
370. ECtHR, 9.11.1999, Application 26449/95 *(Špaček)*, para. 54.
371. Cf. for example Baker, ET 2000, p. 298 (301).
372. Cf. Englisch, StuW 2003, p. 237 et seq.
373. Such a development can already be made out in the case law of the ECJ, because the Court does interpret the basic freedoms also as true freedom rights, at least in areas other than tax law. An illustration is provided by the ruling in the *Carpenter* case where the right to respect for family life was at issue, ECJ, 11.7.2002, case 60/00 *(Carpenter)*, ECR 2002, I-6305.
374. Cf. Farmer, *EC Tax Review* 2003, p. 75 (79).

Annex to Chapter 9: Recent developments in the European Legal Tax Order*

Werner C. Haslehner

I INTRODUCTION

Since the publication of the first edition of this volume, considerable formal and -to a lesser extent - material changes in the setup of the European Legal Order have implicated an unchanged need for a European Legal Tax Order. Legislative constitutional developments entailing both the enlargement to 27 Member States and the further consolidation of the Union, first through the failed attempt of a 'Constitutional Treaty', then through the ratification of the Lisbon Treaty, have to be contrasted with a remarkably changed attitude of the European Court of Justice (ECJ) regarding negative integration in the area of (direct) taxation, which increasingly focuses on possible justifications for unequal treatment by the Member States. Both areas are briefly considered in this update to the analysis of Lang and Englisch. In particular, it will be examined whether the Court of Justice has taken any steps into the direction suggested by the authors to further a European Legal Tax Order based on the ability to pay principle.

II DEVELOPMENTS OF EUROPEAN CONSTITUTIONALISM AND THE EUROPEAN LEGAL TAX ORDER

[A] Legislative Developments: Enlargement, the failed Constitution and the Lisbon Treaty

Since the time of first writing of the above chapter, the European Union has changed in several ways, though not in all respects as expected six years ago. The EU has grown

* This annex updates the previous chapter by Joachim Lang and Joachim Englisch.

to 27 Member States with the accession of Bulgaria and Romania in 2007, arguably increasing tax competition among Member States and thus the pressure to harmonise tax laws. However, the Treaty establishing a Constitution for Europe, intended to bring the EU closer together in substance as well as in form, though signed in 2004, was rejected by popular votes in France and the Netherlands and eventually replaced by the Treaty of Lisbon: Maintaining almost all substantive changes envisaged by the Constitutional Treaty, it removed most of its symbolic features.[1] However, there is no difference between the two and almost no change to the situation under the Treaty of Nice as far as the competences and substantive rules relevant for taxation are concerned. The relevant treaty provisions retain a materially unaltered wording.[2] The only discernible difference to earlier treaties in this respect lies in the repeal of Article 293 EC, which obliges the Member States to engage in negotiations to abolish double taxation within the Community. The consequences of the failure to include a similar provision in the new treaties are, however, unclear: Some scholars claim that it means a loss of competence of the EU to pass legislation relieving double taxation in the internal market,[3] with others taking the opposite position, claiming the deletion has given the EU exclusive competence in that field,[4] and some expecting little to no consequences.[5] As far as effects on the justiciability of situations resulting in double taxation among Member States are concerned, the opinions are equally diverse: Specifically, it has been argued that the repeal strengthens the obligation on the Member States by removing a restriction to the direct effect of the Union objective to abolish double taxation.[6] It appears not very convincing, however, to assume that the original function of Article 293 EC had been to strengthen Member States' autonomy against obligations put on them by other provisions of the Treaties, rather than being an – unjusticiable – obligation on them;[7] it is thus equally unconvincing to assume a strengthened obligation to prevent double taxation after its deletion.[8] Naturally though, the ECJ has not yet had the opportunity to shed light on that question.[9]

1. For an early comprehensive analysis of the Lisbon Treaty see M. Dougan, *Common Market Law Review* 2008, p. 617.
2. M. Nieminen, *Bulletin for International Taxation* 2010, p. 330 (333), noting only one procedural change regarding the possible extension of the freedom to provide services in Article 56 TFEU, i.e. the involvement of the European Parliament.
3. M. Lehner, *British Tax Review* 2005, p. 337 (338 et seq).
4. I. Schwartz and W. Mölls in: von der Groeben/Schwarze, *Kommentar zum EGV/EUV* (2004) Artikel 293 para. 43; undecided L. Cerioni, *Bulletin for International Taxation* 2009, p. 543 (555), who states as one possible consequence the removal of a competence to conclude multilateral conventions by the Member States, thus giving both bilateral treaties and possible harmonizing measures more importance.
5. L. Hinnekens, *Intertax* 2009, p. 602 (606).
6. E.C.C.M. Kemmeren, *EC Tax Review* 2008, p. 156 (157 et seq); similarly L. Cerioni, *Bulletin for International Taxation* 2009, p. 543 (555); different M. Nieminen, *Bulletin for International Taxation* 2010, p. 330 (331 et seq), who detects no material change because of the repeal.
7. B. Knobbe-Keuk, *EC Tax Review* 1994, p. 74 (76); A. de Graaf, *EC Tax Review* 1998, p. 258 (271); P. Pistone, *The Impact of Community Law on Tax Treaties* (2002) p. 77; G. Kofler, *Doppelbesteuerungsabkommen und Europäisches Gemeinschaftsrecht* (2007) p. 381 et seq; M. Nieminen, *Bulletin for International Taxation* 2010, p. 330 (331).
8. L. Hinnekens, *Intertax* 2009, p. 602 (606); O. Marres, *Intertax* 2011, p. 112 (116).
9. As regards the developments on the prohibition of juridical double taxation in the ECJ case law thus far (i.e. before the deletion of Art 293 EC), see *infra* III.D.

[B] Fundamental Rights

[1] EU Charter of Fundamental Rights

The coming into force of the Lisbon Treaty has also resulted in a changed legal value of the Charter of Fundamental Rights of the European Union[10] (ChFR), which is now explicitly put at the same level as the Treaties by Article 6 TEU. The impact of this development remains yet to be seen, although it is expected to be of rather little influence especially as far as the Member States' tax laws are concerned: First, the relevant substantive rights included in the ChFR have long been recognized by the ECJ as fundamental rights in its case law;[11] secondly, the ChFR makes no mention of taxation at all, let alone establish concrete principles for it; thirdly, the applicability of the ChFR to national laws is restricted by Article 51 ChFR to the extent that they are 'implementing Union law'. Though the exact meaning of this is disputed, the applicability of the ChFR in the area of direct taxation is at the very least restricted to exceptional circumstances.[12] By contrast, the influence of the ChFR may prove to be greater in the area of indirect taxation, which is widely regulated by secondary law: Partly because the rights in the ChFR go beyond the scope of general principles of EU law as recognized by the ECJ, partly because the ECJ may be more willing to set stricter boundaries for EU legislative acts on the basis of rights explicitly recognized in the TEU to have the status of supreme primary law. The 'margin of discretion' granted so far to the EU legislator in ECJ case law[13] could be reduced as a consequence, and principles such as fiscal neutrality and taxation according to ability to pay be demanded more forcefully by the judges.

[2] Accession to the ECHR

The Lisbon Treaty also obliges the EU to accede to the European Convention of Human Rights and Fundamental Freedoms (ECHR).[14] This will further formalize the binding nature of the ECHR for any act of EU law; since the ECJ has long recognized these rights to constitute a part of European fundamental rights, which are binding as general principles of EU law[15], that appears to be of little practical relevance. Even in so far as

10. OJ [2010] C 83/02.
11. This is true especially with regard to the right to equal treatment, cf. Articles 20 et seq. ChFR.
12. Only on a very broad understanding of the problematic *ERT-doctrine* could it be argued that all taxation of intra-union cross-border situations has to be considered an act 'within the scope' of EU law, and subsequently establish the need for the interpretation of the fundamental freedoms in accordance with the ability to pay principle as a tax specific formulation of the right to equality. For a discussion and critique of the controversial *'ERT-doctrine'* underlying this question, see M. Huber, *European Public Law* 2008, p. 323.
13. Regarding the ECJ's unsatisfyingly restrained approach in the area of indirect taxation thus far see J. Englisch in: *Traditional and Alternative Routes to European Tax Integration* (2010), p. 231.
14. Article 6 para. 2 TEU.
15. Cf. ECJ 14 May 1974, case 4/73 (*Nold*) ECR 1974, 491, para. 13; ECJ 18 June 1991, case C-260/89 (*ERT*) ECR 1991, I-2925, para. 41; ECJ 6 March 2001, case C-274/99 (*Connolly /*

it may lead to a mandate of the European Court of Human Rights (ECtHR) to review secondary EU law, e.g. the VAT directives, little should be expected from such 'external review', as the ECtHR has, in earlier cases,[16] already accepted a high margin of appreciation for the Union legislator that hardly differs from that applied by the ECJ itself.

[C] Fundamental Freedoms

With respect to the fundamental freedoms as basic 'quasi-constitutional yardstick' for national law, two developments of a more general nature with important implications for national tax laws need to be discussed briefly: First, while the freedoms continue to converge in their dogmatic structure to form a singular principle of non-discrimination of cross-border economic activity and movement, uncertainty regarding their relationship and consequences of their potentially overlapping application has attracted an increasing number of contributions from academic literature and ECJ cases, notably in situations involving third countries. Secondly, recent years have brought increasing discussion regarding the limitation of the application of fundamental freedoms founded in the doctrine of abuse of Union law, with special relevance for abusive practices in the area of taxation.

[1] Relationship and Applicability of multiple freedoms

As the fundamental freedoms are all parts of a general principle of non-discrimination based on nationality, the 'high degree of dogmatic convergence' noted in the original contribution is hardly surprising. Even to the ECJ, for most situations, the question whether one or another freedom would apply seems to be of little concern.[17] Many cross-border transactions come within the scope of more than one freedom, and in general, the ECJ considers them complementary rather than exclusive. Recently, however, the ECJ has aimed to delimit the scope of applicability of the freedoms, especially because of the greater territorial scope of the freedom of capital movement. The ECJ has thus developed a doctrine according to which, in case of a restriction of more than one freedom, only one will be examined, where it is shown that another is 'entirely secondary in relation to the other',[18] and as such the restrictive effect on the

Commission) ECR 2001, I-1611, para. 37; ECJ 22 October 2002, case C-94/00 (*Roquette Frères*) ECR 2002, I-9011, para. 25. See also now Art 6 para. 3 TEU.

16. See e.g. ECtHR 30 June 2005, Application No. 45036/98, especially paras 155 et seq. Strictly speaking, the margin of appreciation is applied to the Member State in question implementing EU law. The ECtHR has, however, accepted that the ECJ provides equivalent protection of fundamental rights.
17. Cf. S. Hemels et al., *EC Tax Review* 2010, p. 19 (20 et seq); A. Cordewener, G.W. Kofler and C.P. Schindler, *European Taxation* 2007, p. 371 (372); W.C. Haslehner, *Internationales Steuerrecht* 2008, p. 565 (570 et seq).
18. ECJ 22 January 2002, case C-390/99 *(Canal Satélite Digital)* ECR 2002, I-607.

other merely is an 'unavoidable consequence of a restriction of the former'.[19] In order to determine thus the primarily affected freedom, the ECJ consistently refers to the purpose of the national legal rule in question.[20] Consequently, legislation covering e.g. specifically permanent establishments or a special parent-subsidiary relationship with definite influence is only examined under Article 49 TFEU and not Article 63, thus being immune to challenges relating to third country situations. Any more generally applicable domestic provision remains subject to scrutiny in light of several freedoms in parallel. Subsequent case law suggests a general priority of the freedom of establishment over the freedom of capital movement by referring to the facts of the case as the decisive criterion to determine the primarily affected freedom,[21] seemingly disregarding the relevance of the purpose of the national legislation.[22] Surprisingly then, in *Glaxo Wellcome*, the ECJ deemed the freedom of capital movement to prevail over the freedom of establishment on the basis that the legislation in question did not envisage an actual establishment, though it did apply to situations of shareholders with definite influence, thus coming within the scope of that freedom as well.[23] This has led to yet more uncertainty,[24] leaving the issue open to debate,[25] though recent decisions point in the – to this author – more convincing direction to regard the purpose of the legislation at issue the decisive factor.[26] A final answer can now be expected from the ECJ in response to the recent preliminary ruling request made by the UK High Court regarding the *FII Group Litigation*-case.[27]

[2] Fundamental Freedoms and the Abuse of EU Law Doctrine

The concept of abuse of law, while in general terms used by the ECJ for over 30 years,[28] has attracted much attention in recent years due to a number of influential decisions in

19. Cf. ECJ 12 September 2006, case C-196/04 *(Cadbury Schweppes)* ECR 2006, I-7995, para. 33; ECJ 3 October 2006, case C-452/04 *(Fidium Finanz)* ECR 2006, I-9521, para. 49.
20. Explicitly so e.g. in ECJ 24 May 2007, case C-157/05 *(Holböck)* ECR 2007, I-4051, para. 22; ECJ 17 September 2009, case C-182/08 *(Glaxo Wellcome)* ECR 2009, I-8591, para. 36; ECJ 21 January 2010, case C-311/08 *(SGI)* ECR 2010, I-487, para. 25, each with references to further cases.
21. Especially ECJ 26 June 2008, case C-284/06 *(Burda)* ECR 2008, I-4571; ECJ 4 June 2009, case C-439/07 *(KBC Bank)* ECR 2009, I-4409; ECJ 18 June 2009, case C-303/07 *(Aberdeen)* ECR 2009, I-5145.
22. S. Hemels et al., *EC Tax Review* 2010 p. 19 (25 et seq).
23. ECJ 17 September 2009, case C-182/08 *(Glaxo Wellcome)* ECR 2009, I-8591, paras 49 et seq.
24. For an overview of the diverging positions of the French, Dutch, German and UK courts see S. Hemels et al., *EC Tax Review* 2010, p. 19 (28 et seq).
25. Cf. J. Englisch, *Intertax* 2010, p. 197 (200 et seq).
26. See, however, ECJ 21 January 2010, case C-311/08 *(SGI)* ECR 2010, I-487, paras 33 et seq., applying a factual test: It is baffling why the ECJ engages in the priority discussion at all, if the mere applicability of the freedom of establishment to the factual circumstances rules out the freedom of capital movement.
27. Pending case, C-35/11, *Test Claimants in the FII Group Litigation (II)*.
28. Cf. R. De la Feria, *Common Market Law Review* 2008, p. 395; equally P. Schammo, *European Law Journal* 2008, p. 351 (358).

the area of (direct and indirect) taxation.[29] The general idea of the concept is that a national of a Member State may not rely on EU law 'improperly to circumvent their national legislation', i.e. '[t]hey must not improperly or fraudulently take advantage of provisions of [Union] law'.[30] While this can certainly be regarded to be a general principle of EU law, the details of what it actually means are far from clear, [31] and it may affect harmonized and non-harmonized areas of taxation differently. As far as the fundamental freedoms are concerned, the principle of prohibition of abuse of law applies primarily as a justification for restrictive anti-avoidance measures relating to direct taxation.[32]The ECJ has, however, limited this defence to 'wholly artificial arrangements'.[33] It might appear more convincing in such circumstances to say that no genuine cross-border economic activity has been carried out, thus taking the situation out of the scope of the fundamental freedoms.[34] However, this approach would fail in situations where not the establishment itself is questioned, but ensuing arrangements, e.g. cross-border payments between connected companies. There, it is necessary to ensure that these arrangements are not restricted in so far as they are genuine and thus protected by the freedoms according to the internal market rationale. The criterion of artificiality, though a concept without clear *ex ante* meaning for all cases, is thus useful to provide an appropriate distinction, allowing Member States to prevent the undermining of their competence, while protecting the freedom of taxpayers to choose among legitimate alternatives for action in a cross-border situation.

III DEVELOPMENTS IN DIRECT TAXATION

This section briefly highlights the most influential judicial developments in respect of the issues on direct taxation identified in Chapter 9 above. In general terms, it is obvious that the ECJ has taken a considerably more cautious approach in striking down national legislation, apparently aware of both the rising discontent among Member States and the inherent shortcomings in the ECJ's power to create a EU legal tax order by way of negative integration alone. This is especially visible since the judgment in the landmark case *Marks & Spencer*. Since then, the ECJ is increasingly inclined to accept defences, which had been seemingly rejected in earlier cases, and to take a less strict approach in determining proportionality, leaving the Member States more leeway to

29. The two leading cases are still ECJ 12 September 2006, case C-196/04 *(Cadbury Schweppes)* ECR 2006, I-7995; and ECJ 21 February 2006, case C-255/02 *(Halifax)* ECR 2006, I-1609.
30. ECJ 12 September 2006, case C-196/04 *(Cadbury Schweppes)* ECR 2006, I-7995, para. 35.
31. For an overview over controversial issues and the range of opinions among scholars see the contributions in R. De la Feria/S. Vogenauer (eds), *Prohibition of Abuse of Law*, Hart Publishing Oxford 2011.
32. It has been pointed out that the ECJ has not explicitly referred to 'abuse of law' in direct tax cases; R. Karimeri, *Intertax* 2011, p. 296 (302). However, the ECJ has considered the question of whether a freedom had been abused by an arrangement, which arguably is a reference to the principle.
33. ECJ 12 September 2006, case C-196/04 *(Cadbury Schweppes)* ECR 2006, I-7995, para. 51; ECJ 13 March 2007, case C-524/04 *(Thin Cap Group Litigation)* ECR 2007, I-2107, para. 72; ECJ 21 January 2010, case C-311/08 *(SGI)* ECR 2010, I-487, para. 65. See further *infra* III.F.1.
34. Cf. W. Schön in: *Comparative Perspectives on Revenue Law* (2008) p. 75 et seq; equally R. Karimeri, *Intertax* 2011, p. 296 (309).

choose between several appropriate measures so long as the choice is not excessively obstructive.[35]

[A] Non-discrimination of non-residents

[1] Foreign Loss Recognition of 'Virtual Residents': The Demise of the Principle of Territoriality?

The ECJ continues to apply the concept of the 'virtual resident' as created in the *Schumacker* case for non-resident taxpayers with regard to personal circumstances,[36] despite the criticism lodged against it in academic literature.[37] It has indeed extended that concept to cover not only tax relief for personal allowances, but to include relief for foreign negative income as well.[38] Insofar as the host state must apply a savings clause for progression in a consistent manner,[39] this is unsurprising and was indeed predicted by LANG and ENGLISCH in their original contribution to this volume.[40] However, the ECJ has extended that view to a deduction of foreign losses from the domestic tax base in the host state in *Renneberg*, disregarding the *territoriality principle* as a valid ground to exclude foreign income.[41] This not only seems to disregard a number of previous cases, especially *Futura Participations*,[42] and the balanced allocation of taxes agreed upon in the bilateral tax treaty between the involved Member States,[43] but may even be problematic as a matter of customary international law, insofar as the host state might be considered unable to recover the relieved losses by taxing subsequent foreign positive income, as there is arguably no sufficient connection to that income.[44] Interestingly, the decisions in *Renneberg* and *Lakebrink* are explicitly based on the need to take the taxpayer's ability to pay into account to extend the reasoning of the

35. Cf. A. Cordewener/G. Kofler/S. Van Thiel, *Common Market Law Review* 2009, p. 1951 (1994 et seq).
36. ECJ 5 July 2005, case C-376/03 *(D)*, ECR 2005, I-5821; ECJ 9 November 2006, case C-520/04 *(Turpeinen)*, ECR 2006, I-10685.
37. See M. Lang, *EC Tax Review* 2009, p. 98 (101 et seq), with further references.
38. ECJ 21 February 2006, case C-152/03 *(Ritter-Coulais)*, ECR 2006, I-1711; ECJ 18 July 2007, case C-182/06 *(Lakebrink)*, ECR 2007, I-6705; ECJ 16 October 2008, case C-527/06 *(Renneberg)*, ECR 2008, I-7735.
39. ECJ 21 February 2006, case C-152/03 *(Ritter-Coulais)*, ECR 2006, I-1711; ECJ 18 July 2007, case C-182/06 *(Lakebrink)*, ECR 2007, I-6705.
40. Cf. *supra*§9.03 A. (COMMENT: In the version of the chapter by Lang and English, which I am referring to, it is labelled Chapter 9, but then the numeration changes from §9.02 to §10.03 – please correct this reference according to the correct numeration of that chapter if necessary).
41. ECJ 16 October 2008, case C-527/06 *(Renneberg)*, ECR 2008, I-7735; for critical review, see E.C.C.M. Kemmeren, *EC Tax Review* 2009, p. 4; G.T.K. Meussen, *European Taxation* 2009, p. 185 et seq.
42. ECJ 15 May 1997, case C-250/95 *(Futura Participations)*, ECR 1995, I-2471.
43. It is also obviously inconsistent with the ECJ's approach to the treatment of foreign losses in the residence state, which it does not require to be relieved immediately. Cf. *infra* III.B.1.
44. Cf. O. Marres, *Intertax* 2011, p. 112 (123 et seq): „[T]he non-discrimination principle overrules any recognition of the allocation of fiscal competence.'

Schumacker doctrine,[45] and may as such be welcomed from the point of view of inter-personal equity, despite their potentially disastrous effects for inter-nation equity. The described problem results, however, not from the extension of loss relief to the host state, but from the lacking safeguard mechanism to ensure a balanced allocation within the limits set by the internal market rationale, i.e. a rule to recapture the loss so relieved. Judicial or legislative adaption of double tax treaties can thus remedy the situation.

Indeed, from the point of view of cross-border taxation based on an EU-wide ability to pay principle, this line of case law is not a step too far, but not far enough, although in the right direction. As criticized in chapter 9 above, where a taxpayer earns income in several member states, but pays no tax in his residence state, a disadvantage may persist. Proportionally allowing personal deductions in each Member State would remedy that situation.[46] This requires equal treatment of all non-resident taxpayers with resident taxpayers in each Member State where they earn *any* income. To be consistent and also to prevent double-non-taxation, this – and a European-wide ability to pay concept – would ultimately require the application of world-wide taxation for non-residents, with appropriate relief from double taxation through bilateral or multilateral agreement.[47]

[2] Withholding Taxation of Non-residents: Three Approaches

As regards potential discriminations relating to the objective ability to pay of non-resident taxpayers, three different lines of cases have arisen in recent years in the context of withholding taxes: First, as regards *active income* derived in a Member State, the ECJ has, following up on its decision in *Gerritse*,[48] ruled in *Scorpio* on the host state's obligation to take expenses related to taxable income into account, requiring, if at all, to levy withholding tax on net rather than gross income.[49] In addition, it held that the imposition of withholding tax on payments to non-residents in itself constitutes discrimination, where no withholding is required from payments to resident taxpayers.[50] It is, however, considered justified by the need to ensure the effective collection of income tax, in particular because at the time of the decision, the Directive on Mutual

45. ECJ 16 October 2008, case C-527/06 *(Renneberg)*, ECR 2008, I-7735, para. 63; ECJ 18 July 2007, case C-182/06 *(Lakebrink)*, ECR 2007, I-6705, para. 34.
46. See e.g. P.J. Wattel, *European Taxation* 2000, p. 210; B.J.M. Terra/P.J. Wattel, *European Tax Law* (2008), p. 804 et seq.
47. As has already been noted by P.J. Wattel, *European Taxation* 2000, p. 210 (221); '[this] possibility is by far the best, because it is the most neutral, the most subsidiary (respect for sovereignty) and the fairest solution'; cf also C. Bardini, *Intertax* 2010, p. 2 (20): 'The application of a European ability-to-pay principle finds its logical obstacle in source taxation, where ability to pay is disregarded'.
48. ECJ 12 June 2003, case C-234/01 *(Gerritse)*, ECR 2003, I-5933.
49. The ECJ has also continued further to establish comparability with regard to deductible expenses on the basis of comparable activities generating income in *Centro Equestro* (ECJ 15 February 2007, C-345/04, paras 23 et seq.)
50. ECJ 3 October 2006, case C-290/04 *(FKP Scorpio Konzertproduktionen)*, ECR 2006, I-9461, paras 33 et seq.

Assistance in the Recovery of Duties[51] had not been extended to cover the taxes at issue.[52] The ECJ is thus effectively allowing a different mode of taxation for non-residents. If upheld in future decisions, this will result in disregarding cash flow disadvantages for the taxpayer as a consequence of earlier tax collection. This coincides with the second type of cases, which concerns passive income: In *Truck Center*[53], the withholding tax levied on cross-border interest in the host state (outside the scope of Directive 2003/49/EC) was found not to be discriminatory in the first place; nor did the ECJ take offence at the lack of a deduction available for connected expenses.[54] This appears irreconcilable with the aforementioned cases. The Court's reasoning is not convincing, either: It essentially denies comparability of residents and non-residents due to their different situation concerning effective supervision.[55] Yet such differences cannot justify taxation on a gross base.[56] If anything, it may, in accordance with *Scorpio*, be considered a *justification* to apply a different mode of taxation – as long as the tax is substantively not higher than in the domestic situation;[57] the acceptance of the remaining cash flow disadvantage is then actually consistent with the earlier case. In the author's view, the judgment ought to be understood in this way and thus distinguished from the third line of cases, regarding withholding taxation of outbound-dividends following *Denkavit* and *Amurta*.[58] In these decisions, the ECJ considered it discriminatory to levy a withholding tax on dividends paid to non-resident shareholders, even where an equal amount of withholding tax was levied on domestic recipients, because only in case of the latter, but not the former, an effective credit for the tax was granted by the state of residence of the distributing company. There is no contradiction with *Truck Center*: After all, the fundamental freedoms require *national treatment*; consequently, where the domestic tax situation is different for interest and dividends, it is hardly surprising to find different requirements for cross-border payments as well. However, in the *Denkavit* and *Amurta* line of cases, the non-resident shareholder faced a substantive tax charge, which the resident shareholder did not have to bear, thus resulting in effective discrimination. Interestingly, the

51. Council Directive 76/308/EEC as amended by Directive 2001/44/EC.
52. It has been noted to be unclear whether a withholding tax would still be appropriate following the entry into force of Directive 2001/44/EC, see D. Molenaar/H. Grams, *European Taxation* 2007, p. 63 (66); CFE Opinion Statement, *European Taxation* 2009, p. 491 (495 et seq); M. Lang, *Steuer & Wirtschaft International* 2007, p. 17 (24).
53. ECJ 22 December 2008, case C-282/07 *(Truck Center)*, ECR 2008, I-10767.
54. Cf. L. De Broe/N. Bammens, *EC Tax Review* 2009, p. 131 (136); M. Lang, *EC Tax Review* 2009, p. 98 (112).
55. ECJ 22 December 2008, case C-282/07 *(Truck Center)*, ECR 2008, I-10767, para. 48. The other reasons given, i.e. the role of the state as the source rather than resident state (para. 42) as well as the different tax charge (para. 43), are even less convincing.
56. Different treatment has to be proportionately different, i.e. reflect the difference of the two situations compared. The lack of cost-deduction also appears to contradict ECJ 19 January 2006, case C-265/04 *(Bouanich)*, ECR 2006, I-923.
57. To this end, cf. ECJ 9 November 2006, case C-520/04 *(Turpeinen)*, ECR 2006, I-10685, which, in addition, implies the relevance of the Mutual Assistance and Recovery Directives (77/799/EEC and 76/308/EEC) to disregard the justification.
58. ECJ 14 December 2006, case C-170/05 *(Denkavit Internationaal)*, ECR 2006, I-11949; ECJ 8 November 2007, case C-379/05 *(Amurta)*, ECR 2007, I-9569.

ECJ has indicated a new cross-border justification[59] for these cases: The Member State may be justified in levying the excessive withholding tax charge, where the disadvantage resulting from it is compensated by a credit in the other Member State on the basis of a bilateral tax treaty[60] provided that the initial disadvantage is fully neutralized.[61] The ECJ has thus created yet another situation where it deviates from the 'single country approach' to consider the tax systems of two Member States together.[62] Even if this compensation is successful,[63] as in the other cases on withholding taxation, a cash flow disadvantage would, however, remain.[64]

It can be derived from these cases that the ECJ has not fully embraced an approach based on ability to pay for non-residents in respect of their taxable income in the host Member State; especially insofar as it disregards cash flow disadvantages. With regard to higher taxes beyond mere cash flow disadvantages, the case law is however mostly consistent in demanding equal taxation of equally taxable income.

[B] Non-discrimination of Foreign-Source Income

[1] Foreign Loss Relief: 'Final' Losses

Foreign loss relief has probably attracted most contributions in both case law and academic literature on EU tax law in recent years: Ever since *Marks & Spencer*, the question whether losses incurred in another Member State through either subsidiary or permanent establishment have to be taken into account to reduce the tax base of the parent or head office in the residence country, under what circumstances and to what extent, remained at the forefront of interest of European tax lawyers.[65] In *Marks &*

59. It should be noted that the ECJ has decided in its latest judgments that such compensation of possible disadvantages effectively achieves compliance with the fundamental freedoms by undoing the latent discrimination, rather than (only) justifying discrimination. See ECJ 19 November 2009, Case C-540/07 *(Commission / Italy)*, ECR 2009, I-10983, para. 53; ECJ 22 November 2010, Case C-199/10 *(Secilpar)*, para. 39. The dogmatic foundations for that approach are however not entirely clear. See further G. Kofler, *Bulletin for International Taxation* 2011, p. 684 (686 et seq.).
60. ECJ 14 December 2006, case C-170/05 *(Denkavit Internationaal)*, ECR 2006, I-11949, paras 44 et seq; ECJ 8 November 2007, case C-379/05 *(Amurta)*, ECR 2007, I-9569, paras 79 et seq.
61. ECJ 19 November 2009, case C-540/07 *(Commission / Italy)*, ECR 2009, I-10983, para. 37.
62. For criticism of this approach see *supra* §9.03 F.3.iv.; G. Bizioli, *European Taxation* 2009, p. 133 (135); D. Weber, *Intertax* 2006, p.585 (601 et seq); M. Lang, *European Taxation* 2008, p. 67 (72); other scholars have, however, endorsed the approach, in particular with respect to the argument that the compensation would only suffice where it can be understood as part of the source state's domestic rules as part of the tax treaty; see, e.g. G. Kofler, *Doppelbesteuerungsabkommen und Europäisches Gemeinschaftsrecht* (2007) p. 601 et seq; F. Vanistendael. *EC Tax Review* 2008, p. 52 (60 et seq). For a detailed recent analysis see G. Kofler, *Bulletin for International Taxation* 2011, p. 684.
63. On the inherent limits of this justification, see J. Englisch, *Intertax* 2010, p. 197 (217 et seq) with additional references.
64. Cf. G.T.K. Meussen, *European Taxation* 2007, p. 244 (245); T. Pons, *European Taxation* 2007, p. 214 (219).
65. For some recent contributions to that topic, see A. Cordewener, *EC Tax Review* 2011, p. 58; O. Marres, *Intertax* 2011, p. 112; M. Vascega/S. Van Thiel, *European Taxation* 2010, p. 33; W.C. Haslehner. *Bulletin for International Taxation* 2010, p. 33; R. Kok, *Intertax* 2010, p. 663; T.

Spencer, the ECJ established the principle that foreign losses have to be taken into account in the resident state where no relief is available in the other Member State.[66] This obligatory relief of so-called 'final losses', which has subsequently been extended from the context of corporate groups to foreign losses incurred by permanent establishments,[67] mirrors the 'always-somewhere' approach[68] applied for the consideration of personal circumstances following the *Schumacker* and *De Groot* line of cases.[69] To this extent, it is equally unconvincing, insofar as taxation according to ability to pay is – as well as the correctly understood non-discrimination principle – opposed to burden the taxpayer with cash flow disadvantages from the time-lag between the incurring of losses and their 'finality' as a mere consequence of the application of the principle of territoriality and an allegedly supra-European allocation of taxing rights.[70] The more convincing approach would thus be to demand cross-border loss relief to be given by the home state to temporary losses as well, and to recapture those losses where relief would later be available in the host Member State.

However, not only is the 'final loss' approach unconvincing from a doctrinal point of view, it is also difficult to apply in practice, as the determination of when a loss has to be considered 'final' is subject to much uncertainty.[71] It is clear that time limits to loss carry-forwards or other peculiarities in the law of the host Member State will not lead to 'final' losses.[72] This has to be supported: If one accepts the above notion that any loss ought to be given immediate relief, the question turns on when the home state is allowed to apply a recapture mechanism. It would indeed undermine the power of a Member State to determine the tax base, if it was barred from taking foreign profits subsequent to a relieved foreign loss into account in an attempt to achieve a balanced result for both taxpayer and the state. Neither non-discrimination nor a European ability to pay principle would require more: If the taxpayer ends up with no relief in either state in such situation, this is indeed a consequence of the tax law in the Member State of source, i.e. a disparity from the home state point of view. [73] However, if loss relief was available for residents in the source state, it would result in discrimination there; if it was not, the complete lack of a loss carry-forward for all taxpayers could violate a *national* constitutional ability to pay principle.

Mkrtchyan, *Bulletin for International Taxation* 2009, p. 586; A.D. Nugroho, *EC Tax Review* 2009, p. 29; G.T.K. Meussen, *European Taxation* 2009, p. 361, each with further references.

66. ECJ 13 December 2005, case C-446/03 *(Marks & Spencer)*, ECR 2005, I-10837, para. 55.
67. ECJ 28 February 2008, case C-293/06 *(Deutsche Shell)*, ECR 2008, I-1129; ECJ 15 May 2008, case C-414/06 *(Lidl Belgium)*, ECR 2008, I-3601.
68. See further B.J.M. Terra/P.J. Wattel, *European Tax Law* (2008) p. 733 et seq.
69. O. Marres, *Intertax* 2011, p. 112 (119).
70. Cf. W.C. Haslehner, *Bulletin for International Taxation* 2010, p. 33 (43 et seq).
71. For a recent analysis, see A. Cordewener, *EC Tax Review* 2011, p. 58 et seq, with references to national case law trying to implement the concept.
72. This can be inferred especially from ECJ 23 October 2008, case C-157/07 *(KR Wannsee)*, ECR 2008, I-8061, para. 49.
73. Insofar correct A. Cordewener, *EC Tax Review* 2011, p. 58 (61); this does not, however, create frictions with *Renneberg*, which only obliges the source state to give national treatment based on worldwide taxation: Where the 'foreign loss' does not translate into a domestic loss as determined in accordance with national rules, it would equally not have to be taken into account.

Most recently, the validity of the 'final loss' doctrine has come to be questioned following judgments of the ECJ with no mentioning of this rule of last resort for loss relief.[74] However, insofar as this would mean disregarding foreign losses altogether and unconditionally accepting a unilateral allocation of those losses to the state of source, it cannot, as should be clear from the arguments above, be accepted.[75]

[2] Foreign Capital Income: Credit and Exemption

The ECJ has further developed its approach to the taxation of inbound dividends in the shareholder residence state and the necessary relief to be granted:[76] In general, residents receiving domestic and foreign dividends are considered comparable, thus requiring equal treatment in principle.[77] This has led the ECJ to demand Member States to extend their mechanisms to relieve economic double taxation applied in the domestic situation to cross-border dividends,[78] including situations where the state of residence of the distributing company is resident in a third country.[79] However, the ECJ appears to be inconsistent insofar as it allows Member States to choose freely among relief mechanisms, by accepting the credit and exemption method to be essentially equivalent,[80] in complete disregard of different compliance burdens, which may in practice be tantamount to a denial of relief.[81] This is surprising insofar as the ECJ allows Member States to justify a disadvantage based on the need to maintain the effectiveness of fiscal controls without scrutinizing its proportionality. Even apart from that criticism, the case law also reveals a very formal approach to decide on cross-border dividends tax systems, especially when taking decisions regarding juridical double taxation into perspective, which is consistently ruled to be beyond the reach of the fundamental freedoms.[82] This arguably fails to reflect economic reality as it gives

74. ECJ 18 July 2007, case C-231/05 *(Oy AA)*, ECR 2007, I-6373; ECJ 25 February 2010, case C-337/08 *(X Holding)*, ECR 2010, I-1215.
75. For strong criticism of the approach in *X Holding*, cf. M. Vascega/S. Van Thiel, *European Taxation* 2010, p. 334 et seq.
76. For a recent comprehensive critique see J. Englisch, *Intertax* 2010, p. 197.
77. As regards the basis for this comparability and related criticism see already the original contribution by J. Lang and J. Englisch, *supra*§9.03 B.
78. Most recently, ECJ 6 March 2007, case C-292/04 *(Meilicke)*, ECR 2007, I-1835; ECJ 10 February 2011, cases C-436/08 and C-437/08 *(Haribo and Österreichische Salinen)*; ECJ 30 June 2011, case C-262/09 *(Meilicke)*; ECJ 15 September 2011, case C-310/09 *(Accor)*; following up on its decisions in *Lenz* and *Manninen*.
79. ECJ 12 December 2006, case C-446/04 *(FII Group Litigation)*, ECR 2006, I-11753, paras 58 et seq; ECJ 10 February 2011, cases C-436/08 and C-437/08 *(Haribo and Österreichische Salinen)*, not yet reported, paras 105 et seq.
80. See ECJ 12 December 2006, case C-446/04 *(FII Group Litigation)*, ECR 2006, I-11753, para. 53; ECJ 10 February 2011, cases C-436/08 and C-437/08 *(Haribo and Österreichische Salinen)*, not yet reported, paras 90, 95 et seq. For limits to this equivalence, see T. Bieber/W.C. Haslehner/G.W. Kofler/C.P. Schindler, *European Taxation* 2008, p. 583 (587).
81. As Smit notes, the ECJ apparently wants to rely on market forces to overcome administrative constraints for the taxpayer, see D. Smit, *European Taxation* 2011, p. 275 (278). In the same vein, Opinion of AG Kokott, 11 November 2010, cases C-436/08 and C-437/08 *(Haribo and Österreichische Salinen)*, paras 58 et seq.
82. ECJ 14 November 2006, case C-513/04 *(Kerckhaert and Morres)*, ECR 2006, I-10967; ECJ 24 May 2008, case C-194/06 *(Orange European Smallcap Fund)*, ECR 2008, I-3747.

Member States the opportunity to reach the same economic result by changing the method of levying taxes,[83] and is thus opposed to consistent taxation based on the ability to pay principle.

[C] Neutrality of Legal Form

With regard to the disputed obligation of Member States to treat different forms of secondary establishment equally, the ECJ has clarified that the different treatment of a foreign subsidiary as compared to a foreign PE does not lead to forbidden discrimination from the perspective of the home Member State,[84] while it may be different for the host Member State.[85] While in the latter case, such *horizontal* comparison[86] is of little consequence compared to the usual approach[87] and thus not very controversial, it is debatable whether the ECJ is right in treating foreign subsidiaries and PEs as incomparable from the home state perspective in all circumstances; especially, where these are treated without distinction domestically.[88]

[D] International Double Taxation

The irrelevance of international juridical double taxation is firmly established in recent case law,[89] despite strong academic support to consider the abolition of double taxation not only – as the ECJ readily concedes[90] – an objective of EU law, but a requirement of the fundamental freedoms as a consequence of it being a restrictive and factually discriminatory 'double burden'.[91] To be sure, the ECJ does not deny the detrimental

83. Cf. D. Weber, *Intertax* 2006, p.585 (601 et seq); T. Spaas/A. Weyn, *EC Tax Review* 2009, p. 53 (63); J. Englisch, *Intertax* 2010, p. 197 (209); B.J.M. Terra/P.J. Wattel, *European Tax Law* (2008) p. 813; M.J. Graetz/A.C. Warren, *Common Market Law Review* 2007, p. 1577 (1613).
84. ECJ 6 December 2007, case C-298/05 *(Columbus Container Services)*, ECR 2007, I-10451, para. 53; ECJ 4 June 2009, cases C-439/07 and C-499/07 *(KBC Bank)*, ECR 2009, I-4409, para. 80; ECJ 25 February 2010, case C-337/08 *(X Holding)*, ECR 2010, I-1215, paras 37 et seq.
85. ECJ 23 February 2006, case C-253/03 *(CLT-UFA)* ECR 2006, I-1831, paras 14 and 22 et seq.; see A. Schnitger, *European Taxation* 2004, p. 522; see also the Opinion of AG Kokott, 19 November 2009, case C-337/08 *(X Holding)*, paras 58 et seq., explaining the different situation between home state and host state.
86. It should be noted that two very different types of comparison are covered under that label: i.e. two non-residents domiciled in the same state, exercising different kinds of secondary establishment; and two non-residents domiciled in different countries, both exercising the same freedom in the same way. See further on the horizontal comparison test in various shapes M. Lang, *EC Tax Review* 2009, p. 98 (104); M. Lang, *Steuer & Wirtschaft International* 2011, p. 154.
87. J. Englisch, *Intertax* 2010, p. 197 (213).
88. M. Vascega/S. Van Thiel, *European Taxation* 2010, p. 334 (343 et seq).
89. ECJ 14 November 2006, case C-513/04 *(Kerckhaert and Morres)*, ECR 2006, I-10967, paras 18 et seq.; ECJ 24 May 2008, case C-194/06 *(Orange European Smallcap Fund)*, ECR 2008, I-3747; ECJ 12 February 2009, case C-67/08 *(Block)*, ECR 2009, I-883, paras 28 et seq.; ECJ 16 July 2009, case C-128/08 *(Damseaux)*, ECR 2009, I-6823, paras 26 et seq.; see also ECJ 15 April 2010, case C-96/08 *(CIBA)*, ECR 2010, I-2911.
90. ECJ 16 July 2009, case C-128/08 *(Damseaux)*, ECR 2009, I-6823, para. 28.
91. See, e.g. *supra* §9.03 D.; J. Englisch, *Intertax* 2005, p. 310 (323); S. Van Thiel, *Free Movement of Persons and Income Tax Law* (2002) p. 331; G.K. Fibbe/A.C.G.A.C. De Graaf in: *Essays in*

effect of double taxation on the internal market, but it deems it to be beyond its powers to allocate responsibility and an obligation to provide for relief on a particular Member State, as the Treaties do not lay down the criteria necessary for such assessment.[92] The ECJ does not consider it appropriate to make Member States jointly and severally responsible for the lack of coordination of their tax rules either, and essentially denies the relevance of international tax principles or even applicable double tax treaties, which could provide guidelines at least for some cases.[93] The case law thus remains unsatisfactory in respect of the ability to pay principle.

[E] Most-Favoured-Nation Treatment

Equally, the ECJ did not follow scholarly suggestions to understand the fundamental freedoms as a guarantee to most-favoured nation treatment, but instead rejected that notion in a number of cases.[94] This is in line with the position of LANG and ENGLISCH in their analysis,[95] and certainly correct in light of the focus of the fundamental freedoms on a *vertical* comparison to provide for 'national treatment'. However, the reasoning of the ECJ is problematic insofar as it accepts comparability of two non-residents domiciled in different Member States in principle, yet subsequently rejects it on the basis of the special reciprocal nature of a bilateral tax treaty. It should also be noted that the question of a most-favoured-nation treatment in the *D*-case specifically arose as a consequence of the denial of national treatment, which should apply to all non-residents, thus eliminating the issue in the first place.[96] The ECJ has also subsequently denied the application for most-favoured-nation treatment in the outbound-situation by disregarding pleas for a *horizontal* comparison in *Columbus*,[97] while considering that approach on other occasions.[98]

Honour of Maarten Ellis (2005) p. 237; G.W. Kofler, *Doppelbesteuerungsabkommen und Europäisches Gemeinschaftsrecht* (2007) p. 154 et seq; F. Vanistendael, *EC Tax Review* 2008, p. 52 (61 et seq); G.W. Kofler/R. Mason, *Columbia Journal of European Law* 2007, p. 63 (79); G. Kofler in: *Double Taxation within the European Union* (2011) p. 97 (123 et seq).

92. ECJ 16 July 2009, case C-128/08 *(Damseaux)*, ECR 2009, I-6823, para. 33; see G. Kofler, *Highlights & Insights on European Taxation* 2009, p. 21 (28).
93. Cf. *supra* §9.03 D.; for a recent in-depth analysis of potential criteria see A. Rust in: *Double Taxation within the European Union* (2011) p. 137 et seq.
94. ECJ 5 July 2005, case C-376/03 *(D)*, ECR 2005, I-5821; ECJ 27 October 2005, C-8/04 *(Bujara)* – case removed from register due to withdrawn preliminary ruling request; ECJ 12 December 2006, case C-374/04 *(ACT Group Litigation)*, ECR 2006, I-11673; for a critical appraisal see e.g. D. Weber, *Intertax* 2005, p. 429; S. Van Thiel, *Intertax* 2005, p. 454; G.W. Kofler/C.P. Schindler, *European Taxation* 2005, p. 530; A. Cordewener/E. Reimer, *European Taxation* 2006, p. 291; S. Van Thiel, *European Taxation* 2007, p. 263; G. Kofler, *Doppelbesteuerungsabkommen und Europäisches Gemeinschaftsrecht* (2007) p. 781 et seq.
95. *Supra* §9.03 E.
96. The same is arguably true for the decision in *ACT Group Litigation*. In favour of the extension of all forms of shareholder relief to non-resident shareholders e.g. J. Englisch, *Intertax* 2010, p. 197 (212 et seq).
97. ECJ 6 December 2007, case C-298/05 *(Columbus Container Services)*, ECR 2007, I-10451.
98. Cf. M. Lang, *EC Tax Review* 2009, p. 98 (104 et seq); M. Lang, *Steuer & Wirtschaft International* 2011, p. 154.

An outcome similar to most-favoured-nation treatment can also result from the element of consistency inherent in the fiscal coherence justification under the ECJ jurisprudence: Where a Member State has forgone the presumed strict link of a tax advantage with a corresponding disadvantage in the bilateral tax treaty with any other state, the justification fails with respect to non-residents from all other Member States.[99] This apparent most-favoured-nation requirement is, however, only a consequence of the obligation to provide for national treatment of a non-resident taxpayer in the first place.

[F] Justifications for Unequal Taxation

As mentioned in the beginning of this section and as visible from the particular decisions of the ECJ in direct tax cases, the ECJ has changed its initially strict attitude towards unequal tax rules in Member States to gradually allow Member States greater leeway by way of accepting justifications. Three grounds of justification effectively accepted in recent judgments are briefly highlighted below, leaving aside the 'effectiveness of fiscal supervision', which can justify more onerous information requirements and a strict burden of proof of the taxpayer, but should not be accepted as a justification for a higher tax burden.[100]

[1] Combating Tax Avoidance

The most recent developments in the area of the ECJ's acceptance of measures to combat abusive behaviour of taxpayers can be described in four stages: First, the continued application of the *wholly artificial* criterion as the limit to the justification in principle,[101] secondly, the development of criteria explaining that concept in respect of CFC rules,[102] thirdly, the extension of the justification beyond rules targeting purely artificial measures by coupling it with the need to preserve a balanced allocation of

99. See A. Cordewener/E. Reimer, *European Taxation* 2006, p. 291 (306); for a different opinion, see *supra* §9.03 F.3.iv.
100. The ECJ appears to be more relaxed and allows different modes of taxation by disregarding cash flow effects (cf. cases cited *supra* III.A.2.on withholding taxation) and in relation to third countries: ECJ 18 December 2007, case C-101/05 *(A)*, ECR 2007, I-11531, paras 60 et seq. In respect of the latter, the ECJ is however too lenient in applying the proportionality test: The taxpayer should have the chance to provide proof for his position regardless of whether an agreement between the Member State and the third state on exchange of information exists; this may include the responsibility of the taxpayer to have the third country's tax authority validate information provided by him, if so required.
101. ECJ 12 September 2006, case C-196/04 *(Cadbury Schweppes)* ECR 2006, I-7995, para. 51; ECJ 13 March 2007, case C-524/04 *(Thin Cap Group Litigation)* ECR 2007, I-2107, para. 72; ECJ 21 January 2010, case C-311/08 *(SGI)* ECR 2010, I-487, para. 65.
102. ECJ 12 September 2006, case C-196/04 *(Cadbury Schweppes)* ECR 2006, I-7995, para. 67: Whether the CFC 'physically exists in terms of premises, staff and equipment'. Further guidance as to the allowed features of anti-avoidance legislation and the burden of proof can be derived from ECJ 23 April 2008, case C-201/05 *(CFC and Dividend Group Litigation)*, ECR 2008, I-2875, paras 81, 85.

taxing power,[103] and fourthly the re-establishment of the criterion of artificiality in the proportionality test in the context of the application of the arm's length standard to transfer pricing.[104]

[2] Fiscal Coherence

Fiscal coherence[105] famously is the oldest accepted tax specific justification and is discussed at great length in the contribution by LANG and ENGLISCH, who criticize it as being too narrow and not adequately taking into account the need for standardizations within a domestic tax system.[106] While it is not discernible that the ECJ has changed its narrow approach to the concept, it has nonetheless found practical application in recent cases.[107] However, in *Papillon*, the justification ultimately failed on proportionality grounds, and in *Krankenheim Wannsee*, the ECJ unconvincingly[108] assumed the existence of discriminatory treatment, which it subsequently found justified. Little new can be derived from those decisions, apart from the fact that Member States can still claim fiscal coherence as a defence.[109]

[3] Balanced Allocation of Taxing Power

The balanced allocation of taxation is the youngest and most commonly raised ground of justification in recent cases before the ECJ. It has initially been accepted only in combination with other arguments,[110] especially the prevention of the double use of losses and of tax avoidance in general, subsequently with only one additional justification, and finally as a self-sufficient justification in its own right.[111] It remains,

103. ECJ 13 December 2005, case C-446/03 *(Marks & Spencer)*, ECR 2005, I-10837, paras 49 and 51; ECJ 18 July 2007, case C-231/05 *(Oy AA)*, ECR 2007, I-6373, para. 63; ECJ 15 May 2008, case C-414/06 *(Lidl Belgium)*, ECR 2008, I-3601, para. 41; ECJ 21 January 2010, case C-311/08 *(SGI)*, ECR 2010, I-487, para. 66.
104. ECJ 21 January 2010, case C-311/08 *(SGI)* ECR 2010, I-487, para. 71; see further P. Baker, *Intertax* 2010, p. 194 (195); G. Meussen, *European Taxation* 2010, p. 245. For detailed analysis see England and Wales Court of Appeal (Civil Division) of 18 February 2011, *Test Claimants in the Thin Cap Group Litigation v. HMRC*, [2011] STC 738 para. 57 (holding in substance that compliance with Art. 9 OECD model convention means compliance with the fundamental freedoms).
105. The above analysis still used the term 'fiscal cohesion', which was also used by the ECJ in the English version of earlier Judgment: However, the term 'coherence' should be used exclusively: Its meaning reflects better what the ECJ is looking for, it is equivalent to terms used consistently in French (*cohérence*), Italian (*coerenza*), Spanish (*coherencia*) and German (*Kohärenz*), and 'cohesion' has a specific use in another context (EU regional policy).
106. Cf. *supra*§9.03 F.3.iv.
107. ECJ 27 November 2008, case C-418/07 *(Papillon)*, ECR 2008, I-8947, para. 51; ECJ 23 October 2008, case C-157/07 *(KR Wannsee)*, ECR 2008, I-8061, para. 43.
108. Cf. W. Haslehner, *Bulletin for International Taxation* 2010, p. 33 (40 et seq).
109. A. Cordewener/G. Kofler/S. Van Thiel, *Common Market Law Review* 2009, p. 1951 (1969 et seq).
110. ECJ 13 December 2005, case C-446/03 *(Marks & Spencer)*, ECR 2005, I-10837, para. 51.
111. ECJ 18 July 2007, case C-231/05 *(Oy AA)*, ECR 2007, I-6373, para. 60; ECJ 25 February 2010, case C-337/08 *(X Holding)*, ECR 2010, I-1215, para. 33.

however, multi-faceted and clearly connected to other grounds:[112] Especially, the ECJ shares the concern of Member States to avoid situations where companies would have a free choice where to pay their taxes irrespective of place and jurisdiction relating to the underlying economic activity, thus seriously undermining inter-nation equity. This objective is undoubtedly legitimate, but the ECJ needs to carefully balance it with concerns relating to inter-personal equity in applying the proportionality test, which it fails to do e.g. when disregarding cash-flow disadvantages flowing from the 'symmetric' treatment of foreign profits and losses.

IV DEVELOPMENTS IN INDIRECT TAXATION

As regards the situation of indirect taxes within the EU, only a very brief overview over some developments can be provided here: With regard to the questions on the application of Article 90 EC [now: 110 TFEU] discussed at length in the original chapter, no further insights can be derived from recent case law. Only two topics shall thus be highlighted below: Firstly, the developments relating to the ongoing struggle of the VAT system to deal with tax fraud and the corresponding problem of the protection of legitimate expectations of the taxpayer; secondly, the application of general principle of equality in VAT.

[A] VAT Fraud and Legitimate Expectations

The ECJ has developed a stringent line of case law regarding the relevance of legitimate expectations of taxpayers in the context of VAT fraud as derived from the fundamental principle of legal certainty. According to this jurisprudence, a taxpayer is entitled to a VAT credit (deduction) or exemption even where the objective criteria to obtain that benefit are not fulfilled, insofar as she has complied with all obligations laid down by law and acted in good faith.[113] However, where the taxpayer has not acted in good faith, she may be burdened with VAT as a consequence of the fraudulent actions of a supplier or purchaser, even where the relevant transaction meets the objective criteria of the VAT directive, entitling the taxpayer to relief.[114] Unsurprisingly, the determination of criteria for a taxpayer to act 'in good faith' is of crucial importance, though not yet fully established in case law.[115] This line of cases provides a good example of the complementing nature of legal certainty and equal treatment: The ECJ frequently refers

112. Cf. J. Englisch, *Steuer & Wirtschaft International* 2009, p. 399 et seq.; see also the cases in the context of tax avoidance *supra* III.F.1.

113. ECJ 27 September 2007, case C-409/04 *(Teleos and Others)*, ECR 2007, I-7797, para. 50; ECJ 21 February 2008, case C-271/06 *(Netto Supermarkt)*, ECR 2008, I-771, paras 25 et seq; the ECJ has earlier decided the same in situations where the conditions for a input tax deduction were fulfilled, but fraud committed on other stages within the chain of supplies: ECJ 12 January 2006, case C-354/03 *(Optigen and others)*, ECR 2006, I-483, para. 52; ECJ 11 May 2006, case C-384/04 *(Federation of Technological Industries)*, ECR 2006, I-4191, para. 33.

114. ECJ 6 July 2006, case C-439/04 and C-440/04 *(Kittel and Recolta Recycling)*, ECR 2006, I-6161, para. 59; ECJ 7 December 2010, case C-385/09 *(R)*, paras 51 et seq.

115. For recent contributions see M. Achatz in: *Umsatzsteuer im Europäischen Binnenmarkt* (DStJG 32, 2009), p. 461 et seq; W. Widmann in: *Festschrift J. Lang* (2010), p. 913 et seq.

to the principle of fiscal neutrality (as the VAT-specific implementation of the equality principle) in its decisions, explaining the need to effectively tax all transactions equally. Consequently, from the perspective of the ability to pay principle, this development is welcome, as long as, in the latter cases, an effective double-charge of the same supply is prevented by coordination between the Member States concerned.

[B] The Principle of Equality and VAT

With regard to the principle of equality, its direct applicability as a general principle of EU law in the harmonized area of VAT, specifically expressed in the principle of fiscal neutrality, is firmly established.[116] The ECJ has utilised that principle widely in its interpretation of the VAT directives,[117] but has so far not ruled on potential violations of the directives themselves, where they treat objectively comparable situations differently: This was particularly prominent in *Puffer*,[118] regarding different treatment of taxable and non-taxable persons in respect of their *private* expenditure for home ownership: The ECJ essentially denied comparability based on the role of taxable persons as collectors of VAT, which bears no connection to the disadvantage in question and is clearly at odds with the ability to pay principle.[119] Equally, the ECJ has not followed the call by scholars to subject the VAT system more substantially to the ability to pay principle by demanding an equal burden on the final consumer for comparable goods and services.[120]

116. ECJ 26 May 2005, case C-498/03 *(Kingscrest Associates)*, ECR 2005, I-4427, paras 54 et seq.; ECJ 7 December 2006, case C-240/05 *(Eurodental)*, ECR 2006, I-11479, para. 55; ECJ 10 April 2008, case C-309/06 *(Marks & Spencer)*, ECR 2008, I-2283, para. 49; ECJ 23 April 2009, case C-460/07 *(Puffer)*, ECR 2009, I-3251, para. 53.
117. For examples, see J. Englisch in: *Traditional and Alternative Routes to European Tax Integration* (2010), p. 231 (241).
118. ECJ 23 April 2009, case C-460/07 *(Puffer)*, ECR 2009, I-3251.
119. Critical remarks have been made, e.g. by J. Englisch in: *Traditional and Alternative Routes to European Tax Integration* (2010), p. 231 (242); W. Reiss in: *Festschrift J. Lang* (2010) p. 861 (887). For another example where the ECJ did not subject the VAT directives to the principle of equality, see ECJ 15 July 2010, case C-582/08 *(Commission / United Kingdom)*, ECR 2010, I-7191; for a critical review see W. Haslehner, *Steuer und Wirtschaft* 2012, *forthcoming*.
120. J. Englisch in: *Traditional and Alternative Routes to European Tax Integration* (2010), p. 231 (245); W. Reiss in: *Festschrift J. Lang* (2010) p. 861 (878).

CHAPTER 10

European Union Tax Law and Internal Tax Systems

Gabriel Casado Ollero & Miguel A. Caamaño Anido

§10.01 INTRODUCTION

Despite not revealing anything new by doing so, we must begin by pointing out that the European Union (EU) is, above all, a *Community based on the Rule of Law*; and not only because it is supported by international Treaties, but also due to the fact that that there are hardly any other public bodies which depend so much on law in order to carry out their functions. The EU is, therefore, created by law, and is equipped only with the law it creates (J.V. Louis). '*Although concluded in the form of an international agreement, it nonetheless constitutes the constitutional charter for a Community based on the Rule of Law*', states the Court, with reference to the EEC Treaty (Opinion 1/91, 15 December 1991, on the European Economic Area, paragraph 21).

So, in this EU created by and the creator of law (the EU legal system), alongside the norms which gave rise to it (the founding Treaties) and those that it produces while performing its duties (Secondary EU law), a set of *principles* and *objectives*, along with a *system of values*, usually all encompassed in the expression '*EU acquis*', must be borne in mind.

Taking the *norms*, the *principles*, and the *aims* and *objectives* of the EU as a starting point, the Court of Justice has outlined the characters (primacy and direct efficacy) which have shaped the consolidation of EU law into a system and as a legal system, base law and of legal structure.

The primacy of EU law constitutes the underlying principle of the EU system, as the Court was quick to point out, 'the EEC Treaty has established its own system of law integrated into the legal systems of Member States...and which must be applied by their courts' (judgments of 15 July 1964, case 6/64, Costa-ENEL, and of 13 February 1969, case 14/68, WALT WILHEIM). Hence the Court simultaneously highlights: the *autonomy* of EU law in respect to national law; its *insertion* in the legal system of Member States, and finally, the *primacy* of EU law over the latter.

It is convenient, however, to remember that, although direct efficacy and primacy of EU law are implicit in the Treaties, the foundation and the source of validity of these, and therefore, of secondary EU law, is found in the internal Constitutions of the Member States, as the supranational character which reflects the specific nature of EU law does not mean acknowledging, in this legal system, a base outside the national Constitutions of the States, as the Spanish Constitutional Court has affirmed as of its Judgment 28/1991, of 14 February.

It is not surprising, then, that the first task that European integration places upon any legal operator consists, precisely, of understanding the characteristics of EU law, as a system and as a legal system, and the problems that are raised by its linking (integrating link) to the internal legal system of the Member States.

However, the expansive character and the dynamism of the supranational integration process itself, along with the character that the Court stamps on EU Law, make the task an unfinished one or, in any case, one which cannot be considered completely finished once and for all, as it demands a permanent need for attention to the evolution of EU law and to its growing protagonism and incidence in both the construction and daily use of law (EU and internal) within the Member States.

On the following pages, the intention is to report on the current state of the principal matters and legal problems which make up the reality of EU tax law, beginning with the attribution and competential distribution between the EU and Member States, dealing with the new sources of EU tax law and the demands of the principle of non-discrimination and the fundamental liberties of the EU; the control of State aids; the demands of the principles of proportionality and loyal cooperation; finally concluding with the financial responsibility of the State as a closing clause to the relation between EU law and the national legal systems which, as well as guaranteeing the full efficiency of EU norms, also guarantees the rights of the individuals (EU citizens) to full reparation of damages caused through infringements of the legal system of the EU attributable to the national authorities, and of which Judgment of 23 December 2010, Appeal number 508/2007 of the Spanish Supreme Court is an emblematic example.

§10.02 THE EU AND THE MEMBER STATES FROM THE LEGAL AND COMPETENCE PERSPECTIVES

[A] The Transfer of National Competences to the European Union

Article 93 of the Spanish Constitution authorizes the ratification of Treaties that confer the exercise of competences derived from the Constitution to an international organization or institution through organic law. In this way, through this precept, drawn up specifically with the accession of Spain to the EU in mind, the Spanish Constitution expressly consents through organic law the conferral of sovereign competences, among them legislative power, in favour of EU Institutions.

Article 93 constitutes, as do the homonymous precepts of the Constitutions of the other EU members, the means of legitimacy not only of the European law in force at the moment of the signing of the Act of Accession of each country to the EC (nowadays, the EU), but it continues to be so for each and every one of the Treaty reforms, as was the case in the Single European Act, in the ratification of the Treaty of the EU of 1992, in the Amsterdam ratification in 1997, or in the most recent one, Lisbon. As RUIZ-JARABO COLOMER said (*El juez interno y el Derecho comunitario*, Cuaderno de Estudios Europeos, Madrid, 1993) this type of constitutional precepts 'not only have an organic competence character, regulating a special procedure for the approval of specific international treaties, but they also respond to an essential legal-material demand which is to constitutionally authorize the regulatory competence of the EU, with all the implications and without prejudice to the powers conferred to the national sovereignty.'

The Constitutional Courts of the Member States agree that, once integration has occurred, the internal Constitution is not a valid frame for EU norms, but it is the Treaty itself, whose ratification implements the sovereign process of transfer of the exercise of powers of competences derived from the Constitution, with the limitation that the rules incorporated in virtue of the transfer are compatible with its basic principles and values. If this limitation is respected, the Constitutional means used to sign the Accession Treaty of each State to the EU continues being valid not only to integrate new expressions of EU law (e.g. The Lisbon Treaty) in the regulatory acquis which governs each State, but to also subordinate all internal law to the supremacy of all EU regulation.

This type of enabling clauses on the limitations on sovereignty, such as the one in Article 93 of the Spanish Constitution, has a double function in the structuring of the relations of coexistence between the national legal system and the EU legal system: a purely internal function, i.e. intra-constitutional, and an external function or of international impact. On anticipating self-restriction of State sovereign powers (legislative, executive and judicial in relation to certain material orders) by delegating its exercise to the EU bodies, the constituting legislator deliberately weakens the other constitutional provisions as well as those relative to, for example, the principle of division of powers, the principle of legality and, last but not least, the principle of rule of competence in favour of certain infra-State bodies or entities (as in the case of the sub central entities). The enabling clause becomes the grounds for dispensation from trial over constitutionality which could fall upon EU acts, even in those situations in which the regulating constitutional provisions of the Constitution guarantee processes do not exempt EU norms as a potential object of a constitutional trial.

In its external function, the clause supports the very existence of the EU as an international authority, and especially the exercise of competences by EU bodies, despite the EU not being expressly named in the filing.

All the Member States, with the exception of the United Kingdom, are governed by a rigid formal Constitution. Of all of them, only one has a general clause of conferral of powers to the EU: the Republic of Ireland.

The Irish Constitution of 1937 is an exceptional case, as it does not expressly allow limitations on sovereignty in favour of an international organization, but in contrast, Article 29.4.5 introduced by virtue of the *Third Amendment of the Constitutional Act* of 1972, and revised in 1992, points out that '*No provision of this Constitution invalidates laws enacted, acts done or measures adopted by the State which are necessitated by the obligations of membership of the European Community or of the Communities, or prevents laws enacted, acts done or measures adopted by the European Community or by the Communities or by institutions thereof, or by bodies competent under the Treaties establishing the Communities, from having the force of law in the State.*' This provision supposes that the EU rules contrary to the Constitution are unconstitutional and, excluding unconstitutionality, and its inhibitive effect, guarantees the implementation of the EU Regulations. As far as we are concerned, we do not see confirmation of what is known as 'degree of supra-constitutionality', of a hierarchical, absolute and unconditional nature in the Irish Constitution.

The ten Constitutions which anticipate limitations to sovereignty do so by means of clauses of very different wording: almost elliptical in the case of France; extended and ambiguous in the cases of Greece and Denmark. On the other hand, some Constitutions characterize in precise legal terms the act of limitation as a 'temporary delegation' (Luxemburg), a 'transfer' (Germany and Denmark) or a 'conferral' (Spain and Belgium). Other Constitutions approach the conferral of competences to the EU in vaguer terms, 'consenting' (Italy), 'admitting' (France) the limitations of sovereignty. Note that, without damaging the differences in historical, political and judicial order, none adopts an express prevision of constitutional consent to a transfer of State sovereignty to the EU.

On the other hand, the Constitutional Courts of the Member States have been carrying out a restricted interpretation of the cited transfer of competence clauses. They are frequently considered 'merely organic and procedural' provisions. In other words, they simply allow, grant or transfer 'competences', but do not grant or extend 'rights'. The Constitutional Courts insist that it is simply about a transfer of competences, a limited transfer, and one which must be understood *ex constitutione*.

As the object of this delegation is not unlimited, even if the constitutional clause on which the act of delegation is based does not specify the material limits, the idea of law which lies within each Constitution, and which characterizes it, finds itself translated into a set of irrevocable principles and norms, whose intangibility has not only the nation as a target, but also Europe. Neither the constituting legislator, by incorporating a general sovereignty limitation clause into the Constitution, nor Parliament, by approving the Treaty which delimits the scope of the delegation, can authorize the exercise of a power forbidden to them, which is the violation of fundamental rights or material limitations of the constituting power, whether made explicit in a specific clause, or not.

The very process of integration entails the delegation of increasingly more important spheres of influence of sovereign powers in favour of the EU, as was verified by the Single European Act, and even more so with the Treaty on EU. From the States' point of view, the erosion of the value of the Constitutions as a parameter and the surreptitious modification of the vertical and horizontal distribution of power within the Constitutional frame is a difficult fact to ignore. With good reason, JELLINEK (*Reforma y mutación de la Constitución*, Madrid, CEC, 1991) invoked the concept of

Constitutional change, a change which can result from the effectiveness of the rules, from Parliamentary and political practice, or from the conforming interpretation of the constitutional court. In the case of the EU, the institutional policy of exercise of powers, especially the expansion of EU competences, approved by or consented to by the Member States, and especially by the Court of Justice of the EU case-law, have contributed decisively to this constitutional mutation.

All this explains the reaction of the German Constitutional Courts in the well-known Solange I and II judgments. With relation to the Treaty, and bearing in mind the limitation of sovereign powers which its ratification supposes, the German Constitutional Court dealt with the matter of the conciliation between the statute of the sovereign State and the development of the institutional-competential model of the EU with marked emphasis. Our aim here is not to discuss the well-known German Constitutional Court's judgment of 12 October 1993, but to simply highlight those conclusions which, preceded by a remarkable richness in its reasoning, link the conferral of competences to the sovereign means of power:

- The EU is not a State, but a 'union of States', always subject to the principle of competence of conferral. In short, the EU lacks competence in competence matters (kompetenz-kompetenz).
- The assumption by the EU of new functions and powers depends on the revision of the constituting Treaties, a process which assures the prevalence of the States' will and guarantees the democratic principle as the Parliament's competence to approve, or not, the ratification law is guaranteed.
- The Member States are the 'Lords of the Treaties', and their fundamental power of self-entailment guarantees them the statute of sovereign State.
- The Constitutional Court expressly criticized the generous application of Article 308 of the old EC Treaty which is the practice of implicit powers, as well as an interpretation in accordance with criteria of beneficial effect. The German Constitutional Court concludes by asserting that an amending interpretation of a competence rule 'does not have a binding effect on Germany', granting itself the same right to review the 'legal acts by European bodies' in order to verify whether they 'respect the limits of sovereignty conferred'.

We must draw attention to one final matter dealt with here: the material limits to European integration.

From a not only meditated but, also, contextualized reading of the transfer of competence clauses in the different constitutional texts of the Member States in favour of the EU, it is not easy to reach the conclusion that such material limits to the power of integration exist. Rather, it seems that the clauses have been drawn up with the deliberate intention of allowing any type of conferral of competences to international organizations for material reasons, so much so that only in certain cases do they establish certain conditions, but not material limits, with the following exceptions:

- The Swedish and Norwegian Constitutions expressly establish material limits to the conferral of competences: a constitutional reform.

- Article 29, section 2.3 of the Irish Constitution expressly 'constitutionalised' the authorization of Ireland's accession to the European Communities.

As a result, however, of the constitutional reforms that some countries (clearly, Germany—new Article 23 of the West German Basic Law-, France and Portugal) have seen themselves obliged to undertake, on account of the ratification of the Maastricht Treaty, some material limits to integration have appeared in the constitutional texts.

However, as PÉREZ TREMPS (*Constitución Española y Comunidad Europea*, Cuadernos de Estudios Europeos, Civitas-Fundación Universidad Empresa, Madrid, 1994) clarifies, the fact that there are almost no express constitutionalised limits does not mean that they do not exist. Political practices and, especially, a number of countries' constitutional case-law has demonstrated that material barriers to the process of integration do exist. Focusing on the limits which directly and specifically affect the power of integration, it can be seen that they are all more or less directly linked to the same idea of State sovereignty: first, the constitutionally protected fundamental rights; and second, determined principles and values, equally established in the Constitution, which form the very essence of the democratic system.

In the countries around us we can find, in one shape or another, both the invocation of fundamental rights and the principles and values of the democratic system as inviolable in all processes of supranational integration:

- Recalling the cited judgment of the German Constitutional Court Solange I, 1974, Article 24 of the Basic Law deals with the transfer of the sovereignty rights to interstate institutions. That cannot be interpreted literally. Article 24 of the Basic Law, like any other constitutional norm of similar nature, must be understood and interpreted in the context of the Basic Law as a whole. This implies that it does not open the way to modifying the Basic Law, which forms the base of its identity without modifying the Basic Law itself. But Article 24 of the Basic Law prevents a Treaty reform threatening the identity of the Basic Law of the Federal Republic by means of an invasion of its constituting structures.
- The well-known judgment of the Italian Constitutional Court *Frontini* (case 183/1973), points out, based on Article 11 of the Constitution, limitations on sovereignty have been consented to only to obtain the objectives therein specified; and it must be excluded that said limitations can carry, for EEC organs, an inadmissible power to violate the fundamental principles of our constitutional regulations, or the inalienable human rights.
- The French Constitutional Council has also established respect to fundamental rights as a constitutionally inescapable requirement in any process which involves transfer of sovereignty.

Both the theory and the actual constitutional texts have used very diverse expressions to refer to the inviolable values and principles of the supranational body of the EU: 'fundamental structures of the Fundamental Rule', 'fundamental principles of constitutional order', 'essential values of the democratic structure', or in other words, 'constitutional principles of the democratic system'. Ultimately, we are faced with nothing but different formulae to define the limits of each constitutional State when joining the EU, all of which form a link with the protection of fundamental rights and with the core values of the democratic system.

[B] The Current Situation of the Distribution of Competences between the EU and the Member States

As we have pointed out above, the sphere of the relations between the EU and the Member States is defined by the principle of conferral of competences (Article 5 of the consolidated version of the Treaty on EU - Official Journal 30 March, 2010, points out that '*Under of the principle of conferral, the Community shall act within the limits of the competences conferred upon it by the Member States in the Treaties to attain the objectives set out therein. Competences not conferred upon the Community in the Treaties remain within the Member States*') which derives from the principle of assumed aims and objectives.

However, despite all that has been said about this principle of competence of conferral, what is certain is that there has been a gradual extension of secondary EU rules – and not only with the approval of the Court of Justice, but frequently through Member States' initiative, usually agreed upon after periods in which one of them occupied the Presidency of the EU – to spheres which would have difficult justification from the initial 'competences of conferral' approach. It is likewise verifiable that EU law has been having an extraordinary influence, perhaps out of 'excessive' respect to the principles of supremacy and of direct effect, on the legal systems of the Member States, and never inversely, frequently causing the non-application of precepts of the legal systems considered contrary to the first.

A sizeable part of this widening of EU powers, be they regulatory or executive, is related to the criteria of the Court of Justice which states that the specific competences which all action taken by EU institutions must be supported by does not necessarily have to be a direct result of the specific provisions of the Treaty, but can also be deduced implicitly from the provisions.

There's no doubt, as CONSTANTINESCO states (*Compétences et pouvoirs dans les Communautés Européennes*, Paris, LGDJ, 1974, p.93), (likewise, GUY ISSAC. Droit Communautaire général, 3rd ed. Paris, Masson, 1992) that material provisions are those that define the EU's functions, powers and spheres of action. Note that matters and competences are not functionally equivalent concepts as, from the interpretation of the norms of competence, the material scope or the object of the functions and powers of the EU are extracted.

The material provision has, in short, an autonomous enabling function, (see M.L DUARTE, *La teoría de los poderes implícitos e a delimitaçao de competências entre a Uniao europeia e os Estados-membros*, Lex, Lisboa, 1997) i.e. it is an adequate and operative legal base, as long as its interpretation can answer the following questions: What is the sphere of activity that composes EU competence? What is the objective to be achieved? What types of powers are available to achieve this objective? What type of action should be adopted? What is at stake is to determine the extension of EU competences and the strength of EU powers in the diverse areas which the implementation of the Treaties reaches. This brief summary on the function and characteristic content of the material provisions and of the norms of competence is nothing more than the final result of an analysis of the Treaties.

However, at this point it is necessary to show that the widening process of the EU competences in detriment of the Member States reaching a turning point after the Maastricht Treaty which, in our opinion, has altered the tendency which we have been speaking about. This Treaty is a milestone, opening up a stage of 'competence retrocession' i.e. recovering competences in favour of the Member States, which had been transferred to the EU, for legal and political reasons.

As motives of a legal nature, the following can be mentioned:

1. The cited judgment of the German Constitutional Court, 12 October 1993, regarding the ratification of the Treaty on EU. As we have already seen in this judgment, which questions the competences that the EU hoped to assume as a consequence of the ratification of the Maastricht Treaty, the German Constitutional Court expressly reserved the competence to control the legality of the execution of the Treaty, with the purpose of verifying at all times that the Institutions of the new EU did not exceed the assumption of competences nor the exercise of powers derived from the new Treaty.
2. Advisory Opinion 1/94 on the WTO (World Trade Organization), where Article 133 of the EC Treaty was interpreted restrictively, narrowing the hopes of homogenization which the cited precept proposed upon entering into tariff agreements, export policies, trade protection measures, especially the antidumping and State aid measures.
3. Advisory Opinion 2/94, 28 March 1996, of the European Court of Justice on the possible ratification of the European Convention on Human Rights by the EU. In its reasoning, the Court of Justice, without denying that according to settled case-law, the fundamental rights form part of the general principles of law and the respect towards them is guaranteed by the Court of Justice, as well as the fact that the respect of human rights is a requirement for the legality of EU acts, concluded, nevertheless, that in the current state of EU law, the EU lacks the competence to join the European Convention of Human Rights.

As for political reasons, eventually 'constitutionalised', for the change in expansive tendencies of competences transferred by the States to the EU, the first to be mentioned must be the principle of subsidiarity.

The current Article 5 of the Treaty on the EU (Official Journal, 30 March 2010), after pointing out in the first paragraph that the EU will act within the limits of the competences that the Treaty confers, and within the objectives likewise assigned, states in the third paragraph, that in the spheres that are not of its exclusive competence, the EU shall intervene according to the principle of subsidiarity, but in so far as the objectives of the intended action cannot be sufficiently reached by Member

States, and consequently, can be better reached due to the dimension or, by the action considered at EU level.

On its practical aspect, the principle of subsidiarity does not operate as a prerequisite, but as an element which must be taken into account by all the institutions and advisory bodies that intervene in the decision process. This would explain that the Protocols annexed to the Treaties establish the requirement to state reasons for the acts in the light of the principle, turning to 'qualitative, or whenever possible, quantitative indicators' which justify that the desired aim can be better reached with it at EU level.

Likewise, it is worth pointing out the clarity of some messages incorporated into the

Protocol as well as into the Inter-institutional Agreement between the European Parliament, Council and Commission on the implementation of the principles of subsidiarity and proportionality:

- the principle of subsidiarity must offer guidance as to how the competences conferred by the Treaty must be exercised at EU level;
- subsidiarity is a dynamic concept and must be applied according to the objectives highlighted by the Treaty. EU intervention is allowed to increase, always within the limits of its competences, when the circumstances demand it and inversely, to restrict or abandon it when it is no longer justified;
- every regulating proposal must be justified in such a way that it complies with the principles of subsidiarity and proportionality, as well as the reasons, by means of qualitative and quantitative indicators, of why an EU aim can be better reached at EU level than internally by each Member State;
- the EU shall legislate only in as far as is necessary, opting for Directives rather than Regulations, and framework Directives over the previous;
- all possible modification of a text by the Commission, proceeding from Parliament or the Council, in as much as it contains a modification in the sphere of EU intervention, shall be accompanied by proof of respect towards the principles of non-excessiveness in the exercise of competences, subsidiarity, and proportionality.

As stated previously, there seems to be an inevitable conclusion, and that is that the EU, like the European Communities before, does not possess ownership, nor can its exercise be damaged due to demands typical of EU integration, of a competence to define or determine its own functions and powers, and decide about other aspects of self- organization. The EU does not have the 'competence of competences' ('*kompetenz-kompetenz*'). Its creation by means of a voluntary act of sovereignty by the Member States makes the EU a derived entity, but limited as a consequence of the vocation of the States towards the potential full exercise of powers. In other words, due to the way it was created, the nature of the process of review of its statute and above all, due to the reversible and specific character of the conferral of powers, the opinion, that even today has numerous supporters, which recognizes the EU as a primary political power, is not legally defensible.

§10.03 THE ATYPICAL SOURCES OF EU TAX LAW

As we have pointed out elsewhere (CAAMAÑO ANIDO Y CALDERÓN CARRERO, *Globalización económica y poder tributario:¿hacia un nuevo Derecho Tributario?*, Civitas, REDF, n°14, abril-junio 2002) the effect of economic globalization on the current 'tax systems' has manifested itself in, amongst others, the emergence of 'new sources' of tax law. The main characteristic of these 'new sources' lies in the fact that they are configured, fundamentally, following different principles from the classic taxation principles, and on the other hand, in that they are generally generated outside, and without intervention of, direct and/or decisive, national Parliaments. Among the 'new sources' it is worth mentioning, due to their growing importance, double taxation agreements, soft-law, the principles devised by the OECD's Committee on Fiscal Affairs and some of the precepts of the WTO treaties.

In the sphere of the EU, alongside the 'typical EU acts' referred to in Article 249 of the TFEU (Regulations and Directives), the EU institutions often adopt, with increasing frequency, other acts which receive different names (communications, decisions, declarations, recommendations, codes of conduct, and so on) to which theory refers to as atypical acts.

Within the context of atypical acts is where the so-called soft-law, currently of great use to the ECOFIN and the European Commission in tax matters, should be placed.

The legal instrument chosen to channel the Commission's latest specific measures and short-term proposals (Communication regarding the elimination of tax obstacles in cross-border pensions, Communication regarding the imposition of dividends received by natural persons in the internal market, Communications regarding the activity of the EU Transfer Pricing Forum, and so on) is none other than soft-law.

BORCHARDT (and more concisely, but along the same line, SNYDER *Soft Law and Institutional Practice*, EUI Working Paper Law, n°5, 1993) (WELLENS & BORCHARDT: *Soft Law in European Community Law*, European Law Review, n°14, 1989) and U. MÖRTH have defined soft law as '*the rules of conduct that find themselves on the legally non-binding level (in the sense of enforceable and sanctionable through international responsibility) but which according to the intention of its authors indeed do possess legal scope, which has to be further defined in each case. Such rules do not have in common a uniform standard of intensity as far as their legal scope is concerned, but they do have in common that they are directed at (intention of the authors) and do have as effect (through international law), that the conduct of States, international organizations and individuals is influenced by these rules, however without containing international legal rights and obligations*' (Soft Law and New Modes of EU Governance - A Democratic Problem? Darmstadt, November 2005).

There are many diverse reasons upon which the EU institutions base their arguments to justify the use of soft-law. First, it has been justified on the base of the principle of subsidiarity, a principle which, besides appearing in the title of Article 5.3 of the Treaty, has been interpreted in the sphere of regulatory activity in the sense that the EU must legislate only as far as is necessary, in such a way that, on equal terms, directives would be preferred to regulations, framework directives to specific measures, and with a preference to non-binding measures, such as recommendations, when they are adequate. Voluntary codes of conduct shall also be adopted, when they are sufficient.

There is no doubt, however, that the use of non-legislative approaches could be an additional measure to progress in the tax sphere. We must even admit, as the theory points out, that the use of instruments, especially Commission recommendations, directives or interpretative notes result in involving the participation of the European Parliament in the 'quasi-legislative' process, which mitigates, even if partially, a certain 'democratic deficit' (or 'crisis in the principle of legality', which we deal with in another chapter) which reflects the common and usual channel of the production of regulations at an EU level.

Third, the non-binding instruments of the EU can serve as points of reference to the legislative activity of the Member States in those cases in which, having recognized competences in certain matters to the EU, it still has not acted. By way of example, the non-binding recommendations which the Commission adopted in the area of cross-border workers or SMEs (latent internal competence and implicit potential competence) which, despite not generating a legal obligation amongst the Members to respect them, did, however, through analogy to the position of the Court of Justice which stated that the national Courts must not ignore those recommendations when they resolve disputes, give the idea that Member States cannot legislate in such a way that moves away from the objectives of the said recommendations is justifiable (if interpreted in this way they would constitute a standstill) and even that the States are obliged to consult the Commission before adopting any national legislation or bilateral Treaty.

Likewise, soft-law can contribute to the development of new tax norms in those cases in which the Court has declared the previous ones illegal. In the area of bilateral tax agreements that Member States enter into among themselves and with third countries, for example, the action of both the Commission and the case-law of the Court of Justice acquire a determining relevance.

In short, the use of soft-law allows points of reference to be given in areas such as corporate taxation in which the competences of the Council are debatable and debated, in a way that it not only demonstrates the problems derived from a lack of coordination in the way a legal person's income is dealt with (hampering of trade and trans border activity in the internal market, erosion of international competiveness of European firms, with the corresponding loss of resources), but it sets the guidelines for the tendencies which the legislation of the Member States must follow in order to offer efficiency and favour business competitiveness in the EU. The most illustrative example is that of Recommendation of 23 October 2001, which contains a strategy aimed at providing companies a consolidated tax base for Corporate Taxation for their EU based activities, and in which the Commission raises interesting points on subjects such as how to regulate the so-called 'European society', covering direct and indirect participation in the Directive on parent companies and their subsidiaries, introducing or expanding bilateral or multilateral programmes of previous agreements on determining transfer pricing at the heart of company groups, the improvement of the Arbitration Convention, giving its resolutions a binding character, and even a final aspiration of drawing up, in the long run, an EU version of the OECD agreement model and of its comments (or at least certain articles) which fulfil the specific requirements of the accession to the EU.

It can also be argued, as MARTIN JIMENEZ indicates (*Towards Corporate Tax Harmonization in the European Community*, Series on International Taxation n°22, Kluwer: The Hague, London and Boston, 1999) which follows BOTHE (*Legal and Non-legal Norms- A meaningful Distinction in International Relations?* in 11 Netherlands Yearbook of International Law 65) and THÖMMES (*Imputation systems to be adapted to the Internal Market*, Intertax n°12, 1995) that the Member States could be more receptive to soft-law than to hard-law as it allows them to maintain a certain amount of freedom and avoids the rigidity of the legal obligations of hard-law. Proof of this is the reaction to the recommendations of the Ruding Report of some Member States, who were less reticent than the Commission to adopt some of this Committee's recommendations. Such was the case, for example, of Spain and Germany, who took into account some of those recommendations in their corporate income tax reforms. Another example is the Code of Good Conduct in matters of corporate taxation, whose form, i.e. of mere good conduct, was thought by the Council to be the best option in order to avoid the rigidity and inflexibility of approving it as a Directive.

However, the legal theory has highlighted some of the problems that derive from the use, and abuse, of soft-law.

For WELLENS AND BORCHARDT (*Soft law in European Community Law*, op.cit.) the real paradox stems from the fact that the soft-law instruments not only allow the Commission to do what it has no right to do using hard-law, but that those soft-law instruments can turn into hard-law, evading the control of the Council and, basically, the procedure anticipated in the Treaty to enact hard-law norms. The activity of the Court of Justice is fundamental to the process of transformation of soft-law into hard-law. From the moment that the Court of Justice uses rules of soft-law as a legal base of a ruling, the norm's soft-law nature adopts the nature and character of hard-law. In this way, the paradox of subsidiarity can close the circle when the Court of Justice appears on the scene: the Commission can produce a soft-law norm that would not have been approved by the Council through the usual legislative procedure, and when threatened with a leap into the Court of Justice or, even, taking a Member State to the Court of Justice, the effects of the soft-law norm are very similar to those of a hard-law measure.

What is more, in the area of direct taxation, another inconvenience, which has been indicated with respect to the use of soft-law, stems from the lack of control of abuses from the Commission when employing this technique. It is much easier to avoid the harshness to which the system of conferral of competences submits regulatory acts via the Council's hard-law through the Commission's recommendations and instructions.

What has also been highlighted is the fact that soft-law derived from the Commission is frequently an exclusive product of the Commission's government employees, a bureaucratic product full of technical imperfections and whose quality suffers due to the distance that exists between it and economic and corporate reality.

§10.04 THE CRISIS OF THE PRINCIPLE OF LEGALITY

As is known, in all regulations that attempt to organize a pluralist democracy in accordance with the principle of distribution of powers, the law constitutes the most genuine and representative expression of the will of the people. The law is a norm dictated by Parliament, an organ of popular representation chosen by universal suffrage. The law means, then, a curb to Administration intervention in financial activity, providing a greater degree of legal safeguards to the regulatory process. In this way, the law clearly endorses the end of the system of relations between the Administration and the taxpayer as a power relation, to provide guarantees that are nowadays proper of any legal obligation relation.

The accession of any State to the EU, however, with the consequent adoption of its laws, primary and secondary, entails a noticeable transformation of the pillars on which the principle of legality rests, as neither European constitutional law nor the Regulations or EU Directives, all of them sources, as is known, of Tax law, obey the fundamental idea, at least in the way that we have put forward, of the principle of legality. It does not seem necessary at this moment to go into the relation between EU and internal regulations of each Member State, the direct effect and the supremacy of the former over the latter, non-contractual responsibility of the States' failure to comply with EU regulations, nor the autonomous character of these, circumstances which justify its 'singularity' as much as its subsistence as an authentic—and autonomous—legal system (vid., for all, PESCATORE, *L'ordre juridique des Communautés Européennes*, Liaja, 1975). However, as we shall now see, making a distinction between primary EU law and secondary EU law, the organic competence and the source of regulatory production of the former finds difficult adaptation within the classic assumptions of the principle of legality.

As is known, primary EU law is made up by the constituting Treaties of the Communities, with their Protocols and Annexes, and the Treaties which modify them, especially the Treaties of the EU, all of which are an integral part of what can be considered Constitutional EU law. Each Treaty, as J.V LOUIS points out (*Les réglements de la CEE*, Brussels, Univ.Presses, 1969) organizes the production of legal norms and shapes a different legal system of competences, while it establishes specific structure and institutional functioning rules for each Community, although it is clear that the TFEU is considered the core of EU law, and similarly, the interpretative rule for the other Treaties.

This primary law, formally made up by, as we have seen, classic legal-international instruments, forms, as the Court of Justice of the Communities expressed in its Report 1/91, the constitutional charter of a based on the Rule of Law, and besides enjoying a hierarchical supremacy over 'secondary' law, forms part of the internal regulations as a consequence of the parliamentary ratification process which it is subject to in every Member State. The parliamentary ratification process endows these legal instruments with the due constitutional legitimacy in a way that they avoid the demands of the principle of legality.

It is more difficult to reach the same conclusion, however, in the case of the so-called secondary law. It constitutes the regulatory acts dictated by the EU organs and, as is known, the regulations and directives carry special relevance in tax matters. With regard to this, despite the consolidated version (Official Journal of 30 March 2010) of the Treaty on EU establishing in Article 14.1 that *'The European Parliament shall, jointly with the Council, exercise legislative and budgetary functions'*, the new Article 223.2 of the TFEU explains that *'All rules or conditions relating to the taxation of Members or former Members shall require unanimity within the Council'*. Little has changed, despite the reforms introduced to the Treaty on EU after the Lisbon Treaty and in the Treaty on the Functioning of the EU, in relation to the judgment that must be made about the presence (or, more precisely, absence) of 'right to self-imposition by the sovereign nation' in relation to the Regulations and the Directives regarding secondary law.

The first, as is known, have general scope, and will be obligatory in all their elements and directly applicable in each Member State. The regulations are published in the Official Journal of the EU and come into force on the date which is stated in them, or failing this, twenty days after their publication. From that moment on, they are norms of a binding content, which directly create rights and obligations for the individuals without the need of an internal transformation or introduction process. So, as a directly applicable norm in the Member States, and with direct effect and supremacy over internal regulations, the EU Regulations on tax matters have been integrated into our law in such a way that, from the perspective of principle of legality, this principle is left weakened. They are not laws in the strict sense, nor are they, which is even more relevant, dictated by organs chosen through a process of popular election, which would endow them with due 'democratic legitimacy'. Professor VANISTENDAEL emphatically insists in his *No European Taxation without European representation* (EC Tax Review, nº3, 2000) that the solution to the representational deficit in the European organs endowed with powers of regulation does not stem from the suppression of the rule of unanimity in the Council, but that it is necessary and urgent for the representatives of the European taxpayers to have an active role through the institution of Parliament reserved.

In fact, the regulations which have had more impact on our internal tax regulations (Regulations of the 27 January and 11 September 1992, 10 January 1996 and especially 2913/92, by which the EU Customs Code is approved) have been dictated by the European Council, and it is well-known that the Council, far from being an organ of popular representation, is an organ whose organic structure has a diplomatic character, being composed of a representative of ministerial rank from each Member State, authorized to involve the government of each Member State (Article 146). Note that with such composition, it is the EU institution whose competence it is to dictate the largest part of secondary EU law, i.e. authentic legislative power. In these cases, Parliament, the only institution which represents the people of the Member States and which, therefore, provides the due democratic legitimacy to the institutional structure of the EU, holds no more than a mere advisory function. Let us recall that despite the consolidated version (OJ of the 30 March 2010) of the Treaty on EU establishing in Article 14.1 that *'The European Parliament shall, jointly with the Council, exercise legislative and budgetary functions'*, the new Article 233.2 of the TFEU establishes the *lex specialis* in virtue of which *'All rules or conditions relating to the taxation of Members or former Members shall require unanimity within the Council'*.

The legislative power, at least in the Regulations on tax matters, corresponds to the Council - and by nothing less than unanimity, i.e. with the right of veto in favour of any of the EU Members - an organ which, as we have seen, at least from a constitutionalist perspective suffers from what a certain scholarly sector [DEHOLSSE, *European Institutional Architecture after Amsterdam: Parliamentary system or Regulatory Structure?*, Common Market Law Review, vol.351998; GIL ROBLES, *Le nouvel équilibre institutionnel de l'Union européenne*, available on hhtp://www.iue.it/General/EUI-review] calls 'institutional democratic deficit'.

When we highlight the role that law has reserved in the legal-financial sphere, its origin is always present, i.e. to constitute a sign of the power of self-imposition of the State, an origin which - without damaging the bridge that Article 93 of the Spanish Constitution, and the homonymous precepts of the other Member States build in this respect - cannot be said of these other norms (EU Regulations) which, besides, enjoy a higher position than the internal systems on the hierarchy, and whose efficacy is direct and immediate. Suffice to recall judgments 19/1987 and 23/1993 of the Spanish Constitutional Court *(as occurs with other principles of legality present in the Constitution the sphere of this one here established is none other than the attempt to ensure that the regulation of a determined area of vital importance for people depends exclusively on the will of those who represent them...this guarantee to self government of the community which is encoded in state law (Article 133.1) is also in our democratic constitutional state a consequence of equality and, due to that, the preservation of basic equality of every citizens position, no less relevant than the very system. (Article 2 of the Constitution))* to realize that the classic approach of the principle of legality is in need of a review in light of what we have mentioned about the EU Regulations.

The effect that we have been advocating about EU Regulations is especially illustrative in the case of Customs Law, regulated by virtue of the Council Regulation 2913/1992, of 12 October 1992, by virtue of which the EU Customs Code is approved, and the Commission Regulations 2454/1993 of 2 July 1993, by which certain provisions for the application of the Regulations previously cited are determined. These norms, especially the first (the Customs Code) arise out of the intention to exclusively legally order (with the exception of certain very specific sectoral dispositions, also announced by the EU Institutions, relative to agricultural or trade policies) the current customs norm, i.e. the general norms and procedures that guarantee the application of the import tariff measures and of other types established on an EU scale in the framework of the interchange of goods between Member States and third countries, including agricultural and commercial policy measures. So, in the cited dispositions the circumstances that we previously advocated of the regulations coincide specifically, which is that they have general scope, are obligatory in all their components and what is especially relevant, that they are applicable in each Member State without their incorporation to internal law depending on any need of ratification or publication. Consequently, from our point of view, the only link between the direct effect and the immediate applicability which the regulations and Parliamentary activity enjoy is that which derives from the conferral of competence clauses incorporated into the constitutional texts of the Member States. It is not easy, then, to correspond the demands of the principle of legality, in particular its political function of assuring democracy through the participation of citizens in the establishment of the tax system, with the way the EU regulations are produced, in this case of the complete regulation of the system of custom rights for all EU members.

As we shall later see, in the absence, or at least not visible in the foreseeable future, of the representatives' willingness to exercise regulatory authority through the Council, it is only through the remission clauses of each constitutional text that the principles that justify the use of Regulations in customs, that these matters of secondary EU law will be legitimate (the concept of customs union, of internal market, of the need to assure the correct application of customs regulations and the rights of the economic operators to be treated in a fair manner, all of which are invoked in the Exposicion de Motivos del Reglamento 2913/93) would be superimposed in (or would postpone) the demands derived from the classic concept of the principle of legality.

We shall reach some similar conclusions in the analysis of the regulations announced by the European Institutions in the shape of Directives, and the demands which we already know about the principle in question.

It is certain, in fact, that the Directive, as a norm, 'will bind the target Member State in relation to the desired result to be achieved, leaving, however, the national authorities to choose the way and means', so that it starts as a legal act that initiates a regulatory procedure whose perpetration demands the participation of the internal organs of the Member States. If it were like that, we would have avoided all possible friction which the validity and effectiveness of the Directives suffer with the principle of legality as in the second phase of production of the norm, its incorporation to the internal system and subsequent development by each State, it would receive the sufficient Parliamentary assent, followed by the corresponding official publication.

However, the precisions which the Court of Justice itself has made about that general criteria must not be forgotten. In its order of 23 November 1995, *Asocarne* (C-10/95 P), it clarified that 'even though a directive is, in principle, binding on its addressees, the Member States, a directive normally constitutes an indirect mode of legislating or regulating. Indeed, the Court of Justice has repeatedly classified a directive as a measure having general scope.'

Second, and from the judgment of 5 February 1963, *Van Gend Loos* (C-26/62), the Court of Justice admitted that the directives must be admitted as having direct effect, i.e. the capacity to deploy full effects themselves, creating rights and obligations for all those who could see themselves affected by their scope of application, being able to be invoked before the public authorities (administrative and legal), with respect to those dispositions which are 'clear' and 'sufficiently precise', and whose mandate is 'unconditional'. In such cases, the directive stops being a mere frame-norm, without any prejudice to it being called upon to be developed by the national legislator, to deploy full direct effect.

The Spanish Supreme Court pointed out in a judgment of 3 November 1997 that '*the Court of Justice of the European Communities, in the Sace Judgment: of the 17 December 1979, Ratti, of the 5 April 1979, and Becker of the 19 January 1982 among others, has declared, to this effect, that the sufficiently precise dispositions of a directive can, in absence of a flaw in the internal development legislation, produce a direct effect and be applicable by internal legal systems to the persons that allege them or whom they benefit*'.

Third, after the entry into force of the Amsterdam Treaty, section 6 of the protocol annexed to the TEU and to the TFEU, on the application of the principles of subsidiarity and proportionality, expressly encourages what has been a fact in the last years, that the Directives should be more detailed, fundamentally technical, that they notably restrict the State's margin of interpretation and that they come close to authentic regulation.

As a consequence of what we have noted, at least in respect of those Directive dispositions that fulfil the characteristics demanded by the case-law of the cited case Van Gend Loos – that they are 'clear', and 'sufficiently precise' and whose mandate is 'unconditional' – in the measure their direct efficacy must be recognized, deriving from that the 'inapplicability' of those norms from national law which oppose them, it must be thought that they present the same problems of adjustment as the principle of legality which we advocated in the Regulations. We also state, in this case, that there is no easy harmony between the provisions of the Directives that take direct effect, as we have seen, and the basis and final justification of the cited principle.

Let us recall that the vast majority of the Directives on fiscal matters in force have been dictated by the Council, whose organic composition, of a diplomatic nature, we have already referred to, as well as the 'democratic deficit' which can be attributed to its power to dictate norms endowed with direct effect. If in its most generic formulation, as RODRIGUEZ BEREIJO ('*Jurisprudencia constitutcional y principios de la imposición*' in the collective work *Garantías constitucionales del contribuyente*, Tirant lo blanch, Valencia, 1998) says, the principle of legality constitutes the legal expression of the political principle of rule or supremacy of law, the expression of the general will through the institution responsible for sovereignty, the people represented by Parliament, we fear that the legal system of so many tax concepts established by clear and unconditional norms of the Directives, i.e. norms dictated by an institution of diplomatic nature, will force us to rethink that principle. Without any prejudice to the coverage that the corresponding constitutional clauses of conferral of powers offer to supranational bodies, particularly to the EU, at first glance, it would seem as if the guarantee of self-provision which encloses the principle of legality, i.e. the political function of ensuring citizen's participation in the creation, modification and elimination of taxes, had broken.

It is important to highlight that the vast majority of regulations of the EU have adopted the form of Directive. What is more, a large number of the provisions within them comply with the demands that we have seen for them to be granted direct effect, that is, that they are clear provisions, sufficiently precise and unconditional, such as is deduced from the decisions of the Court of Justice who, in pre-trial or of direct appeal, has declared certain provisions within the internal regulations of a Member State non-adjusted to EU law, based on the fact that they were not in line with determined precepts of a Directive that had not been object of a transposition, or that the norm of transposition was not in keeping with the frame created by it.

This would explain, and it does not seem casuistry that the Court, rather than referring to the principle of legality, invokes the principle of typicity. In the Advocate General's, Mr Jacobs, conclusions on the matter C-111/92, *Lange,* partially reflected in judgment of 2 August 1993, expressly refers to the 'principle of typicity in taxes', and the cited Advocate clarifies that '*even if the imposition of tax is not regarded as a penalty, a corresponding principle of fiscal law (referring typicity) requires that tax should not be imposed in the absence of a specific legislative basis*'.

It has been rightly said (ORÓN MORATAL, *Consecuencias de la integración en las Comunidades Europeas sobre el Derecho Financiero y Tributario,* Civitas, REDF, n°97, enero-marzo 1998) that, from the perspective of the creation of national law, the consequences of harmonization diminish the function of parliaments, not only due to the detail and technicalities employed in the majority of the Directives, and in some cases the non-conformity with concepts of deep rooted tradition within tax law, but because they are compelled to incorporate some norms to the legal system, in the same terms as they have been approved by EU organs according to their system sources, and that only satisfy the principle of legality in its aspect of self-imposition, as in these cases it can be said that rather than legislate, a document is drawn up, like a commissioner for oaths, of an EU text which is integrated into internal regulations bearing the status of law.

§10.05 NON-DISCRIMINATION AND NON-RESTRICTION AT THE SERVICE OF FUNDAMENTAL FREEDOMS

[A] INTRODUCTION

Article 2 of the consolidated version (Official Journal of 30 March 2010) of the Treaty of the EU establishes the aims of the EU. Among others, it includes the establishment of a common market in which barriers to free movement of goods, people, services and capital among Member States are eliminated. As far as Article 18 (ex Article 12 TEC) of the TFEU is concerned, it points out that '*Within the scope of application, and without prejudice to any special provisions contained therein, any discrimination on grounds of nationality shall be prohibited*'

and Article 26 of the TFUE '*The internal market shall comprise an area without internal frontiers in which the free movement of goods, persons, services and capital is ensured in accordance with the provisions of the Treaties*'.

In furtherance of the described aims and objectives, the TFUE itself regulated the way in which this market should be reached. On one hand, by applying a principle of non-discrimination on grounds of nationality, which establishes the obligation that all nationals of Member States receive the same treatment as nationals of other Member States, and which inspires a good part of the Treaty provisions. On the other hand, the TFEU noted a programme of harmonization of norms and functioning of the common market.

In this context, Articles 26 and the following of the TFEU contain, among others, a charter of freedoms, which guarantee the free circulation of goods, workers, businesses, provision of services, and capital and payments.

In accordance with what is established in Article 45 of the TFEU, freedom of movement entails an abolition of all discrimination based on nationality between workers of Member States as regards to employment, remuneration and other conditions of employment.

Without prejudice to the limitations justified on grounds of public order, public security or public health, the freedom of movement shall entail the right,

(a) to accept offers of employment actually made;
(b) to move freely within the territory of Member States for this purpose;
(c) to stay in a Member State for the purpose of employment in accordance with the provisions governing the employment of nationals of that State laid down by law, regulation or administrative action;
(d) to remain in the territory of a Member State after having been employed in that State, subject to conditions which shall be embodied in regulations drawn up by the Commission.

The freedom of establishment, perhaps the one which has originated a more complex and further-reaching case-law, is contemplated in Articles 49 and following of the TFEU. Within the frame of such freedom:

> restrictions on the freedom of establishment of nationals of a Member State in the territory of another Member State shall be prohibited. Such prohibition shall also apply to restrictions on the setting-up of agencies, branches or subsidiaries by nationals of any Member State established in the territory of any Member State.
>
> Freedom of establishment shall include the right to take up and pursue activities as self-employed persons and to set up and manage undertakings, in particular companies or firms.

In agreement with *Avoir Fiscal*, the freedom of establishment implies that '*pursuant to Article 58 of the TFEU, companies or firms formed in accordance with the law of a Member State and having their registered office, central administration or principal place of business within the Union shall have the right to pursue their activity in a Member State through a branch or agency*'.

The freedom to provide services, established in Articles 56, and the following, of the TFEU, presumes the authority of a national Member State to provide services in another Member State's territory or to nationals of another Member State. The cited Article 56 points out that '*restrictions on freedom to provide services within the Union shall be prohibited in respect of nationals of Member States who are established in a Member State other than that of the person for whom the services are intended*'.

The Treaty itself clarifies that the scope of protection comprises '*a) activities of an industrial character; b) activities of a commercial character; c) activities of craftsmen; d) activities of the professions*'. It is necessary, however, that they be services normally provided for remuneration, projecting the sphere of protection over both the service providers and those for whom the services are intended, in as far as they are of a cross-border nature.

The fourth freedom, free movement of capital and payments (Article 63 and the following, TFEU) prohibits any type of restriction on the capital movement (specifically the movements described in Annex I of the Council Directive 88/361/CEE of 24 June 1988) and on payments whether they are between Member States or between Member States and third countries.

TERRA and WATTEL (*European Tax Law*, 5th edn, Kluer Law International, 2008) as well as M.GAMMIE (*The Compatibility of National Tax Principles with the Single Market*, in Vaniestendael Frans (ed.), EU Freedoms and Taxation, EATLP International Tax Series, Vol.2, IBFD, Amsterdam, 2006) underline that the fundamental freedoms result in logic and immediately two different 'powers': (a) the power to access another market (market access—market access principle) and b) the authority, within a determined market to be treated in the same way as a national of that market (market equality). Non-discrimination and non-discrimination on the grounds of nationality results in the power of the nationals '*to compete on the same terms with the products and with local producers, within the single market area*'. It is quite clear that, in the words of GAMMIE, the tax treatment of a specific product or of a determined producer within a specific national market is at stake. From the perspective of each Member State, what is at stake are the rules that regulate the trade in the internal market (internal market rules).

The cited authors shape non-restriction as a matter of market access, which demands a '*lifting of any obstacle to free movement of products and producers between the different national markets of the Member States*'. It is, in short, about discerning if one Member State uses its internal norms in tax matters to create any type of obstacle or to dissuade a person, while exercising a fundamental right, from entering or leaving a market.

Following A CORDEWENER (*The Prohibitions of Discrimination and Restriction Within the Framework of the Fully Integrated Internal Market*, in Vaniestendael Frans (ed.), EU Freedoms and Taxation, EATLP International Tax Series, Vol.2, IBFD, Amsterdam, 2006) it would be worth distinguishing between 'discriminatory restrictions' and 'non-discriminatory restrictions'. Within the latter, there would be a place for a) double burden situations, in which the obstacle to the fundamental freedoms originate from the over taxation by norms proceeding from different regulations and b) absolute burden situations, defined as '*the national measures which, legally or in virtue of their real consequences, result in altering the exercise of a protected activity in terms of the fundamental freedoms making it extremely difficult, when not impossible*'.

The Advocate General GEELHOED (e.g. Conclusions of the 6 April 2006, *Test Claimants in the FII Group Litigation*) likewise differentiates between 'discriminatory measures' and 'quasi restrictive measures'. The former are those in which a less favourable treatment is given between two persons by virtue of their nationality or similar criteria (e.g. residence), while 'quasi restrictive measures' are those which 'inevitably derive from the coexistence of different national tax systems'. For the cited author, only the first constitutes real ills for the EU, possibly contrary to EU regulations.

[B] Case-Law Evolution of the Characteristic Features of the Concept of Fiscally Restrictive Measure

As we have already pointed out elsewhere here, both the unanimity legally demanded for the regulatory action of the Council and the strength and impact which the principle of subsidiarity has been achieving, have transferred the protagonism of the harmonizing process to the Court of Justice. It was precisely in the sphere called principle of non-discrimination on the grounds of nationality that the 'secondary' harmonizing action of the Court acquired greater intensity, and with it an evolution of marked consequences especially on Member States regulations.

Initially, any measure which fulfilled all these conditions was deemed discriminatory: a) that it was a norm; b) that it brought in a differentiated treatment; c) in relation to two factual groups or situations; d) that they were in a fundamentally identical situation, except for their nationality and e) that the non-national group was the object of a less favourable treatment as a direct consequence of the creation of the norm.

This formula, at the initially narrow concept, simply offered protection to those persons intending to carry out an economic activity in a Member State different to their own and who were treated in a different manner to how the host Member State nationals were treated. The intensification of the flow of trade rapidly reflected that the formula was insufficient. The sphere of protection was so limited that the situations in which effective discrimination was not protected by the principle multiplied. Hence, as from the *Sorgiu* judgment, the States worked to widen the scope of the non-discrimination principle, and with *Biehl* and *Commerzbank* the residency criteria is at the same level of protection as that of nationality.

The way in which the Court of Justice tried the discriminatory effect of a tax measure also underwent its own corresponding evolution. The Court of Justice of the EU started by considering that, faced with the differences in treatment between residents and non-residents, discrimination existed if both groups of taxpayers find themselves in the same position when facing the discriminatory norm (*Avoir Fiscal* 1986). However, after this, its rapprochement of its reasoning the principles of International tax law led it to the affirmation that, in general, residents and non-residents do not find themselves in a comparable situation, but that the existence of differentiated tax systems for each of these categories of taxpayers does not constitute discrimination contrary to the TFEU. From this premise, the Court of Justice of the EU, makes an exception for those non-residents who obtain 'all or most' of their income in the State of source of income or State where the activity is carried out (*Schumacker, Wielockx and Gwchwind*).

As case-law has evolved, the existence of two lines of case-law can be detected, one in matters of company taxation and one relative to the taxation of natural persons. The Court of Justice of the EU is more inclined to admit the existence of a discriminatory restriction (comparability) in the sphere of company taxation than when it judges a measure of similar scope but applied to a natural person. In fact, in cases that affect Company Tax, the Court frequently uses the canon of 'comparability' rather than the norm (*Saint-Gobain* and *Baxter*), while in the situations relative to taxes that affect a natural person's income it starts from the non-comparability between residents and non-residents (*Schumacker, Wielockx and Gwchwind*), although on some occasions it has diverted from this (*Asscher, Vestergaard*).

The Court makes it very clear, however, that the prohibition on non-discrimination is operational in matters of substantive nature as of adjectival or procedural nature (*Commerzbank, Hoeschst*).

On the other hand, the EU prohibition is operative not only when the difference in treatment contained in a norm is projected on the non-national or the non-resident (e.g. when the non-resident cannot take advantage of personal and family tax reduction applicable to the resident taxpayers, *Schumacker*) but also when the discrimination within a tax norm projects its efficiency on resident or national taxpayer(s) but indirectly negatively affects the exercise of freedoms of national persons or residents of other Member States. Such has been the case of a resident taxpayer to whom the application of a tax deduction has been denied, for example for the purchase of property and of determined expenses derived from a professional activity due to the fact that the services that generate the right to deduction (home loan or professional services) were provided by a non-resident (*Safir, Vestergaard and Danner*).

Likewise, the EU prohibition on grounds of nationality operates with relation to the differences in protectionist tax measures that host country, i.e. the Member State to which nationals from other Member States move to in order to carry out business activities, to work or professional activities, can adopt. From this perspective, the EU principle of non-discrimination also prohibits differences in tax treatments established in the taxpayer's national or resident State, which create difficulties or place obstacles when exercising EU freedoms (home state discrimination). In this way, for example, the State of residence of an entity cannot adopt tax measures which restrict movement to another Member State's territory with the corresponding change of residence (viz., *Daily Mail*). In this sense, the Court declared that exemptions for possession of business shares included in the capital tax of the Netherlands were contrary to the freedom of establishment in as much as the norm limited the exemption to the shares in resident Dutch entities, in such a way that the exclusion of shares in resident entities (resident) of other Member States from exemption was considered contrary to the freedom of establishment (*Baars*). The same happened in relation to the request of a resident taxpayer in the Netherlands to apply the exemption in order to eliminate the double taxation in relation to different dividends satisfied by Belgian entities: the Court declared that the Dutch norm which excludes the exemption of foreign dividends is contrary to the free movement of capital (*Verkoijen:* principle of national treatment for foreign dividends).

But, as we have shown above, the Court did not stop at this point, but has expanded the scope of protection of the fundamental freedoms to such an extreme that it has given coverage not only to discriminatory procedures but also to any type of restrictive measures of a tax nature, whether direct or indirect. Although the prohibition on 'quantitative restrictions to imports and measures of equivalent effect' arises out of the tax sphere, the case-law of the Court (*Futura Participations*, *Safir* and *ICI*) adopts the criteria by virtue of which the tax norms of the Member States not only must not be discriminatory but cannot restrict the effective exercise of EU freedoms. Taking *Gebhard* as a starting point, the Court formulates the points of reference on which the validity of any internal norm will rest, even if it involves a situation of restriction: a) the inexistence of discrimination; b) the existence of justification in terms of the *rule of reason*; c) the adaptation of the norm; and d) its non-excessiveness in relation to the ends pursued by it.

It is important to emphasize that the concept of restriction was exported from the free movement of goods to the remaining fundamental freedoms, and the analysis of validity to which the Court submits the regulations of the Member States which, perhaps due to the simplicity of its application (comparability) which must always be carried out from the perspective of non-discrimination is avoided, means that nowadays the concept of restriction has more presence in the declarations of the Court than that of non-discrimination.

Together with the situations of discrimination and restriction, what some authors have called disparities can arise, that is, cases that are not a real interference to the fundamental freedoms, so they do not provoke incompatibility with EU regulation. It is, as it can easily be sensed, related to consequences derived from the lack of harmonization of direct taxation of the Member States, which can generate tax advantages (situations of double non-taxation) or disadvantages (double taxation), but that are not considered damaging to the fundamental freedoms.

Despite the negative delimitation of the concept of 'disparity' being made by the Court in *Gilly*, it was in *Schempp* where it made an effort to shape it more clearly. It points out that '*Article 12 EC is not concerned with any disparities in treatment, for persons and undertakings subject to the jurisdiction of the Community, which may result from divergences existing between the various Member States, so long as they affect all persons subject to them in accordance with objective criteria and without regard to their nationality.*' Consequently, the Court of Justice of the EU concludes that '*the Treaty offers no guarantee to a citizen of the Union that transferring his activities to a Member State other than that in which he previously resided will be neutral as regards taxation.*'

On the matter, it is worth mentioning the distinction that the Advocate General GEELHOED (e.g. in the conclusions of the 6 April 2006, *Test Claimants in the FII Group Litigation*) makes between three different types of disparities, i.e. three types of distortion that do not suppose a justifiable interference from the perspective of fundamental freedoms, but which, strictly speaking, hinder the internal market: a) the high administrative workload (the economic operators who carry out their activities in more than one Member State have higher administrative workloads than those who limit their economic activity to the territorial sphere of a single State); b) the workloads derived from the coexistence of different tax schemes (substantive disparities, which arise from the differences in the structure and the content of the tax systems and tax types of each tax); and c) the distribution of the tax competence, as well as the criteria, nowadays under debate, by virtue of which the State of residence is responsible for eliminating double taxation.

[C] The Causes for Justification of Discriminatory and/or Restrictive Measures

The mere knowledge that a norm is discriminatory or restrictive is not sufficient to conclude that it is incompatible with any of the fundamental freedoms. The freedoms do not define spaces of absolute protection, in such a way that an internal norm which reduces or limits those areas of protection could even be considered admissible, as long as said restriction or limitation is justifiable.

We must analyse, therefore, the grounds that the Court has admitted as supporting the adoption by the different Member States of certain discriminatory and/or restrictive measures.

It is worth highlighting, to this effect, that among the grounds for justification that are supported in the provisions of the Treaty are those that have been created by the case-law of the Court in order to theorise what is understood as 'overriding reasons in the general interest' introduced by *Cassi de Dijon*.

[1] Causes of Justification Established in the TFEU

The Treaty establishes that the fundamental freedoms can be limited for reasons of public order, public safety and public health. Such limitations are explicitly referred to in relation to the free movement of people, the freedom of establishment, free movement of services, and the free movement of capital. In the scope of the latter, Article 65.1 (b) the TFEU points out that the States have the 'right' to apply the provisions of their internal tax regulations that establish a difference in treatment between taxpayers that are not in an identical situation, with reference to place of residence or to the place where the capital is invested. The Court of Justice has clarified, however, that this 'right' belonging to the Member States must be object of a restrictive interpretation, in such a way that any internal norm that introduces discrimination or a restriction can only be considered compatible with the EU regulations when 'the difference of treatment refers to situations which are not comparable or are justified by overriding reasons in the general interest' (ECJ Judgment, Jäger, 17 of January, 2008, C-256/06).

[2] Causes of Justification Adopted or Invoked before the Court of Justice of the European Union

Alongside the causes of justification established in the Treaty, there are a number of reasons which have been accepted by the Court of Justice of the EU as justificatory circumstances of the tax provisions that produce discriminatory or restrictive effects. These are the overriding reasons in the general interest, which, despite the Court's initial resistance to admit them, are today susceptible to invocation throughout the European regulations.

[a] Causes of Justification Generally Inadmissible for the Court of Justice of the European Union

One of the main clauses has been the 'loss of tax revenues'. The Court argued, from the start, that this ground for justification could not be admitted as it was not included in the Treaty. From the moment in which, after *Cassis de Dijon*, the Court of Justice of the EU set the basis for its construction, it argued that the loss of tax revenues did not constitute a 'matter of overriding general interest'. This is reiterated in *Verkooijein, Danner, X e Y, De Groot, Lasteyrie du Saillant, Lenz, Manninen, Marks & Spencer, Meilicke, Shwarz* and *Orange*.

Some Member States have also invoked the 'compensation' argument, indicating that the possible disadvantages brought about by the interference that a discriminatory and/or restrictive measure provokes could be compensated for by other advantages to which the affected non-residents could have access to, even if these advantages are not directly related to the interference. The Court has systematically rejected this so-called grounds for justification as of *Avoir Fiscal*, as it did in *Asscher, Saint-Gobain, Eurowings, Verkooijein, De Groot, Lenz and Lakebrink*. As we shall later see, there are examples of more recent case-law that has admitted a complete neutralization of the effects derived from the interference.

The Court has also, repeatedly, rejected that the '*lack of harmonization of direct taxation at community level*' can justify the differences of tax treatment or restrictive measures. In certain cases, Member States argued that certain interference is due to the fact that in the sphere of direct taxation there are no measures that guarantee harmonization of the regulations of Member States, hence the reason for which the obstacles borne by individuals are as a result of that lack of harmonization. The Court has rejected this appeal for the lack of tax harmonization (e.g. *Avoir Fiscal* and *Centros*) based on the fact that 'the respect to the fundamental freedoms, understood as directly applicable norms, cannot depend on acts that should have been adopted by EU institutions.'

The direct applicability of the norms that consecrate EU freedoms, also justifies the rejection of the 'reciprocality' argument i.e. the thesis that the respect to the fundamental liberties would depend on the existence of a bilateral agreement in matters of reduction or elimination of double taxation. The Court has been conclusive in affirming that the respect towards the sphere of protection of the fundamental freedoms must be guaranteed by the State to all citizens of the different Member States and not only to those resident in a State which has signed a specific Agreement for the elimination of double taxation.

Lastly, the Court has also rejected (*Commission/France, Centro di Musicologia Walter Stauffer, Franked* and *Papillon)* that practical difficulties (especially the extension of a determined taxation treatment conceived for internal situations to transnational situations) could justify a restriction of a fundamental freedom protected by the Treaty.

[b] *Grounds for Justification Generally Accepted by the Court of Justice of the European Union*

The first of the grounds for justification of interference in the fundamental freedoms accepted by the Court stems from 'the necessity to guarantee coherence to the tax system.' It is the first overriding reason in the general interest with a specific tax content admitted by the Court.

The admission of these grounds of justification first appears in the *Bachmann* and *Belgian Commission* trials. Despite its express submission by the States and admission by the Court, it has established a set of demands and requisites which have made these grounds for justification practically inapplicable. For the tax norm to be considered 'necessary to guarantee the coherence of the tax system' the following would have to be approved: a) the existence of a direct correlation between a tax advantage and a tax disadvantage; b) that the advantage and disadvantage refer to the same tax; c) that both are projected onto the same taxpayer and; d) that this direct correlation is not questioned by a Double Taxation Agreement.

Despite having been severely restricted by the Court, to such an extent that several authors have considered it inapplicable de facto, it has been recently accepted in *Krankenheim Ruhesitz.* Another of the overriding reasons most frequently invoked by the States to justify interference is 'the fight against tax avoidance and fiscal fraud' and 'the need to guarantee fiscal supervision'.

With reference to the former, the Court has established that, in the sphere of direct taxation, the interests of Member States to adopt anti-abuse measures abstractly prevails over the protection of fundamental freedoms. The Member States must have the capacity to adopt measures, even if they restrict fundamental freedoms, whose aim is to combat both the wholly artificial arrangements and to pursue those taxpayers who use fundamental freedoms as a way to elude the application of internal tax norms. In some initial judgments (e.g. *Avoir Fiscal* and *Biehl*), the Court refused to accept these grounds for justification based on the argument that it was not expressly provided for in the Treaty. Nowadays, in line with case-law initiated with *ICI* (*Metallgesellschaft, Lankhost-Hohorst, Commission/France, Marks and Spencer, Commission/Belgium, Thin Cap Group Litigation, Rewe, OYAA, Elisa, Lammers & Van Cleef, Commission/ Spain* and *Jobra*) its acceptance is free from strife.

Another grounds for justification frequently invoked stems from the 'need to justify the efficiency of the fiscal supervision'. These grounds for justification is usually admitted by the Court in situations in which the interference derives from the insufficient measures, adopted at EU level, which allow the elimination of problems suffered by the Member States as a consequence of the territorial limitations to their power of intervention. The Court has repeatedly considered that the efficiency of fiscal supervision constitutes valid grounds for justification. It established this in *Bachmann, Schumacker, Futura Participations, Baxter, Lankhorst-Hohorst, Commission/France, Lenz, Scorpio, Centro de Musicologia Walter Stauffer, Commission/Denmark, Rewe, Talott, Geurts, A* and in *Heinrich Bawer Verlag.*

Recently, the Court has accepted that an interference measure can have as grounds for justification the 'risk of using double losses'. Furthermore, in *Marks and*

Spencer, this circumstance was invoked and accepted in *Centro Equester Leziria Grande*, *Rewe*, *Commission/Spain* and *Deutsche Shell*.

The Court has also accepted as valid grounds for justification the 'need for a balanced distribution of the power of taxation'. These grounds for justification, notwithstanding references to this in *De Groot* and *Lateyrie du Saliant*, is explicitly accepted in *Marks and Spencer* and is established in *Deutsche Shell*, when the balanced distribution of competences between the different States is referred to as 'a 'legitimate objective', once '*the Member States can set the criteria for distribution of the sovereignty on tax matters, either unilaterally or through bilateral conventions*'. These grounds for justification was finally invoked in *N*, *Cadbury Schweppes*, *Denkavit International*, *Thin Cap Group Litigation*, *Rewe*, *OYAA*, *Amurta*, *Deutsche Shell* and in *Lidl Belgium*.

The Court seems to encourage 'the need to simplify and of transparency of the tax system', even, the 'reduction of administrative costs' as justifiable circumstances to the interference measures to the fundamental freedoms. This is deduced from Haliburton, Turpeinen, and Jäger.

[D] Evaluation of EU Case-Law on the Principle of Non-discrimination

The existence of a legislative process in which the interests of the Member States can be represented and in which each one of them has the right of veto has been conditioning the possibility of reaching a level worthy of harmonization of direct taxation. Under these circumstances, an independent court (the Court) and an entity with powers in the matter of State aid (the European Commission), have contributed decisively in order for the legislation in direct taxation matters of the Member States to progressively adapt to the imperative demands of the common market.

Just as an example, the action of the Court has resulted in that, after *Marks and Spencer*, many of the Member States have modified their legislation so that, within a context of consolidation, the deduction of the losses of permanent establishments in other Member States is allowed. *Lankhorst*, *Thin Cap Group Litigation* and *Lammers & Van Cleeff* provoked serious modifications in the tax systems of the thin capitalization of many Member States. Some of them have resolved to extend the system to include residents (e.g. Germany and France), while others have left the implementation of the anti thin capitalization norm void to the loans between the residents of the EU. *Cadbury Schweppes* introduced important regulatory modifications not only in the United Kingdom, but in Germany—which allows the non-application of anti abuse norms to EU residents when there is a 'genuine economic activity' and there is an effective interchange of information - and in France, which eliminates the anti abuse clauses in economic relations between EU operators except when it deals with 'wholly artificial arrangements'. In the sphere of exit tax, after *Lasteyrie du Salliant* and *N*, a series of legislative reforms have been triggered in the Member States, the first introduced by Sweden, in order to avoid the infringement of the freedom of establishment, as had just been outlined by the Court.

This so-called 'negative (tax) harmonization' led by the Court has likewise contributed to 'communitise' residents' tax norms in addition to those relative to non-residents, in such a way that they end up being compatible with the workings of the internal market and in the effective exercise of the EU freedoms.

However, we must not lose sight of the fact that if the court of the EU does not act, the Member States must coexist with negative harmonization configured casuisticly and in accordance with some principles very distanced from the classic and constitutional principles of taxation. Note that when the Court has had to examine compatibility in relation to national indirect taxation regulatory norms with the TFUE, it has basically reasoned in economic terms, i.e. focusing on the obstacles that the national tax norms generated on the exercise of EU fundamental freedoms. On most occasions, the justifications invoked by national governments on which to base national tax measures, based mainly on traditional taxation principles (taxation interest, fiscal supervision, fraud prevention, protection of the national taxable basis of assessment, supervision of the obligation to pay taxes, territoriality of the tax, etc) are considered insufficient or are even flatly rejected when described as lacking 'relevance to the EU'. This does not mean that the Court does not supervise (indirectly) or protect national taxation principles or 'taxation interest' of the Member States, but that such protection is set aside, as its main function is to protect the effective exercise of EU freedoms and the smooth functioning of the internal market, even if it leads to a second degree harmonization which erodes to a certain degree the taxation principles that configure the tax systems of the Member States.

In any case, as GARCIA PRATS ('The future of income taxation under the EC law requirements' *EC Tax Review*, n°3, 2002) states, the Court examines tax laws from an anti-protectionism taxation principle as the non-discrimination principle, with the aim of making the EU freedoms on which the internal market is maintained effective, in such a way that the designated 'fiscal interest' of the States or the very function of the taxes within the tax system and each Member States' own taxation systems each are hardly taken into account by the Court. It is possible that the objective of obtaining true taxation harmonization of a systematic, coherent and uniform character can only be attained by legislative means (vid. CFE, 'Contribution to the European Convention: institutional changes required with regard to tax policy' *European Taxation*, December 2002) given that legal action is only cast on the obstacles derived from discriminatory or clearly restrictive norms, but it does not deal with or eliminate other tax obstacles (of 'second level') to the correct functioning of the internal market which arise, generally, from the disparity between the tax systems, and which can only be eliminated through the regulatory action of EU institutions.

§10.06 PROTECTION OF THE INTERNAL MARKET THROUGH THE CONTROL OF STATE AIDS

[A] CONCEPT OF STATE AIDS

The prohibition directed at the Member States to establish State aids derives from the need to protect free competition between companies, first expression of the respect to the freedom of movement of goods, as well as the assumption of the functioning of the internal market. Regarding that matter, Article 107 (ex Article 87) of the TFEU stipulates that 'Save as otherwise provided in the Treaties, any aid granted by a Member State or through State resources in any form whatsoever which distorts or threatens to distort competition by favouring certain undertakings or the production of certain goods shall, in so far as it affects trade between Member States, be incompatible with the internal market'.

Although the declaration that a tax advantage distorts, or threatens to distort, free competition and as a consequence, the internal market, corresponds to the Court, the Commission assumes a forthright role in the control of the legality of the aids that the States as well as sub central entities grant to different economic operators. On one hand, it permanently supervises, alongside the Member States, the systems of existing aids, proposing appropriate measures for their adaptation to the functioning and progressive development of the common market (Article 108 of the TFEU). Likewise, it analyses the new aid projects (including the modifications to existing aid) to determine their compatibility, or not, with the internal market (Article 88.3 of the TFEU). In both cases, it corresponds to the Commission to declare its opinion about the existence of a state aid, as well as on the application of the exceptions to the principle of incompatibility of the aids, having at its disposal a wide margin of appreciation.

On the other hand, the Member States have the obligation to notify the Commission of new aid projects as well as the modification of existing aids, without being able to execute them until the Commission's definitive decision is taken. If the aid is not notified or is executed before the formal procedure of study and control has finalized, without prejudice to the eventual opening of an infringement of EU regulations file of the acting Member State by the Commission, it will be understood that the aid is illegal, in such a way that, if it is finally declared incompatible with the common market, the State must adopt all the necessary measures to recuperate the help of its beneficiaries, with the corresponding interests.

From a substantive perspective, although neither Article 107 of the TFEU nor the EC regulation n° 659/1999, norms which also develop the system of State aids, contain a definition of the concept of State aids (see KEPPENNE, J.P, State aids and national courts: definitions and other problems: A case of premature emancipations? Common Market Law Review, n°37, 2000, regarding that matter) a certain agreement exists on the general notes that characterize this figure:

(1) there must be a benefit, limited to an undertaking or group of undertakings;
(2) the benefit must be conceded through state funds, whether from the central State or sub central territorial entities;

(3) it must be a distortioning benefit of the competence or that affects the interchanges between Member States.

However, despite the lack of a legal definition of the bracket 'State aid', the general principle established in Article 107 of the TFEU, transcribed above, has been developed and clarified, also in this case, by the Court of Justice, highest interpreter of EU law, to whose case-law we must turn in order to know the environment of the prohibition that we are examining.

First, it must be borne in mind that, as the Court of Justice points out (judgment 11 November 2004), the 'Court has maintained in several judgments that State aids are qualified by their effects and not based on the causes or the objectives of the measures adopted by Member States'. The importance rests, therefore, on the effects that any selective tax measure provoke, or can provoke, on free competition in order to judge if it violates the EU regulations or not.

The different forms by which selective tax measures can be adopted have been collected in a list by the Commission, and reflected in the Vademecum of 30 September 2008. The latter refers to, amongst others, the suppositions of reduction to the taxable base, accelerated amortization, exceptional provisions, quota deductions, and tax credit. All these suppositions, in as much as they distort, or threaten to distort, competence, can entail a State aid, contrary to EU law. In fact, they can even constitute State aid measures that are not part of the substantive law, but of adjective or procedural law, such as the favourable concession of deferment of payment.

Cited below are a few less obvious examples of transactions which, according to the Commission, could fit into the concept of State aid, provided that it threatens, currently or potentially, free competition:

- the letting or purchasing of State owned lands by an undertaking for a price below the market price;
- the sale of State owned lands by an undertaking at a price above the market price;
- the privileged access of an undertaking to certain infrastructures without the need to pay canons; and
- the obtaining of State venture capital funds by an undertaking under more advantageous conditions than those demanded from a private investor.

The case-by-case approach of the Court of Justice is, in this respect, preceded, or not, by infringement files of EU law under the control of the Commission, very varied and rich, and is, as a consequence, the very configuration of the category of 'selective fiscal measure'.

Let us look at some illustrative examples:

- Selective taxation: In the judgment of the 22 November 2001, the Court reached the conclusion that the establishment of selective taxes, such as the German 'tax on direct sales', in that they are not applied to wholesalers, can be considered an illegitimate State aid.

- The establishment of differentiated taxes: In the judgment of 29 April 2004, the Court described as State aids the establishment of differentiated rates of tax. For the Court, 'the difference between the highest rate and the basic rate will constitute a State aid for the purpose of the Treaty'.
- Deferral of the amount due: In judgment of 19 September of 2000, before a supposition in which the German government admits that 'hidden reserves that would be the object of taxation at a later date were produced', it affirms without any doubt that 'a simple deferral of tax could constitute a State aid'.

In its aim to devise a conceptual framework of the types of State aid, in many judgments the Court turns to the following reasoning which, due to its reiteration, seems clichéd: 'The concept of aid is wider than that of subsidy, given that it is valid to designate not only positive benefits like the subsidy itself, but also interventions which, in different forms, lessen the burden which is normally incurred in the accounts of an undertaking and therefore, without being subsidies in the strict sense have the same nature and produce identical effects'.

In fact, even the Court has used the imperative that derives from Article 107 TFEU to judge the provisions of adjective or procedural law. And it did so in attempting to place within the conceptual framework of State aid none other than the damaging consequences for the Spanish business group Empresas Álvarez (GEA) as a result of the inactivity of the Spanish administration. In the judgment of 14 September 2004, Spain/Commission, C-276/02), the Court analyses from the perspective of the prohibition of State aids the legality of the Decision 2002/935/CE, relative to an advantage which was given to the Spanish group by the passive behaviour of the Social Security and Tax Agency after the conclusion of the release and postponement agreements which it had reached with the public creditors. In the opinion of the Commission, the Spanish authorities had not acted as a 'diligent private creditor' would have done, i.e. they did not do everything possible to recover a part of the taxes (and contributions) owed. The Court, which considers, however, the appeal of annulment lodged by Spain, highlights there was in fact help from the State, contrary to EU law. And reveals (sections 25–26) that it is not the concluded agreements of release and postponement which generate State aid, but the passive behaviour, i.e. the inactivity in the claim of the refund, of the Spanish Administration after the conclusion of such agreements, which grants an advantage to GEA, contrary to the establishing Treaty, in relation to other undertakings.

As professor SOLER ROCH (*Las medidas fiscales selectivas en la jurisprudencia del TJCE sobre ayudas de Estado*, Revista Quincena Fiscal, Aranzadi, nº14, 2006) said, 'the irrelevance of the type of support, derives from the interpretation, as it were, substantialist and functional which identifies the nature of the aid, not in the legal shape or mechanism through which the beneficiary obtains the economic advantage, but precisely, with that same benefit, which is the fundamental effect of the concession, whether it be a transfer, subsidy or a selective tax measure'.

In this way, as we have mentioned before, Article 87 of the TFEU refers to State aids as those 'granted by the States or through State funds, in any shape or form', in its current case-law, the Court extends the concept in such a way that in its judgment of

15 March 1994 it admits that we may be facing these types of infringements of EU regulation even without there having been a 'transfer of State funds'. In effect, it considered, in the aforementioned judgment, that 'a tax exemption which, even not implying a transfer of funds on behalf of the State, places the beneficiaries in a more favourable economic situation than that of other passive subjects, constitutes help from the State for the purposes of the Treaty'. This particular interpretation, and consequent widening of the concept of State aid, has been the object of severe scholarly criticism (vid. BACON, K., *State Aids and General Measures*, Yearbook of European Law, Oxford University Press, 1998; WATHELET, M., and PARTSCH, P.E., *Délimitation des contours de la notion daide d'état en droit communautaire, Les aides d'état en droit communautaire et en droit nacional/national*, Bruylant, Brussels, 1999).

In respect of the subjective element of the concept of State aid, Article 107.1 of the TFEU expressly refers to, as we have seen, undertakings and production of goods. So, for the Court of Justice, public entities can grant constituent advantages in the form of State aids in favour of undertakings of a private nature as well as public undertakings. The Court does not discriminate between undertakings with higher or lower turnover either. In agreement with its theory, 'a tax exemption to public undertakings constitutes State aid for the purpose of the Treaty'. Likewise, 'the relatively modest dimensions of the beneficiary undertaking does not exclude, according to settled case-law, the situation that interchanges between Member States are affected'.

Further to that, the Court has not even reserved the concept of State aid to the aids which fit well in the literal sense of Article 107 of the TFEU, i.e. to those that distort or threaten to distort the competence, favouring certain undertakings. It has not even reserved it for the cases in which the exercise of a determined business activity is favoured, but it admits that an infringement of the EU regulations in such concept as when the target is an entity that does not carry out business activities but provides services of a professional nature.

In the judgment of 10 January 2006, the Court took the wide concept of undertaking which it uses for the purposes of law of competition, taking into account in the same way 'any entity which exercises an economic activity, leaving aside its legal status and its financing arrangements', where it is understood that the offer of goods and services must be considered economic activity in the market, but without excluding that said activity 'is the object of an operator in direct contact with the market, and indirectly of another subject which controls said operator within the frame of an economic unity to which both belong'. In short, as the judgment itself concludes, 'if through control there is direct or indirect participation in the management of the undertaking, it must be considered a participant in the economic activity', in such a way that the aids received that distort or threaten to distort competition can be considered State aids.

Lastly, we have seen that the concept of State aid demands that there is a distortion, or threat of it, of free competition. So, the Court has pointed out that this circumstance is produced when the conceded benefit 'reinforces the position of one undertaking in relation to the undertakings competing in the intra-union exchanges' (Judgment: ECJ of 19 September 2000). On this matter, the Court has made these two interesting findings:

(a) The entity and scope of the damage, real or potential, on free competition, is irrelevant for the purposes when qualifying a benefit which constitutes State aid when it alters the internal market. In the judgment of 6 March 2002, the Court affirms that 'the case-law does not demand that the distortion of competition or the threat of such distortion of the intra-union exchanges are sensitive or fundamental'.

(b) The Court even admits that aids conceded in favour of entities that have not carried out intra-union transactions can be considered as State aids. In the judgment of 15 December 2005, the Court expressly reasoned that it 'is not necessary that the undertaking benefitting from the aid directly participates in inter-union interchanges.

[B] Exceptions to the Concept of State Aids

In its second and third paragraphs, Article 107 of the Treaty clarifies the general criteria by virtue of which selective tax measures are incompatible with EU law,expressly admitting the admissibility of the following with the common market:

(a) aid having social character granted to the individual consumers, provided they are granted without discrimination related to the origin of the products;

(b) aid to repair the damages caused by natural disasters or by other exceptional circumstances.

The following can be considered compatible with the common market, according to each Member State's criteria:

(1) Aid to promote the economic development of areas in which the standard of living is abnormally low or in which there is serious unemployment.

(2) Aid to promote the execution of an important project of common European interest or to remedy a serious disturbance in the economy of a Member State.

(3) Aid to facilitate the development of certain economic activities or of determined economic regions, as long as they do not adversely affect the trading conditions contrary to the common interest.

(4) Aid to promote culture and heritage conservation, also as long as it does not alter the trading conditions contrary to the common interest.

(5) Other categories of aid which are specified by decision of the Council, taken by qualified majority, on a proposal from the Commission.

However, the case-law of the Court has also in this case allowed a reasonably solid theoretical framework on the aptitude and validity of the different grounds for justification of the exceptions to the norm of Article 107 of the TFEU invoked by the EU to be created.

In this regard, we can point out, first, that such as the Court of Justice has repeatedly expressed (e.g. judgment ECJ of 19 of September 2000) 'an abolition of the general principle of incompatibility of State aid with the common market must be object of a strict interpretation'. As a consequence, any possible grounds for justification of establishment by any of the Member States of a selective tax measure will be subject to a restrictive interpretation.

Within this frame, the first of the exceptions assessed by the Court of Justice is relative to the 'nature and structure of the tax system'. In light of that possible grounds for justification, Professor SOLER ROCH (op.cit.) reasons that the problem resides in the reach of this exception: What is understood by nature of the tax system? What is understood by structure? Does it refer to the underlying principles of the system? Does it refer to the coherence and proportion among different taxes that it is made up by? For the cited author, the Court has not gone, in principle, beyond identifying the nature of the tax system as a means of justifying the selective tax measure based on the 'coherence of a specific fiscal measure with the internal logic of the tax system in general'. It may seem obvious that the constitutional principles which govern the tax system should be considered as included in the mentioned exception. However, their invocation is not always determining when validating the selective tax measure. So, in the judgment of 15 July 2004, the Court understood that '*the principles of equality in taxation and economic capacity, despite undoubtedly constituting the bases of the Spanish tax system, do not impose that taxpayers who are in different situations are treated in the same way*'. Of course, in this case, the Court is not opposed to a principle of EU law in favour of national constitutional principles, but it makes it understood that, precisely a strict interpretation of these principles does not justify, and much less obliges the adoption of selective tax measures that create an unjustified discrimination.

A reasoning frequently invoked by the Member States to justify the adoption of selective tax measures stems from the fact that the advantages (or tax benefits) constituted a 'general measure of economic policy'. So, from very early on, the Court ruled out the admission of this type of argument. For the Court, even if the tax measure affects many of the undertakings in a specific sector, or even a whole sector, independently of how important it is, when the measure has not been applied to all the economic operators, it must be considered a state aid, incompatible with the EU regulations, without the fact that it could constitute a 'general measure of economic policy' being valid grounds for justification turning it into a legitimate exception to the state aid regime.

The reaction of the Court of Justice has been identical when faced with the plea of the States of the 'protection of the environment' as a ground for justification of a possible selective tax measure. As an example, the judgment of 29 April 2004 refused to admit 'as a valid exception to abolish the general principle of prohibition of state aids a regulation whose objective is to discipline the conduct of the farmers in order to reduce the consumption of fertilizers and environmental damage to an acceptable level'. In successive decisions the Court's criteria remained unchanged.

The Court also rejected, in two cases in which special tax measures (the so-called 'tax holidays') adopted by the Foral territory of the Basque country, in Spain, were judged, the grounds for justification invoked by the defence, specifically the constitutional protection of territorial tax systems, which enjoyed, and enjoy constitutional protection. The Court considered that this type of protection does not prevail over the implementation of the rules in Article 87.1 of the TFEU (current Article 107), also rejecting the argument put forward by the Foral institutions of the Basque Country according to which the European Commission would have violated the autonomous norms of such institutions incurring in misuse of power through indirect harmonization. On the contrary, the Court (of first instance) maintained that '*the Commission has not committed misuse of power understood as a decision taken with the exclusive, or at least decisive, purpose of reaching different purposes to those declared*'. Subsequently, and in relation to the same matter, the Court expressly rejected the argument according to which 'the Commission would have questioned the regulatory capabilities of the Basque authorities', and also rejected that the special character of the Foral system '*would be included in the exception of state aid justified by the nature and structure of the tax system*'.

We must, finally, highlight, due to its surprising element, the admission that the Court has made, and consequent declaration of compatibility with EU regulation, although with conditions attached, of certain selective tax measures that had supposedly been created with the objective of compensating certain expenses and costs that determined taxpayers had to bear. The Court has admitted these grounds for justification with the condition that the expenses and costs that certain groups of taxpayers will take on the due proportionality with the tax benefit which has been recognized. In the judgment of 22 of November 2001, the Court pointed out that if 'the wholesalers obtain an advantage which is greater than the added costs that they bear due to not being subject to the tax on direct sales, such benefit, in the amount that exceeds said costs, cannot be considered necessary to allow these operators to carry out their mission', circumstance in which, and only in which, said excess constitutes an illegitimate State aid.

§10.07 THE CANON OF PROPORTIONALITY IN EU TAX LAW

One of the principles that has undergone the most development and implementation in the sphere of EU tax law is the principle of proportionality. According to GARCIA PRATS (*Imposición directa, no discriminación y Derecho comunitario,* Tecno, Madrid, 1998) it is debatable whether we are facing an authentic fundamental right as, in his opinion, it is more a guarantee to preserve other rights. For other authors, however, the canon of proportionality constitutes a real general principle of law. Hence, LORENZ (*General Principles of Law: Their elaboration in the Court of Justice of the European Communities,* The American Journal of Comparative Law, 1964) holds that the principle of proportionality has, for a time, been considered by the Court of Justice as a 'structural' principle of EU law. Furthermore, for the cited author, it must be recognized as a fundamental right of the individual.

What is true is that, since 1965, the Court has taken it into account when legality measures of EU acts impose burdens and restraints on the governed. For the Court, the relevance of the canon or proportionality stems from nothing but 'avoiding that the burdens imposed on the governed exceed the necessary measures to satisfy the public interest which is at stake'.

In any case, it is a purely legal principle, having corresponded to the Court of Justice to not only limit its application, but to extend its projection further than the acts and actions of the EU institutions, and not only as an irrevocable principle in the heart of harmonized taxation, as exceptionally allowed by, for example, the Directive 112/2006, in VAT matters, but it is the Court itself who, as we shall see, has shaped it as an authentic general principle of EU law.

We shall now refer to each of the orders on which the action of the principle in question is projected.

[A] The Principle of Proportionality in the Sphere of Harmonized Taxation

The most important milestones of the case-law of the Court in relation to the effect of the principle of proportionality in the sphere of harmonized taxation can be summarized as follows:

- The Court invoked the principle of proportionality as an argument to consider certain formal or adjectival demands (presentation, as a requirement for the exercise of right of reduction of a 'special invoice', the rejection of duplicates of an invoice or substitute documents, the demands of certain previous administrative authorization or declarations previous to the start of the activity, to give just a few examples) as contrary to EU law, which in practice is translated into a refusal of the fundamental exercise of a right (the right to the rebate of the input tax), with the resulting breakdown in the neutrality of the tax.
- Likewise, the Court declared contrary to the principle of proportionality (judgment of the Court of Justice of 18 December 1997, *Molenheide*, joined cases C-286/94, 340/95, 401/95 and 47/96, p1-7281), withholding of VAT returns as cautionary measures, adopted by a Member State in an attempt to avoid fraud and tax avoidance as well as the refusal, with the same intention, of the exercise of the right of deduction.
- Other manifestations of the principle of proportionality stems from when a Member State must, or at least can, choose between various appropriate measures, it will be necessary to turn to the least restrictive. The well-known judge Lord Diplock has put the principle which we are dealing with into simple terms: '*The principle of proportionality prohibits the use of a steam hammer to crack a nut if a nut cracker would do it*'.
- The Court has held that, in general, disproportionate or excessive burdens are not admissible. The intervention of public powers in the sphere of each person's activity must be the least incisive as possible. To judge such disproportion, (excessiveness) it is necessary to compare the benefits produced by the measure adopted with a restricted legal position and legally protected. On this point, and in relation to the acts of verification and

inspection administered by the Commission, the judgment of 21 September 1989, Hoechst, affirms that '*in all legal systems of the Member States the interventions of public institutions in the sphere of activity of each individual, natural or legal, must be based on the law (...); those regulations foresee protection when faced with the arbitrary or disproportionate interventions. The demands of that protection must be admitted as a general principle of Union law.*'

- Also, in the sphere of indirect taxation, for the Court of Justice, the principle of proportionality, as it is deduced by the system of EU law, is opposed to the existence of *iuris et iure* presumptions. The Court reached this relevant conclusion in the already referred to *Molenheide* case (Court judgment of 18 December 1997, joined cases C-286/94, 340/95, 401/95 and 47/96, p I-7281). Before a supposition in which the valid norm expressly allowed a freezing, the Court considered that when a procedure of these characteristics is presented as an exceptional procedure to the common regime of cautionary sequestrations, in the sense that there is a necessary and urgent *iuris et iure* presumption, its necessary, i.e. proportionate, characteristic can be questioned, in order to guarantee the collection of the adequate amounts. In the Court's opinion, it is appropriate to declare that, unlike *iuris tantum* presumptions, a *iuris et iure* presumption goes beyond what is necessary to guarantee an efficient collection and would infringe the principle of proportionality, in that it would not allow the taxable person concerned to offer the opposing proof under the control of the competent judge.
- And, finally, the Court insisted that the principle of proportionality demands that the taxable person concerned has a real opportunity of legal review available. In the PETERBROECK judgment (judgment of the Court of Justice of 14 December 1995, C-312/93.pI-4599) it was pointed out that pursuant to the principle of cooperation laid down in Article 5 of the Treaty, it is for the courts and tribunals of the Member States to ensure the legal protection which individuals derive from the direct effect of Community law.

[B] THE PRINCIPLE OF PROPORTIONALITY IN DIRECT TAXATION.

[1] The Prohibition of 'Wholly Artificial Arrangements'

The Court of Justice entrusted proportionality with, above all other criteria, specifying the limits that each judgment must never exceed from the point of view of the protection of EU liberties. The Court expressly manifested this in *Leur-Bloen* with respect to the anti-abuse clauses. Immediately following that, it established in *Lankhorst-Hohorst* the thesis in virtue of which Member States can adopt the anti-abuse measures that they consider adequate in order to protect their tax system, but said measures will only be admissible if they respect the canon of proportionality, i.e. if they are justified and are in proportion to the objective they pursue.

However, it adopted an expression in *ICI* for the first time that would gain prominence in the control of acts and regulations adopted by the Member States. The expression we are referring to is 'wholly artificial arrangements'. It took on such prominence that the Court even concluded that any measure that was restrictive or interferes in the full exercise of EU freedoms violates the principle of proportionality and, therefore, is contrary to EU law, whenever it pursues situations different to the 'wholly artificial arrangements'.

This canon of proportionality was later invoked in *Lasteyrie du Saillant, Marks and Spencer, Cadbury Schweppes, Thin Cap Group Litigation and in Rewe Zentral-Finanz.*

Despite its 'age', the formula which is invoked nowadays was coined in *Cadbury Schweppes*, in accordance with which interfering measures which, within the non-excessiveness framework, i.e. of proportionality, aim to combat 'behaviour which consists of creating wholly artificial arrangements, lacking economic reality, with the intention of avoiding the tax usually owed on profits generated by activities carried out on national territory' would be legitimate.

As PINTO NOGUEIRA (*Dereito fiscal europeu, O paradigma da proporcionalidade*, Coimbra editora, 2010) points out, the appreciation of 'artificiality' must be done through the appreciation of elements of a subjective and objective purpose.

At a subjunctive level, its application must be limited to those cases in which there is an 'intention to obtain a fiscal benefit', which is verified when ultimately the taxpayer has not respected the purpose and objective pursued by EU freedoms. From the objective perspective, the measure must be directed at structures characterized by 'a lack of real economic link with the foster Member state', which is evidence of the 'degree of physical existence', specifically whether there are installations, personnel or equipment.

In short, those business structures that have no real identity will be 'artificial' (e.g. front companies), but those who carry out an effective activity will not be considered as such, even if their location is due to exclusively fiscal opportunism (vid. VINTHER and WERLAUF, *Tax Motives are Legal Motives*- the Borderline between the use and abuse of the freedom of establishment with reference to the Cadbury Schweppes case – European Taxation, vol. 46, 8, 2006).

[2] The Prohibition of General Clauses, Presumptions and Legal Fictions

The Court first declared itself in the sphere of direct taxation in *Leur-Bloem*. In relation to the Dutch norms which cut out the concept of fusion, the Court concluded that '*the establishment of a norm of general character which automatically excludes certain categories of operations of a determined tax benefit based on objective and 'standardized' criteria (iuris et iure presumptions), would exceed that which is strictly necessary to avoid said fraud or evasion, and would damage the objective pursued by the Directive*'.

The Court does not strive to make a distinction between general clauses, presumptions or fictions. Simply, any measure that constitutes a general clause or the automatic exclusion of a specific category will be considered as excessive and contrary to EU regulation when it imposes, in transnational operations, a bigger sacrifice than that which would be strictly necessary to avoid fraud or abuse.

In the case of the *iuris tantum* presumptions, the Court, as it did thoroughly in *Cadbury Schweppes*, maintained that the admission of the measure usually depends on the degree of proportionality that the channel to adduce evidence to the contrary (in that cause which the proof that the creation of a non-resident entity in territories with low rates of taxation did not have as an objective the movement of profits abroad) keeps with the object of the restrictive measure (income imputation of the undertakings concerned who reside in territories with lower taxation rates than the prevailing national ones).

The Court followed the same argument in relation to anti-thin capitalization, in *Lankhorst-Hohorst, Thin Cap Group Litigation,* and in *Lammers & Van Cleef*. In the latter, the Court concluded that '*those measures that, shielding behind the fight against abuse, end up affecting, in general, any situation in which the parent company has its head office, whatever its justification, outside the territory of the Member State in question, are not acceptable*'.

In more recent judgments, however, the Court has adopted a partially different viewpoint (vid. CORDEWENER, DAHLBERG, PISTONE, RIEMR y ROMANO: *The Tax Treatment of Foreign Losses: Ritter, Marks and Spencer, and the Way Ahead* (part two), European Taxation, May 2004). The Court takes as a starting point the premise by virtue of which the mere exercise of a fundamental freedom cannot be considered as in indication of fraud or evasion. A determined economic activity cannot be described as fraudulent due to the mere circumstance that it is carried out in a transnational context.

In the sphere of exit taxation, the Court (*Lasteyrie du Salliant*, 11 March 2004, C-9/02), after pointing out that '*the transfer of a physical person's tax residence outside the territory of a Member State does not, in itself, imply tax avoidance*', states that '*tax avoidance or evasion cannot be inferred generally from the fact that the tax residence of a physical person has been transferred to another Member State and cannot justify a fiscal measure which compromises the exercise of a fundamental freedom guaranteed by the Treaty*'. The Court concludes by imposing the French exit tax on the canon of proportionality in these terms: '*the exit cannot, without greatly exceeding what is necessary in order to achieve the aim which it pursues, assume an intention to circumvent French tax law on the part of every taxpayer who transfers his tax domicile outside France*'.

[3] The Prohibition of Discretional Interference by the Administration

On the basis that the EU laws cannot depend on any discretional power bestowed on the Administration, the Court rejects the interfering national measures that allow discretional intervention by the Administration. In *Leur-Bloem*, after having shown, as we previously saw, that '*the laying down of a general rule automatically excluding certain categories of operations of the tax advantage, on the base of objective and "standardized" criteria (iuris et de iuri presumptions) would go further than is necessary to avoid said tax fraud or avoidance*' and concludes that '*the situation would be identical if the rule was discretional for the Administration*'.

Even in the sphere of State aids, the discretion in favour of the Administration relative to the acknowledgement of a tax deduction, favours the evidence of the selective character of the measure, as emerges from the judgment *Commission/Spain* (Judgment of ECJ (C-501/00), of 15 June 2004).

[4] The Rule of 'Impossibility'

In *Marks and Spencer* (judgment of 13 September 2005) the Court, judging the British system which subordinated the deduction of intra-group losses to the fact that all the companies of the group had their head office in Great Britain, first formulated what could be called 'rule of necessity' speaking of the three grounds for justification put forward by the British government: a) the balanced sharing of taxation power; b) prevention of double deduction of losses; and c) the risk of tax avoidance. So, the Court adopts the concept of 'impossibility' to resolve the grounds, that is, the measure that impedes the deduction of the group's losses subsidiaries being excessive, i.e. contrary to the principle of proportionality when it is impossible for the non-resident subsidiary to deduct the losses in the State of residence.

The rule of 'impossibility', or first expression of the principle of proportionality (vid. O'SHEA, *Marks and Spencer v Halsey- HM Inspector of Taxes-: Restriction, Justification and Proportionality*, EC Tax Review, vol.15, 2, 2006), is once again *ratio decidendi*, this time with the adjective of 'manifest', in the cases *N* (judgment C-470/04, ECJ of 7 September 2006, relative to the Dutch system which complied with taxation of the latent hidden reserves highlighted when the changing of residence to another Member State), *Rewe Zentralfinanz* (judgment C-347/04, ECJ 29 March 2007, on the deduction of losses suffered by the parent company, resident in Germany, by virtue of the depreciation of the nominal value of its shares in the subsidiaries), in *Deutsche Shell* (judgment C-293/06, ECJ of 28 February 2008, on the chance of deductibility, by the parent company, of the losses generated by a permanent establishment located in Italy), and finally, in *Lidl Belgium* (judgment C-414/06, ECJ of 15 May 2008, with regard to the intention of the applicant company with head office in Germany, to deduce losses by an establishment permanently located in Luxemburg).

[C] The Presence of the Principle of Proportionality in Penalizing Tax Law

In two judgments of 8 June 1994, *Commission/United Kingdom* (cases C-382/92, p. I-2435, section 55, and C-383/92, p.I-2479) the Court pointed out that when EU law does not foresee specific penalties in the case of infringements of its provisions, or it refers, on this point, to national provisions, Article 5 of the Treaty obliges the Member States to adopt the appropriate measures to guarantee the reach and efficiency of EU law. However, the Member States, despite preserving a discretional power in relation to the choice of sanctions, must ensure that the infringements of EU rules are penalized in base conditions and procedures analogous to those applicable to infringements of similar nature and importance (non-discrimination) within national law and that, in any case, confer the penalty an effective character, proportionate and disuasory.

In judgment of 12 June 2001, *Paraskevas* (C-262/99), the Court clarified the following preliminary question: if there is compatibility between the principle of proportionality and a national legislation which establishes, in case of infringement of the temporary imported system laid down by the Directive, a set of sanctions which include, in particular: a) fixed flat-rate fines exclusively in function of the criteria of the cubic capacity of the vehicle, without taking into account its age; b) the payment of rights for an amount which could reach ten times the taxes in question. So, the reasoning of the Court to the raised question can be summarized as follows:

(1) The Court maintains that, first, for a sanction to conform to EU law, it is necessary for the tax or taxes that serve as a base to that penalty conform to and respect EU law. Contrary to that, then, we can conclude that penalties cannot be imposed when there is a non-fulfilment on behalf of a Member State in the regulation or transposition of a specific tax.
(2) Second, the Court establishes that it is the national court which put forward the preliminary question to carry out the consideration pursuant between the internal regulations of a tax with those of the EU regulations, in order to judge the correctness of the imposed penalty.
(3) Third, the Court insists that the administrative or penalty measures cannot exceed what is strictly necessary to obtain the pursued objectives.
(4) Likewise, and here there is an interesting appraisal, the Court points out that the sanction must not be so disproportionate in relation to the seriousness of the infringement that it constitutes an obstacle to the freedoms recognized by the Treaty. In defence of this criteria, it cites judgment of 16 December 1992, *Commission/Greece*.
(5) The Court admits that although determined imperatives of penalty and prevention could justify a national legislation imposing penalties of a certain level of severity, those that constitute an obstacle to the freedoms protected and guaranteed by the Treaty must however be considered disproportionate
(6) A penalty exclusively based on an invariable criteria (e.g. the cubic capacity of a vehicle) could be disproportionate in relation to the seriousness of the infringement, especially when it is linked to another heavy penalty, imposed as a consequence of the same infringement.
(7) The Court points out that the Directive demands that, as far as the principle or amount of the sanction is concerned, the good faith of the person in question is borne in mind. In this case, also, the case-law of the Court obliges us to reflect on determined legal categories, as in the internal regulations of a fair number of Member States' good faith has disappeared as criteria of adjustment of the sanctions, as they have understood that the concurrence of good faith in the conduct of the taxpayer excludes blame, in such a way that the possibility to sanction disappears.

(8) Lastly, the Court's observation about the circumstances that must be taken into account when adjusting the penalties is also relevant: it points out that in the adjustments the difficulty in the interpretation of the norm as well as the determination of the tax system applicable to certain taxable transactions must be included.

§10.08 THE TAX DIMENSION OF THE PRINCIPLE OF LOYAL COOPERATION

The principle of loyal cooperation, also previously known as principle of EU Solidarity (vid. BLANQUET, M., *L'article 5 du Traité C.E.E- Recherche sur les obligations de fidélité des Etats membres de la Communauté*, Bibliothéque de Droit International et Communautaire, Tome 108, Librairie Générale de Droit et de Jurisprudence París 1994) is clarified in Article 4.3 (ex Article 10) of the Treaty of the EU (consolidated version published in the Official Journal of the EU, 30 March 2010). In accordance with it, the Member States will adopt all the general or specific measures to ensure the fulfilment of the obligations resulting from the acts passed by the Institutions of the EU.

The principle of loyal cooperation, as the Treaty on EU calls it, entails three mandates aimed at the Member States. Two of them are positive and one negative, in the sense of what not to do. On one hand, Member States are highly obliged to adopt all the measures, whether general or specific, to ensure the fulfilment of the obligations derived from the Constitution. Second, they are also linked by a positive obligation to adopt all those measures, whether general or specific, which guarantee the fulfilment of the obligations resulting from the acts of the institutions of the EU. On the other hand, the States are subjected to the negative obligation of abstaining from adopting any type of measure that could endanger the achievement of EU objectives. Likewise, for authors such as BLANQUET, KAPTEYN and VERLOREN VAN THEMAAT (*Introduction to the law of the European Communities after the coming into force of the Single European Act*, second edition, Kluwer Deventer, 1989) and TEMPLE LANG (*The duties of national courts under the constitutional law of the European Community*, Dominik Lasok Lecture, University of Exeter, p.536) the cited principle must be interpreted in the sense that it creates an obligation of solidarity between Member States.

For a certain sector of legal commentators, such as DAUSES (*Quelques réflections sur la signification et la portée de l'article 5 du traité CEE*, in Bieber and Ress: Die Dynamik del Europäischen Gemeinschaftsrechts, Baden-Baden 1987) and BLANQUET, KAPTEYN and VERLOREN VAN THEMAAT (op.cit.), there is no doubt that, without taking away merit from the possibilities that are deduced from the principle in question, it has no direct effect. Other authors (e.g. HINNEKENS, L. *Compatibility of bilateral tax treaties with European Community Law*. The rules, 3, EC Tax Review n.4/1994, p. 148), however, maintain that the principle has direct effect when it is evoked to compel States to fulfil the previsions of the Treaties that are directly applicable. They also admit that we are faced with a principle that can be directly invoked by the individuals of Member States when their legitimate rights or interests are affected.

In any case, the case-law, along with the prevailing opinion of most legal theorists, admits that the combined action of the principle of loyal cooperation, in its third term aimed at the States, and the principle of supremacy of EU regulation, be it constitutional or secondary, on the law of Member States, creates a body of obligations whose fulfilment is necessary to the national legislators as the executives and the courts of the Member States. They are all obliged to fulfil the positive mandate of adopting the necessary measures to ensure the fulfilment of EU regulations, as well as the negative one of having to abstain from adopting any measure which interferes in the achievement of the purposes and objectives of the EU.

The effect of the principle of loyal cooperation in Article 4.3 of the Treaty on EU on the distribution of tax sovereignty between the EU and the Member States, gathers importance, an effect which, as the Court of the EU highlighted (e.g. *Deutsche Grammophon*, C- 78/70) will be different depending on the nature of the competence, i.e. if it is exclusive or shared, as well as if the EU has set out its regulatory action in a determined sphere or not.

When the EU has acted in a legislative way, whether in the sphere of exclusive competences (e.g. the common customs tariffs), whether in shared competences but with a high degree of action by the EU, whether it be through harmonized law (as would be the case of VAT, of excise duties, or of tax on the concentration of capital), whether assumption of power through constitutional law (e.g. energy and environmental taxation), the combined action of the principles of supremacy and cooperation in good faith are translated into the States having nothing else but subordinated powers in these orders, i.e. legislative competences subordinated to:

(a) EU legislation being sufficiently incomplete so as to demand development on behalf of the national legislators, and even in order to avoid, in determined fields, areas of legislative gap;
(b) that EU law itself had expressly stated the legislative collaboration of each Member State;
(c) the act of the national legislators is not clearly prohibited by EU law.

In such assumptions, as the Court (ECJ) has highlighted (e.g. *Commission/United Kingdom* (C-804/49) p.1045), if the Union has initiated, but not yet adopted, legislative proposals, the Member States are obliged to not adopt new ones, or to modify the existing national measures, without first consulting the Commission and following its indications. Besides, once the EU has taken the legislative initiative, the national legislator loses power to legislate, or at least to do so with sovereign freedom.

In this way, Article 2 of the Consolidated version of the Treaty on the Functioning of the EU (OJ of 30 March 2010) currently establishes that '*when the Treaties confer on the Union a competence shared with the Member States in a specific area, the Union and the Member States may legislate and adopt legally binding acts in that area. The Member States shall exercise their competence to the extent that the EU has not exercised its competence. The Member States shall again exercise their competence to the extent that the EU has decided to cease exercising its competence*'.

On the other hand, the theory also corresponds to the Court (case 74/69, *Krohn*, paragraph 5) by virtue of which the principle of loyal collaboration can oblige the national legislators to adopt development measures if they are necessary to remove any obstacle to the full establishment of a Norm which organizes any sector of the common market, or in order to give that Norm full effect (*Schee*, C-30/70, parag.10; and *Leonisio*, C-93/71, paras 20–23). It can also bind it when the EU legislator has not managed to adopt legislative measures necessary in defence of any of the EU ends and objectives.

In the assumption that the competences are shared between the EU and the Member States (e.g. the tax system of the company restructuring or of the flow of capital between parent and subsidiary companies), despite the margin of legislative action of the States depending on each particular case on the degree to which the EU has implemented its legislative power, the principle of cooperation obliges them to, on one hand, dictate the corresponding development legislation, and on the other hand, to avoid adopting any decision which is in opposition to the EU norm or that interferes in the execution of the targets and objectives which had inspired it.

It is precisely in the sphere of shared competences that the Court of Justice was generous in listing of the duties and obligations that the Member States must recover of the principle of loyal cooperation of the ex Article 10 (current Article 4.3 of the Treaty on EU). In this way, it has pointed out that the active obligation of the EU partners to adopt the appropriate general or specific measures to ensure the fulfilment of the Constitution and of the acts of the institutions of the EU entails the following:

(a) The obligation to provide the necessary budgetary forecasts in order to achieve it (*Commission/Italy*, C-30/70).
(b) The organization of the administrative procedures that ensure citizens fulfilment of the EU norms.
(c) The configuration of the corresponding legal remedies, should there be a non-fulfilment of each State's obligations.
(d) The corresponding penalizing measures for infringements of EU law, measures whose features, both fundamental and procedural, must be analogous with the penalties derived from the infringements of the internal regulations, and it must also respect in all cases the principle of proportionality, i.e. those must be in any case 'effective, proportionate and merely dissuasive'.
(e) The configuration of the schemes of financial compensation in favour of individuals, taking the refunding of unlawfully paid revenues as a starting point.

On the other hand, the impact of the principle of loyal cooperation on the sharing of the power of taxation between the EU and the Member States is especially relevant in relation to the directly applicable precepts of primary law and with those which directly formulate EU objectives. In effect, there is no doubt that when faced with precepts from which the directly applicable rights of individuals are derived, each Member State must remove or modify those internal norms which are incompatible with the former. But in relation to those provisions of the Treaty from which the directly applicable rights of the individuals derive, that the last conclusion is that such provisions cannot be the object of development by the national legislators in as much as they violate the principle in accordance with such rights derived directly from the Treaties (to the point that secondary EU law is only recognized as having a merely declarative nature of the mandate of primary law). Such has been the criteria in cases such as *Amsterdam Bulb* or *Royer* on interpreting that in these cases secondary law is a mere coordination of the rights conferred to individuals by the Treaties.

Although not all theory is unanimous on the matter, VAN THIEL (*Free movement of persons and Income Tax Law: the European Court in search of principles*, ed. International Bureau of Fiscal Documentation, Doctoral Series, 2002) highlights, in short, a last demonstration of the principle of loyal cooperation of which we have been speaking of: that the national legislators can find themselves, through solidarity, under the obligation of acting should there be a need for an internal legislation which completes the EU regulatory framework, with particular reference to a basic freedom or to an objective recognized by the Treaty. In the sphere of free circulation of professionals, for example, the Court assumed an obligation of the national administrative authorities to carry out the objectives of Article 43 of the Treaty within the limits of existing national law, in the absence of EU legislation on the mutual acknowledgement of diplomas which the cited article requires. Action on behalf of the EU, therefore, would not impede the implementation of Article 47, but certain authors [Cf. CRISHAM, BLECKMANN, STEINDORF, GOOSE (as cited by SOLLNER, R. Art.5 EWG-Vertrag in der Rechtsprechung des Europäischen Gerischtshofes, Europarecht-VÖLKERRECHT Verlag V.Florentz München 1985, pp. 72 and 73). Against: Ipsen (as quoted in SOLLNER, R. Art.5...op.cit.p73)] defended the theory that the Member States were obliged to draw up and approve the legislation which was necessary to guarantee free circulation. An example is the decision on fisheries, in which the Court went even further (e.g. joined cases185 to 204/78, *Van Dam*) as the Court maintained that, in the absence of EU action in a sphere of exclusive EU competence, the Member States have the right and obligation to adopt the corresponding measures to protect the resources of the sea), invoking a legislative obligation of the Member States to fulfil a specific EU objective if the action was adequate and required in the common interest. The Court interpreted Article 4.3 of the Treaty on EU as such, i.e. the efficiency of the principle of loyal cooperation as a requirement to the Member States to avoid a legislative gap by enacting the necessary national legislation which demands the protection of the internal market and the fundamental freedoms.

§10.09 THE EU TAXPAYER'S STATUTE: NON-CONTRACTUAL RESPONSIBILITY OF THE STATES AND REFUNDING OF UNDULY PAID TAXES

[A] THE GENERAL PRINCIPLE OF THE LIABILITY OF THE STATE

The Court has repeatedly manifested that the Treaty on EU has created its own laws and regulations, integrating the legal systems of the Member States and that it imposes itself on their courts, whose subjects are not only the Member States, but also its nationals, and that in the same way it places burdens on the individuals, it also generates rights which become part of its legal legacy. These are created not only when the Treaty confers them explicitly, but also due to the obligations that the Treaty imposes in a well defined manner both to the individuals as well as the Member States and on the EU Institutions (see the judgments of 5 February 1963, *Van Gend en Loos*, C-26/62, p.3, and of the 15 of July 1964, *Costa*, C-6/64, p. 1141).

Within this context, a Court of Justice legal line has been developed, now consolidated, which imposes on the national courts in charge of applying, within the frame of their competences, the provisions of EU law, the obligation of guaranteeing the full effect of such norms, as well as protecting the rights that these confer to individuals (see, especially, the judgment of 9 March 1978, *Simmenthal*, C-106/77, p. 629, (16), and of 19 June 1990, *Factortame*, C-213/89, p.1-2433, (19)).

In the opinion of the Court, the full effect of EU regulations would be questioned and the protection of the rights it recognizes would be weakened if the individuals did not have the possibility of obtaining reparation when their rights had been damaged by a violation of EU law attributable to a Member State.

The obligation of reparation by the Member State is particularly indispensable when the full effect of the EU norms is subordinate to each State adopting a determined action, e.g. executing or surpassing a determined norm, and consequently, the individuals cannot, in the absence of such conduct invoke before the national courts the rights conferred to them by that EU law.

From all this, the Court reaches the relevant conclusion that the principle of the responsibility for damages caused to individuals through violation of EU law which is attributable to the state is inherent in the system of the Treaty (judgment of the Court of Justice of 14 November 1991, *Francovich*, joined cases C-232 and 233/91,.p.I-5357, and 5 March 1996, *Brasserie du Pêcheur*, joined cases, C-46 and 48/93,.p.I-1029, in repeated theory until the most recent judgment of the Court of Justice of 26 January 2010, *Transportes Urbanos y Servicios Generales*, C-118/08).

However, the obligation of the Member States to repair said damages also finds support in Article 4.3 of the consolidated version (OJEU of 30 March 2010) of the Treaty on EU, by virtue of which the Member States must adopt all appropriate general or specific measures to ensure the fulfilment of the obligations which they are responsible for by virtue of EU law. Among those obligations is the obligation to eliminate the unlawful violation of EU law (see, in relation to the analogous provision of Article 86 of the ECSC Treaty, the judgment of 16 December 1960, *C.Humblet*, 6/60, p.1125).

Definitively, for the Court of Justice, the conclusion of everything shown is that EU law imposes the general principle that the Member States are obliged to repair the damages caused to individuals brought about by violations of EU law that are attributable to it (cited judgments of 14 November 1991, *Frankovich*, joined cases C-232 and 233/91, p.I-5357, and of 5 March 1996, *Brasserie du Pêcheur*, joined cases, C-46 and 48/93, p.I-1029).

From another angle, the Advocate General, Mr Tesauro, in the case *Brasserie du Pêcheur* (judgment of ECJ of 5 March 1996, C-46 and 48/93), gives the following reasoning: '*annulment of an unlawful measure or setting aside a law which is inconsistent with a superior parameter of legality is necessary in a state governed by the Rule of Law. At times, however, this is not enough and it may be necessary to, in order to render the protection real and effective, bring into balance also, the financial content of the right which has been impaired, and hence to ensure the damage is made good*'.

[B] Conditions for Incurring the Liability of the State

On the occasion of a preliminary question brought before the Court of Justice, the Italian court asked if a Member State is obliged to repair damages to individuals arising from the non adaptation of national law to the cited Directives, as well as the responsibility of the State for damages arising from an non-fulfilment of the obligations that they are responsible for by virtue of EU law. In the judgment of 26 January 2010, *Transportes Urbanos y Servicios Generales*, C-118/08, the Court reiterated that when, as occurred in the cited case, a Member State did not fulfil the obligation they were responsible for, by virtue of the third paragraph of Article 189 of the Treaty, adopting all the necessary measures to obtain the result pursued by a Directive, the full efficacy of that norm of EU law imposes a right to the corresponding compensation, as long as three conditions are fulfilled:

(1) The first of these conditions is that the result prescribed by the Directive implies the **conferral of rights in favour of the individuals.**
(2) The second requisite stems from the fact that the content of those rights could be identified based on the provisions of the Directive. In other words, that it is a **sufficiently characterized violation.**

In order to determine in which cases a violation of EU law is sufficiently characterized, we must differentiate between the cases in which the violation committed by a Member State consists in having omitted the execution of any EU norm, and those in which the violation was due to the execution being incorrect and, therefore, distorting.

In the former, lack of execution of a norm of EU law, the conduct of omission of any of the Member States is in itself reason enough for the Court to appreciate that the violation is 'sufficiently characterized'. It is, therefore, a clear example of liability of an objective nature. It is sufficient for a Member State's non-implementation of an EU law, which grants rights to the individuals and that offered no doubt of the casuistic relationship between the violation and the damages suffered by the citizen, to dismiss discussion on the State's financial liability.

The second, i.e. when the infringement of EU law does not derive from a non-implementation but from an incorrect execution, and, as such, causes damages to the citizens in so far as that the mistake is translated into the refusal of subjective rights for them, the theory of objective liability begins to lose ground in favour of a position that demands, so as to order the financial penalty of the State, a consideration of a series of circumstances for each particular case. In this case, there is a demand to apply what ALONSO GARCIA (*La responsabilidad de los Estados miembros por infraccion del dercho comunitario*, Cuadernos de Estudios Europeos, Edit. Civitas, 1997) calls the 'sufficiently characterized violation' test.

And it is on this point that the Court of Justice points out some far reaching details. It highlights as elements that the competent court must ponder, for the purpose of determining if the violation is sufficiently characterized, the following points:

(a) the degree of clarity and precision of the violated norm;
(b) the extent of appreciation that the infringed norm leaves the national or EU authorities;
(c) the intentional or involuntary character of the infringement committed or the damage caused;
(d) the excusable or non-excusable character of an error of law;
(e) the circumstance under which the attitudes adopted by a EU Institution could have contributed to the omission;
(f) the adoption or maintenance of national measures or practices contrary to EU law.

When a Member State acts in a sphere in which it has a wide power of right of access, comparable to that EU Institutions have available to them for the application of EU policies, the requisites for it to incur in responsibilities must be, in principle, the same as those on which the EU responsibility depends, in a comparable situation, i.e. that it only incurs in responsibility if the Institution in question has exceeded its authority, in a '*manifest and serious*', in the exercise of its powers (Judgment of 25 May 1978, HLN/Council and Commission, joined cases 83/76, 94/76, 4/77, 15/77 and 40/77, p. 1209, paragraphs 5 and 6).

However, and with it a valuable contribution is made in this regard, the Court says that 'a breach of EU law will clearly be sufficiently serious if it has persisted despite a judgment finding the infringement in question to be established or a preliminary ruling or settled case-law of the Court in the matter, from which it is clear that the conduct in question constituted an infringement'.

(3) Lastly, the third requisite for incurring of liability of the State stems from the fact that there must be a 'causal connection between the non-fulfilment of the obligation that the State is responsible for and the harm suffered by the individuals affected'.

These requisites are sufficient to generate, in favour of the individuals, the Court emphasized, a right to compensation which is directly based on EU law.

The Court confirmed as of *Francovich* an objective system of liability, which would enter into action as a consequence of the mere infringement of EU law, and which would, besides, reach, in principle, all the internal public authorities which enjoy legislative power equally, which would imply the impossibility of invoking, for the purposes of exempting of liability for the non-fulfilment of EU law, the possible limits in the regulations of the Member States.

What is more, with such a list of requirements, the Court establishes a minimum. After having highlighted that the cited requisites (that an EU norm concedes rights in favour of individuals, that the violation is sufficiently characterized and third, that there is a cause and effect relationship between the non-fulfilment of EU law and the damage/harm caused to the individual) are enough to generate, in favour of the individuals, the right to obtain reparation, and adds, and here the Court's references to the minimum, that such right does not exclude, however, '*that the State cannot incur liability under less strict conditions on the basis of national law,*' (Judgment of 5 March 1996, *Brasserie du Pêcheur*, joined cases, C-46 and. 48/93,.p.I-1029).

These two points are clear then, from this first analysis: 1. That, as from the *Frankovich* judgment, the Court leans towards a system of objective responsibility or blamelessness; and that 2. The table of requirements formulated, of necessary concurrence, for the birth of an obligation of full reparation in favour of the citizen, is a table of minimums, as the financial liability of the State can be generated 'by virtue if less restrictive requisites'.

[C] The Procedural Means and the Limitations to Exercise the Right to Financial Restitution

After establishing the right and delimiting the sphere of responsibility of the State for damages caused by virtue of the non-fulfilment of the obligations imposed that the EU regulations imposes, the Court adds that the compensation must be made in favour of the citizens according to the formal and material demands established by the internal law. However, despite the Court assigning the regulations of each Member State the 'procedural forms' necessary to bring to life the right to financial restitution of the damages, it clarifies the following:

(a) On one hand, it points out that the conditions, substantive and formal, established by the diverse national legislation in matters of compensation for damages must not be less favourable than those applied to similar ones of internal nature (principle of equivalence).

(b) On the other, that such substantive and formal conditions cannot be drafted in such a way that they make it practically impossible or excessively difficult to obtain compensation (principle of effectiveness).

In relation to both principles, i.e. of equivalence and effectiveness, the most recent case-law of the Court is very rich in nuances. Some of the most interesting statements are the following:

- In the judgment of the 13 January 2004 (C-453/00), *Kühne & Heinz*, the Court admitted that, in circumstances such as those set out in the preliminary question by the referring court, (a) the existence of the possibility of reviewing firm decision; (b) that the final decision has acquired strength after a legal redress; (c) that the court decision is based on an interpretation of EU law which, in light of a later judgment by the Court, was erroneous; (d) that it had been adopted without complying to the preliminary hearing to the Court; and lastly, (e) that the interested person addresses the administrative body immediately after having learnt about this judgment], the administrative organ that adopted the decision that has acquired strength must re-examine said decision. In other words, the Administration must review the legal situations derived from administrative acts and that had been confirmed by firm court decisions. And it reaches such a conclusion by virtue of an extensive interpretation of the so-called (before the changes introduced in the constituting Treaty by the Treaty of Lisbon) principle of cooperation of Article 10 of the Treaty on EU.
- In the judgment of the 19 September 2006, *i-21 Germany y Arcor*, C-392/04 and C-422/04, the Court clarifies the reach of the theory *Kuhne & Heinz*. In the judgment *i-21 Germany y Arcor* the Court confirms the extraordinary character of the possibility of reviewing administrative acts that had been confirmed by court decision. Its application is not possible, the Court now concludes, when the taxpayer has not exhausted all the remedies available to them, allowing the act to become final with his/her conduct.
- In its judgment of the 12 February 2008, *Willy Kempter KG* (C-2/06), the preliminary question that the Court considers consists in determining if, in order to have the right to a review of a final decision after a judgment of the Court in the terms expressed before, the petitioner must have cited EU law in the main proceedings. The Court of Justice considers, following the conclusions of the Advocate General, that the very wording of the judgment *Kühne and Heitz* does not demand in any way that the claimant is obliged to allege within the frame of its redress of internal law a precept of EU law (section 43).

Let us remember that in accordance with the theory *Kühne & Heitz*, for a review of the final decisions to admitted, the previous fulfilment if the following requisites is necessary: (a) the existence of possibility to review the final decisions in the national regulations; that the final decision which has acquired strength after a national judicial proceeding is based on an interpretation of the EU law that, in the light of a subsequent judgment of the Court, was erroneous and that such interpretation had been adopted by the ad hoc court without proposing the corresponding preliminary question to the Court, and finally, that the taxpayer in question had addressed the administrative institution immediately after having known the Court judgment which highlights the erroneous interpretation of EU law by the Administration and national courts. On the other hand, in *i-21 Germany and Acor* the Court's approach in *Kühne & Heitz* is consolidated and reaffirms that said approach is applied even if the taxpayer has not alleged within the frame of the national proceeding any proceeding of EU law. Neither does it demand that the provision of EU law whose interpretation has been erroneous in the light of a later judgment of the Court has been examined by the national court, but it is sufficient that it 'could have been examined ex officio by it'.

The judgment of the Court of Justice of 26 January 2010, *Transportes urbanos y Servicios Generales SAL* (C-118/08), adds interesting interpretations to its theory. Acknowledging that the liability claims based on the unconstitutionality of a law and those that are based on the incompatibility with EU law have the same objective, namely, the reparation of damage suffered by a person infringed on by an act or omission by the State, the Court concludes that the reparation of the infringement caused by EU law is not subordinate to the judgment that the Court declares with preliminary character the existence of such infringement. The judgment of the Court of 26 January 2010, *Transportes urbanos y Servicios generales*, C-118/08, considerably widens the possibilities of the taxable person to recover taxes unduly paid as a consequence of an infringement of EU legislation with this theory, as the claims can refer to prescribed exercises, as in main case or to assumptions in which there is a final liquidation, administratively or even legally.

Likewise, as MARTIN JIMENEZ (Jurisprudencia del TJUE, Civitas, Revista Española de Derecho Financiero, n° 146, abril-junio 2010) clarifies, it must be borne in mind that the judgment limits itself to dispense with a requirement (the exhausting of all options), established by domestic law, basing its argument on the rule of equivalence. In order to recognize responsibility and, therefore, to obtain the compensation (which will be quantified by the damage, so therefore does not have to be equivalent to the payment or liability to tax) it will be necessary for the violation to be serious. And it should be borne in mind that the national courts have a certain margin of discretion, as the Court has limited itself to establish a series of general criteria or guidelines. Likewise, according to many provisions of internal administrative law, the action of liability should be inserted within a specific period from when the act that provokes the compensation takes place (we understand that, in general, this is from when the Court of Justice issues the judgment). On the other hand, it is interesting to note that the requirement of equivalence, and of effectiveness, is also used in other procedures or actions different from those of financial responsibility of the Administration, as is the process of refunding unduly paid taxes. Therefore, the case-law contained in the judgment of the Court of 26 January 2010 *Transportes Urbanos y Servicios Generales SAL* (C-118/08), in relation to the principle of equivalence, would be transposed to these other procedures, if we understand that such a movement must be carried out in a non-automatic manner, but bearing in mind the particularities, nature and aim of each process. In this sense, FALCON Y TELLA, (*La revision de providencias de apremio dictadas en ejecución de tributos inconstitucionales: la STS de 30 de Octubre de 2009*, Quincena Fiscal, Aranzadi, n°5, 2010) have shown the full application of this case-law to the supposed notices of recovery (bank enforcement orders in order to proceed against the of the tax debtor's wealth) relative to the final liquidations passed with infringement of EU regulations (in comparison to those notices of recovery of full liquidation issued on the base of internal regulations declared illegal).

[D] On the Impossibility of Conditioning the Reparation of the Existence of Blame

One of the matters that the Court also ruled on was whether the national court, pursuant to the national legislation which it applies, can make the reparation of loss or damage conditional upon an intentional or negligent act on the part of the organ of the State responsible for the breach.

The Court, after stating that the concept of blame does not have the same meaning in the different legal systems, recalls that when a Member State is responsible for violation of EU law which acts in the sphere in which it has a power of appraisal to adopt normative options, the recognition of a right to compensation based on EU law is subject to, among others, the requirement that the violation in question is sufficiently characterized without, the Court concludes, the obligation to repair the damages caused to the individuals being conditioned to a requisite, based on the concept of blame, that goes beyond the sufficiently characterized violation of EU law. In effect, to impose a supplementary requisite of such nature would be equivalent to once again questioning the right to compensation that is based on the EU legal order.

Recently, the Court has returned to this matter although from a different perspective. In the judgment of the 13 June 2006, *Traghetti del Mediterraneo,* (C-173/03), the Court was asked if the EU law, and in particular, the principles stated in the judgment of the Court, *Köbler*, were opposed to a national regulations that, on one hand, excludes the responsibility of the Member States for the damages caused to individuals through the violation of EU law committed, not by the legislator, but by a court which resolves as a last resort, in those cases in which said violation stems from a particular interpretation of the facts and of the evidence tested by that court, and on the other hand, limits that responsibility only to cases of intentional fault or serious misconduct on part of the court. As will be observed, the *Köbler* Court judgment concluded that the responsibility for damages caused through violation of EU law can also be demanded in relation to the acts of the judiciary, specifically, when the violation proceeds from the court that settles as a last resort and constitutes a manifest infringement of EU law applicable to the case. The judgment of the ECJ *Traghetti del Mediterraneo* goes beyond that and makes clear that the manifest infringement of EU law, in relation to the courts that resolve as a last resort, can be produced when the national court interprets a EU law in a manifestly erroneous manner, in view of the state of evolution of the case-law of the Court of Justice (*Koblër*), but also when it interprets national law in such a way that, in practice, it supposes a violation of EU law as a consequence of an erroneous interpretation of the facts or the evidence in the case.

With respect to the intensity of the violation and the damage caused, for the Court of Justice a national norm cannot condition the incurrence of the liability of the courts' intentional fault or serious misconduct by the court. As can be easily sensed, this legal line has extremely important effects from the viewpoint of the systems of the various Member States (amongst them, evidently, the Spanish one), since, as is known, on many occasions, the court of last instance (the Supreme Court and the Constitutional Court, in Spain) shows a flagrant lack of understanding of EU law in its judgments, which, after this new legal theory of the Court, opens the doors for affected taxpayers to claim for compensation for the violation of EU law, even without the existence of intentional fault or serious misconduct.

[E] THE ACTUAL EXTENT OF THE REPARATION

The court has established in this respect a number of rules:

(1) The reparation of damages caused to individuals through violation of EU law must be appropriate to the damages suffered, in such a way that it allows the effective protection of their rights.

(2) In absence of EU provisions is this area, it corresponds to each Member State's internal legal system to decide the criteria that will allow to determine the amount of the reparation, on the understanding that they cannot be less favourable than those referring to similar claims based on internal law and that in no case can be articulated in such a way that they make the reparation almost impossible or excessively difficult.

(3) In particular, to determine the recoverable loss, the national court can detect if the damaged party has acted with adequate diligence in order to avoid damage or to lessen its importance, and, if, especially, all the corresponding actions within the law were carried out within good time.

In effect; according to a general principle common to the law systems of all the Member States, the damaged party must provide evidence that reasonable care was adopted in order to limit the magnitude of the damage if they do not want to run the risk of having to bear the damages alone (judgment of 19 May 1992, *Mulder and others/Council and Commission*, joined cases C-104/89 and C-37/90, p.1-3061, section 33).

Likewise, the Court points out that the absolute exclusion, in the concept of irreparable damage, of the loss of profit cannot be admitted should there be a violation of EU law. In effect, absolute exclusion of the loss of profit can suppose the denial of the effective reparation of the damages, a circumstance which the EU law does not admit.

(4) With respect, especially, to the concession of compensation for damages and exemplary damages, the Court of Justice of the EU specifies that in national law this method of reparation is based on the fact that the public authorities have acted in an oppressive, arbitrary or unconstitutional manner. In as far as this behaviour can constitute a violation of, or aggravate, EU law, the concession of compensation for damages of the exemplary damage type within the framework of a relation or action based on EU law cannot be excluded when the right to the compensation in question can be recognized within the framework of a reclamation or similar action based on internal law.

[F] Extent of the Period Covered by Reparation

The Court emphatically states, at the end, that '*The obligation for Member States to make good loss or damage caused to individuals by breaches of Community law attributable to the State cannot be limited to damage sustained after the delivery of a judgment of the Court finding the infringement in question*'.

§10.10 TAX LAW ON PENALTIES FROM THE PERSPECTIVE OF EU LAW

Despite the fact that the different texts that make up the European Constitutional law omit attribution of the power to impose penalties to the Institutions of the EU, both the Court of Justice as well as the General Court have laid the foundations, once again in a casuistic manner, of what the common demands and principles could be in the sphere of penalizing administrative law. We refer to them in the following section (vid. CAAMAÑO ANIDO: *El Derecho tributario sancionador desde la perspectiva del ordenamiento comunitario (I) y (II)*, Revista de Contabilidad y Tributación, CEF, December 2002 and January 2003).

[A] Classification Criteria of the Penalties

In accordance with the legal theory of the General Court (for all, vid. Judgment of 12 July 2001, *Tate & Lyle*), which contributes interesting innovation to the theory of the Court of Justice, the following are circumstances, which must be considered as aggravating circumstances in the assessment of the penalty:

(a) the intrinsic seriousness of the type of infringement;
(b) the duration, whenever possible in virtue of the type of illegal act;
(c) the repetition;
(d) the refusal to cooperate with the responsible investigating body;
(e) the function of the instigator in other economic entities or organs; as well as
(f) the eventual gains illicitly obtained as a result of infringing behaviour.

There is no doubt that in the relation of the listed circumstances, all of which must be pondered on when deciding the amount of the penalty, will motivate serious reflections if we judge them from the perspective of the laws of the Member States, and even more so taking into account that national law must be interpreted in the light of EU legislation – especially the interpretation which the Court in Luxemburg has made of it in virtue of the competence which the Treaty grants it – and bearing in mind the principle whereby the judgments of the Court express an interpretation of a rule abstractly, not limited to the case, but as leading case. Only from this perspective will we be able to place in its reasonable limits, and also in its complete dimension, EU legal theory relative to penalizing tax law.

In certain systems, however, the Court of Justice has surprised us with affirmations whose acceptance a large part of the continental theorists would currently question. In its Judgment of 12 June 2001, *Paraskevas* (C-262/99) it makes the following considerations:

- First, that the individual's good faith must be taken into account in relation to the quantification of the penalty.
- Second, that amongst the circumstances that must be taken into account when graduating the penalties is the difficulty in the interpretation of the norm as well as in the determination of the fiscal regime applicable to determined taxable facts.

In most of the Member States' (legal) systems, neither the first (the good faith of the alleged offender) nor the second (the difficulty of interpreting the norm that typifies the infringements) constitute circumstances that should have a bearing on the reduction of the penalty but are considered exclusive of responsibility.

[B] The Principle of *Ne Bis in idem*

The Court has also constructed its own version of the principle *ne bis in idem*, referring to its theory relative to the exercise of the Administration's power to impose penalties. This is synthesized by the Advocate General, Jean Mischo, in his conclusions on the matter *ICI/Commission*, C-254/99P, in the following way:

- The principle *ne bis in idem* is applicable within the framework of EU penalty law, as a general principle of law, as the Court of First Instance of the European Communities (nowadays General Court) from the legal theory adopted in the judgment of 14 December 1972, *Boehringer Mannheim*, C-7/72, p.I-1281. Said principle has a double dimension: a) it means that a subject cannot be penalized twice on the same facts; and also, b) that proceedings cannot be brought against it twice on the same facts.
- The only exception to the application of the principle *ne bis in idem* is that which is set out in Article 4, section 2, of Protocol 7 of the European Convention on Fundamental Rights and Public Freedoms, in accordance with the reopening of a case being possible, in particular, if a fundamental flaw of the previous procedure can affect the penalizing resolution. To this respect, the explanatory report of the cited Protocol 7 of the aforementioned Convention indicates that its Article 4.2 corresponds to a fundamental flaw, which could influence the result of the lawsuit, but not when the flaw is of a different nature.

[C] Principle of Reasonable Time

In the judgment of 17 December 1998, *Baustahlgewebe/Commission* (C-185/95P, Rec.p.I-8417), the Court, in relation to the consequences of the non-fulfilment of reasonable time for the validity of the contested penalizing act, says in section 49 that it is case-law of the Court of Justice that should there be no evidence that the duration of the procedure would have had incidence in the outcome of the lawsuit, the motive based on the non-fulfilment of reasonable time cannot give rise to the absolute and complete annulment of the act or contested penalizing resolution.

In his eagerness to precisely define the principle of 'reasonable time', the Advocate General Jean Mischo, in his conclusions to the matter *DSM*, clarifies that these two affirmations do not adjust to the case-law of the Court of Justice:

(a) That the violation of the principle of reasonable time would only justify the annulment of the act or penalizing resolution where it also implied a violation of the right of defence of the alleged infringers. *Contrario sensu*, it must be understood that the 'undue delays' have significance of their own as altering circumstances (reductory) of responsibility without them needing to lead to damage to the right to defence of the infringers.

(b) That of when the existence of a violation of rights to defence is not proven, the non-adherence to of the principle of reasonable time lacks incidence on the administrative procedure. As a consequence, for the cited Advocate General the undue delays can cause the invalidity of the penalizing procedure.

[D] Principle of Comparative Equality and Its Effectiveness, Deterrent Effect and Proportionality

The Court of Justice has left, through its well thought out Judgment of 7 December 2000, *José de Andrade* (C.213/99), a synthesis of what must be considered its theory on the principles of comparative equality and proportionality upon the application of penalties. We refer to them below:

- The Court says that in accordance to settled case-law, when an EU norm does not anticipate specific penalties in case of infringement of its previsions or refers to, on this point, the national provisions, Article 5 of the EC Treaty (current Article 10) obliges Member States to adopt all the appropriate measures in order to guarantee the scope and efficacy of EU law. For this purpose, '*while the choice of penalty remains within their discretion they must ensure in particular that infringements of EU law are penalized under conditions, both procedural and substantive, which are analogous to those applicable to infringements of national law of a similar nature and importance, and which, in any event, make the penalty effective, proportionate and dissuasive*'.
- As regards to customs offences, the court has pointed out that in the absence of harmonization of the EU legislation in that field, the Member States are empowered to choose the penalties which appear appropriate to them. They must, however, exercise the power in accordance with EU Law and its

general principles, and consequently with the principle of proportionality (section 20).

The amount of such a penalty must be determined in accordance with the case-law cited, *under conditions which are comparable to those applicable under national law to infringements of the same nature and gravity.* And as an expression of what a certain case-law calls 'the national court as an EU court', the Court of Justice indicated in section 24 of the judgment Siesse that it is for the national court to ascertain in each case if the adopted coercive measure or penalty is in accordance with the cited principles.

[E] The Right to Non-self-incrimination

The case-law of the General Court and the Court of Justice on the right of all taxpayers to not give evidence against oneself and to not confess their guilt can be extracted in the following way:

- According to settled case-law, the General Court states in its judgment of 20 February 2001, *Werke* (T-112/98), the fundamental rights are part of the general principles of law whose respect is guaranteed by the EU courts. For that purpose, the Court of Justice and the Court of First Instance (now General Court) draw inspiration from the constitutional traditions common to the Member States and from the guidelines supplied by international instruments for the protection of human rights on which the Member States have collaborated or to which they are signatories. In that regard, the European Convention on the Protection of Human Rights and Fundamental Rights has special significance. Furthermore, Article F(2) (current Article 6(2)) of the EU states that the EU shall respect fundamental rights, as guaranteed by the Convention on the Protection of Human Rights and as they result from the constitutional traditions common to the Member States, as general principles of EU law.
- In any case, in the judgment of 18 October 1989, *Okem/Commission* (C-374/87, p.3283), the Court of Justice declared, in first instance, that neither the comparative analysis of the national laws nor Article 7 of the of the European Convention for the Protection of Human Rights and Fundamental Freedoms, of 4 November 1950, nor Article 14 of the International Pact for Civil and Political Rights, of 19 December 1966 lead to the conclusion that a general principle of EU law exists that lays down the right to not declare against oneself in favour of legal persons and in the sphere of infringements of an economic nature.

The Court, however, clarifies such affirmation in the following line, pointing out in said judgment that the respect towards the right of defence, a fundamental right of the EU legal system, excludes the possibility of the Commission imposing upon a company, through a Decision of request for information adopted in accordance with section 5 of

Article 11 of Council regulation n°17, of 6 February 1962, First Regulation implementing Articles [85 EC] and [86 EC] (Official Journal 1962, 13, p.204; 08/0 1, p.22), the obligation of replying which implies the existence of an infringement which must be proven by a competent entity in order to penalize:

- The General Advocate, Mr Gulmann, in his Conclusions to the judgment of 10 November 1993, *Otto* (C-60/92, p.I-5683), pointed out the following: From the case-law of the Court of Justice it cannot be inferred that the national Courts, when they apply directly applicable EU laws, must automatically apply the non-written general principles which are an integral part of EU law. Particularly, a general obligation of the national Judges to apply the procedural principles of EU law cannot be deduced from the case-law of the Court of Justice, when the former apply directly applicable EU laws (paragraph 22).
- Judgment of the General Court of 8 March 1995, *Société générale* (T-34/93), states, in relation to the obligation of facilitating information and data, that those obliged are only obliged to give answers relative to 'points of fact'. On the contrary, they are not obliged to facilitate information when what has been asked for are opinions, value judgments, or they have been urged to deliver suppositions or extract conclusions. Only facts, if any, must be communicated to the authorities.
- In the same judgment, the Court states that the obligation also extends to documents, but only pre-existing documents are necessary, not those which it is necessary to recompile.
- From the report by the European Commission for Human Rights published on 30 May 1991, annexed to the European Court Of Human Rights, judgment *Sociedad Stenuit* of 27 February 1992, it is conferred that when every person's right to protection and guarantees of Article 6 of the ECHR are protected, the expression 'every person' refers to both natural and legal persons. The Court ruled in such a way in the judgment *Orkem*, expressly recognizing not only individuals but also legal persons in respect of whom an investigation is carried out, that they can invoke the fundamental rights guaranteed by Article 6.1 of the ECHR.
- The recognition of an absolute right to maintain silence would infringe on the principle of proportionality, in the sense that it would exceed what is necessary to preserve the right to defence of companies and would constitute an unjustified obstacle for the fulfilment, by Administration, of the task of ensuring the respect for EU law, which is assigned by Article 89 of the EC Treaty (judgment of the General Court of 20 February 2001, *Werke*).
- The right to maintain silence can only be granted to an undertaking who receives a decision calling for information in such a way that it would be obliged to give a response which would imply admitting the existence of the infringement whose proof corresponds to the competent organ in charge of hearing the penalizing procedure or of penalizing. It is necessary, then, to

examine each specific case in order to verify when the indicated circumstances are given (judgment of the General Court of 20 February 2001, *Werke*).

- EU law, states the General Court in the previously cited judgment, acknowledges the fundamental principle of the respect of the right to defence, as well as the right to a fair trial (see judgments of the Court of Justice *Baustahlgewebe/Commission*, paragraph 21, and of 28 March 2000, *Krombach*).

It is in application of those principles, which offer protection equivalent to that guaranteed by Article 6 of the Convention, that the Court of Justice and the Court of First Instance have consistently held that the recipient of requests sent by the Commission, have the following rights:

(1) to confine their answers to those questions of purely factual nature;
(2) to produce only pre-existing documents and materials sought; and
(3) that this right is recognized from the first stage of an investigation which could lead to an administrative penalty.

CHAPTER 11

Community Acts and the Internal Public Finance System

Andrea Amatucci

§11.01 OBJECTIVES AND INSTRUMENTS IMPOSED BY THE TREATY ESTABLISHING THE EUROPEAN COMMUNITY

Italian tax legislation currently in force is the result, on the one hand, of the rules and constitutional principles regulating financial matters, and, on the other, it consists, at least in its relevant parts, the results achieved in the adaptation process to the Community Tax Law. We must, therefore, examine the constitutional relevance and content of such process as an intermediate stage of the two analytical studies.

Article 2 of the Treaty of Rome (now Article 3, paragraph 3 of TUE) establishing the European Community,[1] which establishes expressly the objectives pursued in the

1. Cf. Cartou-Clergerie-Gruber-Rambaud, *L'Union européenne*, Paris, 2002; Ferrari Bravo-Moavero Milanesi, *Lezioni di diritto comunitario*, Napoli, 2002; Guizzi, *Manuale di diritto e politica dell'Unione Europea*, Napoli, 2003; Conforti, *Diritto internazionale*, 5th edn, Napoli, 2003; Zanghi, *Istituzioni di diritto dell'Unione Europea*, Torino, 2003, p. 286; Ballarino, *Manuale di diritto dell'Unione Europea*, Padova, 2004; Isaac, *Droit communautaire général*, Paris, 2004; Lenaerts-Van Nuffel, *Constitutional Law of the European Union*, London, 2005; H. Weber-Grellet, *Europäisches Steuerrecht*, München, 2005; Van Gerven, *The European Union*, Oxford, 2005; Daniele L., *Diritto del mercato unico europeo*, Milano 2006; Ferrari Bravo, *Lezioni di diritto comunitario*, Napoli,2006; Frank Schorkopf, *Der Europäische Haftbefehl vor dem Bundesverfassungsgericht*, Mohr Siebeck, 2006; Isaac-Blanquet, *Droit général de l'Union européenne*, Paris, 2006; J. Lüdicke (Hrsg.), *Europarecht –Ende der nationalen Steuersouveränität?*, Köln, 2006; Pocar F., *Diritto dell'Unione e delle Comunità europee*, Milano, 2006; Rideau J., *Droit institutionnel de l'Union et des Communautés européennes*, Paris, 2006; Strozzi G. (a cura di), *Diritto dell'Unione europea – Parte speciale*, Torino, 2006; Wyatt-Dashwood-Dougan-Arnull-Ross-Spaventa, *European Union Law*, London, 2006; Ballarino, *Manuale breve di diritto dell'Unione Europea*, Padova, 2007; Craig-De Burca, *EU Law*, New York, 2007; Dubois-Blumann, *Droit institutionnel del L'Union européenne*, Paris, 2007; J. Dutheil de la Rochère, *Introduction au Droit de l'Union européenne*, Paris, Hachette supérieur, 5th. edn,

above process was amended by the Maastricht Treaty on the European Union of 7 February 1992 and by the Amsterdam Treaty of 2 October 1997.

The objectives contained in Article 2 (now Article 3, paragraph 3 of TUE) are part of the general framework of the general purposes of the European Community: i.e. a harmonious, balanced and sustainable development of economic activities; a high level of employment and social protection; together with a non-inflationary and sustainable, environmentally sound growth. These objectives can be reached, of course, only with a high degree of competitiveness and convergence of economic results; a considerable degree of environmental protection including the improvement of the quality of the environment; the improvement of the standard of living and quality of life, economic and social cohesion as well as solidarity among Member States, as

2007; L. Ferlazzo Natoli, *Lineamenti di diritto tributario*, Milano, 3th edn,2007; Hartley T. C., *The Foundations of European Community Law*, Oxford, 2007; H. Oberdorff, *L' Union européenne*, Presses universitaires de Grenoble, 2007; Mathijsen P., A *Guide to EC Law*, London 2007; P.-Y. Monjal, *Droit de l'Union européenne*, Paris, Dalloz, Connaissance du droit, 2007; R.Wernsmann, in: *Schultze/Zuleeg* (59), §30 (*Steuerrecht*); *FS für J. Isensee*, Heidelberg, 2007; U. Hufeld, *Steuerstaat als Staatsform in Europa*, p. 857; R. Rohatgi, *Basic International Taxation*, New Delhi, 2007; C. Seiler, *Steuerstaat und Binnemarkt*, p. 875; G. Tinelli, *Istituzioni di diritto tributario*, Padova, 2007; H. Alais, Los impuestos aduaneros aregntinos, en *Impuestos sobre el comercio internacional* (coord. V. Uckmar, H. Taveira Torres and A. Altamirano), Ed. Marcial Pons, Bs. As.,2008; R. Asorey, Los tratados internacionales y el ejercicio del poder tributario en América Latina, *Rivista Tributaria e de Finanças Pùblicas*, Ańo 16–80, mayo-junio 2008; E. Baistrocchi, The Use and Interpretation of Tax Treaties in the Emerging World: Theory and Implications, in *British Tax Review*, Issue 4, 2008; Clergerie-Gruber-Rambaud, *L'Union Européenne*, Paris, 2008; N. D'Amati- A. Uricchio, *Corso di diritto tributario*, Padova,2008; Daniele L., *Il diritto dell'Unione Europea*, Milano, 2008; Kapteyn-McDonnell-Mortelmans-Timmermans, *The Law of the European Union and of the European Communities*, Alphen aan den Rijn, 2008; Ben J. M. Terra – Peter J. Wattel, *European Tax Law*, 5th. edn, Kluwer Law International, 2008; P. Craig, G. De Burca, *EU Law: Text, Cases and Materials, Oxford University Press*, 4th.edn, 2008; Y. Doutriaux et C. Lequesne, *Les institutions de l'Union européenne*, coll. Réflexe Europe, Paris, La Documentation française, 7th. edn, 2008; C. Garbarino, *Manuale di tassazione internazionale*, Milano, 2008; J.-L. Mathieu, *L'Union européenne*, Paris, Puf, Que-sais-je?, 8th.edn, 2008; J. Roux, *Droit général de l'Union européenne*, Paris, Lexis-Nexis, Litec, Objectif droit, 2th.edn, 2008; Villani U., *Istituzioni di diritto dell'Unione europea*, Bari, 2008; L. Dubouis et C. Blumann, *Droit matériel de l'Union européenne*, Paris, Montchrestien, 5th.edn, 2009; M. Brombach-krüger, *Wohin entwickelt sich das Europäisches Steuerrecht*? Ubg, 2009; Draetta U., *Elementi di diritto dell'Unione Europea*, Milano, 2009; Dubois-Blumann, *Droit materiel de L'Union européenne*, Paris, 2009; Foster N., *Foster on EU Law*, Oxford, 2009; G. Gaffuri, *Diritto tributario. Parte generale e parte speciale*, Padova, 2009; Gautron J-C., *Droit Européen*, Paris, 2009; F.Haase, *Internationales u. Europäisches Steuerrecht*, Heidelberg, 2009 p. 335; Jan Klabbers, *Treaty conflict and the European union*, Cambridge University press, 2009; Jaqué J. P., *Droit institutionnel de l'Union européenne*, Paris, 2009; Oppermann-Classen-Nettesheim, Europarecht, Munchen, 2009; Strozzi G., *Diritto dell'Unione europea*, Torino, 2009; Ward I., *A critical introduction to European Law*, Cambridge, 2009; Adam-Tizzano, *Lineamenti di diritto dell'Unione europea*, Torino, 2010; Alonso Garcìa R., *Sistema juridico de la Union europea*, Madrid, 2010; D. Chalmers, G. Davies, G. Monti, *European Union Law, Texts and Materials*, Cambridge University Press,2th edn, 2010; U. Draetta, N. Parisi (dir.), *Elementi di diritto dell'Unione europea*, Milano, Giuffré, 2010; Gaja-Adinolfi, *Introduzione al diritto comunitario*, Bari, 2010; Joël Rideau, *Droit institutionnel de l'Union Européenne*, 6th edn, Paris, 2010; J.-L. Quermonne, *Le système politique de l'Union européenne*, Paris, Montchrestien, Clefs, 8th edn. 2010; J. Rideau, *Union européenne. Nature, valeurs et caractères généraux, J.-Cl. Europe Traité*, Fasc. 110, 2010; Tesauro G., *Diritto dell'Unione Europea*, 6rd edn, Padova, 2010; Zanghì C., *Istituzioni di diritto dell'Unione Europea*, Torino, 2010.

well as the coordination among all the components, the reference to structural and territorial features, the lack of discrepancies and inconsistencies and uniformity of features, which represent the conditions for efficient economic development.

This fundamental purpose implies the establishment of a common market[2] and of an economic and monetary union, as well as the implementation of policies and common action as provided in Articles 3 and 4 (former Article 3A). Article 3 (now Article 3, paragraph 4 of TUE) deals with the implications deriving from the creation of a common market and the economic and monetary union. In this context, Article 3, paragraph (h) is concerned with the approximation of national legislations to the extent necessary for the functioning of the single market. Relevant are also the guidelines to guarantee the four fundamental freedoms of movement of people, services, capital and goods among Member States (paragraphs (a), (b), (c), (d)) (now Article 3, paragraph 2 of TUE), in addition to free competition (paragraph (g)) and the strengthening of economic and social cohesion (paragraph (j) (now Article 4, paragraph 2 of TFUE). Under Article 4 (now Article 119 of TFUE). Member States and the Community must adopt an economic policy based on close coordination with the policies undertaken by Member States in the field of the internal market, including the definition of common objectives, in accordance with the principle of an open market economy and free competition. The instruments specified in Article 3 (whose principles have been substantially included in current Articles 3 of TUE and 4 of TFUE) are, as we can see, the result of a deductive process of the means provided in Article 2 (now Article 3, paragraph 3 of TUE).

In particular, the objective of a high level of protection and improvement of the environment together with the standard of living and quality of life makes us think that the rules of the Treaty tend to the achievement of the highest degree of well-being rather than to production throughout the Community. This objective implies that its achievement must not compromise the full protection of human values.[3] This is the context in which the Treaty establishing the European Constitution firmly locates; it was transmitted to the European Council held in Salonica (Greece) on 20 June 2003, and it was subject to negative *referendum*.

---

2. Cf. Varriale, 'Il ravvicinamento delle legislazioni nel Trattato istitutivo della CEE, con riferimento all'Atto unico europeo ed al Trattato di Maastricht', in *Leg. giust.*, 1992, p. 240; La Pergola, 'L'Unione Europea fra mercato comune ed un moderno tipo di confederazione', in *Riv. trim, dir. proc. civ.*, 1993,I;
3. Panebianco, 'I 'nuovi' diritti fra costituzione italiana e carta dell'Unione Europea', in *Dir. Uomo*, 2000, p. 3,46. As regards fundamental freedoms, Cf. Lehner, *Grundfreiheiten im Steuerrecht der EU-Staaten*, volume 23 — *Münchener Schriften zum internationalen Steuerrecht*, edited by Lehner, Munich, 2000; Ferrari Bravo, Di Majo, Rizzo, 'Progetto di carta dei diritti fondamentali dell'Unione Europea', in *Europa e dir. priv.*, 2001, p. 1; *Carta dei diritti fondamentali dell'Unione Europea, commentata con la giurisprudenza della Corte di giustizia CE e della Corte europea dei diritti dell'uomo e con i documenti rilevanti*, Milano, 2001; Ferrari, Azzena, Di Plinio, Levi, Greppi, Loiodice, Ruggeri, Salazar, Spadaro, Troilo, *I diritti fondamentali dopo la carta di Nizza. Il costituzionalismo dei diritti* (AIDC Conference Proceedings: Taormina, June 2001) edited by Ferrari, Milan, 2001; Grabenwarter, *Europäische Menschenrechts Konvention*, Munich, 2003; C. Kaddous, A. Auer (dir.), *Les Principes fondamentaux de la Constitution européenne*, Bâle, Bruxelles, Paris, Liebing & Lichtenham, Bruylant, LGDJ, 2006; A. Albi et J. Ziller, *The European Constitution and National Constitutions*, Kluwer, 2007;

§11.02 SINGLE EUROPEAN ACT, EUROPEAN UNION, MAASTRICHT, AMSTERDAM AND NICE TREATIES AND THE EU ENLARGEMENT TO NEW MEMBER STATES IN 2004

The Single European Act[4] represents the most significant political and institutional reform of the European Community Treaties. The myth of their intangibility was dispelled and the validity of a classical international principle affirmed. The Single European Act turns out to be of a dual nature, since the conventional foundation behind the Treaties emerges clearly again.

Moreover, the Single European Act aims at protecting human rights in line with the spirit and purposes of the national constitutional charters and laws and the European Convention and Social Charter in the same field as promoted by the Council of Europe, and enhances the representative value of the peoples in the Member States. From this point of view, there is no doubt that it can be qualified as having a personalist and popular character.

According to Article 1, paragraph 1, of the Single European Act, the Communities and political cooperation tend to pursue the objective of contributing together towards the achievement of a real progress in the European Union. The aim of the Union is to transform the whole host of relations between Member States of the Community itself and, specifically, to achieve a continuous and progressive integration process in the Community and, in general, a cooperative and organizational structure in Europe. The enhancement of the powers together with the simplified process of their exercise allow the continuous progress of the Union. The Single European Act has a progressive character on the basis of the logical purposes behind the Treaties establishing the EC and the solemn declaration of Stuttgart of 1983.

Article 13 of the Single European Act introduces Article 14 into the Treaty establishing the European Communities, (now Article 26, paragraphs 1 e 2 of TFUE) and provides in paragraphs 1 and 2 that 'The Community shall adopt measures with the aim of progressively establishing the internal market over a period expiring on 31 December 1992. [...] The internal market shall comprise an area without internal frontiers in which the free movement of goods, persons, services and capital is ensured in accordance with the provisions of this Treaty'.

The aim was to establish a deadline for the achievement of the internal market or unified economic area as already indicated in the EC Treaty and completed since 1993 and, in addition, to adopt crucial decisions regarding monetary and social policies at the same time.

The Maastricht Treaty on the European Union broadens the purposes of the European Communities. It is made up of 53 articles divided into seven titles. However, three of these articles – one applying to each of the Treaties establishing the European Communities – provide for substantial amendments to the Treaties referred to before. The notion of a 'European Union' had already been introduced by Article 1, paragraph 1, of the Single European Act, according to which the Communities and political

4. Drafted on 17 and 28 February 1986 and entered into force on 1 July 1987.

cooperation action of Article 30 of this Act 'pursue the objective of contributing together to make it progress in concrete terms'.[5] Yet, the structure of the Union is not clearly outlined; it is simply 'a new stage' of the integration process still underway.

The objectives of the Union are stated in Article 2 of the EU Treaty which amended Articles 2 and 3 of the EC Treaty (now Article 3, paragraph 3 of TUE). They are: promoting a 'balanced and sustainable' economic and social progress through the 'creation of an area without internal borders' and 'the establishment of an economic and monetary Union' which, in due course, would lead to a single currency[6], vigorously asserting 'the Union identity on the international scene' by 'implementing a foreign common and security policy'. As regards the latter objective, however, provisions are made on a 'progressively established common defence policy which could lead towards a common defence'; and the strengthening of the protection of the

5. As regards the effects on tax law Cf. Gallo, 'Mercato unico e fiscalità, aspetti giuridici del coordinamento fiscale', in *Riv. dir. trib. intern.*, 2000, p. 34; Herzig and Griemla, 'Steuerliche Aspekte der europäischen Aktiengesellschaft/Societas Europaea (SE)', in *StuW*, 2002, p. 55, observe that one of the fundamental pillars as regards fiscal aspects are to be found in the *Societas Europaea*. Aa.Vv., *Lo stato della fiscalità nell'Unione europea*, edited by Di Pietro, Ministero dell'Economia e delle Finanze, 2003.

6. Antonio Finocchiaro, the Vice General Director of the Bank of Italy, in *Bollettino Economico*, March 2003, No. 40, observed: 'With the circulation of Euro banknotes and coins starting at the beginning of 2002, the passage to the third stage of the economic and monetary Union has been perfectioned. After four years of adopting the single currency and one year after the *cash changeover* it may be useful to draw up an early balance of the situation with reference to three aspects: the circulation of the new currency; the effects of the replacement of national currencies on prices; and the international role of the Euro.
Any balance of the consequences deriving from the adoption of the single currency cannot be restricted to the analysis of the impact of the new currency on prices. In a wider perspective, however, account should also be taken of the beneficial effects on the economy which are to be collected not only from a higher degree of transparency in the price system, but also from the highest degree of competitive practice in the markets of the euro area and the absence of exchange fluctuations between the countries of the Euroland (the euro area)'.
In *Bollettino Economico* of March 2003, No. 40, at 59, the Bank of Italy examined the state of public finances in the euro area and Italy and noticed that: 'The main countries of the euro area were faced with economic slow-down in the past two years with reduced margins for manoeuvre in government budgets due to insufficient progress in previous years towards reaching threshold balances as required by the Pact on Stability and Growth. Actions to support the economic activity relied on the performance of economic stabilizers and the full deployment of the effects caused by tax relief as provided in previous years.
In 2002, net indebtedness of public administrations in the euro area grew for the second consecutive year totalling 2.2% of gross domestic product against 1.6% in 2001. Net indebtedness in Germany, where proceedings were brought to deal with excessive deficit, equalled 3.6% of GDP. In France, which had received preventive warning, net indebtedness reached 3%.
Italy's net indebtedness equalled 2.3% of GDP, thus decreasing in comparison to 2.6% in 2001 (in the financial assessments made in March 2002 the latter balance equalled 1.4%). The *Forecast and Planning Report (Relazione previsionale e programmatica)* issued in Sept. 2001 provided 0.5% as a final target.
The financial requirements of public administrations, in terms of the net amounts of indebtedness adjustment and divestment, equalled 2.6% against 3.1 % in 2001. Following the reviews made to the net amount of indebtedness in 2001, the requirement surplus over the indebtedness was reduced in 2001 to 0.5 percentage points of the output whereas it was equal to 1.3 points in 2000. Whether it is true that the gap between the two balances went down to 0.3 points in 2002, it will result being considerably higher provided that the effects caused by the measures to mitigate the requirements without affecting indebtedness are excluded.'

rights and interests of the citizens in the contracting Member States by the 'creation of a European citizenship'; and, finally, developing European citizenship as an area in which freedom, security and justice must be ensured. Moreover, Article 2 (now Article 3, paragraph 3 of TUE) adds a further objective designed to 'fully' retain the *acquis communautaire* so as to guarantee the effectiveness and efficiency of the Union's mechanisms and institutions.

Only few of the objectives indicated above are part of the Union's action, whereas others constitute the subject of new or different actions in which the Community has competence to deal with as governed by amended Community treaties. The specific areas in which the Union has powers to act are those of foreign common and security policy, and cooperation in the field of justice and home affairs.

The EU Treaty provides for substantial amendments to the agreements made between the three Communities.

During the Maastricht meeting, it was envisaged to bring a sort of 'harmonization' in the Treaties establishing the three European Communities, to eradicate the most visible differences among them. At the same time the European Communities were renamed 'European Community', so that the three Communities have now been fused.

The amendments to the EC Treaty deal with the creation of a European citizenship; the establishment an effective economic and monetary policy; the vesting the Community with the power to act in the areas of education, culture and public health; the development of trans-European networks in the field of transports, telecommunications and energy; the reviewing of Community policies in the field of research and technological development, environment and economic and social cohesion; providing a 'codification' of Community competences in the field of industrial policy, consumer protection and development cooperation; envisaging stronger actions of unique character in the area of 'social policy'.

The law-making process in the Community has been redesigned. In the EU Treaty a sanctioning system is established to apply against Member States responsible for the infringement of Community law.

The relationship between the Union and the Community appears, however, ambiguous: the Union[7] is in effect distinct from the Community since it is 'established' by the contracting parties of the Treaty, but its relationship with the Communities, in particular the EC – also is unclear.

Although the Union and the Communities are distinct from a formal point of view, they turn out to be interlinked. Following the ratification of the Amsterdam and Nice Treaties,[8] further amended and supplemented provisions were introduced into the EU Treaty.

7. Cassese, 'L'Unione europea come organizzazione pubblica composita', in *Riv. it. dir. pubbl. comun.*, 2000, p. 987.
8. The former was signed on 2 October 1997 and came into force on 9 May 1999. The latter was signed on 26 February 2001 and came into force in 1 February 2003. Pocar and Secchi, *Il Trattato di Nizza e l'Unione Europea*, (in collaboration with ISPI, Altomonte, Baruffi and Passarelli), Milano, 2001.

The Amsterdam Treaty, entered into force on 1 May 1999, and which renumbered the articles of the previous Treaties, brought amendments to the first pillar (Community), the second pillar (European common security policy) and the third pillar (which has now become known as 'Judicial police cooperation in criminal matters').

In this context, the main amendment deals with the 'enhanced cooperation', that is an action whereby only some states are allowed to participate and deal with certain matters which, in turn, leads them to move faster than others along the road of European integration (so called different-speed Europe). Article 11 of the EC Treaty (added to by the Amsterdam Treaty and replaced by the Nice Treaty) (now Article 20, paragraph 2 of TUE), entered into force on 1 February 2003, states in its second paragraph that authorization to proceed towards enhanced cooperation is granted by the Council upon proposal by the Commission, and prior to consultation with the European Parliament.

Enhanced cooperation is the main safeguard value and protects the interests of the Union. It implies that the Union's coherent identity is strengthened on the international scene by virtue of the Treaty of Nice. The Community has the power to conclude international agreements within its field of competence. The condition for such tendency is that Art. 47 UE (already Art. 281 TCE) (now Article 40 of TUE) – revealingly, a norm which now opens the general and final dispositions of the Treaty on the Union –, it involves the possibility of keeping contractual relationships with Third Countries in the overall number of sectors subject to the Treaties. [9]

9. S. Van Raepenbusch, *La réforme institutionnelle du traité de Lisbonne: l'émergence juridique de l'Union européenne, Cah. dr. eur. 2007,* n°5-6; J.-Cl. Gautron, *Le Traité de Lisbonne ou le retour de la real politik, Rev. aff. eur.* 2007–2008/2, p. 163; F. Picod (dir.), *Le traité í. de Lisbonne, Revue des affaires européennes* 2007–2008/2; Baratta R., Le principali novità del trattato di Lisbona, in *Il diritto dell'Unione europea,* 2008, p. 1 ss; Bassanini F., Tiberi G., *Le nuove istituzioni europee: Commento al Trattato di Lisbona,* Bologna, 2008; J.-P. Jacque, *La complexité d'un traité simplifié. Le Traité de Lisbonne et la coexistence des trois traités, Rev. aff. eur.* 2007–2008/3; J.-P. Jacque, *Le traité de Lisbonne: une vue cavalière, RTD eur.* 2008; J.-Cl. Gautron, *Le traité de Lisbonne, mort et transfiguration de la Constitution européenne,* dans *Politeia, Constitution et traité de Lisbonne,* 2008, n° 13; J. A. Giron Larrucea, *El sistema jurídico de la Unión Europea: la reforma realizada en el Tratado de Lisboa,* Valencia, Tirant lo Blanch, 2008; Griller, J. Ziller, *The Lisbon Treaty. EU Constitutionalism without a Constitutional Treaty,* Wien-New York, Springer, 2008; S. C. Sieberson, *Dividing Lines between The European Union And Its Member States: The Impact of the Treaty of Lisbon,* T.M.C. Asser Press, Cambridge University Press, 2008; J. Ziller (dir.), *L'Union européenne, édition du Traité de Lisbonne,* Les notices de la Documentation française, 2008; J. Ziller, *Les nouveaux traités européens: Lisbonne et après,* Paris, Montchrestien, 2008; Triggiani E. (a cura di), *L'Unione europea secondo la riforma di Lisbona,* Bari, 2008; Bilancia P., D'Amico M., *La nuova Europa dopo il Trattato di Lisbona,* Milano, 2009; Y. Bot, *Quelques perspectives aprés Lisbonne, La semaine juridique. Éd. Gén.,* 83, n. 52, 21 December 2009; E. Brosset, Chevallier-Govers, V. Edjaharian, C. Schneider (dir.), *Le traité de Lisbonne: reconfiguration ou déconstitution nalisation de l'Union européenne,* Bruxelles, Bruylant, 2009; Daniele L., (a cura di), Le relazioni esterne dell'Unione europea dopo il Trattato di Lisbona: verso un nuovo equilibrio?, in *Studi sull'integrazione europea* 2009, 7ss.; J.-P. Jacque, Les réformes institutionnelles introduites par le traité de Lisbonne, in E. Brosset, C. Chevallier-Govers, V. Edjahirian, C. Schneider (dir.), *Le traité de Lisbonne: reconfiguration ou déconstitutionnalisation de l'Union européenne,* Bruxelles, Bruylant, 2009; Patrono A., Lucarelli A., *Commentario al Trattato di Lisbona,* Napoli, 2009; A. Pernice, The Treaty of Lisbon: Multilivel Constitutionalism in Action, *Columbia Journal of European Law,* Vol. 15, n.3, 2009, F. Picod, *Le Traité de Lisbonne: una nouvelle chance pour l'Europe, La semaine juridique, Edition gèNèrale,* 2009, n. 52, 21 December; J. Wouters, L.

There are other amendments which simplify such procedures and allow certain policies to have greater effect, facilitating, at the same time, the freedom of movement of Community citizens.

The first phase (1973–1981) of the enlargement process to Denmark, Ireland, the United Kingdom and, later, Greece, was completed within the framework of the Common Market, that is a customs union characterized by the free movement of goods. Moreover, this process of enlargement, in respect of the original number of founding countries of the European Communities, had great importance, since these countries were included in the initial phase regarding the integration process of state economic areas and the harmonization of national legal systems.

The second phase (1986) of the enlargement process to Spain and Portugal, was completed within the framework of the Common Market with regard to the four fundamental freedoms[10] of movement of goods, services, people and capital, thus laying the grounds for cooperation in the field of foreign policy.

This enlargement took place within a notably more advanced integration and harmonization pace, though it was limited to only two states.

The Copenhagen European Council held in 1993 established that 'the adhesion process will take place as soon as an associated country is able to take on the relative obligations by ensuring that the required economic and political conditions are fulfilled'.

The 'criteria' to be fulfilled were an institutional stability as a way to ensure democracy, legality and human rights, as well as the respect and protection of minorities, efficient market economy, capacity to face competitive pressure and market forces within the Union and, lastly, capacity to assume the obligations arising from their membership of the Union, including their adhesion to the objectives of a political, economic and monetary union.

The increasingly higher relevance acquired by the EU's enlargement process induced the European Council to establish the requirements which candidate countries should meet in the third phase of the enlargement. This phase (1995) was extended to quite a restricted number of countries (Austria, Sweden and Finland), but certainly represented an advance in the process of monetary unification.

A rather complex and structured preparatory procedure to the fourth phase of the enlargement to East European countries was set in motion at the same time, taking into account not only the considerable number of Eastern countries applying for EU membership, but also their particular economic and legislative conditions.

The primary purpose of the fourth enlargement phase was to provide the protection of the main EU values and the integral adoption by the acceding new states of the standards, practices and requirements behind the Community *acquis*, the body

Verhey, P. Kiiver (dir.), *European Constitutionalism beyond Lisbon*, Intersentia, 2009; F. Picod, *Le nouveau cadre institutionnel de l'Union européenne*, *La semaine juridique, éd. Gén.* 5 avril 2010, n. 14, L'étude.

10. Englisch, 'Zur Dogmatic der Grundfreiheiten des EGV und ihren ertragsteuerlichen Implikationen', in *StuW*, 2003, p. 88, examines how tax rules may be constrained by such fundamental freedoms.

of EU's law. The aim was to adapt national rules to the Community legal system, in addition to completing the necessary economic, political and social reforms.

At the European Council held in Madrid in 1995, it was pointed out that each candidate country should adapt its own administrative structures so that EU legislation could be correctly implemented in the national legal systems of the Member States through appropriate administrative and judicial structures, indispensable to establishing mutual confidence viewed as the fundamental requirement for EU membership.

The introduction of the fourth enlargement phase, therefore, made the requirements for countries applying for EU membership tighter.

The Helsinki European Council in 1999, established that candidate countries had to 'to share the values and objectives pursued by the European Union as are enshrined in the Treaties'. It was also pointed out, however, that any 'progress towards negotiations must go hand in hand with the progress made towards the integration of the *acquis* in Community legislation and its effective implementation'.

The parallelism between the negotiation procedure between the EU and candidate countries, and the process of adopting the Community *acquis* into national legislation, with a periodical review, was aimed at identifying some of the sectors requiring specific measures to be taken by applicant countries in order to apply the Community *acquis*.

Some programmes were adopted to prepare candidate countries for membership of the Union. The 'Association Agreements', for example, on matters concerning trade, political dialogue, approximation of legislation and other cooperation domains, produced interesting results in industry, environment, transports and customs, in particular. The 'Periodical Reports' drawn by the Brussels Commission and submitted to the EU Council, were, likewise, evidence of the annual progress made by individual applicant countries. 'Accession Partnerships' identified the priorities of the preparatory stages of each candidate country, and the variety of support actions being provided by the EU.

The 'National Plan for the *acquis* adoption', prescribed that candidate countries indicated the way they intended to put into effect the priorities of the accession partnership, and established a detailed outline of the human and financial resources. 'Pre-accession Assistance' was based on action to support agricultural and rural development *(Sapard);* other actions were also co-financed by the European Investment Bank and other international financial institutions. At the same time, this pre-accession programme was based on the *Phare* Programme which is particularly interesting because it has provided assistance to Central and East European countries applying for membership since 1989, making the application of the *acquis* easier thanks to annual financial commitments.

The European Council of Nice in 2000 called upon candidate countries 'to proceed promptly on the path leading to prodomic reforms of membership to the EU'.

A procedure for a 'structured dialogue' started in 2001; the EU, in arranging for the obligations to be imposed on candidate countries, provided them with the necessary support in order for them to develop in their statistical, analytical and planning capacity as fundamental conditions to formulate common political strategies.

In 2001, candidate countries submitted their own 'Pre-accession Economic Plans' which evidenced the evolutionary process of these countries to build their own capacity for making analysis and plans as an essential condition to participate in multilateral surveillance procedures as required by the EU. In particular, macroeconomic and financial stability, budgetary policies and exchange rate regimes were the subject for analysis in that year, and the way in which candidate countries were able to build on their own capacities was significant.

This being the background, and following the Copenhagen summit meeting in December 2002 as well as the voting results of the European Parliament of 9 April 2003, a fourth EU enlargement phase took effect from 1 May 2004 with countries such as Cyprus, Malta, Hungary, Czech Republic, Poland, Slovenia, Slovakia, Estonia, Latvia and Lithuania; the fifth enlargement phase took effect from January 2007 with the accession of Bulgaria and Romania (*Report* of the Commission of 16 May 2006 IP/06/634).

The above phase can only take place if cooperation is started in the economic and technical fields, as well as in such other sectors as: social policy; employment; justice; asylum law; immigration; foreign, security and defence policy.

Such an intensive preparatory process is one which has so far led to a review, rather than a solution of the problems surrounding divergency between the economies and legal systems in ten of the newly acceding Member States, in comparison with the fifteen full Member States of the EU. Therefore, with the EU now extending to East European countries, enlargement constitutes one of the most significant phases compared to the others described above. In fact, it stands as the most relevant phase in quantitative terms because of the size, number of countries, population and geographical area being involved. Here, it may suffice to say that the population throughout the EU has increased by approximately 25% while the EU geographical area has increased by approximately 30%.

The role played by the law-making process in the Community will be essential in the domain of taxes, with a view to achieving the fundamental objectives in the area of economic and social policy within the framework of a harmonious development.

Each Member State can exercise a veto against a tax rule laid down by the Community.

Differences in quantitative terms, which contribute to defining the dimension involved in the enlarged Europe, are such as to lead to a new moderate course or compromise to be chosen in European institutions, thus adding a higher degree of complexity to the whole of decision-making process in Europe. Clearly, the fact that all EU countries (Eastern and Western) are required to cast votes unanimously may well constitute a considerable obstacle to the fiscal policy of the enlarged Union, given that there are great difficulties for the Union of twenty-five states to agree unanimously in such a delicate sector as tax.

The ten new Member States chose to accede to the EU also on account of the substantial financial support they received during and after the convergence process (common agricultural policy; structural funds; development aid; and so forth). Moreover, a similar system would avoid what is known as the 'Eastern coalition' of the ten new Member States.

For the fifteen countries already full members of the European Union, the primary objective in the enlargement process remains fundamentally political in nature.

After joining the monetary union at a later stage, the ten new EU Member States will each be entitled to a representative of their respective government to sit in the Governing Council of the European Central Bank and, hence, be each equally entitled to a voting on decisions regarding reference rates.

The ten new EU Member States, with a high level of growth and structurally higher inflation, could well express their common interests in the field of economic and monetary policy which are different from those shared by the pre-existing fifteen countries.

In the Commission's opinion of 26 January 2000 carrying the title 'Adapting the Institutions To Make A Success Of Enlargement', the announcement was given on the positive contribution of extending the qualified majority voting to taxation, as well as social security.

It is therefore clear, in the Commission's view, that the Union can face this challenge only by upgrading the efficiency of its own decision-making process through recurrent use of qualified majority voting. In this regard, a higher efficiency can be achieved by narrowing the field of application of unanimous voting, as is now provided for under the Treaty. Qualified majority voting comes as appropriate when applied to the instruments which allow for the coordination of national rules.

At the Nice summit held in December 2000, representatives laid the foundations for the relevant institutional changes, and made a proposal for qualified majority voting to extend also to tax matters. It should be pointed out, however, that the Nice Treaty has not yet modified the unanimity rule to apply to tax matters. The efficiency of the decision-making process is one which rests on the 'likelihood of approval' of a similar rule to the contrary by the European Council. This probability is reduced in the Nice Treaty from 8.2 %, with the Council being composed of fifteen member countries, down to 2.1 %, this time with the Council being composed of twenty-five member countries. The simple majority voting procedure is one which, in terms of voting and population distribution, ensures a higher degree of efficiency in the decision-making process, regardless of the number of countries being involved.

The application of the unanimity rule could be regarded as being appropriate well before the current phase of the EU's enlargement. In this framework, the need would be for tax matters to be added to the thirty other Union matters, which should no longer be dealt with by unanimous decision by the Union as provided under the Nice Treaty, rather by qualified majority, as modified by the above Treaty regarding 'vote weighting' which individual Member States are entitled to.

The effect of this would in particular bring advantages to: (a) the power to exercise the four freedoms; (b) the essentially ecological character of measures; (c) the rules concerned with the fight against fraud, evasion and avoidance of tax, and mutual cooperation and assistance between administrative tax authorities in the Member States.

Community tax rules which are directed at the elimination of the obstacles to the exercise of the four freedoms, should be adopted on a qualified majority basis, with the primary purpose of eliminating the effects of discriminatory taxation and avoiding persons being taxed twice over in respect of the same matter (double taxation). Such coordinating rules, should in effect govern exclusively those situations in which the interests of the majority of Member States are affected, and should not have repercussions on merely internal situations.

As observed by the European Commission, the qualified majority voting should be extended to decisions designed to bring an updated and simplified version of Community rules so as to remove distortions to competition, and ensure that the rules currently in force in tax matters are applied in a way which is uniform, simple and transparent.

We hope that the above opinion of the Commission, which has until now been disregarded, will be welcomed as soon as possible, and that the delicate and complex procedure behind the making of Community acts will be streamlined also in tax matters. This streamlining in tax matters is necessary to eliminate gaps between the economic realities existing in the fifteen EU's member countries and those in the ten new EU's Member States.

§11.03 EFFECTS OF SELF-EXECUTING COMMUNITY ACTS ON THE NATIONAL LEGAL SYSTEM

We must now examine the procedure by which the internal legal system is adapted to the international tax law system. The Italian Constitution contains no provision on the ordinary procedure regarding the adaptation process.

Article 10, paragraph 1 of the Constitution, by establishing that the Italian legal system 'shall be in conformity'[11] with the rules of the international system, rules the effect of this special procedure. The international rule, therefore, has no effect on people under domestic jurisdiction, rather it is a national unwritten rule, automatically formed by way of the special procedure, and which has the same legal substance of the international rule which rules in Italian legal system. 'Conformity' with the international system is ensured by the internal rule spontaneously created in the national system.

The formation of rules is therefore in origin international; problems may occur when we must apply these rules to internal factual situations. The correct use of hermeneutic methodologies[12] allows us to better understanding how international tax rules may be in a correct balance with national laws.

11. According to this Article: '*The Italian legal order shall be in conformity with the generally recognized rules of international law*'.
12. The principle of good faith, codified in Art. 18 of the Vienna Convention I, is a principle of international customary law whose existence has been recognized by the International Court of Justice. It is therefore binding on the Community, i.e. this principle is the corollary (in public international law) of the principle to protect legitimate trust which is part of the Community legal system and to which reference may be made by all economic players where an institution has generated realistic hope. When the Community has given its official approval of an international agreement, and when the date of its entering into force is known, economic players can avail of the principle of protection of legitimate trust in the period prior to the entering into force of this international agreement, in order to oppose the adoption by the

Article 10, paragraph 1 of the Constitution covers only the special or reference procedure *(procedimento speciale o di rinvio)* and applies only to certain rules forming the object of this mechanism.

The above constitutional provision covers only general international rules such as customary rules, including general principles recognized by civil nations. It does not apply however to other rules, such as conventional rules or rules established by international organizations.

Article 10, paragraph 1, on the one hand, establishes the essential features of the special or reference procedure while, on the other, gives a privileged position to general international tax rules when they are subject to a similar procedure.

Each State must not invade the sovereignty of another country in the exercise of its own taxing power, as established by a customary rule corollary of international law. Therefore, people enjoying sovereignty under international law are not subject to the taxing power of a State when the same activities are not subject to the jurisdiction of the tax court of that State.

General international tax rules operate in a State system of law to the extent that they are valid within the international Community. Moreover, each legal system provides, at least implicitly, for a process of adaptation to general international tax law.

The rank of unwritten internal tax rules resulting automatically from international rules, is the same that the internal rule has in the hierarchy of legal sources under which the ordinary or special adaptation procedure is conducted.

---

institutions of any act, which has direct effect in relation to them following the entering into force of the agreement, and which is contrary to the provisions of the latter.

Schaumburg, *Internationales Steuerrecht,* 2nd edn, Cologne, 1998, p. 13, examines the prohibitions imposed on individual states by international customary law on tax matters. Cf. Pisano, 'Il rapporto tra norme interne, diritto convenzionale e diritto comunitario', in *Aspetti fiscali delle operazioni internazionali,* edited by Uckmar and Garbarino, Milan, 1995. This is the case of a customary rule which prohibits the state from exercising sea customs inspection powers outside the boundaries of its territorial sea. The correct interpretation of this rule, however, leads one to believe that state tax controls of the territorial sea are forbidden to foreign ships, but not to national ones. In fact, while explicitly imposing such prohibition, the specifically customary rule refers to the general principle whereby ships are subject to the authority of the State to which they belongs.

Cf. Lupi, *Diritto tributario,* 7th edn, Milan, 2000; Laule, 'Die Harmonisierung des europäischen Steuerrechts', in *IstR,* 2001, p. 197; D'Amati, *Diritto tributario,* I, Bari, 2002, p. 26; Ferlazzo Natoli, *Lineamenti di diritto tributario,* Milan, 2002, p. 9; Russo, *Manuale di diritto tributario,* 4th edn, Milan, 2002, p. 74; Falsitta, *Manuale di Diritto tributario,* 4th edn, Padua, 2003, p. 45; Fantozzi, *Il Diritto tributario,* 3rd edn, Turin, 2003, p. 756; Tinelli, *Istituzioni di Diritto tributario,* Padua, 2003, p. 74; Fedele, *Appunti delle lezioni di Diritto tributario,* Torino, 2005; Gaffuri, *Diritto tributario,* 5th edn, Padua, 2006, p. 55; Isaac Guy et Marc Blanquet, Droit général de l'Union européenne, 9th edn, Paris, 2006; D. Wyatt et A. Dashwood, *European Community Law,* Londress, Sweete & Maxwell, 5th edn, 2006; Tesauro (F), *Istituzioni di diritto tributario, parte generale, 9th 2008 e parte speciale 8th 2006,* Torino, p. 81; Macaela Vaerini *Jensen, Exécution du droit communautaire par les E'tats members, Méthode communautaire et nouvelles formes de gouvernance,* Bruxelles, 2007; La Rosa, *Principi di Diritto tributario,* 3rd, Torino, 2009; Manzoni-Vanz, *Il Diritto tributario,* Giappichelli, Torino, 2009; De Mita, *Principi di Diritto tributario,* Milano, 2007; Tinelli, *Istituzioni di Diritto tributario,* 3rd edn, 2010; Padua, Lang, *A European Tax Order based on ability-to-pay,* in this work; Tosi-Baggio, *Lineamenti di Diritto tributario internazionale,* 3-4th, Padova, 2011.

According to Article 10, paragraph 1 of the Constitution, only general international tax law can give rise to constitutional rules of the same substance, since the special procedure specifically applies only to them. The internal tax rule, therefore, resulting directly from the international customary rule, improves the value and extent of our Constitution.

We must now examine in which way the rules of the Community Treaty and its subordinate legal sources may change the national system of law. Issues may arise from the rules of the Community Treaty governing Community complete acts, that is those which fit the purpose of giving rise to the obligations which will operate in the state system only by virtue of the national statute ratifying the Treaty, rather than by the intervention of the state legislative organs.

The first relevant rule is Article 249, paragraph 1, of the EC Treaty (now Article 288, paragraph 1 of TFUE), which states that:

> 'In order to carry out their task and in accordance with the provisions of this Treaty, the European Parliament acting jointly with the Council of the European Union and the Commission of the European Communities [the latter institution carrying this denomination since 8 November 1994] shall make Regulations and issue Directives, take Decisions, make Recommendations or deliver Opinions'.

The second paragraph of the same Article (now Article 288, paragraph 2 of TFUE) deals with the Regulations and states that: 'A Regulation shall have general application. It shall be binding in its entirety and directly applicable to all Member States'. Regulations are effective throughout the Community since they are the ranking legal acts of the Community, and fulfil the function of supplementing and implementing the Treaty rules. A link may be traced between paragraph 4 of Article 249 of the Treaty (now Article 288, paragraph 4 of TFUE), covering merely executive and administrative acts, and Article 256 of the Treaty (now Article 299, paragraph 1 of TFUE) which, in paragraph 1, establishes that: 'Decisions of the Council or of the Commission which impose a pecuniary obligation on persons other than the States, shall be enforceable'.

The inference of this special effect (i.e. enforceability), which makes regulations and Decisions self-executing acts, can also be found in many international conventions, in which it is used in relation to foreign court judgments and other authorities and bodies of the same rank.

The international character of the Community gives way to the problem of adapting the state system of law to conventional international law, that is the question in which way conventional international law (in our case Community rules and acts) can become part of the national legal system, and thus be applied and coordinated with other State rules.

The Treaty rules, such as Article 249 (former Article 189), paragraphs 2 and 4, and Article 256 (former Art. 189) (now respectively Articles 288 e 299 of TFUE), do not concern the ordinary adaptation procedure, that is the creation of internal rules necessary to give rise to the obligations underlying incomplete rules and acts of the Community.

On the contrary, we must examine the special or reference procedure concerning the rules and acts (i.e. Regulations or Decisions) which are complete in all their elements in order to give rise to obligations. In this case, State legislative organs have so far requested by order that such acts and rules to be observed, thus providing them with full application by way of the Italian statute ratifying the Treaty.

Sometimes it is necessary to have executive legal instruments enacted by the Member State's government since, by virtue of Article 10 of the same Treaty (now Article 4 paragraph 3 of TUE), the Member State has the duty to ensure that such instruments (acts) are made executive.[13]

However there are some acts which need no adopting rule. This means that the Community self-executing act is such as to automatically give rise to the adaptation of the national system of law in which the state rule model is received, whereby a domestic person is found to be under the same obligation as provided under the Community act.

Clearly, the effects of this are twofold: first, no infringement is made to the legal autonomy of the States and, second, persons under domestic law are exclusively affected by the national system of law.

§11.04 CONFLICT BETWEEN INTERNAL AND INTERNATIONAL TAX RULES

International fiscal relationships governed by international tax law,[14] the latter resulting from national rules, are sometimes also governed by tax international law,[15] which

13. The Court of Justice, in its ruling of 23 May 1996, in case C-5/94 *Hedley Lomas*, extended the liability of the state to citizens for failing to fulfil their executive power.
Hakenberg, *Grundzüge des europäischen Gemeinschaftsrechts*, 3rd edn, Munich, 2003; Mager-Herrman, *Höchstrichterliche Rechtsprechung zum Europarecht*, Munich, 2003; Von Borrier-Zacker, *Europarecht von A-Z*, 3rd edn, Munich, 2003.
14. Various: Bannock, *Taxation in the European Community*, Paul Chapman, London, 1990; Fantozzi-Vogel, entry 'Doppia imposizione internazionale', in *Digesto*, 4th edn, Torino, 1990; Garbarino, *La tassazione del reddito transnazionale*, Padua, 1990; Tipke, *Die Steuerrechtsordnung*, Cologne, 1993, III, p. 1159; Various, *Non discrimination rules in international taxation*, XLVIIIb, Rotterdam, 1993; Vogel, 'Il diritto tributario internazionale', in *Trattato di diritto tributario*, edited by Amatucci, Padova, 1994, I, 2, p. 691; Id., *Doppelbesteuerungsabkommen*, 2nd edn, 1990; (in English): *On Double Taxation Conventions*, 1991; Fischer, 'Auslegungsziele und Verfassung', in *Die Steuerrechtsordnung, Festschrift für Klaus Tipke* (for the 70th anniversary), Cologne, 1995; Schweitzer-Hummer, *Europarecht*, Neuewied, 1996; Borries-Winkel, *Europaisches Wirtschaftsrecht*, Munich, 1997; Godzierz-Odengahl, *Europarecht-Sammlung hochstrichterlicher Rechtsprechung*, Neuewied, 1997; Schaumburg, *Internationales Steuerrecht*, 2nd edn, Cologne, 1998, p. 41; Uckmar, 'Double Taxation Conventions', in this work.Jacobs (ed.), *Internationale Unternehmensbesteuerung*, Munich, 1999; Grotherr (ed.), *Handbuch der internationalen Steuerplanung*, Herne/Berlin 2000; Kluge, *Das internationale Steuerrecht*, 4th edn, Munich, 2000; Rose, *Grundzüge des internationalen Steuerrechts*, Wiesbaden, 2000; Schaumburg, 'Systemdefizite im internationalen Steuerrecht', in *StuW*, 2000, p. 369; Frotscher, *Internationales Steuerrecht*, Munich, 2001.
The following themes are the subjects of a constant analysis and include contributions appearing also in English in the cited journal *Rivista di diritto tributario internazionale - International Tax Law Review* of La Sapienza University in Rome, founded in 1999, and co-edited by Amatucci, Tejerizo Lopez, Malherbe, Puoti, Sacchetto.
15. Cf. Höhn, *Steuerrecht*, 7th edn, Bern, Stuttgart, Vienna, 1993, p. 533 and Taveira Torres, 'Fiscalidad internaciónal: Tipologia de las normas y ambitos de estudio', in *Informativo, tributario internaciónal*, 1997,73, as regards the international nature of rules which form

international tax law; Schaumburg, *Internationales Steuerrecht,* 2nd edn, Cologne, 1998, p. 3. Along this line, Martín Queralt, Lozano Serrano, Casado Ollero and Tejerizo López, *Curso de Derecho financiero y tributario,* Madrid, 12th edn, 2001, p. 244.

Vogel, 'Il diritto tributario internazionale', in *Trattato di diritto tributario,* edited by Amatucci, in *An-nuario,* Padua, 2001, p. 365, states that international tax law partly restricts and partly modifies national tax laws in relation to the specific features acquired by the facts in the instant tax case arising beyond national borders. Also on this subject: Jacobs, *Steuerliche Vorteilhaftigkeit des Einsatzes von Eigen- oder Fremdkapital bei der internationalen Konzernfinanzierung,* in *StuW,* 1996, p. 26. Cf. Vogel, *Der Grundsatz der Rücksichtnahme im deutschen innerstaatlichen Recht und im Volkerrecht,* in *Festschrift für Wolfgang Ritter,* by Kley, Sunner, Willemsen, Cologne, 1997 and *Unternehmensfinanzierung im internationalen Steuerrecht,* by piltz and Schaumburg, Cologne, 1995; Schaumburg, *Internationales Steuerrecht,* 2nd edn, Cologne, 1998, p. 1. Tipke, *Die Steuerrechtsordnung,* Cologne, 1993, III Vol., p. 1138, considers that legal rules are synonymous with situations arising from law, and defines them as legal sources. These are analysed in relation to legal provisions, which are understood as commands imposed on the citizen in a specific domain and time, and must be guaranteed by the state or local authority. This distinguished author considers that, in the area of tax law, legal rules also typically amount to conventions against double taxation and rules of super-national law. These rules, because they are not irrelevant for the purpose of acquiring the knowledge of the law, can thus be considered as the sources of such knowledge. In this context, Tipke points out that a proper legal rank is established by the Constitution, maintaining that in the logic of the gradual establishment of the legal order, higher ranking rules are derogated to lower ones. However, he specifies that, under Art. 25 of the German Constitution, rules of general international law are transformed into state laws, and thus acquire the value of ordinary law.

In the German legal system, general international tax rules do not acquire the relevance as constitutional rules, but stand on a level of ordinary law as conventional rules or Decisions of international organizations. Cf. Kluge, *Das deutsche internationale Steuerrecht,* Munich, 1992 and Mössner, Baumhoff, Fischer-Lernin, Greif, Henkel, Menck, Plitz, Schröder, Tillmanns, *Steuerrecht internationaltätiger Unternehmer,* Cologne, 1992, 'Staat Wirtschaft Steuern', in *Writings in honour of Karl Heinrich Friauf,* by Wendt, Hofling, Karpen and Oldiges, Heidelberg, 1996.

On the subject of rule groupings in international tax law, see: Schaunburg, *Internationales Steuerrecht,* 2nd edn, Koln, 1998, p. 5; Kluge, *Das internationale Steuerrecht,* Munich, 2000; O.H.Jacobs, *Internationale Unternehmensbesteuerung,* München, 2007; Bächle/Rupp/Ott/Knies, *Internationales Steuerrecht,* Stuttgart, 2008; G. Brähler, *Internationales Steuerrecht,* Wiesbaden, 2009; F. Haase, *Internationales u. Europäisches Steuerrecht,* Heidelberg, 2009; T.Wörsching, *Grundlagen u. Grundstrukturen des Internationalen Steuerrechts,* SteuerStud, 2009; 176.

Burmester, *Grundlagen internationaler Regelungskumulation undKollision, unter besonderer Berücksichtigung des Steuerrechts,* Baden-Baden, 1993, as regards conflicts apparently arising when the internal tax rule influences the formation of the international one; Flick-Piltz, *Internationale Erbfalle,* Munich; *Schriften zum internationalen Steuerrecht,* by Vogel, Book 21, Munich, 1996; *Internationales Umwandlungssteuerrecht,* by Schaumburg and Piltz, vol. II, '*Forum der Internationalen Besteuerung*', Cologne, 1997; Euler, 'Steuerbilanzielle Konsequenzen der internationalisierten Rechnungslegung', in *StuW,* 1998, p. 15.

López, *Curso de Derecho financiero y tributario,* Madrid, 12th edn 2001, p. 244, competition among administrative tax authorities in the states in which they co-exist as part of the overall international order, is one which gives rise to two fundamental problems, particularly in tax matters: double taxation, on the one hand, and international tax evasion, on the other.

Tipke and Lang, *Steuerrecht, 20*th edn Cologne, 2010, pp. 13 and 30, point out that, from the point of view of a legal comparative analysis, the international nature of economic transactions leads legal tax theory into the territory of international and Community law. In addition, they notice that one area of tax law is constituted by international tax law, which not only amounts to a system of national legal rules but also of rules of international law, and that the law of international conventions plays a determining role in tax law and, in particular, the Treaties against double taxations. These Treaties viewed as special rules, amount to – the authors add – general rules of international law, and are placed at a higher hierarchical level compared to is in effect constituted by general international rules and other rules, such as conventional rules or rules established in decisions of international organizations.[16] By virtue of a perfect balance controlled essentially by domestic law, the result is a tax rule to take precedence over others, which basically regulate the same specific and concrete type of tax case.

A proper knowledge of the different force and value of international tax law-based domestic rules compared to tax international rules, makes it possible to understand which one of them may prevail in the event of incompatibility arising from the content of the rules applied to the same factual situation.

However, determining the relationship between several national tax laws governing the same concrete type of tax case is both a delicate and fascinating matter in the present analysis, especially when some of the above laws are the consequential result of an international rule.

Any statute is unlawful if it is in contrast with constitutional rules, which are produced by general international tax law as under Article 10, paragraph 1, of the Constitution, and which at the same time are found to take precedence over the Constitution. This is because it is precisely the Constitution which gives them the character of special constitutional laws, provided of course they do not lead to a violation of fundamental guarantees. Rules formed as a result of general tax international law are, to a greater extent, binding on the national legislator.

The force of any unwritten constitutional rule created automatically, carrying identical content as a general tax international rule, is one which involves written constitutional rules and national laws to cease to exist in their legal efficacy, whenever the latter are found to be incompatible with the former.

---

a tax law. In fact, the general legal principles of international law qualify the logical-legal rule related to the application of the law of *Rechtsmissbrauch*, and the principle of good faith. In the view of Martín Queralt, Lozano Serrano, Casado Ollero and Tejerizo López, *Curso de Derecho financiero y tributario*, Madrid, 17th edn 2006, p. 244, competition among administrative tax authorities in the states in which they co-exist as part of the overall international order, is one which gives rise to two fundamental problems, particularly in tax matters: double taxation, on the one hand, and international tax evasion, on the other.

16. As regards the definition of international organization, Cf. Seidl-Hohenweldern, *Das Recht der internationalen Organisationen einschliesslich der supranationalen Gemeinschaften*, Munich, 1992.
Along these lines, a commercial agreement or convention whereby a state commits itself to balancing tax treatment of goods imported from other states, in line with the treatment agreed upon for similar national goods, must be interpreted in the sense that it tends to facilitate trade exchange within States. However, this agreement can be raised in legal proceedings against the administrative financial authority by national import enterprises and firms. In fact, while the commitment is taken between States, the relation between enterprises/firms and authority, which is of a 'domestic' nature, is one which form the object of the discipline behind the internal unwritten rule having the same content as the automatically produced conventional rule. Cf. *Aspetti fiscali delle operazioni internazionali*, edited by Uckmar and Garbarino, Milan, 1995; Bricker, 'Arbitration Procedures in Tax Treaties', in *Intertax*, 1998, p. 97.
Whenever a rule of Community law is subject to different interpretations, it is necessary to give priority to the one which aids the purposeful effect of the rule.
In case of a divergency among the various language versions of a Community rule, this must be solved by interpreting it in relation to the general economy and the purposes and aims of the legislation which the rule is part of - Court of Justice of the European Communities, 24 February 2000, No. 434/97, *EC Commission v. French Government*, in *Raccolta*, 2000, I, p. 1129.

Similarly, conventional tax rules or rules contained in tax decisions of international organizations (which have been introduced into the Italian law system by way of a special or reference procedure, but which are not provided in Article 10, paragraph 1, of the Constitution) also require that the methodology for interpretation be based on the same balancing elements.

Conventional tax rules, or those contained in a fiscal decision of international organizations, and received into the national system by way of a special or reference procedure, do not directly operate on taxpayers or administrative tax authorities in the Member State; rather, their effect is such as to automatically give rise to a new unwritten law of equal substance affecting taxpayers through the national system of law acting as a filter. These rules do not just determine the creation of constitutional rules but of ordinary laws which acquire the same rank as legislative acts requiring such rules to be made executive in the national law. Therefore, such tax rules give rise to acts having the same substance, whose legal force and value are the same as those imported in ordinary legislation.

However, while guaranteeing observance of conventional or decision-based tax international rules, any statute which requires rules to be made executive in the State system proves to have a particular character and substance, because it is designed to make provision on more specific matters and to apply to a more limited number of taxable persons. Indeed, this character extends to unwritten tax laws which are produced automatically, and which have the same content as conventional rules or rules contained in decisions of international organizations. As a consequence, any tax statute being produced subsequently, which is such as to depart from unwritten statutes, will in the meantime take precedence, given that it will also in this circumstance lead to repudiation of the formal commitments undertaken under international treaties.

In the absence of a provision on discharge from formal international commitments, the statute produced subsequently will be abrogated by an unwritten tax statute previously created, with which it is found to be incompatible.

For these reasons, rules contained in a convention or agreement[17] against double taxation, and introduced into the domestic system by means of a special procedure, are

17. Mössner-Blumenwitz, 'Doppelbesteueuerungs-abkommen und nationales Recht', in *Münchener Schriften zum internationalen Steuerrecht*, edited by Vogel, book 18, Munich, 1995; Scherer, *Doppelbesteuerung und Europäisches Gemeinschaftsrecht*, Munich, 1995; Uckmar, 'Le convenzioni contro le doppie imposizioni con riguardo all'America Latina', in *Dir. eprat. trib.*, 1996, I, p. 1179; Corasaniti, 'L'eliminazione della doppia imposizione nell'ordinamento italiano e nell'ordinamento federale tedesco', in *Dir. e prat. trib.*, 1997, III, p. 433; Debatin-Wassermeyer, *Doppelbesteuerung,*10th edn, Munich, 1997; Wassermeyer, *Doppelbesteuerungsab-kommen*, Munich, 2002; Vogel-Lehner, *Doppelbesteuerungsabkommen*, 4th edn, Munich, 2003;
On double taxations, cf. Schaumburg, *Internationales Steuerrecht*, 2nd edn, Cologne, 1998, p. 585; Altamirano, C. Alejandro, Finalizaciòn del Convenio Argentino Austriaco para evitar la doble imposiciòn (es suficiente la denuncia del Pen o se require una Ley?), in *Diritto e Pratica Tributaria internazionale*, n. 1/2009 and in *Mundo Fiscal*, n. 4, 2008, Calì-Colombia; A. Crazzolara, Società di persone ed applicazione delle convenzioni internazionali contro la doppia imposizione: riflessioni alla luce dell'interpretazione nel sistema tributario tedesco, in *Diritto e Pratica tributaria internazionale*, vol. VII- n. 3, Padova, 2010;

subject to derogation from a subsequently made tax statute, only if the latter is not limited to make different provision on the same (tax) situation, but expressly shows a failure to keep to the intention to meet international commitments already taken.

The conflicting previous statute is derogated from the unwritten tax statute, simply because the latter comes at a subsequent stage. For this reason, every single source of law can modify the conflicting previous one, in so far as it stands on the same level in the hierarchy of legal sources. The fact that the law assumes a 'special' character in the instant case can only strengthen such principle, given that conflicts between rules can only be solved by taking account of their own rank. By way of the

---

Tipke and Lang, *Steuerrecht 20*th edn, Cologne, 2010 p. 170. Martín Queralt, Lozano Serrano, Casado Ollero and Tejerizo López, *Curso de Derecho financiero y tributario,* Madrid, 17th edn, 2006, p. 150, state that, under Art. 96, paragraph I of the Constitution, the Spanish system provides that the international Treaty, which is validly stipulated and published officially, forms part of the domestic order and, as such, it can be modified in the forms provided for under the Treaty itself, as long as it complies with the rules of general international law. Art. 93 of the Spanish Constitution establishes that, by 'organic law' or *ley organica* (covered in Art. 81 of the Constitution in which absolute parliamentary majority is required), stipulation of the Treaties must be authorized so that any international organization or institution may exercise their powers as provided for by the Constitution. Any Treaty which implies burdens on government finance falls into the category of the Treaties requiring prior authorization by the Parliament. Thus, the law authorizing the provision of conventional rules in the Spanish legal system acquires the rank of an organic law as is prescribed in Art. 93 of the Constitution. There are only three subject matters covered by organic law which may be of interest to financial law. Any national legislation which is contrary to Community legislation cannot be applied by the national court. Cf. Court of Justice 4-6-1992 No. 13/91 (in *Rass. avv. st.*, 1992, I, p. 417) and 9-6-1992 No. 228–234 (in *Giust. civ.*, 1993, I, 1389). Under Art. 24 of the Constitution of the German Federal Republic, it is stated as follows: 'the Federation may, by law, transfer sovereign rights to inter-state Institutions'. This Article goes on by providing in Art. 25: 'general rules of international law shall be an integral part of federal law. *They shall prevail over domestic law* and shall constitute subjective rights and instantaneous obligations and duties to federal people' (emphasis added).

Uckmar, 'Double Taxation Conventions', in this work, points out that any State may impose taxes on anyone who is under its jurisdictional authority, including aliens. The author adds that the co-existence of a jurisdictional authority, of which the taxing power is no more than a proper manifestation, may give rise to conflicts in tax jurisdiction, due to the fact that individual States are short of limits to their taxing power.

Moreover, the author affirms that the correct application of rules belonging to independent fiscal systems, based on different principles of nationality, residence and income source, determines positive conflicts in the field of taxation, in particular when the residence State does not coincide with that in which income is produced. Indeed, the State which adopts the principle of the income source, will levy tax on resident and non-resident persons, regarding all types of income produced within their own territory. On the contrary, the State which adopts the residence principle in its own legal system, will only levy tax on persons who are resident within their own territorial jurisdiction, regarding global income, including the income produced abroad. Sometimes the principle of taxation turns out to be the same, but the classification of facts and situations varies. The conflicting definitions can be the cause for double taxation to arise. In order to avoid positive conflicts in the field of taxation, as well as distortions to competition which inevitably arise from them, it is necessary to have recourse to the Treaties against double taxation.

Tipke, *Die Steuerrechtsordnung,* Cologne, 1993, III, p. 1157, affirms that such Treaties do not fall into the category of general rules of international law under Art. 25 of the German Constitution. However, under the ratification law, these treaties acquire the character of domestic legal rules. This is the same phenomenon as applied under Arts 10 and 11 of the Italian Constitution.

ordinary procedure, however, the internal tax law provides for the national system of law to be adapted to international law. In this circumstance, therefore, international tax rules come to be reformulated via formal procedures by the national parliament.

It is possible to apply the internal tax law which does not however stand on the same level as other State laws, when the ordinary procedure is used. This internal statute is in effect distinguished from other State statutes not only because of the reason giving rise to it as a special statute, but also because it locates mid-way between ordinary laws and constitutional rules in the hierarchy of legal sources. Also in this case, the special law is one which abrogates the ordinary law, with which it is incompatible.

The international rule can only be an auxiliary instrument for the interpreter whose task is to reproduce and, if necessary, make the internal tax law more complete, with the consequence that, in the event of a contrast arising in the content of such rule, the internal law will prevail.

If the law resulting from the application of the ordinary procedure differs from the international rule because of a mistake in the interpretative criteria, it will in any case hinder international tax law from being observed. On the contrary, under the special procedure, the mistake will only affect those cases in which an incorrect interpretation was made of the international fiscal rule.

In this sense, the special procedure guarantees that tax international law is observed to a greater extent. Therefore, the character of a special law is also covered by the ordinary law resulting from the application of the ordinary adaptation procedure of a treaty against double taxation.

This ordinary law may be subject to derogation from another subsequent law, to the extent that the latter is an express manifestation of the will to repudiate the underlying international commitment.

Thus, the national tax law produced formally by the national parliament may not, in all circumstances, derogate from a constitutional unwritten rule which reproduces a rule of general international law, given that this is expressly provided in Article 10, paragraph 1, of the Constitution (i.e. special or reference procedure). On the contrary, the said national law may derogate from unwritten laws which reiterate conventional rules, or rules contained in decisions of international organizations (special or reference procedure), or laws of the national parliament which reproduce international rules (ordinary procedure) on condition that, as well as making a separate provision on the subject matter, it includes an express provision not to fulfil the international commitment already made.

However, the unwritten tax rule may derogate from the Constitution if it is such as to reproduce the rule of general international law as per Article 10, paragraph 1, of the Constitution. The unwritten tax law (which reiterates the international conventional or decision-based tax rule, by virtue of the special procedure) and the written tax law (which reproduces an international rule, by virtue of the ordinary procedure) cannot introduce such a derogation, since they amount to special higher ranking laws over ordinary laws, but at the same time ranking lower than the Constitution.

Having clarified the meaning behind the prevalence of the special law over other subsequently incompatible laws, there is the problem of establishing interpretative methods of international tax rules to which the domestic order conforms.

In this regard, one of the most interesting questions revolves around 'qualifications', the purpose of which being to establish the meaning of the text behind an international tax treaty. This text is one in which a particular legal institution is there to be regulated in a different fashion in the law systems of the States which are parties to the treaty. In this context, the proper solution would be not just for *lex fori* to establish the validity of the meaning as used in the legal systems of the contracting state applying the convention or agreement, but to provide sufficient guidance so that expressions used in the convention text may acquire a clear and uniform meaning for the benefit of both contracting states.

As will be observed, this problem is the same as the one posed to the interpreter who has to establish the meaning and scope of a national tax law, in the case when a particular tax institution – which locates in a different branch of the law and needs to be adapted to the legislative ratio – has already been received into the national system of tax laws. Here it is true that the 'qualifying' tax law modifies the institution already received so as to adapt it to its own peculiar principles, in so far as the substantial structure of the institution is not altered, and as such requires a uniform application under the general rules.

Doubts as to the identification of the 'rule to apply in the instant case' may also arise when a national tax law is contrary to a Community original or derivative rule. Here, the same problem is posed in exactly the same terms as with the rules enshrined in the Treaty establishing the EC already examined, including subsequently modified and supplemented versions of the Treaty. On these rules, in fact, because they originate from conventional international sources, the same considerations made about the special or ordinary procedure apply.

Similarly, complete rules enshrined in the agreements between the Union and third countries are binding on Community institutions and Member States, with the result that the relationship between national tax laws and conventional international rules will also come into play.

In this context, the relevant point to be made is about Community derivative rules which are in contrast with tax laws of the State. The function of these rules may be twofold: (1) to constitute the expression of an autonomous taxing power held by the Community, which tends to be manifested not just in the institution of taxes in the relevant legislations but, above all, in the contribution to public tax revenues in the Member States; or (2) to limit, control and harmonies taxing powers in the Member States. In this sense, it is appropriate to examine the effects implied by these rules on the national system of tax law.

In general terms, Community derivative and incomplete tax rules require a national implementation law to be laid down in substantial terms by way of ordinary procedure, this law equally acquiring the character of a special law *sui generis* for the same reasons.

This reasoning, however, does not hold good for Community derivative and complete tax rules given that the Community order ensures that peace and justice are respected among nations, and implies that the sovereignty principle may be restricted under the equality of conditions with other states, as under Article 11 of the Constitution.[18] The substance of this article is similar to the detailed Article 23, paragraph 1, of

18. Uckmar, 'Progetti e possibili soluzioni dell'armonizzazione fiscale dell'Ue', in *Dir. prat. trib.*,1995,I, p. 9; Grotherr, 'Die unterschiedlichen Konzernbesteuerungssysteme in den Mitgliedstaaten der Europäischen Union', in *StuW*, 1996, p. 356; Various, *Steuerrecht im Europäischen Binnenmarkt*, edited by Lehner, Cologne, 1996; Herdegen, *Europarecht*, Munich, 1997; Classen, *EuropaRecht*, 14th edn, 1997; Von Borries Winkel, *Europäisches Wirtschaftsrecht*, Munich, 1997; Laule, 'Die Harmonisierung des europäischen Steuerrechts', *in IstR*, 2001, p. 297.
Tipke, *Die Steuerrechtsordnung*, Cologne, 1993, III, p. 1159, points out that supranational law constitutes not just a part of domestic law nor of international law, but a legal order on its own. This is the correct view which, on account of all differences, inspires the constructs of the relationship between domestic law and Community law.
Micossi, Il *coordinamento europeo in materia fiscale: elementi per un sistema comune*, in *Giur. imp.*, 2000, p. 1381; Aa.Vv., *Coordinamento fiscale nell'Unione europea* (International Conference Proceedings: Stresa, 19–20 May 2000), Milan, 2001: Aa.Vv., *Fiscalità comunitaria*, edited by Roccatagliata and Valente, in *Dir. prat. trib. intern.*, 2001, p. 441; Perrone Capano, *L'Europa tra debolezza dell' euro e crisidello stato fiscale. Una interpretazionefunzionale*, in *Rass. trib.*, 2001, p. 1319;
Weber-Grellet, *Europäisiertes Steuerrecht? Stand und Entwicklung*, in *StuW*, 1995, p. 336.
Cf.Ballarino,Cf. Ballarino, *Manuale di diritto dell'Unione europea*, Padova, 2004.
It is remarkable that the national system contains rules of international tax law which, by infringing such delicate balances, affirm the primacy of domestic law. Art. 128 of the Consolidated Single Text *(t.u.i.r.)*, No. 917, of 22.12.1986 – which reiterates Art. 75 of Presidential Decree No. 597 of 22.9.1973, in establishing that 'the provisions of this Consolidated Single Text, whether they are more favourable to taxpayers, also apply in derogation from international agreements against double taxation' – makes derogable on such matter those ratification laws which are 'special' in character. This rule overturns the relationship existing between unwritten special laws and more favourable incompatible laws, even though the latter were made previously to the former. The constitutional foundation of any special law being inderogable with regard to other subsequent laws, in so far as the latter do not expressly State the aim of depriving the State of international commitments already undertaken, induces us to believe that a doubt indeed exists as to the constitutional legitimacy of Art. 128 of the aforementioned Single Text. This Text would allow the more favourable ordinary tax law even to derogate from the subsequent special law.
Cf. Various, *Doppelbesteuerungsabkommen der Bundesrepublik Deutschland aufdem Gebiet der Steuern vom Einkommen und Vermögen*, edited by vogel, Munich, 1996.
Schaumburg, *Internationales Steuerrecht*, 2nd edn, Cologne, 1998, p. 585, for instance, is able to perceive the existence of two kinds of components behind the law on double taxation: one being of an international and legal character, the other being of a constitutional and European legal character.
When interpreting conventional rules, these may play a different role compared to Community rules. The former rules, in fact, will stand as 'substituting rules' if they are drafted by impulse of Community rules, which act as, or behave as 'supplementary' rules, which then survive over pre-existing Community rules by means of express will of Contracting States.
The relationship between conventional and Community rules sometimes becomes closely connected. Here, an interesting question arises when an international convention was stipulated with a non-EU country by a Member State, this convention however providing for fiscal benefits which exclude citizens of other Member States. It is clear, in this context, that any rule of conventional international law will operate between the contracting third country and the contracting member country and will not automatically extend to other Member States, in that there is no legal foundation behind such extension. Only the Community, by means of a new Treaty with a third country, may carry out such extension. However, the Member State is required to respect the principles enshrined in the EC Treaty such as, prohibiting tax discrimination; respecting the fundamental freedoms of the taxpayer; and providing for the obligation to establish cooperation between administrative tax authorities in order to achieve

the Fundamental German Legislation, introduced under the Law on Constitutional Review of 21 December 1992.[19]

---

the objectives of the Treaty itself. As a consequence, the contracting Member State is required to lay down laws necessary to implement such principles in relation to the stipulated international Convention. Thus, the question is about adapting an international tax rule to other Community rules in the field which have already been received into the same national system. This question then does not mean that a rule must necessarily prevail over another. It rather means to ensure coordination between them in such a way as to bring benefits to individual taxpayers who are not resident in the State stipulating the international convention with a third country, and to allow tax benefits to accrue to its own residents. See: Carmini Mainardi, *Elementi di Diritto tributario comunitario*, Padua, 1996.
Various, *Verrechnungspreisgrundsätze für multinationale Unternehmen und Steuerverwaltungen*, edited by Flick-Wassermyer-Becker, Cologne, 1997.
Casado Ollero, *The Community Legal System and the Internal Tax System*, in this work, maintains that Community law does not stand as an internal law, foreign law, or international law. It rather forms part of the internal system of law of the Member States (Art. 96 of the Spanish Constitution, and Art. 10 of the Italian Constitution). It is a part of international law, but is distinguished from classical or inter-state international law. In this context, therefore, the option may lie either in the notion of the internal law receiving an expansionist meaning to make room for a kind of legal order created well outside national confines, or in the notion of the international law including a kind of legal order which is able to meet the demands for greater integration in the field of sovereign and super-national powers. In addition, Community tax law, seen as a branch of Community law, relies on a double perspective: the whole body of rules and principles which regulate tax activity of the Community, on the one hand, and Community rules and principles which have a direct influence over Member States' legal orders, on the other.
On the distinction between primary Community law, as contained in the Treaty, and secondary Community law, as produced by the Community organs and institutions, Cf. Tipke and Lang, *Steuerrecht*, 20th edn, Cologne, 2010, p. 33.
Cf. List, 'Die Europäisierung des Steuerrechts', in *Festchriftfür W. Leisner*, 1999, p. 109, and Laule, 'Die Harmonisierung des europäischen Steuerrechts', in *IstR*, 2001, p. 297; López-Espadafor, 'El poder tributario de las Comunidades Europeas', in *Rev. Esp. Der. Fin.*, No. 82, 1994.
Art. 11 of the Constitution reads: 'Italy [....] allows, under the equality of conditions for other States, to limit state sovereign powers as a necessary condition to ensure peace and justice among nations'.
Under the current State of Community law, the Community does not have powers to adhere to the European Convention for the Safeguard of Human Rights and Fundamental Freedoms (Court of Justice of the European Communities, 28 March 1996, in *Foro it.*, 1997, IV, 13).

19. Art. 23, para. 1 of the German Constitution, introduced by the constitutional law of 21 December 1992, states that: 'To achieve a united Europe, the German Federal Republic shall participate in the development of the European Union, which is committed to respecting the democratic principles, the rule of law, the welfare and federal State, and respecting the subsidiarity principle, and shall guarantee protection of fundamental rights of the same type as provided for under this Constitution. To this effect, the Federation may devolve sovereign powers through legislation based on the assent by the *Bundesrat.* To establish the European Union, as is in the case of the modifications to the conventional international grounds of Community law and the equivalent provisions which may either entail or allow for modified or supplemented versions of the substance of this fundamental legislation, Art. 79, paras 2 and 3, shall apply. Under this article, it is required that the assent by two thirds be given by the members of the *Bundestag,* with two thirds of voting to be given by the *Bundesrat,* and it is prohibited that the powers given to the *Bundestag* and *Länder* be subject to constitutional review'. On the relations between the Constitution and the European Union, Cf. Kirchhof, 'Die Mitwirkung Deutschlands an der Wirtschafts - und Währungsunion', in Kirchhof, Offerhaus, Schöberle, *Steuerrecht, Verfassungsrecht, Finanzpolitik- Festschrift für Klein,* Cologne, 1994. *Steuern im Verfassungsstaat, Festschrift für Klaus Vogel,* edited by Kirchhof, Birk and Lehner, Munich, 1996, p. 459.

In its ruling of 12 October 1993,[20] the German Constitutional Court stated that the democratic principle by which full powers are recognized to national parliaments, does not preclude individual States from taking part in a Community of States organized in a supranational fashion. However, this type of participation also requires that a legitimacy and authority deriving from the peoples' attitude 'to exert influence' over the various processes leading to the formation of the political will and decisions, be ensured within the Community.

The Community system is able to fulfil sovereign duties by way of the democratic legitimacy, resulting from the links established between European organs and national parliaments within the Community institutional context, and by the European Parliament elected by universal suffrage by the citizens of the Member States. However, the representative principle, which is fully respected according to the Court's view, is one which has begun to intensify in tax matters where legal reservation is applied.

The European Parliament, replacing national parliaments in their respective countries, must in any case regulate the elements forming tax obligations, and cannot delegate this function to other organs.

The relationship between Community and national legal systems should be understood in a way which reflects the connection with Article 10, paragraph 1, of the Constitution examined before.

This constitutional rule, while exclusively referring to general international tax rules, does not take into account Community derivative and complete tax rules. However, by establishing the essential characters underlying the special or reference procedure, the above constitutional rule is instrumental in providing useful indications in order to solve questions related to the effects caused by such procedure, in the case in which it operates on Community derivative and complete tax rules.[21]

---

20. *In EuGRZ,* 1993, p. 429.
On the grounds of this reasoning, the German Constitutional Court, in its ruling of 12 October 1993, rejected the action brought against the law of 28 December 1992 to authorize ratification of the Treaty on the European Union of 7 February 1992, and declared that the action brought against the law on constitutional review of 21 December 1992 was indeed irreceivable. This law, however, introduced Art. 23, para. 1, of the fundamental legislation. Cf. Streinz, 'Verwirklichung der Europäischen Union, Beteiligung und des Bundesrates', in *Grundgesetz-Kommentar,* edited by Sachs, 3rd edn, Munich, 2003, p. 942.
The Spanish Constitutional Court, in its *Declaración* of 1 July 1992, on the need to establish whether or not a conflict arises between Art. 13.2 of the Spanish Constitution and Art. 8 B. 1, paragraph 1, of the Treaty, stated that Art. 93 of the said Constitution allows for limitations of sovereignty in order to exercise the powers deriving from the Constitution, and that the enforcement of such sovereignty entails, for certain effects, specific limitations or restrictions to the powers and competences vested in the Spanish public authorities *(poderes publicos españoles).* The Court also added that such limitations are indispensable provided there is, *de facto,* a substantial devolution (rather than a legal entitlement) of the competences and powers to international organizations or institutions. Lastly, the Court emphasized that the Spanish public authorities are not less subject to the Constitution, given that they exercise their own competence and powers within the framework of international or supra-international relations. This is what lies behind the protection guaranteed in Art. 95 of the Spanish Constitution, the scope of which should not in any way be reduced by Art. 93 of the Constitution itself.
21. Adam R., Le fonti comunitarie, in Tizzano A., (a cura di), *Il diritto privato dell'Unione Europea, I,* Torino 2006, p.43; Mastroianni R., Le direttive comunitarie nel giudizio di costituzionalità, in Daniele L. (a cura di), *La dimensione internazionale ed europea del diritto nell'esperienza della*

Article 10, paragraph 1, of the Constitution, determines the nature of the internal rule produced, while Article 11 defines the way in which the international rule becomes suitable to give rise to an automatic production of internal rules.

In any case, the national taxation law system remains equally involved in by the special or reference procedure which produces Community derivative and complete tax rules, as a result of the sovereignty principle delegated to the Community by individual States. In this context, the national taxation system also 'conforms to' Community derivative and complete tax rules.

However, it is Article 11 of the Constitution itself which allows for a different legal system to be formed by way of the limitations set by the state to its own sovereignty in tax matters. This is because the organic nature of individual legal systems is guaranteed by the fact that they enjoy an autonomous status.

The dual view[22] based on the original and distinguished features characterizing domestic tax law, does not imply that the Community derivative and complete tax rule, which needs not be reproduced in the national legislation, may have a direct incidence on taxpayers and administrative tax authorities, to such an extent that the latter may jointly be considered as final recipients of Community complete rules and national laws.

Corte Costituzionale, Napoli 2006, p. 325; Stile M. T., Il problema del giudicato di diritto interno in contrasto con l'ordinamento comunitario o con la CEDU, in *Dir. com. sc. int.* 2007, p. 237 ss.; Strozzi G., Il sistema normativo, in Chiti M. P. e Greco G. (diretto da), *Trattato di diritto amministrativo europeo, parte generale, I*, Milano 2007, p. 147; Cannizzaro E., Sui rapporti tra sistemi processuali nazionali e diritto dell'Unione europea, *in Il dir. dell'Unione eur.*, 2008, p. 447 ss.; De Pasquale P., Il riparto di competenze tra Unione europea e Stati membri, in *Dir. pubblico comp. ed europeo*, 2008, p.60 ss; Fiengo G., *Gli atti atipici della Comunità europea*, Napoli, 2008; Piva P., *Giudice nazionale e diritto dell'Unione europea*, Napoli 2008; Porchia O., *Principi dell'ordinamento europeo. La cooperazione pluridirezionale*, Bologna, 2008; Amalfitano C., L'acquis communautaire: da esperienza giuridica a fattore di integrazione, in *Il diritto dell'Un. europea*, 2009, p.789; Bisogni-Bronzini-Piecone (a cura di), *La Carta dei diritti fondamentali dell'Unione europea*, Taranto, 2009; Idem, Diritto costituzionale e diritto interno, *Atti del seminario di Roma, aprile 2007*, Milano 2008; Tesauro G., Costituzione e norme esterne, in *Il dir. dell'Unione eur.*, 2009, p. 195 ss.; Brunelli-Pugiotto-Veronesi (a cura di), *Il diritto costituzionale come regola e limite al potere, Scritti in onore di L. Carlassare, vol. I*, Napoli 2009, p. 393 ss.

22. Cf. Donati, *Diritto comunitario e sindacato di costituzionalità*, Milan, 1995, p. 194.

Figure 11.1 Special Procedure: A View

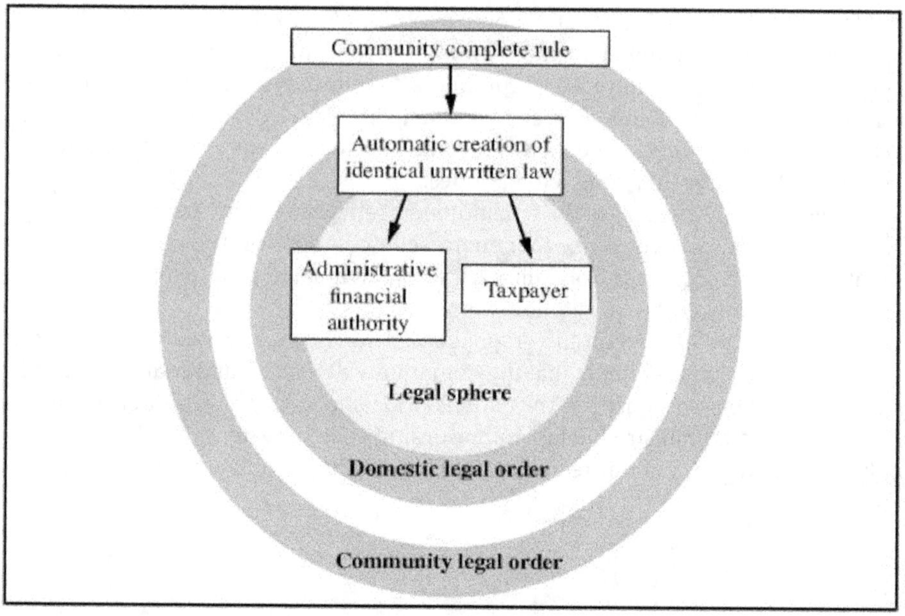

Figure 11.2 Metaphorical View of Special Adaptation Procedure

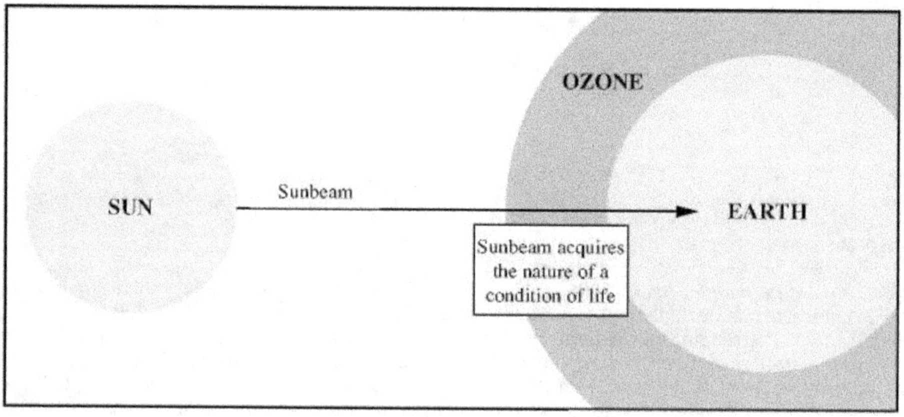

Figure 11.3 Ordinary Procedure: A View

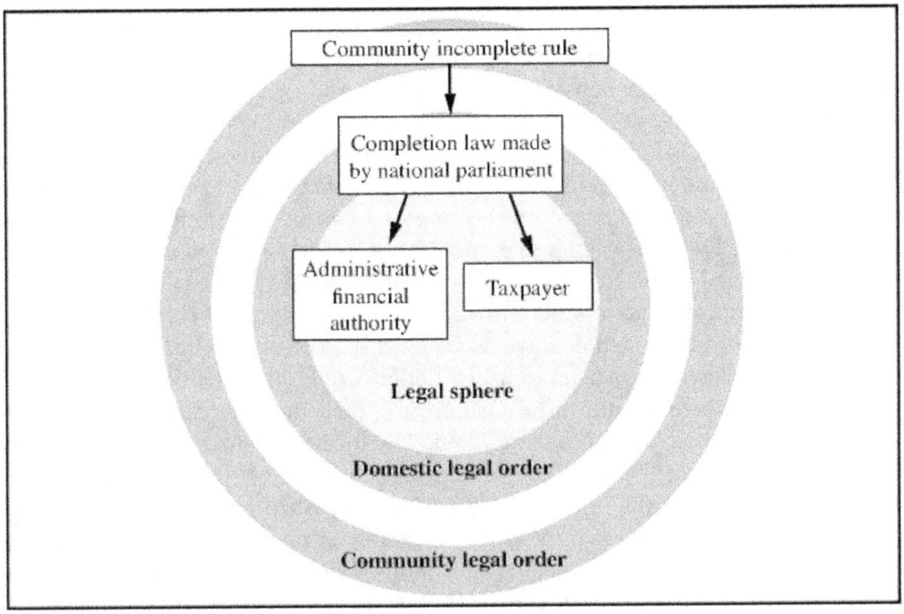

Indeed, the Community derivative and complete tax rule, whose nature is generally derived from Regulations[23] and Decisions, operates by virtue of Article 10, paragraph 1, of the Constitution. This Article, while regulating the special procedure, provides that the internal system must comply with the rules of international law. Therefore, the Community derivative and complete tax rule (contrary to the incomplete one) is filtered through the national legal system and, by virtue of the law ratifying the Treaty, automatically gives rise to a national unwritten special law of equal substance. This law, while producing a direct effect on both taxpayers and administrative tax authorities, will create new rights, duties and obligations as well as tax liability, i.e. it involves the entirety of the elements necessary for the existence of a tax legal relation between individual taxpayers and competent bodies in charge of levying tax. In turn, it is for the state not only to guarantee that such rights are exercised, but also that the duties, obligations and tax obligations are fulfilled.

Thus, while exercising a direct effect, these unwritten laws do not require other Community or national rules to operate.[24] As a result, individual administrative tax authorities and tax courts alike are under an obligation to apply them.

23. In order to make for a uniform interpretation, Council Regulation No. 3330/91 of 7.11.1991, concerning statistical data in the field of goods exchange between Member States, provides in Art. 2 for a preliminary definition of some of the terms used throughout.
24. See EC Court of Justice judgment of 19.11.1991 in joined cases C-6 and 9/90, *Francovich*, rec. I,5357.I,5357.

Similarly, the rules of a Treaty governing tax matters, which are able to produce a direct effect, acquire the character of conventional rules. Therefore, also these rules automatically give rise to a national unwritten law of the same substance.

Among national tax laws, those which are autonomously laid down by the parliament have so far been substantially reduced in number. While the latter laws are not directly or indirectly derived from Community rules, others instead are expressly derived from powers being delegated to Local (Territorial) Authorities *(Enti Locali)*. In exercising its own autonomous law-making power in tax matters, the national parliament is bound by the aims and purposes imposed by the Constitution and the rules established in the Treaty, the latter in particular guaranteeing that economic and social progress is achieved on balanced and sustainable grounds. The basis for this progress lies mainly on improved government finance and a deeply-rooted culture of stability, with the latter to come at a later stage. Consequently, there is no infringement of the principle of legal reservation as established under Article 23 of the Constitution.

Taxpayers are constantly in a position in which they are directly affected by national laws, whether written or unwritten. The former are intended to implement incomplete rules while the latter are intended to automatically reproduce complete rules. However, it is for the interpreter to establish whether a given type of Directive rests on a detailed substance; in other words, whether or not it needs to be supplemented by a given tax law. By imposing obligations on the state, the Directive may only exclusively be invoked against the state (vertical effect) rather than among individuals (horizontal effect). Therefore, by relying on the recognized and well-grounded principle of vertical effect, the taxpayer is legitimized to challenge the financial administrative authority established in the state (this authority being the direct expression of the tax levying power enjoyed by that state) for violation of a Directive which lacks detailed provision and implementation by written law.[25]

25. Tipke, *Die Steuerrechtsordnung*, III, Cologne, p. 1993,1160, defines *EG – Richtlinien* as the instruments of harmonized taxation.
On the subject of harmonization and correspondence between tax legal systems, see the interesting work by Pace, *Sistema di comunicazione fiscale*, Turin, 2000, p. 119.
The failure to apply the Community rule amounts to a violation under the law, and may be raised to bring an action against the Italian *Corte di Cassazione* [Translator's note: this is the court of last resort or highest court from which no appeals are allowed]. Cf. Mazzarella, *Analisi del giudizio per Cassazione*, Padova, 1994, p. 65.
Clearly, the problem with detailed Directives arises in the case of a failure to apply them in line with the time limits and measures prescribed by the national authorities, including those cases in which they [detailed Directives] lack correct or timely implementation. In fact, if they are applied correctly and in time, the effects of detailed Directives will be produced through the various national measures designed to implement them. For this reason, the direct effect of any detailed Directive is intended to fulfil a sanctioning function for the state which failed to implement it. Like the Treaty rules which are addressed to the Member States, the provisions included in a Directive are intended to produce a direct effect, in so far as such provisions imply precise obligations imposed on the state with corresponding rights given to individuals (Cf. Court of Justice judgment of 7.3.1996, case C-192/94, in *Foro it.*, 1996IV, p. 357, with annotation by Barone). Art. 189 of the Treaty does not exclude those legal acts, which are different from Regulations, to produce the same effects. Fulfilment of the obligations on the part of the state would be compromised if individuals were not able to claim the legal effect of such acts, and if national judges were not able to take them on board (action for a preliminary ruling) (cf. Court of Justice judgment of 26.3.1996 case C-392/93, *British Telecommunications*,

Indeed, even when the state is found to have failed in its obligation to implement a non-detailed Directive by written law, the tax levying act issued by the administrative tax authority (and which, in addition, is found to be against the purposes of the Directive) will be unlawful. In these circumstances, however, the burden of the economic sanction applied to the defaulting state to the detriment of individual taxpayers, is one which de facto is transferred to fall upon all of them.

Direct applicability of a complete rule (to include Regulations, on the one hand, and Decisions, detailed Directives, on the other) is distinguished from the direct effect behind an incomplete and non-implemented rule; the former enters the legal frame of the national system only after the court with jurisdiction in the case has proved that the State failed to apply it. The effect of such rule then is to produce an unwritten law of the same substance.

---

in *Foro it.*, 1996, IV, 322, with annotation by Catalano; Court of Justice judgment of 5.3.1996, joined cases C-46 and 48/93, *Factortame,* in *Foro it.*, 1996, IV, p. 185; and, in more general terms, judgment of 23.2.1994, case C-236/92, rec. I-483, items 9 and 10).

See: Tesauro G., Costituzione e norme esterne, in *Il dir. dell'Unione eur.*, 2009, p. 195 ss.

On the horizontal effect, cf. Court of Justice judgment of 14 July 1994, case C-91/92, rec. I,3325, items 21 and 25. Such a reasoning is also confirmed by the Justice Court itself in its judgment of 7 March 1996, case C-192/94, with annotation by Barone, 'L'efficacia diretta delle direttive fra certezza (comunitaria) e fraintendimenti (nazionali)', in *Foro it.*, 1996, IV, p. 338, by stating that: a) a Directive cannot in itself create obligations for individuals to fulfil; b) case law criteria regarding vertical effects exclude the possibility for the state to gain advantage by reason of the state failing to comply with Directives; c) the extension of obligations to relations among individuals (so is the approach taken in Court's case law) means that Directives should be attributed the same effects as implied in Regulations and Decisions; d) if the result to be achieved by the Directive cannot be obtained via interpretative canons, a right to redress the damage caused will be inevitably invoked.

Cf. *Steuerrecht im Europäischen Binnenmarkt,* edited by the German Society of Tax Lawyers and coordinated by Lehner, Cologne, 1996. Tipke and Lang, *Steuerrecht, 20*th edn, Cologne, 2010, p. 33, affirm that the question of the applicability of tax Directives through ordinary legislation should be distinguished from the question as to whether taxpayers should bring a legitimate claim against the national law departing from Directives, thus resulting in taxpayers being unsatisfactorily protected.

See my report on the discretionality powers of administrative tax authorities (subject II) included in the Conference Proceedings of the XVIII *Jornada Latinoamericana de Derecho Tributario, Relatos nacionales,* Montevideo, 1996, p. 437. In this context, it should be noted that any excess of power can be configured as a lack of legitimacy in national legislation which, while not being directly in contrast with Community legislation, may impede or prejudice the Treaty against being constantly observed.

Tipke and Lang, *Steuerrecht, 20*th edn, Cologne, 2010, p. 33, although they take into account tax Directives which – they point out – are applied through legislation, make explicit reference to the constitutional principle. This principle, while also being applied to Community law, is one in which any influence exercised on freedoms and property is deemed to be illegitimate only by law (substantive law). Also, as pointed out by Birkenfeld, in *Umsatzsteuer-Rundschau,* 1993, p. 27, p. 278 and Lohse, *ibid.*, p. 288, no measure is allowed through administrative provisions. The Spanish Constitutional Court, in its judgment No. 28 of 14 February 1991, while also following the reasoning made by Court of Justice, stated that the state, following its adherence to the Treaty establishing the European Community, is bound by Community law which constitutes a legal order *per se,* which is supplemental to the various national legal systems of Member States and, at the same time, imposes its own rules on the jurisdictional bodies in the Member States

Cf. Various, *Unternehmensbesteuerung in EU-Staaten,* edited by Lang, Cologne, 1994; Selling, 'Steuer-harmonisierung im europäischen Binnemarkt', in *IstR,* 2000, p. 417.

Consequently, if state practice is to levy tax on certain types of activity which are deemed non-taxable under a given Community rule, it will often result in sanctions being automatically self-imposed by the state itself, because the tax turns out to be unfeasible in economic terms, and as such will cause the taxable event as prescribed by law to arise in another Member State which, in turn, is observant of the Community rule. Conversely, if tax levy is applied there, the sanction imposed by the Community will consist in a penalty charged on the administrative tax authority to refund the taxpayer of the sum equal to the amount of tax which was unduly collected by the authority under the provisions of Community law.

In no way can discretionary powers be given to administrative tax authorities in the Member States by way of Directives, in spite of the fact that these powers are understood as a way to mediate between the primary interest of the public at large and secondary interests leading to particular choices. Viewed this way, then, in no way can it be assumed that an excess of power exists in the form of a lack of legitimacy of tax levying acts issued by administrative financial authorities.

Thus, while maintaining its own autonomy, the Community system is able to affect taxpayers and administrative financial authorities however always through the internal system of law.

Such a relationship between Community and domestic tax systems coincides with the relationship between international and domestic systems. In fact, the adaptation[26] of the national legal system to the complete rules of the Treaty rests on the constitutional rules themselves. This type of adaptation also rests, however, on the conventional rules from which Directives and Regulations actually derive.

In line with the present analysis, the unwritten tax law being automatically produced is one which repeals any other law with which it is found to be in contrast.

26. Cf. Cartou-Clergerie-Gruber-Rambaud, *L'Union européenne,* Paris, 2002; Ferrari Bravo-Moavero Milanesi, *Lezioni di diritto comunitario,* Napoli, 2002; Guizzi, *Manuale di diritto e politica dell'Unione Europea,* Napoli, 2003; Zanghi, *Istituzioni di diritto dell'Unione Europea,* Torino, 2003; Ballarino, *Manuale di diritto dell'Unione Europea,* Padova, 2004; Isaac, *Droit communautaire général,* Paris, 2004; Lenaerts-Van Nuffel, *Constitutional Law of the European Union,* London, 2005; Van Gerven, *The European Union,* Oxford, 2005; Strozzi, *Diritto dell'Unione Europea,* Torino, 2009; Tesauro G., *Diritto comunitario,* 6th edn, Padova, 2010.

www.ingramcontent.com/pod-product-compliance
Lightning Source LLC
LaVergne TN
LVHW020003031026
849161LV00023B/841
* 9 7 8 9 0 4 1 1 3 7 2 7 2 *